# The American Journey

# The American Journey
## A History of the United States

**SEVENTH EDITION**
Volume 2 (Since 1965)

David Goldfield
*University of North Carolina, Charlotte*

Carl Abbott
*Portland State University*

Virginia DeJohn Anderson
*University of Colorado, Boulder*

Jo Ann E. Argersinger
*Southern Illinois University*

Peter H. Argersinger
*Southern Illinois University*

William L. Barney
*University of North Carolina, Chapel Hill*

Boston   Columbus   Indianapolis   New York   San Francisco   Upper Saddle River
Amsterdam   Cape Town   Dubai   London   Madrid   Milan   Munich   Paris   Montréal   Toronto
Delhi   Mexico City   São Paulo   Sydney   Hong Kong   Seoul   Singapore   Taipei   Tokyo

Editor in Chief: Dickson Musslewhite
Executive Editor: Ed Parsons
Editorial Program Manager: Seanna Breen
Director of Marketing: Brandy Dawson
Executive Marketing Manager: Wendy Albert
Senior Managing Editor: Ann Marie McCarthy
Production Project Manager: Debra A. Wechsler
Senior Operations Supervisor: Mary Fischer
Operations Specialist: Mary Ann Gloriande
Art Director: Maria Lange
Interior Design: Red Kite Project
Cover Design: Maria Lange/
 Red Kite Project
Cover Illustration: Paul Chung

Cover: Eleanor Roosevelt's personal journey took her from a privileged family to the White House. Not content with traditional First Lady duties, she dedicated her life to helping those less fortunate, speaking out against racial discrimination, poverty, and labor injustice to become a prominent figure in her own right. Photo Library of Congress.
Digital Media Editor: Michael Halas
Digital Media Project Manager: Elizabeth Roden Hall
Full-Service Project Management and Composition:
 PreMedia Global USA Inc.
Printer/Binder: R. R. Donnelley / Williard
Cover Printer: Lehigh-Phoenix Color/Hagerstown
Text Font: Minion Pro 10.5 pts

Credits and acknowledgments borrowed from other sources and reproduced, with permission, in this textbook appear on appropriate page within text (or beginning on page C-1).

**Library of Congress Cataloging-in-Publication Data**
Goldfield, David R.
 The American journey : a history of the United States / David Goldfield, University of North Carolina, Charlotte; Carl Abbott, Portland State University; Virginia DeJohn Anderson, University of Colorado, Boulder; Jo Ann E. Argersinger, Southern Illinois University; Peter H. Argersinger, Southern Illinois University; William L. Barney, University of North Carolina, Chapel Hill; — Seventh edition; combined volume.
 pages cm
 ISBN 978-0-205-95852-8 (pbk. : combined) — ISBN 978-0-205-96096-5 (pbk. : v. 1) —
 ISBN 978-0-205-96095-8 (pbk. : v. 2)
 1. United States—History—Textbooks. I. Title.
 E178.1.G614 2013
 973—dc23

                                                                                    2013013884

10 9 8 7 6 5 4 3 2 1

Combined Volume:
ISBN 10: 0205961983


Volume 1:
ISBN 10: 0205961967


Volume 2:
ISBN 10: 0205961975

# Brief Contents

# Contents

# Special Features

## From Then to Now

## Video Series

## Explore . . .

## Maps

# Figures

# Tables

# New to This Edition

Every chapter in the seventh edition of *The American Journey* has been carefully revised to present a briefer, more accessible approach to the material while continuing to emphasize its unique features—chronological organization, geographical literacy, regional balance, and religion.

## Personalize Learning with New MyHistoryLab

This text features full **integration with the new MyHistoryLab**—a rich resource that delivers proven results in helping students succeed, provides engaging experiences that personalize learning, and comes from a trusted partner with educational expertise and a deep commitment to helping students and instructors achieve their goals.

- The **Pearson eText,** with a new streamlined design for tablet devices, lets students access *The American Journey* anytime, anywhere, and any way they want—and they can listen to and download every chapter. Section tabs on the margin of every page make the text much easier to navigate. The new Pearson eText is now fully interactive and links to all the learning resources in the MyLab.
- **Chapter launcher videos** introduce students to the material, helping to engage them even before they begin reading the chapter. Each chapter has a 15-minute segment, comprised of a three-minute overview and three four-minute videos on specific topics. The videos are featured on the second page, directly after the chapter opener.
- In the new **MyHistoryLibrary with audio,** students can read, listen to, annotate, download, and print over 200 of the most commonly assigned primary source documents. These documents can also be annotated by instructors.
- With the new **History Explorer,** students visualize and analyze historical evidence in a powerful mapping resource. The modules cover topics from English Colonization to the Civil Rights Movement, and each contains an assignable exercise with automated assessment. They are also featured in every chapter of the text in a special box.
- The new **automated writing assessment engine** allows students to further explore key topics by responding to them in essay form. The system offers ten formal prompts on standard topics like the American Revolution, the Lewis and Clark expedition, and the New Deal. Each assignment is based on one of MyHistoryLab's engaging **Author Video Lectures**.
- A **personalized study plan** for each student, based on Bloom's Taxonomy, promotes critical thinking skills and helps students succeed in the course and beyond.
- **Assessment** tied to videos, applications, and chapters enables instructors and students to track progress and get immediate feedback. Instructors will be able to find the best resources for teaching their students.

- **MyHistoryLab icons** are paired with images in the text for more thorough integration between the book and online resources.
- The new **Instructor's eText** makes it easier than ever for instructors to access subject-specific resources for class preparation. Housed within MyHistoryLab, it serves as the hub for all available instructor resources—including the new MyHistoryLab Instructor's Guide.
- The new **MyHistoryLab Instructor's Guide** outlines the basic steps for registering and building a course in MyHistoryLab and describes the key resources and assignments available for each chapter of *The American Journey*.
- The **Class Preparation Tool** collects the best class presentation resources in one convenient online destination. Resources include PowerPoint slides, streaming audio and video, audio clips for class tests and quizzes, and all illustrations for creating interactive lectures.

## Engage Students and Improve Critical Thinking

- **Chapter introductory vignettes** provide brief firsthand accounts from individuals who powerfully recount the personal journeys they took in their lives. Each of these "voices" relates to the themes that follow in the chapter.
- **Chapter images** are bigger, visually interesting, and informative. Photographs and pieces of fine art encapsulate emotional and historical meaning. Captions provide valuable information that allows for a fuller understanding of the people who lived the American journey.
- **From Then to Now** relates important issues and events in each chapter to the issues and events of today, letting students see the relevance of history to their lives. This feature also provides thought-provoking visuals to support and enhance the narrative.

## Support Instructors

- **Learning Objective questions** highlight the important issues and themes. Each is linked to one of the chapter's main sections, and they are all emphasized in the chapter overview.
- The **Chapter Review** on the last page addresses all four Learning Objective questions from the beginning of each chapter in brief 50-word answers, summarizing the important issues and themes.
- The **thematic timeline** ending each chapter reinforces the essential points of the narrative, as events are tied to key terms from the text.

# About the Authors

**David Goldfield** is the Robert Lee Bailey Professor of History at the University of North Carolina, Charlotte. A native of Memphis, he grew up in Brooklyn, New York, and attended the University of Maryland. He is the author or editor of sixteen books dealing with the history of the American South, including two works, *Cotton Fields and Skyscrapers: Southern City and Region* (1982) and *Black, White, and Southern: Race Relations and Southern Culture* (1991), nominated for the Pulitzer Prize in history, and both received the Mayflower Award for Non-Fiction. *Still Fighting the Civil War: The American South and Southern History* appeared in 2002 and received the Jules and Frances Landry Prize and was named by *Choice* as an Outstanding Non-fiction Book. His most recent book is *America Aflame: How the Civil War Created a* Nation (2011). Goldfield is the President of the Southern Historical Association (2012–13) and is also the editor of the *Journal of Urban History*. He serves as an expert witness in voting rights and death penalty cases, as a consultant on the urban South to museums and public television and radio, and as an Academic Specialist for the U.S. State Department, leading workshops on American history and culture in foreign countries. He also serves on the Advisory Board of the Lincoln Prize.

**Carl Abbott** is a professor of Urban Studies and Planning at Portland State University. He taught previously in the history departments at the University of Denver and Old Dominion University, and held visiting appointments at Mesa College in Colorado, George Washington University, and the University of Oregon. He holds degrees in history from Swarthmore College and the University of Chicago. He specializes in the history of cities and the American West and serves as co-editor of the *Pacific Historical Review*. His books include *The New Urban America: Growth and Politics in Sunbelt Cities* (1981, 1987), *The Metropolitan Frontier: Cities in the Modern American West* (1993), *Political Terrain: Washington, D. C. from Tidewater Town to Global Metropolis* (1999), *Frontiers Past and Future: Science Fiction and the American West* (2006), and *How Cities Won the West: Four Centuries of Urban Change in Western North America* (2008).

**Virginia DeJohn Anderson** is Professor of History at the University of Colorado at Boulder. She received her B.A. from the University of Connecticut and as a Marshall Scholar earned an M.A. degree at the University of East Anglia in Norwich, England. Returning to the United States, she received her A.M. and Ph.D. degrees from Harvard University. A recipient of fellowships from the American Council of Learned Societies and the National Endowment for the Humanities, she is the author of *New England's Generation* (1991) and *Creatures of Empire: People and Animals in Early America* (2004). She has also published several articles on colonial history, which have appeared in such journals as the *William and Mary Quarterly* and the *New England Quarterly*. Her current book project is tentatively entitled *The Martyr and the Traitor: The Perilous Lives of Moses Dunbar and Nathan Hale in the American Revolution*.

**Jo Ann E. Argersinger** received her Ph.D. from George Washington University and is Professor of History at Southern Illinois University, where she won the George S. and Gladys W. Queen Award for Outstanding Teacher in History. A recipient of fellowships from the Rockefeller Foundation and the National Endowment for the Humanities, she is a historian of U.S. women, labor, and transnational history. Her publications include *Toward a New Deal in Baltimore: People and Government in the Great Depression* (1988), *Making the Amalgamated: Gender, Ethnicity, and Class in the Baltimore Clothing Industry* (1999), and *The Triangle Fire: A Brief History with Documents* (2009). She is currently writing a book entitled *Contested Visions of American Democracy: Public Housing and Citizenship in the International Arena* and working on a video project entitled *Women in America.*

**Peter H. Argersinger** is Professor of History at Southern Illinois University, where he was named Outstanding Scholar by the College of Liberal Arts. He received his B.A. from the University of Kansas and his M.A. and Ph.D. from the University of Wisconsin. He has been a Fellow of the Woodrow Wilson International Center for Scholars in Washington, D.C., and he has received fellowships, grants, and awards from the National Endowment for the Humanities, the American Historical Association, the Organization of American Historians, the Massachusetts Historical Society, and other organizations. Among his books on American political and rural history are *Populism and Politics* (1974), *Structure, Process, and Party* (1992), and *The Limits of Agrarian Radicalism* (1995). His most recent book, integrating legal and political history, is *Representation and Inequality in Late Nineteenth-Century America: The Politics of Apportionment* (2012). His current research focuses on the political crisis of the 1890s.

**William L. Barney** is Professor of History at the University of North Carolina at Chapel Hill. A native of Pennsylvania, he received his B.A. from Cornell University and his M.A. and Ph.D. from Columbia University. He has published extensively on nineteenth-century U.S. history and has a particular interest in the Old South and the coming of the Civil War. Among his publications are *The Road to Secession* (1972), *The Secessionist Impulse* (1974), *Flawed Victory* (1975), *The Passage of the Republic* (1987), *Battleground for the Union* (1989) and *The Making of a Confederate: Walter Lenoir's Civil War* (1997). He is currently finishing an edited collection of essays on nineteenth-century America and a book on the Civil War. Most recently, he has edited *A Companion to 19th-Century America* (2001) and finished *The Civil War and Reconstruction: A Student Companion* (2001).

# Acknowledgments

All of us are grateful to our families, friends, and colleagues for their support and encouragement. Jo Ann Argersinger and Peter Argersinger would like in particular to thank Margaret L. Aust, Rody Conant, Lizzie Gilman, and Ann Zinn; William Barney thanks Pamela Fesmire and Rosalie Radcliffe; Virginia Anderson thanks Fred Anderson, Kim Gruenwald, Ruth Helm, Eric Hinderaker, and Chidiebere Nwaubani; and David Goldfield thanks Frances Glenn and Jason Moscato.

# Supplementary Instructional Materials

| For Instructors | For Students |
|---|---|
| **MyHistoryLab** www.myhistorylab.com<br>**Save Time. Improve Results.**   MyHistoryLab is a dynamic website that provides a wealth of resources geared to meet the diverse teaching and learning needs of today's instructors and students. MyHistoryLab's many accessible tools will encourage students to read their text and help them improve their grade in their course. | **MyHistoryLab** www.myhistorylab.com<br>**Save Time. Improve Results.**   MyHistoryLab is a dynamic website that provides a wealth of resources geared to meet the diverse teaching and learning needs of today's instructors and students. MyHistoryLab's many accessible tools will encourage you to read your text and help you improve your grade in your course. |
| **Instructor's Resource Center**   www.pearsonhighered.com/irc<br>This website provides instructors with additional text-specific resources that can be downloaded for classroom use. Resources include the Instructor's Resource Manual, PowerPoint presentations and the test item file. Register online for access to the resources for *The American Journey*. | **www.coursemart.com**<br>CourseSmart eTextbooks offer the same content as the printed text in a convenient online format—with highlighting, online search, and printing capabilities. You **save 60% over the list price** of the traditional book. |
| **Instructor's Resource Manual**   Available for download at www.pearsonhighered.com/irc, the Instructor's Resource Manual contains chapter outlines, detailed chapter overviews, lecture outlines, topics for discussion, and information about audio-visual resources. | **Books à la Carte**   These editions feature the exact same content as the traditional printed text in a convenient, three-hole-punched, loose-leaf version at a discounted price—allowing you to take only what you need to class. You'll **save 35% over the net price** of the traditional book. |
| **Test Item File**   Available for download at www.pearsonhighered .com/irc, the Test Item File contains more than 1,500 multiple-choice, identification, matching, true-false, and essay test questions and 10–15 questions per chapter on the maps found in each chapter. | **Library of American Biography Series**   www.pearsonhighered. com/educator/series/Library-of-American-Biography/10493.page Pearson's renowned series of biographies spotlighting figures who had a significant impact on American history. Included in the series are Edmund Morgan's *The Puritan Dilemma: The Story of John Winthrop*, B. Davis Edmund's *Tecumseh and the Quest for Indian Leadership*, J. William T. Youngs, *Eleanor Roosevelt: A Personal and Public Life*, and John R. M. Wilson's *Jackie Robinson and the American Dilemma*. |
| **PowerPoint Presentations**   Available for download at www. pearsonhighered.com/irc, the PowerPoints contain chapter outlines and full-color images of maps, figures, and images. | **American Stories: Biographies in United States History**   This two-volume collection of sixty-two biographies provides insight into the lives and contributions of key figures as well as ordinary citizens to American history. Introductions, pre-reading questions, and suggested resources helps students connect the relevance of these individuals to historical events.<br>Volume 1 **ISBN-10: 0131826549 ISBN-13: 9780131826540**;<br>Volume 2 **ISBN-10: 0131826530 ISBN-13: 9780131826533** |

| FOR INSTRUCTORS | FOR STUDENTS |
|---|---|
| **MyTest** www.pearsonmytest.com<br>MyTest is a powerful assessment generation program that helps instructors easily create and print quizzes and exams. Questions and tests can be authored online, allowing instructors ultimate flexibility and the ability to efficiently manage assessments anytime, anywhere! Instructors can easily access existing questions and edit, create, and store using simple drag-and-drop and Word-like controls. | **Penguin Valuepacks**    www.pearsonhighered.com/penguin A variety of Penguin-Putnam texts is available at discounted prices when bundled with *The American Journey, 5/e*. Texts include Benjamin Franklin's *Autobiography and Other Writings*, Nathaniel Hawthorne's *The Scarlet Letter*, Thomas Jefferson's *Notes on the State of Virginia*, and George Orwell's *1984*. |
| **Retrieving the American Past**   (www.pearsoncustom.com, **keyword search | rtap**) Available through the Pearson Custom Library, the *Retrieving the American Past* (RTAP) program lets you create a textbook or reader that meets your needs and the needs of your course. RTAP gives you the freedom and flexibility to add chapters from several best-selling Pearson textbooks, in addition to *The American Journey, 5/e* and/or 100 topical reading units written by the History Department of Ohio State University, all under one cover. Choose the content you want to teach in depth, in the sequence you want, at the price you want your students to pay. | **A Short Guide to Writing About History, 7/e**   Written by Richard Marius, late of Harvard University, and Melvin E. Page, Eastern Tennessee State University, this engaging and practical text helps students get beyond merely compiling dates and facts. Covering brief essays and the documented resource paper, the text explores the writing and researching processes, identifies different modes of historical writing, including argument, and concludes with guidelines for improving style. **ISBN-10: 0205673708; ISBN-13: 9780205673704** |
|  | **Longman American History Atlas**   This full-color historical atlas designed especially for college students is a valuable reference tool and visual guide to American history. This atlas includes maps covering the scope of American history from the lives of the Native Americans to the 1990s. Produced by a renowned cartographic firm and a team of respected historians, the Longman American History Atlas will enhance any American history survey course. **ISBN: 0321004868; ISBN-13: 9780321004864** |

## MyHistoryLab

An online homework, tutorial, and assessment program, MyHistoryLab offers immersive content, tools, and experiences to engage students and help them succeed.

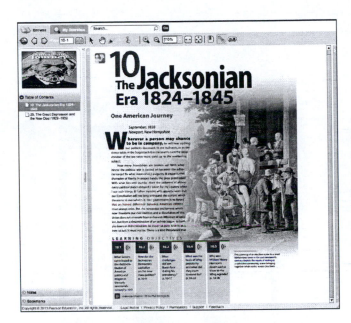

## Pearson eText with Audio

Contained within MyHistoryLab, the Pearson eText enables students to access their textbook online—through laptops, iPads, and tablets. Download the free Pearson eText app to use on tablets. Students may also listen to their text with the Audio eText.

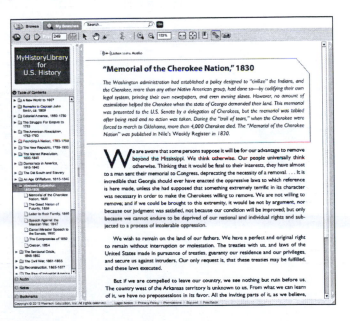

## New MyHistoryLibrary

A new release of Pearson's MyHistoryLibrary contains more than 200 of the most commonly assigned primary source documents, delivered through Pearson's powerful eText platform. Each reading may also be listened to in the Audio eText companion.

## MyHistoryLab Video Series:

Key Topics in US History

This comprehensive video series helps students get up-to-speed on key topics. Correlated to the chapters of *The American Journey*, each video unit reviews key topics of the period, readying students to get the most from the text narrative. The videos feature seasoned historians reviewing the pivotal stories of our past, in a lively format designed to engage and inform.

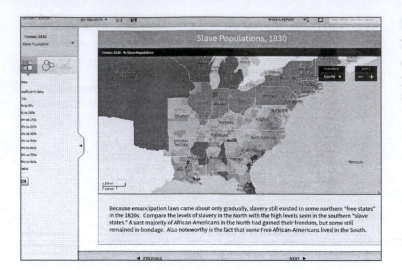

## Explorer

This path-breaking new application in MyHistoryLab enables students to use dynamic maps to understand pivotal events and topics. A unique Explorer application is correlated to each chapter of *The American Journey*.

## Writing Space

MyHistoryLab Writing Space provides the best way to develop and assess concept mastery and critical thinking through writing. Use Writing Space to create, track, and grade writing assignments, access writing resources, and exchange meaningful, personalized feedback quickly and easily. Plus, Writing Space includes integrated access to Turnitin, the global leader in plagiarism prevention.

# Key Supplements & Customer Support

## Annotated Instructor's eText

Contained within MyHistoryLab, the *Annotated Instructor's eText* for your Pearson textbook leverages the powerful Pearson eText platform to make it easier than ever for you to access subject-specific resources for class preparation. The *AI eText* serves as the hub for all instructor resources, with chapter-by-chapter links to PowerPoint slides, content from the Instructor's Manual, and to *MyHistoryLab's* ClassPrep engine, which contains a wealth of history content organized for classroom use.

## Instructor's Manual

The Instructor's Manual for your Pearson textbook contains chapter overviews, discussion questions, and suggested assignments for each chapter, including both general and text-specific content. It also contains a MyHistoryLab syllabus and suggestions for integrating MyHistoryLab into your course.

## PowerPoint Presentations

Strong PowerPoint presentations make lectures more engaging for students. Correlated to the chapters of your Pearson textbook, each presentation includes a full lecture script, discussion questions, a wealth of images and maps, and links to the full array of MyHistoryLab media.

## MyTest Test Bank

Containing a diverse set of multiple choice and essay questions, the MyTest test bank supports a variety of assessment strategies. The large pool of multiple choice questions for each chapter includes factual, conceptual, and analytical questions, so that instructors may assess students on basic information as well as critical thinking.

## Customer Support

Pearson's dedicated team of local representatives will work with you not only to choose course materials but also to integrate them into your class and assess their effectiveness. Moreover, live support for MyHistoryLab users, both educators and students, is available 24/7.

# 16 Reconstruction
## 1865–1877

## One American Journey

A Memoir

*Marianna, Florida 1866*

**The white academy opened** about the same time the church opened the school for the Negro children. As the colored children had to pass the academy to reach the church it was easy for the white children to annoy them with taunts and jeers. The war passed from words to stones which the white children began to hurl at the colored. Several colored children were hurt and, as they had not resented the rock-throwing in kind because they were timid about going that far, the white children became more aggressive and abusive.

One morning the colored children armed themselves with stones and determined to fight their way past the academy to their school. [They] approached the academy in formation whereas in the past they had been going in pairs or small groups. When they reached hailing distance, a half dozen white boys rushed out and hurled their missiles. Instead of scampering away, the colored children not

"A Hunger to Learn." This 1863 watercolor by Henry L. Stephens depicts an elderly African American, probably a former slave, learning to read. The newspaper's headline states, "Presidential Proclamation, Slavery." Learning transcended age among freed blacks in the South.

## LEARNING OBJECTIVE

| 16.1 | 16.2 | 16.3 | 16.4 | 16.5 |
|---|---|---|---|---|
| How did white southerners respond to defeat? p. 451 | Why did black aspirations generate southern white violence? p. 453 | How did Congressional Reconstruction change the status of the former slaves in the South? p. 459 | How were white northerners and the federal government complicit in denying freed slaves the basic rights of American citizenship? p. 468 | How and why did Reconstruction end? p. 473 |

Listen to Chapter 16 on MyHistoryLab

From *The American Journey*, Seventh Edition. Goldfield, Abbott, Anderson, Argersinger, Argersinger and Barney Copyright © 2014 by Pearson Education, Inc. All rights reserved.

# Watch the Video Series on MyHistoryLab

Learn about some key topics related to this chapter with the *MyHistoryLab Video Series: Key Topics in U.S. History.*

**1** **Reconstruction and Its Missed Opportunities: 1865–1877** This overview video introduces critical issues that arose during the post–Civil War period known as Reconstruction, when the former Confederacy was reincorporated into the United States and the freed slaves received their first taste of U.S. citizenship. It examines how presidents Abraham Lincoln, Andrew Johnson, and Ulysses S. Grant dealt with Congress in achieving the goals of Reconstruction, including the constitutional amendments intended to protect the rights of freedmen and the policies to rebuild the South and reconcile it to a stronger federal government.

 Watch on MyHistoryLab

**The Amendments of Freedom** Between 1865 and 1869, Congress passed the Thirteenth, Fourteenth, and Fifteenth Amendments to the Constitution, ending slavery, guaranteeing citizenship, and extending voting rights. This video reveals how these constitutional changes were enacted to protect the citizenship and rights of African Americans, including the formation of agencies such as the Freedman's Bureau. Despite the efforts of the federal government, however, southern states passed Black Codes and engaged in other repressive measures that lasted generations. **2**

Watch on MyHistoryLab 

**3** **Presidential Reconstruction** This video explains how Abraham Lincoln established the precedent of presidential Reconstruction through his legalistic interpretation of the Civil War as an armed rebellion within the United States, thereby enabling himself as commander in chief to control the definition and progress of Reconstruction. His successor, Andrew Johnson, met with stiff resistance from Radical Republicans in Congress who wanted Reconstruction to be a harsh process for the former Confederate states.

 Watch on MyHistoryLab

**The Compromise of 1877** The twelve years of federal occupation and Reconstruction came to an end in the South when its electoral delegates guaranteed Rutherford B. Hayes's victory in the 1876 election in exchange for the withdrawal of the remaining federal troops from the states of the former Confederacy, effectively ending southern Reconstruction. This video examines the Compromise of 1877, the political deal that made Hayes's victory possible. **4**

Watch on MyHistoryLab 

only stood their ground and hurled their missiles but maintained a solemn silence. The white children, seeing there was no backing down as they expected, came rushing out of the academy and charged the colored children.

During some fifteen minutes it was a real tug of war. In the close fighting the colored children got the advantage gradually and began to shove the white children back. As they pressed the advantage the white children broke away and ran for the academy. The colored fighters did not follow them but made it hot for the laggards until they also took to their heels. There were many bruises on both sides, but it taught the white youngsters to leave the colored ones alone thereafter.

T. Thomas Fortune, "Norfolk Journal and Guide," August 20, 1927, reprinted in Dorothy Sterling, ed., *The Trouble They Seen: Black People Tell the Story of Reconstruction*, Doubleday, 1976, pp. 22–24.

## Personal Journeys Online

- N. J. Bell, *Southern Railroad Man*, 1865. A railroad conductor recalls the aftermath of the Civil War and its impact on a white family in Wilmington, North Carolina.
- Adelbert Ames, *Letter from the Republican Governor of Mississippi*, 1875. Letter to his wife expressing frustration at the violence against black voters in his state and his hope for federal intervention.

**T**homas Fortune felt that this incident encapsulated the dilemma of Reconstruction. In the journey from slavery to freedom, education emerged as an important element of full citizenship for African Americans. It was their "ticket" to economic independence, as it was for all Americans. When Thomas realized he could not obtain that ticket in the South, he journeyed north to New York City, where he obtained a job as a printer for the *New York Sun*. New York's gain was the South's loss, a process repeated many times over as talented young black men and women migrated north. It was a double tragedy for the South: losing people who could have rebuilt a shattered region and missing the opportunity to create a society based on racial equality.

Southern whites found the notion of black independence both ludicrous and frightening. Slavery may have ended, but subservience should not, whites believed. The eagerness with which black children (and adults) embraced education implied a pretense of equality, which whites could not accept. They resisted full black citizenship, often violently.

Reconstruction, though, was more than a story of white resistance against black aspirations. What is remarkable about the period is that African Americans continued to press for political, economic, and social rights in the face of withering and often violent white opposition. Most black resistance was futile, as Thomas would eventually discover. But if the failure of African Americans to attain the basic rights of the freedom they won during the Civil War cannot be attributed to their lack of effort and desire, it is also true that southern whites were not the only obstacles along the path of the African American journey from slavery to freedom. Not only did white northerners and the federal government ignore the violence, but they also often condoned or at least rationalized it. Reconstruction was not a southern failure; it was a national disgrace.

The position of African Americans in American society was one of the two great issues of the Reconstruction era. The other great issue was how and under what terms to readmit the former Confederate states. Between 1865 and 1867, under President Andrew Johnson's Reconstruction plan, white southerners pretty much had their way with the former slaves and with their own state governments. Congressional action between 1867 and 1870 attempted to balance black rights and home rule, with mixed results. After 1870, white southerners gradually regained control of their states and localities, often through violence and intimidation, denying black southerners their political gains while Republicans in Washington and white northerners lost interest in policing their former enemies.

By the time the last federal troops left the South in 1877, the white southerners had prevailed. The Confederate states had returned to the Union with all of their rights and many of their leaders restored. And the freed slaves remained in mostly subservient positions with few of the rights and privileges enjoyed by other Americans.

# White Southerners and the Ghosts of the Confederacy, 1865

**16.1** How did white southerners respond to defeat?

**T**o understand how white southerners reacted to black aspirations after the Civil War, it is necessary to understand what whites saw, thought, and felt as they coped with the consequences of their defeat. Confederate soldiers, generals and troops alike, returned to devastated homes. General Braxton Bragg returned to his "once prosperous" Alabama home to find "all, all was lost, except my debts." Bragg and his wife found temporary shelter in a slave cabin. Yeomen farmers, the backbone of the Confederacy, found uprooted fences, farm animals dead or gone, and buildings destroyed. They and their families wandered about in a living nightmare, seeking shelter where they could. They lived in morbid fear of vengeful former slaves or the hated Yankee soldiers wreaking more damage.

Nathaniel Bell, a former Confederate soldier, was lucky enough to get a job on the North Carolina Railroad in 1865. Every two weeks, Bell enjoyed a two-day layover in the coastal city of Wilmington. "On one of these occasions," he wrote, "a small boy and little girl, both pretty children, came to me and asked me for something to eat. I gave them all the meat, bread, potatoes, and syrup that they could carry away. They were very proud of this. They said their father was killed in the war, and that their mother and grandmother were both sick. Some months afterwards I was passing by the same place where I saw the children, and a man got on my train. . . . I asked him about the two children. . . . He said the little boy and girl starved to death."

The casualties of war in the South continued long after the hostilities ceased. These were hardly the only cases of starvation that stalked the defeated region in the months after the surrender. Although soldiers of both sides would experience difficulty in reentering civilian life, the southerner's case was the more difficult because of the economic devastation, the psychological burdens of defeat, and the break-up of families through death, migration, or poverty. Cities such as Richmond, Atlanta, and Columbia lay in ruins; farmsteads were stripped of everything but the soil; infrastructure, especially railroads, was damaged or destroyed; factories and machinery were demolished; and at least 5 million bales of cotton, the major cash crop, had gone up in smoke. Add a worthless currency, and the loss was staggering, climbing into hundreds of billions of dollars in today's currency.

Their cause lost and their society destroyed, white southerners lived through the summer and fall of 1865 surrounded by ghosts, the ghosts of lost loved ones, joyful times, bountiful harvests, self-assurance, and slavery. Defeat shook the basic tenets of their religious beliefs. A North Carolinian cried, "Oh, our God! What sins we must have been guilty of that we should be so humiliated by Thee now!" Some praised God for delivering the South from the sin of slavery. A Virginia woman expressed thanks that "we white people are no longer permitted to go on in such wickedness, heaping up more and more wrath of God upon our devoted heads." But many other white southerners refused to accept their defeat as a divine judgment. How could they, as a devout people, believe that God had abandoned them? Instead, they insisted, God had spared the South for a greater purpose. They came to view the war as the **Lost Cause** and interpreted it, not as a lesson in humility, but as an episode in the South's journey to salvation. Robert E. Lee became the patron saint of this cause, his poignant nobility a contrast to the crassness of the Yankee warlords. White southerners transformed the bloody struggle into a symbol of courage against great odds and piety against sin. Eventually, they believed, redemption would come.

The southern white view of the Civil War (and of Reconstruction) was not a deliberate attempt to falsify history, but rather a need to justify and rationalize the devastation that accompanied defeat. This view, in which the war became the Lost Cause, and Reconstruction became the Redemption, also served to forge a community among white southerners at a time of great unrest. A common religion solidified the bond and sanctified it. The Lost Cause also enabled white southerners to move on with their lives and concentrate on rebuilding their shattered region. The Lost Cause was a historical rationalization that enabled believers to hope for a better future. The regrettable feature of elevating the Civil War to a noble, holy enterprise was that it implied a stainless Old South, a civilization worth fighting and dying for. This new history required the return of the freedmen, if not to the status of slaves, then at least to a lowly place in society. This new history also ignored the savagery of the war by romanticizing the conflict.

**Lost Cause** The phrase many white southerners applied to their Civil War defeat. They viewed the war as a noble cause and their defeat as only a temporary setback in the South's ultimate vindication.

The Lost Cause would exist not merely as a memory, but also as a three-dimensional depiction of southern history, in rituals and celebrations, and as the educational foundation for future generations. The statues of the Confederate common soldier erected typically on the most important site in a town, the courthouse square; the commemorations of Confederate Memorial Day, the birthdays of prominent Confederate leaders, and the reunions of veterans, all marked with flourishing oratory, brass bands, parades, and related spectacles; and the textbooks implanting the white history of the South in young minds and carrying the legacy down through the generations—all of these ensured that the Lost Cause would be not only an interpretation of the past, but also the basic reality of the present and the foundation for the future.

Most white southerners approached the great issues of freedom and reunification with unyielding views. They saw African Americans as adversaries whose attempts at self-improvement were a direct challenge to white people's belief in their own racial superiority, a belief endorsed by white southerners' view of the war and the Old South. A black boy like Thomas Fortune could not dream of success, for the very thought confounded the beliefs of southern whites. White southerners saw outside assistance to black southerners as another invasion. The Yankees might have destroyed their families, their farms, and their fortunes, but they would not destroy the racial order. The war may have ended slavery, but white southerners were determined to preserve strict racial boundaries.

# More than Freedom: African American Aspirations in 1865

**16.2** Why did black aspirations generate southern white violence?

Black southerners had a quite different perspective on the Civil War and Reconstruction, seeing the former as a great victory for freedom and the latter as a time of great possibility. But their view did not matter; it was invisible or, worse, distorted, in books, monuments, and official accounts. If, as the British writer George Orwell later argued, "who controls the present controls the past, and who controls the past controls the future," then the vanishing black perspective is not surprising. The ferocity with which white southerners attempted to take back their governments and their social structure was not only about nostalgia; it was also about power and the legitimacy that power conferred.

And, of course, the black perspective was decidedly different from that of whites. To black southerners the Civil War was a war of liberation, not a Lost Cause. The response of southern whites to black aspirations still stunned African Americans, who believed, naïvely perhaps, that what they sought—education, land, access to employment, and equality in law and politics—were basic rights and modest objectives. The former slaves did not initially even dream of social equality; far less did they plot murder and mayhem, as white people feared. They did harbor two potentially contradictory aspirations. The first was to be left alone, free of white supervision. But the former slaves also wanted land, voting and civil rights, and education. To secure these, they needed the intervention and support of the white power structure.

In 1865, African Americans had reason to hope that their dreams of full citizenship might be realized. They enjoyed a reservoir of support for their aspirations among some Republican leaders. The views of James A. Garfield, Union veteran, U.S. congressman, and future president, were typical of these Republicans. Commenting on the ratification of the Thirteenth Amendment, which abolished slavery, Garfield asked, "What is freedom? Is it the bare privilege of not being chained? . . . If this is all, then freedom is a bitter mockery, a cruel delusion."

**Freedmen's Bureau** Agency established by Congress in March 1865 to provide social, educational, and economic services, advice, and protection to former slaves and destitute whites; lasted seven years.

The first step Congress took beyond emancipation was to establish the Bureau of Refugees, Freedmen, and Abandoned Lands in March 1865. Congress envisioned the **Freedmen's Bureau**, as it came to be called, as a multipurpose agency to provide social, educational, and economic services, advice, and protection to former slaves and destitute white southerners. The bureau marked the federal government's first foray into social welfare legislation. Congress also authorized the bureau to rent confiscated and abandoned farmland to freedmen in 40-acre plots, with an option to buy. This auspicious beginning belied the great disappointments that lay ahead.

## Education

The greatest success of the Freedmen's Bureau was in education. The bureau coordinated more than fifty northern philanthropic and religious groups, which, in turn, established 3,000 freedmen's schools in the South, serving 150,000 men, women, and children.

Initially, single young women from the Northeast comprised much of the teaching force. One of them, 26-year-old Martha Schofield, came to Aiken, South Carolina, from rural Pennsylvania in 1865. Like many of her colleagues, she had joined the abolitionist movement as a teenager and decided to make teaching her life's work. Her strong Quaker beliefs reflected the importance of Protestant Christianity in motivating the young missionaries. When her sponsoring agency, the Pennsylvania Freedmen's Relief Association, folded in 1871, her school closed. Undaunted, she opened another school on her own, and, despite chronic financial problems and the hostility of Aiken's white citizens, she and the school endured. (Since 1953, her school has been part of the Aiken public school system.)

By the time Schofield opened her school in 1871, black teachers outnumbered white teachers in the "colored" schools. The financial troubles of northern missionary societies and white northerners' declining interest in the freedmen's condition opened opportunities for black teachers. Support for them came from black churches, especially the African Methodist Episcopal (AME) Church.

The former slaves crowded into basements, shacks, and churches to attend school. "The children . . . hurry to school as soon as their work is over," wrote a teacher in Norfolk, Virginia, in 1867. "The plowmen hurry from the field at night to get their hour of study. Old men and women strain their dim sight with the book two and a half feet distant from the eye, to catch the shape of the letter. I call this heaven-inspired interest."

At the end of the Civil War, only about 10 percent of black southerners were literate, compared with more than 70 percent of white southerners. Within a decade, black literacy had risen above 30 percent. Joseph Wilson, a former slave, attributed the rise to "this longing of ours for freedom of the mind as well as the body."

Some black southerners went on to one of the thirteen colleges established by the American Missionary Association and black and white churches. Between 1860 and 1880, more than 1,000 black southerners earned college degrees at institutions still serving students today, such as Howard University in Washington, D.C., Fisk University in Nashville, Hampton Institute (now University), Tuskegee Institute, and Biddle Institute (now Johnson C. Smith University) in Charlotte.

Pursuing freedom of the mind involved challenges beyond those of learning to read and write. Many white southerners condemned efforts at "Negro improvement." They viewed the time spent on education as wasted, forcing the former slaves to catch their lessons in bits and pieces between work, often by candlelight or on Sundays. White southerners also harassed white female teachers, questioning their morals and threatening people who rented rooms to them. After the Freedmen's Bureau folded in 1872 and many of the northern societies that supported freedmen's education collapsed or cut back their involvement, education for black southerners became more haphazard.

▶ **Watch the Video** The Schools That the Civil War and Reconstruction Created

The Freedmen's Bureau, northern churches, and missionary societies established more than 3,000 schools, attended by some 150,000 men, women, and children in the years after the Civil War. At first, mostly young white women from the Northeast staffed these schools, as at this one in Georgia. Note the wide age range, which indicates that the thirst for learning spanned generations.

## "Forty Acres and a Mule"

Although education was important to the freed slaves in their quest for civic equality, land ownership offered them the promise of economic independence. For generations, black people had worked southern farms and had received nothing for their labor.

An overwhelmingly agricultural people, freedmen looked to farm ownership as a key element in their transition from slavery to freedom. "Gib us our own land and we take care of ourselves," a Charleston freedman asserted to a northern visitor in 1865. Even before the war's end, rumors circulated through black communities in the South that the government would provide each black family with 40 acres and a mule. These rumors were fueled by General William T. Sherman's **Field Order No. 15** in January 1865, which set aside a vast swath of abandoned land along the South Atlantic coast from the Charleston area to northern Florida for grants of up to 40 acres. The Freedmen's Bureau likewise raised expectations when it was initially authorized to rent 40-acre plots of confiscated or abandoned land to freedmen.

By June 1865, about 40,000 former slaves had settled on Sherman land along the southeastern coast. In 1866, Congress passed the **Southern Homestead Act**, giving black people preferential access to public lands in five southern states. Two years later, the Republican government of South Carolina initiated a land-redistribution program financed by the sale of state bonds. The state used proceeds from the bond sales to purchase farmland, which it then resold to freedmen, who paid for it with state-funded, long-term, low-interest loans. By the late 1870s, more than 14,000 African American families had taken advantage of this program.

**Field Order No. 15** Order by General William T. Sherman in January 1865 to set aside abandoned land along the southern Atlantic coast for 40-acre grants to freedmen; rescinded by President Andrew Johnson later that year.

**Southern Homestead Act** Largely unsuccessful law passed in 1866 that gave black people preferential access to public lands in five southern states.

Land ownership did not ensure financial success. Most black-owned farms were small and on marginal land. The value of these farms in 1880 was roughly half that of white-owned farms. Black farmers also had trouble obtaining credit to purchase or expand their holdings. A lifetime of fieldwork left some freedmen without the managerial skills to operate a farm. The hostility of white neighbors also played a role in thwarting black aspirations. Black farmers often had the most success when groups of families settled together, as in the farm community of Promise Land in up-country South Carolina.

The vast majority of former slaves, however, especially those in the Lower South, never fulfilled their dreams of land ownership. Rumors to the contrary, the federal government never intended to implement a land-redistribution program in the South. General Sherman viewed his field order as a temporary measure to support freedmen for the remainder of the war. President Andrew Johnson nullified the order in September 1865, returning confiscated land to its former owners. Even Republican supporters of black land ownership questioned the constitutionality of seizing privately owned real estate. Most of the land-redistribution programs that emerged after the war, including government-sponsored programs, required black farmers to have capital. But in the impoverished postwar economy of the South, it was difficult for them to acquire it.

Republican Party rhetoric of the 1850s extolled the virtues and dignity of free labor over the degradation of slave labor. Free labor usually meant working for a wage or under some other contractual arrangement. But unlike slaves, according to the then prevailing view, free laborers could enjoy the fruits of their work and might someday become owners or entrepreneurs themselves. It was self-help, not government assistance, that guaranteed individual success. After the war, many white northerners envisioned former slaves assuming the status of free laborers, not necessarily of independent landowners.

Most of the officials of the Freedmen's Bureau shared these views and therefore saw reviving the southern economy as a higher priority than helping former slaves acquire farms. They wanted to both get the crop in the field and start the South on the road to a free labor system. Thus, they encouraged freedmen to work for their former masters under contract and to postpone their quest for land.

At first, agents of the Freedmen's Bureau supervised labor contracts between former slaves and masters. But after 1867, bureau surveillance declined. Agents assumed that both black laborers and white landowners had become accustomed to the mutual obligations of contracts. The bureau, however, underestimated the power of white landowners to coerce favorable terms or to ignore those they did not like. Contracts implied a mutuality that most planters could not accept in their relations with former slaves. As the northern journalist Whitelaw Reid noted in 1865, planters "have no sort of conception of free labor. They do not comprehend any law for controlling laborers, save the law of force."

By the late 1870s, most former slaves in the rural South had been drawn into a subservient position in a new labor system called **sharecropping**. The premise of this system was relatively simple: The landlord furnished the sharecroppers with a house, a plot of land to work, seed, some farm animals, and farm implements and advanced them credit at a store the landlord typically owned. In exchange, the sharecroppers promised the landlord a share of their crop, usually one-half. The croppers kept the proceeds from the sale of the other half to pay off their debts at the store and save or spend as they and their families saw fit. In theory, a sharecropper could save enough to secure economic independence.

But white landlords perceived black independence as both contradictory and subversive. With landlords keeping the accounts at the store, black sharecroppers found that the proceeds from their share of the crop never left them very far ahead. Not all white landlords cheated their tenants, but given the sharecroppers' innocence regarding accounting methods and crop pricing, the temptation to do so was great.

**sharecropping** Labor system that evolved during and after Reconstruction whereby landowners furnished laborers with a house, farm animals, and tools and advanced credit in exchange for a share of the laborers' crop.

## Migration to Cities

Even before the hope of land ownership faded, African Americans looked for alternatives to secure their personal and economic independence. Before the war, the city had offered slaves and free black people a measure of freedom unknown in the rural South. After the war, African Americans moved to cities to find families, seek work, escape the tedium and supervision of farm life, or simply to test their right to move about.

For the same reasons, white people disapproved of black migration to the city. It reduced the labor pool for farms. It also gave black people more opportunities to associate with white people of similar social status, to compete for jobs, and to establish schools, churches, and social organizations, fueling their hopes for racial equality. Between 1860 and 1870, the African American population in every major southern city rose significantly. In Atlanta, for example, black people accounted for one in five residents in 1860 and nearly one in two by 1870. Some freedmen came to cities initially to reunite with their families. Every city newspaper after the war carried advertisements from former slaves seeking their mates and children. In 1865, the Nashville *Colored Tennessean* carried this poignant plea: "During the year 1849, Thomas Sample carried away from this city, as his slaves, our daughter, Polly, and son. . . . We will give $100 each for them to any person who will assist them. . . to get to Nashville, or get word to us of their whereabouts."

Once in the city, freedmen had to find a home and a job. They usually settled on the outskirts of town, where building codes did not apply. Rather than developing one large ghetto, as happened in many northern cities, black southerners lived in small concentrations in and around cities. Sometimes armed with a letter of reference from their former masters, black people went door to door to seek employment. Many found work serving white families, as guards, laundresses, or maids, for very low wages. Both skilled and unskilled laborers found work rebuilding war-torn cities like Atlanta. Frederick Ayer, a Freedmen's Bureau agent in Atlanta, reported to a colleague in 1866 that "many of the whites are making most vigorous efforts to retrieve their broken fortunes and . . . rebuild their dwellings and shops. . . . This furnished employment to a large number of colored people as Masons, Carpenters, Teamsters, and Common Workmen."

Most rural black southerners, however, worked as unskilled laborers. The paltry wages men earned, when they could find work, pushed black women into the workforce. They often had an easier time securing a job in cities as domestics and laundresses. Black men had hoped to assert their patriarchal prerogatives, like white men, by keeping wives and daughters out of the labor market, but necessity dictated otherwise. In both Atlanta and Nashville, black people comprised more than 75 percent of the unskilled workforce in 1870. Their wages were at or below subsistence level. A black laborer in Richmond admitted to a journalist in 1870 that he had difficulty making ends meet on $1.50 a day. "It's right hard," he reported. "I have to pay $15 a month rent, and only two little rooms." His family survived because his wife took in laundry, while her mother watched the children. Considering the laborer's struggle, the journalist wondered, "Were not your people better off in slavery?" The man replied, "Oh, no sir! We're a heap better off now. . . . We're men now, but when our masters had us we was only change in their pockets."

## Faith and Freedom

Religious faith framed and inspired the efforts of African Americans to test their freedom on the farm and in the city. White southerners used religion to transform the Lost Cause from a shattering defeat to a premonition of a greater destiny. Black southerners, in contrast, saw emancipation in biblical terms as the beginning of an exodus from bondage to the Promised Land.

Some black churches in the postwar South had originated during the slavery era, but most split from white-dominated congregations after the war. White churchgoers

The black church was the center of African American life in the postwar urban South. Most black churches were founded after the Civil War, but some, such as the First African Baptist Church in Richmond, shown here in an 1874 engraving, traced their origins to before 1861.

deplored the expressive style of black worship, and black churchgoers were uncomfortable in congregations that treated them as inferiors. A separate church also reduced white surveillance.

The church became a primary focus of African American life. It gave black people the opportunity to hone skills in self-government and administration that white-dominated society denied them. Within the supportive confines of the congregation, they could assume leadership positions, render important decisions, deal with financial matters, and engage in politics. The church also operated as an educational institution. Local governments, especially in rural areas, rarely constructed public schools for black people; churches often served that function.

The desire to read the Bible inspired thousands of former slaves to attend the church school. The church also spawned other organizations that served the black community, such as burial societies, Masonic lodges, temperance groups, trade unions, and drama clubs. African Americans took great pride in their churches, which became visible measures of their progress. The church enforced family and religious values, punishing violators guilty of such infractions as adultery. Black churchwomen, both working class and middle class, were especially prominent in the family-oriented organizations.

The efforts of former slaves in the classroom, on the farm, in cities, and in the churches reflect the enthusiasm and expectations with which black southerners greeted freedom and raised the hopes of those who came to help them. But the majority of white southerners were unwilling to see those expectations fulfilled. For this reason, African Americans could not secure the fruits of their emancipation without the support and protection of the federal government. The issue of freedom was therefore inextricably linked to the other great issue of the era, the rejoining of the Confederacy to the Union, as expressed in federal Reconstruction policy.

# Federal Reconstruction, 1865–1870

**16.3** How did Congressional Reconstruction change the status of the former slaves in the South?

When the Civil War ended in 1865, no acceptable blueprint existed for reconstituting the Union. President Lincoln believed that a majority of white southerners were Unionists at heart, and that they could and should undertake the task of reconstruction. He favored a conciliatory policy toward the South in order, as he put it in one of his last letters, "to restore the Union, so as to make it . . . a Union of hearts and hands as well as of States." He counted on the loyalists to be fair with respect to the rights of the former slaves.

As early as 1863, Lincoln had proposed to readmit a seceding state if 10 percent of its prewar voters took an oath of loyalty to the Union, and it prohibited slavery in a new state constitution. But this Ten Percent Plan did not require states to grant equal civil and political rights to former slaves, and many Republicans in Congress thought it was not stringent enough. In 1864, a group of them responded with the Wade-Davis Bill, which required a majority of a state's prewar voters to pledge their loyalty to the Union and demanded guarantees of black equality before the law. The bill was passed at the end of a congressional session, but Lincoln kept it from becoming law by refusing to sign it (an action known as a "pocket veto").

Lincoln, of course, died before he could implement a Reconstruction plan. His views on reconstructing the Union during the war did not necessarily prefigure how his views would have unfolded after the war. Given his commitment in the Gettysburg Address to promote "a new birth of freedom," it is likely that had white southerners resisted black civil rights, Lincoln would have responded with harsher terms. Above all, Lincoln was a savvy politician: He would not have allowed a stalemate to develop between himself and the Congress, and, if necessary, he would have moved closer to the radical camp. On April 11, 1865, in one of his last pronouncements on Reconstruction, Lincoln stated that he favored a limited suffrage for the freedmen, though he admitted that each state had enough peculiarities that a blanket policy might not work. In a cabinet meeting on April 14, he dismissed an idea for military occupation, though he acknowledged that allowing the states to reconstruct themselves might not work either. In any case, his successor, Andrew Johnson, lacked his flexibility and political acumen.

The controversy over the plans introduced during the war reflected two obstacles to Reconstruction that would continue to plague the ruling Republicans after the war. First, neither the Constitution nor legal precedent offered any guidance on whether the president or Congress should take the lead on Reconstruction policy. Second, there was no agreement on what that policy should be. Proposals requiring various preconditions for readmitting a state, loyalty oaths, new constitutions with certain specific provisions, guarantees of freedmen's rights—all provoked vigorous debate.

President Andrew Johnson, some conservative Republicans, and most Democrats believed that because the Constitution made no mention of secession, the southern states had been in rebellion but had never left the Union, and therefore that there was no need for a formal process to readmit them. Moderate and radical Republicans disagreed, arguing that the defeated states had forfeited their rights. Moderates and radicals parted company, however, on the conditions necessary for readmission to the Union. The radicals wanted to treat the former Confederate states as territories, or "conquered provinces," subject to congressional legislation. Moderates wanted to grant the seceding states more autonomy and limit federal intervention in their affairs while they satisfied the conditions of readmission. Neither group held a majority in Congress, and legislators sometimes changed their positions (see Table 16.1).

**Watch the Video**   The Promise and Failure of Reconstruction

TABLE 16.1 CONTRASTING VIEWS OF RECONSTRUCTION: PRESIDENT AND CONGRESS

| Politician or Group | Policy on Former Slaves | Policy on Readmission of Former Confederate States |
|---|---|---|
| President Johnson | Opposed to black suffrage | Maintained that rebellious states were already readmitted |
| | Silent on protection of black civil rights | Granted pardons and restoration of property to all who swore allegiance to the United States |
| | Opposed to land redistribution | |
| Radical Republicans | Favored black suffrage | Favored treating rebellious states as territories and establishing military districts* |
| | Favored protection of black civil rights | Favored limiting franchise to black people and loyal white people |
| | Favored land redistribution | |
| Moderate Republicans | Favored black suffrage* | Favored some restrictions on white suffrage** |
| | Favored protection of civil rights | Favored requiring states to meet various requirements before being readmitted* |
| | Opposed land redistribution | Split on military rule |

*After 1866.

**True of most but not all members of the group.

## Presidential Reconstruction, 1865–1867

When the Civil War ended in April 1865, Congress was not in session and would not reconvene until December. Thus, the responsibility for developing a Reconstruction policy initially fell on Andrew Johnson, who succeeded to the presidency upon Lincoln's assassination. Johnson seemed well suited to the difficult task. He was born in humble circumstances in North Carolina in 1808. He learned the tailoring trade and struck out for Tennessee as a teenager to open a tailor shop in the eastern Tennessee town of Greenville. Obtaining his education informally, he prospered modestly, purchased a few slaves, and began to pursue politics. He was elected alderman, mayor, state legislator, congressman, governor, and then, in 1856, U.S. senator. Johnson was the only southern senator to remain in the U.S. Senate after secession. This defiant Unionism won him acclaim in the North and credibility among Republican leaders, who welcomed him into their party. During the war, as military governor of Tennessee, he solidified his Republican credentials by advocating the abolition of slavery in Tennessee and severe punishment of Confederate leaders. His views landed him on the Republican ticket as the candidate for vice president in 1864. Indiana Republican congressman George W. Julian, who advocated harsh terms for the South and broad rights for black people, viewed Johnson's accession to the presidency in 1865 as "a godsend."

Most northerners, including many Republicans, approved Johnson's Reconstruction plan when he unveiled it in May 1865. Johnson extended pardons and restored property rights, except in slaves, to southerners who swore an oath of allegiance to the Union and the Constitution. Southerners who had held prominent posts in the Confederacy, however, and those with more than $20,000 in taxable property, had to petition the president directly for a pardon, a reflection of Johnson's disdain for wealthy whites. The plan said nothing about the voting rights or civil rights of former slaves. President Johnson, like many of his northern colleagues, was firm in his belief in the inferiority of African Americans, a status which would make them unfit to vote. As he explained, "it must be acknowledged that in the progress of nations Negroes have shown less capacity for government than any other race of people."

Northern Democrats applauded the plan's silence on these issues and its promise of a quick restoration of the southern states to the Union. They expected the southern states to favor their party and expand its political power. Republicans approved the plan because it restored property rights to white southerners, although some wanted it to provide for black suffrage. Republicans also hoped that Johnson's conciliatory terms might attract some white southerners to the Republican Party.

On the two great issues of freedom and reunion, white southerners quickly demonstrated their eagerness to reverse the results of the Civil War. Although most states accepted President Johnson's modest requirements, several objected to one or more of them. Mississippi and Texas refused to ratify the Thirteenth Amendment, which abolished slavery. Alabama accepted only parts of the amendment. South Carolina declined to nullify its secession ordinance. No southern state authorized black voting. When Johnson ordered special congressional elections in the South in the fall of 1865, the all-white electorate returned many prominent Confederate leaders to office.

In late 1865, the newly elected southern state legislatures revised their antebellum slave codes. The updated **black codes** allowed local officials to arrest black people who could not document employment and residence or who were "disorderly" and sentence them to forced labor on farms or road crews. The codes also restricted black people to certain occupations, barred them from jury duty, and forbade them to possess firearms. Apprenticeship laws permitted judges to take black children from parents who could not, in the judges' view, adequately support them. Given the widespread poverty in the South in 1865, the law could apply to almost any freed black family. Northerners looking for contrition in the South found no sign of it. Worse, President Johnson did not seem perturbed about this turn of events.

The Republican-dominated Congress reconvened in December 1865 in a belligerent mood. When radicals, who comprised nearly half of the Republican Party's strength in Congress, could not unite behind a program, their moderate colleagues took the first step toward a congressional Reconstruction plan. The moderates shared the radicals' desire to protect the former slaves' civil rights. But they would not support land-redistribution schemes or punitive measures against prominent Confederates, and disagreed on extending voting rights to the freedmen. The moderates' first measure, passed in early 1866, extended the life of the Freedmen's Bureau and authorized it to punish state officials who failed to extend equal civil rights to black citizens. But President Johnson vetoed the legislation.

Undeterred, Congress passed the Civil Rights Act of 1866 in direct response to the black codes. The act specified the civil rights to which all U.S. citizens were entitled. In creating a category of national citizenship with rights that superseded state laws, the act changed federal-state relations (and in the process overturned the *Dred Scott* decision). President Johnson vetoed the act, but it became law when Congress mustered a two-thirds majority to override his veto, the first time in American history that Congress passed major legislation over a president's veto.

To keep freedmen's rights safe from presidential vetoes, state legislatures, and federal courts, the Republican-dominated Congress moved to incorporate some of the provisions of the 1866 Civil Rights Act into the Constitution. The **Fourteenth Amendment**, which Congress passed in June 1866, addressed the issues of civil and voting rights. It guaranteed every citizen equality before the law. The two key sections of the amendment prohibited states from violating the civil rights of their citizens, thus outlawing the black codes, and gave states the choice of enfranchising black people or losing representation in Congress. Some radical Republicans expressed disappointment that the amendment, in a reflection of northern ambivalence, failed to give the vote to black people outright.

The amendment also disappointed advocates of woman suffrage, for the first time using the word *male* in the Constitution to define who could vote. Wendell Phillips, a prominent abolitionist, counseled women, "One question at a time. This hour belongs to the Negro." Susan B. Anthony, who had campaigned for the abolition of slavery before the war and helped mount a petition drive that collected 400,000 signatures for the Thirteenth Amendment, founded the American Equal Rights Association in 1866 with her colleagues to push for woman suffrage at the state level.

**black codes** Laws passed by states and municipalities denying many rights of citizenship to free blacks before the Civil War. Also, during the Reconstruction era, laws passed by newly elected southern state legislatures to control black labor, mobility, and employment.

**Fourteenth Amendment** Constitutional amendment passed by Congress in April 1866 incorporating some of the features of the Civil Rights Act of 1866. It prohibited states from violating the civil rights of their citizens and offered states the choice of allowing black people to vote or losing representation in Congress.

((( • 📖 **Read the Document** *Jourdon Anderson, Letter to His Former Master (1865)*

"Selling a Freeman to Pay His Fine at Monticello, Florida." This 1867 engraving shows how the black codes of the early Reconstruction era reduced former slaves to virtually their pre–Civil War status. Scenes like this convinced northerners that the white South was unrepentant and prompted congressional Republicans to devise their own Reconstruction plans.

The Fourteenth Amendment had little immediate impact on the South. Although enforcement of black codes diminished, white violence against black people increased. In the 1870s, several decisions by the U.S. Supreme Court weakened the amendment's provisions. Eventually, however, it would play a major role in securing the civil rights of African Americans.

President Johnson encouraged southern white intransigence by openly denouncing the Fourteenth Amendment. In August 1866, at the start of the congressional election campaign, he undertook an unprecedented tour of key northern states to sell his message of sectional reconciliation to the public. Although listeners appreciated Johnson's desire for peace, they questioned his claims of southern white loyalty to the Union. The president's diatribes against the Republican Congress won him followers in those northern states with a reservoir of opposition to black suffrage. But the tone and manner of his campaign offended many as undignified. In the November elections, the Democrats suffered embarrassing defeats in the North as Republicans managed better than two-thirds majorities in both the House and Senate, sufficient to override presidential vetoes. Radical Republicans, joined by moderate colleagues buoyed by the election results and revolted by the president's and the South's intransigence, seized the initiative when Congress reconvened.

## Congressional Reconstruction, 1867–1870

The radicals' first salvo in their attempt to take control of Reconstruction occurred with the passing over President Johnson's veto of the Military Reconstruction Acts. The measures, passed in March 1867, inaugurated a period known as **Congressional Reconstruction** or Radical Reconstruction. With the exception of Tennessee, the only southern state that had ratified the Fourteenth Amendment and been readmitted to the Union, Congress divided the former Confederate states into five military districts, each headed by a general. The commanders' first order of business was to conduct voter-registration campaigns to enroll black people and to bar white people who had held office before the Civil War and supported the Confederacy. The eligible voters would then elect delegates to a state convention to write a new constitution that guaranteed universal manhood suffrage. Once a majority of eligible voters ratified the new constitution and the Fourteenth Amendment, their state would be eligible for readmission to the Union.

The Reconstruction Acts fulfilled the radicals' three major objectives. First, they secured the freedmen's right to vote. Second, they made it likely that southern states would be run by Republican regimes that would enforce the new constitutions, protect former slaves' rights, and maintain the Republican majority in Congress. Finally, they set standards for readmission that required the South to accept the preeminence of the federal government and the end of slavery. These measures seemed appropriate in view of the war's outcome and the freedmen's status, but white southerners, especially those barred from participation, perceived the state and local governments constructed upon the new basis as illegitimate. Many southern whites would never acknowledge the right of these governments and their officials to rule over them.

To limit presidential interference with their policies, Republicans passed the **Tenure of Office Act**, prohibiting the president from removing certain officeholders without the Senate's consent. Johnson, angered at what he believed was an unconstitutional attack on presidential authority, deliberately violated the act by firing Secretary of War Edwin M. Stanton, a leading radical, in February 1868. The House responded by approving articles of impeachment against a president for the first time in American history. That set the stage for the next step prescribed by the Constitution: a Senate trial to determine whether the president should be removed from office.

Johnson had indeed violated the Tenure of Office Act, a measure of dubious constitutionality even to some Republicans, but enough Republicans felt that his actions fell short of the "high crimes and misdemeanors" standard set by the Constitution for dismissal from office. Seven Republicans deserted their party, and Johnson was acquitted. The seven Republicans who voted against their party did so not out of respect for Johnson but because they feared that a conviction would damage the office of the presidency and violate the constitutional separation of powers. The outcome weakened the radicals and eased the way for Ulysses S. Grant, a moderate Republican, to gain the party's nomination for president in 1868.

The Republicans viewed the 1868 presidential election as a referendum on Congressional Reconstruction. They supported black suffrage in the South but equivocated on allowing African Americans to vote in the North. Black northerners could vote in only eight of the twenty-two northern states, and between 1865 and 1869, white northerners rejected equal suffrage referendums in eight of eleven states. Republicans "waved the bloody shirt," reminding voters of Democratic disloyalty, the sacrifices of war, and the peace only Republicans could redeem. Democrats denounced Congressional Reconstruction as federal tyranny and, in openly racist appeals, warned white voters that a Republican victory would mean black rule. Grant won the election, but his margin of victory was uncomfortably narrow. Reflecting growing ambivalence in the North over

**Congressional Reconstruction** Name given to the period 1867–1870 when the Republican-dominated Congress controlled Reconstruction era policy. It is sometimes known as Radical Reconstruction, after the radical faction in the Republican Party.

**Tenure of Office Act** Passed by the Republican-controlled Congress in 1867 to limit presidential interference with its policies, the act prohibited the president from removing certain officeholders without the Senate's consent. President Andrew Johnson, angered at what he believed to be an unconstitutional attack on presidential authority, deliberately violated the act by firing Secretary of War Edwin M. Stanton. The House responded by approving articles of impeachment against a president for the first time in American history.

The Democratic Party ran an openly racist presidential campaign in 1868. This pro-Republican drawing by noted cartoonist Thomas Nast includes three Democratic constituencies: former Confederate soldiers (note the "CSA" on the belt buckle); the Irish or immigrant vote (note the almost simian depiction of the Irishman); and the well-dressed Democratic presidential candidate, Horatio Seymour, sporting a "5th Avenue" button and waving a wallet full of bills, a reference to the corrupt Democratic politics in New York City. The three have their feet on an African American soldier. In the background, note the "colored orphan asylum" and "southern school" ablaze, and the lynching of black children.

issues of race and federal authority, New York's Horatio Seymour, the Democratic presidential nominee, probably carried a majority of the nation's white vote. Black voters' overwhelming support for Grant probably provided his margin of victory.

The Republicans retained a strong majority in both houses of Congress and managed to pass another major piece of Reconstruction legislation, the **Fifteenth Amendment**, in February 1869. In response to growing concerns about voter fraud and violence against freedmen, the amendment guaranteed the right of American men to vote, regardless of race. Although the amendment provided a loophole allowing states to restrict the right to vote based on literacy or property qualifications, it was nonetheless a milestone. It made the right to vote perhaps the most distinguishing characteristic of U.S. citizenship.

The Fifteenth Amendment allowed states to keep the franchise a male prerogative, angering many in the woman suffrage movement more than had the Fourteenth Amendment. The resulting controversy severed the ties between the movement and Republican politics. Susan B. Anthony broke with her abolitionist colleagues and opposed the

**Fifteenth Amendment** Passed by Congress in 1869, guaranteed the right of American men to vote, regardless of race.

amendment. A fellow abolitionist and woman suffragist, Elizabeth Cady Stanton, charged that the amendment created an "aristocracy of sex." In an appeal brimming with ethnic and racial animosity, Stanton warned that "if you do not wish the lower orders of Chinese, African, Germans and Irish, with their low ideas of womanhood to make laws for you and your daughters . . . awake to the danger . . . and demand that woman, too, shall be represented in the government!" Such language created a major rift in the nascent women's movement.

## Southern Republican Governments, 1867–1870

Away from Washington, the first order of business for the former Confederacy was to draft state constitutions. The documents embodied progressive principles new to the South. They mandated the election of numerous local and state offices. Self-perpetuating local elites could no longer appoint themselves or cronies to powerful positions. The constitutions committed southern states, many for the first time, to public education. Lawmakers enacted a variety of reforms, including social welfare, penal reform, legislative reapportionment, and universal manhood suffrage.

The Republican regimes that gained control in southern states promoted vigorous state government and the protection of civil and voting rights. Three Republican constituencies supported these governments: native whites, native blacks, and northern transplants. The small native white group was mostly made up of yeomen farmers. Residing mainly in the upland regions of the South and long ignored by lowland planters and merchants in state government, they were left devastated by the war. They struggled to keep their land and hoped for an easing of credit and for debt-stay laws to help them escape foreclosure. They wanted public schools for their children and good roads to get their crops to market. Some urban merchants and large planters also called themselves Republicans. They were attracted to the party's emphasis on economic development, especially railroad construction, and would become prominent in Republican leadership after 1867, forming a majority of the party's elected officials.

Collectively, opponents called these native white southerners **scalawags**. Although their opponents perceived them as a unified group, scalawags held a variety of views. Planters and merchants opposed easy debt and credit arrangements and the use of their taxes to support programs other than railroads or port improvements. Yeomen farmers desperately needed the debt and credit legislation to retain their land. And even though they supported public schools and road building, which would require increased state revenues, they opposed higher taxes.

Northern transplants, or **carpetbaggers**, as many southern whites called them, constituted a second and smaller group of southern Republicans. Thousands of northerners came south during and after the war. Many were Union soldiers who simply enjoyed the climate and perhaps married a local woman. Most were drawn by economic opportunity. Land was cheap and the price of cotton high. Although most carpetbaggers had supported the Republican Party before they moved south, few became politically active until the cotton economy nosedived in 1866. Financial concerns were not all that motivated carpetbaggers to enter politics; some hoped to aid the freedmen.

Carpetbaggers never comprised more than 2 percent of any state's population. Most white southerners viewed them as an alien presence, instruments of a hated occupying force. They estranged themselves from their neighbors by supporting and participating in the Republican state governments that most white people despised. In Alabama, local editors organized a boycott of northern-owned shops. Because many of them tended to support extending political and civil rights to black southerners, carpetbaggers were also often at odds with their fellow white Republicans, the scalawags.

African Americans constituted the Republican Party's largest southern constituency. In three states, South Carolina, Mississippi, and Louisiana, they also constituted the majority of eligible voters. They viewed the franchise as the key to civic equality and economic opportunity and demanded an active role in party and government affairs.

Black people began to take part in southern politics even before the end of the Civil War, especially in cities occupied by Union forces. In February 1865, black people in

**scalawags** Southern whites, mainly small landowning farmers and well-off merchants and planters, who supported the southern Republican Party during Reconstruction for diverse reasons; a disparaging term.

**carpetbaggers** Pejorative term to describe northern transplants to the South, many of whom were Union soldiers who stayed in the South after the war.

## From Then to Now

# African American Voting Rights in the South

R ight from the end of the Civil War, white southerners resisted African American voting rights. Black people, with equal determination, used the franchise to assert their equal right to participate in the political process. Black voting rights proved so contentious that Congress sought to secure them with the Fourteenth and Fifteenth Amendments to the U.S. Constitution. But U.S. Supreme Court decisions in *United States v. Cruikshank* (1876) and in the *Civil Rights Cases* (1883) undermined federal authority to protect the rights of freedmen, including voting rights. A combination of violence, intimidation, and legislation effectively disfranchised black southerners by the early twentieth century.

During the 1960s, Congress passed legislation designed to override state prohibitions and earlier court decisions limiting African American voting rights. The key measure, the 1965 Voting Rights Act, not only guaranteed black southerners (and later, other minorities) the right to register and vote but also protected them from procedural subterfuges. These protections proved necessary because of the extreme racial polarization of southern elections.

To ensure African American candidates an opportunity to win elections, the federal government after 1965 insisted that states and localities establish procedures to increase the likelihood of such a result. By the early 1990s, states were being directed to draw districts with majority-black voting populations to ensure African American representation in the U.S. Congress and in state legislatures. The federal government cited the South's history of racial discrimination and racially polarized voting to justify these districts. But white southerners

The Congressional Black Caucus of the 113th Congress (January 3, 2013–January 3, 2015)

Southern black men during Reconstruction went to great lengths to vote and to protect themselves on election day, as these voters fording a stream with rifles aloft attest.

challenged such claims, as they had more than a century earlier, and their challenges proved partially successful in federal court.

As with the First Reconstruction, the U.S. Supreme Court has narrowed the scope of black voting rights in several decisions since the early 1990s. Despite the history of racial discrimination with respect to voting rights, the Court has often championed the standard of "color-blindness," which justices insist was codified in the Fourteenth Amendment. The principle of color-blindness, however wonderful in the abstract, ignores the history of black voting rights from the Reconstruction era to the present. The framers of the Reconstruction Amendments had the protection of the rights of the freedmen in mind (including and especially voting rights) when they wrote those measures.

The issue of African American voting rights in the South, and the degree to which the federal government may or may not intercede to protect those rights, remains as much at issue as it was more than a century ago. In the 2012 presidential election campaign, civil rights advocates charged that the attempts by more than a dozen states throughout the country to purge voter rolls or to require state-issued voter identification, allegedly to prevent voter fraud, weighed disproportionately against minorities, especially African Americans.

### Question for Discussion

- There is considerable debate about whether the U.S. Constitution is color-blind with respect to voting rights. Should it be?

Norfolk, Virginia, gathered to demand a say in the new government that Union supporters were forming in that portion of the state. In April, they created the Colored Monitor Union Club, modeled after regular Republican Party organizations in northern cities, called **Union Leagues**. They demanded "the right of universal suffrage" for "all loyal men, without distinction of color." Black people in other southern cities held similar meetings, seeking inclusion in the democratic process to protect their freedom. Despite white threats, black southerners thronged to Union League meetings in 1867, even forging interracial alliances in states such as North Carolina and Alabama. Focusing on political education and recruitment, the leagues successfully mobilized black voters. In 1867, more than 90 percent of eligible black voters across the South turned out for elections. Black women, even though they could not vote, also played a role. During the 1868 presidential campaign, for example, black maids and cooks in the South wore buttons touting the candidacy of the Republican presidential nominee, Ulysses S. Grant.

**Union League** A Republican Party organization in northern cities that became an important organizing device among freedmen in southern cities after 1865.

Black southerners were not content just to vote; they also demanded political office. White Republican leaders in the South often took the black vote for granted. But on several occasions after 1867, black people threatened to run independent candidates, support rival Democrats, or simply stay home unless they were represented among Republican nominees. These demands brought them some success. The number of southern black congressmen in the U.S. House of Representatives increased from two in 1869 to seven in 1873, and more than 600 African Americans, most of them former slaves from plantation counties, were elected to southern state legislatures between 1867 and 1877.

White fears that black officeholders would enact vengeful legislation proved unfounded. African Americans generally did not promote race-specific legislation. Rather, they supported measures such as debt relief and state funding for education that benefited all poor and working-class people. Like all politicians, however, black officials in southern cities sought to enact measures beneficial to their constituents, such as roads and sidewalks.

During the first few years of Congressional Reconstruction, Republican governments walked a tightrope, attempting to lure moderate Democrats and unaffiliated white voters into the party without slighting the black vote. They used the lure of patronage power and the attractive salaries that accompanied public office. In 1868, for example, Louisiana's Republican governor, Henry C. Warmoth, appointed white conservatives to state and local offices, which he divided equally between Confederate veterans and black people, and repealed a constitutional provision disfranchising former Confederate officials.

Republicans also gained support by expanding the role of state government to a degree unprecedented in the South. Southern Republican administrations appealed to hard-pressed upland white constituents by prohibiting foreclosure and passing stay laws that allowed farm owners additional time to repay debts. They undertook building programs that benefited black and white citizens, erecting hospitals, schools, and orphanages. Stepping further into social policy than most northern states at the time, Republican governments in the South expanded women's property rights, enacted legislation against child abuse, and required child support from fathers of mulatto children. In South Carolina, the Republican government provided medical care for the poor; in Alabama, it provided free legal aid for needy defendants.

Despite these impressive policies, southern Republicans were unable to hold their diverse constituency together. Although the party had some success among white yeoman farmers, the liberal use of patronage failed to attract white conservatives. At the same time, it alienated the party's core supporters, who resented seeing their former enemies rewarded with lucrative offices.

The high costs of their activist policies further undermined the Republicans by forcing them to raise state taxes. In Mississippi, where the Republican government built a public school system for both black and white students, founded a black university, reorganized the state judiciary, built new courthouses and two state hospitals, and pushed through legislation giving black people equal access to public facilities, the state debt soared to $1.5 million between 1869 and 1873. This was in an era in which state budgets rarely exceeded $1 million. Unprecedented expenditures and the liberal use of patronage sometimes resulted in waste and corruption. Problems like these were not limited to the South, but the perception of dishonesty was nonetheless damaging to governments struggling to build legitimacy among a skeptical white electorate.

The excesses of some state governments, high taxes, contests over patronage, and conflicts over the relative roles of white and black party members opened rifts in Republican ranks. Patronage triggered intraparty warfare. Every office secured by a Democrat created a disappointed Republican. Class tensions erupted in the party as economic development policies sometimes superseded relief and social service legislation supported by small farmers. There were differences among black voters too. In the Lower South, divisions that had developed in the prewar era between urban, lighter-skinned free black people and darker, rural slaves persisted into the Reconstruction era. In many southern states, black clergy, because of their independence from white support and their important spiritual and educational role, became leaders. But most preached salvation in the next world rather than equality in this one, conceding more to white people than to their rank-and-file constituents.

# Counter-Reconstruction, 1870–1874

**16.4** How were white northerners and the federal government complicit in denying freed slaves the basic rights of American citizenship?

Republicans might have survived battles over patronage, policy, expenditures, and taxes, but they could not overcome racism and the violence it generated. Racism killed Republican rule in the South because it deepened divisions within the party, encouraged white violence, and eroded support in the North. Southern Democrats discovered that they could use race baiting and racial violence to create solidarity among white people that overrode their economic and class differences. Unity translated into election victories.

Northerners responded to the persistent violence in the South, not with outrage, but with a growing sense of tedium. They came to accept the arguments of white southerners that it was folly to allow black people to vote and hold office, especially since most northern whites would not extend the franchise to African Americans in their own states. Racism became respectable. Noted intellectuals and journalists espoused "scientific" theories that claimed to demonstrate the natural superiority of white people over black people.

By 1874, Americans were concerned with an array of domestic problems that overshadowed Reconstruction. An economic depression left them more preoccupied with survival than racial justice. Corruption convinced many that politics was part of the nation's problems, not a solution to them. With the rest of the nation thus distracted and weary, white southerners reclaimed control of the South.

## The Uses of Violence

Racial violence preceded Republican rule. As African Americans moved about, attempted to vote, haggled over labor contracts, and carried arms as part of the occupying Union forces, they tested the patience of white southerners, to whom any black assertion of equality seemed threatening. African Americans were the face of whites' defeat, of their world turned upside down. If the war was about slavery, then here was the visible proof of the Confederacy's defeat. Many white southerners viewed the term "free black" less as a status than as an oxymoron. The restoration of white supremacy meant the restoration of order and civilization, an objective southern whites would pursue with vengeance.

White paramilitary groups were responsible for much of the violence directed against African Americans. Probably the best-known of these groups was the **Ku Klux Klan**. Founded in Tennessee by six Confederate veterans in 1866, the Klan was initially a social club. Within a year, the Klan had spread throughout the South. In 1867, when black

**Ku Klux Klan** Perhaps the most prominent of the vigilante groups that terrorized black people in the South during Reconstruction Era, founded by Confederate veterans in 1866.

**Read the Document**     Albion W. Tourgee, Letter on Ku Klux Klan Activities (1870)

The Klan directed violence at African Americans primarily for engaging in political activity. Here, a black man, John Campbell, vainly begs for mercy in Moore County, North Carolina, in August 1871.

people entered politics in large numbers, the Klan unleashed a wave of terror against them. Klan nightriders in ghostlike disguises intimidated black communities. The Klan directed much of its violence toward subverting the electoral process. One historian has estimated that roughly 10 percent of all black delegates to the 1867 state constitutional conventions in the South became victims of political violence during the next decade.

By 1868, white paramilitary organizations permeated the South. Violence was particularly severe in election years in Louisiana, which had a large and active black electorate. The most serious example of political violence in Louisiana occurred in Colfax in 1873 when a white Democratic mob attempted to wrest control of local government from Republicans. For three weeks, black defenders held the town against the white onslaught. When the white mob finally broke through, they massacred the remaining black defenders, including those who had surrendered and laid down their weapons. It was the bloodiest peacetime massacre in nineteenth-century America.

Racial violence and the combative reaction it provoked both among black people and Republican administrations energized white voters. Democrats regained power in North Carolina, for example, after the state's Republican governor enraged white voters by calling out the militia to counter white violence during the election of 1870. That same year, the Republican regime in Georgia fell as well. Some Republican governments countered the violence successfully for a time. Governor Edmund J. Davis of Texas, for example, organized a special force of 200 state policemen to round up Klan nightriders. Between 1870 and 1872, Davis's force arrested 6,000 and broke the Klan in

Texas. But other governors hesitated to enforce laws directed at the Klan, fearing that to do so would further alienate white people.

The federal government responded with a variety of legislation. One example was the Fifteenth Amendment. Another was the Enforcement Act of 1870, which authorized the federal government to appoint supervisors in states that failed to protect voting rights. When violence and intimidation persisted, Congress followed with a second, more sweeping measure, the Ku Klux Klan Act of 1871. This law permitted federal authorities, with military assistance, if necessary, to arrest and prosecute members of groups that denied a citizen's civil rights if state authorities failed to do so. The Klan Act was not successful in curbing racial violence, as the Colfax Massacre in 1873 made vividly clear. But with it, Congress, by claiming the right to override state authority to bring individuals to justice, established a new precedent in federal-state relations.

## Northern Complicity

The success of political violence after 1871 reflected both a declining commitment on the part of northern Republicans to support southern Republican administrations and a growing hostility of white northerners to southern black aspirations. The erosion of northern support for Congressional Reconstruction began as early as 1867 when three states, Minnesota, Ohio, and Kansas, defeated black suffrage amendments. Could Congressional Republicans force whites in, say, Alabama, to accept African American voting, when their own constituents in the North opposed the franchise for blacks?

That northern base grew increasingly skeptical about Reconstruction policy in general and assistance to the freedmen in particular. Many Northern Republicans looked around their cities and saw the local political scene infested with unqualified immigrant voters and corruption. New York City's Democratic boss William M. Tweed and his associates bilked the city of an astounding $100 million dollars. When white southerners charged that unqualified blacks and grasping carpetbaggers corrupted the political process in the South, northerners recognized the argument.

Changing perceptions in the North also indicated a convergence of racial views with white southerners. As radical Republican congressman from Indiana George W. Julian admitted in 1865, white northerners "hate the negro." They expressed this hatred in their rejection of black suffrage, in racial segregation of their African American population, and in periodic violence against black residents, such as during the New York draft riots of 1863. Northerners' views were bolstered by prevailing scientific theories of race that "proved" blacks' limited capacities and, therefore, unfitness for either the ballot or skilled occupations.

Northerners also grew increasingly wary of federal power. The emerging scandals of the Grant administration, fueled, it seemed, by government subsidies to railroads and other private businesses, demanded a scaling back of federal power and discretion. When white southerners complained about federal meddling, again, they found resonance in the North.

The excesses and alleged abuses of federal power inspired a reform movement among a group of northern Republicans and some Democrats. In addition, business leaders decried the ability of wealthy lobbyists to influence economic decisions. An influential group of intellectuals and opinion makers lamented the inability of politicians to understand "natural" laws, particularly those related to race. And some Republicans joined the reform movement out of fear that Democrats would capitalize on the turmoil in the South and the political scandals in the North to reap huge electoral victories in 1872.

## Liberal Republicans and the Election of 1872

Liberal Republicans, as the reformers called themselves, put forward an array of suggestions to improve government and save the Republican Party. They advocated civil service reform to reduce reliance on patronage and the abuses that accompanied office

THE IGNORANT VOTE—HONORS ARE EASY

Thomas Nast, "The Ignorant Vote—Honors Are Easy," 1876. Many white northerners drew parallels between the corruption and inefficiency of their local and state governments, supported by immigrant and working-class votes, and similar problems in southern states where African Americans voted. Note the monkey-like portrayal of the Irish immigrant (labeled "white") and the stereotyped black figure.

seeking. To limit government and reduce artificial economic stimuli, the reformers called for tariff reduction and an end to federal land grants to railroads. For the South, they recommended a general amnesty for white people and a return to "local self-government" by men of "property and enterprise."

When the Liberals failed to convince other Republicans to adopt their program, they broke with the party. Taking advantage of this split, the Democrats forged an alliance with the Liberals. Together, they nominated journalist Horace Greeley to challenge Ulysses S. Grant for the presidency in the election of 1872. Grant won resoundingly, helped by high turnout among black voters in the South.

## Economic Transformation

After 1873, the Republican Party in the South became a liability for the national party, especially as Americans fastened on economic issues. The major story of the decade would not be equal rights for African Americans—a long shot even in the heady days following freedom—but the changing nature of the American economy. An overextended banking and credit system generated the Panic of 1873 and caused extensive suffering, particularly among working-class Americans. But the depression masked a remarkable economic transformation as the nation moved toward a national industrial economy.

During the 1870s, the economy grew annually between 4.5 and 6 percent, among the fastest decadal growth rates on record. Consumption grew even faster; Americans purchased more food, more fuel, and more manufactured products than at any other

## ✳ Explore Reconstruction on MyHistoryLab

### HOW DID RECONSTRUCTION AFFECT AFRICAN AMERICANS IN THE SOUTH?

In 1865, at the end of the Civil War, the United States was at a crossroads. The Thirteenth Amendment to the Constitution had freed the slaves of the rebellious eleven states, but questions remained on how to implement the rights of the newly liberated African Americans. Further, leaders were divided on how to reintegrate the war-torn southern states back into the Union. Many white Southerners tried to continue their ways of life while freed African Americans struggled in a society built on segregation. Though the subsequent Fourteenth and Fifteenth Amendments theoretically extended the realm of equality for blacks, in the end, whites in the North and South saw to it that the promises of Reconstruction for African Americans went unfulfilled.

Much hope was placed in the policies of Reconstruction as this allegorical lithograph shows. The reconciliation between the North and South, however, would have a mixed legacy, especially for African Americans.

### RECONSTRUCTION AMENDMENTS TO THE CONSTITUTION

| Amendment | Summary | Date |
|-----------|---------|------|
| Thirteenth | Abolishes slavery | December 6, 1865 |
| Fourteenth | Ensures equal rights and protections to every person born or naturalized in the United States | July 9, 1868 |
| Fifteenth | Prohibits the denial of the right of vote based on race | February 3, 1870 |

SOURCE: United States Constitution

## KEY QUESTIONS   Use **MyHistoryLab** *Explorer* to **answer** these **questions:**

**Analysis ▶▶▶** *How did voting patterns for Republicans evolve during the Reconstruction period?*

Chart voting patterns to understand reasons behind voting trends.

**Comparison ▶▶▶** *How did literacy rates differ between African Americans and Euro-Americans in the South?*

Theorize how this might affect black disenfranchisement.

**Response ▶▶▶** *What was the landholding situation for African Americans at the end of the nineteenth century?*

Map land tenure to see discrepancies with whites.

previous time in the nation's history. Although unemployment was severe, overall, employment grew by 40 percent between 1870 and 1880, and productivity increased at least as fast. This seeming contradiction is explained by the rapid expansion of new industries such as oil refining and meatpacking, and the application of technology in iron and steel production. Technology also eliminated jobs, and those that remained were primarily low-skilled, low-paying positions—painful, to be sure, for those caught in the change, but liberating for those with education and ability who populated a burgeoning middle-management sector of the growing urban middle class.

The depression and the economic transformation occupied center stage in the American mentality of the mid-1870s, at least in the North. Most Americans had mentally forsaken Reconstruction long before the Compromise of 1877 made its abandonment a political fact. The sporadic violence against black and white Republicans in the South, and the cries of help from freedmen as their rights and persons were abused by white Democrats, became distant echoes from another era, the era of the Civil War, now commemorated and memorialized, but no longer an active part of the nation's present and future. Of course, for white southerners, the past was not yet past. There was still work to do.

# Redemption, 1874–1877

**16.5**    How and why did Reconstruction end?

For southern Democrats, the Republican victory in 1872 underscored the importance of turning out larger numbers of white voters and restricting the black vote. They accomplished these goals over the next four years with a surge in political violence, secure in the knowledge that federal authorities would rarely intervene against them. Preoccupied with corruption and economic crisis, and increasingly indifferent, if not hostile, to African American aspirations, most Americans looked the other way. The elections of 1876 confirmed the triumph of white southerners.

In a religious metaphor that matched their view of the Civil War as a lost crusade, southern Democrats called their victory "Redemption" and depicted themselves as **Redeemers**, holy warriors who had saved the South from the hell of black Republican rule. Generations of American boys and girls would learn this interpretation of the Reconstruction era, and it would affect race relations for nearly a century.

**Redeemers** Southern Democrats who wrested control of governments in the former Confederacy from Republicans, often through electoral fraud and violence, beginning in 1870.

## The Democrats' Violent Resurgence

The violence between 1874 and 1876 differed in several respects from earlier attempts to restore white government by force. Attackers operated more openly and more closely identified themselves with the Democratic Party. Mounted, gray-clad, ex-Confederate soldiers flanked Democratic candidates at campaign rallies and "visited" black neighborhoods afterward to discourage black men from voting. With black people intimidated and white people already prepared to vote, election days were typically quiet.

Democrats swept to victory across the South in the 1874 elections. "A perfect reign of terror" redeemed Alabama for the Democrats. The successful appeal to white supremacy inspired a massive white turnout to unseat Republicans in Virginia, Florida (legislature only), and Arkansas. Texas had fallen to the Democrats in 1873. Only South Carolina, Mississippi, and Louisiana, states with large black populations, survived the debacle. But the relentless tide of terror would soon overwhelm them as well.

Democratic leaders in those states announced a "white line" policy, inviting all white men, regardless of party affiliation, to "unite" and redeem the states. They all had the same objective: to eliminate African Americans as a political factor by any means. Black Republicans feared not only for their political future, but also for their lives.

A bold assault occurred in New Orleans in September 1874 when 8,500 White League troops, many of them leading citizens and Confederate veterans, attempted a coup to oust Republican Governor William P. Kellogg and members of his administration. The League's manifesto, promulgated in July 1874, offered a clear indication of its intentions: "Having solely in view the maintenance of our hereditary civilization and Christianity menaced by a stupid Africanization, we appeal to the men of our race . . . to unite with us against that supreme danger . . . in an earnest effort to re-establish a white man's government in this city and the State." These were no mincing words or veiled threats.

The New Orleans Leaguers overwhelmed the city's racially mixed Metropolitan Police Force under the command of former Confederate General James B. Longstreet. The timely arrival of federal troops, ordered to the scene by President Grant, prevented the takeover. The League was more successful in the Louisiana countryside in the weeks preceding the Democratic victory in November 1874. League troops overthrew or murdered Republican officials in eight parishes.

The Democratic victory in Louisiana encouraged a corresponding group, the White Liners, in Mississippi. Blacks dominated the Warren County government headquartered in Vicksburg. Liners demanded the resignations of all black officials including the sheriff, Peter Crosby, a black Union veteran. Republican Governor Adelbert Ames, a native of Maine, ordered the Liners to disperse and granted Crosby's request to raise a protective militia to respond to future threats.

Peter Crosby's efforts to gather a militia force were too successful. An army of several hundred armed African Americans marched in three columns from the surrounding countryside to Vicksburg. Whites responded to the challenge, firing on the militia and tracking down and terrorizing blacks in the city and county over the next ten days. Among the victims were a black Presbyterian minister and several of his congregants kneeling in prayer. Liners killed at least twenty-nine blacks and wounded countless more. Democrats gained control of the county government.

The Vicksburg incident was a rehearsal for Democratic victories in statewide elections in 1875. The *Birmingham News* cheered on the Mississippi White Liners, "We intend to beat the negro in the battle of life, and defeat means one thing—EXTERMINATION." The intimidation worked; the Democrats swept to victory in Mississippi. They would not allow Governor Ames to finish his term, threatening him with impeachment. Fearing for his safety, Ames resigned and fled the state. The South's second war of independence was reaching its climax.

On July 4, 1876, America's one-hundredth birthday, a modest celebration unfolded in Hamburg, South Carolina, a small town in Edgefield County across the Savannah River from Augusta, Georgia. Blacks comprised more than 75 percent of the town's population. They held most of the political offices. An altercation occurred concerning the right of way between the black militia parading in the street and a passing wagon carrying several prominent white residents. When the aggrieved parties met four days later, more than 1,000 armed whites were milling in front of the wooden "armory" where 100 black militiamen had taken refuge. A shot rang out and shattered a second-floor window, and soon a pitched battled was raging. The white attackers fired a cannon that turned most of the building into splinters. As blacks fled, whites tracked them down. The white men also burned homes and shops and robbed residents of the town.

The November election went off in relative calm. In Edgefield County, out of 7,000 potential voters, 9,200 ballots were cast. Similar frauds occurred throughout the state. Still, the result hung in the balance. Both Democrats and Republicans claimed victory and set up rival governments. The following April, after a deal was brokered in Washington between the parties, federal troops were withdrawn from South Carolina and a Democratic government installed in Columbia. The victorious Democrats expelled twenty-four Republicans from the state legislature and elected Matthew C. Butler to the U.S. Senate. Butler had led the white attackers at Hamburg.

## The Weak Federal Response

When Governor Daniel H. Chamberlain could no longer contain the violence in South Carolina in 1876, he asked the president for help. Grant acknowledged the gravity of Chamberlain's situation but would offer him only the lame hope that South Carolinians would exercise "better judgment and cooperation" and assist the governor in bringing offenders to justice "without aid from the federal Government."

Congress responded to blacks' deteriorating status in the South with the Civil Rights Act of 1875 (see Table 16.2). The act, which had no provision for voting rights because Congress presumed the Fifteenth Amendment protected those, prohibited discrimination against black people in public accommodations, such as theaters, parks, and trains, and guaranteed freedmen's rights to serve on juries. Most judges, however, either interpreted the law narrowly or declared it unconstitutional. In 1883, the U.S. Supreme Court agreed and overturned the act, declaring that only the states, not Congress, could redress "a private wrong, or a crime of the individual."

## The Election of 1876 and the Compromise of 1877

Reconstruction officially ended with the presidential election of 1876, in which the Democrat Samuel J. Tilden ran against the Republican Rutherford B. Hayes. When the ballots were counted, it appeared that Tilden, a conservative New Yorker respectable

**Read the Document**  Thirteenth, Fourteenth, and Fifteenth Amendments

**TABLE 16.2** CONSTITUTIONAL AMENDMENTS AND FEDERAL LEGISLATION OF THE RECONSTRUCTION ERA

| Amendment or Legislation | Purpose | Significance |
|---|---|---|
| Thirteenth Amendment (passed and ratified in 1865) | Prevented southern states from reestablishing slavery after the war | Final step toward full emancipation of slaves |
| Freedmen's Bureau Act (1865) | Oversight of resettlement, labor for former slaves | Involved the federal government directly in relief, education, and assisting the transition from slavery to freedom; worked fitfully to achieve this objective during its seven-year career |
| Southern Homestead Act (1866) | Provided black people preferential access to public lands in five southern states | Lack of capital and poor quality of federal land thwarted the purpose of the act |
| Civil Rights Act of 1866 | Defined rights of national citizenship | Marked an important change in federal-state relations, tilting balance of power to national government |
| Fourteenth Amendment (passed 1866; ratified 1868) | Prohibited states from violating the rights of their citizens | Strengthened the Civil Rights Act of 1866 and guaranteed all citizens equality before the law |
| Military Reconstruction Acts (1867) | Set new rules for the readmission of former Confederate states into the Union and secured black voting rights | Initiated Congressional Reconstruction |
| Tenure of Office Act (1867) | Required congressional approval for the removal of any official whose appointment had required Senate confirmation | A congressional challenge to the president's right to dismiss cabinet members; led to President Andrew Johnson's impeachment trial |
| Fifteenth Amendment (passed 1869; ratified 1870) | Guaranteed the right of all American male citizens to vote regardless of race | The basis for black voting rights |
| Civil Rights Act of 1875 | Prohibited racial discrimination in jury selection, public transportation, and public accommodations | Rarely enforced; Supreme Court declared it unconstitutional in 1883 |

| | Precompromise Electoral Vote (%) | Final Electoral Vote (%) | Popular Vote (%) |
|---|---|---|---|
| **RUTHERFORD B. HAYES** **(Republican)** | **165** **(47)** | **185** **(50)** | **4,034,311** **(48)** |
| Samuel J. Tilden (Democrat) | 184 (53) | 184 (50) | 4,288,546 (51) |
| Peter Cooper (Greenback) | – | – | 75,973 (1) |
| Disputed | 20 | | |

**MAP 16.1  THE ELECTION OF 1876** The Democrat Samuel F. Tilden won a majority of the popular vote but eventually fell short of an electoral vote majority when the contested electoral votes of Florida, Louisiana, and South Carolina went to his Republican opponent, Rutherford B. Hayes. The map also indicates the Republicans' failure to build a base in the South after more than a decade of Reconstruction.

enough for northern voters and Democratic enough for white southerners, had won. But despite a majority in the popular vote, disputed returns in three southern states left him with only 184 of the 185 electoral votes needed to win (see Map 16.1). The three states—Florida, South Carolina, and Louisiana—were the last in the South still to have Republican administrations.

Both camps maneuvered intensively in the following months to claim the disputed votes. Congress appointed a fifteen-member commission to settle the issue. Because the Republicans controlled Congress, they held a one-vote majority on the commission.

Southern Democrats wanted Tilden to win, but they wanted control of their states more. They were willing to deal. Hayes intended to remove federal support from the remaining southern Republican governments anyway. It thus cost him nothing to promise to do so in exchange for the contested electoral votes. Republicans also made vague promises to invest in the southern economy and support a southern transcontinental railroad, but these were secondary. What the South wanted most was to be left alone, and that is what it got. The so-called **Compromise of 1877** installed Hayes in the White House and gave Democrats control of every state government in the South. Congress never carried through on the economic promises, and southern Democrats never pressed it to. Southern Democrats emerged the major winners from the Compromise of 1877. President Hayes and his successors into the next century left the South alone.

**Compromise of 1877** The congressional settling of the 1876 election that installed Republican Rutherford B. Hayes in the White House and gave Democrats control of all state governments in the South.

In practical terms, the Compromise signaled the revocation of civil rights and voting rights for black southerners. The Fourteenth and Fifteenth Amendments would be dead letters in the South until well into the twentieth century. On the two great issues confronting the nation at the end of the Civil War, reunion and freedom, the white South had won. It reentered the Union largely on its own terms with the freedom to pursue a racial agenda consistent with its political, economic, and social interests.

## The Memory of Reconstruction

Southern Democrats used the memory of Reconstruction to help them maintain power. Reconstruction joined the Lost Cause as part of the glorious fight to preserve the civilization of the Old South. As white southerners elevated Civil War heroes into saints and battles into holy struggles, they equated Reconstruction with Redemption. White Democrats had rescued the South from black rule and federal oppression. During the next century, whenever southern Democrats felt threatened, they reminded their white constituents of the sacrifices and heroism of the war, the "horrors of Reconstruction," the menace of black rule, and the cruelty of the Yankee occupiers. The southern view of Reconstruction permeated textbooks, films, and standard accounts of the period. By the early 1900s, professional historians at the nation's finest institutions concurred in this view, ignoring contrary evidence and rendering the story of African Americans invisible. By that time, therefore, most Americans believed that the policies of Reconstruction had been misguided and had brought great suffering to the white South. The widespread acceptance of this view allowed the South to maintain its system of racial segregation and exclusion without interference from the federal government.

Memorialists did not deny the Redeemers' use of terror and violence. To the contrary, they praised it as necessary. South Carolina Senator Benjamin R. Tillman, a participant in the Hamburg massacre, stood in front of his Senate colleagues in 1900 and asserted: "We were sorry we had the necessity forced upon us, but we could not help it, and as white men we are not sorry for it, and we do not propose to apologize for anything we have done in connection with it. We took the government away from them [African Americans] in 1876. We did take it. . . . We of the South have never recognized the right of the negro to govern white men, and we never will." The animosity of southern whites toward Republican governments had much less to do with alleged corruption and incompetence than the mere fact of African Americans casting ballots and making laws.

Not all memories of Reconstruction conformed to the theme of redemption. In 1913, John R. Lynch, a former black Republican congressman from Mississippi, published *The Facts of Reconstruction* to "present the other side." He hoped that his book would "bring to public notice those things that were commendable and meritorious, to prevent the publication of which seems to have been the primary purpose of nearly all who have thus far written upon that important subject." But most Americans ignored his book. Two decades later, a more forceful defense, W. E. B. Du Bois's *Black Reconstruction* (1935), met a similar fate. An angry Du Bois attacked the prevailing view of Reconstruction as "one of the most stupendous efforts the world ever saw to discredit human beings, an effort involving universities, history, science, social life and religion."

The national historical consensus grew out of a growing national reconciliation concerning the war, a mutual agreement that both sides had fought courageously and that it was time to move on. Hidden in all the goodwill was the tacit agreement between southern and northern whites that the South was now free to work out its own resolution to race relations. Reconstruction rested on a national consensus of African American inferiority.

There is much to be said in favor of sectional reconciliation as opposed to persistent animosity. There are enough examples in the world today of antagonists in the same country never forgetting or never forgiving their bloody histories. Ideally, Americans could have had *both* healing and justice, but instead they settled for the former.

Frederick Douglass, prescient as ever, worried about the peace that followed the Civil War and what it would mean for race relations: "If war among the whites brought peace and liberty to the blacks, what will peace among the whites bring?"

## Modest Gains

If the overthrow of Reconstruction elicited a resounding indifference from most white Americans, black southerners greeted it with frustration. Their dreams of land ownership faded as a new labor system relegated them to a lowly position in southern agriculture. Redemption reversed their economic and political gains and deprived them of most of the civil rights they had enjoyed under Congressional Reconstruction. Although they continued to vote into the 1890s, they had by 1877 lost most of the voting strength and political offices they held. Rather than becoming part of southern society, they were increasingly set apart from it, valued only for their labor.

Still, the former slaves were better off in 1877 than in 1865. They were free, however limited their freedom. Some owned land; some held jobs in cities. They raised their families in relative peace and experienced the spiritual joys of a full religious life. They socialized freely with relatives and friends, and they moved about. The Reconstruction amendments to the Constitution guaranteed an array of civil and political rights, and eventually these guarantees would form the basis of the civil rights revolution after World War II. But that outcome was long, too long, in the future.

Black southerners experienced some advances in the decade after the Civil War, but these owed little to Reconstruction. Black families functioned as economic and psychological buffers against unemployment and prejudice. Black churches played crucial roles in their communities. Self-help and labor organizations offered mutual friendship and financial assistance. All of these institutions had existed in the slavery era, although on a smaller scale. And some of them, such as black labor groups, schools, and social welfare associations, endured because comparable white institutions excluded black people.

Black people also scored some modest economic successes during the Reconstruction era, mainly from their own pluck. In the Lower South, black per capita income increased 46 percent between 1857 and 1879, compared with a 35 percent decline in white per capita income. Sharecropping, oppressive as it was, represented an advance over forced and gang labor. Collectively, black people owned more than $68 million worth of property in 1870, a 240 percent increase over 1860, but the average worth of each was only $408.

The Fourteenth and Fifteenth Amendments to the Constitution are among the few bright spots in Reconstruction's otherwise dismal legacy. But the benefits of these two landmark amendments did not accrue to African Americans until well into the twentieth century. White southerners effectively nullified the Reconstruction amendments, and the U.S. Supreme Court virtually interpreted them, and other Reconstruction legislation, out of existence.

In the **Slaughterhouse cases** (1873), the Supreme Court contradicted the intent of the Fourteenth Amendment by decreeing that most citizenship rights remained under state, not federal, control. In **United States v. Cruikshank** (1876), the Court overturned the convictions of some of those responsible for the Colfax Massacre, ruling that the Enforcement Act applied only to violations of black rights by states, not individuals. Within the next two decades, the Supreme Court would uphold the legality of racial segregation and black disfranchisement, in effect declaring that the Fourteenth and Fifteenth Amendments did not apply to African Americans. The Civil War had killed secession forever, but states' rights enjoyed a remarkable revival.

As the historian John Hope Franklin accurately concluded, Reconstruction "had no significant or permanent effect on the status of the black in American life. . . . [Black people] made no meaningful steps toward economic independence or even stability."

**Slaughterhouse cases** Group of cases resulting in one sweeping decision by the U.S. Supreme Court in 1873 that contradicted the intent of the Fourteenth Amendment by decreeing that most citizenship rights remained under state, not federal, control.

**United States v. Cruikshank** Supreme Court ruling of 1876 that overturned the convictions of some of those responsible for the Colfax Massacre, ruling that the Enforcement Act applied only to violations of black rights by states, not individuals.

# Conclusion

Formerly enslaved black southerners had entered freedom with many hopes, among the most prominent of which was to be left alone. White southerners, after four bloody years of unwanted attention from the federal government, also longed to be left alone. But they did not include their ex-slaves as equals in their vision of solitude. Northerners, too, began to seek escape from the issues and consequences of the war, abandoning their weak commitment to secure civil and voting rights for black southerners.

White southerners robbed black southerners of their gains and sought to reduce them again to servitude and dependence, if not to slavery. But in the process, the majority of white southerners lost as well. Yeoman farmers missed an opportunity to break cleanly from the Old South and establish a more equitable society. Instead, they allowed the old elites to regain power and gradually ignore their needs. They preserved the social benefit of a white skin at the cost of almost everything else. Many lost their farms and sank into tenancy. Few had a voice in state legislatures or the U.S. Congress. A new South, rid of slavery and sectional antagonism, had indeed emerged—redeemed, regenerated, and disenthralled. But the old South lingered on.

As federal troops left the South, an era of possibility for American society ended, and a new era began. "The southern question is dead," a Charleston newspaper proclaimed in 1877. "The question of labor and capital, work and wages" had moved to the forefront. The chance to redeem the sacrifice of a bloody civil war with a society that fulfilled the promise of the Declaration of Independence and the Constitution for all citizens slipped away. It would take a new generation of African Americans a long century later to revive it.

The journey toward equality after the Civil War had aborted. Reconstruction had not failed. It was overthrown. In the weeks and months after Appomattox, white southerners launched a war against the freedmen and their allies to return white Democrats to power and African Americans to a position of permanent subordination in southern society. The indifferent and often hostile attitudes of white northerners toward blacks played a role in limiting the federal response and ensuring the success of the white South in prosecuting this war. As with the Civil War, the overthrow of Reconstruction was a national tragedy. By 1877, the "golden moment," an unprecedented opportunity for the nation to live up to its ideals by extending equal rights to all its citizens, black and white alike, had passed. Thomas Fortune would leave the South the following year, giving up on fulfilling his dream of full citizenship in the region of his birth. Edward A. Pollard who, more than any other southern white articulated the Lost Cause, wrote in 1867 that, despite the surrender at Appomattox, victory was still possible. If white supremacy could be reestablished, he wrote, then the South "really triumphs in the true cause of the war with respect to all its fundamental and vital issues." And so it did.

**For Suggested Readings go to MyHistoryLab.**

# Chapter Review

## White Southerners and the Ghosts of the Confederacy, 1865

**16.1** How did white southerners respond to defeat? p. 451

White southerners confronted a devastated homeland after the war. In order to cope with defeat and devastation, they rationalized their efforts during the war. The Lost Cause provided personal relief, affirmed their faith, and offered collective justification for their attitudes and policies toward former slaves and northerners.

## More than Freedom: African American Aspirations in 1865

**16.2** Why did black aspirations generate southern white violence? p. 453

Former slaves viewed the war's outcome very differently from their white neighbors. Freedom was just the beginning. They hoped to build productive and independent lives and exercise the rights of citizenship. Their hopes depended to a great extent on how much support they would receive from the federal government.

## Federal Reconstruction, 1865–1870

**16.3** How did Congressional Reconstruction change the status of the former slaves in the South? p. 459

White southerners reacted to President Andrew Johnson's mild Reconstruction program by oppressing the freed slaves and returning leading Confederates to power. Northern voters retaliated in 1866, sending strong Republican majorities to the Congress where members enacted a series of measures to guarantee freedmen's rights and limit the influence of former Rebels.

## Counter-Reconstruction, 1870–1874

**16.4** How were white northerners and the federal government complicit in denying freed slaves the basic rights of American citizenship? p. 468

White southerners responded violently to Congressional Reconstruction, engaging in acts of terror to limit African American participation in southern governments and in economic life. Northern whites grew increasingly indifferent to black aspirations and sympathized with southern white allegations of black fraud and incompetence.

## Redemption, 1874–1877

**16.5** How and why did Reconstruction end? p. 473

The Republican Party, fearing a backlash from their northern constituents, abandoned Reconstruction policy. Paramilitary groups roamed the South in support of white Democratic candidates,

effectively suppressing black political power. The election of 1876 and the subsequent Compromise of 1877 restored white southerners and white supremacy to power in the South.

# Timeline

**1863**
**Federal Reconstruction—** Lincoln proposes his Ten Percent Plan

**1866**
**Federal Reconstruction—** Fourteenth Amendment to the Constitution is passed (ratified 1868)

**1867**
**Federal Reconstruction—** Congress passes Military Reconstruction Acts, Tenure of Office Act

**1869**
**Federal Reconstruction—** Fifteenth Amendment is passed (ratified 1870)

**1871**
**Counter-Reconstruction—** Congress passes Ku Klux Klan Act

**1873**
**Counter-Reconstruction—** Colfax Massacre occurs; U.S. Supreme Court's decision in the *Slaughterhouse* cases weakens the intent of the Fourteenth Amendment

**1874**
**Redemption—** Democrats win off-year elections across the South amid widespread fraud and violence

**1876**
**Redemption—** Outcome of the presidential election between Republican Rutherford B. Hayes and Democrat Samuel J. Tilden is contested

**1877**
**Redemption—** Compromise of 1877 makes Hayes president and ends Reconstruction

# 17 A New South: Economic Progress and Social Tradition 1877–1900

## One American Journey

Anna J. Cooper on the Prospects and Aspirations of Black Women in the 1890s

**T**he colored woman of to-day occupies . . . a unique position in this country. . . . She is confronted by both a woman question and a race problem. . . . While the women of the white race can with calm assurance enter upon the work they feel by nature appointed to do [including reform efforts both inside and outside the home], while their men give loyal support and appreciative countenance to [these] efforts, recognizing in most avenues of usefulness the propriety and the need of woman's distinctive co-operation, the colored woman too often finds herself hampered and shamed by a less liberal sentiment . . . on the part of those for whose opinion she cares most. . . .

## LEARNING OBJECTIVES

| 17.1 ((• | 17.2 ((• | 17.3 ((• | 17.4 ((• |
|---|---|---|---|
| How new was the New South? p. 483 | Why did southern farmers organize? p. 489 | How did urbanization and industrialization affect race and gender relations in the South? p. 492 | How did African Americans respond to the growing violence and legal restrictions whites directed at them? p. 494 |

The economic advance of African Americans in the South during the decades after the Civil War against great odds provided one of the more inspiring success stories of the era. But it was precisely this success, as depicted here at Dr. McDougald's Drug Store in Georgia, in 1900, that infuriated whites who believed that the African Americans' place in the South resided in menial and subservient occupations.

From *The American Journey*, Seventh Edition. Goldfield, Abbott, Anderson, Argersinger, Argersinger and Barney Copyright © 2014 by Pearson Education, Inc. All rights reserved.

##  Watch the Video Series on MyHistoryLab

Learn about some key topics related to this chapter with the *MyHistoryLab Video Series: Key Topics in U.S. History.*

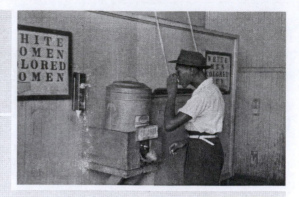

**1** **The New South: 1877–1900** Although the South had suffered the first total war, this gave the former Confederate states the opportunity not only to rebuild their cities, but also to rebuild and expand the factories and railroads they had lacked during the Civil War.
As this video shows, although the South began to industrialize and urbanize after Reconstruction, as it became more entrepreneurial and the role of women expanded outside the home, it remained essentially an agricultural economy, and for many African Americans the New South quickly returned to the racial prejudice and persecution of the Old.

⊙ **Watch** on **MyHistoryLab**

**Southern Farmers' Alliance** As the price of cotton and other commodities fell and their indebtedness to creditors rose, growers—first in Texas and then in other states—formed the Southern Farmers' Alliance in the late 1870s. This video discusses the Alliance and how it sponsored farmers' cooperatives to provide members with seed, supplies, equipment, and credit at low interest rates. The Alliance not only protected farmers with smaller operations from bankruptcy, but it also provided them with political clout and a sense of community. **2**

**Watch** on **MyHistoryLab** ⊙

**3** **Women's Groups** In addition to church groups and the Women's Christian Temperance Unions, southern white middle-class women joined book clubs, self-improvement societies, and reform groups, such as those devoted to suffrage and preserving the morals of workingmen and women. African American women in southern cities also formed clubs and organizations to improve the life of their people. However, as this video reveals, little contact existed between these white and black women's groups, which might have provided a venue for racial reconciliation.

⊙ **Watch** on **MyHistoryLab**

**Legalized Segregation** This video examines how southern lawmakers gradually instituted a system of legalized segregation, known as "Jim Crow laws," and the disfranchisement of black Americans. The system became reinforced and greatly expanded with the Supreme Court's *Plessy v. Ferguson* "separate-but-equal" decision, which ruled against a black plaintiff who had challenged a state's segregation law. **4**

**Watch** on **MyHistoryLab** ⊙

You do not find the colored woman selling her birthright for a mess of pottage. . . . It is largely our women in the South to-day who keep the black men solid in the Republican Party. The black woman can never forget, however lukewarm the party may to-day appear, that it was a Republican president who struck the manacles from her own wrists and gave the possibilities of manhood to her helpless little ones; and to her mind a Democratic Negro is a traitor and a time-server.

To be a woman in a . . . [new] age carries with it a privilege and an opportunity never implied before. But to be a woman of the Negro race in America, and to be able to grasp the deep significance of the possibilities of the crisis, is to have a heritage, it seems to me, unique in the ages. In the first place, the race is young and full of the elasticity and hopefulness of youth. All its achievements are before it. . . . Everything to this race is new and strange and inspiring. There is a quickening of its pulses and a glowing of its self-consciousness. Aha, I can rival that! I can aspire to that!

I can honor my name and vindicate my race! Something like this, it strikes me, is the enthusiasm which stirs the genius of young Africa in America; and the memory of past oppression and the fact of present attempted repression only serve to gather momentum for its irrepressible power. . . . What a responsibility then to have the sole management of the primal lights and shadows! Such is the colored woman's office. She must stamp weal or woe on the coming history of this people. May she see her opportunity and vindicate her high prerogative.

Anna J. Cooper,
*A Voice from the South,* 1892

Anna Julia Cooper, *A Voice from the South* (Xenia, OH: Aldine Printing House, 1892), pp. 134–135, 138–140, 142–145. The book may be accessed from the Internet: http://docsouth.unc.edu/church/cooper/cooper.html.

## Personal Journeys Online

- Booker T. Washington, *Atlanta Compromise Address,* 1895. Speech in which Washington accepts segregation and disfranchisement of southern blacks in return for white southerners' economic assistance.
- W. E. B. Du Bois, *Of Mr. Booker T. Washington and Others,* 1903. Du Bois declares that Washington's compromise places African Americans in the South on a journey to failure.

**A**nna J. Cooper undertook an incredible journey that took her from slavery at her birth in Raleigh, North Carolina, in 1858, to a doctoral degree at the Sorbonne in Paris, France, and to a prominent career as an educator. Throughout her life she remained a firm believer in the role that women, especially black women, should play in striking down both white supremacy and male domination. In 1892, Dr. Cooper published *A Voice from the South,* excerpted here. The book appeared at a time when the first African American generation raised in freedom produced a relatively prosperous, educated middle class intent on challenging the limits of race in the New South. The assertiveness of this generation alarmed their white counterparts, who launched a campaign of violence and repression, mainly directed at black men.

By the early 1900s, Cooper was living in Washington, DC, and had immersed herself in the woman suffrage movement and the promotion of female education. She would live to see the dawn of a new racial and gender era in the South and in America, but the journey would take many years and many lives. Cooper died at the age of 106 in 1964.

# The "Newness" of the New South

**17.1** How new was the New South?

**A**nna J. Cooper's journey looked forward to a brighter, if elusive, future for African Americans, women in particular. White southerners marched backward toward an idealized past whose elements they hoped to restore as faithfully as possible, especially those related to race and gender. At the same time, they projected an image of progress, touting economic and technological advances, welcoming investment, and promoting benign race relations and a docile labor force. The progress was genuine, but only within the framework of white supremacy. When the idea of white supremacy proved insufficient to sustain order, white southerners resorted to legislation and violence. The New South, as one observer noted, was merely "the Old South under new conditions." By the early 1900s, the South had traveled farther away from the American journey than at any time in its history. The rest of the nation followed the detour as well.

On the surface, this did not seem to be the case. Southerners and other Americans between 1877 and 1900 were building railroads, erecting factories, creating new industries, and moving to towns and cities. The results in the South were more modest than elsewhere, but still significant in terms of where the region had been before the Civil War. The factories did not dramatically alter the South's rural economy, however, and the towns and cities did not make it an urban region. The changes, nonetheless, brought political and social turmoil, emboldening black people like Cooper to assert their rights, encouraging women to work outside the home and pursue public careers, and frightening some white men. The backlash would be significant.

The New South's "newness" was to be found primarily in its economy, not in its social relations, although the two were complementary. After Reconstruction, new industries absorbed tens of thousands of first-time industrial workers from impoverished rural areas. Southern cities grew faster than those in any other region of the country. A burst of railroad construction linked these cities to one another and to the rest of the country, giving them increased commercial prominence. Growing in size and taking on new functions, cities extended their influence into the countryside with newspapers, consumer products, and new values. But this urban influence had important limits. It did not bring electricity, telephones, public health services, or public schools to the rural South. It did not greatly broaden the rural economy with new jobs. And it left the countryside without the daily contact with the outside world that fostered a broader perspective.

The Democratic Party dominated southern politics after 1877, significantly changing the South's political system. Through various deceits, Democrats purged most black people and some white people from the electoral process and suppressed challenges to their leadership. The result was the emergence by 1900 of the **Solid South**, a period of white Democratic Party rule that lasted into the 1950s.

**Solid South** The one-party (Democratic) political system that dominated the South from the 1890s to the 1950s.

Although most southern women remained at home or on the farm, piecing together families shattered by war, some enjoyed new options after 1877. Middle-class women in the cities, both white and black, became increasingly active in civic work and reform. They organized clubs, preserved and promoted memories of the war, lobbied for various causes, and assumed regional leadership on a number of important issues. Tens of thousands of young white women from impoverished rural areas found work in textile mills, in city factories, or as servants. These new options posed a challenge to prevailing views about the role of women but ultimately did not change them.

The status of black southerners changed significantly between 1877 and 1900. The members of the first generation born after emancipation sought more than just freedom as they came of age. They also expected dignity and self-respect and the right to work, to vote, to go to school, and to travel freely. White southerners responded to the new challenge in the same manner they responded immediately after the war, with violence and restrictive legislation. By 1900, black southerners found themselves more isolated from white southerners and with less political power than at any time since 1865. Despite these setbacks, they succeeded, especially in the cities, in building a rich community life and spawning a vibrant middle class, albeit in a restricted environment.

## An Industrial and Urban South

Southerners manufactured very little in 1877, less than 10 percent of the national total. By 1900, however, they boasted a growing iron and steel industry, textile mills that rivaled those of New England, a world-dominant tobacco industry, a timber-processing industry that helped make the South a leading furniture-manufacturing center, and the beginnings of an industry that would transform not only the South but also the nation: oil. A variety of regional enterprises also rose to prominence, among them the maker of what would become the world's favorite soft drink, Coca-Cola.

**Steel Mills and Textiles.** Birmingham, barely a scratch in the forest in 1870, exemplified one aspect of what was new about the New South. Union soldiers and engineers fighting their way south during the Civil War found rich deposits of coal and iron in the Appalachian hills stretching from West Virginia to north Alabama. The problem lay not in mining these mineral riches, but in transporting them to the growing cities of America and the world. The frenzy of railroad construction in the South after the war solved the problem of access, and Birmingham benefited, utilizing the minerals to fire furnaces and make steel. Within a decade, its iron and steel mills were belching the smoke of progress across the northern Alabama hills.

By 1889, Birmingham had surpassed the older southern iron center of Chattanooga, Tennessee, and was preparing to challenge Pittsburgh, the nation's preeminent steel-making city. Although hampered by discriminatory freight rates and pricing, the "Magic City," as locals called it because it had materialized from virtually nothing, grew from 3,000 residents in 1880 to an astounding population of 130,000 thirty years later, making it one of the South's largest cities.

The southern textile industry also experienced significant growth during the 1880s. Although the South had manufactured cotton products since the early decades of the nineteenth century, chronic shortages of labor and capital kept the industry small. In the 1870s, however, several factors drew local investors into textile enterprises. The population of the rural South was rising, but farm income was low, ensuring a steady supply of cheap labor. Cotton was plentiful and cheap. Mixing profit and southern

📖 **Read the Document**   **Mill Workers Comment on the New South (1887, 1889)**

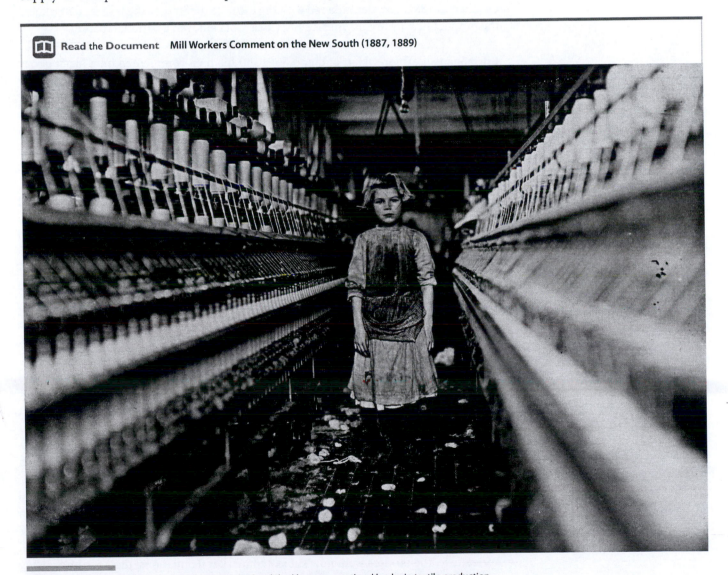

The face of southern industry. By the early 1900s, the South had become a national leader in textile production, relying on cheap labor, especially women and young children, such as this young girl depicted here in a Lewis Hine photograph at the Globe Cotton Mill in August, Georgia, 1909. She stands in a grimy dress between two large looms. The floor is littered with cotton lint that is harmful to the lungs. Hine took such photographs to call attention to the evil of child labor. To hard-pressed southern families who could not sustain themselves on the farm, these industrial jobs were literally life-saving, but at a terrible cost to the health, education, and welfare of their children.

patriotism, entrepreneurs promoted a strong textile industry as a way to make the South less dependent on northern manufactured products and capital. By 1900, the South had surpassed New England to become the nation's foremost textile-manufacturing center.

**Tobacco and Coca-Cola.** The South's tobacco industry, like its textile industry, predated the Civil War. Virginia was the dominant producer, and its main product was chewing tobacco. The discovery of bright-leaf tobacco, a strain suitable for smoking in the form of cigarettes, changed Americans' tobacco habits. In 1884, James B. Duke installed the first cigarette-making machine in his Durham, North Carolina, plant. By 1900, Duke's American Tobacco Company controlled 80 percent of all tobacco manufacturing in the United States.

Although not as important as textiles or tobacco in 1900, a soft drink developed by an Atlanta pharmacist named Dr. John Pemberton eventually became the most renowned southern product worldwide. Pemberton developed the drink, a mixture of oils, caffeine, coca leaves, and cola nuts, in his backyard in an effort to find a good-tasting cure for headaches. He called his concoction Coca-Cola. It was not an overnight success, and Pemberton, short of cash, sold the rights to it to another Atlantan, Asa Candler, in 1889. Candler tinkered with the formula to improve the taste and marketed the product heavily. By the mid-1890s, Coca-Cola enjoyed a national market.

**Oil.** Spanish explorer Hernando do Soto and his men commented on a black gooey substance that washed up on the beaches of east Texas during their sixteenth-century exploration of the area. By the late nineteenth century, the oil industry was already underway in western Pennsylvania and John D. Rockefeller was accumulating a fortune for his Standard Oil Company. But as with steel, ultimately, and far more successfully, the oil business soon moved south. The knowledge of a great reservoir of oil underneath the salt domes of east Texas was general. The problem lay in developing the technology to extract the resource and then to transport it. Captain A. F. Lucas, an army engineer, persuaded the wealthy Mellon family of Pittsburgh to bankroll his drill and scheme to penetrate the salt dome at a place called Spindletop near Beaumont, Texas, in January 1901. When the drill bit broke through the dome, oil gushed 120 feet into the air and filled 100,000 barrels a day for a week. Galveston, Texas, with its access to the Gulf of Mexico, seemed the logical beneficiary of this discovery were it not for a devastating hurricane—the greatest natural disaster in American history—that flattened the city in 1900. Houston leaped into the breach, building railroads and dredging a bayou that gave ships access to the Gulf of Mexico. The small Texas town would become the largest city in the South.

**Railroads and Growth.** Railroads were the key catalysts of southern industrial growth. Southern railroad construction boomed in the 1880s, outpacing the rest of the nation. Overall, southern track mileage doubled between 1880 and 1890, with the greatest increases in Texas and Georgia. In 1886, the southern railroads agreed to conform to a national standard for track width, firmly linking the region into a national transportation network and ensuring quick and direct access for southern products to the booming markets of the Northeast.

The railroad not only penetrated previously inaccessible regions rich in natural resources, but it also connected many formerly isolated small southern farmers to national and international agricultural markets. At the same time, it gave them access to a whole new range of products, from fertilizers to fashions. Drawn into commercial agriculture, the farmers were now subject to market fluctuations, their fortunes rising and falling with the market prices for their crops. To an extent unknown before the Civil War, the market now determined what farmers planted, how much credit they could expect, and on what terms.

The railroad also opened new areas of the South to settlement and tourism. In 1892, according to one guidebook, Florida was "in the main inaccessible to the ordinary tourist, and unopened to the average settler." But railroad construction boomed in the state in the 1890s, and by 1912 there were tourist hotels as far south as Key West. Railroads also penetrated the Appalachian Mountains, not only expanding markets for farmers but also opening the area to outside timber and coal-mining interests.

## The Limits of Industrial and Urban Growth

Rapid as it was, urban and industrial growth in the South barely kept pace with that in the booming North (see Chapter 18). Between 1860 and 1900, the South's share of the nation's manufacturing increased only marginally from 10.3 percent to 10.5 percent, and its share of the nation's capital declined slightly from 11.5 percent to 11 percent. About the same percentage of people worked in manufacturing in the southern states east of the Mississippi in 1900 as in 1850. Between 1860 and 1880, the per capita income of the South declined from 72 percent of the national average to 51 percent, and by 1920 it had recovered to only 62 percent.

A weak agricultural economy and a high rural birthrate depressed wages in the South. Southern industrial workers earned roughly half the national average manufacturing wage during the late nineteenth century. Business leaders promoted the advantages of this cheap labor to northern investors.

**Effects of Low Wages.** Despite their attractiveness to industrialists, low wages undermined the southern economy in several ways. Poorly paid workers did not buy much, keeping consumer demand low and limiting the market for southern manufactured goods. They also could not provide much tax revenue, restricting the southern states' ability to fund services like public education. As a result, investment in education lagged in the South. Per-pupil expenditure in the region was at least 50 percent below that of the rest of the nation in 1900. North Dakota, not a wealthy state, spent ten times more per pupil than North Carolina, not the poorest state in the South.

Finally, low wages kept immigrants, and the skills and energy they brought with them, out of the South. Between 1860 and 1900, during one of the greatest waves of immigration the United States has yet experienced, the foreign-born population of the South actually declined from about 10 percent to less than 2 percent.

**Limited Capital.** Why did the South not do better? Why did it not benefit more from the rapid expansion of the national economy in the last three decades of the nineteenth century? The simple answer is that, despite its growing links to the national economy, the South remained a region apart.

The Civil War had wiped out the South's capital resources, leaving it, in effect, an economic colony of the North. Northern goods flowed into the South, but northern capital, technology, and people did not. Northern-based national banks emerged in the wake of the Civil War to fund northern economic expansion. The South, in contrast, had few banks, and they lacked sufficient capital reserves to fuel an equivalent expansion. In 1880, Massachusetts alone had five times as much bank capital as the entire South.

With limited access to other sources of capital, the South's textile industry depended on thousands of small investors in towns and cities. These investors avoided risk and shunned innovation. Most textile operations remained small-scale. The average southern firm in 1900 was capitalized at $11,000, compared with an average of $21,000 elsewhere.

The lumber industry, the South's largest, typified the shortcomings of southern economic development in the late nineteenth century. It also reflected the lack of concern about the natural environment. As a nascent conservation movement took hold in the North, southerners continued to view the natural environment as a venue for economic exploitation. The lumber industry required little capital, relied on unskilled labor, and processed its raw materials on site. After clear-cutting (i.e., felling all the trees) in one region, sawmills moved quickly to the next stand of timber, leaving behind a bare landscape, rusting machinery, and a workforce no better off than before. This process, later repeated by the coal-mining industry, inflicted environmental damage on once remote areas such as Appalachia, and displaced their residents.

The tobacco industry avoided some of the problems that plagued other southern enterprises. James B. Duke's American Tobacco Company was so immensely profitable that he became, in effect, his own bank. With more than enough capital to install the latest technology in his plants, Duke bought out his competitors. He then diversified into electric power generation, investing in an enterprise that became the Southern Power Company in 1905 (and later the Duke Power Company). He also endowed what became Duke University.

Southern industry fit into a narrow niche of late-nineteenth-century American industrialization. With an unskilled and uneducated workforce, poor access to capital and technology, and a weak consumer base, the South processed raw agricultural products and produced cheap textiles, cheap lumber products, and cheap cigarettes. "Made in the South" became synonymous with bottom-of-the-line goods. In the North, industrialization usually occurred in an urban context and promoted rapid urban growth. In the South, textile mills were typically located in the countryside, often in mill villages where employers could easily recruit families and keep them isolated from the distractions and employment alternatives of the cities. The timber industry similarly remained a rural-based enterprise. Tobacco manufacturing helped Durham and Winston, North Carolina, grow, but they remained small compared to northern industrial cities.

## Farms to Cities: Impact on Southern Society

If industrialization in the South was limited compared to the North, it nonetheless had an enormous impact on southern society. Keep in mind that the North had the highest rate of industrial development in the Western world during the late nineteenth century. Perhaps the more appropriate comparison would be between the South at the end of the Civil War and the South in 1900. The impact of industry becomes more substantial from that perspective.

In the southern Piedmont, for example, textile mills transformed a portion of the farm population into an industrial workforce. Failed farmers moved to textile villages to earn a living. Entire families secured employment and often a house in exchange for their labor. Widows and single young men also moved to the mills, usually the only option outside farm work in the South. Nearly one-third of the textile-mill labor force by 1900 consisted of children under the age of 14 and women.

In 1880, southern towns often did not differ much from the countryside in appearance, economy, religion, and outlook. Over the next twenty years, the gap between town and country widened. By 1900, a town in the New South would boast a business district and more elegant residences than before. It would have a relatively prosperous economy and more frequent contact with other parts of the country. Its influence would extend into the countryside. Mail, the telegraph, the railroad, and the newspaper brought city life to the attention of farm families. In turn, farm families visited nearby towns and cities more often.

The urban South drew the region's talented and ambitious young people. White men moved to cities to open shops or take jobs as bank clerks, bookkeepers, merchants, and salesmen. White women worked as retail clerks, telephone operators, and office personnel. Black women filled the growing demand for laundresses and domestic servants. And black men also found prospects better in towns than on the farm, despite a narrow and uncertain range of occupations available to them. The excitement that drew some southerners to their new cities repelled others. To them, urbanization and the emphasis on wealth, new technology, and display represented a second Yankee conquest. The cities, they feared, threatened to infect the South with northern values, undermining southern grace, charm, faith, and family.

Country people held ambivalent views of the city. Farm children looked forward to the Saturday excursion to town, when they would gaze into shop windows, watch people rushing about, wonder at the workings of electricity, and drink a "Co-Cola" at the drugstore. Their parents shared some of this excitement but experienced apprehension as well. They were disturbed by the easy blurring of class and racial distinctions in town and offended by the scorn with which town folk sometimes treated them.

White southerners in town and country, who not long before had lived similar lives, grew distant. Small landholding white farmers and their families had fallen on hard times. The market that lured them into commercial agriculture threatened to take away their independence. They faced the loss of their land and livelihood. Their way of life no longer served as the standard for the South. New South spokesmen promoted cities and industries and ordered farmers to get on board the train of progress before it left the station without them.

## The Southern Environment

Railroads and industry affected not only the lives of rural southerners, but also their landscape. In terms of economic development, if there was one thing in which the New South matched the North it was the awful toll these took on the environment. At one time, a squirrel could travel from Virginia to Alabama without ever touching the ground—until the lumber industry moved south after the Civil War. Southerners had used the forests to build homes, fences, and outbuildings for generations before the war. But as late as 1880, much of the South's virgin forests of hardwood and long-leaf pines still stood. In the 1890s, railroads pierced these forests and steam-powered machines hauled cut logs for waiting rail cars to feed the growing cities of America. By 1900, one out of five southern industrial workers labored in the timber industry. Lumber companies clear-cut the land, and then moved on to the next stand of trees to do the same. Soil erosion and chronic flooding were the consequences of timbering in the South.

The railroad's penetration of Appalachia brought the banjo and black workers from the lowland South, and removed the iron ore and coal. But it left behind a gouged landscape, polluted streams, and sick miners. Appalachian landowners were complicit in these depredations, selling their birthrights to northern coal, iron, and railroad interests. Little wonder that in the upstart towns and cities of the South, often the most prominent structure by the turn of the century was the railroad terminal. And in these cities, particularly those with industry such as Birmingham and Chattanooga, smoke meant progress. The New South had mimicked the North quite well in its inattention to the environmental fallout from economic development.

It did not take much prognostication for farm families to see what was happening around and to them: declining prices for what they grew, greater profits for city-based enterprises, tainted drinking water and destroyed landscapes, and unforgiving banks. It was not the case that rural southerners longed for the past; they wanted to embrace the future and the consumer products now suddenly available to them that would moderate their lives. They only wanted a fair shot to take advantage of modern America; instead, they believed that the very forces that had brought progress to their land could bring ruin to them.

# The Southern Agrarian Revolt

**17.2** Why did southern farmers organize?

Even more than before the Civil War, cotton dominated southern agriculture between 1877 and 1900. And the economics of cotton brought despair to cotton farmers. The size of the cotton crop continued to set annual records after 1877. Fertilizers revived supposedly exhausted soils in North and South Carolina, turning them white with cotton. The railroad opened new areas for cultivation in Mississippi and eastern Texas. But the price of cotton fell while the price of fertilizers, agricultural tools, food, and most other necessities went up (see Figure 17.1). As a result, the more cotton the farmers grew, the less money they made.

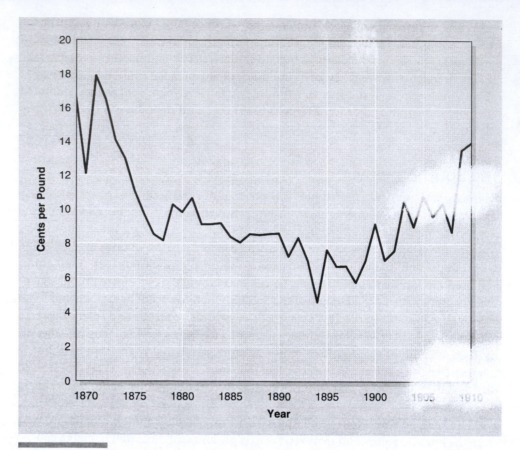

**FIGURE 17.1 THE PRICE OF COTTON, 1869–1910** The steadily declining price of cotton after the Civil War, from 18 cents a pound to 5 cents a pound by the early 1890s, reflected extreme overproduction. Behind the numbers lay an impoverished rural South.

SOURCE: U.S. Department of Commerce, *Historical Statistics of the United States: Colonial Times to 1957.*

## Cotton and Credit

The solution to this agrarian dilemma seemed simple: Grow less cotton. But that course was not possible for several reasons. In a cash-poor economy, credit ruled. Cotton was the only commodity instantly convertible into cash and thus the only commodity accepted for credit. Food crops generated less income per acre than cotton. Local merchants, themselves bound in a web of credit to merchants in larger cities, accepted cotton as collateral. As cotton prices plummeted, the merchants required their customers to grow more cotton to make up the difference. Trapped in debt by low cotton prices and high interest rates, small landowning farmers lost their land in record numbers. Just after the Civil War, less than one-third of white farmers in the South were tenants or sharecroppers. By the 1890s, nearly half were.

## Southern Farmers Organize, 1877–1892

As their circumstances deteriorated, southern farmers fought back. They had lived a communal life of church, family, and kin. Now they would widen the circle of their community to include other farmers sharing the same plight. These were not naïve country folk; most owned their own land and participated in the market economy. They just wanted to make the market fairer, to lower interest rates and ease credit, to regulate railroad freight rates, and to keep the prices of necessities in check.

But these goals required legislation that neither the federal government nor southern state governments were inclined to support. Therefore, southern farmers came together to address common grievances related to pricing, credit, and tax policies. The most powerful agricultural reform organization, the **Southern Farmers' Alliance,**

**Southern Farmers' Alliance** The largest of several organizations that formed in the post-Reconstruction South to advance the interests of beleaguered small farmers.

originated in Texas in the late 1870s. Alliance-sponsored farmers' cooperatives provided their members with discounts on supplies and credit. Members also benefited from marketing their cotton crops collectively.

The Alliance was still very much a Texas organization in 1887 when Charles W. Macune, a Wisconsin native, became its driving force. Macune sent a corps of speakers to create a network of southern cooperatives. Within two years, the Alliance had spread throughout the South and into the North and West. By 1890, it claimed more than a million members. With the exception of a few large landowners and some tenant farmers, almost all were small farmers who owned their own land. The success of the Alliance reflected both the desperate struggle of these small farmers to keep their land and the failure of other organizations to help them. The Alliance lobbied state legislatures to fund rural public schools. To increase the sense of community, the Alliance sponsored picnics, baseball games, and concerts.

The Alliance became for many small farmers a surrogate government and church in a region where public officials and many mainline Protestant ministers ignored their needs. It imposed strict morality on its members, prohibiting drinking, gambling, and sexual misconduct. Alliance leaders criticized the many Baptist, Methodist, and Presbyterian ministers who had strayed from the traditional emphasis on individual salvation and were defending a status quo that benefited large planters and towns. Cyrus Thompson, the president of the North Carolina Alliance and a prominent Methodist, declared in 1889 that "the church today stands where it has always stood, on the side of human slavery."

Some Alliance members left their churches for new religious groups. The Holiness movement, which began in the North before the Civil War, revived among Texas farmers in the mid-1880s. Holiness disciples advocated simple dress, avoided coffee and pork, and swore off all worldly amusements. The members of the Church of God, which was founded in the mountains of Tennessee and North Carolina in 1886, similarly sought to cleanse themselves of secular evils. The new churches promoted a vision of an egalitarian South. They accepted women on an equal basis, and occasionally black people as well. As many as a third of Holiness preachers were women.

Unlike some of the new religious movements, however, the Alliance did not accept black members. Black farmers formed the first **Colored Farmers' Alliance** in Texas in 1886. The Colored Alliance had fewer landowners and more tenants and sharecroppers in its ranks than the white organization. It concerned itself with issues relevant to this constituency, such as higher wages for cotton pickers. In 1891, the Colored Alliance attempted a region-wide strike over farm wages but was unable to enforce it in the worsening southern economy.

**Colored Farmers' Alliance** An organization of southern black farmers formed in Texas in 1886 in response to the Southern Farmers' Alliance, which did not accept black people as members.

The white Alliance had better results with a protest over price fixing. To protect cotton shipped to market, farmers wrapped it in a burlap-like material called jute. In 1888, jute manufacturers combined to raise the price from 7 cents to as much as 14 cents a yard. The Alliance initiated a jute boycott throughout the South, telling farmers to use cotton bagging as an alternative. The protest worked, forcing the chastened jute manufacturers to offer farmers their product at a mere 5 cents per yard.

**Storing Cotton.** This success encouraged Macune to pursue a more ambitious project. Low cotton prices and a lack of cash kept farmers poor. To address these problems, Macune proposed his **subtreasury plan**. Alliance members were to store their crops in a subtreasury (i.e., warehouse), keeping their cotton off the market until the price rose. In the meantime, the government would loan the farmers up to 80 percent of the value of the stored crops at a low interest rate of 2 percent per year. This arrangement would free farmers from merchants' high interest rates and crop liens. Macune urged Alliance members to endorse political candidates who supported the subtreasury scheme. Many Democratic candidates for state legislatures throughout the South did endorse it and were elected, with Alliance backing, in 1890. Once in office, however, they failed to deliver.

**subtreasury plan** A program promoted by the Southern Farmers' Alliance in response to low cotton prices and tight credit. Farmers would store their crop in a warehouse until prices rose, in the meantime borrowing up to 80 percent of the value of the stored crops from the government at a low interest rate.

The failure of the subtreasury plan, combined with a steep drop in cotton prices after 1890, undermined the Alliance. Its cooperatives collapsed as crop liens cut down

**Populist Party** A major third party of the 1890s, formed on the basis of the Southern Farmers' Alliance and other organizations, mounting electoral challenges against Democrats in the South and the Republicans in the West.

small landowners as though with scythes. Desperate Alliance leaders merged their organization with a new national political party in 1892, the People's Party, better known as the **Populist Party**. The Populists appropriated the Alliance program and challenged Democrats in the South and Republicans in the West. The merger reflected desperation more than calculation. As we will see in Chapter 20, the Populists stirred up national politics between 1892 and 1896. In the South, they challenged the Democratic Party, sometimes courting Republicans, including black voters.

# Women in the New South

**17.3** How did urbanization and industrialization affect race and gender relations in the South?

Just as farm women found their voices in the Alliance movement of the 1880s, a growing group of middle-class white and black urban women entered the public realm and engaged in policy issues. In the late-nineteenth-century North, women became increasingly active in reform movements, including woman suffrage, labor legislation, social welfare, and city planning. Building on their antebellum activist traditions, northern women, sometimes joining with men, sought to improve the status of women.

Because the antebellum reform movements included abolitionism, they had made little headway in the South. As a result, southern women had a meager reform tradition to build on. The war also left them ambivalent about independence. With husbands, fathers, and brothers dead or incapacitated, many women had to care for themselves and their families in the face of defeat and deprivation. Some determined never again to depend on men. Others, responding to the stress of running a farm or business, would have preferred less independence.

The response of southern white men to the war also complicated women's efforts to improve their status. Southern men had been shaken by defeat. They had lost the war and placed their families in peril. Many responded with alcoholism and violence. To regain their self-esteem, they recast the war as a noble crusade rather than a defeat. And they imagined southern white women as paragons of virtue and purity who required men to defend them. Demands for even small changes in traditional gender roles would threaten this image. Southern women understood this and never mounted an extensive reform campaign like their sisters in the North. Some middle-class women were openly hostile to reform, and others adopted conservative causes more inclined to reinforce the role of men in southern society than to challenge it.

Despite such limitations, middle-class southern women found opportunities to broaden their social role and enter the public sphere in the two decades after 1880. They found these opportunities primarily in the cities, where servants, stores, and schools freed them of many of the productive functions, such as making clothing, cooking, and childcare, that burdened their sisters in the country and kept them tied to the home.

## Church Work and Preserving Memories

Southern women waded warily into the public arena, using channels men granted them as natural extensions of the home, such as church work. By the 1880s, evangelical Protestant churches had become prominent in many aspects of southern life. Women took advantage of the church's prominence to build careers using the moral gravity of church affiliation to political advantage. Most of the major reform efforts in the South during this era emanated from the church, and from the women for whom church work was an approved role for their gender.

The movement to found home mission societies, for example, was led by single white women in the Methodist Church. Home missions promoted industrial education among the poor and helped working-class women become self-sufficient. The home mission movement reflected an increased interest in missionary work in white southern evangelical churches. Laura Haygood, an Atlantan who had served as a missionary in China, founded a home mission in Atlanta when she returned in 1883. Lily Hammond, another Atlantan, extended the mission concept when she opened settlement houses in black and white neighborhoods in Atlanta in the 1890s. **Settlement houses**, pioneered in New York in the 1880s, promoted middle-class values in poor neighborhoods and provided them with a permanent source of services. In the North, they were privately sponsored. In the South, they were supported by the Methodist Church and known as Wesley Houses, after John Wesley, the founder of Methodism.

Religion also prompted southern white women to join the **Women's Christian Temperance Union (WCTU)**. The first southern local was organized in Laura Haygood's church in Atlanta in 1880. Temperance reform, unlike other church-inspired activities, involved women directly in public policy. Women framed temperance and the prohibition of alcohol as a family issue—alcohol ruined families, victimizing innocent women and children. WCTU members visited schools to educate children about the evils of alcohol, addressed prisoners, and blanketed men's meetings with literature. As a result, they became familiar with the South's abysmal school system and its archaic criminal justice system. They soon began advocating education and prison reform as well as legislation against alcohol.

By the 1890s, many WCTU members realized that they could not achieve their goals unless women had the vote. Rebecca Latimer Felton, an Atlanta suffragist and WCTU member, reflected the frustration of her generation of southern women in an address to working women in 1892: "But some will say, you women might be quiet, you can't vote, you can't do anything! Exactly so, we have kept quiet for nearly a hundred years hoping to see relief come to the women of this country, and it hasn't come."

Rebecca Felton's own career highlighted the essentially conservative nature of the reform movement among middle-class white women in the New South. She fought for childcare facilities and sex education, as well as compulsory school attendance, and she pushed for the admission of women to the University of Georgia. But she strongly supported textile operators over textile workers and defended white supremacy. She had no qualms about the lynching of black men, executing them without trial "a thousand times a week if necessary" to preserve the purity of white women. In 1922, she became the first woman member of the U.S. Senate. By any definition, Felton was a reformer, but like most middle-class southern women, she had no interest in challenging the class and racial inequities of the New South.

The dedication of southern women to commemorating the memory of the Confederate cause also indicates the conservative nature of middle-class women's reform in the New South. Ladies' Memorial Associations formed after the war to ensure the proper burial of Confederate soldiers and suitable markings for their graves. The associations joined with men to erect monuments to Confederate leaders and, by the 1880s, to the common soldier. These activities reinforced white solidarity and constructed a common heritage for all white southerners regardless of class or location. By the 1890s, women were planning monuments in prominent civic spaces in the urban South. Their efforts sparked interest in city planning and city beautification. A new organization, the United Daughters of the Confederacy (UDC), appeared in 1894 to preserve southern history and honor its heroes.

## Women's Clubs

A broader spectrum of southern middle-class women joined women's clubs than joined church-sponsored organizations or memorial associations. Most women's clubs began in the 1880s as literary or self-improvement societies that had little interest in reform. By 1890, most towns and cities boasted at least several women's clubs and perhaps a federated club organization. But by that time, some clubs and their members had also begun to discuss political issues, such as child labor reform, educational improvement, and prison reform.

**settlement houses** A multipurpose structure in a poor neighborhood that offered social welfare, educational, and homemaking services to the poor or immigrants, usually under private auspices and directed by middle-class women.

**Women's Christian Temperance Union (WCTU)** Women's organization whose members visited schools to educate children about the evils of alcohol, addressed prisoners, and blanketed men's meetings with literature.

The activities of black women's clubs paralleled those of white women's clubs. Most African American women in southern cities worked as domestics or laundresses. Black women's clubs supported daycare facilities for working mothers and settlement houses in poor black neighborhoods modeled after those in northern cities. Atlanta's Neighborhood Union, founded by Lugenia Burns Hope in 1908, provided playgrounds and a health center and obtained a grant from a New York foundation to improve black education in the city. Black women's clubs also established homes for single black working women to protect them from sexual exploitation, and they worked for woman suffrage.

Only rarely, however, as at some meetings of the Young Women's Christian Association (YWCA) or occasional meetings in support of prohibition, did black and white club members interact. Some white clubwomen expressed sympathy for black women privately, but publicly they maintained white solidarity. Most were unwilling to sacrifice their own reform agenda to the cause of racial reconciliation.

The primary interest of most southern white women's clubs was the plight of young white working-class and farm women. This interest reflected the growing number of such women in the workforce. Single and adrift in the city, many worked for low wages, and some slipped into prostitution. The clubs sought to help them make the transition from rural to urban life or to improve their lives on the farm. To this end, they focused on child labor reform and on upgrading public education.

# Settling the Race Issue

**17.4** How did African Americans respond to the growing violence and legal restrictions whites directed at them?

The assertiveness of a new generation of African Americans in the 1880s and 1890s, especially in urban areas, provided the impetus and opportunity for white leaders to secure white solidarity. To counter black aspirations, white leaders enlisted the support of young white southerners, convincing them that the struggle for white supremacy would place them beside the larger-than-life heroes of the Civil War generation. African Americans resisted the resulting efforts to deprive them of their remaining freedoms. Although some left the South, many more built new lives and communities within the restricted framework white southerners allowed them.

## The Fluidity of Southern Race Relations, 1877–1890

Race relations remained remarkably fluid in the South between the end of Reconstruction and the early 1890s. Despite the departure of federal troops and the end of Republican rule, many black people continued to vote and hold office. Some Democrats even courted the black electorate. Although segregation ruled in churches, schools, and in some organizations and public places after the Civil War, black people and white people continued to mingle, do business with each other, and often maintain cordial relations.

In 1885, T. McCants Stewart, a black journalist from New York, traveled to his native South Carolina, expecting a rough reception once his train headed south from Washington, DC. To his surprise, the conductor allowed him to remain in his seat while white riders sat on baggage or stood. He provoked little reaction among white passengers when he entered the dining car. Some of them struck up a conversation with him. In Columbia, South Carolina, Stewart found that he could move about with no restrictions. "I can ride in first-class cars. . . . I can go into saloons and get refreshments even as in New York. I can stop in and drink a glass of soda and be more politely waited upon than in some parts of New England."

Other black people corroborated Stewart's experiences in different parts of the South. During the 1880s, black people joined interracial labor unions and continued to be active in the Republican Party. They engaged in business with white people. In the countryside, African Americans and white people hunted and fished together, worked side by side at sawmills, and traded with each other. Cities were segregated more by class than by race, and people of both races sometimes lived in the same neighborhoods. To be sure, black people faced discrimination in employment and voting and random retaliation for perceived violations of racial barriers. But the barriers were by no means fixed.

## The White Backlash

The black generation that came of age in this environment demanded full participation in American society. For many in the generation of white southerners who came of age in this period, however, this assertiveness rankled. These young white people, raised on the myth of the Lost Cause, were continually reminded of the heroism and sacrifice of their fathers during the Civil War. For them, black people replaced the Yankees as the enemy; they saw it as their mission to preserve white purity and dominance.

The South's deteriorating rural economy and the volatile politics of the late 1880s and early 1890s exacerbated the growing tensions between assertive black people and threatened white people. So too did the growth of industry and cities in the South. In the cities, black and white people came into close contact, competing for jobs and jostling each other for seats on streetcars and trains. Racist rhetoric and violence against black people accelerated in the 1890s.

## Lynch Law

In 1892, three prominent black men, Tom Moss, Calvin McDowell, and William Stewart, opened a grocery on the south side of Memphis, an area with a large African American population. The People's Grocery prospered, while a white-owned store across the street struggled. The proprietor of the white-owned store, W. H. Barrett, was incensed. He obtained an indictment against Moss, McDowell, and Stewart for maintaining a public nuisance. Outraged black community leaders called a protest meeting at the grocery, during which two people made threats against Barrett. Barrett learned of the threats, notified the police, and warned the gathering at the People's Grocery that white people planned to attack and destroy the store. Nine sheriff's deputies, all white, approached the store to arrest the men who had threatened Barrett. Fearing Barrett's threatened white assault, the people in the grocery fired on the deputies, unaware who they were, and wounded three. When the deputies identified themselves, thirty black people surrendered, including Moss, McDowell, and Stewart, and were imprisoned. Four days later, deputies removed the three owners from jail, took them to a deserted area, and shot them dead.

The men at the People's Grocery had violated two of the unspoken rules that white southerners imposed on black southerners to maintain racial barriers: They had prospered, and they had forcefully challenged white authority. During 1892, a year of political agitation and economic depression, 235 **lynchings** occurred in the South. White mobs lynched nearly 2,000 black southerners between 1882 and 1903. During the 1890s, lynchings occurred at the rate of 150 a year. Most lynchers were working-class whites with rural roots, who were struggling in the depressed economy of the 1890s and enraged at the fluidity of urban race relations. The men who murdered Moss, McDowell, and Stewart, for example, had recently moved to Memphis from the countryside, where they had been unable to make a living farming.

The most common justification for lynching was the presumed threat posed by black men to the sexual virtue of white women. Sexual "crimes" could include remarks, glances, and gestures. Yet only 25 percent of the lynchings that took place in the thirty years after 1890 had an alleged sexual connection. Certainly, the men of the People's

**lynchings** Executions, usually by a mob, without trial.

((• 📖 **Read the Document**   Ida B. Wells-Barnett, False Accusations, from *A Red Record* (1895)

Lynching became a public spectacle, a ritual designed to reinforce white supremacy. Note the matter-of-fact satisfaction of the spectators at this gruesome murder of a black man.

Grocery had committed no sex crime. Lynchers did not carry out their grisly crimes to end a rape epidemic; they killed to keep black men in their place and to restore their own sense of manhood and honor.

Ida B. Wells, who owned a black newspaper in Memphis, used her columns to publicize the People's Grocery lynchings. The great casualty of the lynchings, she noted, was her faith that education, wealth, and upright living guaranteed black people the equality and justice they had long sought. The reverse was true. The more black people succeeded, the greater was their threat to white people. She investigated other lynchings, countering the claim that they were the result of assaults on white women. When she suggested that, on the contrary, perhaps some white women were attracted to black men, the white citizens of Memphis destroyed her press and office. Exiled to Chicago, Wells devoted herself to the struggle for racial justice.

What was striking about this carnival of lynching from the 1890s onward was its orchestrated cruelty and the involvement of large segments of the white community. Postcards and bootlegged photographs of the events showed men, women, and even children gathering as if for a Sunday picnic, surrounding the mutilated corpse. The elevation of white men as the protector for weak women was one reason for the spectacle, but, more important, lynching reinforced white solidarity and reiterated (especially to blacks) that white supremacy ruled the South with impunity.

# Explore Racial Violence in the United States, 1880–1930, on MyHistoryLab

## WHAT WAS THE RELATIONSHIP BETWEEN RACIAL INEQUALITY AND VIOLENCE IN THE SOUTH DURING THE EARLY 1900s?

Though slaves were freed by the Thirteenth Amendment, the promises of equality offered to African Americans during Reconstruction under the Fourteenth and Fifteenth Amendments did not last long or went unfulfilled. White southerners worked to ensure that African Americans remained subordinate in the South. This system of discrimination used in part legal loopholes to disenfranchise African Americans, though outright violence was also employed to maintain white control. Some white southerners used lynching against African Americans who threatened the status quo. Victims were generally accused of some—often exaggerated—crime and subsequently hanged without a

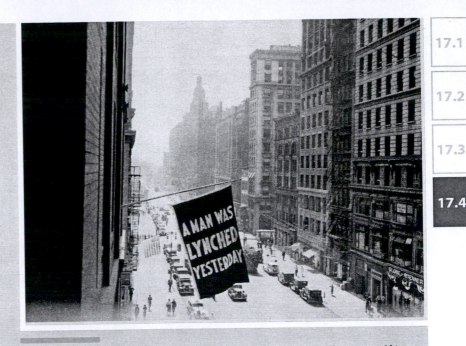

This flag was flown from the New York City headquarters of the NAACP whenever an African American had been lynched—summary execution without trial—in the South, a practice that continued into the 1930s.

trial. Lynching became a tool to maintain the social, political, and economic dominance of white southerners over African American communities.

### TOTAL LYNCHINGS IN SELECTED STATES, 1900–1931

| State | Total |
| --- | --- |
| Alabama | 132 |
| Arkansas | 127 |
| Florida | 170 |
| Georgia | 302 |
| Louisiana | 172 |
| Mississippi | 285 |
| Texas | 201 |

SOURCE: Lynchings by States and Counties in the United States 1900 to 1931, Research Department, Tuskegee Institute, http://memory.loc.gov/.

## KEY QUESTIONS  Use MyHistoryLab *Explorer* to answer these questions:

**Analysis ▶▶▶** *In what regions of the South were lynchings most common?*

Consider the reasons behind such patterns.

**Consequence ▶▶▶** *How did white literacy rates correspond to the frequency of lynchings in particular areas?*

Explore the relationship between these two elements.

**Response ▶▶▶** *How did local economic patterns affect the prevalence of lynchings?*

Consider connections between land ownership and violence against African Americans.

**segregation** A system of racial control that separated the races, initially by custom but increasingly by law, during and after Reconstruction.

**disfranchisement** The use of legal means to bar individuals or groups from voting.

## Segregation by Law

Southern white lawmakers sought to cement white solidarity and ensure black subservience in the 1890s by instituting **segregation** by law and the **disfranchisement** of black voters. Racial segregation restricting black Americans to separate and rarely equal public facilities had prevailed nationwide before the Civil War. After 1870, the custom spread rapidly in southern cities.

During the same period, many northern cities and states, often in response to protests by African Americans, were ending segregation. Roughly 95 percent of the nation's black population, however, lived in the South. Integration in the North, consequently, required white people to give up very little to black people. And as African American aspirations increased in the South during the 1890s while their political power waned, they became more vulnerable to segregation by law at the state level. At the same time, migration to cities, industrial development, and technologies such as railroads and elevators increased the opportunities for racial contact and muddled the rules of racial interaction.

Much of the new legislation focused on railroads, a symbol of modernity and mobility in the New South. Local laws and customs could not control racial interaction on interstate railroads. White passengers objected to black passengers' implied assertion of economic and social equality when they sat with them in dining cars and first-class compartments. Black southerners, by contrast, viewed equal access to railroad facilities as a sign of respectability and acceptance. When southern state legislatures required railroads to provide segregated facilities, black people protested.

Segregation laws required the railroads to provide "separate but equal" accommodations for black passengers. Railroads balked at the expense involved in doing so and provided black passengers with distinctly inferior facilities. Many lines refused to sell first-class tickets to black people and treated them roughly if they sat in first-class seats or tried to eat in the dining car. In 1890, Homer Plessy, a light-skinned black Louisianan, refused to leave the first-class car of a railroad traveling through the state. Arrested, he filed suit, arguing that his payment of the first-class fare entitled him to sit in the same first-class accommodations as white passengers. He claimed that under his right of citizenship guaranteed by the Fourteenth Amendment, neither the state of Louisiana nor the railroad could discriminate against him on the basis of color. The Constitution, he claimed, was color-blind.

*Plessy v. Ferguson* Supreme Court decision holding that Louisiana's railroad segregation law did not violate the Constitution as long as the railroads or the state provided equal accommodations.

The U.S. Supreme Court ruled on the case, *Plessy v. Ferguson*, in 1896. In a seven-to-one decision, the Court held that Louisiana's railroad segregation law did not violate the Constitution as long as the railroads or the state provided equal accommodations for black passengers. Justice Henry B. Brown, a native of Michigan, spoke for the majority, expressing social opinions common among whites at the time. "Social prejudices," he wrote, may not be "overcome by legislation," and lawmakers were "powerless to eradicate racial instincts." As for the Fourteenth Amendment's guarantee of equal rights, Brown wrote that the amendment did not require "an enforced commingling of the two races," and, in fact, such interaction would worsen race relations. He concluded, "If one race be inferior to the other socially, the Constitution of the United States cannot put them upon the same plane." The decision left unclear what "equal" meant. The only justice to vote against the decision was John Marshall Harlan, a Kentuckian and former slave owner. In a stinging dissent, he predicted that the decision would result in an all-out assault on black rights.

Harlan's was a prophetic dissent. Both northern and southern states enacted new segregation laws in the wake of *Plessy v. Ferguson*. In practice, the separate facilities for black people these laws required, if provided at all, were rarely equal.

**Jim Crow laws** Segregation laws that became widespread in the South during the 1890s.

The segregation statutes came to be known collectively as **Jim Crow laws**, after the blackface stage persona of Thomas Rice, a white northern minstrel-show performer in the 1820s. Reflecting white stereotypes of African Americans, Rice had caricatured Crow as a foolish, elderly, lame slave who spoke in an exaggerated dialect. The purpose of these laws was not only to separate the races, but also to humiliate blacks and reinforce white supremacy. Separation was never equal. William Jefferson White, a black journalist and educator in Augusta, Georgia, wrote at the turn of the twentieth century that the segregation laws represented a concerted effort "to humiliate the colored people. They speak of the Negro in this day of freedom, just as they spoke of them in the days of slavery."

Economic segregation followed social segregation. Before the Civil War, black men had dominated such crafts as carpentry and masonry. By the 1890s, white men were replacing them in these trades and excluding them from new ones, such as plumbing and electrical work. Trade unions, composed primarily of craft workers, began systematically to exclude African Americans. Although the steel and tobacco industries hired black workers, most other manufacturers turned them away. Confined increasingly to low or unskilled positions in railroad construction, the timber industry, and agriculture, black people underwent deskilling, a decline in workforce expertise, after 1890. With lower incomes from unskilled labor, they faced reduced opportunities for better housing and education.

## Disfranchisement

With economic and social segregation came political isolation. The authority of post-Reconstruction Redeemer governments had rested on their ability to limit and control the black vote. Following the political instability of the late 1880s and the 1890s, however, white leaders determined to disfranchise black people altogether, thereby reinforcing white solidarity and eliminating the need to consider black interests. Obstacles loomed—the Fifteenth Amendment, which guaranteed freedmen the right to vote, and a Republican-dominated Congress—but with a national consensus emerging in support of white supremacy, they proved easy to circumvent. Support for disfranchisement was especially strong among large landowners in the South's plantation districts, where heavy concentrations of black people threatened their political domination. Urban leaders, especially after the turmoil of the 1890s, looked on disfranchisement as a way to stabilize politics and make elections more predictable.

The movement to reduce or eliminate the black vote in the South began in the 1880s and continued through the early 1900s (see Table 17.1). Democrats enacted a variety of measures to attain their objectives without violating the letter of the Fifteenth Amendment. They complicated the registration and voting processes. States enacted **poll taxes**, requiring citizens to pay to vote. They adopted the secret ballot, which confused and intimidated illiterate black voters accustomed to using ballots with colors to identify parties. States set literacy and educational qualifications for voting or required prospective registrants to "interpret" a section of the state constitution. To avoid disfranchising poor, illiterate white voters with these measures, states enacted **grandfather clauses**, granting the vote automatically to anyone whose grandfather could have voted prior to 1867 (the year Congressional Reconstruction began). The grandfathers of most black men in the 1890s had been slaves, ineligible to vote.

Tennessee was the first state to pass disfranchising legislation. In 1889, it required the secret ballot and a poll tax in four cities, Nashville, Memphis, Chattanooga, and Knoxville, where African Americans often held the balance of power. A year later, Mississippi amended its constitution to require voters to pass a literacy test and to prove that they "understood" the state constitution. The laws granted the registrar wide latitude in interpreting the accuracy of the registrant's understanding. When a journalist asked an Alabama lawmaker if Jesus Christ could pass his state's "understanding" test, the legislator replied, "That would depend entirely on which way he was going to vote."

Lawmakers sold white citizens on franchise restrictions with the promise that they would apply only to black voters and would scarcely affect white voters. This promise proved untrue. Alarmed by the Populist uprising, Democratic leaders used disfranchisement to gut dissenting parties. During the 1880s, minority parties in the South consistently polled an average of 40 percent of the statewide vote; by the mid-1890s, the figure had diminished to 30 percent despite the Populist insurgency. Turnout dropped even more dramatically. In Mississippi, for example, voter turnout in gubernatorial races during the 1880s averaged 51 percent; during the 1890s, it was 21 percent. Black turnout in Mississippi, which averaged 39 percent in the 1880s, plummeted to near zero in the 1890s. Overall turnout, which averaged 64 percent during the 1880s, fell to only 30 percent by 1910.

**poll taxes** Taxes imposed on voters as a requirement for voting.

**grandfather clauses** Rule that required potential voters to demonstrate that their grandfathers had been eligible to vote; used in some southern states after 1890 to limit the black electorate.

((• ▭ **Read the Document**  Booker T. Washington, Atlanta Exposition Address (1895)

TABLE 17.1 THE MARCH OF DISFRANCHISEMENT ACROSS THE SOUTH, 1889–1908

| Year | State | Strategies |
|---|---|---|
| 1889 | Florida | Poll tax |
| 1889 | Tennessee | Poll tax |
| 1890 | Mississippi | Poll tax, literacy test, understanding clause |
| 1891 | Arkansas | Poll tax |
| 1893, 1901 | Alabama | Poll tax, literacy test, grandfather clause |
| 1894, 1895 | South Carolina | Poll tax, literacy test, understanding clause |
| 1894, 1902 | Virginia | Poll tax, literacy test, understanding clause |
| 1897, 1898 | Louisiana | Poll tax, literacy test, grandfather clause |
| 1899, 1900 | North Carolina | Poll tax, literacy test, grandfather clause |
| 1902 | Texas | Poll tax |
| 1908 | Georgia | Poll tax, literacy test, understanding clause, grandfather clause |

## History and Memory

Whites codified white supremacy in laws, enforced it with violence, and institutionalized it on the landscape and in the history books. Not only did history immortalize the Lost Cause and the Redemption, but it also served a more contemporary purpose. It endorsed white supremacy and justified actions carried out in its name. By the early 1900s, a statue of a Confederate soldier stood guard over courthouse squares throughout the South, silent witness to sacrifice and restoration. In Richmond, the capital of the Confederacy became a shrine. Down the wide boulevard of Monument Avenue, the statues of the war heroes marched. By 1900, only three monuments paid tribute to black soldiers, and none was in the South. African Americans were as absent in the landscape as they were in the textbooks.

## A National Consensus on Race

White southerners openly segregated, disfranchised, and lynched African Americans, and twisted the historical record beyond recognition without a national outcry for the same reasons they were able to overthrow Reconstruction. The majority of Americans in the 1890s subscribed to the notion that black people were inferior to white people and deserved to be treated as second-class citizens. Contemporary depictions of black people show scarcely human stereotypes: black men with bulbous lips and bulging eyes, fat black women wearing turbans and smiling vacuously, and black children contentedly eating watermelon or romping with jungle animals. Among the widely read books of the era was *The Clansman,* a glorification of the rise of the Ku Klux Klan. D. W. Griffith transformed *The Clansman* into an immensely popular motion picture epic under the title *Birth of a Nation.*

Intellectual and political opinion in the North bolstered southern policy. So-called scientific racism purported to establish white superiority and black inferiority on biological grounds. Northern-born professional historians reinterpreted the Civil War and Reconstruction in the white South's favor. Harvard's Charles Francis Adams Jr. chided colleagues who disregarded the "fundamental, scientific facts" that, he claimed, demonstrated black inferiority. The *New York Times,* summarizing this national consensus in 1903, noted that "practically the whole country" supported the "southern solution" to the race issue, because "there was no other possible settlement."

These views permeated Congress, which made no effort to block the institutionalization of white supremacy in the South after 1890, and the courts, which upheld discriminatory legislation. As the white consensus on race emerged, the status of African Americans slipped in the North as well as the South. Although no northern states threatened to deny black citizens the right to vote, they did increase segregation. The

"Uncle Rastus" promoting Cream of Wheat. The national consensus on race included the belief among whites that African Americans were inferior. Black caricatures became common in the new advertising media, exaggerating the physical features and alleged lack of intelligence of black people as indicated here in the ungrammatical endorsement. Uncle Rastus made his first appearance in 1890. Such images enabled the South to control its black population through legislation and violence without interference from outside authorities. Uncle Rastus was modeled after Frank L. White, a Chicago chef who was paid five dollars to pose for the ad. With only slight modifications, Uncle Rastus continues to represent Cream of Wheat to this day.

booming industries of the North generally did not hire black workers. Antidiscrimination laws on the books since the Civil War went unenforced. In 1904, 1906, and 1908, race riots erupted in Springfield, Ohio; Greensburg, Indiana; and Springfield, Illinois, matching similar disturbances in Wilmington, North Carolina; and Atlanta, Georgia.

## Responses of the Black Community

American democracy had, it seemed, hung out a "whites only" sign. How could African Americans respond to the growing political, social, and economic restrictions on their lives? Given white America's hostility, protest proved ineffective, even dangerous. African Americans organized more than a dozen boycotts of streetcar systems in the urban South between 1896 and 1908 in an effort to desegregate them, but not one succeeded. The Afro-American Council, formed in 1890 to protest the deteriorating conditions of black life, accomplished little and disbanded in 1908. W. E. B. Du Bois organized an annual Conference on Negro Problems at Atlanta University beginning in 1896, but it produced no effective plan of action.

The fact that few in the white community, North or South, took up their cause, and the fact that federal courts endorsed the exclusionary legislation hampered black efforts. The array of power against them discouraged but did not deter persistent black efforts to challenge white supremacy. They mounted, for example, a vigorous attack on disfranchisement. When 160 South Carolina delegates gathered to amend the state constitution in 1895, the six black delegates among them mounted a passionate but futile defense of their right to vote. The protesters understood that once blacks became invisible in the political arena, they would disappear from public policy. Public expenditures for black public schools, for example, plummeted drastically after disfranchisement.

The protests helped to develop black self-help organizations and also to maintain self-respect and dignity in a very trying environment. African Americans also resorted to humor. A popular story circulating in southern black neighborhoods in the early twentieth century told of a black man arrested for running a red light. As the defendant explained to the judge, "Lord, boss, I sho' thought them green lights was for the white folks and the red lights was for us cullud folks."

A few black people chose to leave the South. In 1879, Benjamin "Pap" Singleton, a Nashville real estate agent, led several thousand black migrants to Kansas. Henry McNeal Turner of Georgia, an African Methodist Episcopal (AME) bishop, promoted migration to Liberia, but only a few hundred made the trip in the late 1870s, Turner not included, and most of them returned disappointed. Most black people who moved in the 1890s stayed within the South, settling in places like Mississippi, Louisiana, and Texas, where they could find work with timber companies or farming new lands that had opened to cotton and rice cultivation.

In southern cities, African Americans attempted to counter their growing invisibility in politics and society by using public space to express their solidarity and contributions to American society. These events also served to present a different narrative of southern history from the one southern whites were building with their monuments, heritage groups, and school books.

New Year's Day, the anniversary of the Emancipation Proclamation (see Chapter 15), was probably the most-celebrated date on the black calendar in the South. Blacks also celebrated Washington's birthday in February, using that occasion to remind their communities that their ancestors had fought alongside white patriots to secure the nation's independence. Lincoln's birthday also occurred in February, and many black communities celebrated that anniversary, adding to it the purported birthday of Frederick Douglass (February 18), all of which played a role in the designation by black scholar Carter G. Woodson of February as Black History Month in 1926. The Fourth of July was another celebration divided by the color line, as southern blacks marked the event, but not whites until the 1890s.

African Americans marked these milestones with parades, parties, and picnics. They added church anniversaries and the founding dates of their benevolent societies to the holiday calendar as well.

That these events also contained more than a hint of protest is evident from the ritual of blacks in Richmond, Virginia, in the 1890s of gathering at the imposing equestrian statue of Robert E. Lee on stately Monument Avenue. They did not seek to honor the general, but rather to highlight his defeat at the hands of the Union army, which included African American soldiers.

Orators were key figures at all of these celebrations, as they were at white events. Speakers reminded listeners about the heroism of black Civil War soldiers, about great black leaders such as Frederick Douglass, and about the importance of not succumbing to despair.

Yet, by the end of the nineteenth century, African Americans in the South faced great obstacles. They confronted not only a battery of laws and the ever-present threat of violence, but also a national consensus that relegated them to a permanent second-class citizenship. The *New York Times,* the leading Republican Party newspaper of the era, printed an editorial in May 1900 that summarized northern attitudes toward segregation and disfranchisement. "Northern men . . . no longer denounce the suppression of the Negro vote [in the South] as it used to be denounced in the reconstruction days. The necessity of it under the supreme law of self-preservation is candidly recognized."

While the northern press endorsed white supremacy, Congress repealed all of the federal election laws, easing the way for disfranchisement. Given the racial climate, it is remarkable that African Americans built communities, maintained self-respect and dignity, and developed a small, though influential middle class.

**An Urban Middle Class.**   Black people withdrew to develop their own rich community life within the restricted confines white society permitted them. Particularly in the cities of the South, they could live relatively free of white surveillance and even white contact. In 1890, fully 70 percent of black city dwellers lived in the South; and between 1860 and 1900, the proportion of black people in the cities of the South rose from one in six to more than one in three. The institutions, businesses, and families that black people had begun painstakingly building during Reconstruction continued to grow, and in some cases flourish, after 1877.

By the 1880s, a new black middle class had emerged in the South. Urban-based, professional, business-oriented, and serving a primarily black clientele, its members fashioned an interconnected web of churches, fraternal and self-help organizations, families, and businesses. Black Baptists, AME, and AME Zion churches led reform efforts that sought to eliminate drinking, prostitution, and other vices in black neighborhoods.

African American fraternal and self-help groups, led by middle-class black people, functioned as surrogate welfare organizations for the poor. Fraternal orders also served as the seedbed for such business ventures as the North Carolina Mutual Life Insurance Company, founded in Durham in 1898. Within two decades, North Carolina Mutual became the largest black-owned business in the nation and helped transform Durham into the "capital of the black middle class."

The African American middle class worked especially hard to improve black education (see Figure 17.2). Declining black political power encouraged white leaders to

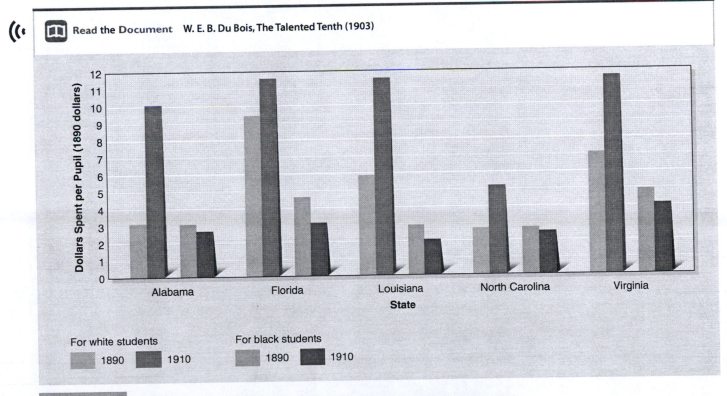

((• 📖 **Read the Document**   W. E. B. Du Bois, The Talented Tenth (1903)

For white students
1890   1910

For black students
1890   1910

**FIGURE 17.2 DISFRANCHISEMENT AND EDUCATIONAL SPENDING IN THE SOUTH, 1890–1910**
By barring black people from the political process, franchise restrictions limited their access to government services. Educational expenditures, which increased for white people but decreased for black people following disfranchisement, provide one measure of the result.

SOURCE: Robert A. Margo, "Disfranchisement, School Finance, and the Economics of Segregated Schools in the United States South, 1890–1910," Ph.D diss., Harvard University, 1982.

reduce funding for black public education. Black students in cities had only makeshift facilities; those in the countryside had almost no facilities. By the early 1900s, the student–teacher ratio in Nashville's segregated school system was 33 to one for white schools but 71 to one for black schools. To improve these conditions, black middle-class leaders solicited educational funds from northern philanthropic organizations.

**Black Women's Roles.** After disfranchisement, middle-class black women assumed an even more pivotal role in the black community. While men could only protest at their peril, or utilize the indirect method of celebrations to express their humanity, black women, by virtue of their gender, had more latitude of expression; and, like Anna J. Cooper, they used it. They often used their relations with prominent white women and organizations such as the WCTU and the YWCA to press for public commitments to improve the health and education of African Americans. Absent political pressure from black men, and given the danger of African American males asserting themselves in the tense racial climate after 1890, black women became critical spokespersons for their race.

Black middle-class women joined together in clubs and performed an array of social services for their communities. Some of these services were coordinated from

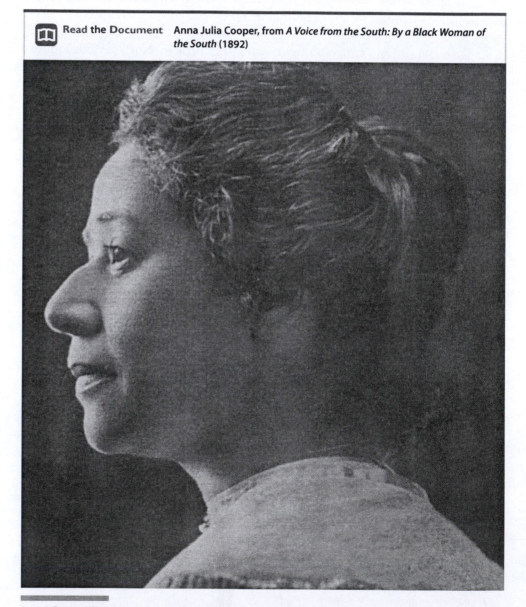

**Read the Document** Anna Julia Cooper, from *A Voice from the South: By a Black Woman of the South* (1892)

Anna J. Cooper. Like many educated black, middle-class women in the 1890s, she expressed the optimistic view that education, hard work, and building a sense of community would overcome white prejudice and legal restrictions.

the Washington, DC, headquarters of the National Association of Colored Women (NACW), a federal of black women's clubs founded in 1896 with Mary Church Terrell as its president. The NACW, like its white counterpart, the General Federation of Women's Clubs, established in 1887, was a middle-class organization that focused on helping poor women and children. The NACW slogan, "Lifting as We Climb," encapsulated the dual purposes of middle-class black reform. Like white women's clubs, initial activities of black women's clubs focused on self-improvement and then moved in ever wider circles to the broader community. Given the close connection between history and identity, black women used the past to educate and edify, just like the male orators at celebratory events.

As the black urban population surged in the South during the 1890s, club women directed more of their activities toward poor blacks, single women, and school children in the cities, again, similar to the efforts of white club women. Quietly, black women replaced the Confederate school curriculum in favor of a broader, more positive instruction. One black teacher, Mamie Garvin Fields, recalled teaching her students in this period "America the Beautiful" and the Pledge of Allegiance. "My school was in the United States, after all, and not the Confederacy."

Black club women also shared with their white sisters the belief that the first postwar generation would cast the mold for the race and the South for decades to come. They possessed a sense of mission and obligation that enabled them to pool the limited resources of the black community and provide an array of social and educational services that no one else would have provided. We can marvel at the exuberance and confidence with which black educator Anna J. Cooper approached the challenges of an era that broke the dreams of many African Americans in the South.

The extension of black club work into rural areas of the South, where the majority of the African American population lived, to educate families about hygiene, nutrition, and childcare, anticipated similar efforts among white women after 1900. But unlike their white counterparts, these middle-class black women worked with limited resources in a context of simmering racial hostility and political and economic impotence. In response, they nurtured a self-help strategy to improve the conditions of the people they sought to help. One of the most prominent African American leaders of the late nineteenth and early twentieth centuries, Booker T. Washington, adopted a similar approach to racial uplift.

**Booker T. Washington's Accommodation.** Born a slave in Virginia in 1856, Washington and his family worked in the salt and coal mines of West Virginia after the Civil War. Ambitious and flushed with the postwar enthusiasm for advancement that gripped freedmen, he enrolled in Hampton Normal and Agricultural Institute, the premier black educational institution in the South. Washington worked his way through Hampton, graduated, taught for a time, and then, in 1881, founded the Tuskegee Institute for black students in rural Alabama. Washington thought that his students would be best served if they learned a trade and workplace discipline. By learning industrial skills, he maintained, black people could acquire self-respect and economic independence. As a result, Tuskegee emphasized vocational training over the liberal arts.

Washington argued that African Americans should accommodate themselves to segregation and disfranchisement until they could prove their economic worth to American society. In exchange for this accommodation, however, white people should help provide black people with the education and job training they would need to gain their independence. Washington articulated this position, known as the **Atlanta Compromise**, in a speech at the Atlanta Cotton States and International Exposition in 1895. Despite his conciliatory public stance, Washington secretly helped to finance legal challenges to segregation and disfranchisement. The social and economic realities of the South, meanwhile, frustrated his educational mission. Increasingly, black people were shut out of the kinds of jobs for which Washington hoped to train them. Facing a depressed rural economy and growing racial violence, they had little prospect of advancement.

**Atlanta Compromise** Booker T. Washington's policy accepting segregation and disfranchisement for African Americans in exchange for white assistance in education and job training.

505

## From Then to Now
# The Confederate Battle Flag

M emories of the Civil War and Reconstruction formed a crucial part of southern civic and religious culture from the late nineteenth century onward. White southerners perceived themselves and the rest of the nation through the lens of the heroic Lost Cause and the alleged abuses of Reconstruction, and the symbols associated with those events took on the status of icons. During the 1890s, the memory industry that white political and religious leaders had promoted since the end of the war became institutionalized. Organizations such as the United Daughters of the Confederacy and the Sons of Confederate Veterans strove to educate a new generation of white southerners on the sacrifices of the war generation, bolstering white supremacy through racial segregation and disfranchisement. The Confederate battle flag emerged from this process as an icon of the Lost Cause and a symbol of white supremacy.

Confederate Battle Flag at 1917 Reunion of Confederate veterans.

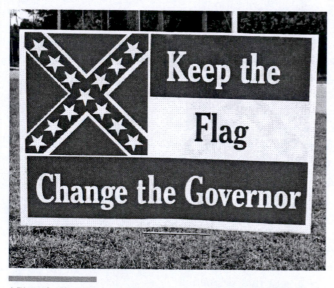

A "Keep the Flag. Change the Governor" political sign is shown in a yard in Louisville, Mississippi, October 9, 2003. Two years after Mississippi voters decided to keep a Confederate battle emblem on their state banner, the flag had again become an issue in the governor's race. In a television ad, Republican gubernatorial nominee Haley Barbour said Democratic governor Ronnie Musgrove "attacked" the state flag when he insisted on giving voters a chance to decide the banner's design in 2001. Barbour's campaign office in Yazoo City, Mississippi, was also distributing "Keep the Flag. Change the Governor" campaign materials. Barbour won the election.

The Confederate battle flag was displayed mostly at veterans' reunions and only rarely on other public occasions until the late 1940s, that is, when civil rights for African Americans reemerged as a national issue. Proponents argued that the battle flag represented heritage, not hate. Opponents denounced it as a symbol of white supremacy. Controversies and referenda over the display and location of battle flags and the design of state flags flared in South Carolina, Georgia, and Mississippi from 1999 through 2004, and an NAACP boycott of South Carolina over the battle flag persists to this day. When people in other parts of the country sometimes remark that white southerners are still fighting the Civil War, it is controversies like the one over the battle flag that they have in mind.

But the controversy is less about the past than it is about the way we use history to shape our understanding of the society we live in and our vision of its future. At issue is not just history, but whose history. In this sense the flag controversy can at least generate positive dialogue. Even so, in the interests of reconciliation, it may be time for southerners to follow Robert E. Lee's final order to his men and "Furl the flag, boys."

### Question for Discussion

- Is the current conflict over the Confederate battle flag a reflection of differing views of history or does it derive from present-day issues?

**W. E. B. Du Bois Attacks the Atlanta Compromise.** Another prominent African American leader, W. E. B. Du Bois, challenged Washington's acceptance of black social inequality. Born in Massachusetts in 1868, Du Bois was the first African American to earn a doctorate at Harvard. Du Bois promoted self-help, education, and black pride. A gifted teacher and writer, he taught at Atlanta University and wrote eighteen books on various aspects of black life in America. In *The Souls of Black Folk,* published in 1903, he described the strengths of black culture and attacked Washington's Atlanta Compromise. Du Bois was a cofounder, in 1910, of the **National Association for the Advancement of Colored People (NAACP)**, an interracial organization dedicated to restoring African American political and social rights.

**National Association for the Advancement of Colored People (NAACP)** Interracial organization cofounded by W. E. B. Du Bois in 1910 dedicated to restoring African American political and social rights.

Despite their differences, which reflected their divergent backgrounds, Washington and Du Bois agreed on many issues. Both had reservations about allowing illiterate black people to vote, and both believed that black success in the South required some white assistance. But it became apparent to Du Bois that "the best white people" did not care to elevate black southerners. In 1906, after a bloody race riot in Atlanta, Du Bois left the South, a decision millions of black southerners would make over the next two decades.

## Conclusion

On the surface, the South was more like the rest of the nation in 1900 than at any other time since 1860. Southern cities hummed with activity, and industries from textiles to steel dotted the southern interior. Young men and women migrated to southern cities to pursue opportunities unavailable to their parents. Advances in the production and marketing of cigarettes and soft drinks would soon make southern entrepreneurs and their products household names. Southerners ordered fashions from Sears, Roebuck catalogs and enjoyed electric lights, electric trolleys, and indoor plumbing as much as other urban Americans.

Americans idealized the South—not the urban industrial South, but a mythical South of rural grace and hospitality. National magazines and publishers rushed to print stories about this land of moonlight and magnolias, offering it as a counterpoint to the crowded, immigrant-infested, factory-fouled, money-grubbing North. It was this fantasy South that white people in both the North and the South imagined as they came to a common view on race and reconciled their differences. Northern journalists offered admiring portraits of such southern heroes as Robert E. Lee, of whom one declared in 1906, "the nation has a hero to place beside her greatest." The Republican-dominated Congress agreed to care for the graves of the Confederate dead and ordered the return to the South of captured Confederate flags. White southerners cultivated national reconciliation but remained fiercely dedicated to preserving the peculiarities of their region: a one-party political system, disfranchisement of African Americans, and segregation by law. Though the region's urban and industrial growth was impressive, deep rural poverty and low urban wages restricted the development of a vigorous consumer-oriented economy that characterized the North.

How one viewed the New South depended on one's vantage point. White northerners accepted at face value the picture southerners painted for them of a chastened and prosperous, yet still attractive, region. Middle-class white people in the urban South enjoyed the benefits of a national economy and a secure social position. Middle-class white women enjoyed increased influence in the public realm, but not to the extent of their northern sisters. And the institutionalization of white supremacy gave even poor white farmers and factory workers a place in the social hierarchy a rung or two above the bottom.

For black people, the New South proved a crueler ruse than Reconstruction. No one now stepped forward to support their cause and stem the erosion of their economic independence, political freedom, and civil rights. Yet they did not give up the American dream, nor did they give up the South for the most part. Black men, and especially black women built communities and worked as best they could to challenge restrictions on their freedom.

The New South was thus both American and southern. It shared with the rest of the country a period of rapid urban and industrial growth. But the legacy of war and slavery still lay heavily on the South, manifesting itself in rural poverty, segregation, and black disfranchisement. The burdens of this legacy would limit the attainments of both black and white southerners for another half century, until Americans finally rejected racial inequality as an affront to their national ideals. America allowed the South to take another path, and the South took the nation on a long detour until the despised African righted the way.

**For Suggested Readings go to MyHistoryLab.**

# On MyHistoryLab

## Chapter Review

### The "Newness" of the New South

 **17.1** How new was the New South? p. 483

Southern cities and industries grew impressively after the Civil War, especially when compared to the overwhelmingly rural nature of the Old South. However, a struggling agricultural sector and low wages in factories limited the South's economic potential. Economic development did not overturn, but rather reinforced the South's racial and gender relations.

### The Southern Agrarian Revolt

**17.2** Why did southern farmers organize? p. 489

Declining prices for cotton and the rising costs of fertilizers and food created an economic vise for southern farmers. Small landowners and sharecroppers in particular suffered. In the decades after Reconstruction, southern farmers joined together to provide mutual aid, community, and, eventually, a political platform to air their grievances.

### Women in the New South

**17.3** How did urbanization and industrialization affect race and gender relations in the South? p. 492

Working through their churches and clubs, middle-class black and white women addressed a range of issues in the postwar South. Working separately, they each focused on family-related causes such as temperance and education. White women also led on preserving Civil War memories and black women on uplifting the less fortunate members of their race.

### Settling the Race Issue

 **17.4** How did African Americans respond to the growing violence and legal restrictions whites directed at them? p. 494

As the first generation of African Americans born in freedom came of age in the 1880s, they asserted the rights of that freedom. Whites reacted to preserve the verdict of Redemption. The result was a rise in lynching and the legalization of segregation and disfranchisement, all of which blacks contested, usually unsuccessfully.

## Timeline

**1872** The "Newness" of the New South—Texas and Pacific Railway connects Dallas to eastern markets

**1880** Women in the New South—First southern local of the Women's Christian Temperance Union is formed in Atlanta

**1881** Settling the Race Issue—Booker T. Washington establishes Tuskegee Institute

**1883** Women in the New South—Laura Haygood founds the home mission movement in Atlanta

**1886** The "Newness" of the New South—Dr. John Pemberton creates Coca-Cola

**1887** The Southern Agrarian Revolt—Charles W. Macune expands the Southern Farmer's Alliance from its Texas base to the rest of the South

**1890** Settling the Race Issue—Mississippi becomes the first state to restrict black suffrage with literacy tests

**1894** Women in the New South—United Daughters of the Confederacy is founded

**1895** Settling the Race Issue—Booker T. Washington delivers his "Atlanta Compromise" address

**1907** The "Newness" of the New South—Pittsburgh-based U.S. Steel takes over Birmingham's largest steel producer

# 18 Industry, Immigrants, and Cities 1870–1900

## One American Journey

A Young Girl Describes Her Journey from Russia to the Ship That Will Take Her to America

**W**e were homeless, **houseless,** and friendless in a strange place. We had hardly money enough to last us through the voyage for which we had hoped and waited for three long years. We had suffered much that the reunion we longed for might come about; we had prepared ourselves to suffer more in order to bring it about, and had parted with those we loved, with places that were dear to us in spite of what we passed through in them, never again to see them, as we were convinced, all for the same dear end. With strong hopes and high spirits that hid the sad parting, we had started on our long journey. And now we were checked so unexpectedly but surely. . . . When my mother had recovered enough to speak, she began to argue with the *gendarme,* telling him our story and begging him to be kind. The children were frightened and all but I cried. I was only wondering what would happen. . . . Here we had been taken to a lonely place; . . . our things were taken away, our friends separated from us; a man came to

Photographer Lewis Hine's portrait of a young Jewish woman arriving from Russia at Ellis Island in 1905. Like hundreds of thousands of other immigrants who passed through the portals of New York harbor, this young woman's expression carries the hope, fear, and remembrance that touched her fellow wanderers as they embarked on their new life in America.

## LEARNING OBJECTIVES

**18.1** ((•
How did workers respond to the changing demands of the workplace in the late nineteenth century? p. 511

**18.2** ((•
What kinds of communities did new immigrants create in America? p. 522

**18.3** ((•
How did the new cities help to create the new middle class? p. 531

((• Listen to Chapter 18 on MyHistoryLab

From *The American Journey*, Seventh Edition. Goldfield, Abbott, Anderson, Argersinger, Argersinger and Barney Copyright © 2014 by Pearson Education, Inc. All rights reserved.

#  Watch the Video Series on MyHistoryLab

Learn about some key topics related to this chapter with the *MyHistoryLab Video Series: Key Topics in U.S. History.*

**1** **The Rise of an Industrial Giant: 1865–1900** During the decades following the Civil War, the United States experienced rapid growth in both industrial development and urban expansion. This video surveys the new industries, products, businesses, organizational models, and an increasing population that combined to create fantastic wealth and a middle class as well as the overcrowding of cities, pollution, and social and economic inequities.

**Watch** on **MyHistoryLab**

**The Gilded Men** Robber Barons or Captains of Industry? In this video industrialists, financiers, and other capitalists of the late nineteenth century, such as Andrew Carnegie, John D. Rockefeller, and J. P. Morgan, are profiled. Not only did they build industrial empires and make the United States a dominant economic power, but they also accumulated vast wealth in very few hands in ways never before seen in human history.

**Watch** on **MyHistoryLab** **2**

**3** **The New American City** The growth of industry during the Gilded Age went hand in hand with the expansion of urban centers in the northeastern and midwestern United States. American cities remained attractive destinations for immigrants as well as for newcomers from the rural regions of the United States who wished to take advantage of the greater economic opportunities that urban life afforded. However, as this video makes clear, these new opportunities and challenges changed the face of American cities forever.

**Watch** on **MyHistoryLab**

**The Making of a Consumer Culture** This video looks at the second industrial revolution and the consumer culture it brought with it in the form of new gadgets, labor-saving devices, ready-to-wear clothes, fast food, and similar conveniences and choices. It also examines the new system of consumer credit and the many kinds of retail outlets, such department stores, dime stores, and mail-order catalogs, that were a part of the making of the American consumer paradise. **4**

**Watch** on **MyHistoryLab**

inspect us, as if to ascertain our full value; strange-looking people driving us about like dumb animals, helpless and unresisting; children we could not see crying in a way that suggested terrible things; ourselves driven into a little room where a great kettle was boiling on a little stove; our clothes taken off, our bodies rubbed with a slippery substance that might be any bad thing; a shower of warm water let down on us without warning. . . . We are forced to pick out our clothes from among all the others, with the steam blinding us; we choke, cough, entreat the women to give us time; they persist, "Quick! Quick!, or you'll miss the train!", Oh, so we really won't be murdered! They are only making us ready for the continuing of our journey, cleaning us of all suspicions of dangerous sickness. Thank God! . . .

Oh, what solemn thoughts I had! How deeply I felt the greatness, the power of the scene! The immeasurable distance from horizon to horizon; . . . the absence of any object besides the one ship; . . . I was conscious only of sea and sky and something I did not understand. And as I listened to its solemn voice, I felt as if I had found a friend, and knew that I loved the ocean.

Mary Antin

Mary Antin, *The Promised Land*
(Boston: Houghton Mifflin Co., 1912), chap. VIII.

## Personal Journeys Online

- *Young Chinese immigrant memoir*, 1882. A Chinese immigrant recalls his migration to America and his early days in San Francisco.
- *Letters of Negro Migrants*, 1917. Letters from southern black migrants to the North back home.

**M**ary Antin, a 13-year-old Jewish girl from Russia, describes her family's perilous journey from persecution in tsarist Russia to the ship that would take her from Hamburg, Germany, to faraway America. In 1894, Mary and her mother and sisters set out from their village to join her father in Boston.

Millions of European immigrants made similar journeys across the Atlantic (as did Chinese and Japanese immigrants, across the Pacific), a trip fraught with danger, unpredictable detours, occasional heartbreak, the sundering of family ties, and the fear of the unknown. So powerful was the promise of American life for the migrants that they willingly risked these obstacles to come to the United States. For Mary, America did indeed prove to be *The Promised Land*, as she titled her emigration memoir, published in 1912. At the age of 15, she published her first poem in the *Boston Herald* and, after attending Barnard College in New York City, she wrote on immigrant issues, lectured widely, and worked for Theodore Roosevelt's Progressive Party. She fought against immigration-restriction legislation and promoted public education as the main channel of upward mobility for immigrants.

Mary and her family were part of a major demographic and economic transformation in the United States between 1870 and 1900. Rapid industrial development changed the nature of the workforce and the workplace. Large factories staffed by semiskilled laborers displaced the skilled artisans and small shops that had dominated American industry before 1870. Industrial development also accelerated urbanization. Between the Civil War and 1900, the proportion of the nation's population living in cities, swelled by migrants from the countryside and immigrants from Europe and Asia, increased from 20 to 40 percent, a rate of growth twice that of the population as a whole. During the 1880s alone, more than 5 million immigrants came to the United States, twice as many as in any previous decade.

The changes in American life were exhilarating for some, tragic for others. New opportunities opened as old opportunities disappeared. Vast new wealth was created, but poverty increased. New technologies eased life for some but left others untouched. It would be the great dilemma of early-twentieth-century America to reconcile these contradictions and satisfy the American quest for a decent life for all within the new urban-industrial order.

Late-nineteenth-century America is often called the **Gilded Age**. The term is taken from the title of a novel by Mark Twain that satirizes the materialistic excesses of the day. It serves as a shorthand description of the shallow worship of wealth, and the veneer of respectability and prosperity covering deep economic and social divisions, that characterized the period. Even so, an array of opportunities opened for more Americans than at any other previous time in the nation's history.

**Gilded Age** Term applied to late-nineteenth-century America that refers to the shallow display and worship of wealth characteristic of that period.

# New Industry

**18.1** How did workers respond to the changing demands of the workplace in the late nineteenth century?

**B**etween 1870 and 1900, the United States transformed itself from an agricultural nation, a nation of farmers, merchants, and artisans, into the world's foremost industrial power, producing more than one-third of the world's manufactured goods. By the early twentieth century, factory workers made up one-fourth of

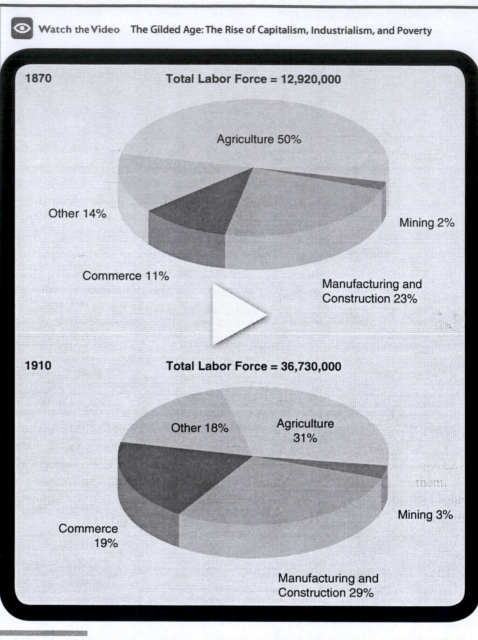

**Watch the Video** The Gilded Age: The Rise of Capitalism, Industrialism, and Poverty

1870        **Total Labor Force = 12,920,000**

Agriculture 50%

Other 14%

Mining 2%

Commerce 11%

Manufacturing and Construction 23%

1910        **Total Labor Force = 36,730,000**

Other 18%

Agriculture 31%

Mining 3%

Commerce 19%

Manufacturing and Construction 29%

**FIGURE 18.1 CHANGES IN THE AMERICAN LABOR FORCE, 1870–1910** The transformation of the American economy in the late nineteenth century changed the nature and type of work. By 1910, the United States was an urban-industrial nation with a matching workforce that toiled in factories and commercial establishments (including railroads) and, less frequently, on farms.

SOURCE: U.S. Department of Labor

the workforce, and agricultural workers had dropped from a half to less than a third (see Figure 18.1).

Although the size of the industrial workforce increased dramatically, the number of firms in any given industry shrank. Mergers, changes in corporate management and the organization of the workforce, and a compliant government left a few companies in control of vast segments of the American economy. Workers, reformers, and eventually government challenged this concentration of economic power.

## Inventing Technology: The Electric Age

Technology played a major role in transforming factory work and increasing the scale of production. Steam engines, and later electricity, freed manufacturers from dependence on water power. Factories no longer had to be located by rivers. Technology also enabled managers to substitute machines for workers, skewing the balance of power in the workplace toward employers. And it transformed city life, making available a host of new conveniences.

By the early twentieth century, electric lights, appliances, ready-made clothing, and store-bought food eased middle-class life. Electric trolleys whisked clerks, salespeople, bureaucrats, and bankers to new urban and suburban subdivisions. Electric streetlights lit up city streets at night. Amusement parks drew crowds with mechanical attractions scarcely imaginable a generation earlier. Movies entertained the masses. As the historian and novelist Henry Adams put it at the turn of the century, "In the essentials of life . . . the boy of 1854 stood nearer [to] the year one than to the year 1900."

For much of the nineteenth century, the United States was dependent on the industrial nations of Europe for technological innovation. In the late nineteenth century, the United States changed from a technology borrower to a technology innovator. By 1910, a million patents had been issued in the United States, 900,000 of them after 1870.

Nothing represented this shift better than Thomas A. Edison's development of a practical electric light bulb and electric generating system. Edison's invention transformed electricity into a new and versatile form of industrial energy. It also reflected a change in the relationship between science and technology. Until the late nineteenth century, advances in scientific theory usually followed technological innovation, rather than the other way around. Techniques for making steel, for example, developed before scientific theories emerged to explain how they worked. Textile machinery and railroad technology developed similarly. In contrast, a theoretical understanding of electricity preceded its practical use as a source of energy. Scientists had been experimenting with electricity for half a century before Edison unveiled his light bulb in 1879. Edison's research laboratory at Menlo Park, New Jersey, also established a model for corporate-sponsored research and development that would rapidly increase the pace of technological innovation.

Electricity conquered space and the night. The yellow glow of incandescent bulbs, the whiz of trolleys, and the rumble of elevated railways energized the Bowery, an emerging entertainment district in lower Manhattan, at the end of the nineteenth century.

Edison's initial success touched off a wave of research and development in Germany, Austria, Great Britain, France, and the United States. Whoever could light the world cheaply and efficiently held the key to an enormous fortune. Ultimately, the prize fell not to Edison but to Elihu Thomson, a high school chemistry teacher in Philadelphia. Leaving teaching to devote himself to research full-time, Thomson founded his own company and in 1883 moved to Connecticut, where he experimented with transformers and electric trolley equipment. Thomson purchased Edison's General Electric Company in 1892 and established the country's first corporate research and development division. His scientists produced what was then the most efficient light bulb design, and by 1914, General Electric was producing 85 percent of the world's light bulbs.

Following this precedent, other American companies established research and development laboratories. Standard Oil, U.S. Rubber, the chemical giant Du Pont, and the photographic company Kodak all became world leaders in their respective industries because of innovations their laboratories developed.

The process of invention that emerged in the United States gave the country a commanding technological lead. But the modernization of industry that made the United States the world's foremost industrial nation after 1900 reflected organizational as well as technological innovation. As industries sought efficient ways to apply technology and expand their markets within and beyond national borders, their workforces expanded, and their need for capital mounted. Coping with these changes required significant changes in corporate management.

## The Corporation and Its Impact

The modern corporation provided the structural framework for the transformation of the American economy. A corporation is an association of individuals that is legally authorized to act as a fictional "person" and thus relieves its individual members of certain legal liabilities. A key feature of a corporation is the separation of ownership from management. A corporation can raise capital by selling ownership shares, or stock, to people who have no direct role in running it.

The corporation had two major advantages over other forms of business organization that made it attractive to investors. First, unlike a partnership, which dissolves when a partner dies, a corporation can outlive its founders. This durability permits long-term planning. Second, a corporation's officials and shareholders are not personally liable for its debts. If it goes bankrupt, they stand to lose only what they have invested in it.

As large corporations emerged in major American industries, they had a ripple effect on the economy. To build plants, merge with or acquire other companies, develop new technology, and hire workers, large corporations needed huge supplies of capital. They turned to the banks to help meet these needs, and the banks grew in response. The corporations stimulated technological change as they looked for ways to speed production, improve products, and lower costs. As they grew, they generated jobs.

Large industrial corporations also changed the nature of work. By the early twentieth century, control of the workplace was shifting to managers, and semiskilled and unskilled workers were replacing skilled artisans. These new workers, often foreign-born, performed repetitive tasks for low wages.

Because corporations usually located factories in cities, they stimulated urban growth. Large industrial districts sprawled along urban rivers and rail lines. By 1900, fully 90 percent of all manufacturing occurred in cities.

Two organizational strategies, vertical integration and horizontal integration, helped successful corporations reduce competition and dominate their industries. **Vertical integration** involved the consolidation of all functions related to a particular industry, from the extraction and transport of raw materials to manufacturing and finished-product distribution and sales. Vertical integration reduced a company's dependence on outside suppliers, cutting costs and delays.

**vertical integration** The consolidation of numerous production functions, from the extraction of the raw materials to the distribution and marketing of the finished products, under the direction of one firm.

The meatpacking industry provides a good example of vertical integration. Meat is perishable and cannot be transported long distances without refrigeration. To reach eastern markets, cattlemen had to ship live animals in cattle cars from western ranges to major rail centers like Chicago. Since only 40 percent of a steer is edible, shippers were paying freight charges for a lot of commercially useless weight. In addition, some animals died in transit, and many lost weight.

Gustavus Swift, a Boston native who moved to Chicago in 1875, realized that refrigerated railway cars would make it possible to ship butchered meat, eliminating the need to transport live cattle. He invented a refrigerated car but could not sell it to the major railroads because they feared losing their substantial investment in cattle cars and pens. Swift had the cars built himself and convinced a Canadian railroad with only a small stake in cattle shipping to haul them to eastern markets. He established packinghouses in Omaha and Kansas City near the largest cattle markets, built refrigerated warehouses at key distribution points, and hired a sales force to convince eastern butchers of the quality of his product. He now controlled the production, transportation, and distribution of his product, the essence of vertical integration. By 1881, he was shipping $200,000 worth of beef a week. Competitors soon followed his example.

**Horizontal integration** involved the merger of competitors in the same industry. John D. Rockefeller's Standard Oil Company pioneered horizontal integration in the 1880s. He began investing in Cleveland oil refineries by his mid-twenties and formed Standard Oil in 1870. Using a variety of tactics, including threats, deceit, and price wars, Rockefeller rapidly acquired most of his competitors. Supported by investment bankers like J. P. Morgan, Standard Oil controlled 90 percent of the nation's oil refining by 1890. Acquiring oil fields and pipelines as well as refineries, it achieved both vertical and horizontal integration. Rockefeller's dominant position allowed him to impose order and predictability on the industry, ensuring a continuous flow of profits. He closed inefficient refineries, opened new ones, and kept his operations up to date with the latest technologies.

**horizontal integration** The merger of competitors in the same industry.

The invention of the internal combustion engine and the growth of automobile and truck manufacturing after 1900 suddenly made an inconsequential by-product of the refining process, gasoline, an indispensable fuel. By that time, the refining and production of oil had spread to Texas and Oklahoma, with the discovery of oil at Spindletop Hill, near Beaumont, Texas. The Texas oil fields dwarfed the Pennsylvania basin and soon surpassed their eastern rivals in output, spawning towns from the Gulf Coast to the Permian Basin in West Texas, and new companies such as the Texas Oil Company (Texaco) and Gulf Oil, breaking Rockefeller's near-monopoly. The petroleum industry represented one of the earliest shifts of industrial wealth from the Northeast and Midwest to the South and Southwest.

The concentration of industry in the hands of a few powerful corporate monopolies, or **trusts**, as they came to be known, alarmed many Americans. Giant corporations set prices, influenced politicians, and threatened to restrict opportunities for small entrepreneurs like the shopkeepers, farmers, and artisans who abounded at mid-century. Impersonal and governed by profit, the modern corporation challenged the ideal of the self-made man and the belief that success and advancement would reward hard work. These concerns eventually prompted the federal and state governments to respond with antitrust and other regulatory laws (see Chapters 20 and 21).

**trusts** A combination of corporations cooperating in order to reduce competition and control prices.

The entrepreneurs operated in an environment that allowed them free reign. They had access to capital, markets, and technology. And when they did not, they created it. Above all, they were innovators generating untold wealth that supported not only lavish lifestyles but also a broadening middle class. The integration of the nation's transportation and communication infrastructure, the managerial revolution that rationalized the operation of geographically distant units and large and diverse workforces, and the application of continuous flow production, pioneered in flour mills long before Henry Ford adapted it to car manufacturing, were a few of the innovations entrepreneurs devised to make their operations more efficient and profitable in the postwar years.

The large corporation changed how Americans lived their daily lives. People moved to cities in unprecedented numbers. They purchased goods that did not exist or that had limited distribution prior to the Civil War. They worked in an environment where management and labor became ever more distinct. And they established new consumption patterns in purchasing and furnishing their dwellings and in their leisure activities. Their lives revolved around family, work, and leisure. They were modern Americans.

## The Changing Nature of Work

The growth of giant corporations was a mixed blessing. The corporations provided abundant jobs, but they firmly controlled working conditions, especially for those who worked with their hands instead of their brains.

As late as the 1880s, shops of skilled artisans were responsible for most manufacturing in the United States. Since mid-century, however, industrialists had been introducing ways to simplify manufacturing processes so that they could hire low-skilled workers. This deskilling process accelerated in the 1890s in response to new technologies, new workers, and workplace reorganization. Mechanization and technological innovation did not reduce employment, although they did eliminate some jobs, most of them skilled. On the contrary, the birth of whole new industries—steel, automobiles, electrical equipment, cigarettes, food canning, and machine tools—created a huge demand for workers. Innovations in existing industries, like railroads, similarly spurred job growth.

Ironically, it was a shortage of skilled workers as much as other factors that encouraged industrialists to mechanize. Unskilled workers cost less than the scarce artisans. And with massive waves of immigrants arriving from Europe and Asia between 1880 and 1920 (joined after 1910 by migrants from the American South), the supply of unskilled workers seemed limitless.

**Low Salaries and Long Hours.**   The new workers shared little of the wealth generated by industrial expansion and enjoyed few of the gadgets and products generated by the new manufacturing. Nor did large corporations put profits into improved working conditions. In 1881, on-the-job accidents maimed or killed 30,000 railroad workers. Safety equipment existed that could have prevented many of these injuries, but the railroads refused to purchase it. At a U.S. Steel plant in Pittsburgh, injuries or death claimed one out of every four workers between 1907 and 1910. In Chicago's meat plants, injuries were commonplace. Workers grew careless from fatigue and long-term exposure to the extreme temperatures of the workplace. Meat cutters working rapidly with sharp knives often sliced fingers off their numb hands. Upton Sinclair wrote, in his novel *The Jungle* (1906), a chronicle of the killing floors of meatpacking plants in Chicago, "It was to be counted as a wonder that there were not more men slaughtered than cattle."

Factory workers typically worked 10 hours a day, six days a week in the 1880s. Steel workers put in 12 hours a day. The mills operated around the clock, so once every two weeks, when the workers changed shifts, one group had to take a "long turn" and stay on the job for 24 hours.

Long hours affected family life. By Sunday, most factory workers were too tired to do more than sit around home. During the week, they had time only to eat and sleep. Workers lived as close to the factory as possible, to reduce the time and expense of getting to work. The environment around many factories, however, was almost as unwholesome as the conditions inside. A visitor to Pittsburgh in 1884 noticed "a drab twilight" hanging over the areas around the steel mills, where "gas-lights, which are left burning at mid-day, shine out of the murkiness with a dull, reddish glare." Industrial wastes fouled streams and rivers around many plants. The factories along the Cuyahoga River in Cleveland turned that waterway into an open sewer by the turn of the century.

Big factories were not characteristic of all industries after 1900. In some, like the "needle," or garment, trade, operations remained small-scale. But salaries and working conditions in these industries were, if anything, worse than in the big factories. The garment industry was dominated by small manufacturers who assembled clothing for retailers from cloth provided by textile manufacturers. The manufacturers squeezed workers into small, cramped, poorly ventilated **sweatshops**. These might be in attics or lofts or even in the workers' own dwellings. Workers pieced together garments on the manufacturers' sewing machines. A government investigator in Chicago in the 1890s described one sweatshop in a three-room tenement where the workers, a family of eight, both lived and worked: "The father, mother, two daughters, and a cousin work together making trousers at seventy-five cents a dozen pairs. . . . They work seven days a week. . . . Their destitution is very great."

**sweatshops** Small, poorly ventilated shops or apartments crammed with workers, often family members, who pieced together garments.

## Child Labor

Child labor was common in the garment trade and other industries. Shocked reformers in the 1890s told of the devastating effects of factory labor on children's lives, citing cases like that of a 7-year-old girl whose legs were paralyzed and deformed because she toiled "day after day with little legs crossed, pulling out bastings from garments."

Industries that employed many children were often dangerous, even for adults. In the gritty coal mines of Pennsylvania, breaker boys, youths who stood on ladders to pluck waste matter from coal tumbling down long chutes, breathed harmful coal dust all day. Girls under 16 made up half the workforce in the silk mills of Scranton and Wilkes-Barre, Pennsylvania. Girls with missing fingers from mill accidents were a common sight in those towns.

By 1900, Pennsylvania and a few other states had passed legislation regulating child labor, but enforcement of these laws was lax. Parents desperate for income often lied about their children's age, and government officials were often sympathetic toward mill or mine owners, who paid taxes and provided other civic benefits.

## Working Women

Women accompanied children into the workforce outside the home in increasing numbers after 1870. The comparatively low wages of unskilled male workers often required women family members to work as well. Between 1870 and 1920, the number of women and children in the workforce more than doubled.

Like child labor, the growing numbers of women in the workforce alarmed middle-class reformers. They worried about the impact on family life and on the women themselves. Streets in working-class districts teemed with unsupervised children. Working-class men were also concerned. The trend toward deskilling favored women. Employers, claiming that women worked only for supplemental money, paid them less than men. A U.S. Department of Labor commissioner asserted that women worked only for "dress or pleasure." In one St. Louis factory in 1896, women received $4 a week for work for which men were paid $16 a week.

Most women worked out of economic necessity. In 1900, fully 85 percent of wage-earning women were unmarried and under the age of 25. They supported siblings and contributed to their parents' income. A typical female factory worker earned $6 a week in 1900. On this wage, a married woman might help pull her family up to subsistence level. For a single woman on her own, however, it allowed little more, in the writer O. Henry's words, "than marshmallows and tea." Her lodging rarely consisted of more than one room.

Over time, more work options opened to women, but low wages and poor working conditions persisted. Women entered the needle trades after widespread introduction of the sewing machine in the 1870s. Factories gradually replaced sweatshops in the garment industry after 1900, but working conditions improved little.

On the factory floor, young women had less room for negotiation because the customer was far removed from the manufacturing process, but they banded together, sometimes in labor unions after 1900, to demand and receive concessions from management. Working women, no less than working men, refused to be inanimate recipients of bosses' decrees and working conditions. And if a young woman could obtain some basic skills, other opportunities loomed as well.

The introduction of the typewriter transformed office work, dominated by men until the 1870s, into a female preserve. Women were alleged to have the dexterity and tolerance for repetition that the new technology required. But they earned only half the salary of the men they replaced. Middle-class parents saw office work as clean and honorable compared with factory or sales work. Consequently, clerical positions drew growing numbers of native-born women into the urban workforce after 1890.

By the turn of the century, women were gaining increased access to higher education. Coeducational colleges were rare, but by 1900 there were many women-only institutions. By 1910, women comprised 40 percent of all American college students, compared to 20 percent in 1870. Despite these gains, many professions, including those of physician and attorney, remained closed to women. Men still accounted for more than 95 percent of all doctors in 1900. Women also were rarely permitted to pursue doctoral degrees.

Most women college graduates found employment in such "nurturing" professions as nursing, teaching, and library work. Between 1900 and 1910, the number of trained women nurses increased sevenfold. In response to the growing problems of urban society, a relatively new occupation, social work, opened to women. There were 1,000 women social workers in 1890 and nearly 30,000 by 1920. Reflecting new theories on the nurturing role of women, school boards after 1900 turned exclusively to female teachers for the elementary grades. Despite these gains, women's work remained segregated. More than 90 percent of all wage-earning women in 1900 worked at occupations in which women comprised the great majority of workers.

Some reforms meant to improve working conditions for women reinforced this state of affairs. Protective legislation restricted women to "clean" occupations and limited their ability to compete with men in other jobs. Women also confronted negative stereotypes. Most Americans in 1900 believed a woman's proper role was to care for home and family. The single working woman faced doubts about her virtue. The system of "treating" on dates reinforced stories about loose salesgirls, flirtatious secretaries, and easy factory workers. Newspapers and magazines published exposés of working girls descending into prostitution. These images encouraged sexual harassment at work, which was rarely punished.

Still, for a girl growing up after the Civil War, there were many more possibilities open to her than before. Louisa May Alcott's *Little Women* appeared in 1868 and became the biggest-selling novel since Harriet Beecher Stowe's *Uncle Tom's Cabin*. If any indicator existed to summarize the difference between the overheated 1850s' imagery of sin and salvation and the postwar era's promise and economic prosperity, it was the transition from Stowe to Alcott. Of the four March girls in Alcott's novel, Josephine, who preferred the masculine-sounding "Jo," became a writer. Meg, a governess, dreamed of acting; Amy, a schoolgirl, hoped to become a great painter. Beth, the only March girl who did not imagine a career outside the home, died prematurely of unknown causes.

## Responses to Poverty and Wealth

Concerns about working women merged with larger anxieties about the growing numbers of impoverished workers in the nation's cities during the 1890s and the widening gap between rich and poor. While industrial magnates flaunted their fabulous wealth, working men and women led hard lives on meager salaries and in crowded dwellings. In his exposé of poverty in New York, *How the Other Half Lives* (1890), the Danish-born urban reformer Jacob Riis wrote that "the half that is on top cares little for the struggles, and less for the fate of those who are underneath so long as it is able to hold them there and keep its own seat."

Inadequate housing was the most visible badge of poverty. Crammed into four- to six-story buildings on tiny lots, **tenement** apartments in urban slums were notorious

**tenements** Four- to six-story residential dwellings, once common in New York, built on tiny lots without regard to providing ventilation or light.

The new industrial age created great wealth and abject poverty, and the city became the stage upon which these hard economic lessons played out. Here a "modest" Fifth Avenue mansion in turn-of-the-century New York City; farther downtown, Jacob Riis found this tenement courtyard.

SOURCE: Getty Images Inc., Hulton Archive Photos. Photograph by Jacob A. Riis, 22 Baxter Street Court. The Jacob A. Riis Collection, Museum of the City of New York.

for their lack of ventilation and light. Authorities did nothing to enforce laws prohibiting overcrowding for fear of leaving people homeless. The population density of New York's tenement district in 1894 was 986.4 people per acre, the highest in the world at the time. (Today, the densest areas of American cities rarely exceed 400 people per acre, and only Calcutta, India, and Lagos, Nigeria, approach the crowding of turn-of-the-century New York; today Manhattan has 84 residents per acre.)

One early attempt to deal with these conditions was the settlement house. The settlement house movement, which originated in England, sought to moderate the effects of poverty through neighborhood reconstruction. New York's Neighborhood Guild, established in 1886, was the first settlement house in the country; Chicago's **Hull House**, founded in 1889 by Jane Addams, a young Rockford (Illinois) College graduate, became the most famous. Addams had visited settlement houses in England and thought the idea would work well in American cities.

**Hull House** Chicago settlement house that became part of a broader neighborhood revitalization project led by Jane Addams.

**The Gospel of Wealth.**    Late-nineteenth-century political ideology discouraged more comprehensive efforts to remedy urban poverty until the Progressive Era (discussed in Chapter 21). According to the **Gospel of Wealth**, a theory popular among industrialists, intellectuals, and some politicians, any intervention on behalf of the poor was of doubtful benefit. Hard work and perseverance, in this view, led to wealth. Poverty, by implication, resulted from the flawed character of the poor.

A flawed attempt to apply Charles Darwin's theory of biological evolution to human society emerged as a more common justification than the Gospel of Wealth for

**Gospel of Wealth** Thesis that hard work and perseverance lead to wealth, implying that poverty is a character flaw.

18.1

18.2

18.3

**Social Darwinism** The application of Charles Darwin's theory of biological evolution to society, holding that the fittest and wealthiest survive, the weak and the poor perish, and government action is unable to alter this "natural" process.

**Horatio Alger stories** A series of best-selling tales about young rags-to-riches heroes first published in 1867 stressing the importance of neat clothes, cleanliness, thrift, and hard work. The books also highlighted the importance of chance in getting ahead and the responsibility of those better off to serve as positive role models.

**Great Uprising** Unsuccessful railroad strike of 1877 to protest wage cuts and the use of federal troops against strikers; the first nationwide work stoppage in American history.

the growing gap between rich and poor. According to the theory of **Social Darwinism**, the human race evolves only through competition. The fit survive, the weak perish, and humanity moves forward. Wealth reflects fitness; poverty, weakness. For governments or private agencies to interfere with this natural process is futile. Thus, Columbia University president Nicholas Murray Butler, claiming that "nature's cure for most social and political diseases is better than man's," warned against charity for the poor in 1900.

The era's popular literature contributed to the notion that the individual, armed with his wits and a determination to work hard, was responsible for his own fate. The press circulated stories of self-made men. Luxuries, such as suburban residences, carriages, and household appliances, came within the grasp of the growing urban middle class. Moving up the economic ladder, even dramatic improvement in one's status, seemed not only possible but probable.

Few cultural icons contributed to these sentiments more than the **Horatio Alger stories**. Alger captured the country's imagination beginning in the late 1860s with a series of best-selling stories about rags-to-riches heroes. He was an unlikely hero himself. Born in Massachusetts in 1832 in a comfortable family, he overcame a stuttering defect to climb the academic ladder and enter Harvard's Divinity School, where he graduated as a Unitarian minister in 1860. In 1866, allegations that he had molested two children forced him to resign from the ministry and move to New York City, where he began his writing career.

In New York, Alger saw an opportunity to atone for his sins and save the children of the city. The result was his first rags-to-riches novel, *Ragged Dick,* published in 1867. Dick shines shoes for his meager living and sleeps on the streets. One day he overhears a conversation between a wealthy businessman and his newly arrived nephew. Dick volunteers to show the young lad about the city. His contact with the nephew opens Dick to another life and to a desire to succeed, which he does after improving his personal habits and having another chance encounter with a wealthy businessman.

Many workers, however, unlike Alger's character, could not afford to wait for a chance encounter to lift themselves out of poverty.

## Workers Organize

Wild swings in the business cycle, the fluctuation between periods of growth and contraction in the economy, aggravated tensions between labor and management. Two prolonged depressions, one beginning in 1873 and the other in 1893, threw as many as 2 million laborers out of work. Skilled workers, their security undermined by deskilling, were hit particularly hard. Their hopes of becoming managers or starting their own businesses disappearing, they saw the nation "drifting," as a carpenter put it in 1870, "to that condition of society where a few were rich, and the many very poor."

Beginning after the Civil War and continuing through World War I, workers fought their loss of independence to industrial capital by organizing and striking (see Table 18.1). Violence often accompanied these actions such as in the railroad strike of 1877, sometimes referred to as the **Great Uprising**. The four largest railroads, in the midst of a depression and in the wake of a series of pay cuts over the preceding four

### TABLE 18.1 WORKERS ORGANIZE

| Organization | History | Strategies |
|---|---|---|
| Knights of Labor | Founded in 1869; open to all workers; declined after 1886 | Disapproved of strikes; supported an array of labor reforms, including cooperatives; favored broad political involvement |
| American Federation of Labor | Founded in 1886; open only to craft-workers and organized by craft; hostile to blacks and women; became the major U.S. labor organization after 1880s | Opposed political involvement; supported a limited number of labor reforms; approved of strikes |

years, agreed to slash wages yet again. When Baltimore & Ohio Railroad workers struck in July to protest the cut, President Rutherford B. Hayes dispatched federal troops to protect the line's property. The use of federal troops infuriated railroad workers throughout the East and Midwest, and they stopped work. Violence erupted in Pittsburgh when the state militia opened fire on strikers and their families, killing twenty-five, including a woman and three children. As news of the violence spread, so did the strike, as far as Galveston, Texas, and San Francisco. Over the next two weeks, police and federal troops continued to clash with strikers. By the time this first nationwide work stoppage in American history ended, more than 100 had been killed. The wage cuts remained.

The **Knights of Labor**, a union of craft workers founded in Philadelphia in 1869, grew dramatically after the Great Uprising under the leadership of Terence V. Powderly. Reflecting the views of many skilled workers, the Knights saw "an inevitable . . . conflict between the wage system of labor and [the] republican system of government." Remarkably inclusive for its time, the Knights welcomed black workers and women to its ranks. Victories in several small railroad strikes in 1884 and 1885 boosted its membership to nearly 1 million workers by 1886.

In that year, the Knights led a movement for an 8-hour workday. Ignoring the advice of the national leadership to avoid strikes, local chapters staged more than 1,500 strikes involving more than 340,000 workers. Employers fought back. They persuaded the courts to order strikers back to work and used local authorities to arrest strikers for trespassing or obstructing traffic. In early May 1886, police killed four unarmed workers during a skirmish with strikers in Chicago. Rioting broke out when a bomb exploded at a meeting in Haymarket Square to protest the slayings. The bomb killed seven policemen and four strikers and left 100 people wounded. Eight strike leaders were tried for the deaths, and despite the lack of evidence linking them to the bomb, four were executed.

The Haymarket Square incident, and a series of disastrous walkouts that followed it, weakened the Knights of Labor. By 1890, it had fewer than 100,000 members. Thereafter, the **American Federation of Labor (AFL)**, founded in 1886, became the major organizing body for skilled workers.

The AFL was much less ambitious, and less inclusive, than the Knights of Labor. Led by a British immigrant, Samuel Gompers, it emphasized **collective bargaining**, negotiations between management and union representatives, to secure workplace concessions. The AFL also discouraged political activism. With this business unionism, the AFL proved more effective than the Knights of Labor at meeting the needs of skilled workers, but it left out the growing numbers of unskilled workers, black workers, and women workers, to whom the Knights had given a glimmer of hope.

Rather than including all workers in one large union, the AFL organized skilled workers by craft. It then focused on a few basic workplace issues important to each craft. The result was greater cohesion and discipline. In 1889 and 1890, more than 60 percent of AFL-sponsored strikes were successful, a remarkable record in an era when most strikes failed. Responding to this success, employers determined to break the power of craft unions just as they had destroyed the Knights. In 1892, Andrew Carnegie dealt the steelworkers' union a major setback in the Homestead strike. Carnegie's manager, Henry Clay Frick, announced to workers at Carnegie's Homestead plant in Pennsylvania that he would negotiate only with workers individually and not renew the union's collective bargaining contract. Expecting a strike, Frick locked the union workers out of the plant and hired 300 armed guards to protect the nonunion ("scab") workers he planned to hire in their place. Union workers, with the help of their families and unskilled workers, seized control of Homestead's roads and utilities. In a bloody confrontation, they drove back Frick's forces. Nine strikers and seven guards died. But Pennsylvania's governor called out the state militia to open the plant and protect the nonunion workers. After four months, the union capitulated. With this defeat, skilled steelworkers lost their power on the shop floor. Eventually, mechanization cost them their jobs.

**Knights of Labor** Labor union founded in 1869 that included skilled and unskilled workers irrespective of race or gender.

**American Federation of Labor (AFL)** Union formed in 1886 that organized skilled workers along craft lines and emphasized a few workplace issues rather than a broad social program.

**collective bargaining** Representatives of a union negotiating with management on behalf of all members.

In 1894, workers suffered another setback in the Pullman strike, against George Pullman's Palace Sleeping Car Company. The strike began when the company cut wages for workers at its plant in the "model" suburb it had built outside Chicago, without a corresponding cut in the rent it charged workers for their company-owned housing. When Pullman rejected their demands, the workers appealed for support to the American Railway Union (ARU), led by Eugene V. Debs. On behalf of the Pullman strikers, Debs ordered a boycott of any trains with Pullman cars, disrupting train travel in several parts of the country. The railroads claimed to be innocent victims of a local dispute, and with growing public support, they fired workers who refused to handle trains with Pullman cars. Debs called for all ARU members to walk off the job, crippling rail travel nationwide. When Debs refused to honor a federal court injunction against the strike, President Cleveland, at the railroads' request, ordered federal troops to enforce it. Debs was arrested, and the strike and the union were broken.

These setbacks, and the depression that began in 1893, left workers and their unions facing an uncertain future. But growing public opposition to the use of troops, the high-handed tactics of industrialists, and the rising concerns of Americans about the power of big business sustained the unions. Workers would call more than 22,000 strikes over the next decade, the majority of them union-sponsored. Still, no more than 7 percent of the American workforce was organized by 1900. By that time, a dramatic change in the industrial workforce was afoot. As the large factories installed labor- and time-saving machinery, unskilled foreign-born labor flooded onto the shop floor. Immigrants transformed not only the workplace, but also the cities where they settled and the nation many eventually adopted. In the process, they changed themselves.

# New Immigrants

**18.2** What kinds of communities did new immigrants create in America?

The late nineteenth century was a period of unprecedented worldwide population movements. The United States was not the only New World destination for the migrants of this period. Many also found their way to Brazil, Argentina, and Canada. The scale of overseas migration to the United States after 1870, however, dwarfed all that preceded it. Between 1870 and 1910, the country received more than 20 million immigrants. Before the Civil War, most immigrants came from northern Europe. Most of the new immigrants, by contrast, came from southern and eastern Europe. Swelling their ranks were migrants from Mexico and Asia, as well as internal migrants moving from the countryside to American cities (see Map 18.1).

## Old World Backgrounds

The people of southern and eastern Europe had long been accustomed to migrating within Europe on a seasonal basis to find work to support their families. In the final quarter of the nineteenth century, however, several factors drove migrants beyond the borders of Europe and into the Western Hemisphere.

A growing rural population combined with unequal land distribution to create economic distress in late-nineteenth-century Europe. With land ownership concentrated in increasingly fewer hands, more and more people found themselves working ever smaller plots as laborers rather than owners.

For Russian Jews, religious persecution compounded economic hardship. After the assassination of Tsar Alexander II in 1881, which was falsely blamed on Jews, the government sanctioned a series of violent attacks on Jewish settlements; these attacks were known as **pogroms**. At the same time, the government forced Jews into fewer towns, deepening their poverty and making them easier targets for violence.

**pogroms** Government-directed attacks against Jewish citizens, property, and villages in tsarist Russia beginning in the 1880s; a primary reason for Russian Jewish migration to the United States.

18.1

18.2

18.3

Number of Immigrants

| | |
|---|---|
| From Asia | 700,000 |
| Main groups | |
| Chinese | 370,000 |
| Japanese | 275,000 |
| From Canada | 2,200,000 |
| From Europe | 30,000,000 |
| Main groups | |
| Germans | 5,000,000 |
| Irish | 4,500,000 |
| Italians | 4,500,000 |
| Poles | 2,600,000 |
| English | 2,600,000 |
| Jews | 2,000,000 |
| From Latin America | 900,000 |

**MAP 18.1 PATTERNS OF IMMIGRATION, 1820–1914** The migration to the United States was part of a worldwide transfer of population that accelerated with the industrial revolution and the accompanying improvement in transportation.

Chinese and Japanese immigrants also came to the United States in appreciable numbers for the first time during the late nineteenth century. Most Chinese immigrants came from Canton in South China, a region of great rural poverty. They worked on railroads and in mines throughout the West and as farm laborers in California. Many eventually settled in cities such as San Francisco, where they established residential enclaves referred to as Chinatowns. The Chinese population in the United States peaked at about 125,000 in 1882.

Japanese began immigrating to the United States in the late 1880s, driven by a land shortage even more acute than the one in Europe. The first wave came by way of Hawaii to work on farms in California, taking the place of Chinese workers who had moved to the cities. By 1900, there were some 50,000 Japanese immigrants in the United States, nearly all on the West Coast.

Some immigrants came from right across our borders. In the late nineteenth century, Mexicans came across the border to work on the ranches and cotton farms of South and West Texas. Unlike their counterparts from Asia and Europe, these migrants settled primarily in rural areas. Whether on farms, in squalid quarters in the barrios of El Paso or San Antonio, or in the smaller urban centers in South Texas, such as Laredo, living and working conditions were harsh. By the turn of the century, Mexican laborers in urban areas began to organize into unions.

Wherever they came from, most migrants saw their route as a two-way highway. They intended to stay only a year or two, long enough to earn money to buy land or, more likely, to start a business back home and improve life for themselves and their families. Roughly half of all immigrants to the United States between 1880 and World War I returned to their country of origin. Some made several round-trips. Jews, unwelcome in the lands they left, were the exception. No more than 10 percent of Jewish immigrants returned to Europe, and very few Jews from Russia, who accounted for almost 80 percent of Jewish immigrants after 1880, went back home.

Most of the newcomers were young men. (Jews, again, were the exception: Reflecting their intention to stay in their new home, they tended to migrate in families.)

Hope for a new generation. Victoria de Ortiz came to Nebraska with her family around 1915 to escape the turmoil in Mexico and, like millions of other immigrants of that era, to make a better life for herself and her family. The black lines are part of the photograph.

Immigrants easily found work in the nation's booming cities. The quickest way to make money was in the large urban factories, with their voracious demands for unskilled labor. Except for the Japanese, few immigrants came to work on farms after 1880.

By 1900, women began to equal men among all immigrant groups as young men who had decided to stay sent for their families. In a few cases, entire villages migrated, drawn by the good fortune of one or two compatriots, a process called **chain migration**. The success of Francesco Barone, a Buffalo tavern owner, induced 8,000 residents of his former village in Sicily to migrate to that city, many arriving on tickets Barone purchased.

Immigrants tended to live in neighborhoods among people from the same homeland. The desire of the new immigrants to retain their cultural traditions led contemporary observers to doubt their ability to assimilate into American society. Even sympathetic observers, such as social workers, marveled at the utterly foreign character of immigrant districts.

## Cultural Connections in a New World

Immigrants maintained their cultural traditions through the establishment of religious and communal institutions. Charitable organizations were frequently connected to religious institutions. The church or synagogue became the focal point for immigrant neighborhood life. Much more than a place of worship, it was a school for transmitting Old World values and language to American-born children. The church or synagogue also functioned as a recreational facility and a gathering place for community leaders. In Jewish communities, associations called *landsmanshaften* arranged for burials, jobs, housing,

**chain migration** Process common to many immigrant groups whereby one family member brings over other family members, who in turn bring other relatives and friends and occasionally entire villages.

# ✳ Explore Foreign-Born Population on MyHistoryLab

## HOW DID IMMIGRANTS REDEFINE THE UNITED STATES IN THE SECOND HALF OF THE 1800s?

Immigrants to the United States have been key in the country's settlement and growth, and their numbers between 1860 and 1900 stand out in particular. By the end of the century, immigrants made up a considerable percentage of the population of certain parts of the country. Many immigrants concentrated together in distinct geographic communities as particular settlement patterns emerged in many regions. Newcomers often tried to hang on to their own languages and customs while integrating their often American-born children into U.S. society and culture. Thus, those from foreign lands had a great impact on the development of the United States.

This book illustration provides a glimpse of street life in New York's Chinatown in the 1890s.

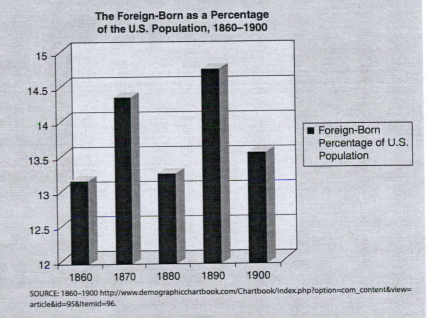

The Foreign-Born as a Percentage of the U.S. Population, 1860–1900

■ Foreign-Born Percentage of U.S. Population

SOURCE: 1860–1900 http://www.demographicchartbook.com/Chartbook/index.php?option=com_content&view=article&id=95&Itemid=96.

**KEY QUESTIONS**   Use **MyHistoryLab** *Explorer* to **answer** these **questions:**

**Analysis ▶▶▶** *Where did immigrant communities settle?*
Map these trends to understand what factors might help explain immigration patterns.

**Response ▶▶▶** *What areas had a high percentage of native-born children of immigrants?*
Imagine what this might mean for the composition of the U.S. population.

**Cause ▶▶▶** *How did the quality of land farmed by immigrants compare to that of native-born farmers?*
Map improved farmland to consider the reasons behind this pattern.

Mulberry Street, New York, 1905. The vibrant, predominantly Russian Jewish Lower East Side of New York at first reflected more the culture of the homeland than of the United States. Language, dress, ways of doing business, keeping house, and worshiping—all followed Old World patterns. Gradually, thanks especially to the influence of school-age children, a blend of Russian Jewish and American traditions emerged.

and support for the sick, poor, and elderly. Because religious institutions were so central to their lives, immigrant communities insisted on maintaining control over them.

Religious institutions played a less formal role among Chinese and Japanese neighborhoods. For them, the family functioned as the source of religious activity and communal organization. Chinatowns were organized in clans of people with the same surname. An umbrella organization called the Chinese Consolidated Benevolent Association emerged; it functioned like the Jewish *landsmanshaften.* A similar association, the Japanese Association of America, governed the Japanese community in the United States. This organization was sponsored by the Japanese government, which was sensitive to mistreatment of its citizens abroad and anxious that immigrants set a good example. The Japanese Association, unlike other ethnic organizations, actively encouraged assimilation and stressed the importance of Western dress and learning English.

Ethnic newspapers, theaters, and schools supplemented associational life for immigrants. These institutions reinforced Old World culture while informing immigrants about American ways. Thus, the *Jewish Daily Forward,* first published in New York in 1897, reminded readers of the importance of keeping the Sabbath while admonishing them to adopt American customs.

## The Job

If immigrant culture provided newcomers with a supportive environment, work offered the ultimate reward for coming to America. All immigrants perceived the job as the way to independence and as a way out, either back to the Old World or into the larger American society.

Immigrants typically got their first job with the help of a countryman. Italian, Chinese, Japanese, and Mexican newcomers worked with contractors who placed them in jobs. These middlemen often provided housing, loans, and other services for recent arrivals. Other immigrant groups, such as Poles and Russian Jews, often found work through their ethnic associations or village or family connections. Family members sometimes exchanged jobs with one another.

The type of work available to immigrants depended on their skills, the local economy, and local discrimination. Mexican migrants to southern California, for example, concentrated in railroad construction. Mostly unskilled, they replaced Chinese laborers when the federal government prohibited Chinese immigration after 1882. Mexicans built the interurban rail lines of Los Angeles in 1900 and established communities at their construction camps. Los Angeles businessmen barred Mexicans from other occupations. Similarly, Chinese immigrants were confined to work in laundries and restaurants within the boundaries of Los Angeles's Chinatown.

The Japanese who came to Los Angeles around 1900 were forced into sectors of the economy that native-born white people had either shunned or failed to exploit. The Japanese turned this discrimination to their benefit when they transformed the cultivation of market-garden crops into a major agricultural enterprise. By 1904, Japanese farmers owned more than 50,000 acres in California. George Shima, who came to California from Japan in 1889 with a little capital, made himself the "Potato King" of the Sacramento Delta. By 1913, Shima owned 28,000 acres of farmland.

Stereotypes also channeled immigrants' work options, sometimes benefiting one group at the expense of another. Jewish textile entrepreneurs, for example, sometimes hired only Italians because they thought them less prone to unionization than Jewish workers. Other Jewish bosses hired only Jewish workers, hoping that ethnic loyalty would overcome the lure of the unions. Pittsburgh steelmakers preferred Polish workers to the black workers who began arriving in northern cities in appreciable numbers after 1900. This decision began the decades-long tradition of handing down steel mill jobs through the generations in Polish families.

Like their native-born counterparts, few married immigrant women worked outside the home, but unlike the native-born, many Italian and Jewish women did piecework for the garment industry in their apartments. Unmarried Polish women often worked in factories or as domestic servants. Japanese women, married and single, worked with their families on farms. Until revolution in China in 1911 began to erode traditional gender roles, married Chinese immigrant women typically remained at home.

The paramount goal for many immigrants was to work for themselves rather than for someone else. Some immigrants, like George Shima, parlayed their skills and a small stake into successful businesses. Most new arrivals, however, had few skills, and no resources beyond their wits, with which to realize their dreams. Major banks at the time were unlikely to extend even a small business loan to a budding ethnic entrepreneur. Family members and small ethnic-based community banks provided the initial stake for most immigrant businesses. Many of these banks failed, but a few prospered. For example, the Bank of Italy, established by Amadeo Pietro Giannini in San Francisco in 1904, eventually grew into the Bank of America, today one of the nation's largest financial institutions.

Immigrants could not fully control their own destinies in the United States, any more than native-born Americans could. The vagaries of daily life, including death, disease, and bad luck, thwarted many immigrants' dreams. Hard work did not always ensure success. Add to these the difficulty of cultural adjustment to an unfamiliar environment, and the newcomer's confident hopes could fade quickly. Almost all immigrants, however, faced an obstacle that by its nature white native-born Americans did not. They faced it on the job, in the city at large, and even in their neighborhoods: the anti-foreign prejudice of American nativism.

## Nativism

Despite the openness of America's borders in the nineteenth century, and contrary to the nation's reputation as a refuge from foreign persecution and poverty, immigrants did not always receive a warm reception. Ben Franklin groused about the "foreignness" of German immigrants during the colonial era. From the 1830s to 1860, nativist sentiment, directed mainly at Irish Catholic immigrants, expressed itself in occasional violence and job discrimination. Anti-immigrant sentiment gave rise to an important political party, the Know-Nothings, in the 1850s.

**nativism** Favoring the interests and culture of native-born inhabitants over those of immigrants.

When immigration revived after the Civil War, so did anti-foreign sentiment. But late-nineteenth-century **nativism** differed in two ways from its antebellum predecessor. First, the target was no longer Irish Catholics, but the even more numerous Catholics and Jews of southern and eastern Europe, people whose languages and usually darker complexions set them apart from the native-born majority. Second, late-nineteenth-century nativism had a pseudo-scientific underpinning. As we saw in Chapter 17, "scientific" racism of the period maintained that some people are inherently inferior to others. There was, in this view, a natural hierarchy of race. At the top, with the exception of the Irish, were northern Europeans, especially those of Anglo-Saxon ancestry. Below them in descending order were French, Slavs, Poles, Italians, Jews, Asians, and Africans. Social Darwinism, which justified the class hierarchy, reinforced scientific racism.

When the "inferior" races began to arrive in the United States in significant numbers after 1880, nativists sounded the alarm. A prominent Columbia University professor wrote in 1887 that Hungarians and Italians were "of such a character as to endanger our civilization." Nine years later, the director of the U.S. census warned that eastern and southern Europeans were "beaten men from beaten races. They have none of the ideas and aptitudes which fit men to take up readily and easily the problem of self-care and self-government." The result of unfettered migration would be "race suicide."

Such sentiments generated proposals to restrict foreign immigration. The treatment of the Chinese provided a precedent. Chinese immigrants had long worked for low wages, under harsh conditions, in mining and railroad construction in the West. Their different culture and their willingness to accept low wages provoked resentment among native- and European-born workers. Violence against Chinese laborers increased during the 1860s and 1870s. In 1870, the Republican-dominated Congress passed the Naturalization Act, which limited citizenship to "white persons and persons of African descent." The act was specifically intended to prevent Chinese from becoming citizens, a ban not lifted until 1943, but it affected other Asian groups also. The Chinese Exclusion Act of 1882, passed following another decade of anti-Chinese pressure, made the Chinese the only ethnic group in the world that could not immigrate freely into the United States.

Labor competition also contributed to the rise of another anti-immigrant organization. A group of skilled workers and small businessmen formed the American Protective Association (APA) in 1887 and claimed half a million members a year later. The APA sought to limit Catholic civil rights in the United States to protect the jobs of Protestant workingmen.

The Immigration Restriction League (IRL), formed in 1894 in the midst of a depression, took a more modest and indirect approach. The IRL proposed to require prospective immigrants to pass a literacy test that most southern and eastern Europeans would presumably fail. The IRL ultimately failed to have its literacy requirement enacted. The return of prosperity and the growing preference of industrialists for immigrant labor put an end to calls for formal restrictions on immigration for the time being. Less than thirty years later, however, Congress would enact major restrictive legislation aimed at southern and eastern European immigrants. In the meantime, IRL propaganda encouraged northern universities to establish quotas limiting the admission of new immigrants, especially Jews.

Immigrants and their communal associations fought attempts to restrict immigration. The Japanese government even hinted at violent retaliation if Congress ever enacted restrictive legislation on Japanese similar to that imposed on the Chinese. But most immigrants believed that the more "American" they became, the less prejudice they would encounter. Accordingly, leaders of immigrant groups stressed the importance of assimilation.

Assimilation connotes the loss of one culture in favor of another. The immigrant experience of the late nineteenth and early twentieth centuries might better be described

Read the Document   Lee Chew, "Life of a Chinese Immigrant" (1903)

THROWING DOWN THE LADDER BY WHICH THEY ROSE.

"Throwing Down the Ladder by Which They Rose," Thomas Nast's 1870 attack on nativism. White workers, many of them immigrants themselves, objected to labor competition from Chinese immigrants and eventually helped to persuade Congress to pass the Chinese Exclusion Act in 1882.

as a process of adjustment between old ways and new. It was a dynamic process that resulted in entirely new cultural forms. The Japanese, for example, had not gone to Los Angeles to become truck farmers, but circumstances led them to that occupation, and they used their cultural heritage of hard work, strong family ties, and sober living to make a restricted livelihood successful. Sometimes economics and the availability of alternatives resulted in modifications of traditions that nonetheless maintained their spirit. In the old country, Portuguese held *festas* every Sunday honoring a patron saint. In New England towns, they confined the tradition to their churches instead of parading through the streets. And instead of baking bread themselves, Portuguese immigrant women were happy to buy all the bread they needed from local bakers.

Despite the antagonism of native-born white people toward recent immigrants, the greatest racial divide in America remained that between black and white. Newcomers quickly caught on to this distinction and sought to assert their "whiteness" as a common bond with other European immigrant groups and a badge of acceptance into the larger society. Nativists, however, often lumped immigrants into the "black" category. The word *guinea,* for example, which originally referred to African slaves, emerged as a derogatory epithet for Italians and, occasionally, Greeks, Jews, and Puerto Ricans. When the Louisiana legislature debated disfranchisement in 1898, a lawmaker explained that "according to the spirit of our meaning when we speak of 'white man's government,' Italians are as black as the blackest negro in existence." For immigrants, therefore, becoming "white," distancing themselves from African American culture and people, was often part of the process of adjusting to American life, especially as increasing numbers of black southerners began moving to northern cities.

## Roots of the Great Migration

Nearly 90 percent of African Americans still lived in the South in 1900, most in rural areas. Between 1880 and 1900, however, black families began to move into the great industrial cities of the Northeast and Midwest. They were drawn by the same economic promise that attracted overseas migrants and were pushed by growing persecution in the South. Job opportunities probably outweighed all other factors in motivating what became known as the **Great Migration**.

**Great Migration** The mass movement of African Americans from the rural South to the urban North, spurred especially by new job opportunities during World War I and the 1920s.

In most northern cities in 1900, black people typically worked as common laborers or domestic servants. They competed with immigrants for jobs, and in most cases they lost. Immigrants even claimed jobs that black workers had once dominated, such as barbering and service work in hotels, restaurants, and transportation.

Black women had very few options in the northern urban labor force outside of domestic service, although they earned higher wages than they had for similar work in southern cities. The retail and clerical jobs that attracted young working-class white women remained closed to black women. Employers rejected them for any job involving direct contact with the public.

The lack of options black migrants confronted in the search for employment matched similar frustrations in their quest for a place to live. Even more than foreign immigrants, they were restricted to segregated urban ghettos. Small black ghettos existed in antebellum northern cities. As black migration to northern cities accelerated after 1900, the pattern of residential isolation became more pronounced. The black districts in northern cities were more diverse than those in southern cities. Migration brought rural southerners, urban southerners, and West Indians together with the black northerners already living there. People of all social classes lived in these districts.

The difficulties that black families faced to make ends meet paralleled in some ways those of immigrant working-class families. Restricted job options, however, limited the income of black families, even with black married women five times more likely to work than married white women. In black families, moreover, working teenage children were less likely to stay home and contribute their paychecks to the family income.

Popular culture reinforced the marginalization of African Americans. Vaudeville and minstrel shows, popular urban entertainments around 1900, featured songs belittling black people and black characters with names like Useless Peabody and Moses Abraham Highbrow. Immigrants frequented these shows and absorbed the culture of racism from them. The new medium of film perpetuated the negative stereotypes.

In the North as in the South, African Americans sought to counter the hostility of the larger society by building their own communal institutions. An emerging middle-class leadership sought to develop black businesses. Despite these efforts, chronic lack of capital kept black businesses mostly small and confined to the ghetto. Immigrant groups often pooled extended-family capital resources or tapped ethnic banks. With few such resources at their disposal, black businesses failed at a high rate. Most black people worked outside the ghetto for white employers. Economic marginalization often attracted unsavory businesses—dance halls, brothels, and bars—to black neighborhoods.

Other black institutions proved more lasting than black businesses. In Chicago in 1891, black physician Daniel Hale Williams established Provident Hospital, the nation's first interracially staffed hospital, with the financial help of wealthy white Chicagoans. Although it failed as an interracial experiment, the hospital thrived, providing an important training ground for black physicians and nurses.

# New Cities

**18.3** How did the new cities help to create the new middle class?

Despite the hardships associated with urban life, the American city continued to act, in the words of the contemporary novelist Theodore Dreiser, as a "giant magnet." Immigration from abroad and migration from American farms to the cities resulted in an urban explosion during the late nineteenth century (see Map 18.2). In 1850, six cities had a population exceeding 100,000; by 1900, thirty-eight did. In 1850, only 5 percent of the nation's population lived in cities of more than 100,000 inhabitants; by 1900, the figure was 19 percent. The nation's population tripled between 1860 and 1920, but the urban population increased ninefold. Of the 1,700 cities listed in the 1900 census, fewer than 2 percent even existed in 1800.

In Europe, a few principal cities, such as Paris and Berlin, absorbed most of the urban growth during this period. In the United States, by contrast, growth was more evenly distributed among many cities. Despite the relative evenness of growth, a distinctive urban system had emerged by 1900, with New York and Chicago anchoring an urban-industrial core extending in a crescent from New England to the cities bordering the Great Lakes. This region included nine of the nation's ten largest cities in 1920. Western cities like Denver, San Francisco, and Los Angeles emerged as dominant urban places in their respective regions but did not challenge the urban core for supremacy. Southern cities, limited in growth by low consumer demand, low wages, and weak capital formation, were drawn into the orbit of the urban core.

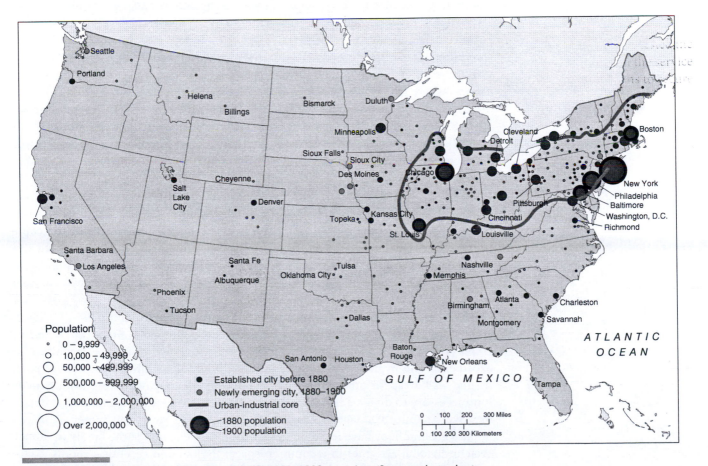

**MAP 18.2 THE GROWTH OF AMERICAN CITIES, 1880–1900** Several significant trends stand out on this map. First is the development of an urban-industrial core, stretching from New England to the Midwest, where the largest cities were located. And second is the emergence of relatively new cities in the South and West, reflecting the national dimensions of innovations in industry and transportation.

Urban growth highlighted the growing divisions in American society. The crush of people and the emergence of new technologies expanded the city outward and upward as urban dwellers sorted themselves by social class and ethnic group. While the new infrastructure of water and sewer systems, bridges, and trolley tracks kept steel mills busy, it also fragmented the urban population by allowing settlements well beyond existing urban boundaries. The way people satisfied their needs for food, clothing, and shelter stimulated the industrial economy while distinguishing one class from another. Although urban institutions emerged to counter these divisive trends, they could not overcome them completely.

## Centers and Suburbs

The centers of the country's great cities changed in scale and function in this era, achieving a prominence some would eventually lose in the twentieth century. Downtowns expanded up and out as tall buildings arose, monuments to business and finance, creating towering urban skylines. Residential neighborhoods were pushed out, leaving the center dominated by corporate headquarters and retail and entertainment districts.

Corporate heads administered their empires from downtown, even if their factories were located on the urban periphery or in other towns and cities. Banks and insurance companies clustered in such financial centers as Atlanta's Five Points district to service the corporations. Department stores and shops clustered in retail districts in strategic locations along electric trolley lines.

As retail and office uses crowded out dwellings from the city center, a new phenomenon emerged: the residential neighborhood. Advances in transportation technology, first the horse-drawn street railway and, by the 1890s, the electric trolley, eased commuting for office workers. Some in the growing and increasingly affluent middle class left the crowded, polluted city altogether to live in new residential suburbs. These people did not abandon the city; they still looked to it for its jobs, schools, libraries, and entertainment, but they rejected it as a place to live, leaving it to the growing ranks of working-class immigrants and African Americans. This pattern contrasted with that of Europe, where the middle class remained in the city.

The suburb emerged as the preferred place of residence for the urban middle class after 1870. As early as 1873, Chicago boasted nearly 100 suburbs with a combined population of more than 50,000. The ideals that had promoted modest suburban growth earlier in the nineteenth century—privacy, aesthetics, and home ownership—became increasingly important to the growing numbers of middle-class families after 1880. Consider the Russells of Short Hills, New Jersey. Short Hills lay 18 miles by railroad from New York City. William Russell, his wife Ella Gibson Russell, and their six children moved there from Brooklyn in the late 1880s, seeking a "pleasant, cultured people whose society we could enjoy" and a cure for Russell's rheumatism. Russell owned and managed a small metal brokerage in New York and enjoyed gardening, reading, and socializing with his new neighbors. Ella Russell cared for their six children with the help of a servant and also found time for several clubs and charities.

The design of the Russell home reflected the principles Catharine Beecher and Harriet Beecher Stowe outlined in their suburban home bible, *American Woman's Home* (1869). The kitchen, according to Beecher and Stowe, should be organized for expedience and hygiene. The home's utilities should be confined to a central core, freeing wall areas for other functions. The new technology of central heating made it unnecessary to divide a house into many small rooms, each with its own fireplace or stove. Taking advantage of this change, Beecher and Stowe recommended that a home's ground floor have fewer but larger rooms, to encourage the family to pursue their individual activities in a common space. Parlors and reception rooms disappeared, along with such former standards as the children's wing, the male "smoking room," and the female parlor.

The once-prevailing view that women were too frail for vigorous exercise was changing. Thus, the entire Russell family was to be found enjoying the tennis, swimming, and skating facilities at the Short Hills Athletic Club. Because the community bordered on undeveloped woodland traversed by trails, "wheel clubs" appeared in the 1880s to organize families for bicycle outings. The emphasis on family togetherness also reflected the changing role of men in late-nineteenth-century society. Women's roles also broadened, as Ella Russell's club work attested.

Suburbs differed, not only from the city, but also from one another. With the growth after 1890 of the electric trolley, elevated rail lines, and other relatively inexpensive forms of commuter travel, suburbs became accessible to a broader spectrum of the middle class. The social structure, architecture, and amenities of suburbs varied, depending on the rail service and distance from the city. The commuter railroad remained popular among people like the Russells who could afford the time and expense of commuting to and from the city center.

The suburb underscored the growing fragmentation of life in and around American cities in the late nineteenth century. Residence, consumer habits, and leisure activities reflected growing social and class divisions. Yet, at the same time, the growing materialism of American society promised a common ground for its disparate ethnic, racial, and social groups.

## The New Middle Class

From the colonial era, America's urban middle class had included professionals, physicians, lawyers, ministers, educators, editors, as well as merchants, shopkeepers, and skilled artisans (until they dropped from the middle class in the late nineteenth century). In the late nineteenth century, industrial technology and urban growth expanded the urban middle class to include salespeople, factory supervisors, managers, civil servants, technicians, and a broad range of "white-collar" office workers, such as insurance agents, bank tellers, and legal assistants. This newer middle class set national trends in residential patterns, consumption, and leisure.

The more affluent members of the new middle class, like the Russells, repaired to new subdivisions within and outside the city limits. Simple row houses sheltered the growing numbers of clerks and civil servants who remained in the city. These dwellings contrasted sharply with the crowded one- or two-room apartments that confined the working class. Rents for these apartments ran as much as $3 a week, at a time when few workers made more than $9 or $10.

## A Consumer Society

The new middle class transformed America into a consumer society. In earlier times, land had been a symbol of prestige. Now it was consumer goods. And the new industries obliged with a dazzling array of merchandise and technologies. By 1910, the new middle class lived in all-electric homes with indoor plumbing. A typical kitchen might include an electric coffeepot, a hot plate, a chafing dish, and a toaster. The modern city dweller worked by the clock, not by the sun. Eating patterns changed: Cold packaged cereals replaced hot meats at breakfast; fast lunches of Campbell's soup, "a meal in itself," or canned stews weaned Americans from the heavy lunch. Jell-O appeared in the 1890s, touted as America's "most quick and easy" dessert. In Nashville at the same time, Joel Cheek ground and blended coffee beans in his store for customers' convenience. He convinced the city's Maxwell House Hotel to serve his new concoction, and in 1907, when President Theodore Roosevelt visited the hotel and drained his cup, he turned to Cheek and declared that the coffee was "good to the very last drop." A slogan and Maxwell House coffee were born.

The middle class liked anything that saved time: trolleys, trains, electric razors, vacuum cleaners. The telephone replaced the letter for everyday communication; it was quicker and less formal. By 1900, some 1.4 million phones were in service, and many middle-class homes had one. Observers wondered if the telephone would eventually make written communication obsolete.

The middle class liked its news in an easy-to-read form. Urban tabloids multiplied after 1880, led by Joseph Pulitzer's *New York World* and William Randolph Hearst's *New York Journal*. The newspapers organized the news into topical sections, used bold headlines and graphics to catch the eye, ran human interest stories to capture the imagination, inaugurated sports pages to attract male readers, and offered advice columns for women. And they opened their pages to a wide range of attractive advertising, much of it directed to women, who did about 90 percent of the shopping in American cities by 1900.

As the visual crowded out the printed in advertising, newspapers, and magazines, these materials became accessible to a wider urban audience. Although mainly middle class in orientation, the tabloid press drew urban society together with new features such as the comic strip, which first appeared in the 1890s, and heart-rending personal sagas drawn from real life. Immigrants, who might have had difficulty reading

((• 📖 **Read the Document**    Thorstein Veblen, from *The Theory of Leisure Class* (1899)

Window shopping at Marshall Field's department store, Chicago, 1909. The large department store led the transformation of downtown to retail and office space. Large window displays directed their advertising primarily to women who comprised most of the shoppers by the early 1900s.

small-type newspapers, received their initiation into the mainstream of American society through the tabloids.

In a similar manner, the department store, essentially a middle-class retail establishment, became one of the city's most democratic forums and the focus of the urban downtown after 1890. Originating in the 1850s and 1860s with the construction of retail palaces such as Boston's Jordan Marsh, Philadelphia's Wanamaker & Brown, New York's Lord & Taylor, and Chicago's Marshall Field, the department store came to epitomize the bounty of the new industrial capitalism. At the time of the Philadelphia Exposition in 1876, only thirty or so department stores existed; by 1920, there were thousands. They exuded limitless abundance with their extensive inventories, items for every budget, sumptuous surroundings, and efficient, trained personnel.

At first, most department store customers were middle-class married women. Not expected to work and with disposable income and flexible schedules, these women had the means and time to wander department store aisles. The stores catered to their tastes, and the current emphasis on home and domesticity, with such items as prefabricated household furnishings, ready-made clothing, toys, and stationery. Department stores maintained consumers' interest with advertising campaigns arranged around holidays like Easter and Christmas, the seasons, and the school calendar. Each event required new clothing and accessories, and the ready-made clothing industry changed fashions accordingly.

Soon the spectacle and merchandise of the department store attracted shoppers from all social strata, not just the middle class. Although many less affluent women came merely to "window-shop," some came to buy. After 1890, department stores increasingly hired young immigrant women to cater to their growing foreign-born clientele.

The department store, the turn-of-the-century shopping mall, provided inexpensive amusement for young working-class people, especially immigrants. Mary Antin recalled how she and her teenage friends and sister would spend their Saturday nights patrolling "a dazzlingly beautiful palace called a 'department store.'" It was there that Mary and her sister "exchanged our hateful homemade European costumes . . . for real American machine-made garments, and issued forth glorified in each other's eyes."

By 1900, department stores had added sporting goods and hardware sections and were attracting customers from a wide social spectrum. When Wanamaker's introduced a "bargain room" in 1888, other retail stores, including Filene's famous "Automatic Bargain Basement" in Boston, followed suit.

## The Growth of Leisure Activities

The expanding floor space devoted to sporting goods reflected the growth of leisure in urban society. And like other aspects of that society, leisure and recreation both separated and cut across social classes. The leisure activities of the wealthy increasingly removed them from the rest of urban society. As such sports as football became important extracurricular activities at Harvard, Yale, and other elite universities, intercollegiate games became popular occasions for the upper class to congregate and, not incidentally, to discuss business. The elite also gathered at the athletic clubs and country clubs that emerged as open spaces disappeared in the city. High fees and strict membership criteria kept these clubs exclusive.

Middle-class urban residents could not afford country clubs, but they rode electric trolleys to the end of the line to enjoy suburban parks and bicycle and skating clubs. Reflecting the emphasis on family togetherness in late-nineteenth-century America, both men and women participated in these sports. Bicycling in particular became immensely popular.

If college football was the rage among the elite, baseball was the leading middle-class spectator sport. Organized baseball originated among the urban elite before the

Civil War. The middle class took over the sport after the war. Baseball epitomized the nation's transition from a rural to an urban-industrial society. Reflecting rural tradition, it was played on an expanse of green, usually on the outskirts of the city. It was leisurely; unlike other games, it had no time limit. Reflecting industrial society, however, it had clearly defined rules and was organized into leagues. Professional leagues were profit-making enterprises, and, like other enterprises, they frequently merged. Initially, most professional baseball games were played on weekday afternoons, making it hard for working-class spectators to attend. After merging with the American Association in 1883, the National League adopted some of its innovations to attract more fans, including beer sales, cheap admission, and, despite the objections of Protestant churches, Sunday games.

The tavern, or saloon, was the workingman's club. Typically an all-male preserve, the saloon provided drink, cheap food, and a place to read a newspaper, socialize, and learn about job opportunities. Advances in refrigeration in the 1870s allowed large breweries such as Anheuser-Busch and Pabst to distribute their product nationwide. Alcoholism was a severe problem in cities, especially, though not exclusively, among working-class men, fueling the Prohibition movement of the late nineteenth century.

Amusement parks, with their mechanical wonders, were another hallmark of the industrial city. Declining trolley fares made these parks accessible to the working class

**Read the Document** Richard K. Fox, *Coney Island Frolics* (1883)

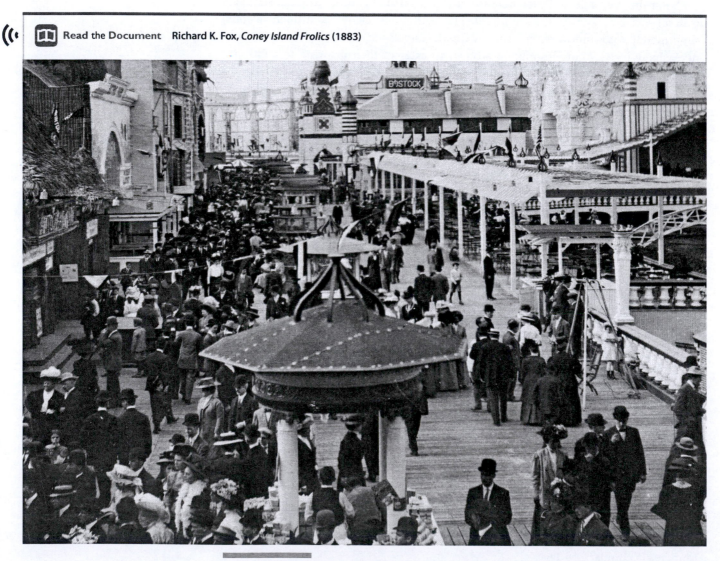

Amusement for the masses. Better transportation, more leisure time, and disposable income fueled escapes such as Luna Park in Coney Island, Brooklyn, a place where people could come together and have fun in a relatively controlled environment.

around 1900. Unlike taverns, they provided a place for working-class men and women to meet and date.

The most renowned of these parks was Brooklyn's Coney Island. In 1897, George C. Tilyou opened Steeplechase Park on Coney Island. He brought an invention by George Washington Ferris, a giant rotating vertical wheel, equipped with swinging carriages, to the park from Chicago, and the Ferris wheel quickly became a Coney Island signature. Together with such attractions as mechanical horses and 250,000 of Thomas Edison's light bulbs, Steeplechase dazzled patrons with its technological wonders. It was quickly followed by Luna Park and Dreamland, and the Coney Island attractions became collectively known as "the poor man's paradise." Immigrant entrepreneurs, seeing a good thing, flocked to Coney Island to set up sideshows, pool halls, taverns, and restaurants. One German immigrant opened a small café serving sausages that he named "frankfurters" after his native Frankfurt. Locals called them "Coney Island hots" or "hot dogs" because they resembled the dachshund, a German-bred dog.

After 1900, the wonders of Coney Island began to lure people from all segments of an increasingly diverse city. Sightseers came from around the world. Notables such as Herman Melville, Mark Twain, and even Sigmund Freud (what did he think of Dreamland?) rubbed shoulders with factory workers, domestics, and department store clerks. In much the same manner, baseball was becoming a national pastime as games attracted a disparate crowd of people with little in common but their devotion to the home team.

Increasing materialism had revealed great fissures in American urban society by 1900. Yet places like department stores, baseball parks, and amusement parks provided democratic spaces for some interaction. Newspapers and schools also offered diverse groups the vicarious opportunity to share similar experiences.

## The Ideal City

For all its problems, the American city was undeniably the locus of the nation's energy; in some ways, with the passing of the frontier, it competed with the West in the national imagination as the environment where possibility was boundless. John Dewey, on his first encounter with Chicago in 1894, sensed this energy and wrote to his wife back home, "Chicago is the place to make you appreciate at every turn the absolute opportunity which chaos affords. . . . I had no conception that things could be so much more phenomenal & objective than they are in a country village." This sense of limitless energy and innovation appeared most notably in urban skylines where skyscrapers reached heavenward as graceful cathedrals of commerce. The tall buildings bespoke a confidence that declared even the sky was not the limit.

There was great interest in creating clean cities, harmonious with nature, and with aesthetic and cultural amenities. The early suburb of Riverside, Illinois (1868), produced a generation of planned communities with these attributes. These planned towns coincided with a growing conservation movement that also included protecting the natural environment from the sprawl of urban growth. Few landscapes expressed this new urban ideal better than the 1893 World's Columbian Exposition in Chicago, a World's Fair to celebrate the 400th anniversary of the European discovery of America (though delays caused the Fair to open one year later). The Fair demonstrated how with foresight, planning, and copious funds, it was possible to create a safe and aesthetic urban environment, quite different from the gritty industrial city just beyond its borders. Dubbed the White City, the exposition epitomized cleanliness, grandeur, beauty, and order in its architecture. That it was sheer fantasy, a temporary respite from the reality beyond the gates, did not faze the millions who attended. The White City represented the possibility, and in America, anything was possible.

# From Then to Now
# Green Cities

Large-scale urbanization and industrialization in the late nineteenth century inspired the early environmental conservation movement. The impact of growth affected the natural environments within and outside cities and created health problems for urban residents. Even before the 1880s, civic leaders had attempted to "soften" the harsh urban environment, first through the construction of rural cemeteries and then through parks, such as Frederick Law Olmsted's Central Park which opened in 1857.

Others believed that creating new urban environments rather than attempting to improve upon the older cities could incorporate the best practices for healthy and natural living spaces. The emergence of suburban planned communities (such as Short Hills, New Jersey, where the Russells resided) connected to cities by steam railroads became popular after the Civil War. The planned suburban town movement culminated with the design of Radburn, New Jersey, literally 45 minutes from Broadway. Its inspiration was the loss of farmland and wooded areas to the rapid expansion of New York City and its suburbs. Even at the height of its settlement, however, no more than 3,000 people lived in the community before suburban New Jersey engulfed it by World War II.

The contemporary example of the redesigned and environmentally sensitive city is called "The New Urbanism" by its creators, the Cuban American design team of Anders Duany and Elizabeth Plater-Zyberk, and it, too, emphasized new communities at first, with the development of Seaside on the Florida Panhandle in 1980. Unlike earlier new towns, Seaside is far from any major urban center. Seaside features higher densities than most suburbs and building in harmony with the natural environment. The town and its "back-to-the-future" Victorian architecture proved wildly popular and spawned countless imitations.

Seaside's principles have enjoyed a vigorous reinterpretation as part of a broad urban renewal since the late 1990s featuring attributes the city has always offered such as light rail; cultural, leisure, and educational amenities; and a mixture of housing types in a more secure environment than was the case a generation ago. These New Urban attributes have flourished best in those cities that have successfully made the transition to a postindustrial, high-tech economy that attracts highly educated, affluent, and creative people. The New Urbanism has not solved poverty, segregation, or blight, but it has helped to reinvigorate parts of urban America and enhance the movement to create "green" cities.

Aerial view of Central Park, 1957. You can see clearly the design elements of Frederick Law Olmsted and his colleague, Calvert Vaux: the landscaping, the winding roads, and the ponds that make the park an oasis in the midst of America's largest city.

Seaside, Florida. The prototype for the New Urbanism. Its high-density Victorian architecture harks back to an allegedly simpler time of community, security, and proximity to nature. This pedestrian-friendly town contains numerous urban amenities and includes an extensive environmental conservation program.

**Question for Discussion**

- Is it possible to be "green" and "equitable" in the modern city?

## Conclusion

The new industrial order, the changing nature of work, the massive migrations of populations from the countryside and abroad, and the rise of great cities changed the American landscape in the late nineteenth century. By 1900, the factory worker and the department store clerk were more representative of the new America than the farmer and small shopkeeper. Industry and technology had created thousands of new jobs, but they also eliminated the autonomy many workers had enjoyed and limited their opportunities to advance. The individual journey from farms and small towns to large cities, and from Europe, Asia, and Latin America to the United States, became a collective journey, moving America further along toward becoming a modern urban and industrial nation, with all of the accompanying ills, but also with all of its possibilities.

Immigrants thronged to the United States to realize their dreams of economic and religious freedom. They found both to varying degrees but also discovered a darker side to the promise of American life. The great cities thrilled newcomers with their possibilities and their abundance of goods and activities. But the cities also bore witness to the growing divisions in American society. As the new century dawned, the prospects for urban-industrial America seemed limitless, yet the stark contrasts that had appeared persisted and deepened.

Still, it would be wrong to depict the nation in 1900 as merely a larger and more divided version of what it had been in 1870. Although sharp ethnic, racial, and class differences persisted, the nation seemed better poised to address them in 1900 than it had a quarter century earlier. Labor unions, ethnic organizations, government legislation, and new urban institutions promised ways to remedy the worst abuses of the new urban-industrial economy.

**For Suggested Readings go to MyHistoryLab.**

# Chapter Review

## New Industry

**18.1** How did workers respond to the changing demands of the workplace in the late nineteenth century? p. 511

Between 1870 and 1900, the United States transformed itself from an agricultural nation into the world's foremost industrial power, producing more than one-third of the world's manufactured goods. By the latter date, factory workers made up one-fourth of the workforce, and agricultural workers had dropped from a half to less than a third.

## New Immigrants

**18.2** What kinds of communities did new immigrants create in America? p. 522

The scale of overseas migration to the United States after 1870 dwarfed all that preceded it. Between 1870 and 1910, the country received more than 20 million immigrants. Most of the new immigrants arrived from southern and eastern Europe, in contrast to the earlier migration from northern Europe.

## New Cities

**18.3** How did the new cities help to create the new middle class? p. 531

As with industry and migration, cities grew to unprecedented scale. In 1850, six cities had a population exceeding 100,000; by 1900, thirty-eight did. The new cities were showcases for American technology and consumer goods. Cities expanded geographically, providing opportunities for the growing middle class, but also increasing social and racial disparities.

# Timeline

**1869**
New Industry—The Knights of Labor is founded in Philadelphia

1869

**1870**
New Industry—John D. Rockefeller organizes the Standard Oil Company

1870

**1876**
New Industry—The Centennial Exposition opens in Philadelphia

1876

**1877**
New Industry—The Great Uprising railroad strike, the first nationwide work stoppage in the United States, provokes violent clashes between workers and federal troops

1877

**1879**
New Industry—Thomas Edison unveils the electric light bulb

1879

**1882**
New Immigrants—Congress passes the Chinese Exclusion Act

1882

**1886**
New Industry—Riot in Chicago's Haymarket Square breaks the Knights of Labor; American Federation of Labor is formed

1886

**1892**
New Industry—General Electric opens the first corporate research and development division in the United States

1892

**1894**
New Industry—Pullman Sleeping Car Company strike fails

1894

# 19 Transforming the West
## 1865–1890

## One American Journey

### Official Photographer of Union Pacific Records Completion of First Transcontinental Railroad

After a pleasant ride of about six miles we attained a very high elevation, and, passing through a gorge of the mountains, we entered a level, circular valley, about three miles in diameter, surrounded on every side by mountains. The track is on the eastern side of the plain, and at the point of junction extends in nearly a southwest and northeast direction. Two lengths of rails are left for today's work.... At a quarter to nine A.M. the whistle of the C.P. [Central Pacific Railroad] is heard, and soon arrives, bringing a number of passengers.... Two additional trains arrive from the East. At a quarter to eleven the Chinese workmen commenced leveling the bed of the road with picks and shovels, preparatory to placing the ties.... At a quarter past eleven the Governor's train arrived. The engine was gayly decorated with little flags and ribbons, the red, white, and blue. At 12 P.M. the rails were laid, and the iron spikes driven. The last tie that was laid is 8 feet long, 8 inches wide, and 6 inches thick. It is of California laurel, finely polished, and is ornamented with a silver escutcheon bearing the following inscription: "The last tie laid on the Pacific Railroad, May 10th, 1869"....

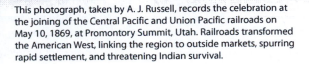

This photograph, taken by A. J. Russell, records the celebration at the joining of the Central Pacific and Union Pacific railroads on May 10, 1869, at Promontory Summit, Utah. Railroads transformed the American West, linking the region to outside markets, spurring rapid settlement, and threatening Indian survival.

## LEARNING OBJECTIVES

**19.1** What were the main objectives of federal Indian policy in the late nineteenth century? p. 543

**19.2** How did the mining and timber industries of the West change over the course of the second half of the nineteenth century? p. 549

**19.3** What factors contributed to the development of the range-cattle industry? p. 554

**19.4** How did new technology contribute to the growth of Western agriculture? p. 559

Listen to Chapter 19 on MyHistoryLab

##  Watch the Video Series on MyHistoryLab

Learn about some key topics related to this chapter with the *MyHistoryLab Video Series: Key Topics in U.S. History.*

**1** **The Meaning of the American West** The West, as this video makes clear, held a special place in the American imagination and culture from the nation's very inception. The West epitomized a new start, making one's fortune, and testing oneself against nature. For Native Americans, however, and the environment, such dreams and ambitions led to genocide, subjugation, and ecological damage that can never be repaired.

**Watch on MyHistoryLab**

**The Transcontinental Railroad** This video surveys the construction and realization of the transcontinental railroad, which linked the Atlantic and Pacific coasts, as well as the enormous influences that railroads had on changing the life and economy of the United States in the nineteenth century. **2**

Watch on MyHistoryLab

**3** **The Dawes Act** The Dawes Act of 1887 was part of the U.S. government's assault on Indian values and Indian lands. This video examines how the law sought to break up tribes and promote Americanization by allotting some reservation land to individual Indians as private property. It also authorized the government to open the remaining tribal lands not so allocated to white settlement.

 Watch on MyHistoryLab

The point of contact is 1,085 4/5 miles from Omaha, leaving 690 miles for the C.P. portion of the work. The engine Jupiter, of the C.P., and engine 119, of the U.P.R.R. [Union Pacific Railroad] moved up within thirty feet of each other. . . . Three cheers were given for the Government of the United States, for the railroad, for the President, for the Star Spangled Banner, for the laborers, and for those who furnished the means respectively. The four spikes, two gold and two silver, were furnished by Montana, Idaho, California, and Nevada. They were about seven inches long, and a little larger than the iron spike. Dr. Harkness, of Sacramento, on presenting to Governor Stanford a spike of pure gold, delivered a short and appropriate speech. The Hon. F.A. Tuttle, of Nevada, presented Dr. Durant with a spike of silver, saying: 'To the iron of the East, and the gold of the West, Nevada adds her link of silver to span the continent and wed the oceans.'. . . The two locomotives then moved up until they touched each other, . . . and at one P.M., under an almost cloudless sky, and in the presence of about one thousand one hundred people, the completion of the greatest railroad on earth was announced.

Andrew J. Russell, "The Completion of the Pacific Railroad," *Frank Leslie's Illustrated Newspaper*, June 5, 1869.

## Personal Journeys Online

**A**ndrew J. Russell's short journey on the morning of May 10, 1869, from Ogden to Promontory Summit, Utah, enabled him to document what he called "the completion of the greatest work of the age, by which this vast continent is spanned, from ocean to ocean, by the iron path of travel and commerce." The transcontinental railroad itself symbolized the classic American journey, a people and a nation moving westward.

The construction of the transcontinental railroad set a precedent for western development. The two railroads that met in a desolate sagebrush basin were huge corporate enterprises, not individual efforts, and corporations would dominate western growth as much as they did eastern industrialization. The crowd of onlookers had good reason to give three cheers for the federal government, for it played a crucial role in railroad construction, as in virtually all aspects of western development. Congress had authorized the Union Pacific and Central Pacific to build the railroad link, given them the right-of-way for their tracks, and provided huge land grants and financial subsidies.

The railroads' dependence on capital investment, engineering knowledge, technological innovations, and labor skills also typified western development. Their labor forces both reflected and reinforced the region's racial and ethnic diversity. European immigrants, Mexicans, Paiute Indians, both male and female, and especially Chinese, recruited in California and Asia, chiseled the tunnels through the mountains, built the bridges over the gulches, and laid the ties and rails across the plains. But Russell had the Chinese workers step back so as not to appear in the famous photographs he took at Promontory, an indication of the racism that marred so many western achievements.

Laying track as quickly as possible to collect the subsidies awarded by the mile, the railroad corporations adopted callous and reckless construction tactics, resulting in waste, deaths (perhaps as many as a thousand Chinese), and environmental destruction, all consequences that would similarly characterize other forms of economic development in the West. And as with most American undertakings in the West, the construction provoked conflict with the Cheyenne, Sioux, and other tribes.

The most important feature of the railroad, however, was that traffic moved in both directions. The transcontinental and subsequent railroads helped move soldiers, miners, cattle raisers, farmers, merchants, and other settlers into the West, but they also enabled the West to send precious metals, livestock, lumber, and wheat to the growing markets in the East. Thus the railroad both integrated the West into the rest of the nation and made it a crucial part of the larger economic revolution that transformed America after the Civil War.

# Subjugating Native Americans

**19.1**    What were the main objectives of federal Indian policy in the late nineteenth century?

**T**he initial obstacle to exploiting the West was the people already living there, who used its resources in their own way and held different concepts of progress and civilization. As whites pressed westward, they attempted to subjugate the Indians, displace them from their lands, and strip them of their culture.

## Tribes and Cultures

Throughout the West, Indians had adapted to their environment, developing subsistence economies ranging from simple gathering to complex systems of irrigated agriculture. Each activity encouraged their sensitivity to the natural world, and each had social and political implications.

In the Northwest, abundant food from rich waters and dense forests gave rise to complex and stable Indian societies. Tillamooks, Chinooks, and other tribes developed artistic handicrafts, elaborate social institutions, and a satisfying religious life. At the opposite environmental extreme, in the dry and barren Great Basin of Utah and Nevada, Shoshones and Paiutes ate grasshoppers and other insects to supplement their diet of rabbits, mice, and other small animals. Such harsh environments restricted the size, strength, and organizational complexity of societies.

In the Southwest, the Pueblos dwelled in permanent towns of adobe buildings and practiced intensive agriculture. Because tribal welfare depended on maintaining complex irrigation systems, the Zunis, Hopis, and other Pueblos emphasized community solidarity rather than individual ambition. Town living encouraged social stability and the development of effective governments, elaborate religious ceremonies, and creative arts.

The most numerous Indian groups lived on the Great Plains. The largest of these tribes were the Lakota, or Sioux, who ranged from western Minnesota through the Dakotas; the Cheyenne and Arapaho, who controlled much of the central plains between the Platte and Arkansas rivers; and the Comanches, preeminent on the southern plains. Two animals dominated the lives of these peoples: the horse, which enabled them to move freely over the plains and to use the energy stored in the valuable grasses, and the buffalo, which provided meat, hides, bones, and horns for tools, and a focus for spiritual life.

**Clashing Values.**   Despite their diversity, all tribes were resilient, thanks especially to procedures, rituals, and beliefs devised over generations to ensure tribal identity and stability. All emphasized community welfare over individual interest. They based their economies on subsistence rather than profit. They tried to live in harmony with nature to ward off sickness, injury, death, or misfortune. And they were intensely religious, absorbed with the need to establish proper relations with supernatural forces that linked human beings with all other living things. By thus living in what the Navajos called "the blessing way," Indians achieved both physical and spiritual contentment. The connections among these basic values appeared in the frequent religious rituals regulating hunting and in the Indians' attitude toward land, which they regarded, like air and water, as part of nature to be held and used communally, not as an individual's personal property from which others could be excluded.

White and Indian cultural values were incompatible. Disdaining Native Americans and their religion, whites condemned them as "savages" to be converted or exterminated. Rejecting the concept of communal property, most settlers demanded land for the exclusive use of ambitious individuals. Ignoring the need for natural harmony, they followed their own culture's goal of extracting wealth from the land for a market economy.

## Federal Indian Policy

The government had in the 1830s adopted the policy of separating whites and Indians (see Chapter 10). Eastern tribes were moved west of Missouri and resettled on land then scorned as "the Great American Desert," unsuitable for white habitation and development. This division presumed a permanent frontier with perpetual Indian ownership of western America. It collapsed in the 1840s, when the United States acquired Texas, California, and Oregon, and migrants crossed Indian lands to reach the West Coast. Rather than curbing white entry into Indian country, the government built forts along the overland trails and ordered the army to punish Indians who threatened travelers.

White migration devastated the Indians, already competing among themselves for the limited resources of the Plains. Migrants' livestock destroyed crucial timber and pastures along streams in the semiarid region; trails disrupted buffalo grazing patterns and eliminated buffalo from tribal hunting ranges. The Plains Indians also suffered from diseases the white migrants introduced. Smallpox, cholera, measles, whooping cough, and scarlet fever, for which Indians had no natural immunity, swept through the tribes, killing up to 40 percent of their population. Emigrants along the Platte River routes came across "villages of the dead."

By the early 1850s, white settlers sought to occupy Indian territory. Recognizing that the Great American Desert could support agriculture, they demanded the removal of the Indians. Simultaneously, railroad companies developed plans to lay tracks across the plains. To promote white settlement, the federal government decided to relocate the tribes to separate and specific reserves. In exchange for accepting such restrictions, the tribes were promised annual payments of livestock, clothing, and other materials. To implement this policy, the government negotiated treaties extinguishing Indian rights to millions of acres (see Map 19.1) and ordered the army to keep Indians on their assigned reservations.

But the treaties, often coerced or misleading, so disadvantaged the tribes that one historian has termed them "instruments of chicanery and weapons of aggression." White

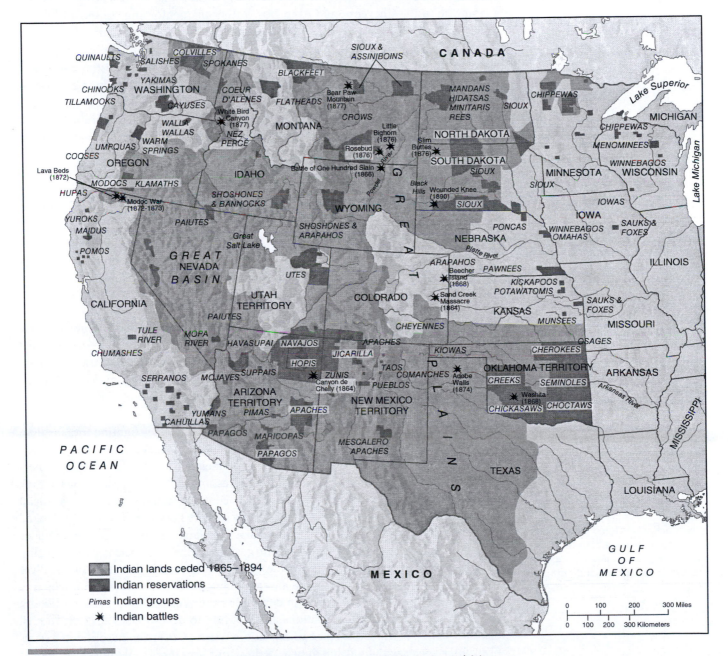

**MAP 19.1 INDIAN LAND CESSIONS, 1860–1894** As white people pushed into the West to exploit its resources, Indians were steadily forced to cede their lands. By 1900 they held only scattered parcels, often in areas considered worthless by white people. Restricted to these reservations, tribes endured official efforts to suppress Indian customs and values.

negotiators sometimes omitted from the formal documents provisions that Indians had insisted upon or included others specifically rejected, and at times Congress sharply reduced the annual payments or the size of the reservations promised in the treaties.

## Warfare and Dispossession

Most smaller tribes accepted the government's conditions, realizing that their survival depended upon accommodation to American power. Many larger tribes resisted. From the 1850s to the 1880s, warfare engulfed the advancing frontier. Indians sometimes initiated conflict, especially in the form of small raids, but invading Americans bore ultimate responsibility for these wars. As General Philip Sheridan declared of the Indians: "We took away their country and their means of support, broke up their mode of living, their habits of life, introduced disease and decay among them, and it was for this and against this that they made war. Could anyone expect less?"

One notorious example of white aggression occurred in 1864, at Sand Creek, Colorado. Gold discoveries had attracted a flood of white settlers onto land only recently guaranteed to the Cheyenne and Arapahos. Rather than enforcing the Indians' treaty rights, however, the government compelled the tribes to relinquish their lands, except for a small tract designated as the Sand Creek reservation. But white settlers wanted to eliminate the Indian presence altogether. John Chivington, a Methodist minister who had organized Denver's first Sunday school, led a militia force to the Sand Creek camp of a band of Cheyenne under Black Kettle, an advocate of peace and accommodation. An American flag flew over the camp. Under Chivington's orders to "kill and scalp all, big and little," the militia attacked Black Kettle's sleeping camp without warning. With howitzers and rifles, the soldiers fired into the camp and then assaulted any survivors with swords and knives. One white trader later described the helpless Indians: "They were scalped, their brains knocked out; the [white] men used their knives, ripped open women, clubbed little children, knocked them in the head with their guns, beat their brains out, mutilated their bodies in every sense of the word."

The **Sand Creek Massacre** appalled many easterners. The Cheyenne, protested the commissioner of Indian affairs, were "butchered in cold blood by troops in the service of the United States." Westerners, however, justified the brutality as a means to secure their own opportunities. One western newspaper demanded, "Kill all the Indians that can be killed. Complete extermination is our motto."

Other tribes were more formidable. None was more powerful than the Sioux, whose military skills had been honed in conflicts with other tribes. An army offensive against the Sioux in 1866 failed completely. Entire units deserted in fear and frustration; others were crushed by the Sioux. General William T. Sherman, who had marched through Georgia against Confederates, knew that the odds were different in the West. Fifty Plains Indians, he declared, could "checkmate" 3,000 soldiers. General Philip Sheridan calculated that the army suffered proportionately greater losses fighting Indians than either the Union or the Confederacy had suffered in the Civil War.

With the army unable to defeat the Sioux and their allies, and with many easterners shocked by both the military's indiscriminate aggression and the expense of the fighting, the government sought peace. Describing white actions as "uniformly unjust," a federal peace commission in 1868 negotiated the **Treaty of Fort Laramie**, in which the United States abandoned military posts and trails on Sioux territory, one of the few times Indians forced whites to retreat. The United States also guaranteed the Sioux permanent ownership of the western half of South Dakota and the right to inhabit and hunt in the Powder River country in Wyoming and Montana, an area to be henceforth closed to all white people.

The army was a key institution in developing the West. It built roads, undertook scientific activities, distributed rations and clothing to destitute settlers, settled civil disputes, and even supervised the earliest national parks. Government contracts to supply military posts with food, building materials, uniforms, grain, and horses promoted freight companies, commercial development, and agriculture.

But the army's primary role was military, and its leaders were bitter about the Sioux victory. Turning to the southern plains, they adopted a devastating new strategy: winter

**Sand Creek Massacre** The near annihilation in 1864 of Black Kettle's Cheyenne band by Colorado troops under Colonel John Chivington's orders to "kill and scalp all, big and little."

**Treaty of Fort Laramie** The treaty acknowledging U.S. defeat in the Great Sioux War in 1868 and supposedly guaranteeing the Sioux perpetual land and hunting rights in South Dakota, Wyoming, and Montana.

A hide painting depicting the U.S. Army's 1870 winter attack on an unsuspecting Piegan village on the Marias River in Montana. The Army killed 173 people, mostly women and children, in this massacre of a "friendly" village; its intended target was another Indian village, seventeen miles away.

campaigns directed at villages. Winter impaired Indian mobility by depleting food sources for both people and ponies, while the army could draw upon stocks of supplies, equipment, and animals. And attacks on villages, inevitably causing heavy casualties among women and children, might demoralize warriors, as Sherman said, "by making them feel we can reach their families and property." The Seventh Cavalry initiated the strategy in a surprise attack on a Cheyenne winter camp on the Washita River in Oklahoma. Colonel George A. Custer reported that his troops killed 103 men and, "in the excitement," many women and children as well. They then destroyed the tribe's 875 horses, its lodges and clothing, and its "whole supply" of food. Any survivors would be impoverished and starving in the bitter weather. By such offensives, the army secured the southern plains by 1875.

Momentum soon shifted on the northern plains as well. Peace had prevailed for several years after the Fort Laramie Treaty, but in 1872, the Northern Pacific Railroad began to build westward on a route that would violate Sioux territory. Rather than stopping the railroad, the government sent an army to protect the surveyors. Sherman drew up plans for the war that he expected the construction to provoke. He regarded railroad expansion as the most important factor in defeating the Indians, for it would allow troops to travel as far in a day as they could march in weeks. Other technological developments, from the telegraph to rapid-fire weapons, also undercut the skills of the Indian warrior.

The destruction of the buffalo also threatened Native Americans. From 1872 to 1874, white hunters killed 4 million buffalo. Railroad survey and construction parties disrupted grazing areas, and hunters working for the railroads killed hordes of buffalo, both to feed construction crews and to prevent the animals from obstructing rail traffic. Hide hunters slaughtered even more of the beasts for their skins, leaving the bodies to rot. Federal officials encouraged the buffalo's extermination because it would destroy the Indians' basis for survival.

The climactic provocation of the Sioux began in 1874, when Custer led an invasion to survey the Black Hills for a military post and to confirm the presence of gold. Thousands of white miners then illegally poured onto Sioux land. Ignoring Sioux demands that the government enforce the Fort Laramie Treaty, the army insisted that the Indians leave their Powder River hunting grounds. When the Sioux refused, the army attacked. The Oglala Sioux, under Crazy Horse, repulsed one prong of this offensive at the Battle

**Battle of the Little Bighorn** Battle in which Colonel George A. Custer and the Seventh Cavalry were defeated by the Sioux and Cheyenne under Sitting Bull and Crazy Horse in Montana in 1876.

of the Rosebud in 1876 and then joined a larger body of Sioux under Sitting Bull and their Cheyenne and Arapaho allies to overwhelm a second American column, under Custer, at the **Battle of the Little Bighorn**.

But the Indians could not follow up their dramatic victory. They had to divide their forces to find fresh grass for their horses and to hunt for food. Not similarly handicapped but supplied and equipped by an industrializing nation, the U.S. Army relentlessly pursued the separate bands to exhaustion. "Wherever we went," said one Oglala holy man, "soldiers came to kill us." Most bands capitulated in the winter of 1876–1877. In the end, the conquest of the northern plains came, not through any decisive victory, but through attrition and the inability of the traditional Indian economy to support resistance to the technologically and numerically superior white forces.

In the Southwest, the Navajos and the Comanches were subdued, as the Sioux had been, by persistent pursuit that prevented them from obtaining food. The last to submit were the Apaches, under Geronimo. In 1886, he and thirty-six followers, facing 5,000 U.S. troops, finally surrendered. Geronimo and other Apaches were sent to a military prison in Florida; the tribes were herded onto barren reservations. The Oglala chief Red Cloud concluded of the white invasion: "They made us many promises, more than I can remember, but they never kept but one. They promised to take our land, and they took it."

## Life on the Reservation: Americanization

Conquering the tribes and seizing their land were only the initial objectives of government policy. The next goal was to require Indians to adopt white ways, instilled by education and religion and enforced when necessary by the military. This goal did not involve assimilation but merely "Americanization," an expression of cultural conquest.

The government received aid from many Christian denominations, which had long proposed nonviolent methods of controlling Indians. Reformers wanted to change Indian religious and family life, train Indian children in Protestant beliefs, and force Indians to accept private ownership and market capitalism.

Confined to reservations, Indians were a captive audience for white reformers. Furthermore, with their very survival dependent on government rations and annual payments stipulated by treaties, Indians were "compelled by sheer necessity," as one federal official said, to accept government orders "or starve." Government agents of the Bureau of Indian Affairs used their power to undermine tribal authority and destroy traditional Indian government, prohibiting tribal councils from meeting and imprisoning tribal leaders.

White activists sought to destroy Indian religion because it was "pagan" and because it helped Indians resist assimilation. Protestant religious groups persuaded the Bureau of Indian Affairs to frame a criminal code prohibiting tribal religious practices. Established in 1884, the code remained in effect until 1933. To enforce the ban, the government withheld rations and disrupted the religious ceremonies that transmitted traditional values. In 1890, to suppress the Ghost Dance religion, the army even used artillery and killed at least 200 Sioux men, women, and children at Wounded Knee, South Dakota, in what became known as the **Wounded Knee Massacre**.

**Wounded Knee Massacre** The U.S. Army's brutal winter massacre in 1890 of at least 200 Sioux men, women, and children as part of the government's assault on the tribe's Ghost Dance religion.

The government and religious groups also used education to eliminate Indian values and traditions. They isolated Indian children from tribal influences at off-reservation boarding schools. Troops often seized Indian children for these schools, where they were confined until after adolescence. The schoolchildren were forced to speak English, attend Christian services, and profess white American values.

Finally, the government and the religious reformers imposed the economic practices and values of white society on Indians. Government agents taught Indian men how to farm and distributed agricultural implements, but Indians could not farm successfully on reservation lands that whites had already rejected as unproductive. Whites, however, believed that the real obstacle to economic prosperity for the Indians was their rejection of private property. The Indians' communal values, the reformers argued, inhibited the pursuit of personal success that lay at the heart of capitalism. As one Bureau of Indian Affairs official declared, Indians must be taught to be more "mercenary and ambitious to obtain riches."

Dressed in their school uniforms, Indian children sit under the U.S. flag. Government and missionary schools sought to promote "Americanization" and suppress native cultures. Such education, said one member of Congress, "is the solution of the vexed Indian problem."

To force such values on Indians, Congress in 1887 passed the **Dawes Act**, which divided tribal lands among individual Indians. One Caddo chief complained to U.S. officials: "You are attempting to change our customs and entail ruin on my people." Western settlers also supported the law because it provided that reservation lands not allocated to individual Indians would be opened to white settlers. Under this "reform," the amount of land held by Indians declined by more than half by 1900. The Dawes Act, noted one Sioux chief, was "only another trick of the whites." White acquisition and exploitation of Indian land thus seemed to be the only constant in the nation's treatment of Native Americans.

Certainly assimilation scarcely succeeded. Some Indians did accept Christianity, formal education, and new job skills in attempting to adapt to their changing world. But often they employed such knowledge in another strategy of resistance, lecturing and lobbying to reform Indian policies or working to curtail the economic exploitation of their tribes. Other Indians, when they returned from school to their reservations, simply went "back to the blanket," as disgusted white critics called their reversion to traditional ways. Most Indians resented assimilationist efforts, clinging to their own values and rejecting as selfish, dishonorable, and obsessively materialistic those favored by whites. As Big Bear, a chief of the Otoe-Missouria, defiantly declared, "You cannot make white men of us. That is one thing you can't do." But if it was not yet clear what place Native Americans would have in America, it was at least clear by 1900 that they would no longer stand in the way of western development.

**Dawes Act** An 1887 law terminating tribal ownership of land and allotting some parcels of land to individual Indians with the remainder opened for white settlement.

# Exploiting the Mountains: Mining and Timber

**19.2**    How did the mining and timber industries of the West change over the course of the second half of the nineteenth century?

n the later nineteenth century, the West experienced several stages of economic development that transformed the environment, produced economic and social conflict, and integrated the region into the modern national economy. The first stage of development centered on mining, which attracted eager prospectors into the mountains in search of gold and silver. They founded communities, stimulated the railroad construction that brought further development, and contributed to the disorderly heritage of the frontier. But few gained the wealth they expected.

## Rushes and Mining Camps

The first important gold rush in the Rocky Mountains came in Colorado in 1859. More than 100,000 prospectors crowded into Denver and nearby mining camps. Simultaneously, the discovery of the famous Comstock Lode in Nevada produced booming mining camps like Virginia City. Strikes in the northern Rockies followed in the 1860s. Boise and Lewiston in Idaho and Helena in Montana became major mining centers, and other camps prospered briefly before fading into ghost towns. The last gold rush came in 1874 in the Black Hills of South Dakota, where the roaring mining camp of Deadwood flourished. Later, other minerals shaped frontier development: silver in Nevada, silver and lead in Colorado and Idaho, silver and copper in Arizona and Montana.

Mining camps were often isolated by both distance and terrain. They frequently consisted only of flimsy shanties, saloons, crude stores, dance halls, and brothels, all hastily built by entrepreneurs. Such towns reflected the speculative, exploitive, and transitory character of mining. And yet they did contribute to permanent settlement by encouraging agriculture, industry, and transportation in the surrounding areas.

The camps had an unusual social and economic structure. Their population was overwhelmingly male. In 1860, for example, about 2,300 men and only 30 women lived in the Nevada camps of Virginia City and Gold Hill. Women found far fewer economic opportunities than men did on the mining frontier. Some became prospectors themselves; in Montana, women, "skirts hiked up," were reported working claims. But most stayed within conventional domestic spaces. Several opened lodging houses or hotels. Those with less capital worked as seamstresses and cooks and took in washing. The few married women often earned more than their husbands by boarding other miners willing to pay for the trappings of family life.

But the largest source of paid employment for women was prostitution, a flourishing consequence of the gender imbalance and the limited economic options for women. Mary Josephine Welch, an entrepreneurial Irish immigrant, settled in Helena in 1867 and established the Red Light Saloon, the first of many saloons, dance halls, and brothels that she owned and operated. Most women who engaged in such activities, however, were far less successful. Many who entered brothels already suffered from economic hardship or a broken family; some Chinese women were virtually sold into prostitution. By the 1890s, as men gained control of the vice trade from the madams, violence, suicide, alcoholism, disease, drug addiction, and poverty overcame most prostitutes.

**Saloon Society.** The gender imbalance in the mining camps also made saloons prevalent among local businesses. An 1879 business census of Leadville, Colorado, reported 10 dry-goods stores, 4 banks, and 4 churches, but 120 saloons, 19 beer halls, and 118 gambling houses. Saloons were social centers in towns where most miners lived in crowded and dirty tents and rooming houses. But the male-dominated saloon society of the mining camps generated social conflict. One observer reported that men, "unburdened by families, drink whenever they feel like it, whenever they have money to pay for it, and whenever there is nothing else to do. . . . Bad manners follow, profanity becomes a matter of course. . . . Excitability and nervousness brought on by rum help these tendencies along, and then to correct this state of things the pistol comes into play." Disputes over mining claims could become violent, adding to the disorder. The California mining town of Bodie experienced twenty-nine killings between 1877 and 1883, a homicide rate higher than that of any U.S. city a century later. But such killings occurred only within a small group of males—young, single, surly, and armed—who were known as the Badmen of Bodie. Daily life for most people was safe.

**Collective Violence.** Indeed, personal and criminal violence, which remains popularly associated with the West, was less significant than collective violence. This, too, affected

Read the Document   John Lester, "Hydraulic Mining" (1873)

Opening restaurants and boarding houses, some women earned money from their domestic skills in mining camps.

mining camps and was aggravated by their ethnic and racial diversity. Irish, Germans, English, Chinese, Australians, Italians, Slavs, and Mexicans, among others, rushed into the mining regions. In many camps, half the population was foreign-born. The European immigrants who sometimes encountered nativist hostility in the East experienced less animosity in the West, but nonwhite minorities often suffered. Whites frequently drove Mexicans and Chinese from their claims or refused to let them work in higher-paid oc-cupations in the mining camps. The Chinese had originally migrated to the California gold fields and thereafter spread to the new mining areas of the Rockies and the Great Basin, where they worked in mining when possible, operated laundries and restaurants, and held menial jobs like hauling water and chopping wood. In 1870, more than a quar-ter of Idaho's population and nearly 10 percent of Montana's were Chinese. Where they were numerous, the Chinese built their own communities and maintained their customs.

But racism and fear of economic competition sparked hostility and violence against the Chinese almost everywhere. In Colorado, town leaders boasted of having driven all Chinese out of Leadville by 1879, and whites destroyed Denver's Chinatown in 1880. The worst anti-Chinese violence occurred in Rock Springs, Wyoming, in 1885 when whites killed 28 Chinese workers and drove away all 700 residents from the local Chinatown. Although the members of the mob were well known, the grand jury, speaking for the white majority, found no cause for legal action: "Though we have examined a large number of witnesses, no one has been able to testify to a single criminal act com-mitted by any known white person." Such community sanction for violence against racial minorities made mob attacks one of the worst features of the mining camps.

## Labor and Capital

New technology had dramatic consequences for both miners and the mining industry. Initially, mining was an individual enterprise in which miners used simple tools, such as picks, shovels, and wash pans, to work shallow surface deposits known as placers. Placer mining attracted prospectors with relatively little capital or expertise, but surface deposits were quickly exhausted. More complex and expensive operations were needed to reach the precious metal buried in the earth.

Hydraulic mining, for example, required massive capital investment to build reservoirs, ditches, and troughs to power high-pressure water cannons that would pulverize hillsides and uncover the mineral deposits. Quartz, or lode, mining, sometimes called hard-rock mining, required still more money, technology, and time to sink a shaft into the earth, timber underground chambers and tunnels, install pumps to remove underground water and hoists to lower men and lift out rock, and build stamp mills and smelters to treat the ore.

Such complex, expensive, and permanent operations necessarily came under corporate control. Often financed with eastern or British capital, the new corporations integrated the mining industry into the larger economy. Hard-rock mining produced more complex ores than could be treated in remote mining towns, but with the new railroad network, they were shipped to smelting plants as far away as Kansas City and St. Louis and then to refineries in eastern cities. Western ores thus became part of national and international business.

**Effects of Corporate Mining.**    While corporate mining helped usher the mining frontier into a more stable period, it had disturbing effects. Its impact on the environment was horrendous. Hydraulic mining washed away hillsides, depositing debris in canyons and valleys to a depth of 100 feet or more, clogging rivers and causing floods, and burying thousands of acres of farmland. Such damage provoked an outcry and eventually led to government regulation. Fewer westerners worried about sterile slag heaps or the toxic fumes that belched from smelters and killed vegetation. They were the signs of progress. "The thicker the fumes," declared one proud Butte newspaper, "the greater our financial vitality."

Corporate mining also hurt miners, transforming them into wage workers with restricted opportunities. "It is useless to say that here all have an equal chance," conceded a Colorado newspaper in 1891. Miners' status declined as new machinery, such as power drills, reduced the need for skilled laborers and enabled employers to hire cheaper workers from eastern and southern Europe. Mining corporations, moreover, did little to protect miners' health or safety. Miners died in cave-ins, explosions, and fires, or from the great heat and poisonous gases in underground mines. Others contracted silicosis, lead poisoning, or other diseases or were crippled or killed by machines.

**Unions and Union Busting.**    To protect themselves, miners organized unions. These functioned as benevolent societies, aiding injured miners or their survivors, establishing hospitals and libraries, and providing an alternative to the saloons with union halls serving as social centers. Unions also promoted miners' interests by striking against wage cuts and campaigning for mine safety. They convinced states to pass mine safety laws and, beginning in the 1880s, to appoint mine inspectors. The chief role of these state officials was, in the words of a Colorado inspector, to decide "How far should an industry be permitted to advance its material welfare at the expense of human life?"

The industry itself, however, often provided the answer to this question, for mining companies frequently controlled state power and used it to crush unions. Thus, in 1892, in the Coeur d'Alene district of Idaho, mining companies locked out strikers and imported a private army, which battled miners in a bloody gunfight. Management next persuaded the governor and the president to send in the state militia and the U.S. Army. State officials then suppressed the strike and the union by confining all union members and their sympathizers in stockades. When mining companies in Utah, Colorado, and Montana pursued the same aggressive tactics, the local miners' unions in the West united for strength and self-protection. In 1893, they formed one of the nation's largest and most militant unions, the Western Federation of Miners.

Violence and conflict were attributable not to frontier lawlessness but to the industrialization of the mines. Both management's tactics—blacklisting union members, locking out strikers, obtaining court injunctions against unions, and using soldiers against workers—and labor's response mirrored conditions in the industrial East. In sum, western mining, reflecting the industrialization of the national economy, had been transformed from a small-scale prospecting enterprise characterized by individual initiative and simple tools into a large-scale corporate business characterized by impersonal management, outside capital, advanced technology, and wage labor.

## Lumber Companies and Lumberjacks

Less famously, the lumber industry developed in a pattern similar to that of mining. Before the mid-nineteenth century, lumbering was an occupation often combined with farming, as farmers cleared their fields and sold their timber to small local mills. But industrialization, urbanization, and the expansion of settlement westward opened vast new markets for lumber, and large lumber companies began to develop, first in the Great Lakes region and then in the Far West, where mining and railroads required massive amounts of timber. The mines of Nevada's Comstock Lode, which used 600 million feet of timber to support their tunnels, became known as "the tomb of the forests of the Sierras"; railroads needed even more wood for bridges, stations, fuel, and especially railroad ties. Lumber companies in Washington, Oregon, and California soon supplied these needs as well as entered the global economy by shipping lumber to Latin America, China, and throughout the Pacific Basin.

Initially, loggers simply cut timber from the public domain and floated the logs downstream to coastal sawmills. The Secretary of the Interior complained that whole fleets of ships were "carrying timber stolen from the public lands to be sold in foreign countries, immense tracts being devastated that some robbers might fill their pockets." By the 1880s the shorelines of rivers and harbors had been stripped, and the industry—and its environmental ravages—began to move inland, seeing in the timber of the mountains what one journalist described as "a mine of wealth." To exploit that wealth, the California Redwood Company, the Pacific Lumber Company, and other corporations adopted vertical integration by adding to their logging operations and mills their own timberlands, company railroads and ocean ships for transporting timber, and marketing offices. When acquiring vast tracts of forest land, some companies engaged in blatant fraud, one seizing 100,000 acres of public land and then thwarting federal investigators by bribing, beating, and kidnapping witnesses. Other companies purchased their lands from those the government had granted to railroads, climaxing at the end of the century when the Weyerhaeuser Corporation bought 900,000 acres of Douglas fir forest land in Washington. Smaller operations were squeezed out by these expanding capital costs, together with technological changes as logging became increasingly mechanized and as mills shifted from handsaws to steam-powered circular and band saws.

Environmental costs also increased. As steam engines replaced ox teams in moving logs, they intensified the damage to forests, smashing young trees, uprooting ground cover, and breaking the soil. The short-sighted but profitable adoption of clear-cutting left ghastly, barren hillsides; rampant erosion soon polluted streams. In the mill towns, unnumbered tons of sawdust were simply burned, a wasteful practice that also polluted the air. Such abuses prompted a growing demand to protect the region's timberlands, and in the 1890s the government established forest reserves in Oregon's Cascade Mountains and Washington's Olympic Peninsula. Effective conservation, however, awaited the twentieth century.

**Life and Labor.**   Working and living conditions for lumberjacks and mill hands were poor. Loggers, like miners, tended to be young, single, and immigrants, particularly from Scandinavia and Canada's Maritime Provinces. Management also hired Chinese and Japanese mill workers, although nativist white mobs drove Asians out of Tacoma and other lumber centers in the 1880s. Nevertheless, companies actively recruited such workers, which helped keep wages low for hard and dangerous work. Loggers were crushed by falling trees or maimed by crosscut saws; mill hands worked over giant, unprotected saw blades and inhaled sawdust 12 hours a day. In Washington, the industry

Workers and a "steam donkey" in the forests of Washington. These steam engines could drag large logs to railroads for shipment to sawmills, but sometimes their sparks caused destructive forest fires and their boilers exploded, making such power logging extremely dangerous.

had five times more fatal accidents than any other. Lumber camps and mill towns were often company owned. "Food was poor and crudely prepared," one worker recalled, and company housing was "crudely built bunkhouses with rude double-deck bunks, infested with bedbugs and sometimes lice. There were no washhouses, no recreation facilities." Small-scale spontaneous strikes sometimes occurred, especially over bad food and harsh foremen, and some lumber workers joined the Knights of Labor in the 1880s. But the isolated locales of logging camps and mill towns—and the workers' dependence on their employers for both room and board—gave lumber companies great power and restrained strikes and unionism.

Such conditions produced high worker turnover, and seasonal unemployment further contributed to workers' lack of security. Returning to coastal cities to line up another job, lumberjacks often let off steam in the skid row neighborhoods of Seattle or Portland. This gave them the reputation of disreputable and unreliable riffraff rather than hardworking men living difficult lives, and it contributed to management's contempt for them.

Despite such growing problems, the lumber industry emerged as a major contributor to the economic development of the West. In 1899, the *Pacific Lumber Trade Journal* proudly reported that much of Washington's economy and two-thirds of its workers depended upon lumbering. Such regional pride, however, did not obscure the reality that lumbering, like mining, largely depended on the national and international economy for capital, markets, and technology nor the growing realization that corporate success often came at the expense of individual opportunity.

## Using the Grass: The Cattle Kingdom

**19.3**    What factors contributed to the development of the range-cattle industry?

The development of the range-cattle industry opened another stage of exploitation of the late-nineteenth-century West. It reflected the needs of an emerging eastern urban society, the economic possibilities of the grasslands of the Great Plains, the technology of the expanding railroad network, and the requirements of corporations and capital. It also brought "cow towns" and urban development to the West. The fabled cowboy, though essential to the story, was only a bit player.

## Cattle Drives and Cow Towns

The cattle industry originated in southern Texas, where the Spanish had introduced cattle in the eighteenth century. Developed by Mexican ranchers, "Texas longhorns" proved well adapted to the plains grasslands. As industrial expansion in the East and Midwest enlarged the urban market for food, the potential value of Texas steers increased. And the extension of the railroad network into the West opened the possibility of tapping that market. The key was to establish a shipping point on the railroads west of the settled farming regions, a step first taken in 1867 by Joseph McCoy, an Illinois cattle shipper. McCoy selected Abilene, Kansas, in his words "a very small, dead place, consisting of about one dozen log huts." But Abilene was also the western railhead of the Kansas Pacific Railroad and was ringed by lush grasslands for cattle. Texans opened the **Chisholm Trail** through Indian Territory to drive their cattle northward to Abilene. Within three years, a million and a half cattle reached Abilene, divided into herds of several thousand, each directed by a dozen cowhands on a "long drive" taking two to three months.

**Cow Town Life.**   The cattle trade attracted other entrepreneurs who created a bustling town. As both railroads and settlement advanced westward, a series of other cow towns—Ellsworth, Wichita, Dodge City, Cheyenne—attracted the long drives, cattle herds, and urban development.

As with the mining camps, the cow towns' reputation for violence was exaggerated. They adopted gun-control laws, prohibiting the carrying of handguns within city limits, and established police forces to maintain order. The towns regulated, rather than prohibited, prostitution and gambling, for merchants viewed these vices as necessary to attract the cattle trade. Thus, the towns taxed prostitutes and gamblers and charged high fees for liquor licenses. By collecting such "sin taxes," Wichita was able to forgo general business taxes, thereby increasing its appeal to prospective settlers.

Not all cow towns became cities like Wichita; most, like Abilene, dwindled into small towns serving farm populations. But cow towns, again like mining camps, contributed to the growth of an urban frontier. Railroads often determined the location and development of western cities, providing access to markets for local products, transporting supplies and machinery for residents, and attracting capital for commercial and industrial expansion. When railroads reached El Paso, Texas, for example, the city became a shipping point for cattle but then built its own packinghouses and opened smelters to process Arizona ores. Its Mexican workers clustered in barrios and developed their own religious and social organizations, just as San Francisco's Chinese did in Chinatown or European immigrants did in eastern cities. This urbanization demonstrated how western developments paralleled those in older regions. The West, in fact, had become the most urban region in the nation by 1890, with two-thirds of its population living in communities of at least 2,500 people.

## Rise and Fall of Open-Range Ranching

The significance of the long drive to the cow towns faded as cattle raising expanded beyond Texas. Indian removal and extension of the railroads opened land for ranching in Kansas, Nebraska, Wyoming, Colorado, Montana, and the Dakotas. Cattle reaching Kansas were increasingly sold to stock these northern ranges rather than for shipment to the packinghouses. Ranches soon spread across the Great Plains and into the Great Basin, the Southwest, and even eastern Oregon and Washington. This expansion was helped by the initially low investment that ranching required. Calves were cheap, and grass was mostly free. Ranchers did not buy, but merely used, the grazing lands of the open range, which was public land. It sufficed to acquire title to the site for a ranch house and a water source, because controlling access to water in semiarid lands gave effective control of the surrounding public domain. Ranchers thus needed to invest only in horses, primitive corrals, and bunkhouses. Their labor costs were minimal: They

**Chisholm Trail** The route followed by Texas cattle raisers driving their herds north to markets at Kansas railheads.

hired cowboys in the spring to round up new calves for branding and in the fall to herd steers to market.

By the early 1880s, the high profits from this enterprise and an expanding market for beef attracted speculative capital and reshaped the industry. Eastern and European capital flooded the West, with British investors particularly prominent. Some investors went into partnership with existing ranchers, providing capital in exchange for expertise and management. Wisconsin investors formed the Three Rivers Land and Cattle Company of New Mexico, for example, by buying into a ranch owned by Susan Barber, whom they then employed as general manager. Barber was unusual in the male-dominated industry, but the managerial skills she demonstrated were necessary for success. On a larger scale, British and American corporations acquired, expanded, and managed huge ranches. The Swan Land and Cattle Company controlled a tract in Wyoming 130 miles long and 40 to 100 miles wide, with more than 100,000 head of cattle.

**Effects of Corporate Control.**   Large companies soon dominated the industry, just as they had gained control of mining. Cattle companies often worked together to enhance their power, especially by restricting access to the range and by intimidating small competitors. Some large companies illegally enclosed the open range, building fences to exclude newcomers and minimize labor costs by reducing the number of cowboys needed to control the cattle. One Wyoming newspaper complained: "Some morning we will wake up to find that a corporation has run a wire fence about the boundary lines of Wyoming, and all within the same have been notified to move."

Such tensions sometimes exploded in instances of social violence as serious as those that disrupted the mining frontier. Attempts by large ranchers to fence off public lands in Texas provoked the Fence-Cutters War of 1883–1884. Montana's largest cattlemen organized an armed force known as "Stuart's Stranglers" and, in America's worst vigilante violence, killed more than a hundred people they viewed as challenging their power.

The corporate cattle boom overstocked the range and threatened the industry itself. Overgrazing replaced nutritious grasses with sagebrush, Russian thistle, and other plants that livestock found unpalatable. Droughts in the mid-1880s further withered vegetation and enfeebled the animals. Millions of cattle starved or froze to death in terrible blizzards in 1886 and 1887. These ecological and financial disasters destroyed the open-range cattle industry. The surviving ranchers reduced their operations, restricted the size of their herds, and tried to ensure adequate winter feed by growing hay. To further reduce their dependence on natural vegetation, they introduced drought-resistant sorghum and new grasses; to reduce their dependence on rainfall, they drilled wells and installed windmills to pump water.

## Cowhands and Capitalists

One constant in the cattle industry was the cowboy, but his working conditions and opportunities changed sharply over time and corresponded little to the romantic image of a dashing individual free of social constraints. Cowboys' work was hard, dirty, seasonal, tedious, sometimes dangerous, and poorly paid. Many early cowboys were white southerners unwilling or unable to return home after the Civil War. Black cowhands made up perhaps 25 percent of the trail-herd outfits. Many others, especially in Texas and the Southwest, were Mexicans. Indeed, Mexicans developed most of the tools, techniques, and trappings that characterized the cattle industry: from boots, chaps, and the "western" saddle to roundups and roping. As the industry expanded northward, more cowboys came from rural Kansas, Nebraska, and neighboring states.

Initially, in the frontier-ranching phase dominated by the long drive, cowboys were seasonal employees who worked closely with owners. Often the sons or neighbors of ranchers, they frequently expected to become stock raisers themselves. They typically

📖 **Read the Document** Perspectives on the American Cowboy (1884, 1886)

Cowboys gather around the chuck wagon at the XIT Ranch in Texas. Poor pay and arduous work defined the lives of most cowboys.

enjoyed the rights to "maverick" cattle, putting their own brand on unmarked animals they encountered, and to "run a brand," or own their own cattle while working for a ranch. These informal rights provided opportunities to acquire property and move up the social ladder.

As ranching changed with the appearance of large corporate enterprises, so did the work and work relationships of cowhands. The power and status of employer and employees diverged, and the cowboys' traditional rights disappeared. Employers redefined mavericking as rustling and prohibited cowhands from running a brand of their own. One cowboy complained that these restrictions deprived a cowhand of his one way "to get on in the world." But that was the purpose: Cowboys were to be workers, not potential ranchers and competitors. To increase labor efficiency, some companies prohibited their cowboys from drinking, gambling, and carrying guns.

**Unions and Strikes.** Cowboys sometimes responded to these structural transformations the same way skilled workers in the industrial East did, by forming unions and striking. The first strike occurred in Texas in 1883, when the Panhandle Stock Association, representing large operators, prohibited ranch hands from owning their own cattle and imposed a standard wage. More than 300 cowboys struck seven large ranches. Ranchers evicted the cowboys, hired scabs, and used the Texas Rangers to drive the strikers from the region.

Other strikes also failed because corporate ranches and their stock associations had great influence and cowhands faced long odds in their efforts to organize. They were isolated across vast spaces and had little leverage in the industry. Members of the Northern New Mexico Cowboys Union, formed in 1886, recognized their weakness. After asking employers for "what we are worth after many years' experience," they conceded, "We are dependent on you."

The transformation of the western cattle industry and its integration into a national economy dominated by corporations thus made the cherished image of cowboy independence and rugged individualism more myth than reality. One visitor to America in the late 1880s commented: "Out in the fabled West, the life of the 'free' cowboy is as much that of a slave as is the life of his Eastern brother, the Massachusetts mill-hand. And the slave-owner is in both cases the same, the capitalist."

# ✳ Explore the New Economy of the West, 1850–1893 on MyHistoryLab

## WHAT NEW ECONOMIC PATTERNS EMERGED IN THE WEST?

The second half of the 1800s brought quick expansion of the United States into the West. Railroads quickly spread across the region, spurring town development and creating a giant national marketplace that stretched from coast to coast. The federal government established post offices through the West to help further connect the nation. Settlers streamed from the East in search of cheap land on which to raise their crops and livestock. The West became an important agricultural region as farm products then moved along the railroad network linking western towns with eastern and international markets.

This patriotic lithograph, titled "Across the Continent—Westward the Course of Empire Takes Its Way," represents the expansion into the American West made possible by the nation's first transcontinental railway, which was completed in 1869.

## GROWING POPULATION IN THE WEST

|  | 1860 | 1890 |
| --- | --- | --- |
| Montana | N/A | 142,924 |
| Idaho | N/A | 88,548 |
| Wyoming | N/A | 62,555 |
| Colorado | 34,277 | 413,249 |
| New Mexico | 93,516 | 160,282 |
| Arizona | N/A | 88,243 |
| Utah | 40,273 | 210,779 |
| Nevada | 6,857 | 47,355 |
| Washington | 11,594 | 357,232 |
| Oregon | 52,465 | 317,704 |
| California | 379,994 | 1,213,398 |
| Kansas | 107,206 | 1,428,108 |
| Nebraska | 28,841 | 1,062,656 |
| North Dakota | N/A | 190,983 |
| South Dakota | 4,837 | 348,600 |

SOURCE: "United States Resident Population by State", http://lwd.dol.state.nj.us/labor/lpa/census/1990/poptrd1.htm.

## KEY QUESTIONS Use MyHistoryLab *Explorer* to answer these questions:

**Cause ▶▶▶** *How did railroad expansion shape population growth in the West?*

Map the growth of the railroad network and the development of western towns and cities.

**Analysis ▶▶▶** *How did western agriculture develop during the late 1800s?*

Map the importance of agricultural commodities produced in the West.

**Response ▶▶▶** *How did the federal government's presence manifest itself as settlers moved west?*

Trace the spread of post offices.

# Working the Earth: Homesteaders and Agricultural Expansion

**19.4**  How did new technology contribute to the growth of Western agriculture?

Even more than ranching and mining, agricultural growth boosted the western economy and bound it tightly to national and world markets. In this process, the government played a significant role, as did the railroads, science and technology, eastern and foreign capital, and the dreams and hard work of millions of rural settlers. The development of farming produced remarkable economic growth, but it left the dreams of many unfulfilled.

## Settling the Land

To stimulate agricultural settlement, Congress passed the most famous land law, the **Homestead Act** of 1862 (see Table 19.1). The measure offered 160 acres of land free to anyone who would live on the plot and farm it for five years. The act promised opportunity and independence to ambitious farmers. The governor of Nebraska exclaimed, "What a blessing this wise and humane legislation will bring to many a poor but honest and industrious family."

**Homestead Act**  Law passed by Congress in 1862 providing 160 acres of land free to anyone who would live on the plot and farm it for five years.

**Limits of the Homestead Act.**  However, prospective settlers found less land open to public entry than they expected. Federal land laws did not apply in much of California and the Southwest, where Spain and Mexico had previously transferred land to private owners. Elsewhere, the government had given away millions of acres to railroads or authorized selling millions more for educational and other purposes. Moreover, other laws provided for easy transfer of public lands to cattle companies, to other corporations exploiting natural resources, and to land speculators.

Thus, settlers in Kansas, Nebraska, Minnesota, and the Dakotas in the late 1860s and early 1870s often found most of the best land unavailable for homesteading and much of the rest remote from transportation facilities and markets. Although 375,000 farms were claimed by 1890 through the Homestead Act, a not insignificant number, most settlers had to purchase their land.

The Homestead Act also reflected traditional eastern conceptions of the family farm, which were inappropriate in the West. A farm of 160 acres would have suited conditions in eastern Kansas or Nebraska, but farther west, larger-scale farming was necessary. And the law ignored the need for capital—for machinery, buildings, livestock, and fencing—that was required for successful farming. Without such capital, said California's governor in 1881, farming "would bring defeat to the man of humble means."

**TABLE 19.1  GOVERNMENT LAND POLICY**

| Legislation | Result |
| --- | --- |
| Railroad land grants (1850–1871) | Granted 181 million acres to railroads to encourage construction and development |
| Homestead Act (1862) | Gave 80 million acres to settlers to encourage settlement |
| Morrill Act (1862) | Granted 11 million acres to states to sell to fund public agricultural colleges |
| Other grants | Granted 129 million acres to states to sell for other educational and related purposes |
| Dawes Act (1887) | Allotted some reservation lands to individual Indians to promote private property and weaken tribal values among Indians; offered remaining reservation lands for sale to whites (by 1906, some 75 million acres had been acquired by whites) |
| Various laws | Permitted direct sales of 100 million acres by the Land Office |

**Promoting Settlement.** Nevertheless, many interests promoted settlement. Newspaper editors trumpeted the prospects of their region. Land companies, eager to sell their speculative holdings, sent agents through the Midwest and Europe to encourage migration. Steamship companies, hoping to sell transatlantic tickets, advertised the opportunities in the American West across Europe. Religious and ethnic groups encouraged immigration. The Scandinavian Immigration Society generated both publicity and settlers for Minnesota; the Hebrew Emigrant Aid Society established Jewish agricultural colonies in Kansas and North Dakota. Mormons organized the Perpetual Emigrating Fund Company, which helped more than 100,000 European immigrants settle in Utah and Idaho. Their agricultural communities, relying on communal cooperation under church supervision, succeeded where individual efforts often failed in developing this region.

Most important, railroad advertising and promotional campaigns attracted people to the West. Not only would railroads profit from selling their huge land reserves to settlers, but a successful agricultural economy would produce crops to be shipped east and a demand for manufactured goods to be shipped west on their lines. The railroads therefore advanced credit to prospective farmers, provided transportation assistance, and extended technical and agricultural advice.

Thus encouraged, migrants poured into the West, occupying and farming more acres between 1870 and 1900 than Americans had in the previous 250 years (see Figure 19.1). Farmers settled in every region. Most, however, streamed into the Great Plains states, from the Dakotas to Texas.

Whites predominated in the mass migration, but African Americans initiated one of its most dramatic episodes, a millenarian folk movement they called the Exodus. Seeking to escape the misery and repression of the post-Reconstruction South, these poor "Exodusters" established several dozen black communities in 1879 in Kansas and Nebraska on the agricultural frontier.

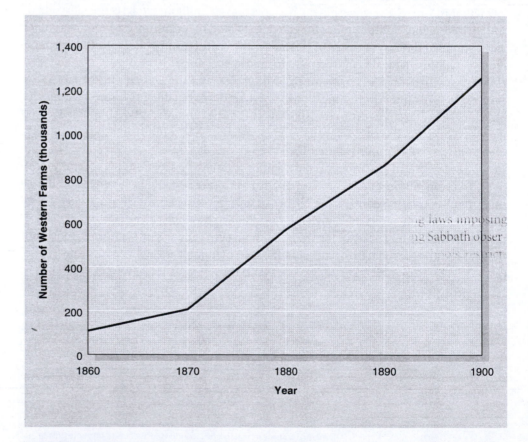

**FIGURE 19.1  THE GROWTH OF WESTERN FARMING, 1860–1900** Indian removal, railroad expansion, and liberal land policies drew farm families into the West from much of Europe as well as the East. Technological innovations like barbed wire and farm machinery soon enabled them to build farms, but economic, social, and environmental challenges remained.

SOURCE: Historical Statistics of the United States (1975).

Many settlers came from other countries, bringing with them not only their own attitudes toward the land but also special crops, skills, settlement patterns, and agricultural practices. Peasants from Norway, Sweden, and Denmark flocked to Minnesota. Germans, Russians, and Irish put down roots across Texas, Kansas, Nebraska, and the Dakotas. French, Germans, and Italians developed vineyards, orchards, and nurseries in California, where Chinese farm workers made fruit and vegetable production successful by providing both the knowledge and the labor of diking, ditching, and irrigating fields and their skill in cultivating, harvesting, and packing produce. Although poorly paid and often the object of racist attacks, the Chinese, as the *Pacific Rural Press* marveled, transformed California agriculture. After the Chinese Exclusion Act in 1882 (see Chapter 18), Japanese and then Mexican farm workers gradually became the basis of the state's low-wage migrant labor force. As one large fruit grower explained, "we have so degraded" farm labor that white Americans avoided the work. Many Mexicans also entered Texas, some as temporary harvest labor, others as permanent residents. By 1890, many western states had substantial foreign-born populations; North Dakota's exceeded 40 percent, and California's was nearly as high. Immigrants often settled together in separate ethnic communities, held together by their church, and attempted to preserve their language and customs rather than be assimilated.

**Hispanic Losses.**   Migrants moved into the West in search of opportunity, which they sometimes seized at the expense of others already there. In the Southwest, Hispanics had long lived in village communities largely outside a commercial economy, farming small tracts of irrigated land and herding sheep on communal pastures. As Anglos, or white Americans, arrived, their political and economic influence undermined traditional Hispanic society. Congress restricted the original Hispanic land grants to only the villagers' home lots and irrigated fields, throwing open most of their common lands to newcomers. Hispanic title was confirmed to only 2 million of the 37.5 million acres at stake. Anglo ranchers and settlers manipulated the federal land system to control these lands.

Spanish Americans resisted these losses in court or through violence. One militant group, organized as *Las Gorras Blancas* ("the White Caps"), staged night raids to cut fences erected by Anglo ranchers and farmers and to attack the property of railroads, the symbol of the encroaching new order. Such resistance, however, had little success.

As their landholdings shrank, Hispanic villagers could not maintain their pastoral economy. Few turned to homesteading, for that would have required dispersed settlement and abandoning the village and its church, school, and other cultural institutions. Thus many Hispanics became seasonal wage laborers in the Anglo-dominated economy, sometimes working as stoop labor in the commercial sugar-beet fields that

Mexican-American ranch family, Mora Valley, New Mexico Territory, 1895. Anglo-dominated development often displaced such families from their traditional lands and turned them into wage-laborers.

emerged in the 1890s, sometimes working on the railroads or in the mines. Women also participated in the new labor market, working as cooks and domestic servants in railroad towns and mining camps. Such seasonal labor enabled Hispanics to preserve their villages and retain some cultural autonomy, but they had little influence over the larger processes of settlement and development that restricted their opportunities and bound them to the western and national economy.

## Home on the Range

In settling the West, farm families encountered many difficulties, especially on the Great Plains, where they had to adapt to a radically new environment. The scarcity of trees on the plains meant that there was little wood for housing, fuel, and fencing. Until they had reaped several harvests and could afford to import lumber, pioneer families lived in houses made of sod. Though inexpensive and sturdy, sod houses were also dark and dirty. Snakes, mice, and insects often crawled out of the walls and roofs.

**Women's Work.** Within these rough houses, women worked to provide food, clothing, and medicine to ensure the family's survival. Their efforts were greatly constrained by the harsh environment. For fuel, families often had to rely on buffalo or cattle "chips," dried dung. The scarcity of water also complicated women's domestic labor. They often had to transport water over long distances, pulling barrels on "water sleds" or carrying pails on neck yokes. They melted snow for wash water and used the same water over again for different chores. Where possible, they also helped to dig wells by hand.

Some women farmed the land themselves. Single women could claim land under the Homestead Act, and in some areas, women claimants made up 18 percent of the total and succeeded more frequently than men in gaining final title. At times, married women operated the family farm by themselves while their husbands worked elsewhere to earn the money needed for seeds, equipment, and building supplies.

**Isolation and Community.** Isolation and loneliness troubled many early settlers on the plains. Women especially suffered because they frequently had less contact with other people than farm men, who conducted their families' business in town and participated in such public activities as political meetings. One farm woman complained that "being cut off from everybody is almost too much for me."

Over time, conditions improved. As population increased, women in particular worked to bind isolated households into communities by organizing social activities and institutions. They held fairs, dances, and picnics and established churches, schools, and libraries, thereby gaining both companionship and a sense of purpose.

Churches, in turn, also promoted community. Indeed, many were "union" churches, open to people of all denominations. In addition to holding religious services,

Read the Document Emma Hill, *Settling in Kansas* (1873)

Sunday school meeting in Custer County, Nebraska, in 1888. Sunday schools were important social as well as religious institutions on the Great Plains, where, as one newspaper reported, rural families often felt like "strangers in a strange land."

revivals, and camp meetings, churches were often the center of social life, especially by sponsoring sociables and children's organizations. "However great may have been the need for salvation," one plains woman recalled, "the need for recreation was given preference." Nondenominational Sunday schools helped bind together differing nationalities and church preferences, and because they did not require the services of an ordained minister, they often enabled women to initiate and lead community activities.

Other institutions also encouraged community action. Rural families created their own agricultural cooperatives and other economic and social organizations, like local Grange lodges. External developments also served the rural population. Rural Free Delivery, for example, eventually brought letters, newspapers, magazines, and advertisements to farm families' doorsteps; mail-order companies made available to farm people such helpful goods as stoves, sewing machines, and shoes. Such changes helped incorporate westerners into the larger society.

## Farming the Land

Pioneer settlers had to make daunting adjustments to develop the agricultural potential of their new land. Advances in science, technology, and industry made such adjustments possible. The changes not only reshaped the agricultural economy but also challenged traditional rural values and expectations.

**Growing Crops.** Fencing was an immediate problem, for crops needed protection from livestock. But without timber, farmers could not build wooden fences. Barbed wire, developed in the mid-1870s, solved the problem. By 1900, farmers were importing nearly 300 million pounds of barbed wire each year from eastern and midwestern factories.

The aridity of most of the West also posed difficulties. In California and Colorado, settlers used streams fed by mountain snow packs to irrigate land. Elsewhere, enterprising farmers developed variants of the "dry farming" practices that the Mormons had introduced in Utah to maximize the limited rainfall. Some farmers erected windmills to pump underground water. The scarce rainfall also discouraged the cultivation of many of the crops that supported traditional general agriculture and encouraged farmers to specialize in a single cash crop for market. Gradually, many plains farmers adopted the drought-resistant Turkey Red variety of hard winter wheat that German Mennonites had introduced into Kansas. Government agencies and agricultural colleges contributed to the success of such adaptations, and private engineers and inventors also fostered agricultural development. Related technological advancements included grain elevators that would store grain for shipment and load it into rail cars mechanically and mills that used corrugated, chilled-iron rollers rather than millstones to process the new varieties of wheat.

Mechanization and technological innovations made possible the large-scale farming practiced in semiarid regions. Farmers required special plows to break the tough sod, new harrows to prepare the soil for cultivation, grain drills to plant the crop, and harvesting and threshing machines to bring it in. Thanks to more and better machines, agricultural efficiency and productivity shot up. By the 1890s, machinery permitted the farmer to produce eighteen times more wheat than hand methods had. Nearly 1,000 corporations were manufacturing agricultural machinery to meet the demands of farmers, who purchased implements in steadily mounting quantities.

**Growing Tensions.** These developments reflected both the expansion of agriculture and its increasing dependence on the larger society. Western commercial farmers needed the high demand of eastern and midwestern cities and the expanding world market. The rail network provided essential transportation for their crops; the nation's industrial sector produced necessary agricultural machinery. Banks and loan companies extended the credit and capital that allowed farmers to take advantage of mechanization and other new advances; and many other businesses graded, stored, processed, and sold their crops. In short, because of its market orientation, mechanization, and specialization, western agriculture relied on other people or impersonal forces as it was incorporated into the national and international economy.

## From Then to Now
# The Legacy of Indian Americanization

T he assumptions, objectives, and failures of the Americanization policies of the nineteenth century continue to affect American Indians more than a century later. Although periodically modified (see Chapter 25), these policies long persisted, as did their consequences. In the 1970s official investigations reported that the continuing attempts of the Bureau of Indian Affairs to use education to force Indians into an Anglo-American mold "have been marked by near total failure, haunted by prejudice and ignorance." Similarly, the conditions on reservations in the nineteenth century foreshadowed those a century later. Today, Indians rank at the bottom on almost all measures of economic well-being and suffer the highest rates of infant mortality, pneumonia, and suicide. The U.S. Commission on Civil Rights reported in 2003 that Indians endured a "quiet crisis" of poverty, discrimination, and unmet promises.

Indian culture, however, did not succumb to either the pressure to Americanize or these miserable conditions. In the words of a Shoshone writer, "Indian history didn't end in the 1800s. Indian cultures . . . evolve, grow, and continually try to renew themselves."

In recent decades, Indian peoples have begun to reclaim their past and assert control over their future. Dramatic protests have called attention to serious grievances while Indians also have moved to regain control of the institutions that define their cultural identity. They have established community schools and colleges that preserve traditions while opening new opportunities; they have built tribal museums and visitor centers in order to shape the presentation of their histories and cultures. New laws and court decisions have assured Indian religious freedom, land ownership, and water rights.

Dramatically symbolizing Indians' success in preserving their cultural heritage and keeping it vibrant for future generations was the 2004 opening of the National Museum of the American Indian on the Mall in Washington, DC. "What we really want visitors to understand," said its director, a Cheyenne, "is that we survived" both conquest and Americanization. "We are still here, making vital contributions."

**Question for Discussion**

- In what ways does the historical experience of Native Americans differ from that of other minority groups in the United States?

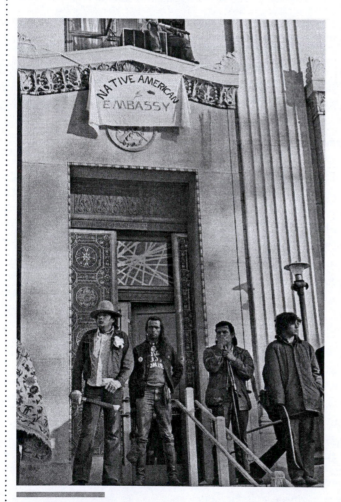

Indian protesters temporarily seized control of the Bureau of Indian Affairs building in Washington, DC, in 1972.

A government boarding school, designed to isolate Indian youth from their culture, looms over the old tribal lodgings on the Pine Ridge Reservation in 1891.

When conditions were favorable—good weather, good crops, and good prices—western farmers prospered. Too often, however, they faced adversity. In the 1870s, periodic droughts and grasshopper plagues brought crop failures. Descending in what one woman described as a "cloud so dense that the sun was obscured and the earth was in darkness," grasshoppers ate crops, clothing, and bedding; they attacked sod houses and chewed woodwork and furniture. State and federal governments appropriated public funds and private relief organizations distributed food, clothing, and seed to aid destitute farm families.

In the late 1880s, drought coincided with a slump in crop prices. The large European market that had encouraged agricultural expansion in the 1870s and early 1880s contracted after 1885, when several nations erected trade barriers to U.S. commodities. More important, America's production competed with that from Argentina, Canada, Australia, and Russia, and a world surplus of grain drove prices steadily downward. The average price of wheat dropped from $1.19 a bushel in 1881 to only $0.49 in 1894.

Squeezed between high costs for credit, transportation, and manufactured goods and falling agricultural prices, western farmers faced disaster. They responded by lashing back at their points of contact with the new system. They especially condemned the railroads, believing that the companies charged excessive and discriminatory freight rates.

Farmers similarly censured the grain elevators in the local buying centers. Often owned by eastern corporations, including the railroads, elevators allegedly exploited their local monopoly to cheat farmers by fixing low prices or misrepresenting the quality of wheat. A Minnesota state investigation found that systematic fraud by elevators cost farmers collectively a massive sum. Farmers also denounced the bankers and mortgage lenders who had provided the credit for them to acquire land, equipment, and machinery. Much of the money had come from eastern investors seeking the higher interest rates in the West. With failing crops and falling prices, however, the debt burden proved calamitous, and beginning in 1889, many farms were foreclosed.

Stunned and bitter, western farmers concluded that their problems arose because they had been incorporated into the new system, an integrated economy directed by forces beyond their control. And it was a system that did not work well. "There is," one of them charged, "something radically wrong in our industrial system. There is a screw loose."

## Conclusion

In a few decades, millions of people had migrated westward in search of new opportunities. With determination, ingenuity, and hard work they had settled vast areas, made farms and ranches, built villages and cities, brought forth mineral wealth, and imposed their values on the land. These were remarkable achievements, though tempered by the shameful treatment of Indians and the often destructive exploitation of natural resources. But if most westerners took pride in their accomplishments, and a few enjoyed wealth and power, many also grew discontented with the new conditions they encountered as the "Wild" West receded.

Railroad expansion, population movements, eastern investment, corporate control, technological innovations, and government policies had incorporated the region fully into the larger society. Indians experienced this incorporation most thoroughly and most tragically, losing their lands, their traditions, and often their lives; the survivors were dependent on the decisions and actions of interlopers determined to impose "Americanization," the name itself implying the adoption of national patterns. Cowboys, lumberjacks, and miners also learned that the frontier merely marked the cutting edge of eastern industrial society. All were wageworkers, often for corporations controlled by eastern capital, and if industrial technology directly affected miners and lumberjacks more than cowhands, none could escape integration into the national economy by managerial decisions, transportation links, and market forces. Most settlers in the West were farmers, but they too learned that their distinctive environment did not insulate them from assimilation into larger productive, financial, and marketing structures.

Western developments, in short, reflected and interacted with those of eastern industrial society. The processes of incorporation drained away westerners' hopes along with their products, and many of the discontented would demand a serious reorganization of relationships and power. Led by angry farmers, they turned their attention to politics and government, where they encountered new obstacles and opportunities.

**For Suggested Readings go to MyHistoryLab.**

## Chapter Review

### Subjugating Native Americans

**19.1** What were the main objectives of federal Indian policy in the late nineteenth century? p. 543

Native Americans held different cultural, religious, and economic values from those of white people, who insisted that Indians be pushed aside in order to achieve their own culture's goal of exploiting nature for a market economy. Brutal warfare, legal chicanery, and technological developments forced Indians onto reservations, but efforts to "Americanize" them were less successful.

### Exploiting the Mountains: Mining and Timber

**19.2** How did the mining and timber industries of the West change over the course of the second half of the nineteenth century? p. 549

The mountains of the West attracted those eager to exploit its minerals and timber. As both resources became more difficult to access, requiring greater capital, organization, and technology, corporations supplanted individuals in the search for wealth, company towns replaced rough mining and logging camps, and work became increasingly dangerous and environmentally destructive.

### Using the Grass: The Cattle Kingdom

**19.3** What factors contributed to the development of the range-cattle industry? p. 554

The range-cattle industry developed in response to the growing needs of the Eastern urban society for food and the ability of the expanding railroad network to deliver it. Based upon the open range, the industry spread from Texas across the West and increasingly became a corporate endeavor in which the fabled cowboy had little autonomy and less opportunity.

### Working the Earth: Homesteaders and Agricultural Expansion

**19.4** How did new technology contribute to the growth of Western agriculture? p. 559

Agricultural growth boosted the West's economy and bound it to national and world markets. The Homestead Act and land speculators encouraged settlement; barbed wire, windmills, and women's activism mitigated an unfamiliar environment; mechanization expanded productivity; and railroads and elevators linked crops to markets. Farmers' increasing dependence on the larger society, however, produced economic instability and unrest.

## Timeline

**1858**
**Mountains**—Gold is discovered in Colorado and Nevada — 1858

**1862**
1862 — **Agricultural Expansion**—Homestead Act is passed

**1864**
**Native Americans**—Militia slaughters Cheyenne at Sand Creek, Colorado — 1864

**1867**
1867 — **Cattle Kingdom**—Cattle drives make Abilene the first cow town

**1868**
**Native Americans**—Fort Laramie Treaty is signed — 1868

**1869**
1869 — **Cattle Kingdom**—First transcontinental railroad is completed

**1874**
**Agricultural Expansion**—Turkey Red wheat is introduced in Kansas; barbed wire is patented — 1874

**1876**
1876 — **Native Americans**—Indians devastate U.S. troops in the Battle of the Little Bighorn

**1890**
**Native Americans**—Government troops kill 200 Sioux at Wounded Knee, South Dakota — 1890

**1893**
1893 — **Mountains**—Western Federation of Miners is organized

# 20 Politics and Government 1877–1900

## One American Journey

### A Newspaper Reporter Describes a Campaign Parade in Indiana

**T**he **largest political procession of the season** in Fort Wayne, so far, was that of the Republicans Saturday night. They turned out in very large numbers and paraded on the principal streets preparatory to the speaking which came later at the Rifles' armory.

The following were in line:

First Regiment Band
Railroad Men's Club
Soldiers' and Sons' Union Club
Tippecanoe Club
Chase Club
Lincoln Club
McKinley Club
Colored Drum Corps
Colored Republicans' Club
Republican Voters

The McKinley Club wore tin hats and the Tippecanoe club carried torches that spouted fire at intervals. One of the prettiest illuminations was the railroad lantern light of the Railroad Men's Republican club. The numerous lights of the colors used in the railway service make as pretty a sight as can be seen anywhere.

In the late nineteenth century, parades like this Republican one in Canton, Ohio, in 1896 were popular features of a participatory political culture dominated by political parties and intense partisanship.

## LEARNING OBJECTIVES

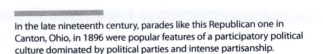

| 20.1 | 20.2 | 20.3 | 20.4 |
|---|---|---|---|
| How did parties shape late-nineteenth-century politics? p. 570 | What explains the weakness and inefficiency of late-nineteenth-century government? p. 575 | How effective was government in addressing the problems of America's industrializing economy? p. 577 | What factors contributed to the rise and fall of the Populist Party? p. 583 |

Listen to **Chapter 20** on MyHistoryLab

From *The American Journey*, Seventh Edition. Goldfield, Abbott, Anderson, Argersinger, Argersinger and Barney Copyright © 2014 by Pearson Education, Inc. All rights reserved.

# Watch the Video Series on MyHistoryLab

Learn about some key topics related to this chapter with the *MyHistoryLab Video Series: Key Topics in U.S. History.*

**1** **Political Life in the Late Nineteenth Century** With much of the North dominated by the Republican Party, the Solid South in the pocket of the Democrats, and both parties controlling big-city machines and state houses across the nation, politics in the late nineteenth century was as partisan as politics is today. This video surveys a quarter century of campaigns, elections, and issues that absorbed the American public and even spawned third parties as well as special-interest organizations representing industrialists, farmers, workers, and reformers during a period when government was often too weak and divided to keep up with a rapidly modernizing and changing nation.

Watch on MyHistoryLab

**A Weak Presidency—An Inefficient Congress** The presidents of late-nineteenth-century America were unlike the presidents of recent history. They viewed their duties as mainly administrative and made little effort to reach out to the public or to exert legislative leadership. Even President Grant, who had wielded great power during the Civil War, often deferred to the authority of the legislative branch. This video also looks at Congress, which, despite its power, was often hamstrung by procedural rules, fierce partisanship, and limited perspectives.

Watch on MyHistoryLab

**3** **The Rise of Federal Regulation** The rapid and often destructive growth of corporate power in the late nineteenth century spurred growing public demands for Congress to curtail business abuses. This video explores the first legislation of what would become the sophisticated federal regulatory policy of the present, including the Interstate Commerce Act of 1887 and the Sherman Antitrust Act of 1890, and the first regulatory agency, the Interstate Commerce Commission.

Watch on MyHistoryLab

**Populist Party** During the 1890s, grievances and concerns of both the rural farm population and the urban working class led to the formation of a new political party, the People's Party, which championed currency reform, regulation of railroads and industry, and expanded, participatory democracy. This video examines the party's origins and issues, as well as its nomination of the Democratic candidate William Jennings Bryan as its candidate for president in the 1896 election. **4**

Watch on MyHistoryLab

Most of the clubs were in fine uniforms and made a grand appearance. Numerous banners and transparencies announcing mottoes of the campaign were carried. One banner bore the words, "Cleveland's record—Glad Lincoln was shot—Pronounced the war a failure."

The great parade was viewed by thousands of people who thronged the streets all along the line of march.

The hall was crowded and the meeting was most enthusiastic. Music was furnished by the band and Emerson quartette of Huntington. . . . The quartette just took the cake. Anything more enjoyable and mirth-provoking than their glees rendered as they render them would be hard to find. After music by the quartette, which was enthusiastically encored, Dr. Stemen, the presiding officer, introduced the speaker of the evening, Hon. L.R. Stookey, of Warsaw, Ind. Mr. Stookey is a ready and rapid speaker. He paid a glowing tribute to the soldiers, and referred in scathing terms to Grover Cleveland's treatment of them and his insulting vetoes of pension bills. He spoke . . . [of a law providing for election supervisors at the polls] and what we ask is that it shall apply without limitation north and south whenever there is an attempt or danger of attempt, to deny equal rights of all to cast their free ballot and have it counted as cast.

When he concluded the Emerson quartette gave another selection and responded to an encore. The audience then began to call loudly for "You," "You." Mr. A.J. You, our candidate for congress, was then introduced and made a stirring address. Mr. You has been speaking nearly every day and evening and is holding out first rate and proving himself one of the most popular candidates in the field.

He was repeatedly and enthusiastically cheered during his speech. Another selection by the quartette, and the house resounded with calls for "Brown," "Brown." Rev. W.H. Brown, for years the pastor of the A.M.E. church, of this city, took the platform and, though he protested that the hour was too late to permit another speech, made it clearly evident in the course of a twenty minute speech that the colored people of the country understand the situation and intend to stand by the party that broke the chains and gave freedom to the slave. The meeting then adjourned to music by the Glee club.

*Fort Wayne* (Ind.) *Weekly Gazette,* October 20, 1892

## Personal Journeys Online

- Susan B. Anthony, *Speech to the National American Woman Suffrage Association,* 1894. Asking Congress for political justice.
- Henry Vincent, *Marching through Iowa,* 1894. The journey of Kelly's "industrial army."
- William Jennings Bryan, *Campaigning across America,* 1896. Bryan's own account of his famous presidential campaign.

**T**he *Fort Wayne Weekly Gazette,* a fiercely Republican newspaper, proudly reported on the activities of the local Republicans in Indiana during the political campaign in 1892. Their grand torchlight parade through the streets of Fort Wayne, the thronging and enthusiastic crowds, the lengthy and bombastic speeches—all illustrate much about U.S. politics in the late nineteenth century. Parties mobilized ardently partisan voters into a politics of participation, which included political clubs, campaign festivities, and record-high turnouts on election day. The pageantry and hoopla made politics a major source of popular entertainment for Republicans and Democrats alike. But the extreme campaign rhetoric and outright misrepresentation of opponents indicated the intensity of partisan emotions. So did the military-style campaign, with uniformed marchers organized into companies, brigades, and divisions; with signs, slogans, and speeches referring to soldiers and the Civil War; with rallies held in armories. These campaign features also pointed to the enduring importance of the Civil War as a basis for partisan divisions and loyalties and marked electoral politics as a rough-and-tumble masculine business.

At the same time, contemporary issues did matter. Stookey's stump appeal for election supervisors to protect voters' rights at the polls pointed to an important policy issue while hinting at the sometimes violent nature of elections, including the suppression of voters. It also emphasized that suffrage was often a contested issue.

The prominent role of Rev. Brown, the content of his speech, and the participation of the Colored Drum Corps and the Colored Republicans' Club in the parade show that partisan divisions in the United States overlapped with racial, religious, and other social divisions. Black voters, for instance, would "stand by the party that broke the chains and gave freedom to the slave." The journey to the polls, symbolized by the parade through Fort Wayne, invoked the most basic beliefs and values of Americans.

While the *Gazette* lavished praise on the Republican campaign and "our candidate" and ridiculed the opposition, its Democratic counterpart, the *Fort Wayne Sentinel*, extolled the success of the Democratic campaign, the enthusiasm of Democratic crowds, the integrity of Democratic candidates, and the despicable nature of the Republican Party. Such partisanship permeated journalism as well as nearly all aspects of public life, including government agencies.

These features of late-nineteenth-century politics would eventually be transformed in significant ways. But while they endured, they shaped not only campaigns and elections but also the form and role of government. Only a national crisis in the 1890s would finally cause some Americans to demand more of their political leaders and institutions.

# The Structure and Style of Politics

**20.1**    How did parties shape late-nineteenth-century politics?

Politics in the late nineteenth century was an absorbing activity. Campaigns and elections expressed social values as they determined who held the reins of government. Political parties dominated political life. They organized campaigns, controlled balloting, and held the unswerving loyalty of most of the electorate. While the major parties worked to maintain a sense of unity and tradition among their followers, third parties sought to activate those the major parties left unserved. Other Americans looked outside the electoral arena to achieve their political goals.

## Campaigns and Elections

Political campaigns and elections generated remarkable public participation and enthusiasm. They constituted a major form of entertainment at a time when recreational opportunities were limited. Marching in torchlight parades, as in Fort Wayne, attending party meetings and conventions, listening to lengthy speeches appealing to group loyalties and local pride, gathering at the polls to watch the voting and the counting, celebrating victory and drowning the disappointment of defeat—all these provided social enjoyment and defined popular politics.

Virtually all men participated in politics. In many states, even immigrants not yet citizens were eligible to vote and flocked to the polls. African Americans voted regularly in the North and irregularly in the South before being disfranchised at the end of the century. Overall, turnout was remarkably high, averaging nearly 80 percent of eligible voters in presidential elections between 1876 and 1900, a figure far greater than ever achieved thereafter (see Figure 20.1).

Political parties mobilized this huge electorate. They kept detailed records of voters, transported them to the polls, saw that they were registered where necessary, and sometimes even paid their poll taxes or naturalization fees to make them eligible. With legal regulations and public machinery for elections negligible, parties dominated the campaigns and elections. Until the 1890s, most states had no laws to ensure secrecy in voting, and balloting often took place in open rooms or on sidewalks. Election clerks and judges were not public officials but partisans chosen by the political parties.

Nor did public authorities issue official ballots. Instead voters used party tickets—strips of paper printed by the parties—listing only the names of the candidates of the party issuing them and varying in size and color. Casting a ballot thus revealed the voter's party allegiance. Tickets were distributed by paid party workers known as peddlers or hawkers, who stationed themselves near the polls, each trying to force his ticket on prospective voters. Fighting and intimidation were so commonplace at the polls that one state supreme court ruled in 1887 that they were "acceptable" features of elections.

**FIGURE 20.1  VOTER TURNOUT IN PRESIDENTIAL ELECTIONS, 1876–1924** The exciting partisan politics of the late nineteenth century produced very high voter turnouts, but as party competition declined and states enacted more restrictive voter regulations, popular participation in elections fell in the twentieth century.

SOURCE: Federal Register, National Archives and Records Administration, http://www.archives.gov/federal-register/electoral-college/historical.html

As the court recognized, the open and partisan aspects of the electoral process did not necessarily lead to election fraud, however much they shaped the nature of political participation. In these circumstances, campaigns and elections provided opportunities for men to demonstrate publicly their commitment to their party and its values, thereby reinforcing their partisan loyalties.

Although women could not vote in national elections, they too exhibited their partisanship in this exciting political environment. Women wrote partisan literature, sponsored rallies, and gave campaign speeches. Sometimes they acted together with men; other times they worked through separate women's organizations. J. Ellen Foster established the Woman's National Republican Association in 1888 and built it into an organizing machine for the Republican Party with state and local clubs. The partisanship of its members was so deeply embedded that they remained loyal Republicans even when the party repudiated woman suffrage. "What discourages me about women," noted suffragist Susan B. Anthony, was that they care more for "[their] political party . . . than for [their] own political rights."

## Partisan Politics

A remarkably close balance prevailed between the two major parties in the elections of this era. Democrats and Republicans had virtually the same level of electoral support, one reason they worked so hard to get out the vote (see Map 20.1). Control of the presidency and Congress shifted back and forth. Rarely did either party control both branches of government at once.

The party balance gave great influence to New York, New Jersey, Ohio, and Indiana, whose evenly divided voters controlled electoral votes that could swing an election either way. Both parties tended to nominate presidential and vice presidential candidates from those states to woo their voters. The parties also concentrated campaign funds and strategy on the swing states. When Republican presidential candidate James Garfield of Ohio carried Indiana by 6,000 votes, and the nation by 9,000 out of 9.2 million cast in 1880, his victory was the outcome not of a contest over great issues but of carefully organized, tightly balanced parties mobilizing their supporters.

**Party Loyalty.**   Interrelated regional, ethnic, religious, and local factors determined the party affiliations of most Americans. Economic issues, although important to the

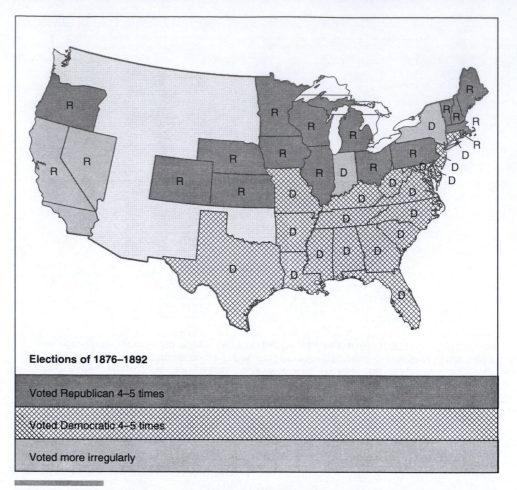

Elections of 1876–1892

Voted Republican 4–5 times

Voted Democratic 4–5 times

Voted more irregularly

**MAP 20.1  THE TWO-PARTY STALEMATE OF THE LATE NINETEENTH CENTURY** Strong parties, staunch loyalties, and an evenly divided electorate made for exciting politics but often stalemated government in the late nineteenth century. Most states voted consistently for one of the major parties, leaving the few swing states like New York and Indiana the scenes of fierce partisan battles.

politics of the era, generally did not decide party ties. Farmers, for example, despite their many shared economic concerns, affiliated with both major parties. Like religious belief and ethnic identity, partisan loyalty was largely a cultural trait passed from parents to children, a situation that helps to explain the electoral stability of most communities.

Republicans were strongest in the North and Midwest, where they benefited from their party's role as the defender of the Union in the Civil War. But not all northerners voted for the Grand Old Party, or GOP. The Republican Party appealed primarily to old-stock Americans and other Protestants, including those of German and Scandinavian descent. African Americans, loyal to the party that had emancipated and enfranchised the slaves of the South, also supported the GOP where they could vote. Democrats were strongest in the South, where they stood as the defenders of the traditions of the region's white population. But Democrats also drew support in the urban Northeast, especially from Catholics and recent immigrants.

**Party Identities.**   Each major party consisted of a complex coalition of groups with differing traditions and interests. This internal diversity often provoked conflict and threatened party stability. To hold its coalition together, each party identified itself with a theme that appealed broadly to all its constituents, while suggesting that it was menaced by the members and objectives of the opposing party.

Republicans identified their party with nationalism and national unity and attacked the Democrats as an "alliance between the embittered South and the slums of the Northern cities." They combined a "bloody shirt" appeal to the memories of the Civil War with campaigns for immigration restriction and cultural uniformity. Seeing a threat to American society in efforts by Catholic immigrants to preserve their ethnic and cultural traditions, for example, Republican legislatures in several states in the 1880s and 1890s enacted laws regulating parochial schools, the use of foreign languages, and alcohol consumption.

Democrats portrayed themselves as the party of limited government and "personal liberties," a theme that appealed to both the racism of white southerners and the resentment immigrants felt about the nativist meddling of Republicans. The Democrats' commitment to personal liberties had limits. They supported the disfranchisement of African Americans, the exclusion of Chinese immigrants, and the dispossession of American Indians. Nevertheless, their emphasis on traditional individualism and localism proved popular.

The partisan politics of both major parties culminated in party machines, especially at the local level. Led by powerful bosses, such as the Democrat Richard Croker of New York and the Republican George Cox of Cincinnati, the machines controlled not only city politics but also municipal government. Party activists used well-organized ward clubs to mobilize working-class voters, who were rewarded with municipal jobs and baskets of food or coal doled out by the machine. Such assistance was often necessary, given the lack of public welfare systems, but to buy votes the machine also sold favors. Public contracts and franchises were peddled to businesses whose high bids covered kickbacks to the machine.

**Third Parties.**    The partisan politics of the era left room for several third parties, organized around specific issues or groups. The **Prohibition Party** persistently championed the abolition of alcohol but also supported electoral reforms such as woman suffrage, economic reforms such as railroad regulation and income taxes, and social reforms including improved race relations. The **Greenback Party** of the 1870s denounced "the infamous financial legislation which takes all from the many to enrich the few." Its policies of labor reform and currency inflation (to stimulate and democratize the economy) attracted supporters from Maine to Texas. Other significant third parties included the Anti-Monopoly Party, the Union Labor Party, and, most important, the People's or **Populist Party** of the 1890s. Although third parties often won temporary success at the local or regional level, they never permanently displaced the major parties or undermined traditional voter allegiances.

**Prohibition Party** A venerable third party still in existence that has persistently campaigned for the abolition of alcohol but has also introduced many important reform ideas into American politics.

**Greenback Party** A third party of the 1870s and 1880s that garnered temporary support by advocating currency inflation to expand the economy and assist debtors.

**Populist Party** A major third party of the 1890s, also known as the People's Party. Formed on the basis of the Farmers' Alliance and other reform organizations, it mounted electoral challenges against the Democrats in the South and the Republicans in the West.

## Associational Politics

Much political activity was neither partisan nor electoral. Associations of like-minded citizens, operating as pressure groups, played an increasingly important role in late-nineteenth-century politics. These organizations worked to achieve public policies beneficial to their members. Farmers organized many such groups, most notably the Patrons of Husbandry, known familiarly as the Grange (see Chapter 17). Its campaign for public regulation of the rates charged by railroads and grain elevators helped convince midwestern states to pass the so-called **Granger laws**. Labor organizations often pursued ambitious political agendas as well. Adopting nonpartisan tactics, the New Jersey Federation of Trades and Labor Unions drafted bills to require improved working conditions, testified before legislative committees, and marshaled delegations of workers to lobby for the measures.

Industrialists also formed pressure groups. Organizations such as the American Iron and Steel Association and the American Protective Tariff League lobbied Congress for high tariff laws and made campaign contributions to friendly politicians of both parties. At the state level, business groups used their political clout to block the reform efforts of farmers and workers, sometimes in the legislatures but otherwise in the courts. Declaring that "lawmakers are too frequently influenced by public clamor and agitation for the cure of so-called social wrongs," the Illinois Manufacturers' Association in 1895 persuaded the Illinois Supreme Court to overturn a law establishing the 8-hour day for working women and girls.

A small group of conservative reformers known derisively as **Mugwumps** (the term derives from the Algonquian word for "chief") devoted most of their effort to campaigning for honest and efficient government through civil service reform. Other

**Granger laws** State laws enacted in the Midwest in the 1870s that regulated rates charged by railroads, grain elevator operators, and other middlemen.

**Mugwumps** Elitist and conservative reformers who favored sound money and limited government and opposed tariffs and the spoils system.

Read the Document   Proceedings of the Thirteenth Session of the National Grange of the Patrons of Husbandry (1879)

The Grange rejected partisanship but not politics. This sympathetic cartoon shows a Granger trying to warn Americans blindly absorbed in partisan politics of the dangers of onrushing industrialization.

pressure groups focused on cultural politics. The rabidly anti-Catholic American Protective Association, for example, agitated for laws restricting immigration, taxing church property, and inspecting Catholic religious institutions.

Christian lobbyists committed their political energies to demanding laws that view of personal moral behavior. They campaigned for laws requiring vance (no entertainment, work, or travel on Sundays) and Bible reading in schools, restricting divorce on scriptural grounds, and prohibiting gambling and other "sinful" activities. The greatest success for such Christian lobbyists was the Comstock Law, passed by Congress in 1873, which outlawed the possession or sale of "obscene" materials, including any contraceptive information or devices. Directly affecting the lives of many Americans, the Comstock Law clearly revealed the importance of this type of political activism.

**Women as Activists.**   Women also sought power and influence through associational politics. Susan B. Anthony and others formed groups to lobby Congress and state legislatures for constitutional amendments extending the right to vote to women. The leading organizations merged in 1890 as the **National American Woman Suffrage Association.** Despite the opposition of male politicians of both major parties, suffragists had succeeded by the mid-1890s in gaining full woman suffrage in four western states—Wyoming, Colorado, Idaho, and Utah—and partial suffrage (the right to vote in school elections) in several other states, east and west.

**National American Woman Suffrage Association** The organization, formed in 1890, that coordinated the ultimately successful campaign to achieve women's right to vote.

Other women shaped public issues through social service organizations. Although the belief that women belonged in the domestic sphere limited their involvement in electoral politics, it furnished a basis for political action focused on welfare and moral reform. With petition campaigns, demonstrations, and lobbying, women's social service organizations sought to remedy poverty and disease, improve education and recreation, and provide day nurseries for the children of working women.

Women also combined domesticity and politics in the temperance movement. Alcoholism, widespread in U.S. society, was regarded as a major cause of crime, wife abuse, and broken homes. The temperance movement thus invoked women's presumed moral superiority to address a real problem that fell within their accepted sphere. The Woman's Christian Temperance Union (WCTU) gained a massive membership by campaigning for restrictive liquor laws. It helped secure prohibition or local-option laws in a dozen states and was particularly successful in persuading legislatures to require temperance education in the public schools.

Under the leadership of Frances Willard, the WCTU built on traditional women's concerns to develop an important critique of American society. Reversing the conventional view, Willard argued that alcohol abuse was a result, not a cause, of poverty and social disorder. Under the slogan of "Home Protection," the WCTU inserted domestic issues into the political sphere with a campaign for social and economic reforms far beyond temperance. It pushed for improved health conditions, reached out to the Knights of Labor to support workplace reforms, and lobbied for federal aid to education, particularly as a means to provide schooling for black children in the South. It eventually supported woman suffrage as well, on the grounds that women needed the vote to fulfill their duty to protect home, family, and morality.

# The Limits of Government

**20.2**  What explains the weakness and inefficiency of late-nineteenth-century government?

Despite the popular enthusiasm for partisan politics and the persistent pressure of associational politics, government in the late nineteenth century was neither active nor productive by present standards. The receding governmental activism of the Civil War and Reconstruction years coincided with a resurgent belief in localism and **laissez-faire** policies. In addition, a Congress and presidency divided between the two major parties, a small and inefficient bureaucracy, and judicial restraints joined powerful private interests to limit the size and objectives of the federal government.

**laissez-faire** The doctrine that government should not intervene in the economy, especially through regulation.

## The Weak Presidency

The presidency was a weak and restricted institution. The impeachment of President Johnson at the outset of Reconstruction had undermined the office. President Grant clearly subordinated it to the legislative branch by deferring to Congress on appointments and legislation. Other factors contributed as well. The men who filled the office between 1877 and 1897—Republicans Rutherford B. Hayes (1877–1881), James A. Garfield (1881), and Chester A. Arthur (1881–1885); Democrat Grover Cleveland (1885–1889 and 1893–1897); and Republican Benjamin Harrison (1889–1893)—were all honest and generally capable. Each had built a solid political record at the state or federal level. But they were all conservatives, with a narrow view of the presidency, and proposed few initiatives. They viewed their duties as chiefly administrative and made little effort to reach out to the public or to exert legislative leadership.

The presidency was also hampered by its limited control over bureaus and departments, which responded more directly to Congress, and by its small staff, consisting of no more than a half dozen secretaries, clerks, and telegraphers. As Cleveland complained, "If the President has any great policy in mind or on hand he has no one to help him work it out."

## The Inefficient Congress

Congress was the foremost branch of the national government. It exercised authority over the federal budget, oversaw the cabinet, debated public issues, and controlled legislation. Its members were often state and national party leaders, who were strong-willed and, as one senator conceded, "tolerated no intrusion from the President or from anybody else."

But Congress was scarcely efficient. Its chambers were noisy and chaotic, and members rarely devoted their attention to the business at hand. The repeated shifts in party control impeded effective action. So, too, did the loss of experienced legislators to rapid turnover. In some Congresses, a majority of members were first-termers. Procedural rules, based on precedents from a simpler time and manipulated by determined partisans, hindered congressional action. Some rules restricted the introduction of legislation; others prevented its passage. The most notorious rule required that a quorum be not only present but voting. When the House was narrowly divided along party lines, the minority could block all business simply by refusing to answer when the roll was called.

But as a nationalizing economy required more national legislation, the amount of business before Congress grew relentlessly (see Figure 20.2). The expanding scale of congressional work prompted a gradual reform of procedures and the centralization of power in the Speaker of the House and the leading committees. These changes did not, however, create a coherent program for government action.

## The Federal Bureaucracy and the Spoils System

Reflecting presidential weakness and congressional inefficiency, the federal bureaucracy remained small and limited in the late nineteenth century. There were little more than 50,000 government employees in 1871, and three-fourths of them were local postmasters scattered across the nation.

The system for selecting and supervising federal officials had developed gradually in the first half of the century. Known as the spoils system, its basic principle was that victorious politicians awarded government jobs to party workers, often with little regard for qualifications, and ousted the previous employees. Appointees then typically promised part of their salary and time to the political interests of their patron or party.

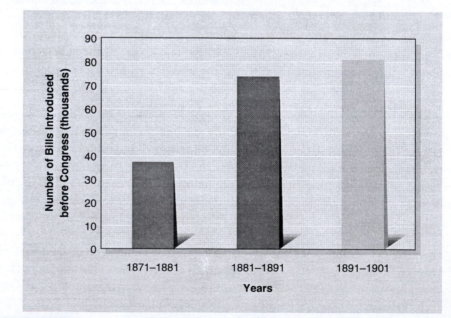

**FIGURE 20.2 INCREASE IN CONGRESSIONAL BUSINESS, 1871–1901** Industrialization, urbanization, and western expansion brought increased demands for government action, but the party stalemate, laissez-faire attitudes, and inefficient public institutions often blocked effective responses.

SOURCE: Library of Congress, 42nd to 56th Congress, Washington, DC.

The spoils system played a crucial role in all aspects of politics. It enabled party leaders to strengthen their organizations, reward loyal party service, and attract the political workers needed to mobilize the electorate. Supporters described it as a democratic system that offered opportunities to many citizens and prevented the emergence of an entrenched bureaucracy.

Critics, however, charged that the system was riddled with corruption, abuse, and inefficiency. Rapid turnover bred instability; political favoritism bred incompetence. Certainly, the spoils system was ineffective for filling positions that required special clerical skills or scientific expertise. Even worse, the spoils system absorbed the president and Congress in unproductive conflicts over patronage.

## Inconsistent State Government

State governments were more active than the federal government. Considered closer and more responsible to the people, they had long exercised police power and regulatory authority. They collected taxes for education and public works, and they promoted private enterprise and public health. Still, they did little by today's standards. Few people thought it appropriate for government at any level to offer direct help to particular social groups. Some state governments contracted in the 1870s and 1880s, following the wartime activism of the 1860s, and new state constitutions restricted the scope of public authority.

Nonetheless, state governments gradually expanded their role in response to the stresses produced by industrialization. Following the lead of Massachusetts in 1869, most states had by the turn of the century created commissions to investigate and regulate industry. Public intervention in other areas of the economy soon followed. One observer noted in 1887 that state governments enacted many laws and established numerous state agencies in "utter disregard of the laissez-faire principle." In Minnesota, for example, the state helped farmers by establishing a dairy commission, prohibiting the manufacture or sale of margarine, creating a bureau of animal industry, and employing state veterinarians. It also regulated railroads and dangerous occupations, prohibited racial discrimination in inns, and otherwise protected the public welfare.

Not all such agencies and laws were effective, nor were all state governments as diligent as Minnesota's. Southern states, especially, lagged, and one midwesterner complained that his legislature "meets in ignorance, sits in corruption, and dissolves in disgrace every two years." Still, the widening scope of state action represented a growing acceptance of public responsibility for social welfare and economic life and laid the foundation for more effective steps in the early twentieth century.

# Public Policies and National Elections

**20.3** How effective was government in addressing the problems of America's industrializing economy?

Several great issues dominated the national political arena in the late nineteenth century, including civil service reform, tariffs, and business and financial regulation. Rarely, however, did these issues clearly and consistently separate the major political parties. Instead, they divided each party into factions along regional, interest, and economic lines. As a consequence, these leading issues often played only a small role in determining elections and were seldom resolved by government action.

## Civil Service Reform

Reform of the spoils system emerged as a prominent issue during the Hayes administration. Mugwumps and other reformers wanted a professional civil service, based on merit and divorced from politics. They wanted officeholders to be selected on the basis

Read the Document    Pendleton Civil Service Act (1883)

In this 1881 cartoon, the evil spirit of partisanship threatens a government clerk hesitating to kick back an assessed portion of his salary to the party in power. Civil service reformers wanted to eliminate political factors in staffing the federal bureaucracy.

of competitive written examinations and protected from removal on political grounds. They expected such a system to promote efficiency, economy, and honesty in government. But they also expected it to increase their own influence and minimize that of "mere politicians." Other Americans rejected the Mugwump perspective. The *New York Sun* denounced "the proposition that men shall be appointed to office as the result of examinations in book learning and that they shall remain in office during life.... We don't want an aristocracy of office-holders in this country."

President Hayes favored civil service reform but did not fully renounce the spoils system. He rewarded those who had helped to elect him, permitted party leaders to name or veto candidates for the cabinet, and insisted that his own appointees contribute funds to Republican election campaigns. But he rejected the claims of some machine leaders and office seekers and struck a blow for change when he fired Chester A. Arthur from his post as New York customs-house collector after an investigation pronounced Arthur's patronage system as characterized by "ignorance, inefficiency, and corruption."

The weakness of the civil service reformers was dramatically underscored in 1880 when the Republicans, to improve their chances of carrying the crucial state of New York, nominated Arthur for vice president on a ticket headed by James Garfield of Ohio. They won, and Garfield immediately found himself enmeshed in the demands of the unreformed spoils system. Within a few months of his inauguration in 1881, Garfield was assassinated by a disappointed and crazed office seeker, and Arthur became president.

Public dismay over this tragedy finally spurred changes in the spoils system. In 1883 Congress passed the **Pendleton Civil Service Act**, prohibiting federal employees from soliciting or receiving political contributions from government workers and creating the Civil Service Commission to administer competitive examinations to applicants for government jobs. The act gave the commission jurisdiction over only about 10 percent of federal positions but provided that presidents could extend its authority. And subsequent presidents did so, if sometimes only to prevent their own appointees from being turned out by a succeeding administration. A professional civil service free from partisan politics gradually emerged, strengthening the executive branch's ability to handle its increasing administrative responsibilities.

The new emphasis on merit and skill rather than party ties opened new opportunities to women. Federal clerks had long been nearly exclusively male, but by the early 1890s, women held a third of the clerical positions in the executive departments in Washington. These workers constituted the nation's first substantial female clerical labor force. Their work in public life challenged the conventional belief that a woman's ability and personality limited her to the domestic sphere.

## The Political Life of the Tariff

Americans debated heatedly over tariff legislation throughout the late nineteenth century. This complex issue linked basic economic questions to partisan, ideological, and regional concerns. Tariffs on imported goods provided revenue for the federal government and protected American industry from European competition. They promoted industrial growth but often allowed favored industries to garner high profits. By the 1880s, tariffs covered 4,000 items and generated more revenue than the government needed to carry on its limited operations.

Reflecting its commitment to industry, the Republican Party vigorously championed protective tariffs. Party leaders also claimed that American labor benefited from tariff protection. "Reduce the tariff, and labor is the first to suffer," declared William McKinley of Ohio. Most Democrats, by contrast, favored tariff reduction, a position that reflected their party's relatively laissez-faire outlook. They argued that lower tariffs would encourage foreign trade and, by reducing the treasury surplus, minimize the temptation for the government to pursue activist policies. They pointed out the discriminatory effects of high tariffs, which benefited some interests, such as certain manufacturers, but hurt others, such as some farmers, while raising the cost of living for all (see Table 20.1).

The differences between the parties, however, were often more rhetorical than substantial. They disagreed only about how high tariffs should be and what interests they should protect. Congressmen of both parties voted for tariffs that would benefit their districts. A Democratic senator from Indiana, elected on a campaign pledge to reduce tariffs, summed up the prevailing rule succinctly: "I am a protectionist for every interest which I am sent here by my constituents to protect."

In the 1884 campaign, the Republican presidential candidate, James G. Blaine, maintained that prosperity and high employment depended on high tariffs. The Democrats' platform endorsed a lowered tariff, but their candidate, New York governor Grover Cleveland, generally ignored the issue. Unable to address this and other important issues, both parties resorted to scandal mongering. Democrats exploited Blaine's image as a beneficiary of the spoils system, and Republicans exposed Cleveland as the father of an illegitimate child. One observer called the election "a more bitter, personal, and disgusting campaign than we have ever seen."

**Pendleton Civil Service Act** An 1883 law that reformed the spoils system by prohibiting government workers from making political contributions and creating the Civil Service Commission to oversee their appointment on the basis of merit rather than politics.

Read the Document Interstate Commerce Act (1887)

TABLE 20.1 ARGUMENTS IN THE TARIFF DEBATES

| Area Affected | High-Tariff Advocates | Low-Tariff Advocates |
| --- | --- | --- |
| Industry | Tariffs promote industrial growth. | Tariffs inflate corporate profits. |
| Employment | Tariffs stimulate job growth. | Tariffs restrict competition. |
| Wages and prices | Tariffs permit higher wages. | Tariffs increase consumer prices. |
| Government | Tariffs provide government revenue. | Tariffs violate the principle of laissez-faire and produce revenues that tempt the government to activism. |
| Trade | Tariffs protect the domestic market. | Tariffs restrict foreign trade. |

Cleveland continued to avoid the tariff issue for three years after his election, until the growing treasury surplus and rising popular pressure for tariff reduction prompted him to act. He devoted his entire 1887 annual message to attacking the "vicious, inequitable, and illogical" tariff, apparently making it the dominant issue of his 1888 reelection campaign. Once again, however, the distinctive political attribute of the period—intense and organized campaigning between closely balanced parties—forced both Democrats and Republicans to blur their positions. Cleveland proposed a Democratic platform that ignored his recent message and did not even use the word *tariff*, and he named high-tariff advocates to manage his campaign. Cleveland won slightly more popular votes than his Republican opponent, Benjamin Harrison of Indiana, but Harrison carried the electoral college, indicating the decisive importance of strategic campaigning, local issues, and large campaign funds rather than great national issues.

The triumphant Republicans raised tariffs to prohibitive levels with the McKinley Tariff Act of 1890. McKinley praised the law as "protective in every paragraph and American on every page," but it provoked a popular backlash that helped return the Democrats to power. Still, the Democrats made little effort to push tariff reform. The *Atlanta Constitution* mused about such tariff politics in a bit of doggerel.

> It's funny 'bout this tariff, how they've lost it or forgot;
> They were rushing it to Congress once; their collars were so hot
> They could hardly wait to fix it 'till we harvested a crop;
> Was it such a burnin' question that they had to let it drop?

## The Beginnings of Federal Regulation

While business leaders pressed for protective tariffs and other public policies that promoted their interests, they otherwise used their ample political influence to ensure governmental laissez-faire. Popular pressure nonetheless compelled Congress to take the first steps toward the regulation of business with the passage of the Interstate Commerce Act in 1887 and the Sherman Antitrust Act in 1890.

The rapid growth of great corporations and their disruptive effects on traditional practices and values profoundly alarmed the public (see Chapter 18). Popular concern focused first on the railroads, the preeminent symbol of big business. Both farm groups and business shippers complained of discriminatory rates levied by railroads. Consumers condemned the railroads' use of pooling arrangements to suppress competition and raise rates. The resulting pressure was responsible for the Granger laws enacted in several midwestern states in the 1870s to regulate railroad freight and storage rates. At first, the Supreme Court upheld this legislation, ruling in *Munn v. Illinois* (1877) that state governments had the right to regulate private property when it was "devoted to a public use." But in 1886, the Court ruled in *Wabash, St. Louis, and Pacific Railway Company v. Illinois* that only the federal government could regulate interstate commerce. This decision effectively ended state regulation of railroads but simultaneously increased pressure for congressional action. With the support of both major parties, Congress in 1887 passed the **Interstate Commerce Act**.

The act prohibited rebates, discriminatory rates, and pooling and established the **Interstate Commerce Commission (ICC)** to investigate and prosecute violations. The ICC was the first federal regulatory agency. But its powers were too limited to be effective. Railroads continued their objectionable practices and frustrated the commission by refusing to provide required information and endlessly appealing its orders to a conservative judiciary. In its first fifteen years, only one court case was decided in favor of the ICC.

Many people saw railroad abuses as indicative of the dangers of corporate power in general and demanded a broader federal response. As with railroad regulation, the first antitrust laws—laws intended to break up or regulate corporate monopolies—were passed by states. Exposés of the monopolistic practices of such corporations as Standard Oil forced both major parties to endorse national antitrust legislation during the campaign of 1888. In 1890, Congress enacted the **Sherman Antitrust Act** with only a single vote in opposition. But this near unanimity concealed real differences over the desirability and purpose of the law. Although it emphatically prohibited any combination in restraint of trade (any attempt to restrict competition), the law was vaguely written and too weak to prevent abuses. The courts further weakened the act, and presidents of both parties made little effort to enforce it. Essentially still unfettered, large corporations remained a threat in the eyes of many Americans.

## The Money Question

Persistent wrangling over questions of currency and coinage made monetary policy the most divisive political issue. Despite the sometimes arcane and difficult nature of the money question, millions of Americans adopted positions on it and defended them with religious ferocity.

Creditors, especially bankers, as well as conservative economists and many business leaders favored limiting the money supply. They called this a **sound money** policy and insisted that it would ensure economic stability, maintain property values, and retain investor confidence. Farmers and other debtors complained that this deflationary monetary policy would depress already low crop prices, drive debtors further into debt, and restrict economic opportunities. They favored expanding the money supply to match the country's growing population and economy. They expected this inflationary policy to raise prices, stimulate the economy, reduce debt burdens, and increase opportunities.

The conservative leadership of both major parties supported the sound money policy, but their rank-and-file membership, especially in the West and the South, included many inflationists. As a result, the parties avoided confronting each other on the money issue.

The conflict between advocates of sound money and inflation centered on "greenbacks" and silver coinage. During the Civil War, the government had issued $450 million in greenbacks, paper money backed only by its credit, not by gold or silver, the traditional basis of currency. In 1875, sound money advocates in Congress enacted a deflationary law that withdrew some greenbacks from circulation and required that the remainder be convertible into gold. This action forced the money issue into electoral politics. Outraged inflationists organized the Greenback Party. They charged that the major parties had "failed to take the side of the people" and instead supported the "great moneyed institutions." The Greenbackers polled more than a million votes in 1878 and elected fourteen members of Congress, nearly gaining the balance of power in the House. As the 1870s depression faded, however, so did interest in the greenback issue, and the party soon withered.

**The Silver Issue.** Inflationists then turned to the silver issue, which would prove more enduring and disruptive. Historically, the United States had been on a bimetallic standard, using both gold and silver as the basis of its currency. But after the 1840s, the market price of silver rose above the currency value assigned to it by the government.

**Interstate Commerce Act** The 1887 law that expanded federal power over business by prohibiting pooling and discriminatory rates by railroads and establishing the first federal regulatory agency, the Interstate Commerce Commission.

**Interstate Commerce Commission (ICC)** The first federal regulatory agency, established in 1887 to oversee railroad practices.

**Sherman Antitrust Act** The first federal antitrust measure, passed in 1890; sought to promote economic competition by prohibiting business combinations in restraint of trade or commerce.

**sound money** Misleading slogan that referred to a conservative policy of restricting the money supply and adhering to the gold standard.

## From Then to Now
# Regulatory Government

F ew things about the federal government in the nineteenth century seem more removed from contemporary life than the limited role it played in American society. A writer in 1884 observed that the government affected the typical American "very rarely, and only at points of very little importance to him. . . . His interests and his activities are entirely beyond its scope, and there is hardly any serious interest of his life which is affected by it."

Since then, however, the government has assumed new responsibilities, providing new public services and adding departments and agencies. Such growth derived from social and economic changes, political parties and pressure groups, and government officials themselves. Most importantly, the impact of industrialization and corporate power created political pressures that led the federal government toward a regulatory role. The Interstate Commerce Commission, established in 1887, was the first regulatory agency. In the early twentieth century, new programs and agencies began regulating food, drugs, agricultural markets, and banking and business practices. The Great Depression of the 1930s led to additional agencies, regulating economic activities from stock exchanges to working conditions. Still later, Congress expanded the regulatory focus by creating such agencies as the Occupational Safety and Health Administration (1970).

New issues also prompted federal regulation. Growing threats to the environment, for example, led to the Environmental Protection Agency (1970) while threats of terrorism generated security agencies and regulations after September 11, 2001. Emerging technologies similarly produced regulatory responses, from the Federal Communications Commission (1934) for radio and television to the Nuclear Regulatory Commission (1974) for atomic power.

The governmental journey to a regulatory role was not a straight one. While most Americans supported such agencies as practical responses to changing conditions, others complained about the growing size of the government or the taxation necessary to carry out these public responsibilities. Periodically, demands for "deregulation," especially from business and its political allies, persuaded the government to stop enforcing some regulations, as in the 1920s and 1980s, or even to repeal them. (The ICC itself was abolished in 1995.) But such deregulation usually demonstrated why the laws and agencies had been adopted in the first place. Terminating 1930s regulations on financial institutions, for instance, contributed to the recklessness and fraud that led to the Great Recession of 2007–2010, spurring calls for "re-regulation."

**Question for Discussion**

- What varying roles does government regulation play and how have they changed over time?

To protect the nation from terrorism, by 2010 the federal Transportation Security Administration used full-body scanners for airline passengers, a governmental intrusion into private life overwhelmingly supported in public opinion polls.

Depicting corporate power as threatening popular liberty, this cartoon posed the question, "What are you going to do about it?" The American answer, beginning with the ICC in 1887, was government regulation.

Silver miners and owners began to sell the metal for commercial use rather than to the government for coinage, and little silver money circulated. In 1873, Congress passed a law "demonetizing" silver, thereby making gold the only standard for U.S. currency. Gold-standard supporters hoped that the law would promote international trade by aligning U.S. financial policy with that of Great Britain, which insisted on gold-based currency. But they also wanted to prevent new silver discoveries in the American West from expanding the money supply.

Indeed, silver production soon boomed, flooding the commercial market and dropping the value of the metal. Dismayed miners wanted the Treasury Department to purchase their surplus silver on the old terms and demanded a return to the bimetallic system. More important, the rural debtor groups seeking currency inflation joined in this demand, seeing renewed silver coinage as a means to reverse the long deflationary trend in the economy. Many passionately denounced the "Crime of '73" as a conspiracy of eastern bankers and foreign interests to control the money system to the detriment of ordinary Americans.

Again, both major parties equivocated. Eastern conservatives of both parties denounced silver; southerners and westerners demanded **free silver**, meaning unlimited silver coinage. By 1878, a bipartisan coalition succeeded in passing the Bland-Allison Act. This compromise measure required the government to buy and coin at least $2 million of silver a month. However, the government never exceeded the minimum, and the law had little inflationary effect.

**free silver** Philosophy that the government should expand the money supply by purchasing and coining all the silver offered to it.

After hard times hit rural regions in the late 1880s, inflationists secured passage of the Sherman Silver Purchase Act of 1890. The Treasury now had to buy a larger volume of silver and pay for it with treasury notes redeemable in either gold or silver. But this, too, produced little inflation, because the government did not coin the silver it purchased, redeemed the notes only with gold, and, as increased silver production depressed bullion prices further, had to spend less and less to buy the stipulated amount of silver. Debtors of both parties remained convinced that the government favored the "classes rather than the masses." Gold-standard advocates (again, of both parties) were even less happy with the law and planned to repeal it at their first opportunity. The division between the two groups was deep and bitter.

# The Crisis of the 1890s

**20.4**   What factors contributed to the rise and fall of the Populist Party?

In the 1890s, social, economic, and political pressures created a crisis for both the political system and the government. A third-party political challenge generated by agricultural discontent disrupted traditional party politics. A devastating depression spawned social misery and labor-management violence. Changing public attitudes led to new demands on the government and a realignment of parties and voters. These developments, in turn, set the stage for important political, economic, and social changes in the new century.

## Farmers Protest Inequities

The agricultural depression that engulfed the Great Plains and the South in the late 1880s brought misery and despair to millions of rural Americans. Falling crop prices and rising debt overwhelmed many people already exhausted from overwork and alarmed by the new corporate order. "At the age of 52 years, after a long life of toil, economy, and self-denial, I find myself and family virtual paupers," lamented one Kansan. His family's farm, rather than being "a house of refuge for our declining years, by a few turns of the monopolistic crank has been rendered valueless." To a large extent, the farmers' plight stemmed from bad weather and international overproduction of farm products. Seeking relief, however, the farmers naturally focused on the inequities of railroad discrimination, tariff favoritism, a restrictive financial system, and apparently indifferent political parties.

**Credit Inequities.**   Angry farmers particularly singled out the systems of money and credit that worked so completely against agricultural interests. Government rules for national banks directed credit into the urbanized North and East at the expense of the rural South and West and prohibited loans on farm property and real estate. As a result, farmers had to turn to other sources of credit and pay higher interest rates. In the West, farmers borrowed from mortgage companies to buy land and machinery, but declining crop prices made it difficult for them to pay their debts, and mortgage foreclosures then crushed the hopes of many. In the South, the credit shortage interacted with the practices of cotton marketing and retail trade to create the sharecropping system, which trapped more and more farmers, black and white, in a vicious pattern of exploitation. Moreover, the government's policies of monetary deflation worsened the debt burden for all farmers.

**Freight Rates and Tariffs.** Farmers protested other features of the nation's economic system as well. Railroad freight rates were two or three times higher in the West and South than in the North and East. The near-monopolistic control of grain elevators and cotton brokerages in rural areas left farmers feeling exploited. Protective tariffs on agricultural machinery and other manufactured goods further raised their costs. The failure of political parties and the government to devise effective regulatory and antitrust measures or to correct the inequities in the currency, credit, and tariff laws capped the farmers' anger. By the 1890s, many were convinced that the nation's economic and political institutions were aligned against them.

**Farmers' Alliance** A broad mass movement in the rural South and West during the late nineteenth century, encompassing several organizations and demanding economic and political reforms; helped create the Populist Party.

**Farmers Organize.** In response, farmers turned to the **Farmers' Alliance**, the era's greatest popular movement of protest and reform. Originating in Texas, the Southern Farmers' Alliance spread throughout the South and across the Great Plains to the Pacific coast. African American farmers organized the Colored Farmers' Alliance. The Northwestern Farmers' Alliance reached westward and northward from Illinois to Nebraska and Minnesota. In combination, these groups constituted a massive grassroots movement committed to economic and political reform.

Often propelling the movement, moreover, was a religious fervor rooted in rural evangelical soil. Many Alliance members saw farmers' economic and political problems, and their solutions, in moral terms. They decried industrial capitalism as violating Christian ethics, for "under competitive life Americans have, like heathen, strove with one another and preyed upon their neighbor." The exploitation of farmers and workers, abuses of monopolies, inequitable money and banking laws, casual cruelties of Social Darwinism—all were "contrary to the fundamental principles of Christianity." By contrast, Alliance principles were "directly in harmony with true religion." In their struggle for reform, then, "the battle is between God's people and the worshippers of the golden calf."

The Farmers' Alliance restricted membership to men and women of the "producing class" and urged them to stand "against the encroachments of monopolies and in opposition to the growing corruption of wealth and power." At first, the Alliance organized farmers' cooperatives to market crops and purchase supplies. Although some co-ops worked well, most soon failed because of the opposition of established business interests. Railroads suppressed Alliance grain elevators by refusing to handle their wheat. In Leflore County, Mississippi, when members of the Colored Farmers' Alliance shifted their trade to an Alliance store, local merchants provoked a conflict in which state troops killed twenty-five black farmers, including the local leaders of the Colored Alliance.

The Alliance also developed ingenious proposals to remedy rural credit and currency problems. In the South, the Alliance pushed the subtreasury system, which called on the government to warehouse farmers' cotton and advance them credit based on its value (see Chapter 17). In the West, the Alliance proposed a system of federal loans to farmers, using land as security. This land-loan scheme, like the subtreasury system, would have expanded the money supply while providing immediate relief to distressed farmers. These proposals were immensely popular among farmers, but the major parties and Congress rejected them. The Alliance also took up earlier calls for free silver, government control of railroads, and banking reform, again to no avail. Denouncing the

A lawyer and spellbinding orator, Mary Elizabeth Lease became famous for several aphorisms, including an exhortation to farmers to "raise less corn and more *Hell!*" She explained her speaking prowess by saying "My tongue is loose at both ends and hung on a swivel."

indifference of the major parties and the institutions of government, William A. Peffer, the influential editor of the Alliance newspaper the *Kansas Farmer,* declared that the "time has come for action. The people will not consent to wait longer. . . . The future is full of retribution for delinquents."

## The People's Party

In the West, discontented agrarians organized independent third parties to achieve reforms the major parties had ignored. State-level third parties appeared in the elections of 1890 under many names. All eventually adopted the labels "People's" or "Populist," which were first used by a Kansas party formed by members of the Farmers' Alliance, the Knights of Labor, the Grange, and the old Greenback Party. The new party's campaign, marked by grim determination and fierce rhetoric, set the model for Populist politics and introduced many of the movement's leaders. These people, women as well as men, were earnest organizers and powerful orators. One was *Kansas Farmer* editor Peffer. Others included "Sockless Jerry" Simpson, Annie Diggs, and Mary E. Lease.

The Populist parties proved remarkably successful. They gained control of the legislatures of Kansas and Nebraska and won congressional elections in Kansas, Nebraska, Minnesota, and South Dakota. Their victories came at the expense of the Republicans, who had traditionally controlled politics in these states, and contributed to a massive defeat of the GOP in the 1890 midterm elections. Thereafter, Populists won further victories throughout the West. In the mountain states, where their support came more from miners than from farmers, they elected governors in Colorado and Montana. On the Pacific Coast, angry farmers found allies among urban workers in Seattle, Tacoma, Portland, and San Francisco, where organized labor had campaigned for reform since the 1880s. The Populists elected a governor in Washington, congressmen in California, and legislators in all three states. Even in the Southwest, where territorial status limited political activity, Populist parties emerged. In Oklahoma, the party drew support from homesteaders and tenant farmers; in Arizona, from miners and railroad workers; in New Mexico, from small stockraisers and poor Hispanics.

With their new political power, Populists enacted reform legislation in many western states. New laws regulated banks and railroads and protected debtors by capping interest rates and restricting mortgage foreclosures. Others protected unions and mandated improved workplace conditions. Still others made the political system more democratic. Populists were instrumental, for example, in winning woman suffrage in Colorado and Idaho, although the united opposition of Democrats and Republicans blocked their efforts in other states.

In the South, the angry farmers did not initially form third parties but instead attempted to seize control of the dominant Democratic Party by forcing its candidates to pledge support to the Alliance platform. The rural southern electorate then swept these "Alliance Democrats" into office. But most of these Democrats then repudiated their Alliance pledges and remained loyal to their party and its traditional opposition to governmental activism. Betrayed again by the political system, disgruntled Alliance members began organizing their own Populist parties, but they faced obstacles that western farmers did not. A successful challenge to the entrenched Democrats would require the political cooperation of both white and black farmers, but that would expose Populists to demagogic attacks from Democrats for undermining white supremacy, frightening away potential white supporters. The *Baton Rouge Advocate*, for example, warned its readers that Populists were "the most dangerous and insidious foe of white supremacy."

Some southern Populists, black and white, did appeal for racial cooperation in political if not social action. In Texas, John B. Rayner, the "silver tongued orator of the colored race," spoke to racially mixed audiences across the state and helped shape the Texas Populist platform calling for "equal justice and protection under the law to all citizens without reference to race, color, or nationality." In Georgia, Populist leader Tom Watson supported a biracial party organization and counseled whites to accept blacks as partners in their common crusade. "You are kept apart," Watson told black and white southerners, "that you may be separately fleeced of your earnings. You are made to hate each other because upon that hatred is rested the keystone of the arch of financial despotism which enslaves you both."

But steeped in racism, most white southerners recoiled from the prospect of interracial unity. And for their part, most black people remained loyal to the Republican Party for its role in abolishing slavery and for the few patronage crumbs the party still threw their way. Moreover, primarily tenants and farm laborers, their interests were not identical to those of white land-owning farmers who formed the core of the Populist Party. Unwilling or unable to mobilize black voters and largely unsuccessful in dislodging white voters from the Democratic Party, Populists in the South achieved but limited political success, making significant inroads only in the legislatures of Texas, Alabama, and Georgia, and sending Tom Watson to Congress.

**National Action.** Populists soon realized that successful reform would require national action. They met in Omaha, Nebraska, on July 4, 1892, to organize a national party and nominated former Greenbacker James B. Weaver for president. The party platform, known as the **Omaha Platform**, rejected the laissez-faire policies of the old parties: "We believe that the powers of government, in other words, of the people, should be expanded . . . to the end that oppression, injustice, and poverty shall

**Omaha Platform** The 1892 platform of the Populist Party repudiating laissez-faire and demanding economic and political reforms to aid distressed farmers and workers.

# ✳ Explore the Populist Movement on MyHistoryLab

## WHAT IMPACT DID THE POPULIST MOVEMENT HAVE ON AMERICAN POLITICS?

In the last decades of the 1800s, farmers faced serious difficulties. They suffered from declining commodity prices, increasing debt, and monetary deflation. When the major parties ignored their plight, discontented agrarians in the South and West organized a mass reform movement, the Farmers' Alliance. Joined by some labor organizations, the Alliance then created a new political party, the People's (or Populist) Party, which demanded government action to regulate the economy and reform the money and banking system. The People's Party nominated James B. Weaver for president in the 1892 election. Although he lost, the party carried several western states and elected hundreds of legislators and other officials. When a harsh depression began in 1893, the Populists attempted to broaden their appeal by stressing the issue of silver inflation. But in 1896 the Democratic Party adopted the silver issue as its own and nominated the liberal William

This Republican cartoon attempted to frighten conservative Democrats by depicting William Jennings Bryan as the head of the Populist Party, swallowing their own party in 1896. Actually, Bryan was a Democrat, and his nomination by the Populists left them swallowed by the Democratic Party.

Jennings Bryan, leaving the Populists with little alternative to nominating Bryan themselves and submerging their party in a fusion campaign with the Democrats. Bryan's loss to Republican William McKinley then left the Populists in complete disorder, and their party withered away. Yet the influence of the People's Party persisted, for it had contributed to an important realignment of the major parties and had raised issues that would continue to shape state and national politics.

### PRESIDENTIAL ELECTION RESULTS: 1892

| Candidate | Party | Popular Vote |
|---|---|---|
| Grover Cleveland | Democratic | 5,551,833 |
| Benjamin Harrison | Republican | 5,179,244 |
| James B. Weaver | People's | 1,041,028 |

### PRESIDENTIAL ELECTION RESULTS: 1896

| Candidate | Party | Popular Vote |
|---|---|---|
| William McKinley | Republican | 7,108,480 |
| William J. Bryan | Democratic/ People's | 6,511,495 |

SOURCE: http://www.archives.gov/federal-register/electoral-college/scores.html#1892; Library of Congress

## KEY QUESTIONS    Use MyHistoryLab *Explorer* to answer these questions:

**Consequence ▶▶▶** *How did the average value of farmland change over this period?*

Chart these changes to consider their impact on national politics.

**Analysis ▶▶▶** *How did the People's Party fare in various elections?*

Consider the overall larger political influence of the People's Party.

**Response ▶▶▶** *In what regions was support for the People's Party strongest?*

Map geographical distribution of Populist support.

Read the Document The People's Party Platform (1892)

VOL. 20 NO. 503        JUNE 6 1891        PRICE 10 CENTS.

*Judge*

ENTERED AT THE POST OFFICE AT NEW YORK AS SECOND-CLASS MATTER.    COPYRIGHT 1891 BY THE JUDGE PUBLISHING CO.

A PARTY OF PATCHES.
Grand Balloon Ascension—Cincinnati, May 20th, 1891.

Established interests ridiculed the Populists unmercifully. This hostile cartoon depicts the People's Party as an odd assortment of radical dissidents committed to a "Platform of Lunacy."

eventually cease in the land." It demanded government ownership of the railroads and the telegraph and telephone systems, a national currency issued by the government rather than by private banks, the subtreasury system, free silver, a graduated income tax, and the redistribution to settlers of land held by railroads and speculative corporations. Accompanying resolutions endorsed the popular election of senators, the secret ballot, and other electoral reforms to make government more democratic and responsive to popular wishes.

The Populists left Omaha to begin an energetic campaign. Weaver toured the western states and with Mary Lease invaded the Democratic stronghold of the South where some Populists tried to mobilize black voters. Southern Democrats, however, used violence and fraud to intimidate Populist voters and cheat Populist candidates out of office. Some local Populist leaders were murdered, and Weaver was driven from the South. One Democrat confessed that Alabama's Populist gubernatorial candidate "carried the state, but was swindled out of his victory . . . with unblushing trickery and corruption." Southern Democrats also appealed effectively to white supremacy, undermining the Populist effort to build a biracial reform coalition.

Elsewhere, too, Populists met disappointment. Midwestern farmers unfamiliar with Alliance ideas and organization ignored Populist appeals and stood by their traditional political allegiances. So did most eastern working-class voters, who learned little of the Populist program beyond its demand for inflation, which they feared would worsen their own conditions.

The Populists lost the election but showed impressive support. They garnered more than a million votes, carried several western states, and won hundreds of state offices throughout the West and in pockets of the South. Populist leaders immediately began working to expand their support, to the alarm of both southern Democrats and northern Republicans.

## The Challenge of the Depression

The emergence of a significant third-party movement was but one of many developments that combined by the mid-1890s to produce a national political crisis. A harsh and lengthy depression began in 1893, cruelly worsening conditions not only for farmers but for most other Americans. Labor unrest and violence engulfed the nation, reflecting workers' distress but frightening more comfortable Americans. The persistent failure of the major parties to respond to serious problems contributed mightily to the growing popular discontent. Together these developments constituted an important challenge to America's new industrial society and government.

Although the Populists lost in 1892, the election nonetheless reflected the nation's spreading dissatisfaction. Voters decisively rejected President Harrison and the incumbent Republicans in Congress, putting the Democrats in control of Congress and Grover Cleveland back in the White House. But the conservative Cleveland was almost oblivious to the mounting demand for reform. He delivered an inaugural address championing laissez-faire and rejecting government action to solve social or economic problems.

Cleveland's resolve was immediately tested when the economy collapsed in the spring of 1893. Railroad overexpansion, a weak banking system, tight credit, and plunging agricultural prices all contributed to the disaster. So too did a depression in Europe, which reduced American export markets and prompted British investors to sell their American investments for gold. Hundreds of banks closed, and thousands of businesses, including the nation's major railroads, went bankrupt. By winter, 20 percent of the labor force was unemployed, and the jobless scavenged for food in a country that had no public unemployment or welfare programs.

Churches, local charity societies, and labor unions tried to provide relief but were overwhelmed. Most state governments offered little relief beyond encouraging private charity to the homeless. In Kansas, however, the Populist governor insisted that traditional laissez-faire policies were inadequate: "It is the duty of government to protect the weak, because the strong are able to protect themselves." Cleveland disagreed and showed little sympathy for the struggling. The functions of the government, he said, "do not include the support of the people."

**Appeals for Federal Action.** If Cleveland and Congress had no idea how the federal government might respond to the depression, other Americans did. Jacob Coxey, a Populist businessman from Ohio, proposed a government public-works program for the unemployed to be financed with paper money. This plan would improve the nation's infrastructure, create jobs for the unemployed, and provide an inflationary stimulus to counteract the depression's deflationary effects. In short, Coxey advocated positive government action to combat the depression. Elements of his plan would be adopted for mitigating economic downturns in the twentieth century; in 1894, it was too untraditional for Congress to consider.

Coxey organized a march of the unemployed to Washington as "a petition with boots on" to support his ideas. Coxey and his followers marched through the industrial

**Coxey's Army** A protest march of unemployed workers, led by Populist businessman Jacob Coxey, demanding inflation and a public-works program during the depression of the 1890s.

towns of Ohio and Pennsylvania and into Maryland, attracting attention and support. The excited press dubbed the movement **Coxey's Army**, but its formal name was the Commonweal of Christ, and it was suffused with religious rhetoric and symbolism as it called for compassion and assistance for those in distress.

Other "industrial armies" of the unemployed also set out for the capital. Some formed in eastern cities from Boston to Baltimore and in southern cities like Birmingham and Houston, but far larger ones organized in the western cities of Denver, San Francisco, and Seattle. Five hundred marchers from Los Angeles captured a train to cross the Southwest and were feted and fed by townspeople from Tucson to El Paso. When the Southern Pacific uncoupled the train's locomotive and left them stranded in West Texas, the governor of Texas threatened to hold the railroad responsible for murder "by torture and starvation." Texas citizens quickly raised funds to speed the army on to St. Louis. From there it marched to Washington on foot.

The sympathy and assistance with which Americans greeted these industrial armies reflected more than anxiety over the depression and unemployment. As one economist noted, what distinguished Populists and Coxeyites from earlier reformers was their appeal for federal action. Their substantial public support suggested a deep dissatisfaction with the failure of the government to respond to social and economic needs.

Nonetheless, the government acted to suppress Coxey. When he reached Washington with 600 marchers, police and soldiers arrested him and his aides, beat sympathetic bystanders in a crowd of 20,000, and herded the marchers into detention camps. Unlike the lobbyists for business and finance, Coxey was not permitted to reach Congress to deliver his statement urging the government to assist "the poor and oppressed."

**Protecting Big Business.** The depression also provoked labor turmoil. In 1894, there were some 1,400 industrial strikes, involving nearly 700,000 workers, the largest number of strikers in any year in the nineteenth century. Cleveland had no response except to call for law and order. One result was the government's violent suppression of the Pullman strike (see Chapter 18).

In a series of decisions in 1895, the Supreme Court strengthened the bonds between business and government. First, it upheld the use of a court-ordered injunction to break the Pullman strike. As a result, injunctions became a major weapon for courts and corporations against labor unions, until Congress finally limited their use in 1932. Next, in *United States v. E. C. Knight Company,* the Court gutted the Sherman Antitrust Act by ruling that manufacturing, as opposed to commerce, was beyond the reach of federal regulation. Finally, the Court invalidated an income tax that agrarian Democrats and Populists had maneuvered through Congress. The conservative Court rejected the reform as an "assault upon capital." A dissenting justice noted that the decision gave vested interests "a power and influence" dangerous to the majority of Americans. Not until 1913, and then only with an amendment to the Constitution, would it be possible to adopt an equitable system of taxation.

Surveying these developments, farmers and workers increasingly concluded that the government protected powerful interests while ignoring the plight of ordinary Americans. Certainly the callous treatment shown to workers contrasted sharply with Cleveland's concern for bankers as he managed the government's monetary policy in the depression. Cleveland blamed the economic collapse on the Sherman Silver Purchase Act, which he regarded as detrimental to business confidence and a threat to the nation's gold reserve. He persuaded Congress in 1893 to repeal the law, enraging southern and western members of his own party. These Silver Democrats condemned Cleveland for betraying the public good to "the corporate interests."

Cleveland's policy failed to end the depression. By 1894, the Treasury began borrowing money from Wall Street to bolster the gold reserve. These transactions benefited a syndicate of bankers headed by J. P. Morgan. It seemed to critics that an indifferent

Cleveland was helping rich bankers profit from the nation's economic agony. "A set of vampires headed by a financial trust has control of our destiny," cried one rural newspaper.

## The Battle of the Standards and the Election of 1896

The government's unpopular actions, coupled with the unrelenting depression, alienated workers and farmers from the Cleveland administration and the Democratic Party. In the off-year elections of 1894, the Democrats suffered the greatest loss of congressional seats in American history. Populists increased their vote by 42 percent, making especially significant gains in the South. But the real beneficiaries of the popular hatred of Cleveland and his policies were the Republicans. Denouncing Cleveland's "utter imbecility," they gained solid control of Congress as well as state governments across the North and West. All three parties began to plan for the presidential election of 1896.

As hard times persisted, the silver issue came to overshadow all others. Some Populist leaders, hoping to broaden the party's appeal, began to emphasize silver rather than the more radical but divisive planks of the Omaha Platform. Many southern and western Democrats, who had traditionally favored silver inflation, also decided to stress the issue, both to undercut the Populists and to distance themselves and their party from the despised Cleveland.

**McKinley and the Republicans.** William McKinley, governor of Ohio and author of the McKinley Tariff Act of 1890, emerged as the front-runner in a crowd of hopeful Republican presidential candidates. His candidacy benefited particularly from the financial backing and political management of Mark Hanna, a wealthy Ohio industrialist. Hanna thought that McKinley's passion for high tariffs as the key to revived prosperity would appeal to workers as well as to industry and business. The Republicans nominated McKinley at their 1896 convention. Their platform called for high tariffs but also endorsed the gold standard, placating eastern delegates but prompting several western Silver Republicans to withdraw from the party.

**Bryan and the Silverites.** When the Democratic convention met, embattled supporters of the gold standard soon learned that the silver crusade had made them a minority in the party. With a fervor that conservatives likened to "scenes of the French Revolution," the Silver Democrats revolutionized their party. They adopted a platform repudiating Cleveland and his policies and endorsing free silver, the income tax, and tighter regulation of trusts and railroads. A magnificent speech supporting this platform by William Jennings Bryan helped convince the delegates to nominate him for president.

Holding their convention last, the Populists faced a terrible dilemma. The Democratic nomination of Bryan on a silver platform undercut their hopes of attracting disappointed reformers from the major parties. Bryan, moreover, had already worked closely with Nebraska Populists, who now urged the party to endorse him rather than split the silver vote and ensure the victory of McKinley and the gold standard. Other Populists argued that fusing—joining with the Democrats—would cost the Populists their separate identity and subordinate their larger political principles to the issue of free silver. After anguished discussion, the Populists nominated Bryan for president.

**Money and Oratory.** The campaign was intense and dramatic, with each side demonizing the other. Eastern financial and business interests contributed millions of dollars to Hanna's campaign for McKinley. Standard Oil alone provided $250,000, about the same amount as the Democrats' total national expenses. Hanna used these funds to organize an unprecedented campaign. Shifting the emphasis from parades

William Jennings Bryan in 1896. A powerful orator of great human sympathies, Bryan was adored by his followers as "the majestic man who was hurling defiance in the teeth of the money power." Nominated three times for the presidency by the Democrats, he was never elected.

to information, Republicans issued 250 million campaign documents in a dozen languages, warning of economic disaster should Bryan be elected and the bimetallic standard be restored, but promising that McKinley's election would finally end the depression. Republicans were aided by a national press so completely sympathetic that many newspapers not only shaped their editorials but distorted their news stories to Bryan's disadvantage.

Lacking the Republicans' superior resources, the Democrats relied on Bryan's superb speaking ability and youthful energy. Bryan was the first presidential candidate to campaign systematically, speaking hundreds of times to millions of voters. By contrast, McKinley stayed home in Canton, Ohio, where he conducted a "front porch" campaign. But Hanna brought groups of Republicans from all over the country to visit McKinley every day, and McKinley reiterated his simple promise of prosperity.

In the depression, that appeal proved enough. As the Democratic candidate, Bryan was, ironically, burdened with the legacy of the hated Cleveland administration. The intense campaign brought a record voter turnout. McKinley won decisively by capturing the East and Midwest as well as Oregon and California (see Map 20.2 on page 594). Bryan carried the traditionally Democratic South and the mountain and plains states, where Populists and silverites dominated. But by subordinating other popular grievances to silver, he failed to gain support among industrial workers in the cities of the East and Midwest.

This Republican campaign poster of 1896 depicts William McKinley standing on sound money and promising a revival of prosperity. The depression of the 1890s shifted the electorate into the Republican column.

The elections of 1894 and 1896 ended the close balance between the major parties. Cleveland's failures, coupled with an economic recovery in the wake of the election of 1896, gained the Republicans a reputation as the party of prosperity and industrial progress, firmly establishing them in power for years to come. By contrast, the Democratic Party receded into an ineffectual sectional minority dominated by southern conservatives, despite Bryan's liberal views.

The People's Party simply dissolved. Demoralized by fusion with the Democrats, who had earlier violently repressed them, many southern Populists dropped out of politics. The Democrats' disfranchisement laws, directed at discontented poor whites as well as poor blacks, further undermined the Populists in the South. In the West, the silver tide of 1896 carried many Populists into office, but with their party collapsing, they had no hope of reelection. By 1898, the Populist Party had virtually disappeared. Its reform legacy, however, proved more enduring. The issues it raised would continue to shape state and national politics.

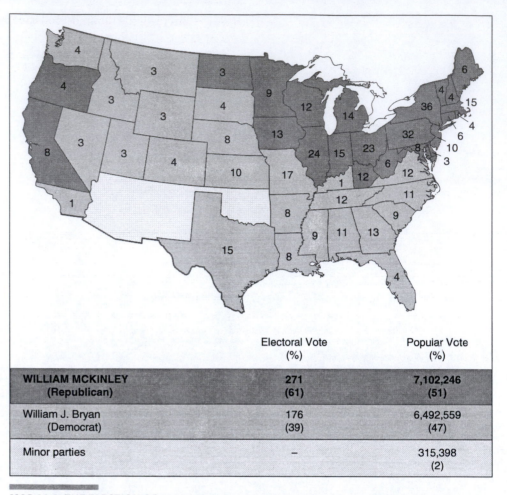

| | Electoral Vote (%) | Popular Vote (%) |
|---|---|---|
| **WILLIAM MCKINLEY** (Republican) | **271** **(61)** | **7,102,246** **(51)** |
| William J. Bryan (Democrat) | 176 (39) | 6,492,559 (47) |
| Minor parties | – | 315,398 (2) |

**MAP 20.2  THE ELECTION OF 1896** William Jennings Bryan carried most of the rural South and West, but his free silver campaign had little appeal to more urban and industrial regions, which swung strongly to Republican candidate William McKinley.

McKinley plunged into his presidency. Unlike his predecessors, he had a definite, if limited, program, consisting of tariff protection, sound money, and overseas expansion. He worked actively to see it through Congress and to shape public opinion, thereby helping establish the model of the modern presidency. He had promised prosperity, and it returned, although not because of the record high tariff his party enacted in 1897 or the Currency Act of 1900, which firmly established the gold standard. Prosperity returned, instead, because of reviving markets and a monetary inflation that resulted from the discovery of vast new deposits of gold in Alaska, Australia, and South Africa. The silverites had recognized that an expanding industrial economy required an expanding money supply. Ironically, the new inflation was greater than the inflation that would have resulted from free silver. With the return of prosperity and the decline of social tensions, McKinley easily won reelection in 1900, defeating Bryan a second time.

## Conclusion

In late-nineteenth-century America, politics and government often seemed at cross-purposes. Political contests were exciting events, absorbing public attention, attracting high voter turnout, and often raising issues of symbolic or substantive importance. Closely balanced political parties commanded the zealous support of their constituents and wielded power and influence. The institutions of government, by contrast, were limited in size, scope, and responsibility. A weakened presidency and an inefficient Congress, hampered by a restrictive judiciary, were often unable to resolve the very issues that were so dramatically raised in the political arena. The persistent disputes over tariff and monetary policy illustrate this impasse. But the issue that most reflected it was civil service reform. The patronage system provided the lifeblood of politics but also disrupted government business.

Localism, laissez-faire, and other traditional principles that shaped both politics and government were becoming increasingly inappropriate for America's industrializing society. New challenges were emerging that state and local governments could not effectively solve on their own. The national nature of the railroad network, for example, finally brought the federal government into the regulatory arena, however imperfectly, with the Interstate Commerce Act of 1887. Both the depression of the 1890s and the popular discontent articulated most clearly by the Populist rejection of laissez-faire underscored the need for change and discredited the limited government of the Cleveland administration.

By the end of the decade, the political system had changed. The Republicans had emerged as the dominant party, ending the two-party stalemate of previous decades. Campaign hoopla in local communities, like the elaborate parade and ceremonies in Fort Wayne described at the beginning of this chapter, had given way to information-based campaigns directed by and through national organizations. A new, activist presidency was emerging. And the disruptive currency issue faded with the hard times that had brought it forth. Still greater changes were on the horizon. The depression and its terrible social and economic consequences undermined traditional ideas about the responsibilities of government and increased public support for activist policies. The stage was set for the Progressive Era.

**For Suggested Readings go to MyHistoryLab.**

# Chapter Review

## The Structure and Style of Politics

**20.1** How did parties shape late-nineteenth-century politics? p. 570

Parties dominated political life, organizing campaigns, controlling balloting, and staffing government offices. By appealing to group loyalties, they also mobilized a huge electorate and created a politics of mass participation and high turnout. Virtually all men participated, and although women could not vote, they were active as both partisans and members of pressure groups.

## The Limits of Government

**20.2** What explains the weakness and inefficiency of late-nineteenth-century government? p. 575

Government in the late nineteenth century was neither active nor productive by present standards; localism and laissez-faire attitudes dominated. A restrained presidency and an inefficient Congress, hampered further by partisan differences, combined with a small and ineffective federal bureaucracy and a restrictive judiciary to limit the size and objectives of government.

## Public Policies and National Elections

**20.3** How effective was government in addressing the problems of America's industrializing economy? p. 577

Policy issues often were not partisan issues; therefore, they rarely determined elections or were resolved. Civil service reform only gradually curtailed the spoils system. Tariff policies produced heated debates but little change. Under popular pressure, both parties endorsed business regulation, but without practical effect. The divisive money question generated only inconclusive legislation.

## The Crisis of the 1890s

**20.4** What factors contributed to the rise and fall of the Populist Party? p. 583

Agricultural discontent sparked a third-party protest movement. The Populist rejection of laissez-faire together with a severe depression and labor unrest produced a political crisis and undermined traditional ideas of the responsibilities of government. McKinley's victory over Bryan in the 1896 election established the Republicans as the party of prosperity and progress.

# Timeline

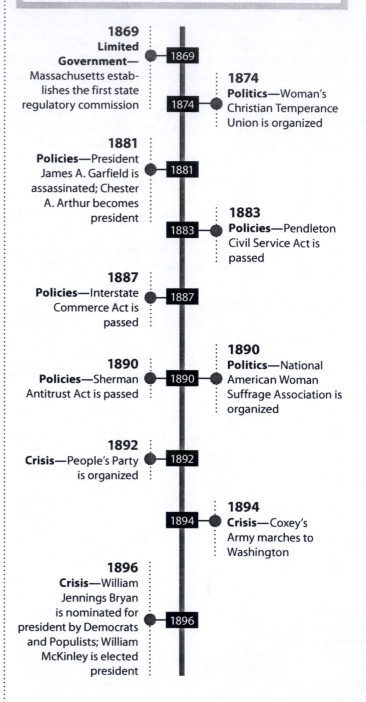

**1869**
**Limited Government—** Massachusetts establishes the first state regulatory commission

1869

**1874**
**Politics—**Woman's Christian Temperance Union is organized

1874

**1881**
**Policies—**President James A. Garfield is assassinated; Chester A. Arthur becomes president

1881

**1883**
**Policies—**Pendleton Civil Service Act is passed

1883

**1887**
**Policies—**Interstate Commerce Act is passed

1887

**1890**
**Policies—**Sherman Antitrust Act is passed

1890

**1890**
**Politics—**National American Woman Suffrage Association is organized

**1892**
**Crisis—**People's Party is organized

1892

**1894**
**Crisis—**Coxey's Army marches to Washington

1894

**1896**
**Crisis—**William Jennings Bryan is nominated for president by Democrats and Populists; William McKinley is elected president

1896

# 21 The Progressive Era 1900–1917

## One American Journey

### A Famous Union Organizer Recalls Her March to Protest Child Labor

**I**n the spring of 1903, I went to Kensington, Pennsylvania, where 75,000 textile workers were on strike. Of this number at least 10,000 were little children. The workers were striking for more pay and shorter hours. Every day little children came into Union Headquarters, some with their hands off, some with the thumb missing, some with their fingers off at the knuckle. They were stooped little things, round shouldered and skinny. Many of them were not over ten years of age. . . .

We assembled a number of boys and girls one morning in Independence Park and from there we arranged to parade with banners to the court house where we would hold a meeting.

A great crowd gathered in the public square in front of the city hall. I put the little boys with their fingers off and hands crushed and maimed on a platform. I held up their mutilated hands and showed them to the crowd and made the

Women march in support of Mother Jones in Trinidad, Colorado. Dramatic tactics and careful organizing like those that marked this parade often helped secure reform in the Progressive Era.

| 21.1 | 21.2 | 21.3 | 21.4 | 21.5 |
|------|------|------|------|------|
| What values and beliefs bound progressives together? p. 600 | How did progressives respond to the social challenges of industrializing America? p. 606 | How did progressives change American politics and government? p. 613 | How did Theodore Roosevelt's view of the presidency shape his administration? p. 618 | How did Woodrow Wilson's view of the role of government change during his presidency? p. 623 |

Listen to Chapter 21 on MyHistoryLab

From *The American Journey*, Seventh Edition. Goldfield, Abbott, Anderson, Argersinger, Argersinger and Barney Copyright © 2014 by Pearson Education, Inc. All rights reserved.

# ◉ Watch the Video Series on MyHistoryLab

Learn about some key topics related to this chapter with the
*MyHistoryLab Video Series: Key Topics in U.S. History.*

**1** The Progressive Era: 1900–1916  This video is an introduction to
the progressives and the Progressive Era of the early twentieth
century. Ranging from politicians and social workers to
educators and journalists, the progressives were reformers who
believed the problems of American society could be solved by
efficiency, organization, and the power of government.

◉ Watch on MyHistoryLab

**Theodore Roosevelt**  Theodore Roosevelt is profiled in this video. The very model of the progressive
politician, Roosevelt championed many of the progressive causes from his position as president.
An avid outdoorsman, he established national parks and expanded national forests to advance
conservation. To prevent corporate abuses and defend the public interest, he worked to expand federal
supervision and regulation of business.

**2**

Watch on MyHistoryLab

 **3** Industrial Workers of the World   This video describes how the dangers of the late-nineteenth-century
industrial workplace, especially in mining, and other unfair labor practices inspired socialists and
anarchists to found a universal worker organization known as the Industrial Workers of the World
(IWW), whose members were known to its detractors as "Wobblies" for their radical ideas.

◉ Watch on MyHistoryLab

**Nineteenth Amendment**  The successful adoption of the Nineteenth Amendment to the Constitution
in 1920 achieved women's suffrage in the United States. This video explores the background of the
movement to give women the right to vote, especially the work of two groups, the National American
Woman Suffrage Association and the National Woman's Party.

**4**

Watch on MyHistoryLab ◉

statement that Philadelphia's mansions were built on the broken bones, the quivering hearts, and
drooping heads of these children. . . .

I [then] decided to go with the children to see President Roosevelt to ask him to have
Congress pass a law prohibiting the exploitation of childhood. I thought that President Roosevelt
might see these mill children and compare them with his own little ones spending the summer at
the seashore at Oyster Bay. . . .

Everywhere [en route] we had meetings, showing with little children the horrors of
child labor. . . . [In Princeton, New Jersey,] a great crowd gathered, professors and students,
and the people; and I told them that the rich robbed these little children of any education of the lowest order that they might send their sons and daughters to places of higher
education. . . .

[In New York City] I told an immense crowd of the horrors of child labor in the mills . . . and I
showed them Gussie Rangnew, a little girl from whom all the childhood had gone. Her face was
like an old woman's. Gussie packed stockings in a factory, eleven hours a day for a few cents a
day. . . . [I said,] "Fifty years ago there was a cry against slavery and men gave up their lives to stop

the selling of black children on the block. Today the white child is sold for two dollars a week to the manufacturers."

...We marched down to Oyster Bay but the president refused to see us and he would not answer my letters. But our march had done its work. We had drawn the attention of the nation to the crime of child labor. And while the strike of the textile workers in Kensington was lost and the children driven back to work, not long afterward the Pennsylvania legislature passed a child labor law that kept thousands of children home from the mills.

*The Autobiography of Mother Jones.* Originally published in 1937
by Charles H. Kerr Publishing Company, Chicago, IL.

## Personal Journeys Online

- Washington Gladden, *The World Is Beginning to See*, 1909. Social Gospeler Washington Gladden's view of the ethical journey underlying the progressive reform impulse.
- Al Smith, *Enacting Reform Legislation*, 1929. Smith's account of overcoming opposition to reform laws in the wake of the Triangle Fire in 1911.

**T**he sweet-faced, white-haired "Mother" Jones was nearly 70 years old when she led "the children's crusade" in 1903. Born Mary Harris in Ireland, she had survived famine, emigration, hard labor, and the horrible deaths of her husband and their four children. Indomitable, she had become a celebrated union organizer and powerful orator against what she saw as the economic injustices of America.

The journey of Mother Jones, with Gussie Rangnew and other maimed children, from Kensington, Pennsylvania, to Oyster Bay, New York, was thus just part of her legendary life journey. But it also illustrated critical features of life in the **Progressive Era.** Important movements challenged traditional relationships and attitudes—here involving working conditions, unregulated industrial development, concepts of opportunity and childhood itself—and often met strong resistance and only limited success. "Progressives" seeking change investigated problems, proposed solutions, organized their supporters, and attempted to mobilize public opinion—just as Mother Jones sought to do. And rather than rely only on traditional partisan politics, reformers adopted new political techniques, including lobbying and demonstrating as nonpartisan pressure groups. Reform work, begun at the local and state levels where the campaign against child labor had already met some success, inexorably moved to the national level as the federal government expanded its authority and became the focus of political interest. Finally, Mother Jones's march revealed the exceptional diversity of the progressive movement, for she and her followers were marching, in part, against the seemingly indifferent Theodore Roosevelt, perhaps the most prominent progressive.

The issue of child labor, then, did not define progressivism. Indeed, in a sense, there was no "progressive movement," for progressivism had no unifying organization, central leadership, or consensus on objectives. Instead, it represented the coalescing of different and sometimes even contradictory movements that sought changes in the nation's social, economic, and political life. But reformers did share certain convictions. They believed that industrialization and urbanization had produced serious social disorders, from city slums to corporate abuses. They believed that new ideas and methods were required to correct these problems. In particular, they rejected the ideology of individualism in favor of broader concepts of social responsibility, and they sought to achieve social order through organization and efficiency. Finally, most progressives believed that government itself, as the organized agent of public responsibility, should address social and economic problems.

**Progressive Era** An era in the United States (roughly between 1900 and 1917) in which important movements challenged traditional relationships and attitudes.

# The Ferment of Reform

**21.1**  What values and beliefs bound progressives together?

The diversity of progressivism reflected the diverse impulses of reform. Reformers responded to the tensions of industrialization and urbanization by formulating programs according to their own interests and priorities. Nearly every movement for change encountered fierce opposition. But in raising new issues and proposing new ideas, progressives helped America grapple with the problems of industrial society (see Table 21.1).

## The Context of Reform: Industrial and Urban Tensions

The origins of progressivism lay in the crises of the new urban-industrial order that emerged in the late nineteenth century. The severe depression and mass suffering of the 1890s, the labor violence and industrial armies, and the political challenges of Populism and an obviously ineffective government shattered the complacency that many middle-class Americans had felt about their nation and made them aware of social and economic inequities that rural and working-class families had long recognized. Many Americans began to question the validity of Social Darwinism and the laissez-faire policies that had justified unregulated industrial growth. They began to reconsider the responsibilities of government and, indeed, of themselves for social order and betterment.

By 1900, returning prosperity had eased the threat of major social violence, but the underlying problems intensified. Big business, which had disrupted traditional economic relationships in the late nineteenth century, suddenly became bigger in a series of mergers between 1897 and 1903, resulting in huge new business combinations. Such gigantic corporations threatened to squeeze opportunities for small firms and workers, dominate markets, and raise social tensions. They also inspired calls for public control.

Industrial growth affected factory workers most directly. Working conditions were difficult and often dangerous. Most workers still toiled 9 to 10 hours a day; steelworkers and textile employees worked 12-hour shifts. Wages were minimal; an economist

**TABLE 21.1  MAJOR PROGRESSIVE ORGANIZATIONS AND GROUPS**

| Group | Activity |
| --- | --- |
| Social Gospel movement | Urged churches and individuals to apply Christian ethics to social and economic problems |
| Muckrakers | Exposed business abuses, public corruption, and social evils through investigative journalism |
| Settlement House movement | Attempted through social work and public advocacy to improve living and working conditions in urban immigrant communities |
| National Consumers' League (1898) | Monitored businesses to ensure decent working conditions and safe consumer products |
| Women's Trade Union League (1903) | United working women and their middle-class allies to promote unionization and social reform |
| National Child Labor Committee (1904) | Campaigned against child labor |
| Country Life movement | Attempted to modernize rural social and economic conditions according to urban-industrial standards |
| National American Woman Suffrage Association | Led the movement to give women the right to vote |
| Municipal reformers | Sought to change the activities and structure of urban government to promote efficiency and control |
| Conservationists | Favored efficient management and regulation of natural resources rather than uncontrolled development or preservation |

((• 📖 Read the Document    John Spargo, from *The Bitter Cry of the Children* (1906)

21.1

21.2

21.3

21.4

21.5

The famous photographer Lewis Hine extensively documented child labor. These boys worked in a Pennsylvania coal mine, earning 39 cents for a 10-hour day.

in 1905 calculated that 60 percent of all adult male breadwinners made less than a living wage. Family survival, then, often required women and children to work, often in the lowest-paid, most exploited positions. Poor ventilation, dangerous fumes, open machinery, and the absence of safety programs threatened not only workers' health but their lives as well. Such conditions were gruesomely illustrated in 1911, when a fire killed 146 workers, most of them young women, trapped inside the factory of the Triangle Shirtwaist Company in New York because management had locked the exits. The United States had the highest rate of industrial accidents in the world. Half a million workers were injured and 30,000 killed at work each year. These terrible conditions cried out for reform.

Other Americans saw additional social problems in the continuing flood of immigrants who were transforming America's cities. From 1900 to 1917, more than 14 million immigrants entered the United States. Most of the arrivals were so-called new immigrants from southern and eastern Europe, rather than the British, Irish, Germans, and Scandinavians who had arrived earlier. Several hundred thousand Japanese also arrived, primarily in California, as did increasing numbers of Mexicans. Crowding into urban slums, immigrants overwhelmed municipal sanitation, education, and fire protection services. Many native-born Americans considered the predominantly Catholic and Jewish newcomers a threat to social stability and cultural identity and so demanded programs to reform either the urban environment or the immigrants themselves.

**Social Gospel movement** Movement created by reform-minded Protestant ministers seeking to introduce religious ethics into industrial relations and appealing to churches to meet their social responsibilities.

## Church and Campus

Many groups, drawing from different traditions and inspirations, responded to these economic and social issues. Reform-minded Protestant ministers were especially influential, creating the **Social Gospel movement**, which sought to introduce religious ethics into industrial relations and appealed to churches to meet their social responsibilities. Washington Gladden, a Congregational minister in Columbus, Ohio, was one of the earliest Social Gospelers. Shocked in 1884 by a bloody strike crushed by wealthy members of his own congregation, Gladden began a ministry to working-class neighborhoods that most churches ignored. He endorsed unions and workers' rights and proposed replacing a cruelly competitive wage system with profit sharing. In *Christianity and the Social Crisis* (1907), Walter Rauschenbusch, a Baptist minister who had served impoverished immigrants in New York, argued that Christians should support social reform to alleviate poverty, slums, and labor exploitation.

The Social Gospel was part of an emerging liberal movement in American religion. Scholars associated with this movement discredited the literal accuracy of the Bible and emphasized instead its general moral and ethical lessons. As modernists, they abandoned theological dogmatism for a greater tolerance of other faiths and became more interested in social problems. By linking reform with religion (as "applied Christianity," in the words of Washington Gladden), the Social Gospel movement gave progressivism a powerful moral drive and an ethical justification for government intervention to improve the social order.

Scholars in the social sciences also gradually helped turn public attitudes in favor of reform by challenging the laissez-faire views of the Social Darwinists and traditional academics. In *Applied Sociology* (1906), Lester Ward called for social progress through rational planning and government intervention rather than through unrestrained and unpredictable competition. Economists rejected laissez-faire principles in favor of state action to accomplish social evolution. Industrialization, declared economist Richard T. Ely, "has brought to the front a vast number of social problems whose solution is impossible without the united efforts of church, state, and science."

## Muckrakers

**muckraking** Journalism exposing economic, social, and political evils, so named by Theodore Roosevelt for its "raking the muck" of American society.

Journalists also spread reform ideas by developing a new form of investigative reporting known as **muckraking**. Technological innovations had recently made possible the mass circulation of magazines, and editors competed to attract an expanding urban readership. Samuel S. McClure sent his reporters to uncover political and corporate corruption for *McClure's Magazine*. Sensational exposés sold magazines, and soon *Cosmopolitan, Everybody's,* and other journals began publishing investigations of business abuses, dangerous working conditions, and the miseries of slum life.

Muckraking novels also appeared. *The Octopus* (1901), by Frank Norris, dramatized the Southern Pacific Railroad's stranglehold on California's farmers, and *The Jungle* (1906), by Upton Sinclair, exposed the nauseating conditions in Chicago's meatpacking industry. Such muckraking aroused indignant public demands for reform.

## The Gospel of Efficiency

Many progressive leaders believed that efficiency and expertise could control or resolve the disorder of industrial society. President Theodore Roosevelt praised the "gospel of efficiency." Like many other progressives, he admired the success of corporations in applying management techniques to guide economic growth. Drawing from science and technology as well as from the model of the corporation, many progressives attempted to manage or direct change efficiently. They used scientific methods to collect extensive data and relied on experts for analysis and recommendations. "Scientific management," a concept often used interchangeably with "sound business management," seemed the key to eliminating waste and inefficiency in government, society, and industry.

Business leaders especially advocated efficiency, order, and organization. Industrialists were drawn to the ideas of Frederick Taylor, a proponent of scientific management, for cutting factory labor costs. Taylor proposed to increase worker efficiency through imposed work routines, speedups, and mechanization. Workers, Taylor insisted, should "do what they are told promptly and without asking questions. . . . It is absolutely necessary for every man in our organization to become one of a train of gear wheels." By assigning workers simple and repetitive tasks on machines, Taylorization made their skills expendable and enabled managers to control the production, pace of work, and hiring and firing of personnel. Stripped of their influence and poorly paid, factory workers shared little of the wealth generated by industrial expansion and scientific management. When labor complained, one business leader declared that unions failed "to appreciate the progressivism of the age."

Sophisticated managers of big business saw some forms of government intervention as another way to promote order and efficiency. In particular, they favored regulations that could bring about safer and more stable conditions in society and the economy. Government regulations, they reasoned, could reassure potential consumers, open markets, mandate working conditions that smaller competitors could not provide, or impose systematic procedures that competitive pressures would otherwise undercut.

## Labor Demands Its Rights

Industrial workers with different objectives also hastened the ferment of reform. Workers resisted the new rules of efficiency experts and called for improved wages and working conditions and reduced work hours. They and their middle-class sympathizers sought to achieve some of these goals through state intervention, demanding laws to compensate workers injured on the job, curb child labor, and regulate the employment of women. Sometimes they succeeded. After the Triangle Shirtwaist fire, for example, urban politicians with working-class constituencies created the New York State Factory Commission and enacted dozens of laws dealing with fire hazards, machine safety, and wages and hours for women.

Workers also organized unions to improve their lot. The American Federation of Labor (AFL) claimed 4 million members by 1920, recruiting mainly skilled workers, particularly native-born white males. New unions organized the factories and sweatshops where most immigrants and women worked. Despite strong employer resistance, the International Ladies Garment Workers Union (1900) and the Amalgamated Clothing Workers (1914) organized the garment trades, developed programs for social and economic reforms, and led their members—mostly young Jewish and Italian women—in spectacular strikes.

A still more radical union tried to organize miners, lumberjacks, and Mexican and Japanese farm workers in the West, black dockworkers in the South, and immigrant factory hands in New England. Founded in 1905, the Industrial Workers of the World (IWW), whose members were known as "**Wobblies**," used sit-down strikes, sit-ins, and mass rallies, tactics adopted by other industrial unions in the 1930s and the civil rights movement in the 1960s.

**Wobblies** Popular name for the members of the Industrial Workers of the World (IWW).

## Extending the Woman's Sphere

Women reformers and their organizations played a key role in progressivism. Women responded not merely to the human suffering caused by industrialization and urbanization but also to related changes in their own status and role. By the early twentieth century, more women than before were working outside the home—in the factories, mills, and sweatshops of the industrial economy and as clerks in stores and offices. In 1910, more than one-fourth of all workers were women, increasing numbers of them married. Their importance in the workforce and participation in unions and strikes challenged assumptions that woman's "natural" role was to be a submissive housewife.

Shrinking family size, labor-saving household equipment, and changing social expectations also enabled middle-class women to find more time and opportunities to pursue activities outside the home.

The women's clubs that had begun multiplying in the late nineteenth century became seed-beds of progressive ideas in the early twentieth century. Often founded for cultural purposes, women's clubs soon adopted programs for social reform and gave their members a route to public influence. In 1914, an officer of the General Federation of Women's Clubs proudly declared that every cause for social reform had "received a helpful hand from the clubwomen."

Women also joined or created other organizations that pushed beyond the limits of traditional domesticity. "Woman's place is in the home," observed one progressive, but "no longer is the home encompassed by four walls." By threatening healthy and happy homes, urban problems required that women become "social housekeepers" in the community. The National Consumers' League, founded in 1898, tried to protect both women wage earners and middle-class housewives by monitoring stores and factories to ensure decent working conditions and safe products. The Women's Trade Union League (WTUL, founded in 1903) united working women and their self-styled middle-class "allies" to unionize women workers and eliminate sweatshop conditions.

Although most progressive women stressed women's special duties and responsibilities as social housekeepers, others began to demand women's equal rights. In 1914, for example, critics of New York's policy of dismissing women teachers who married formed a group called the Feminist Alliance and demanded "the removal of all social, political, economic and other discriminations which are based upon sex, and the award of all rights and duties in all fields on the basis of individual capacity alone." With these new organizations and ideas, women gave important impetus and direction to the reform sentiments of the early twentieth century.

## Trans-Atlantic Influences

A major source of America's progressive impulse lay outside its borders. European nations were already grappling with many of the problems that stemmed from industrialization and urbanization, and they provided guidance, examples, and possible solutions. Progressive reformers soon learned that America's political, economic, and social structures made it necessary to modify, adapt, or even abandon these imported ideas, but their influence was obvious.

University study in Europe taught Americans the limits of their traditional laissez-faire attitudes and the possibilities of state action. Trained in Germany, the economist Richard T. Ely returned to academic posts in America to teach that government "is the agency through which we must work." International influences were especially strong in the Social Gospel movement, symbolized by William T. Stead, a British social evangelist, whose idea of a "Civic Church" (a partnership of churches and reformers) captured great attention in the United States. Muckrakers not only exposed American problems but also looked for foreign solutions. *Everybody's* sent Charles E. Russell around the world in 1905 to describe the social advances in Europe and New Zealand.

By 1912, American consumer activists, trade unionists, factory inspectors, and feminists regularly participated in international conferences on labor legislation, child welfare, social insurance, and housing reform and returned home with new ideas and strategies. State governments organized commissions to analyze European policies and agencies for lessons that might be applicable in the United States.

## Socialism

The growing influence of socialist ideas also promoted the spirit of progressivism. Socialism never attracted a large following in the United States, but its criticism of the industrial economy gained increasing attention in the early twentieth century. American socialists condemned social and economic inequities, criticized limited government, and demanded public ownership of railroads, utilities, and communications. They also campaigned for tax reforms, better housing, factory inspections, and recreational facilities for all.

The most prominent socialist was the dynamic and engaging Eugene V. Debs. An Indiana labor leader who had converted to socialism while imprisoned for his role in the 1894 Pullman strike, Debs had evangelical energy and a generous spirit. He decried what he saw as the dehumanization produced by industrial capitalism and hoped for an egalitarian society where everyone would have the opportunity "to develop the best there is in him for his own good as well as the good of society."

In 1901, Debs helped organize the Socialist Party of America; thereafter, he worked tirelessly to attract followers to a vision of socialism deeply rooted in American political and religious traditions. In the next decade, the party won many local elections, especially in Wisconsin and New York, where it drew support from German and Russian immigrants, and in Oklahoma, where it attracted poor tenant farmers.

Most progressives considered socialist ideas too drastic. Nevertheless, socialists contributed importantly to the reform ferment, not only by providing support for reform initiatives but often also by prompting progressives to push for changes to undercut increasingly attractive radical alternatives.

## Opponents of Reform

Not all Americans supported progressive reforms. Social Gospelers, for example, faced opposition from Protestant traditionalists emphasizing what they termed fundamental beliefs. Particularly strong among evangelical denominations with rural roots, these **fundamentalists** stressed personal salvation rather than social reform. "To attempt reform in the black depths of the great city," said one, "would be as useless as trying to purify the ocean by pouring into it a few gallons of spring water." Indeed, the urban and industrial crises that inspired Social Gospelers to preach reform drove many evangelical leaders to endorse social and political conservatism. The evangelist Billy Sunday denounced labor unions, women's rights, and business regulation as violating traditional values and condemned the Social Gospel as "godless social service nonsense."

Muckrakers also encountered opposition. Business interests, angered by exposés of corporate abuse and corruption, attacked the muckrakers. Business groups such as the American Bankers' Association accused muckrakers of promoting socialism. Major corporations like Standard Oil created public relations bureaus to improve their image and identify business, not its critics, with the public interest. Advertising boycotts discouraged magazines from running critical stories, and credit restrictions forced some muckraking journals to suspend publication. By 1910, the heyday of muckraking was over.

Labor unions likewise encountered resistance. Led by the National Association of Manufacturers, business groups denounced unions as corrupt and radical, hired thugs to disrupt them, organized strike-breaking agencies, and used blacklists to eliminate union activists. The antiunion campaign peaked in Ludlow, Colorado, in 1914, when John D. Rockefeller's Colorado Fuel and Iron Company used armed guards and the state militia to shoot and burn striking workers and their families. The courts aided employers by issuing injunctions against strikes and prohibiting unions from using boycotts, one of their most effective weapons.

Progressives campaigning for government intervention and regulation also met stiff resistance. Many Americans objected to what they considered unwarranted interference in private economic matters. Again, the courts often supported these attitudes. In *Lochner v. New York* (1905), the Supreme Court even overturned a maximum-hours law on the grounds that it deprived employers and employees of their "freedom of contract." Progressives continually struggled against such opponents, and progressive achievements were limited by the persistence and influence of their adversaries.

**fundamentalists** Religious conservatives who believe in the literal accuracy and divine inspiration of the Bible.

# Reforming Society

**21.2** How did progressives respond to the social challenges of industrializing America?

With their varied motives and objectives, progressives worked to transform society by improving living conditions, educational opportunities, family life, and social and industrial relations (see Table 21.2). They sought what they called social justice, but their plans for social reform sometimes also smacked of social control. Organized women dominated the movement to reform society, but they were supported, depending on the goal, by Social Gospel ministers, social scientists, urban immigrants, labor unions, and even some conservatives eager to regulate personal behavior.

## Settlement Houses and Urban Reform

The spearheads for social reform were settlement houses—community centers in urban immigrant neighborhoods. Reformers created 400 settlement houses, largely modeled after Hull House in Chicago, founded in 1889 by Jane Addams. Settlement houses often reflected the ideals of the Social Gospel. "A simple acceptance of Christ's message and methods," wrote Addams, "is what a settlement should stand for." In the South, Methodists, led by the Woman's Board of Home Missions, dominated the settlement movement and often combined social services and evangelism. Outside the South, however, most settlements were secular institutions, avoiding religion to gain the trust of Catholic and Jewish immigrants.

Settlements were generally led and staffed by middle-class young women, seeking to alleviate poverty and do useful professional work when most careers were closed to them. Settlement work did not immediately violate prescribed gender roles because it initially focused on the "woman's sphere"—family, education, domestic skills, and cultural "uplift." Settlement workers, however, soon saw that the root problem for immigrants was widespread poverty that required more than changes in individual behavior. Unlike earlier reformers, they regarded many of the evils of poverty as products of the social environment rather than of moral weakness. Thus, they campaigned for stricter

**TABLE 21.2  MAJOR LAWS AND CONSTITUTIONAL AMENDMENTS OF THE PROGRESSIVE ERA**

| Legislation | Effect |
|---|---|
| New York Tenement House Law (1901) | Established a model housing code for safety and sanitation |
| Newlands Act (1902) | Provided for federal irrigation projects |
| Hepburn Act (1906) | Strengthened the Interstate Commerce Commission |
| Pure Food and Drug Act (1906) | Regulated the production and sale of food and drug products |
| Meat Inspection Act (1906) | Authorized federal inspection of meat products |
| Sixteenth Amendment (1913) | Authorized a federal income tax |
| Seventeenth Amendment (1913) | Mandated the direct popular election of senators |
| Underwood-Simmons Tariff Act (1913) | Lowered tariff rates and levied the first regular federal income tax |
| Federal Reserve Act (1913) | Established the Federal Reserve System to supervise banking and provide a national currency |
| Federal Trade Commission Act (1914) | Established the FTC to oversee business activities |
| Harrison Act (1914) | Regulated the distribution and use of narcotics |
| Smith-Lever Act (1914) | Institutionalized the county agent system |
| Keating-Owen Act (1916) | Indirectly prohibited child labor |
| Eighteenth Amendment (1919) | Instituted prohibition |
| Nineteenth Amendment (1920) | Established woman suffrage |

building codes to improve slums, better urban sanitation systems to enhance public health, public parks to revive the urban environment, and laws to protect women and children.

The crusades of settlement workers for sanitation and housing reform demonstrated the impact that social reformers often had on urban life. Settlement worker Mary McDowell gained renown as the "Garbage Lady" for her successful campaign against the open garbage dumps and polluted sewers in Chicago. Lawrence Veiller used settlement workers to investigate housing conditions in New York's congested slums and agitate for improvements. In 1901, the New York Tenement House Law incorporated his proposals to limit the size of tenements and require toilet facilities, ventilation, and fire protection and became a model for other cities.

## Protective Legislation for Women and Children

While settlement workers initially undertook private efforts to improve society, many reformers eventually concluded that only government intervention could achieve social justice. The maiming and killing of children in industrial accidents made it "inevitable," Addams said, "that efforts to secure a child labor law should be our first venture into the field of state legislation." The National Child Labor Committee, organized in 1904, led the campaign to curtail child labor. Reformers documented the problem with extensive investigations and also benefited from the public outrage stirred by Mother Jones's "children crusade" and by socialist John Spargo's muckraking book *The Bitter Cry of the Children* (1906). They had to overcome stiff resistance from manufacturers who used child labor, conservatives who opposed government action as an intrusion into family life, and some poor parents who needed their children's income. In 1900, most states had no minimum working age; by 1914, every state but one had such a law. Effective regulation, however, required national action, for many state laws were weak or poorly enforced.

Social reformers also lobbied for laws regulating the wages, hours, and working conditions of women and succeeded in having states from New York to Oregon pass maximum-hours legislation. After the Supreme Court upheld such laws in *Muller v. Oregon* (1908), thirty-nine states enacted new or stronger laws on women's maximum hours between 1909 and 1917. Eight midwestern and western states set minimum wages for women, but few other states followed.

Protective legislation for women posed a troubling issue for reformers. In California, for example, middle-class clubwomen favored protective legislation on the grounds of women's presumed weakness. They wanted to preserve "California's potential motherhood." More radical progressives, as in the socialist-led Women's Trade Union League of Los Angeles, supported such legislation to help secure economic independence and equality in the labor market for women, increase the economic strength of the working class, and serve as a precedent for laws improving conditions for all workers.

Progressive Era lawmakers adopted the first viewpoint. They limited protective legislation to measures reflecting the belief that women needed paternalist protection, even by excluding them from certain occupations. Laws establishing a minimum wage for women, moreover, usually set a wage level below subsistence rates. Rather than ensuring women's economic independence, then, protective legislation in practice reinforced women's subordinate place in the labor force.

Protective legislation for male workers scarcely existed. Both lawmakers and judges rebuffed demands for the protection of all workers while approving reforms that endorsed inequality. Only in very dangerous industries did male workers gain much protection, due primarily to the relentless efforts of labor unions. The Western Federation of Miners persuaded several states that the extraordinary occupational hazards of mining—cave-ins, explosions, poisonous gasses, silicosis and other diseases—required laws regulating hours and conditions of work.

Social justice reformers forged the beginnings of the welfare state in further legislation. Prompted by both humanitarian and paternalistic urgings, many states began

(( Read the Document   Jane Addams, from *Twenty Years at Hull House* (1910)

Julia Lathrop, Jane Addams, and Mary McDowell in Washington, DC, in 1913. Important figures in Chicago settlement houses, these women gained national influence by expanding their activities to encompass a wide range of reform activities.

in 1910 to provide "mothers' pensions" to indigent widows with dependent children. Twenty-one states, led by Wisconsin in 1911, enacted workers' compensation programs, ending the custom of holding workers themselves liable for injuries on the job.

Compared to the social insurance programs in Western Europe, however, these were feeble responses to the social consequences of industrialization. Proposals for health insurance, unemployment insurance, and old-age pension programs went nowhere. Business groups and other conservative interests curbed the movement toward state responsibility for social welfare.

## Reshaping Public Education

Concerns about child labor overlapped with increasing attention to the public schools. The rapid influx of immigrants, as well as the demands of the new corporate workplace, generated interest in education not only as a means of advancement but also as a tool for assimilation and the training of future workers.

Between 1880 and 1920, compulsory school attendance laws, kindergartens, age-graded elementary schools, professional training for teachers, vocational education, parent-teacher associations, and school nurses became standard elements in American education. School reformers regarded these measures as both educationally sound and important for countering slum environments. As Jacob Riis contended, the kindergartner would "rediscover . . . the natural feelings that the tenement had smothered." Others supported the kindergarten as "the earliest opportunity to catch the little Russian, the little Italian, the little German, Pole, Syrian, and the rest and begin to make good American citizens of them."

Public education in the South lagged behind. Northern philanthropy and southern reformers brought some improvements after 1900, as per capita expenditures for education doubled, school terms were extended, and high schools spread across the region. But the South frittered away its limited resources on a segregated educational system that shortchanged both races. Black southerners particularly suffered, for the new programs increased the disparity in funding for white and black schools. South Carolina spent twelve times as much per white pupil as per black pupil.

Racism also underlay important changes in the schooling of Native Americans. The earlier belief that education would promote equality and facilitate assimilation gave way to a conviction that Indians were inferior and fit merely for manual labor. Educators now rejected the notion of a common school education for Indian children in favor of manual training that would enable Indians to fill menial jobs and whites to "turn their attention to more intellectual employments." Educators also renounced the practice of integrating Indian children into previously all-white classrooms, a policy begun in 1891. Critics futilely noted that limiting Indian children to a rudimentary and segregated education merely doomed them to the margins of American society.

## Challenging Gender Restrictions

Most reformers held fairly conservative, moralistic views about sexuality and gender roles, but a small group of influential women sharply challenged conventional ideas about the social role of women. In critiquing women's subordinate status in society and articulating the case for full female equality, these women began self-consciously to refer to themselves as "feminists."

In *Women and Economics* (1898) and subsequent writings, Charlotte Perkins Gilman maintained that a communally organized society, with cooperative kitchens, nurseries, laundries, and housekeeping run by specialists, would free women from domestic drudgery and enable them to fulfill productive roles in the larger society while being happier wives and better mothers. Emma Goldman, a charismatic speaker (and celebrated anarchist), delivered lectures attacking marriage as legalized prostitution rather than a partnership of independent equals and advocating birth control as a means to willing and "healthy motherhood and happy child-life."

Margaret Sanger, a public-health nurse and an IWW organizer, soon made the struggle for reproductive rights her personal crusade. Sanger saw in New York's immigrant neighborhoods the plight of poor women worn out from repeated pregnancies or injured or dead from self-induced knitting-needle abortions. Despite federal and state laws against contraceptives, Sanger began promoting birth control as a way to avert such tragedies. Prohibiting contraceptives meant "enforced motherhood," Sanger declared. "Women cannot be on an equal footing with men until they have full and complete control over their reproductive function."

Sanger's crusade attracted support from many women's and labor groups, but it also infuriated those who regarded birth control as a threat to the family and morality. Indicted for distributing information about contraception, Sanger fled to Europe. Other women took up the cause, forming the National Birth Control League in 1915 to campaign for the repeal of laws restricting access to contraceptive information and devices.

## Reforming Country Life

Although most progressives focused on the city, others sought to reform rural life, both to modernize its social and economic conditions and to integrate it more fully into the larger society. They worked to improve rural health and sanitation, to replace inefficient one-room schools with modern consolidated ones under professional control, and to extend new roads and communication services into the countryside. To further these goals, President Theodore Roosevelt created the Country Life Commission in 1908. The country lifers had a broad program for social and economic change, involving expanded government functions, activist government agencies staffed by experts, and the professionalization of rural social services.

Agricultural scientists, government officials, and many business interests also sought to promote efficient, scientific, and commercial agriculture. A key innovation was the county-agent system: The U.S. Department of Agriculture and business groups placed an agent in each county to teach farmers new techniques and to encourage changes in the rural social values that had previously spawned the Populist radicalism that most progressives decried. The Smith-Lever Act (1914) provided federal subsidies for county agents throughout the country.

Few farmers, however, welcomed these efforts. As one Illinois county agent said in 1915, "Farmers, as a whole, resent exceedingly those forces which are at work with missionary intent trying to uplift them." School consolidation meant the loss of community control of education; good roads would raise taxes and chiefly benefit urban business interests. Besides, most farmers believed that their problems stemmed not from rural life, but from industrial society and its nefarious trusts, banks, and middlemen. Rural Americans did not want their lives revolutionized.

Even so, rural people were drawn into the larger urban-industrial society during the Progressive Era. Government agencies, agricultural colleges, and railroads and banks steadily tied farmers to urban markets. Telephones and rural free delivery of mail lessened countryside isolation but quickened the spread of city values. Improved roads and the coming of the automobile eliminated many rural villages and linked farm families directly with towns and cities. Consolidated schools wiped out the social center of rural neighborhoods and carried children out of their communities, eventually encouraging an ever-growing migration to the city.

## Moral Crusades and Social Control

Moral reform movements, although often appearing misguided or unduly coercive today, generally reflected the progressive hope to protect people in a debilitating environment. In practice, however, these efforts to shape society tended toward social control. Moreover, these efforts often meshed with the restrictive attitudes that conservative Americans held about race, religion, immigration, and morality. The result was widespread attempts to restrict certain groups and control behavior.

**Controlling Immigrants.** Many Americans wanted to limit immigration for racist reasons. Nativist agitation in California prompted the federal government to secure restrictions on Japanese immigration in 1907. Californians, including local progressives, also hoped to curtail the migration of Mexicans.

Nationally, public debate focused on restricting the flow of new immigrants from southern and eastern Europe. Some labor leaders believed that immigration held down wages and impeded unionization; many sociologists thought it created serious social problems; other Americans disliked the newcomers on religious, cultural, or ethnic grounds. Many backed their prejudice with a distorted interpretation of Darwinism, labeling the Slavic and Mediterranean peoples "inferior races." In 1917 nativists persuaded Congress to require a literacy test for admission, expecting it to exclude such immigrants.

Other nativists demanded the "Americanization" of immigrants already in the country. The Daughters of the American Revolution sought to inculcate loyalty, patriotism, and conservative values. Settlement workers and Social Gospelers promoted a gentler kind of Americanization through English classes and home mission campaigns, but they too attempted to transfer their own values to the newcomers. In Texas, settlements targeted Mexican immigrants under the slogan "Americanizing and Christianizing."

**Prohibition.** Closely linked to progressives' worries about immigrants was their campaign for **prohibition**. This movement engaged many of the progressives' basic impulses. Social workers saw liquor as a cause of crime, poverty, and family violence; employers blamed it for causing industrial accidents and inefficiency; Social Gospel ministers condemned the "spirit born of hell" because it impaired moral judgment and behavior. But also important was native-born Americans' fear of new immigrants—"the dangerous classes, who are readily dominated by the saloon." Many immigrants, in fact, viewed liquor and the neighborhood saloon as vital parts of daily life, and so prohibition became a focus of nativist hostility, cultural conflict, and Americanization pressures. In the South, racism also figured prominently. Alexander McKelway, the southern secretary for the National Child Labor Committee, endorsed prohibition as a way to maintain social order and white supremacy.

Protestant fundamentalists stoutly supported prohibition, working through the Anti-Saloon League, founded in 1893. Their nativism and antiurban bias surfaced in demands for prohibition to "flush out the cesspools of cities and so save civilization from pollution."

With these varied motivations, prohibitionists campaigned for local and state laws against the manufacture and sale of alcohol. Beginning in 1907, they proved increasingly successful, especially in the South and Midwest. By 1917, twenty-six states had prohibition laws. Congress then approved the **Eighteenth Amendment**. Ratified in 1919, it made prohibition the law of the land.

Less controversial were drives to control or prohibit narcotics and cigarettes. Patent (over-the-counter) medicines commonly contained opium, heroin, and cocaine (popularly used for hay fever), and physicians known as "dope doctors" openly dispensed drugs to paying customers. Fears that addiction was spreading in "the fallen and lower classes" prompted Congress in 1914 to pass the Harrison Act, prohibiting the distribution and use of narcotics for other than medicinal purposes. The Anti-Cigarette League of America, organized in 1899 and having 300,000 members by 1901, led the charge against "the devil's toothpicks." Many states soon restricted cigarettes, but such laws were rarely enforced and were often repealed within a few years.

**Suppressing Prostitution.** Reformers also sought to suppress the "social evil" of prostitution. Like crowded slums, sweatshops, and child labor, the "vice districts" where prostitution flourished were seen as part of the exploitation and disorder in the industrial cities. Women's low wages as factory workers and domestic servants explained some of the problem, as a muckraking article entitled "The Daughters of the Poor" pointed out. But nativism spurred public concern, as when New York officials insisted that most brothel owners, some of whom "have been seducers of defenseless women all their lives," were foreign-born.

The response to prostitution was typical of progressivism: investigation and exposure, a reliance upon experts—boards of health, medical groups, clergy—for recommendations, and enactment of new laws. State and municipal legislation abolished the "red-light" districts previously tolerated, and a federal law, the Mann Act of 1910, prohibited the interstate transport of women "for immoral purposes."

**Regulating Entertainment** Some progressives sought to control new forms of popular entertainment emerging in the cities that differed from the church socials, Sunday-school picnics, and other older forms of recreation that revolved around the community and family. Commercial entertainments like dance halls and nickelodeons not only brought young men and women together without family supervision, but,

**prohibition** A ban on the production, transportation, and sale of liquor, achieved temporarily through state laws and the Eighteenth Amendment.

**Eighteenth Amendment** Constitutional revision, adopted in 1919, that prohibited the production and sale of alcohol in the United States.

in seeming to emphasize sex and sexuality, also flaunted middle-class notions of propriety. Condemning movie theaters as "recruiting stations of vice," progressives successfully campaigned to prohibit unaccompanied children from theaters and to establish censorship boards that cut from films any hint of smoking, drinking, or other "improper" behavior. Chicago in 1906 banned any films depicting "crime, criminals, and immoral scenes which appeal to small boys and weak-minded adults." Reacting against ragtime music and suggestive dances, the Juvenile Protective Association and other progressive organizations publicized "Rules for Correct Dancing" and persuaded cities to regulate dance halls.

Such efforts had only mixed success, but California vividly illustrated the progressive pursuit of social control and moral reform. The state assembly, described as "a legislature of progressive cranks," prohibited gambling, card-playing, and prizefighting. Los Angeles—influenced by the aptly named Morals Efficiency League—banned premarital sex and introduced censorship of art. One critic in 1913 complained that the reformers' "frenzy of virtue" made "Puritanism . . . the inflexible doctrine of Los Angeles."

## For Whites Only?

Racism permeated the Progressive Era. In the South, progressivism was built on black disfranchisement and segregation. Like most white southerners, progressives believed that racial control was necessary for social order and that it enabled reformers to address other social problems. Such reformers also invoked racism to gain popular support for their objectives. In Georgia, for instance, child labor reformers warned that while white children worked in the Piedmont textile mills, black children were going to school: Child labor laws and compulsory school attendance laws were necessary to maintain white supremacy.

Governors Hoke Smith of Georgia and James Vardaman, "the White Chief," of Mississippi typified the link between racism and reform in the South. These men supported progressive reforms but also viciously attacked black rights. Their racist demagogy incited antiblack violence throughout the South.

Even in the North, race relations deteriorated. Civil rights laws went unenforced, restaurants and hotels excluded black customers, and schools were segregated. A reporter in Pennsylvania found that "this disposition to discriminate against Negroes has greatly increased within the past decade." Few progressives expressed concern for such racial inequities. Even most Social Gospel ministers ignored the issue, as did the muckrakers. And antiblack race riots exploded in New York in 1900 and in Springfield, Illinois—Abraham Lincoln's hometown—in 1908.

**Black Activism.** Although most white progressives promoted or accepted racial discrimination, and most black southerners had to adapt to it, black progressive activism was growing. Even in the South, some African Americans struggled to improve conditions. In Atlanta, for example, black women created progressive organizations and established settlement houses, kindergartens, and daycare centers. On a broader scale, in twenty-five cities from Richmond to San Antonio, African Americans engaged in massive boycotts against segregated streetcars between 1900 and 1906. They had only limited success, but their efforts demonstrated a persisting commitment to reforming society.

In the North, African Americans more openly criticized discrimination and rejected Booker T. Washington's philosophy of accommodation. Ida Wells-Barnett, the crusading journalist who had fled the South for Chicago (see Chapter 17), became nationally prominent for her militant protests against racial injustices. She also agitated for woman suffrage and organized kindergartens and settlement houses for Chicago's black migrants.

Still more important was W. E. B. Du Bois, who campaigned tirelessly against all forms of racial discrimination. In 1905, Du Bois and other black activists met in Niagara

📖 **Read the Document** Platform Adopted by the National Negro Committee (1909)

The Flanner House, a black settlement house in Indianapolis, provided the black community with many essential services, including health care. In addition to this baby clinic, pictured in 1918, it established a tuberculosis clinic at a time when the city's public hospitals refused to treat black citizens afflicted with the disease.

SOURCE: Indiana Historical Society, M0513.

Falls, Canada, to make plans to promote political and economic equality. In 1910, this **Niagara Movement** joined with a small group of white reformers, including Jane Addams, to organize the National Association for the Advancement of Colored People (NAACP). The NAACP sought to overthrow segregation and establish equal justice and educational opportunities. As its director of publicity and research, Du Bois launched an influential magazine, *The Crisis,* to shape public opinion. "Agitate," he counseled, "protest, reveal the truth, and refuse to be silenced." By 1918, the NAACP had 44,000 members in 165 branches. Two generations later, it would successfully challenge the racial discrimination that most early-twentieth-century white progressives either supported or tolerated.

**Niagara Movement** African American group organized in 1905 to promote racial integration, civil and political rights, and equal access to economic opportunity.

# Reforming Politics and Government

**21.3** How did progressives change American politics and government?

Progressives of all kinds worked to reform politics and government. But their political activism was motivated by different concerns, and they sometimes pursued competing objectives. Many wanted to change procedures and institutions to promote greater democracy and responsibility. Others hoped to improve the efficiency of government, eliminate corruption, or increase their own influence. All justified their objectives as necessary to adapt the political system to the nation's new needs.

## Woman Suffrage

One of the most important achievements of the era was woman suffrage. The movement had begun in the mid-nineteenth century, but suffragists had been frustrated by the prevailing belief that women's proper sphere was the home and the family. Males dominated the public sphere, including voting. Woman suffrage, especially when

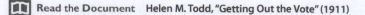

Read the Document    Helen M. Todd, "Getting Out the Vote" (1911)

Carrying ballot boxes on a stretcher to ridicule American pretensions to a healthy democracy without woman suffrage, these activists marched in a dramatic parade in New York City in 1915. Combining such tactics with traditional appeals to patriotism and women's moral purity, woman suffragists eventually achieved the greatest democratic reform of the Progressive Era.

championed as a step toward women's equality, seemed to challenge the natural order of society, and it generated much opposition.

Most women progressives viewed suffrage as the key issue of the period. Already taking active leadership in broad areas of public affairs—especially by confronting and publicizing social problems and then lobbying legislators and other officials to adopt their proposed solutions—they thought it ridiculous to be barred from the ballot box. But most of all, the vote meant power, both to convince politicians to take seriously their demands for social reforms and to participate fully in electoral as in other forms of politics, thereby advancing the status of women.

In the early twentieth century, suffragists began to outflank their traditional opposition. Under a new generation of leaders, such as Carrie Chapman Catt and Harriot Stanton Blatch, they adopted activist tactics, including parades, mass meetings, and "suffrage tours" by automobile. They also organized by political districts and attracted working women and labor unions. By 1917, the National American Woman Suffrage Association had more than 2 million members.

Some suffrage leaders adopted new arguments to gain more support. Rather than insisting on the justice of woman suffrage or emphasizing equal rights, they spoke of the special moral and maternal instincts women could bring to politics if allowed to vote. Many suffragists, particularly among working-class groups, remained committed to the larger possibilities they saw in suffrage, but the new image of the movement increased public support by appealing to conventional views of women.

Gradually, the suffrage movement began to prevail (see Map 21.1). In 1910, Washington became the first state since the mid-1890s to approve woman suffrage, followed by California in 1911 and Arizona, Kansas, and Oregon in 1912. Suffragists also campaigned for a federal constitutional amendment to grant women the vote, and women sent petitions and organized pilgrimages to Washington from across the country. By 1919, thirty-nine states had established full or partial woman suffrage, and Congress finally approved an amendment. Ratified by the states in 1920, the **Nineteenth Amendment** marked a critical advance in political democracy.

**Nineteenth Amendment**
Constitutional revision that in 1920 established women citizens' right to vote.

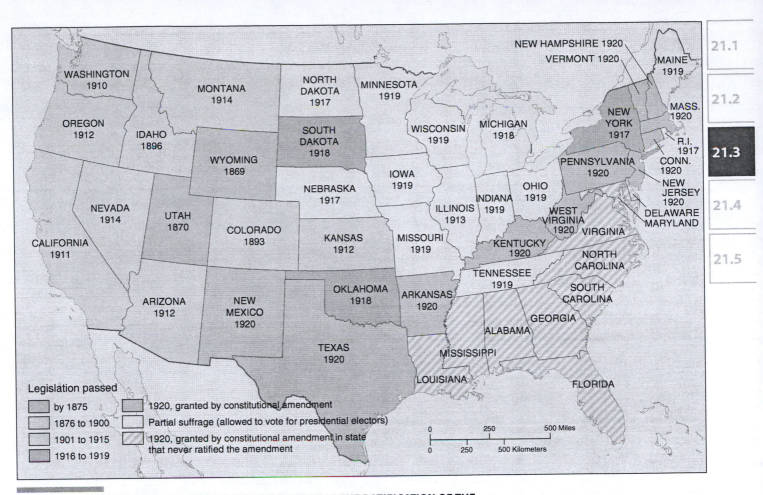

**MAP 21.1  WOMAN SUFFRAGE IN THE UNITED STATES BEFORE THE RATIFICATION OF THE NINETEENTH AMENDMENT** Beginning with Wyoming in 1869, woman suffrage slowly gained acceptance in the West, but women in the South and much of the East got the ballot only when the Nineteenth Amendment was ratified in 1920.

## Electoral Reform

Other electoral reforms changed the election process and the meaning of political participation. The so-called **Australian ballot** adopted by most states during the 1890s provided for official ballots and secret voting, freeing voters from intimidation and discouraging vote buying and other corruption.

**Australian ballot** Secret voting and the use of official ballots rather than party tickets.

Government responsibility for the ballot soon led to public regulation of other parts of the electoral process previously controlled by parties. Beginning with Mississippi in 1902, nearly every state provided for direct primaries to remove nominations from the boss-ridden caucus and convention system. Many states also reformed campaign practices.

These reforms weakened the influence of political parties. Their decreasing ability to mobilize voters was reflected in a steady decline in voter participation, from 79 percent in 1896 to 49 percent in 1920. These developments had ominous implications, for parties and voting had traditionally linked ordinary Americans to their government. As parties slowly contracted, nonpartisan organizations and pressure groups, promoting narrower objectives, gained influence. The U.S. Chamber of Commerce, for instance, organized in 1912 to lobby for business goals. Many of these special-interest groups represented the same middle- or upper-class interests that had led the attack on parties. Their organized lobbying would steadily give them greater influence over government and contribute to the declining popular belief in the value of voting or participation in politics.

Disfranchisement more obviously undermined American democracy. In the South, Democrats—progressive and conservative alike—eliminated not only black voters but also many poor white voters from the electorate through poll taxes, literacy tests, and other restrictions. Republicans in the North adopted educational or literacy tests in ten states, enacted strict registration laws, and gradually abolished the right of aliens to

# ✳ Explore the Age of Progressivism on MyHistoryLab

## WHAT MARKED THE PROGRESSIVE ERA IN THE UNITED STATES?

In the first couple decades of the 1900s, the Progressive movement played an important role in American politics. To define the movement is difficult because it was composed of numerous different reform movements, ranging from one calling for the establishment of safety regulations for food to another advocating the creation of new national parks. Its believers stretched across political party lines. The main unifying feature of the progressives was the belief in the power of government to improve society. Two progressive campaigns

This storefront office in Cleveland, Ohio, as well as its signage, shows how well organized the woman suffrage movement had become by 1912. Here women show their support for an amendment to the state constitution to give them the right to vote. The right to vote in national elections would not come until 1920, with the ratification of the Nineteenth Amendment to the U.S. Consituton.

in particular—the movement for woman suffrage and another for the prohibition of spirituous liquors—marked the period. Both campaigns were successful, though Prohibition, which was extremely controversial, failed in the end. Most presidential candidates of the major parties during the period were progressives, although after his 1908 election, Taft came to be recognized as more a conservative than a progressive.

## PROGRESSIVE CANDIDATES FOR PRESIDENT

| Election | Republican Party | Democratic Party | Progressive Party | Socialist Party of America |
|---|---|---|---|---|
| 1900 | **William McKinley** | William Jennings Bryan* | | |
| 1904 | **Theodore Roosevelt*** | Alton B. Parker | | Eugene V. Debs |
| 1908 | **William Howard Taft*** | William Jennings Bryan* | | Eugene V. Debs |
| 1912 | William Howard Taft | **Woodrow Wilson*** | Theodore Roosevelt* | Eugene V. Debs |
| 1916 | Charles E Hughes* | **Woodrow Wilson*** | | |
| 1920 | **Warren G. Harding** | James M. Cox* | | |

Winner is in bold.

Asterisk indicates progressive candidate.

SOURCE: National Archives and Record Administration, http://www.archives.gov/federal-register/electoral-college/scores.html#1892.

**KEY QUESTIONS** Use **MyHistoryLab** *Explorer* **to answer** these **questions:**

**Analysis ▶▶▶** *Along what lines did the regional vote for president fall during this period?*

Consider the role of Progressivism in national politics.

**Response ▶▶▶** *Where were Prohibition laws more common?* Map the popularity of the ban on alcohol.

**Consequence ▶▶▶** *How did opinions on woman suffrage differ by region?* Chart the development of legislation granting women's right to vote across states.

vote. These restrictions reflected both the progressives' anti-immigrant prejudices and their obsessions with social control and with purifying politics and "improving" the electorate. Such electoral reforms reduced the political power of ethnic and working-class Americans, often stripping them of their political rights and means of influence.

## Municipal Reform

Antiparty attitudes also shaped progressives' efforts to reform municipal government, which they regarded as inefficient and corrupt, at least partly because of the power of urban political machines. Muckrakers had exposed crooked alliances between city bosses and business leaders that resulted in wasteful or inadequate municipal services. In some cities, urban reformers attempted to break these alliances and improve public services. Socialist mayors, elected in hundreds of towns and cities, successfully championed public ownership of utilities.

More elitist progressives changed the structure of urban government by replacing ward elections, which could be controlled by the neighborhood-based city machine, with at-large elections. To win citywide elections required greater resources and therefore helped swell middle-class influence at the expense of the working class. So did nonpartisan elections, which reformers introduced to weaken party loyalties.

Urban reformers developed two other structural innovations: the city commission and the city manager. Both attempted to institutionalize efficient, businesslike government staffed by professional administrators. By 1920, hundreds of cities had adopted one of the new plans, which business groups often promoted. Again, then, reform often shifted political power from ethnic and working-class voters, represented however imperfectly by partisan elections, to smaller groups with greater resources.

## Progressive State Government

Progressives also reshaped state government. Some tried to democratize the legislative process, regarding the legislature—the most important branch of state government in the nineteenth century—as ineffective and even corrupt, dominated by party bosses and corporate influences. The Populists had first raised such charges in the 1890s and proposed two novel solutions. The **initiative** enabled reformers to propose legislation directly to the electorate, bypassing an unresponsive legislature; the **referendum** permitted voters to approve or reject legislative measures. South Dakota Populists established the first system of "direct legislation" in 1898, and progressives adopted these innovations in twenty other states between 1902 and 1915.

Other innovations also expanded the popular role in state government. The **Seventeenth Amendment**, ratified in 1913, provided for the election of U.S. senators directly by popular vote instead of by state legislatures. Beginning with Oregon in 1908, ten states adopted the **recall**, enabling voters to remove unsatisfactory public officials from office.

As state legislatures and party machines were curbed, dynamic governors such as Robert La Follette in Wisconsin, Charles Evans Hughes in New York, and Hiram Johnson in California pushed progressive programs into law. Elected governor in 1900, "Fighting Bob" La Follette turned Wisconsin into "the laboratory of democracy." Overcoming fierce opposition from "stalwart" Republicans, La Follette established direct primaries, railroad regulation, the first state income tax, workers' compensation, and other important measures before being elected to the U.S. Senate in 1906. La Follette also stressed efficiency and expertise. The Legislative Reference Bureau that he created to advise on public policy was staffed by university professors. He used regulatory commissions to oversee railroads, banks, and other interests. Most states followed suit, and expert commissions became an important feature of state government, gradually gaining authority at the expense of elected local officials.

"Experts" were presumed to be disinterested and therefore committed to the general welfare. In practice, however, regulators were subject to pressures from competing

**initiative** Procedure by which citizens can introduce a subject for legislation, usually through a petition signed by a specific number of voters.

**referendum** Submission of a law, proposed or already in effect, to a direct popular vote for approval or rejection.

**Seventeenth Amendment** Constitutional change in 1913 that established the direct popular election of U.S. senators.

**recall** The process of removing an official from office by popular vote, usually after using petitions to call for such a vote.

interest groups, and some commissions became captives of the very industries they were supposed to control. This irony was matched by the contradiction between the expansion of democracy through the initiative and referendum and the increasing reliance on nonelected professional experts to set and implement public policy. Such inconsistencies emphasized the complex mixture of ideas, objectives, and groups that were reshaping politics and government.

# Theodore Roosevelt and the Progressive Presidency

**21.4** How did Theodore Roosevelt's view of the presidency shape his administration?

When an anarchist assassinated William McKinley in 1901, Theodore Roosevelt entered the White House, and the progressive movement gained its most prominent leader. The son of a wealthy New York family, Roosevelt had pursued a career in Republican politics, serving as a New York legislator, U.S. civil service commissioner, and assistant secretary of the navy. After his exploits in the Spanish-American War (see Chapter 22), he was elected governor of New York in 1898 and vice president in 1900. Roosevelt's flamboyance and ambitions made him the most popular politician of the time, and enabled him to dramatize the issues of progressivism and to become the first modern president.

## TR and the Modern Presidency

Roosevelt rejected the limited role of Gilded Age presidents. He believed that the president could do anything to meet national needs that the Constitution did not specifically prohibit. "Under this interpretation of executive power," he later recalled, "I did and caused to be done many things not previously done." Indeed, the expansion of government power and its consolidation in the executive branch were among his most significant accomplishments.

Rather than defer to Congress, Roosevelt exerted legislative leadership. He spelled out his policy goals in more than 400 messages to Congress, sent drafts of bills to Capitol Hill, and intervened to win passage of "his" measures. Some members of Congress resented his "executive arrogance" and "dictatorship." Roosevelt generally avoided direct challenges to the conservative Old Guard Republicans who controlled Congress, but his activities helped shift the balance of power within the national government.

Roosevelt also reorganized the executive branch. He believed in efficiency and expertise, which he attempted to institutionalize in special commissions and administrative procedures. To promote rational policymaking and public management, he staffed the expanding federal bureaucracy with able professionals. Here, too, he provoked opposition. The president, complained one Republican, was "trying to concentrate all power in Washington . . . and to govern the people by commissions and bureaus."

Finally, Roosevelt encouraged the development of a personal presidency by exploiting the public's interest in their exuberant young president. He established the first White House press room and skillfully handled the mass media. His endless and well-reported activities, from playing with his children in the White House to wrestling, hiking, and horseback riding, made him a celebrity, known as TR or Teddy. The publicity not only kept TR in the spotlight but also enabled him to mold public opinion.

## Roosevelt and Labor

TR demonstrated his vigorous new approach to the presidency in handling a coal strike in 1902. Members of the United Mine Workers Union walked off their jobs, demanding higher wages, an 8-hour day, and recognition of their union. The mine owners closed the mines and waited for the union to collapse. But led by John Mitchell, the strikers held their ranks. The prospect of a freezing winter frightened consumers. Management's stubborn arrogance, which contrasted with the workers' orderly conduct and willingness to negotiate, hardened public opinion against the owners.

Although his legal advisers told him that the government had no authority to intervene, Roosevelt invited both the owners and the union leaders to the White House and declared that the national interest made government action necessary. Mitchell agreed to negotiate with the owners or to accept an arbitration commission appointed by the president. The owners, however, refused even to speak to the miners and demanded that Roosevelt use the army to break the union, as Cleveland had done in the Pullman strike in 1894.

Roosevelt was not a champion of labor, and he had favored shooting the Pullman strikers. But as president, he believed his role was to mediate social conflict for the public good. Roosevelt announced that he would use the army to seize and operate the mines, not to crush the union. Reluctantly, the owners accepted the arbitration commission they had previously rejected. The commission gave the miners a 10 percent wage increase and a 9-hour day, but not union recognition, and permitted the owners to raise coal prices by 10 percent. Roosevelt described his intervention as simply giving both labor and management a "square deal." It also set important precedents for an active government role in labor disputes and a strong president acting as a steward of the public.

## Managing Natural Resources

Federal land policy had helped create farms and develop transportation, but it had also ceded to speculators and business interests much of the nation's forests, mineral deposits, water power sites, and grazing lands. Reckless exploitation of these resources alarmed a new generation that believed the public welfare required the **conservation** of natural resources through efficient and scientific management. Conservationists achieved early victories in the Forest Reserve Act (1891) and the Forest Management Act (1897), which authorized the federal government to withdraw timberlands from development and to regulate grazing, lumbering, and hydroelectric sites in the forests (see Map 21.2).

Roosevelt built on these beginnings and on his friendship with Gifford Pinchot to make conservation a major focus of his presidency. Pinchot had been trained in French and German scientific forestry practices. Appointed in 1898 to head the new Division of Forestry (renamed the Forest Service in 1905), he brought rational management and regulation to resource development. With his advice, TR used presidential authority to triple the size of the forest reserves to 150 million acres, to set aside another 80 million acres valuable for minerals and petroleum, and to establish dozens of wildlife refuges. In 1908, Roosevelt held a White House conference that led to the creation of the National Conservation Commission, forty-one state conservation commissions, and widespread public support for conservation.

Not everyone, of course, agreed with TR's conservationist policies. Some favored **preservation**, hoping to set aside land as permanent wilderness, whereas Roosevelt favored a scientific and efficient rather than uncontrolled use of resources. Pinchot declared, "Wilderness is waste." Preservationists won some victories, saving a stand of California's giant redwoods and helping to create the National Park Service in 1916, but more Americans favored the utilitarian emphasis of the conservationists.

Other interests opposed conservation completely. While some of the larger timber and mineral companies supported conservation as a way to guarantee long-run profits, smaller western entrepreneurs often cared only about quick returns. Many westerners, moreover, resented having easterners make key decisions about western growth and saw conservation as a perpetuation of this colonial subservience. Many ranchers refused to pay federal grazing fees. Colorado arsonists set forest fires to protest the creation of forest reserves.

But westerners were happy to take federal money for expensive irrigation projects that private capital would not underwrite. They favored the 1902 National Reclamation Act, which established what became the **Bureau of Reclamation**. Its engineers were to

**conservation** The efficient management and use of natural resources, such as forests, grasslands, and rivers, as opposed to preservation or uncontrolled exploitation.

**preservation** Protecting forests, land, and other features of the natural environment from development or destruction, often for aesthetic appreciation.

**Bureau of Reclamation** Federal agency established in 1902 providing public funds for irrigation projects in arid regions.

**MAP 21.2 THE GROWTH OF FEDERAL RESERVES, INCLUDING LEADING NATIONAL PARKS AND NATIONAL FORESTS** Rapid exploitation of the West prompted demands to preserve its spectacular scenery and protect its remaining forests. In 1872 Yellowstone became the first National Park, and the National Forest system began in the 1890s. Conservation became increasingly important during the Progressive Era but often provoked Western hostility.

construct dams, reservoirs, and irrigation canals, and the government was to sell the irrigated lands in tracts no larger than 160 acres. With massive dams and networks of irrigation canals, it reclaimed fertile valleys from the desert, but by not enforcing the 160-acre limitation, it helped create powerful corporate farms in the West.

Westerners also welcomed Roosevelt's conservationist emphasis on rational development when it restricted Indian control of land and resources. He favored policies breaking up many reservations to open the land to whites for "efficient" development and diverting Indian waters to growing cities like Phoenix. Tribal protests were ignored.

## Corporate Regulation

Nothing symbolized Roosevelt's active presidency better than his popular reputation as a "trust buster." TR regarded the formation of large business combinations favorably, but he realized he could not ignore the public anxiety about corporate power. Rather than invoking "the foolish antitrust law," he favored government regulation to prevent corporate abuses and defend the public interest. "Misconduct," not size, was the issue.

Roosevelt filed lawsuits against some "bad trusts," including the Northern Securities Company, a holding company controlling the railroad network of the Northwest. For TR, this action was an assertion of government power that reassured a worried public and encouraged corporate responsibility. In 1904, the Supreme Court ordered the dissolution of the Northern Securities Company. Ultimately, Roosevelt brought forty-four antitrust

# From Then to Now
# The Environmental Movement

Many of the issues that concern environmentalists to-day were first raised by the conservationists and pres-ervationists of the Progressive Era. Led by Theodore Roosevelt, conservationists favored the planned and regulated management of America's natural resources for the public ben-efit. In contrast, preservationists—like John Muir, who founded the Sierra Club in 1892—sought to protect wilderness from any development whatsoever. Opposing both were those who championed the uncontrolled development of public lands.

Decades later, public concern over polluted rivers, oil spills, and urban smog gave birth to the environmental move-ment, which drew on the legacy of both the conservation and preservation movements but had wider interests and broader support than either. Beginning in the 1970s, Congress passed laws to protect endangered species, reduce pollution, limit the use of pesticides, and control hazardous waste. The Environmental Protection Agency became the largest federal regulatory agency.

Again, however, as during the Progressive Era, efforts to protect the environment encountered opposition from propo-nents of unrestricted development, especially in the West. In the Sagebrush Rebellion in the 1980s, some westerners con-demned "outside" federal regulation and tried to seize control of public lands for private exploitation. One oil company dis-missed catastrophic oil spills as merely "Mother Earth letting some oil come out." And four Republican presidents from the West—Californians Richard Nixon and Ronald Reagan and Texans George Bush and George W. Bush, all closely tied to oil

Theodore Roosevelt and John Muir, here on a 1903 camping trip in Yosemite, championed public responsibility for the nation's scenic and other natural resources.

and real estate interests—sought in varying degrees to curtail environmental policies, agencies, and budgets, even to deny the existence of global warming, and to oppose environmental protection as inconsistent with economic growth. This repudia-tion of Theodore Roosevelt's conservationism reflected the shift of the party's base to the Sunbelt. As one presidential adviser said, "Conservation is not in the Republican ethic."

Congress, the courts, and the public, however, generally resisted efforts to weaken environmental policy. Debate is sure to continue over the cost and effectiveness of specific policies, but Americans are increasingly inclined to stand with Theodore Roosevelt and John Muir in looking to the federal government for effective action to resolve environmental problems.

**Question for Discussion**

- How do differing economic and political attitudes under-lie the conflicting stances of Americans toward environ-mental issues?

Former Vice President Al Gore won the Nobel Peace Prize for helping direct attention to the dangers of global warming.

suits against business combinations, but except for a few like Standard Oil, he avoided the giant firms. Many of the cases had inconclusive outcomes, but Roosevelt was more inter-ested in establishing a regulatory role for government than in breaking up big businesses.

Elected president in his own right in 1904 over the colorless and conservative Democratic candidate, Alton B. Parker, Roosevelt responded to the growing popular demand for reform by pushing further toward a regulatory government. He proposed legislation "to work out methods of controlling the big corporations without paralyz-ing the energies of the business community." In 1906, Congress passed the Pure Food

621

((• 📖 **Read the Document**   Herbert Croly, *The Promise of American Life* (1914)

**THE CROWN PRINCE.**

Critics of Roosevelt's expansion of presidential power often depicted him as assuming a monarchical role, as when he used his influence to select William Howard Taft as his successor.

and Drug Act, the Meat Inspection Act, and the Hepburn Act, which expanded the authority of the Interstate Commerce Commission (ICC) over railroads. All three were compromises between reformers seeking serious government control of the industries involved and political defenders and lobbyists of the industries themselves.

Despite the compromises and weaknesses in the three laws, TR contended that they marked "a noteworthy advance in the policy of securing federal supervision and control over corporations." In 1907 and 1908, he pushed for an 8-hour workday, stock market regulation, and inheritance and income taxes. Republican conservatives in Congress blocked such reforms, and tensions increased between the progressive and conservative wings of the party.

## Taft and the Insurgents

TR handpicked his successor as president: a loyal lieutenant, William Howard Taft. If Roosevelt thought that Taft would be a successful president, continuing his policies and holding the Republican Party together, he was wrong. Taft's election in 1908, over

Democrat William Jennings Bryan in his third presidential campaign, led to a Republican political disaster.

Taft did preside over important progressive achievements. His administration pursued a more active and successful antitrust program than Roosevelt's. He supported the Mann-Elkins Act (1910), which extended the ICC's jurisdiction to telephone and telegraph companies. Taft set aside more public forest lands and oil reserves than Roosevelt had. He also supported a constitutional amendment authorizing an income tax, which went into effect in 1913 under the **Sixteenth Amendment**. One of the most important accomplishments of the Progressive Era, the income tax would provide the means for the government to expand its activities and responsibilities.

Nevertheless, Taft soon alienated progressives and floundered into a political morass. His problems were twofold. First, the Republicans were divided. Midwestern reform Republicans, led by La Follette, clashed with conservative Republicans, led by Senator Nelson Aldrich of Rhode Island. Second, Taft was politically inept. He was unable to mediate between the two Republican factions, and the party split apart.

Reformers wanted to restrict the power of the speaker of the House, "Uncle Joe" Cannon, a reactionary who systematically blocked progressive measures and loudly declared, "I am goddamned tired of listening to all this babble of reform." After seeming to promise support, Taft backed down when conservatives threatened to defeat important legislation. The insurgents in Congress eventually restricted the speaker's powers, but they never forgave what they saw as Taft's betrayal. The tariff also alienated progressives from Taft. He had campaigned in 1908 for a lower tariff to curb inflation, but when they introduced tariff reform legislation, the president failed to support them, and Aldrich's Senate committee added 847 amendments, many of which raised tariff rates. Taft justified his inaction as avoiding presidential interference with congressional business, but this position clashed with TR's example and the reformers' expectations. Progressives concluded that Taft had sided with the Old Guard against real change.

This perception solidified when Taft stumbled into a controversy over conservation. Gifford Pinchot had become embroiled in a complex struggle with Richard Ballinger, Taft's secretary of the interior. Ballinger, who was closely tied to western mining and lumbering interests, favored private development of public lands. When Pinchot challenged Ballinger's role in a questionable sale of public coal lands to a J. P. Morgan syndicate, Taft upheld Ballinger and fired Pinchot. Progressives concluded that Taft had repudiated Roosevelt's conservation policies.

Republican progressives determined to replace Taft, whom they now saw as an obstacle to reform. In 1911, the National Progressive League organized to champion La Follette for the Republican nomination in 1912. But Taft's political blunders increasingly angered Roosevelt, who began to campaign for the Republican nomination himself. In thirteen state primaries, he won 278 delegates, to only 46 for Taft. But most states did not then have primaries; as a result, Taft was able to dominate the Republican convention and win renomination. Roosevelt's forces formed a third party—the Progressive Party—and nominated the former president. The Republican split almost guaranteed victory for the Democratic nominee, Woodrow Wilson.

**Sixteenth Amendment**
Constitutional revision in 1913 that authorized a federal income tax.

21.1

21.2

21.3

21.4

21.5

# Woodrow Wilson and Progressive Reform

**21.5**   How did Woodrow Wilson's view of the role of government change during his presidency?

The pressures for reform called forth many new leaders. The one who would preside over progressivism's culmination, and ultimately its collapse, was Woodrow Wilson. Elected president in 1912 and 1916, he mediated among differing progressive views to achieve a strong reform program, enlarge the power of the executive branch, and make the White House the center of national politics.

# The Election of 1912

Despite the prominence of Roosevelt and La Follette, progressivism was not simply a Republican phenomenon. In Congress, Democrats more consistently supported reform measures than did Republicans, and the Democratic leader William Jennings Bryan surpassed Roosevelt as a persistent advocate of significant reform. As the Republicans quarreled during Taft's administration, Democrats pushed progressive remedies and achieved major victories in the state and congressional elections of 1910. To improve the party's chances in 1912, Bryan announced that he would step aside. The Democratic spotlight shifted to the governor of New Jersey, Woodrow Wilson.

Wilson combined public eloquence with a cold personality; he balanced a self-righteousness that led to stubborn inflexibility with an intense ambition that permitted the most expedient compromises. Wilson first entered public life as a conservative, steeped in the limited-government traditions of his native South. As president of Princeton University, beginning in 1902, he became a prominent representative of middle-class respectability and conservative causes. In 1910, New Jersey's Democratic bosses selected him for governor to head off the progressives. But once in office, Wilson championed popular reforms and immediately began to campaign as a progressive for the party's 1912 presidential nomination.

Wilson's progressivism differed from that of Roosevelt in 1912. TR emphasized a strong government to promote economic and social order. He defended big business as inevitable and healthy provided that government control ensured that it would benefit the entire nation. Roosevelt called this program the **New Nationalism**, reflecting his belief in a powerful state and a national interest. He also supported demands for social welfare, including workers' compensation and the abolition of child labor.

Wilson was horrified by Roosevelt's vision. His **New Freedom** program rejected what he called TR's "regulated monopoly." Wilson wanted "regulated competition," with the government's role limited to breaking up monopolies through antitrust action and preventing artificial barriers like tariffs from blocking free enterprise. Wilson opposed social welfare legislation as paternalistic and beyond the proper scope of the federal government, which he hoped to minimize. (This position, shot back the alarmed Roosevelt, meant the repeal of "every law for the promotion of social and industrial justice.")

Roosevelt's endorsement of social legislation attracted many women into political action. As Jane Addams observed, "their long concern for the human wreckage of industry has come to be considered politics." The Progressive Party also endorsed woman suffrage, accepted women as convention delegates, and pledged to give women equal representation on party committees.

Despite his personal popularity, however, TR was unable to add progressive Democrats to the Republicans who followed him into the Progressive Party, and thus was doomed to defeat. Other reform voters embraced the Socialist candidate, Eugene V. Debs, who captured 900,000 votes—6 percent of the total. Taft played little role in the campaign.

Wilson won an easy electoral college victory, though he received only 42 percent of the popular vote and fewer popular votes than Bryan had won in any of his three campaigns (see Map 21.3). Roosevelt came in second, Taft third. The Democrats also gained control of Congress, giving Wilson the opportunity to enact his New Freedom program.

# Implementing the New Freedom

As president, Wilson built on Roosevelt's precedent to strengthen executive authority. He proposed a full legislative program and worked forcefully to secure its approval. When necessary, he appealed to the public for support, ruthlessly used patronage, or compromised with conservatives. With such methods and a solid Democratic majority, Wilson gained approval of important laws.

Wilson turned first to the traditional Democratic goal of reducing the high protective tariff, the symbol of special privileges for industry. He forced through the **Underwood-Simmons Tariff Act** of 1913, the first substantial reduction in duties since before the Civil War. The act also levied the first income tax under the recently

**New Nationalism** Theodore Roosevelt's 1912 program calling for a strong national government to foster, regulate, and protect business, industry, workers, and consumers.

**New Freedom** Woodrow Wilson's 1912 program for limited government intervention in the economy to restore competition by curtailing the restrictive influences of trusts and protective tariffs, thereby providing opportunities for individual achievement.

**Underwood-Simmons Tariff Act** The 1913 reform law that lowered tariff rates and levied the first regular federal income tax.

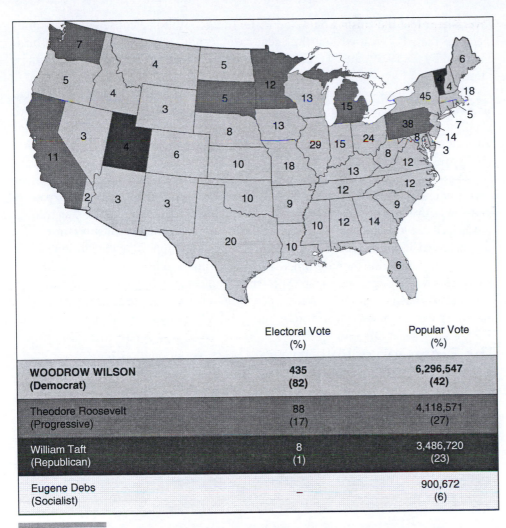

| | Electoral Vote (%) | Popular Vote (%) |
|---|---|---|
| **WOODROW WILSON** (Democrat) | **435** **(82)** | **6,296,547** **(42)** |
| Theodore Roosevelt (Progressive) | 88 (17) | 4,118,571 (27) |
| William Taft (Republican) | 8 (1) | 3,486,720 (23) |
| Eugene Debs (Socialist) | — | 900,672 (6) |

**MAP 21.3 THE ELECTION OF 1912** The split within the Republican Party enabled Woodrow Wilson to carry most states and become president even though he won only a minority of the popular vote.

ratified Sixteenth Amendment. Conservatives condemned the "revolutionary" tax, but it was designed simply to compensate for lower tariff rates. The top tax rate paid by the wealthiest was a mere 7 percent.

Wilson next reformed the nation's banking and currency system, which was inadequate for a modernizing economy. Wilson skillfully maneuvered a compromise measure through Congress, balancing the demands of agrarian progressives for government control with the bankers' desires for private control. The **Federal Reserve Act** of 1913 created twelve regional Federal Reserve banks that, although privately controlled, were to be supervised by the Federal Reserve Board, appointed by the president. The law also provided for a flexible national currency and improved access to credit. Serious problems remained, but the new system promoted the progressive goals of order and efficiency and fulfilled Wilson's New Freedom principle of introducing limited government regulation while preserving private business control.

Wilson's third objective was new legislation to break up monopolies. Initially, he supported the Clayton antitrust bill, which prohibited unfair trade practices and sharply restricted holding companies. But when business leaders and other progressives strenuously objected, Wilson reversed himself. Opting for continuous federal regulation rather than for the dissolution of trusts, Wilson endorsed the creation of the **Federal Trade Commission (FTC)** to oversee business activity and prevent illegal restrictions on competition.

The Federal Trade Commission Act of 1914 dismayed many of Wilson's early supporters because it embraced the New Nationalism's emphasis on positive regulation. Roosevelt's 1912 platform had proposed a federal trade commission; Wilson now accepted what he had earlier denounced as a partnership between trusts and the

**Federal Reserve Act** The 1913 law that revised banking and currency by extending limited government regulation through the creation of the Federal Reserve System.

**Federal Trade Commission (FTC)** Government agency established in 1914 to provide regulatory oversight of business activity.

government that the trusts would dominate. Indeed, Wilson's conservative appointments to the FTC ensured that the agency would not seriously interfere with business, and by the 1920s, the FTC had become virtually a junior partner of the business community.

The fate of the Clayton antitrust bill after Wilson withdrew his support reflected his new attitude toward big business. Congressional conservatives gutted the bill with crippling amendments before permitting it to become law in 1914. As one senator complained, "It is a sort of legislative apology to the trusts, delivered hat in hand, and accompanied by assurances that no discourtesy is intended."

These measures indicated the limited nature of Wilson's vision of reform. In fact, he now announced that no further reforms were necessary—astonishing many progressives whose objectives had been completely ignored. Wilson refused to support woman suffrage and helped kill legislation abolishing child labor and expanding credits to farmers. He demonstrated his indifference to issues of social justice by supporting the introduction of racial segregation within the government itself. Government offices, shops, restrooms, and restaurants were all segregated; employees who complained were fired. Federal officials in the South discharged black employees. One Georgia official promised that there would be no more government jobs for African Americans: "A Negro's place is in the cornfield."

## The Expansion of Reform

Wilson had won in 1912 only because the Republicans had split. By 1916, Roosevelt had returned to the GOP, and Wilson realized that he had to attract some of TR's former followers. Wilson therefore abandoned his opposition to social and economic reforms and promoted measures he had previously condemned. But he had also grown in the White House and now recognized that some problems could be resolved only by positive federal action.

Woodrow Wilson at his desk in the White House. A strong president, Wilson led Congress to enact sweeping and significant legislation.

To assist farmers, Wilson in 1916 convinced Congress to pass the Federal Farm Loan Act. This law, which Wilson himself had earlier rejected twice, provided farmers with federally financed long-term agricultural credits. The Warehouse Act of 1916 improved short-term agricultural credit. The Highway Act of 1916 provided funds to construct and improve rural roads through the adoption of the dollar-matching principle by which the federal government would expand its power over state activities in the twentieth century.

Wilson and the Democratic Congress also reached out to labor. Wilson signed the Keating-Owen Act prohibiting the interstate shipment of products made by child labor. In 1902, Wilson had denounced Roosevelt's intervention in the coal strike, but in 1916 he broke a labor-management impasse and averted a railroad strike by helping pass the Adamson Act establishing an 8-hour day for railroad workers. Wilson also pushed the Kern-McGillicuddy Act, which achieved the progressive goal of a workers' compensation system for federal employees. Together, these laws marked an important advance toward government regulation of the labor market.

Wilson also promoted activist government when he nominated Louis Brandeis to the Supreme Court. Known as "the people's lawyer," Brandeis had successfully defended protective labor legislation before the conservative judiciary. The nomination outraged conservatives, including William Howard Taft and the American Bar Association. Brandeis was the first Jew nominated to the Court, and anti-Semitism motivated some of his opponents. Wilson overcame a vicious campaign against Brandeis and secured his confirmation.

By these actions, Wilson brought progressivism to a culmination of sorts and consolidated reformers behind him for a second term. Less than a decade earlier, Wilson the private citizen had assailed government regulation and social legislation; by 1916, he had guided an unprecedented expansion of federal power. His own personal and political journey symbolized the development of progressivism.

## Conclusion

In the early twentieth century, progressive reformers responded to the tensions of industrial and urban development by moving to change society and government. Rejecting the earlier emphasis on individualism and laissez-faire, they organized to promote social change and an interventionist state. Programs and laws to protect women, children, and injured workers testified to their compassion; the creation of new agencies and political techniques indicated their interest in order and efficiency; campaigns to end corruption, whether perceived in urban political machines, corporate influence, drunkenness, or "inferior" immigrants, illustrated their self-assured vision of the public good.

Progressivism had its ironies and paradoxes. It called for democratic reforms—and did achieve woman suffrage, direct legislation, and popular election of senators—but helped disfranchise black southerners and northern immigrants. It advocated social justice but often enforced social control. It demanded responsive government but helped create bureaucracies largely removed from popular control. It endorsed the regulation of business in the public interest but forged regulatory laws and commissions that tended to aid business. Some of these seeming contradictions reflected the persistence of traditional attitudes and the need to accommodate conservative opponents; others revealed the progressives' own limitations in vision, concern, or nerve.

Nonetheless, both the successes and the failures of progressivism revealed that the nature of politics and government had changed significantly. Americans had come to accept that government action could resolve social and economic problems, and the role and power of government expanded accordingly. The emergence of an activist presidency, capable of developing programs, mobilizing public opinion, directing Congress, and taking forceful action, epitomized this key development.

These important features would be crucial when the nation fought World War I, which brought new challenges and dangers to the United States. The Great War would expose many of the limitations of progressivism and the naïveté of the progressives' optimism.

**For Suggested Readings go to MyHistoryLab.**

# Chapter Review

## The Ferment of Reform

**21.1** What values and beliefs bound progressives together? p. 600

Progressives were a diverse collection of reformers convinced that industrialization and urbanization had produced serious social disorders, from city slums to corporate abuses and government corruption. Rejecting older ideologies of individualism and laissez-faire in favor of broader concepts of social responsibility, they sought social order and justice through private organizations and government actions.

## Reforming Society

**21.2** How did progressives respond to the social challenges of industrializing America? p. 606

Progressives worked to transform society by improving urban and rural living conditions, enacting protective legislation for women and children, reorganizing schools, and reforming family, social, and industrial relations. Racism marred some efforts, as did coercive efforts to limit immigration, impose prohibition, or regulate entertainment. Conservative opposition blocked others.

## Reforming Politics and Government

**21.3** How did progressives change American politics and government? p. 613

Many progressives worked to advance democracy through achieving woman suffrage, popular election of senators, direct legislation, and direct primaries. Others sought to combat perceived corruption by restricting political parties and electorates and to increase government efficiency by institutionalizing nonelected professional experts to set and implement public policy.

## Theodore Roosevelt and the Progressive Presidency

**21.4** How did Theodore Roosevelt's view of the presidency shape his administration? p. 618

Seeking a strong government to promote the national interest, Theodore Roosevelt both expanded government power and consolidated it in the executive branch. He pressured Congress to enact reforms; mediated labor disputes for the public good; acted as steward of the public in the conservation of natural resources; and pursued a regulatory role toward business.

## Woodrow Wilson and Progressive Reform

**21.5** How did Woodrow Wilson's view of the role of government change during his presidency? p. 623

Wilson initially favored limiting government to promoting competition through antitrust action and lowered tariffs, while opposing social welfare legislation or specific reforms to aid aggrieved groups. Eventually, he adopted Roosevelt's emphasis on positive regulation,

in the Federal Trade Commission, and also pursued legislation expanding government's reach by assisting farmers, helping workers, and building highways.

# Timeline

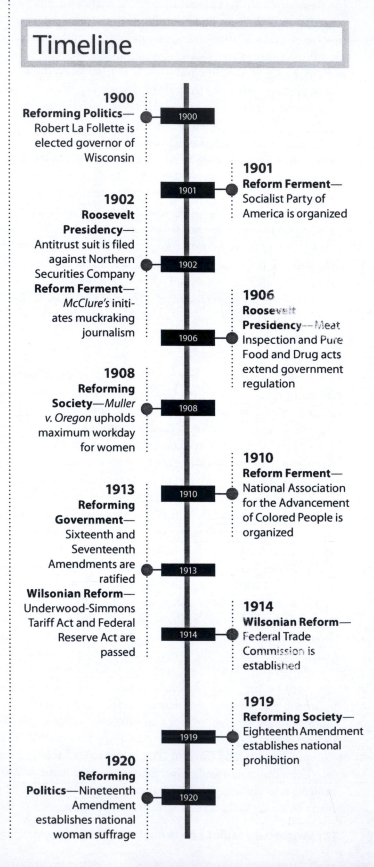

**1900**
**Reforming Politics—** Robert La Follette is elected governor of Wisconsin

1900

**1901**
**Reform Ferment—** Socialist Party of America is organized

1901

**1902**
**Roosevelt Presidency—** Antitrust suit is filed against Northern Securities Company
**Reform Ferment—** *McClure's* initiates muckraking journalism

1902

**1906**
**Roosevelt Presidency—** Meat Inspection and Pure Food and Drug acts extend government regulation

1906

**1908**
**Reforming Society—** *Muller v. Oregon* upholds maximum workday for women

1908

**1910**
**Reform Ferment—** National Association for the Advancement of Colored People is organized

1910

**1913**
**Reforming Government—** Sixteenth and Seventeenth Amendments are ratified
**Wilsonian Reform—** Underwood-Simmons Tariff Act and Federal Reserve Act are passed

1913

**1914**
**Wilsonian Reform—** Federal Trade Commission is established

1914

**1919**
**Reforming Society—** Eighteenth Amendment establishes national prohibition

1919

**1920**
**Reforming Politics—** Nineteenth Amendment establishes national woman suffrage

1920

# 22 Creating an Empire 1865–1917

## One American Journey

The U.S. Military Governor of Occupied Cuba Views Cuban-American Relations

*Havana, Cuba, October 1901*

**When the Spanish-American war was declared** the United States . . . assumed a position as protector of the interests of Cuba. It became responsible for the welfare of the people, politically, mentally, and morally. The mere fact of freeing the island from Spanish rule has not ended the care which this country should give. . . . The effect will be to uplift the people, gaining their permanent friendship and support and greatly increasing our own commerce. At present there are two million people requiring clothing and food, for but a small proportion of the necessaries of life are raised on the island. It is folly to grow food crops when sugar and tobacco produce such rich revenues in comparison. The United States should supply the Cubans with their breadstuffs, even wine, fruit, and vegetables, and

## LEARNING OBJECTIVES

| 22.1 (( | 22.2 (( | 22.3 (( | 22.4 (( | 22.5 (( |
|---|---|---|---|---|
| What arguments were made in favor of American expansion in the late nineteenth century? p. 632 | What were the most important consequences of the Spanish-American War? p. 638 | What opportunities and obstacles did American expansionists find in Asia? p. 644 | What was the nature of U.S. involvement in Latin America? p. 646 | Why did the United States take a larger role in Europe at the beginning of the twentieth century? p. 654 |

After the Spanish-American War, Uncle Sam seemed to face a controversial choice: Follow traditional policies such as the Monroe Doctrine or travel down the "Imperial Highway."

From *The American Journey*, Seventh Edition. Goldfield, Abbott, Anderson, Argersinger, Argersinger and Barney Copyright © 2014 by Pearson Education, Inc. All rights reserved.

#  Watch the Video Series on MyHistoryLab

Learn about some key topics related to this chapter with the *MyHistoryLab Video Series: Key Topics in U.S. History.*

**1** The American Empire  The United States is that rare exception in history where a former colony becomes a major imperial power. This video discusses America's territorial ambitions. It also profiles two U.S. secretaries of state responsible for achieving them—William H. Seward, who purchased Alaska from the Russian Empire, and James G. Blaine, who promoted an expansionist policy that eventually made the United States an imperial power.

 Watch on MyHistoryLab

Coup in Hawaii  The McKinley Tariff Act had the unintended effect of leading to a coup that ended the reign of Queen Liliuokalani and an independent Hawaii. This video reveals how American sugar growers and other foreign interests deposed the queen, whose move toward more control over her country threatened the duty-free export of sugar to the mainland.

Watch on MyHistoryLab **2**

**3** The Spanish-American War  The Spanish-American War of 1898 is the stuff of colorful battles and personalities, such as Theodore Roosevelt's Rough Riders and Admiral Dewey's victory in Manila Bay. However, the war resulted from an intense determination to establish an overseas presence for the young nation—to establish and protect trade, provide ports and coal stations for its shipping, and the like. This video looks at how the proponents of U.S. imperialism and international power took advantage of the weakest colonial power, the kingdom of Spain, and won from it control of numerous island territories.

 Watch on MyHistoryLab

War in the Philippines  In winning the Spanish-American War, not only did the United States gain possession of the Philippines, but it also inherited a war of independence, as this video reveals. It discusses how U.S. administrators and soldiers quickly cast aside high-minded principles and morals to engage in a bloody guerilla war with Filipino freedom fighters.

Watch on MyHistoryLab **4**

should clothe the people. . . . The money received for their crops will be turned over in a great measure in buying supplies from the United States. . . .

Naturally the manufacturers of the United States should have precedence in furnishing machinery, locomotives, cars, and rails, materials for buildings and bridges, and the wide diversity of other supplies required, as well as fuel for their furnaces. With the present financial and commercial uncertainty at an end the people of the island will . . . come into the American market as customers for products of many kinds.

The meeting of the Constitutional Convention on November 5th will be an event in Cuban history of the greatest importance, and much will depend upon the action and outcome of this convention as to our future control of the island. . . . I considered it unwise to interfere, and I have made it a settled policy to permit the Cubans to manage every part of their constitution-making.

This has been due to my desire to prevent any possible charge of crimination being brought against the United States in the direction of their constitutional affairs. . . .

There is no distrust of the United States on the part of the Cubans, and I know of no widespread antipathy to this country, its people, or its institutions. There are, of course, a handful of malcontents, as there must be in every country. . . .

I could not well conceive how the Cubans could be otherwise than grateful to the United States for its efforts in their behalf. . . . In the brief time since the occupation of the island by American troops the island has been completely rehabilitated—agriculturally, commercially, financially, educationally, and governmentally. This improvement has been so rapid and so apparent that no Cuban could mistake it. To doubt in the face of these facts that their liberators were not still their faithful friends would be impossible.

Major-General Leonard Wood, "The Future of Cuba," *The Independent* 54 (January 23, 1902): 193–194; idem, "The Cuban Convention," *The Independent* 52 (November 1, 1900): 265–266.

## Personal Journeys Online

- Josiah Strong, *Our Country*, 1885. An appeal for Anglo-Saxon imperialism by an American minister.
- Charles Denby, *Shall We Keep the Philippines?* 1898. An argument for an economic empire by an American diplomat.
- Vincent F. Howard, *Imperialism*, 1900. A poem denouncing the imperialist journey.

**G**eneral Leonard Wood's reports on Cuba, which was then under his control as military governor, captured the complex mixture of attitudes and motives that underlay the journey of the United States from a developing nation to a world power. Plans for economic expansion, a belief in national mission, a sense of responsibility to help others, scarcely hidden religious impulses and racist convictions—all combined in an uneasy mixture of self-interest and idealism.

Wood himself had taken a symbolic journey in American expansionism. His earlier career had been on the American southwestern frontier with the troops chasing the Apache under Geronimo, but in 1898, he and Theodore Roosevelt organized the Rough Riders cavalry to participate in the Spanish-American War in Cuba. As Wood wrote on a transport ship headed for that Spanish colony: "[T]his is the first great expedition our country has sent overseas and marks the commencement of a new era in our relations with the world." Upon Spain's surrender, Cuba came under U.S. military occupation, and Wood was appointed military governor of the island.

The tension between what a friend of Wood's called the "righteous" and the "selfish" aspects of expanding American influence was but scarcely concealed in Wood's reports. United States rule had fulfilled paternalistic or humanitarian instincts to improve Cuba's economy, schools, and sanitation while at the same time "naturally" making American business interests the beneficiaries of this reorganization of Cuban life. Wood's claim that he was not interfering with Cuba's constitutional convention was disingenuous, for he had already limited those who could participate as voters or delegates and was even then devising means to restrict the convention's autonomy. And in his repeated insistence that the Cubans were grateful for the intervention of "their faithful friends," the Americans, Wood obviously protested too much: Cubans, as well as Filipinos, Puerto Ricans, and others, rarely perceived American motives or American actions as positively as did Wood and other proponents of American expansion. Victory in the Spanish-American War had provided the United States with an extensive empire, status as a world power, and opportunities and problems that would long shape U.S. foreign policy.

# The Roots of Imperialism

What arguments were made in favor of American expansion in the late nineteenth century?

**imperialism** The policy and practice of exploiting nations and peoples for the benefit of an imperial power either directly through military occupation and colonial rule or indirectly through economic domination of resources and markets.

The United States had a long-established tradition of expansion across the continent. Indeed, by the 1890s, Republican Senator Henry Cabot Lodge of Massachusetts boasted that Americans had "a record of conquest, colonization, and territorial expansion unequalled by any people in the nineteenth century." Lodge now urged the country to build an overseas empire, emulating the European model of **imperialism** based on the acquisition and exploitation of colonial possessions. Other Americans favored a less formal empire, in which U.S. interests and influence would be ensured through extensive trade and investments rather than through military occupation. Still others advocated a cultural expansionism in which the nation exported its ideals and institutions. All such expansionists could draw from many sources to support their plans (see Table 22.1, Rationales for Imperialism).

## Ideological and Religious Arguments

Scholars, authors, politicians, and religious leaders provided interlocking ideological arguments for the new imperialism. Some intellectuals, for example, invoked Social Darwinism, maintaining that the United States should engage in a competitive struggle for wealth and power with other nations. "The survival of the fittest," declared one writer, was "the law of nations as well as a law of nature." As European nations expanded into Asia and Africa in the 1880s and 1890s, seeking colonies, markets, and raw materials, these advocates argued, the United States had to adopt similar policies to ensure national success.

Related to Social Darwinism was a pervasive belief in racial inequality and in the superiority of people of English, or Anglo-Saxon, descent. To many Americans, the industrial progress, military strength, and political development of England and the United States were proof of an Anglo-Saxon superiority that carried with it a responsibility to extend the blessings of their rule to less able people. As a popular expression put it, colonialism was the "white man's burden," carrying with it a duty to aid and uplift other peoples. Such attitudes led some expansionists to favor imposing American ideas and practices on other cultures regardless of their own values and customs.

Reflecting this aggressiveness, as well as Darwinian anxieties, some Americans endorsed expansion as consistent with their ideals of masculinity. Forceful expansion would be a manly course, relying upon and building strength and honor among American males. Men who confronted the challenges of empire would thereby improve their ability to compete in the international arena. "Pride of race, courage, manliness," predicted one enthusiast, would be both the causes and the consequences of an assertive foreign policy.

## TABLE 22.1  RATIONALES FOR IMPERIALISM

| Category | Beliefs |
| --- | --- |
| Racism and Social Darwinism | The conviction that Anglo-Saxons were racially superior and should dominate other peoples to ensure national success, establish international stability, or benefit the "inferior" races by imposing American ideas and institutions on them |
| Righteousness | The conviction that Christianity, and a supporting American culture, should be aggressively spread among the benighted peoples of other lands |
| Mahanism | The conviction, following the ideas advanced by Alfred Thayer Mahan, that U.S. security required a strong navy and economic and territorial expansion |
| Economics | A variety of arguments holding that American prosperity depended on acquiring access to foreign markets, raw materials, and investment opportunities |

Read the Document    Josiah Strong, from *Our Country* (1885)

22.1

22.2

22.3

22.4

22.5

Emily Hartwell, an American missionary, and her Chinese converts ("Bible Women") in the Foochow Mission in 1902. American missionaries wanted to spread the Gospel abroad but inevitably spread American influence as well. Hartwell used the ethnocentric and militant rhetoric of the imperialism of righteousness in appealing to Americans for money and prayers for her "picket duty on the very outskirts of the army of the Lord."

American missionaries also promoted expansionist sentiment. Hoping to evangelize the world, American religious groups increased the number of Protestant foreign missions sixfold from 1870 to 1900. Women in particular organized foreign missionary societies and served in the missions. Missionaries publicized their activities throughout the United States, generating support for what one writer called the "imperialism of righteousness." Abroad they pursued a religious transformation that often resembled a cultural conversion, for they promoted trade, developed business interests, and encouraged westernization through technology and education as well as religion. Sometimes, as in the Hawaiian Islands, American missionaries even promoted annexation by the United States.

Indeed, the American religious press endlessly repeated the themes of national destiny, racial superiority, and religious zeal. The Reverend J. H. Barrows in early 1898 lectured on the "Christian conquest of Asia," suggesting that American Christianity and commerce would cross the Pacific to fulfill "the manifest destiny of the Christian Republic." Missionaries contributed to the imperial impulse by describing their work, as Barrows did, in terms of the conquest of enemy territory. Thus, while missionaries were motivated by what they considered to be idealism and often brought real benefits to other lands, especially in education and health, religious sentiments reinforced the ideology of American expansion.

## Strategic Concerns

Other expansionists were motivated by strategic concerns, shaped by what they saw as the forces of history and geography. America's location in the Western Hemisphere,

633

**Mahanism** The ideas advanced by Alfred Thayer Mahan, stressing U.S. naval, economic, and territorial expansion.

its coastlines on two oceans, and the ambitions and activities of other nations, particularly Germany and Britain, convinced some Americans that the United States had to develop new policies to protect and promote its national security and interests. Alfred Thayer Mahan, the president of the Naval War College, emphasized the importance of a strong navy for national greatness in his book *The Influence of Sea Power upon History*. To complement the navy, Mahan proposed that the United States build a canal across the Isthmus of Panama to link its coasts, acquire naval bases in the Caribbean and the Pacific to protect the canal, and annex Hawaii and other Pacific islands to promote trade and service the fleet. The United States must "cast aside the policy of isolation which befitted her infancy," Mahan declared, and "begin to look outward."

**Mahanism** found a receptive audience. President Benjamin Harrison declared in 1891 that "as to naval stations and points of influence, we must look forward to a departure from the too conservative opinions which have been held heretofore." Still more vocal advocates of Mahan's program were a group of nationalistic Republicans, predominantly from the Northeast. They included politicians like Henry Cabot Lodge and Theodore Roosevelt, journalists like Whitelaw Reid and Albert Shaw, and diplomats and lawyers like John Hay and Elihu Root. One British observer concluded that Mahan's influence served "as oil to the flame of 'colonial expansion' everywhere leaping into life."

Even so, Mahan was not solely responsible for the large-navy policy that was popular among imperialists. Its origins went back to 1881, when Congress established the Naval Advisory Board, which successfully lobbied for larger naval appropriations. An extensive program to replace the navy's obsolete wooden ships with modern cruisers and battleships was well under way by 1890, when Mahan's book appeared. The United States soon possessed the formidable navy the expansionists wanted. This larger navy, in turn, demanded strategic bases and coaling stations.

## Economic Designs

One reason for the widespread support for a larger navy was its use to expand and protect America's international trade. Nearly all Americans favored economic expansion through foreign trade. Such a policy promised national prosperity: more markets for manufacturers and farmers, greater profits for merchants and bankers, more jobs for workers. Far fewer favored the acquisition of colonies that was characteristic of European imperialism. As one diplomat declared in 1890, the nation was more interested in the "annexation of trade" than in the annexation of territory.

The United States had long aggressively fostered American trade, especially in Latin America and East Asia. As early as 1844, the United States had negotiated a trade treaty with China, and ten years later a squadron under Commodore Matthew Perry had forced the Japanese to open their ports to American products. In the late nineteenth century, the dramatic expansion of the economy caused many Americans to favor more government action to open foreign markets to American exports. Said a naval officer trying to open Korea to U.S. products in 1878, "At least one third of our mechanical and agricultural products are now in excess of our wants, and we must *export* these products or *deport* the people who are creating them."

Exports, especially of manufactured goods, which grew ninefold between 1865 and 1900, did increase greatly in the late nineteenth century. Still, periodic depressions fed the fears of overproduction. The massive unemployment and social unrest that accompanied these economic crises also provided social and political arguments for economic relief through foreign trade.

In the depression of the 1890s, with the secretary of state seeing "symptoms of revolution" in the Pullman strike and Coxey's Army of unemployed workers, the interest in foreign trade became obsessive. More systematic government efforts to promote trade seemed necessary, a conclusion strengthened by new threats to existing American markets. In that tumultuous decade, European nations raised tariff barriers against American products, and Japan and the European imperial powers began to restrict commercial opportunities in the areas of China that they controlled. Many American leaders decided that the United States had to adopt decisive new policies or face economic catastrophe.

## First Steps

Despite the growing ideological, strategic, and economic arguments for imperialism, the government only fitfully interested itself in foreign affairs before the mid-1890s. It did not pursue a policy of isolationism from international affairs, for the nation maintained normal diplomatic and trade ties and at times vigorously intervened in Latin America and East Asia. But in general the government deferred to the initiative of private interests, reacted haphazardly to outside events, and did little to create a professional foreign service. In a few bold if inconsistent steps, however, the United States moved to expand its influence.

**Seward and Blaine.** Two secretaries of state, William H. Seward, secretary under presidents Abraham Lincoln and Andrew Johnson (1861–1869), and James G. Blaine, secretary under presidents James Garfield and Benjamin Harrison (1881, 1889–1892), laid the foundation for a larger and more aggressive U.S. role in world affairs. Seward possessed an elaborate imperial vision, based on his understanding of commercial opportunities, strategic necessities, and national destiny. His interest in opening East Asia to American commerce and establishing American hegemony over the Caribbean anticipated the subsequent course of American expansion. Seward purchased Alaska from Russia in 1867, approved the navy's occupation of the Midway Islands in the Pacific, pushed American trade on a reluctant Japan, and repeatedly tried to acquire Caribbean naval bases (see Map 22.1). His policy of expansion, however, as

**MAP 22.1 UNITED STATES EXPANSION IN THE PACIFIC, 1867–1899** Pursuing visions of a commercial empire in the Pacific, the United States steadily expanded its territorial possessions as well as its influence there in the late nineteenth century.

635

one observer noted, "went somewhat too far and too fast for the public," and many of his plans fizzled.

Blaine was an equally vigorous, if inconsistent, advocate of expansion. He worked to extend what he called America's "commercial empire" in the Pacific and to ensure U.S. sovereignty over any canal in Panama, insisting that it be "a purely American waterway to be treated as part of our own coastline." He also attempted to induce Latin American nations to import manufactured products from the United States rather than Europe; but, wary of economic subordination to the colossus of the north, they rejected Blaine's plans.

If U.S. officials were increasingly assertive toward Latin America and Asia, however, they remained little involved in Europe and wholly indifferent to Africa, which the European powers were then carving up into colonies. In short, despite some important precedents for the future, much of American foreign policy remained undeveloped, sporadic, and impulsive.

**Hawaii.** Blaine regarded Hawaii as "indispensably" part of "the American system." Although Hawaii continued to be ruled by native monarchs, U.S. influence grew steadily, particularly as Americans arrived to establish sugar plantations and eventually dominate the economy. Treaties in 1875 and 1887 integrated the islands into the American economy and gave the United States control over Pearl Harbor on the island of Oahu. In 1887, the United States rejected a proposal from Britain and France for a joint guarantee of Hawaii's independence and endorsed a new Hawaiian constitution that gave political power to wealthy white residents. The obvious next step was U.S. annexation.

Several factors soon impelled American planters to bid for annexation. The McKinley Tariff Act of 1890 effectively closed the U.S. market to Hawaiian sugar, threatening their economic ruin. At the same time, Queen Liliuokalani moved to restore native control of Hawaiian affairs. To ensure market access and protect their political authority, the American planters decided to seek annexation to the United States. In 1893, they overthrew the queen. John Stevens, the American diplomatic representative, ordered U.S. marines to help the rebels, then declared an American protectorate over the new Hawaiian government, and wired Washington: "The Hawaiian pear is now fully ripe, and this is the golden hour for the United States to pluck it." A delegation from the new provisional government, which did not include any native Hawaiians, went to Washington to draft a treaty for annexation. President Harrison signed the pact but could not get Senate approval before the new Cleveland administration took office.

After an investigation convinced him that Hawaiians were "for the Queen, against the provisional Government, and against annexation," Grover Cleveland apologized to the queen for the "flagrant wrong" done her by the "reprehensible conduct" of U.S. diplomats and troops. But the American-dominated provisional government refused to step down, and Cleveland's rejection of annexation set off a noisy debate in the United States.

Many Republicans strongly supported annexation, which they regarded as merely the first step toward making the Pacific "an American ocean, dominated by American commercial enterprise for all time." Some also invoked racial imperialism, maintaining that annexation would both fittingly reward the enterprising white residents of Hawaii and provide an opportunity to civilize native Hawaiians.

Democrats generally opposed annexation. They doubted, as Missouri Senator George Vest declared, whether the United States should desert its traditional principles and "venture upon the great colonial system of the European powers." The Hawaiian episode of 1893 thus foreshadowed the arguments over imperialism at the end of the century and emphasized the policy differences between Democrats and the increasingly expansionist Republicans.

COATING.

The old horse was too slow for Uncle Sam.

As other imperial powers look on, the United States abandons its traditional principles to rush headlong into world affairs. Uncle Sam would not always find it a smooth ride.

**Chile and Venezuela.** American reactions to developments in other countries in the 1890s also reflected an increasingly assertive national policy and excitable public opinion. In 1891, American sailors on shore leave in Chile became involved in a drunken brawl that left two of them dead, seventeen injured, and dozens in jail. Encouraged by a combative navy, President Harrison threatened military retaliation against Chile, provoking an outburst of bellicose nationalism in the United States. Harrison relented only when Chile apologized and paid an indemnity.

A few years later, the United States again threatened war over a minor issue but against a more formidable opponent. In 1895, President Cleveland intervened in a boundary dispute between Great Britain and Venezuela over British Guiana. Cleveland was motivated not only by the long-standing U.S. goal of challenging Britain for Latin American markets but also by ever more expansive notions of the Monroe Doctrine and the authority of the United States. He urged Congress to establish a commission to determine the boundary and enforce its decision by war if necessary. As war fever swept the United States, Britain agreed to U.S. arbitration, recognizing the limited nature of the issue that so convulsed Anglo-American relations.

Cleveland's assertion of U.S. hemispheric dominance angered Latin Americans, and their fears deepened when the United States decided arbitration terms with Britain without consulting Venezuela, which protested before bowing to American pressure. The United States had intervened less to protect Venezuela from the British bully than to advance its own hegemony. The further significance of the Venezuelan crisis, Captain Mahan noted, lay in its "awakening of our countrymen to the fact that we must come out of our isolation . . . and take our share in the turmoil of the world."

# The Spanish-American War

**22.2** What were the most important consequences of the Spanish-American War?

The forces pushing the United States toward imperialism and international power came to a head in the Spanish-American War. Cuba's quest for independence from the oppressive colonial control of Spain activated Americans' long-standing interest in the island. Many sympathized with the Cuban rebels' yearning for freedom, others worried that disorder in Cuba threatened their own economic and political interests, and some thought that intervention would increase the influence of the United States in the Caribbean and along key Pacific routes to Asian markets. But few foresaw that the war that finally erupted in 1898 would dramatically change U.S. relationships with the rest of the world and give the United States a colonial empire.

## The Cuban Revolution

The last major European colony in Latin America, Cuba held an economic potential that attracted American business interests and a strategic significance for any Central American canal. In the late nineteenth century, American investors expanded their economic influence in Cuba, while Cubans themselves rebelled repeatedly but unsuccessfully against increasingly harsh Spanish rule.

Cuban discontent erupted again in 1895 in a classic guerrilla war, with the rebels controlling the countryside and the Spanish army the towns and cities. American economic interests were seriously affected, for both Cubans and Spaniards destroyed American property and disrupted American trade. But the brutality with which Spain attempted to suppress the revolt promoted American sympathy for the Cuban insurgents. Determined to cut the rebels off from their peasant supporters, the Spanish herded most civilians into "reconcentration camps," where tens of thousands died of starvation and disease.

American sympathy was further aroused by the sensationalist **yellow press**. To attract readers and boost advertising revenues, the popular press of the day adopted bold headlines, fevered editorials, and real or exaggerated stories of violence, sex, and corruption. A circulation war helped stimulate interest in a Cuban war. Failure to intervene to protect the innocent from Spanish lust and cruelty, insisted the yellow journalists, would be dishonorable and cowardly.

The nation's religious press, partly because it reflected the prejudice of many Protestants against Catholic Spain, also advocated American intervention. One religious newspaper endorsed an American war against Spain as God's instrument for attacking "that system of iniquity, the papacy." Another promised that if war came, "every Methodist preacher will be a recruiting officer" for the military. The *Catholic Herald* of New York sarcastically referred to the "bloodthirsty preachers" of the Protestant churches, but such preachers undeniably influenced American opinion against Spain.

As the Cuban rebellion dragged on, more and more Americans advocated intervention to stop the carnage, protect U.S. investments, or uphold various principles. In the election of 1896, both major parties endorsed Cuban independence.

## Growing Tensions

In his 1897 inaugural address, President William McKinley outlined an expansionist program ranging from further enlargement of the navy to the annexation of Hawaii and the construction of a Central American canal, but his administration soon focused on Cuba. McKinley's principal complaint was that chronic disorder in Cuba disrupted American investments and agitated public opinion. Personally opposed to military

**yellow press** A deliberately sensational journalism of scandal and exposure designed to attract an urban mass audience and increase advertising revenues.

intervention, McKinley first used diplomacy to press Spain to adopt reforms that would settle the rebellion. In late 1897, Spain modified its brutal military tactics and offered limited autonomy to Cuba. But Cubans insisted on complete independence, a demand that Spain rejected.

Relations between the United States and Spain deteriorated. On February 15, 1898, the U.S. battleship *Maine* blew up in Havana harbor, killing 260 men. The Spanish were not responsible for the tragedy, which a modern naval inquiry has attributed to an internal accident. But many Americans agreed with Theodore Roosevelt, the assistant secretary of the navy, who called it "an act of dirty treachery on the part of the Spaniards" and told McKinley that only war was "compatible with our national honor."

Popular anger was inflamed, but the sinking of the *Maine* by itself did not bring war, though it did restrict McKinley's options and pressure him to be more assertive toward Spain. Other pressures soon began to build on the president. Increasingly, business interests favored war as less disruptive than a volatile peace that threatened their investments. And Republicans, although hesitant to suggest "war for political reasons," warned McKinley that inaction on Cuba endangered their prospects in the fall elections.

At the end of March 1898, McKinley sent Spain an ultimatum. He demanded an armistice in Cuba, an end to the reconcentration policy, and the acceptance of American arbitration, which implied Cuban independence. Again Spain made concessions, abolishing reconcentration and declaring a unilateral armistice. But McKinley had already begun war preparations. He submitted a war message to Congress on April 11, asking for authority to use force against Spain. Congress declared war on Spain on April 25, 1898.

A few national leaders welcomed the war as a step toward imperialism, but there was little popular support for an imperialist foreign policy. Most interventionists were not imperialists, and Congress added the **Teller Amendment** to the war resolution, disclaiming any intention of annexing Cuba and promising that Cubans would govern themselves. Congress also refused to approve either a canal bill or the annexation of Hawaii. Nevertheless, the Spanish-American War did turn the nation toward imperialism.

**Teller Amendment** A congressional resolution adopted in 1898 renouncing any American intention to annex Cuba.

## War and Empire

The decisive engagement of the war took place not in Cuba but in another Spanish colony, the Philippines, and it involved the favored tool of the expansionists, the new navy (see Map 22.2). In 1897, McKinley had approved plans for an attack on the Philippines in the event of war with Spain. Once war was declared, Commodore George Dewey led the U.S. Asiatic squadron into Manila Bay and destroyed the much weaker Spanish fleet on May 1, 1898. This dramatic victory galvanized expansionist sentiment in the United States. With Dewey's triumph, exulted one expansionist, "We are taking our proper rank among the nations of the world. We are after markets, the greatest markets now existing in the world." To expand this foothold in Asia, McKinley ordered troops to the Philippines, postponing the military expedition to Cuba itself.

Dewey's victory also precipitated the annexation of Hawaii, which had seemed unlikely only weeks before. Annexationists now pointed to the islands' strategic importance as stepping stones to Manila. "To maintain our flag in the Philippines, we must raise our flag in Hawaii," the *New York Sun* contended. In July, Congress approved annexation, a decision welcomed by Hawaii's white minority. Native Hawaiians solemnly protested this step taken "without reference to the consent of the people of the Hawaiian Islands." Filipinos would soon face the same American imperial impulse.

Military victory also came swiftly in Cuba, once the U.S. Army finally landed in late June. Victory came despite bureaucratic bungling in the War Department, which left the army poorly led, trained, and supplied. More than 5,000 Americans died of diseases and accidents brought on by such mismanagement; only 379 were killed in battle. State militias supplemented the small regular army, as did volunteer units, such as the famous Rough Riders, a cavalry regiment of cowboys and eastern dandies organized by Leonard Wood and Theodore Roosevelt.

**MAP 22.2 THE SPANISH-AMERICAN WAR** The United States gained quick victories in both theaters of the Spanish-American War. Its naval power proved decisive, with Commodore Dewey destroying one enemy fleet in the Philippines, and a second U.S. naval force cutting off the Spanish in Cuba.

Although the Rough Riders captured public attention, other units were more effective. The 10th Negro Cavalry, for example, played the crucial role in capturing San Juan Hill, a battle popularly associated with the Rough Riders. Nevertheless, the Rough Riders gained the credit, thanks in part to Roosevelt's self-serving and well-promoted account of the conflict, which one humorist proposed retitling *Alone in Cuba*.

United States naval power again proved decisive. In a lopsided battle on July 3, the Spanish squadron in Cuba was destroyed, isolating the Spanish army and guaranteeing its defeat. United States forces then seized the nearby Spanish colony of Puerto Rico without serious opposition. Humbled, Spain signed an armistice ending the war on August 12.

## The Treaty of Paris

The armistice required Spain to accept Cuban independence, cede Puerto Rico and Guam (a Pacific island between Hawaii and the Philippines) to the United States, and allow the Americans to occupy Manila, pending the final disposition of the Philippines at a formal peace conference. The acquisition of Puerto Rico and Guam indicated the expansionist nature the conflict had assumed for the United States. So did the postponement of the Philippine issue. McKinley knew that delay would permit the advocates of expansion to build public support for annexation.

McKinley defended his decision to acquire the Philippines with self-righteous imperialist rhetoric, promising to extend Christian influence and American values. But he was motivated primarily by a determination to use the islands to strengthen America's political and commercial position in East Asia. Moreover, he believed the Filipinos poorly suited to self-rule, and he feared that Germany or Japan might seize the Philippines if the United States did not. Meeting in Paris in December, American and

Read the Document    William McKinley, Speech on the Decision on the Philippines (1900)

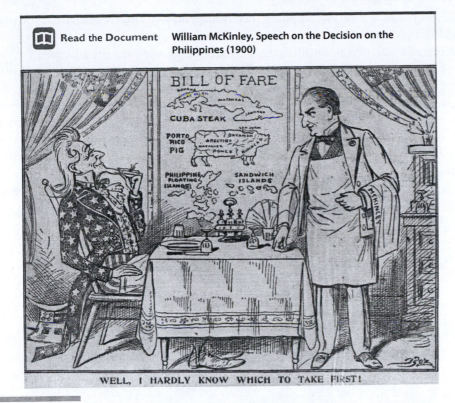

Uncle Sam considers the expansionist menu offered by President McKinley. The Sandwich Islands (Hawaii) were only the appetizer.

Spanish negotiators settled the final terms for peace. Spain agreed—despite Filipino demands for independence—to cede the Philippines to the United States.

The decision to acquire the Philippines sparked a dramatic debate over the ratification of the Treaty of Paris. Imperialists invoked the familiar arguments of economic expansion, national destiny, and strategic necessity, while asserting that Americans had religious and racial responsibilities to advance civilization by uplifting backward peoples. *The United States Investor* demanded the Philippines as "a base of operations" in East Asia; other economic expansionists warned that "our commercial rivals in the Orient" would grab the islands if the United States did not. *The Presbyterian Banner* spoke for a nearly unanimous religious press in describing U.S. acquisition as a "duty in the interest of human freedom and Christian progress." And some imperialists argued that conquering and holding the Philippines as a colony would create among Americans the "physical manhood" and "character of force" presumably necessary in the international Darwinian struggle.

Opponents of the treaty raised profound questions about national goals and ideals. They included such prominent figures as the civil-service reformer Carl Schurz, the steel baron Andrew Carnegie, the social reformer Jane Addams, the labor leader Samuel Gompers, and the author Mark Twain. Their organizational base was the Anti-Imperialist League, which campaigned against the treaty, distributing pamphlets, petitioning Congress, and holding rallies. The League's criticisms reflected a conviction that imperialism was a repudiation of the moral and political traditions embodied in the Declaration of Independence. The acquisition of overseas colonies, they argued, conflicted with the nation's commitment to liberty and its claim to moral superiority.

But other arguments were less high-minded. Many anti-imperialists objected to expansion on the racist grounds that Filipinos were inferior and inassimilable. Gompers feared that cheap Asian labor would undercut the wages and living standards of American workers. The *San Francisco Call,* representing California-Hawaiian sugar interests, wanted no competition from the Philippines.

Finally, on February 6, 1899, the Senate narrowly ratified the treaty. All but two Republicans supported the pact; most Democrats opposed it, although several voted in favor after William Jennings Bryan suggested that approval was necessary to end the war and detach the Philippines from Spain. Thereafter, he hoped, a congressional resolution would give the Filipinos their independence. But, by a single vote, the Republicans defeated a Democratic proposal for Philippine independence once a stable government had been established; the United States would keep the islands.

Bryan attempted to make the election of 1900 a referendum on "the paramount issue" of imperialism, promising to free the Philippines if the Democrats won. But other issues determined the outcome. Some of the most ardent anti-imperialists were conservatives who remained loyal to McKinley because they could not tolerate Bryan's economic policies. Republicans also benefited from the prosperity the country experienced under McKinley after the hard 1890s, and they played on the nationalist emotions evoked by the war, especially by nominating the "hero of San Juan Hill," Theodore Roosevelt, for vice president. Bryan lost again, as in 1896, and under Republican leadership, the United States became an imperial nation.

**Read the Document** Frederick Bancroft, ed., Platform of the American Anti-Imperialist League (1898)

Republicans countered William Jennings Bryan's attempt to make imperialism an issue in 1900 by wrapping themselves in patriotism and the American flag. "Take Your Choice," a cartoon from *Judge* magazine, posed President McKinley raising Old Glory over the Philippines with a disheveled and frantic Bryan chopping down the symbol of American pride and power.

# ✳ Explore the Spanish-American War on MyHistoryLab

## HOW DID THE UNITED STATES BUILD AN OVERSEAS EMPIRE IN THE 1890s?

By the end of the 1800s, American territorial expansion had reached across the continent. This territory was not "free land" but territory that formerly belonged to Native Americans. During the last decade of the century, the United States began to acquire an empire overseas. The country obtained many of its new possessions in 1899 through defeating Spain in a war the previous year. From the perspectives of the inhabitants of these territories, U.S. victory in the war meant trading one imperial master, Spain, for another as the territories of the United States spread from the Caribbean Sea across the Pacific Ocean.

One of the pivotal events in the Spanish-American War of 1898 and the conquest of Cuba was the capture of the blockhouse on San Juan Hill by American forces—including Col. Theodore Roosevelt's cavalry unit, the "Rough Riders"—on July 2, 1898.

### U.S. TERRITORIAL ACQUISITIONS, 1890s

| Location | Year | From |
|----------|------|------|
| Hawaii | 1898 | Annexation |
| Cuba | 1899 | Spain |
| Puerto Rico | 1899 | Spain |
| Guam | 1899 | Spain |
| Philippines | 1899 | Spain |

SOURCE: Library of Congress
http://www.loc.gov/rr/hispanic/1898/chronology.html.

**KEY QUESTIONS**   Use **MyHistoryLab** *Explorer* **to answer** these **questions:**

**Analysis** ▶▶▶ *Where and how did the Spanish-American War unfold?*

Map the war's major battles.

**Response** ▶▶▶ *How did American territorial claims change between 1790 and 1900?*

Map the expansion of the United States, paying particular attention to the trends of the 1890s.

**Comparison** ▶▶▶ *What were domestic attitudes toward the new overseas empire?*

See how American expansion was represented at home.

# Imperial Ambitions: The United States and East Asia, 1899–1917

**22.3** What opportunities and obstacles did American expansionists find in Asia?

n 1899, as the United States occupied its new empire, Assistant Secretary of State John Bassett Moore observed that the nation had become "a world power.... Where formerly we had only commercial interests, we now have territorial and political interests as well." American policies to promote these expanded interests focused first on East Asia and Latin America, where the Spanish-American War had provided the United States with both opportunities and challenges. In Asia, the first issue concerned the fate of the Philippines, but looming beyond it were American ambitions in China, where other imperial nations had their own goals.

## The Philippine-American War

Filipino nationalists, like the Cuban insurgents, were already fighting Spain for their independence before the sudden American intervention. The Filipino leader, Emilio Aguinaldo, welcomed Dewey's naval victory as the sign of a de facto alliance with the United States; he then issued a declaration of independence and proclaimed the Philippine Republic. His own troops captured most of Luzon, the Philippines' major island, before the U.S. Army arrived. But the Filipinos' optimism declined as American officials acted in an increasingly imperious manner toward them, first refusing to meet with the "savages" and then ridiculing Aguinaldo and "his so-called government." When the Treaty of Paris provided for U.S. ownership rather than independence, Filipinos felt betrayed. Their initial vision of a "liberating America," wrote one Filipino, had been but a "beautiful fiction"; now they endured only "cruel disenchantment." Mounting tensions erupted in a battle between American and Filipino troops outside Manila on February 4, 1899, sparking a long and brutal war.

Ultimately, the United States used nearly four times as many soldiers to suppress the Filipinos as it had to defeat Spain in Cuba and, in a tragic irony, employed many of the same brutal methods for which it had condemned Spain. United States military commanders adopted ever harsher measures, often directed at civilians, who were crowded into concentration camps in which perhaps 200,000 died. American troops often made little effort to distinguish between soldiers and noncombatants, viewing all Filipinos with racial antagonism. After reporting one massacre of a thousand men, women, and children, an American soldier declared, "I am in my glory when I can sight my gun on some dark skin and pull the trigger."

A California newspaper defended such U.S. atrocities with remarkable candor: "There has been too much hypocrisy about this Philippine business. . . . Let us all be frank. WE DO NOT WANT THE FILIPINOS. WE DO WANT THE PHILIPPINES. All of our troubles in this annexation matter have been caused by the presence in the Philippine Islands of the Filipinos. . . . The more of them killed the better. It seems harsh. But they must yield before the superior race."

The overt racism of the war repelled African Americans. John Mitchell, a Virginia editor, condemned all the talk of "white man's burden" as deceptive rhetoric for brutal acts that could not be "defended either in moral or international law."

Other Americans also denounced the war. The Anti-Imperialist League revived, citing the war as proof of the corrosive influence of imperialism on the nation's morals and principles. Women figured prominently in mass meetings and lobbying efforts to have the troops returned, their moral stature further undercutting the rationale for colonial wars. By 1902, the realities of imperial policy—including American casualties far exceeding those of the Spanish-American War—disillusioned most of those who had clamored to save Cuba.

By that time, however, the American military had largely suppressed the rebellion, and the United States had established a colonial government headed by an American governor general appointed by the president. Filipino involvement in the government was limited on educational and religious grounds. Compared to the brutal war policies, U.S. colonial rule was relatively benign, though paternalistic. William Howard Taft, the first governor general, launched a program that brought the islands new schools and roads, a public health system, and an economy tied closely to both the United States and a small Filipino elite. Independence would not come for nearly half a century.

## China and the Open Door

America's determined involvement in the Philippines reflected its preoccupation with China. By the mid-1890s, other powers threatened prospects for American commercial expansion in China. Japan, after defeating China in 1895, annexed Formosa (Taiwan) and secured economic privileges in the mainland province of Fukien (Fujian); the major European powers then competed aggressively to claim other areas of China as their own exclusive **spheres of influence**.

**spheres of influence** Regions dominated and controlled by an outside power.

These developments alarmed the American business community. It was confident that, given an equal opportunity, the United States would prevail in international trade because of its efficient production and marketing systems. But the creation of exclusive spheres of influence limited the opportunity to compete. In early 1898, business leaders organized the Committee on American Interests in China to lobby Washington to promote American trade in the shrinking Chinese market. The committee's efforts influenced McKinley's decision to acquire the Philippines, but the Philippines, in the words of Mark Hanna, were only a "foothold"; China was the real target.

In 1899, the government moved to advance American interests in China. Without consulting the Chinese, Secretary of State John Hay asked the imperial powers to maintain an **Open Door** for the commercial and financial activities of all nations within their Chinese spheres of influence. Privately, Hay had already approved a plan to seize a Chinese port for the United States, if necessary to join in the partition of China, but equal opportunity for trade and investment would serve American interests far better. It would avoid the expense of military occupation, avert further domestic criticism of U.S. imperialism, and guarantee a wider sphere for American business.

**Open Door** American policy of seeking equal trade and investment opportunities in foreign nations or regions.

The other nations replied evasively, except for Russia, which rejected the Open Door concept. In 1900, an anti-foreign Chinese nationalist movement known as the Boxers laid siege to the diplomatic quarter in Beijing. The defeat of the Boxer Rebellion by a multinational military force, to which the United States contributed troops, again raised the prospect of a division of China among the colonial powers. Hay sent a second Open Door note, reaffirming "the principle of equal and impartial trade" and respect for China's territorial integrity.

Despite Hay's notes, China remained a tempting arena for imperial schemes. But the Open Door became a cardinal doctrine of American foreign policy in the twentieth century, a means by which the United States sought to dominate foreign markets. The United States promoted an informal or economic empire, as opposed to the traditional territorial colonial empire identified with European powers. Henceforth, American economic interests expected the U.S. government to oppose any developments that threatened to close other nations' economies to American penetration and to advance "private enterprise" abroad.

## Rivalry with Japan and Russia

At the turn of the twentieth century, both the Japanese and the Russians were more deeply involved in East Asia than was the United States. Japan and Russia expressed little support for the Open Door, which they correctly saw as favoring American interests over their own. But in pursuing their ambitions in China, the two countries came into conflict with each other. Alarmed at the threat of Russian expansion in Manchuria and Korea, Japan in 1904 attacked the Russian fleet at Port Arthur and defeated the Russian army in Manchuria.

American sympathies in the Russo-Japanese War lay with Japan, for the Russians were attempting to close Manchuria to foreign trade. President Theodore Roosevelt privately complained that a reluctant American public opinion meant that "we cannot fight to keep Manchuria open." He welcomed the Japanese attack in the belief that "Japan is playing our game." But he soon began to fear that an overwhelming Japanese victory would threaten American interests as much as Russian expansionism did, so he skillfully mediated an end to the war. In the Treaty of Portsmouth in 1905, Japan won control of Russia's sphere of influence in Manchuria, half the Russian island of Sakhalin, and recognition of its domination of Korea.

The treaty marked Japan's emergence as a great power, but, ironically, it worsened relations with the United States. Anti-American riots broke out in Tokyo. The Japanese people blamed Roosevelt for obstructing further Japanese gains and blocking a Russian indemnity that would have helped Japan pay for the war. Tensions were further aggravated by San Francisco's decision in 1906 to segregate Asian and white schoolchildren. Japan regarded this as a racist insult, and Roosevelt worried that "the infernal fools in California" would provoke war. Finally, he persuaded the city to rescind the school order in exchange for his limiting Japanese immigration, which lay at the heart of California's hostility. Under the **Gentlemen's Agreement**, worked out through a series of diplomatic notes in 1907 and 1908, Japan agreed to deny passports to workers trying to come to the United States, and the United States promised not to prohibit Japanese immigration overtly or completely.

**Gentlemen's Agreement** A diplomatic agreement in 1907 between Japan and the United States curtailing but not abolishing Japanese immigration.

The United States and Japan entered into other agreements aimed at calming their mutual suspicions in East Asia but failed to mend the deteriorating relationship. Increasingly, Japan began to exclude American trade from its territories in East Asia and to press for further control over China. General Leonard Wood complained that the Japanese "intend to dominate Asia as we do the Americas." Elihu Root, Roosevelt's secretary of state, insisted that the Open Door and American access had to be maintained but asserted also that the United States did not want to be "a protagonist in a controversy in China with Russia and Japan or with either of them." The problem was that the United States could not sustain the Open Door without becoming a protagonist in China. This paradox would plague American foreign policy in Asia for decades.

# Imperial Power: The United States and Latin America, 1899–1917

**22.4**   What was the nature of U.S. involvement in Latin America?

n Latin America, where no major powers directly challenged American objectives as Japan and Russia did in Asia, the United States was more successful in exercising imperial power (see Map 22.3). In the two decades after the Spanish-American War, the United States intervened militarily in Latin America no fewer than twenty times to promote its own strategic and economic interests (see Table 22.2). Policymakers believed that these goals required restricting the influence of European nations in the region, building an isthmian canal under U.S. control, and establishing the order thought necessary for American trade and investments to expand. Intervention at times achieved these goals, but it often ignored the wishes and interests of Latin Americans, provoked resistance and disorder, and aroused lasting ill will.

## U.S. Rule in Puerto Rico

Well before 1898, expansionists had advocated acquiring Puerto Rico because of its strategic location in the Caribbean. Military invasion during the Spanish-American

Read the Document    Platt Amendment (1901)

**MAP 22.3 THE UNITED STATES IN THE CARIBBEAN** For strategic and economic reasons, the United States repeatedly intervened in the Caribbean in the first three decades of the twentieth century. Such interventions protected the U.S. claim to dominance but often provoked great hostility among Latin Americans.

TABLE 22.2 U.S. INTERVENTIONS IN LATIN AMERICA, 1891–1934

| Country | Type of Intervention | Year |
|---|---|---|
| Chile | Ultimatum | 1891–1892 |
| Colombia | Military intervention | 1903 |
| Cuba | Occupation | 1898–1902, 1906–1909, 1912, 1917–1922 |
| Dominican Republic | Military and administrative intervention | 1905–1907 |
| | Occupation | 1916–1924 |
| Haiti | Occupation | 1915–1934 |
| Mexico | Military intervention | 1914, 1916–1917 |
| Nicaragua | Occupation | 1912–1925, 1927–1933 |
| Panama | Acquisition of Canal Zone | 1904 |
| Puerto Rico | Military invasion and territorial acquisition | 1898 |

War and the Treaty of Paris brought the island under American control, with mixed consequences. A military government improved transportation and sanitation and developed public health and education. But to the dismay of Puerto Ricans, who had been promised that American rule would bestow "the advantages and blessings of enlightened civilization," their political freedoms were curtailed.

In 1900, the United States established a civil government, but it was under U.S. control, with popular participation even less than under Spain. In the so-called Insular Cases (1901), the Supreme Court upheld the authority of Congress to establish an inferior status for Puerto Rico as an "unincorporated territory" without promise of statehood. Disappointed Puerto Ricans pressed to end this colonial status, some advocating independence, others statehood or merely greater autonomy. This division would continue for decades to come. In 1917, the United States granted citizenship and greater political rights to Puerto Ricans, but their island remained an unincorporated territory under an American governor appointed by the president.

Economic development also disappointed most islanders, for American investors quickly gained control of the best land and pursued large-scale sugar production for the U.S. market. The landless peasants struggled to survive as workers on large plantations. By 1929, the new governor—ironically, Theodore Roosevelt, Jr.—found that under the domination of American capital, "poverty was widespread and hunger, almost to the verge of starvation, common." Increasingly, Puerto Ricans left their homes to seek work in the United States.

## Cuba as a U.S. Protectorate

Despite the Teller Amendment, the Spanish-American War did not leave Cuba independent. McKinley opposed independence and distrusted the Cuban rebels. Many Americans considered Cubans racial inferiors, and one U.S. general in Cuba snorted, "Why those people are no more fit for self-government than gun-powder is for hell." Accordingly, a U.S. military government was established in the island. Only in 1900, when the Democrats made an issue of imperialism, did McKinley move toward permitting a Cuban government. He summoned a Cuban convention to draft a constitution under the direction of the American military governor, General Leonard Wood. Reflecting the continuing U.S. fear of Cuban autonomy, the constitution restricted suffrage on the basis of property and education, leaving few Cubans with the right to vote.

Even so, before removing its troops, the United States wanted to ensure its control over Cuba. It therefore made U.S. withdrawal contingent on Cuba's adding to its constitution the provisions of the **Platt Amendment**, drawn up in 1901 by the U.S. secretary of war. The Platt Amendment restricted Cuba's autonomy in diplomatic relations with other countries and in internal financial policies, required Cuba to lease naval bases to the United States, and most important, authorized U.S. intervention to maintain order and preserve Cuban independence. As General Wood correctly observed, "There is, of course, little or no independence left Cuba under the Platt Amendment."

Cubans resented this restriction on their sovereignty, and to preserve American influence, the United States sent troops into Cuba three times between 1906 and 1917 (Roosevelt admitted his recurrent itch to "wipe its people off the face of the earth"). During their occupations of Cuba, the Americans modernized its financial system, built roads and schools, and developed a public-health and sanitation program that eradicated the deadly disease of yellow fever. But most Cubans thought that these material benefits did not compensate for their loss of political and economic independence. The Platt Amendment remained the basis of U.S. policy toward Cuba until 1934.

## The Panama Canal

The Spanish-American War intensified the long American interest in a canal through Central America to eliminate the lengthy and dangerous ocean route around South America. Its commercial value seemed obvious, but the war emphasized its strategic importance.

**Platt Amendment** A stipulation the United States had inserted into the Cuban constitution in 1901 restricting Cuban autonomy and authorizing U.S. intervention and naval bases.

McKinley declared that a canal was now "demanded by the annexation of the Hawaiian Islands and the prospective expansion of our influence and commerce in the Pacific."

Theodore Roosevelt moved quickly to implement McKinley's commitment to a canal after becoming president in 1901. He was convinced that a strong presidential role was as important in foreign affairs as in domestic politics. Neither Congress nor "the average American," he believed, took "the trouble to think carefully or deeply" about international affairs. Roosevelt's canal diplomacy helped establish the assertive presidency that has largely characterized U.S. foreign policy ever since.

First, Roosevelt persuaded Britain to renounce its treaty right to a joint role with the United States in any canal venture. Where to build the canal was a problem. One possibility was Nicaragua, where a sea-level canal could be built. Another was Panama, then part of Colombia. A canal through Panama would require an elaborate system of locks. But the French-owned Panama Canal Company had been unsuccessfully trying to build a canal in Panama and was now eager to sell its rights to the project before they expired in 1904.

📖 **Read the Document**    **Theodore Roosevelt, from the Third Annual Message to Congress (1903)**

"I RATHER LIKE THAT IMPORTED AFFAIR."

The *Puck* cartoonist criticizes Theodore Roosevelt's aggressive foreign policy by depicting him in his Rough-Rider uniform and indicating his preference for the crown of European imperialism over the simple American hats of previous presidents.

In 1902, Congress directed Roosevelt to purchase the French company's claims for $40 million and build the canal in Panama if Colombia ceded a strip of land across the isthmus on reasonable terms. Otherwise, Roosevelt was to negotiate with Nicaragua for the alternative route. In 1903, Roosevelt pressed Colombia to sell a canal zone to the United States for $10 million and an annual payment of $250,000. Colombia, however, rejected the proposal, fearing the loss of its sovereignty in Panama and hoping for more money. After all, when the Panama Canal Company's rights expired, Colombia could then legitimately collect the $40 million so generously offered to the company.

Roosevelt was furious. After threatening "those contemptible little creatures" in Colombia, he began writing a message to Congress proposing military action to seize the isthmus of Panama. Instead of using direct force, however, Roosevelt worked with Philippe Bunau-Varilla, a French official of the Panama Canal Company, to exploit long-smoldering Panamanian discontent with Colombia. Roosevelt's purpose was to get the Canal Zone, Bunau-Varilla's to get the American money. Roosevelt ordered U.S. naval forces to Panama; from New York, Bunau-Varilla coordinated a revolt against Colombian authority directed by officials of the Panama Railroad, owned by Bunau-Varilla's canal company. The bloodless "revolution" succeeded when U.S. forces prevented Colombian troops from landing in Panama, although the United States was bound by treaty to maintain Colombian sovereignty in the region. Bunau-Varilla promptly signed a treaty accepting Roosevelt's original terms for a canal zone and making Panama a U.S. protectorate, which it remained until 1939. Panamanians themselves denounced the treaty for surrendering sovereignty in the zone to the United States, but the United States took formal control of the Canal Zone in 1904 and completed construction of the Panama Canal in 1914.

Many Americans were appalled by what the *Chicago American* called Roosevelt's "rough-riding assault upon another republic over the shattered wreckage of international law and diplomatic usage." But others, as *Public Opinion* reported, wanted a "canal above all things" and were willing to overlook moral questions and approve the acquisition of the canal zone as simply "a business question." Roosevelt himself boasted, "I took the Canal Zone and let Congress debate," but his actions generated resentment among Latin Americans that rankled for decades.

## The Roosevelt Corollary

To protect the security of the canal, the United States increased its authority in the Caribbean. The objective was to establish conditions there that would both eliminate any pretext for European intervention and promote American control over trade and investment. The inability of Latin American nations to pay their debts to foreign lenders raised the possibility of European intervention, as evidenced by a German and British blockade of Venezuela in 1903 to secure repayment of debts to European bankers. "If we intend to say hands off to the powers of Europe," Roosevelt concluded, "then sooner or later we must keep order ourselves."

Toward that end, in 1904, Roosevelt announced a new policy, the so-called **Roosevelt Corollary** to the Monroe Doctrine. "Chronic wrongdoing," he declared, would cause the United States to exercise "an international police power" in Latin America. The Monroe Doctrine had expressed American hostility to European intervention in Latin America; the Roosevelt Corollary attempted to justify U.S. intervention and authority in the region. Roosevelt invoked his corollary immediately, imposing American management of the debts and customs duties of the Dominican Republic in 1905. Commercial rivalries and political intrigue in that poor nation had created disorder, which Roosevelt suppressed for both economic and strategic reasons. Financial insolvency was averted, popular revolution prevented, and possible European intervention forestalled.

Latin Americans vigorously resented the United States' unilateral claim to authority. By 1907, the so-called Drago Doctrine (named after Argentina's foreign minister) was incorporated into international law, prohibiting armed intervention to collect

**Roosevelt Corollary** President Theodore Roosevelt's policy asserting U.S. authority to intervene in the affairs of Latin American nations; an expansion of the Monroe Doctrine.

THE BIG STICK IN THE CARIBBEAN SEA

The Roosevelt Corollary proclaimed the intention of the United States to police Latin America. Enforcement came, as this cartoon shows, with Roosevelt and subsequent presidents sending the U.S. Navy to one Caribbean nation after another.

debts. Still, the United States would continue to invoke the Roosevelt Corollary to advance its interests in the hemisphere.

## Dollar Diplomacy

Roosevelt's successor as president, William Howard Taft, hoped to promote U.S. interests in less confrontational ways. He proposed "substituting dollars for bullets"—using government action to encourage private American investments in Latin America to supplant European interests, promote development and stability, and earn profits for American bankers. Under this **dollar diplomacy**, American investments in the Caribbean increased dramatically during Taft's presidency from 1909 to 1913, and the State Department helped arrange for American bankers to establish financial control over Haiti and Honduras.

But Taft did not shrink from employing military force to protect American property or to establish the conditions he thought necessary for American investments. In fact, Taft intervened more frequently than Roosevelt had, with Nicaragua a major target. In 1909, Taft sent U.S. troops there to aid a revolution fomented by an American mining corporation and to seize the Nicaraguan customs houses. Under the new government, American bankers then gained control of Nicaragua's national bank, railroad, and customs service. To protect these arrangements, U.S. troops were again dispatched in 1912. To control popular opposition to the American client government, the marines remained in Nicaragua for two decades. Military power, not the social and economic improvement promised by dollar diplomacy, kept Nicaragua's minority government stable and subordinate to the United States.

Dollar diplomacy increased American power and influence in the Caribbean and tied underdeveloped countries to the United States economically and strategically. By 1913, American investments in the region had grown dramatically, and Americans had captured more than 50 percent of the foreign trade of Costa Rica, Cuba, the Dominican Republic, Guatemala, Haiti, Honduras, Nicaragua, and Panama. But this policy failed to improve conditions for most Latin Americans. United States officials remained primarily concerned with promoting American control and extracting American profits from the region. Not surprisingly, dollar diplomacy proved unpopular in Latin America.

**dollar diplomacy** The U.S. policy of using private investment in other nations to promote American diplomatic goals and business interests.

651

# From Then to Now
# The Panama Canal

On December 31, 1999, almost a century after the United States took control of the Panama Canal Zone, Panama reclaimed it. "The canal is ours," proclaimed Panamanian president Mireya Moscoso, as her country's flag was raised over the canal area, resolving a contentious and complex issue.

From the beginning, Panamanians denounced the 1903 treaty—"the treaty that no Panamanians signed"—that had given the United States a perpetual lease and American sovereignty over a strip of land that divided their country in two. For many decades, the United States rejected the repeated Panamanian demands for an end to this "Yankee colonialism" over the Canal Zone, with one U.S. senator explaining, "We stole it fair and square." But in the 1960s and 1970s, the United States began negotiating the return of the Canal Zone to Panama, motivated less by concerns about Panamanian discontent than by conclusions that the canal was no longer of such strategic significance that the United States needed to maintain perpetual control and exclusive jurisdiction over it. Besides, the canal was gradually becoming obsolete, too small to accommodate ever-larger ships.

A treaty in 1978 returned jurisdiction over the Canal Zone to Panama but left the United States responsible for operating and defending the canal until December 31, 1999. During the 1990s, Panama gradually assumed territorial and legal jurisdiction over the canal, with Panamanian administrators and workers assuming responsibilities previously held by Americans. Shortly after celebrating the final transfer of authority, Panamanian officials began planning to modernize the canal, and in 2007 Panama started a massive construction project to double the canal's capacity and thereby facilitate international trade and provide much needed revenue for the country. The new sets of locks are expected to be completed by 2014, one hundred years after the canal first opened.

**Question for Discussion**

- Why did Americans and Panamanians hold such contrasting views of the Canal Zone and its importance?

Both critics and admirers saw the Panama Canal as topping Roosevelt's imperial crown.

President Mireya Moscoso celebrated Panama's regaining control of the Canal Zone in 1999.

## Wilsonian Interventions

Taking office in 1913, the Democrat Woodrow Wilson repudiated the interventionist policies of his Republican predecessors. He promised that the United States would "never again seek one additional foot of territory by conquest" but would instead work to promote "human rights, national integrity, and opportunity" in Latin America.

Nonetheless, Wilson soon became the most interventionist president in American history. Convinced that the United States had to expand its exports and investments abroad and that U.S. dominance of the Caribbean was strategically necessary, he also held the racist belief that Latin Americans were inferior and needed paternalistic guidance from the United States. In providing that guidance, through military force if necessary, Wilson came close to assuming that American principles and objectives were absolutes, and that different cultural traditions and national aspirations were simply wrong. His self-righteousness and determination to transform the behavior of other peoples led his policies to be dubbed "missionary diplomacy," but they also contained elements of Roosevelt's commitment to military force and Taft's reliance on economic power.

**Caribbean Interventions.**   In 1915, Wilson ordered U.S. marines to Haiti to preserve "gravely menaced" American interests. The United States saved and even enhanced those interests by establishing a protectorate over Haiti and drawing up a constitution that increased U.S. property rights and commercial privileges. The U.S. Navy selected a new Haitian president, granting him nominal authority over a client government. Real authority, however, rested with the American military, which controlled Haiti until 1934, protecting the small elite who cooperated with American interests and exploited their own people. As usual, American military rule improved the country's transportation, sanitation, and educational systems, but the forced-labor program that the United States adopted to build such public works provoked widespread resentment. In 1919, marines suppressed a revolt against American domination, killing more than 3,000 Haitians.

Wilson also intervened elsewhere in the Caribbean. In 1916, when the Dominican Republic refused to cede control of its finances to U.S. bankers, Wilson ordered the marines to occupy the country. The marines ousted Dominican officials, installed a military government to rule "on behalf of the Dominican government," and ran the nation until 1924. In 1917, the United States intervened in Cuba, which remained under American control until 1922.

**Interfering with Mexico.**   Wilson also involved himself in the internal affairs of Mexico. The lengthy dictatorship of Porfirio Díaz had collapsed in 1911 in revolutionary disorder. The popular leader Francisco Madero took power and promised democratic and economic reforms that alarmed both wealthy Mexicans and foreign investors, particularly Americans. In 1913, General Victoriano Huerta seized control in a brutal counterrevolution backed by the landed aristocracy and foreign interests. Appalled by the violence of Huerta's power grab and aware that opponents had organized to reestablish constitutional government, Wilson refused to recognize the Huerta government.

Hoping to bring the Constitutionalists to power, Wilson authorized arms sales to the forces led by Venustiano Carranza, pressured other nations to deprive Huerta of foreign support, and blockaded the Mexican port of Vera Cruz. In 1914, Wilson exploited a minor incident to have the marines attack and occupy Vera Cruz. This assault damaged his image as a promoter of peace and justice, and even Carranza and the Constitutionalists denounced the American occupation as unwarranted aggression. After Carranza toppled Huerta, Wilson shifted his support to Francisco ("Pancho") Villa, who seemed more susceptible to American guidance. But Carranza's growing popular support in Mexico and Wilson's preoccupation with World War I in Europe finally led the United States to grant de facto recognition to the Carranza government in 1915.

Villa then began terrorizing New Mexico and Texas, hoping to provoke an American intervention that would undermine Carranza. In 1916, Wilson ordered troops under General John J. Pershing to pursue Villa into Mexico, leading Carranza to fear a permanent U.S. occupation of northern Mexico. Soon the American soldiers were fighting the Mexican army rather than Villa's bandits. On the brink of full-fledged war, Wilson finally ordered U.S. troops to withdraw in January 1917 and extended full recognition to the Carranza government. Wilson lamely defended these steps as showing that the United States had no intention of imposing on Mexico "an order and government of our own choosing." That had been Wilson's original objective, however. His aggressive tactics had not merely failed but also embittered relations with Mexico.

# Engaging Europe: New Concerns, Old Constraints

**22.5** Why did the United States take a larger role in Europe at the beginning of the twentieth century?

hile the United States expanded its power in Latin America and strove to increase its influence in Asia in the early twentieth century, it also took a larger role in Europe. Its traditional policy of noninvolvement, however, remained popular with many Americans and constituted an important restraint upon the new imperial nation.

Responding to the lopsided outcome of the Spanish-American War, European nations immediately began to adjust their policies to take into account the evident power of the United States. German officials even considered seeking an alliance in order to strengthen Germany in Europe. But Germany's rival, Great Britain, moved quickly to resolve all possible disputes with the United States and thereby establish a basis for long-term cooperation. Britain's support for the American annexation of the Philippines and its decision in 1901 to accede to American control of the projected Panama Canal were early examples of this policy. These steps not only abetted the expansionist ambitions of the United States but also enabled Britain to focus more of its attention and fleet on the North Atlantic against the growing German navy. By 1905, only a decade after Britain and the United States seemed on the verge of war over Venezuela, British and American diplomats agreed that their nations' interests were "absolutely identical and that the more closely we can work together, the better it will be for us and the world at large."

Roosevelt also cautiously intervened in European affairs, convinced that it was in the nation's interests "to keep matters on an even keel in Europe." The great European powers were aligning themselves into rival blocs: the Entente of Britain and France (and sometimes Russia) and the Alliance of Germany and Austria-Hungary (and sometimes Italy). When France and Germany quarreled over the control of Morocco in 1906, Roosevelt helped arrange an international conference at Algeciras, Spain, to resolve the crisis. While placating Germany, American diplomats then helped uphold France's claims, upon its pledge to maintain an open door in Morocco, a pledge the United States would later use to insist upon securing petroleum and commercial opportunities. Roosevelt had helped preserve the balance of power in Europe while advancing what he saw as America's own interests.

Eager to ensure stability, American leaders also engaged Europeans in efforts to promote arbitration of international disputes. In 1899, the United States participated in the First Hague Peace Conference, which created the Permanent Court of Arbitration. Roosevelt helped arrange a second Hague conference in 1907. It did not accept American proposals for compulsory arbitration, but it led to another conference in 1909 which issued the Declaration of London codifying international law for maritime war and establishing the rights of neutral nations. And Roosevelt, Taft, and Wilson negotiated dozens of arbitration or conciliation treaties providing for submitting international disputes to the Hague Court.

However, public opinion and Senate opposition, rooted in older perspectives toward involvement in world affairs, persistently restricted the effectiveness of these efforts. Although the treaties themselves had broad loopholes, the Senate insisted upon further restricting the possible questions to be arbitrated and reserved for itself the right to approve every particular decision to arbitrate. These restrictive views, grumbled Roosevelt and Taft, rendered the treaties ineffective; they would shortly cause Wilson still greater difficulty. The irony of this impasse was symbolized by Senator Henry Cabot Lodge, who regularly championed an imperial role for the United States while also endorsing the traditional American isolationist stance toward European power politics. In criticizing a proposed treaty a few years before World War I, Lodge declared, "we have no concern with the wars of Europe."

## Conclusion

By the time of Woodrow Wilson's presidency, the United States had been expanding its involvement in world affairs for half a century. Several themes had emerged from this activity: increasing American domination of the Caribbean, continuing interest in East Asia, the creation of an overseas empire, and the evolution of the United States into a major world power.

Underlying these developments was an uneasy mixture of ideas and objectives. The American involvement in the world reflected a traditional, if often misguided, sense of national rectitude and mission. Generous humanitarian impulses vied with ugly racist prejudices as Americans sought both to help other peoples and to direct them toward U.S. concepts of religion, sanitation, capitalist development, and public institutions. American motives ranged from ensuring national security and competing with European colonial powers to the conviction that the United States had to expand its economic interests abroad.

But if imperialism, both informal and at times colonial, brought Americans greater wealth and power, it also increased tensions in Asia and contributed to anti-American hostility and revolutionary ferment in Latin America. In addition, it entangled the United States in the Great Power rivalries that would ultimately result in two world wars.

**For Suggested Readings go to MyHistoryLab.**

# Chapter Review

## The Roots of Imperialism

**22.1** What arguments were made in favor of American expansion in the late nineteenth century? p. 632

Many Americans proposed expanding U.S. influence in the world. Some favored aggressively building a colonial empire, but most preferred a less formal hegemony, achieved through extensive trade and investments or a cultural expansionism in which the nation exported its ideals and institutions. Only fitfully, however, did government officials pursue an active foreign policy before the 1890s.

## The Spanish-American War

**22.2** What were the most important consequences of the Spanish-American War? p. 638

For economic, political, and ideological reasons, the United States expanded Cuba's quest for independence into the Spanish-American War. Military victory in turn propelled the United States into an imperial role. Hawaii was annexed, Puerto Rico incorporated, Cuba occupied, and the Philippines acquired, although many Americans vigorously protested imperialism as a repudiation of American political and moral ideals.

## Imperial Ambitions: The United States and East Asia, 1899–1917

**22.3** What opportunities and obstacles did American expansionists find in Asia? p. 644

The United States waged a brutal war to suppress Filipino aspirations for independence and to secure a foothold in East Asia. It advanced American commercial and financial expansion in China by opposing exclusive spheres of interest and insisting upon an Open Door policy. Competing Japanese and Russian interests in China, however, threatened to obstruct U.S. dominance.

## Imperial Power: The United States and Latin America, 1899–1917

**22.4** What was the nature of U.S. involvement in Latin America? p. 646

After the Spanish-American War, the United States frequently intervened in Latin America to promote its own strategic and economic interests. It restricted European influence in the region, built the Panama Canal, and established control over many nations, through military occupation, client governments, or dollar diplomacy. Such policies ignored the wishes and interests of Latin Americans and provoked lasting ill will.

## Engaging Europe: New Concerns, Old Constraints

**22.5** Why did the United States take a larger role in Europe at the beginning of the twentieth century? p. 654

After demonstrating its power in the Spanish-American War, the United States tentatively took a larger role in Europe. Although increasingly aligned with Britain, it participated in new efforts to preserve the balance of power and to promote arbitration of international disputes. Public opinion and Senate opposition, however, restricted the effectiveness of these ventures.

# Timeline

**1890**
**Imperialist Roots**—Alfred Thayer Mahan publishes *The Influence of Sea Power upon History*

**1890**

**1893**
**Imperialist Roots**—Harrison signs but Cleveland rejects a treaty for the annexation of Hawaii

**1893**

**1898**
**Spanish-American War**—Spanish-American War is fought and Hawaii is annexed

**1898**

**1899**
**Imperial Ambitions**—Open Door note is issued

**1899**

**Engaging Europe**—First Hague Peace Conference is held

**1899–1902**
**Imperial Ambitions**—Philippine-American War is fought

**1899–1902**

**1904**
**Imperial Power**—United States acquires the Panama Canal Zone; Roosevelt Corollary is announced

**1904**

**1906**
**Engaging Europe**—United States participates in Algeciras Conference

**1906**

**1906–1934**
**Imperial Power**—United States occupies several Latin American countries

**1906–1934**

# 23 America and the Great War 1914–1920

## One American Journey

### President Wilson Calls for a Declaration of War on Germany

**P**roperty can be paid for; the lives of peaceful and innocent people cannot be. The present German submarine warfare against commerce is a warfare against mankind. . . . It is a war against all nations. . . . Each nation must decide for itself how it will meet it. . . . There is one choice we cannot make, we are incapable of making: we will not choose the path of submission and suffer the most sacred rights of our nation and our people to be ignored or violated. The wrongs against which we now array ourselves are no common wrongs; they cut to the very roots of human life. . . . Neutrality is no longer feasible or desirable where the peace of the world is involved and the freedom of its peoples, and the menace to that peace and freedom lies in the existence of autocratic governments backed by organized force which is controlled wholly by their will, not the will of the people. The world must be made safe for democracy. Its peace must be planted upon the tested foundations of political liberty.

## LEARNING OBJECTIVES

| 23.1  | 23.2 | 23.3 | 23.4 |
|---|---|---|---|
| Why were Americans so reluctant to get involved in World War I? p. 659 | How did the war effort threaten civil liberties? p. 665 | What hopes did Wilson have for the Treaty of Versailles? p. 671 | What challenges did America face in the aftermath of the war? p. 679 |

In World War I, government posters exhorted Americans to increase industrial and agricultural production, buy war bonds, and suppress dissent.

 Listen to Chapter 23 on MyHistoryLab

From *The American Journey*, Seventh Edition. Goldfield, Abbott, Anderson, Argersinger, Argersinger and Barney Copyright © 2014 by Pearson Education, Inc. All rights reserved.

#  Watch the Video Series on MyHistoryLab

Learn about some key topics related to this chapter with the *MyHistoryLab Video Series: Key Topics in U.S. History.*

**1** **World War I** How did the United States get involved in a global conflict far from American shores in Western Europe? This video answers this question by exploring the roots of World War I and how European imperialism challenged America's economic interests. Although President Woodrow Wilson embraced American participation in the war as a way to positively effect eventual peace, his goal was largely frustrated.

**◉ Watch on MyHistoryLab**

**A World and a Nation in Upheaval** This video examines the controversial issue of American policies in World War I, which favored Great Britain and forced a German response that almost guaranteed U.S. entry into the war on the side of the Allied powers. The discussion highlights such contributory factors as submarine warfare and the sinking of the *Lusitania* as well as the discovery of the Zimmerman Telegram.

**Watch on MyHistoryLab ◉** **2**

**3** **The United States at War** When the United States entered World War I, it faced a tremendous challenge in getting its military and society onto a war footing. This video covers such topics as the formation of the American Expeditionary Force, mobilization of industry and the home front, the military draft, and the suppression of the language and culture of German Americans to achieve national unity.

**◉ Watch on MyHistoryLab**

**Winning a Hard-Fought Peace** In brokering the peace between the victorious Allies and the defeated Central Powers, Woodrow Wilson faced many challenges abroad and at home, as the video shows. The U.S. Senate proved reluctant to join the new League of Nations, and Wilson's primary war objective failed tragically. **4**

**Watch on MyHistoryLab ◉**

There are, it may be, many months of fiery trial and sacrifice ahead of us. It is a fearful thing to lead this great peaceful people into war, into the most terrible and disastrous of all wars, civilization itself seeming to be in the balance. But the right is more precious than the peace, and we shall fight for the things which we have always carried nearest our hearts. . . . To such a task we can dedicate our lives and our fortunes, everything that we are and everything that we have, with the pride of those who know that the day has come when America is privileged to spend her blood and her might for the principles that gave her birth and happiness and the peace she has treasured.

Excerpted from President Woodrow Wilson's Request for Declaration of War,
April 2, 1917.
Woodrow Wilson Presidential Library.

## Personal Journeys Online

- Jane Addams, *Peace and Bread in Time of War,* 1922. Describing the transition of President Wilson from an advocate of peace to one of war.
- Letter from former president Theodore Roosevelt to Sir Edward Grey, 1915. Promoting American preparedness and support of the Allies.

**E** **scorted by the U.S. cavalry** on the evening of April 2, 1917, Woodrow Wilson drove through a misty rain eerily illuminated by searchlights down Pennsylvania Avenue to Capitol Hill to deliver his war address. Throughout the day the Emergency Peace Federation had frantically lobbied Congress, but sentiment in both houses was growing for war. Mounted police with drawn sabers held back silent crowds as Wilson asked Congress to declare war on Germany, a war, many insisted, that had little popular support. Even Wilson conceded that the war he requested would sow death, misery, and reaction throughout the nation but also threatened "the firm hand of repression" against disloyalty—anticipating battles at home as well as abroad. When Wilson promised to make the world "safe for democracy," many members of Congress, waving small American flags, broke into cheers, and Senator Lodge personally congratulated Wilson.

On April 4, Senator Robert La Follette delivered a three-hour speech denouncing the president's call for war as a dangerous and reckless journey for the American nation. But La Follette's well-known oratorical talents proved unable to sway the forces for war in Congress. Indeed, his speech aroused such anger in the Senate chamber that he was handed a noose as he exited the room. Both the Senate and the House overwhelmingly supported Wilson's request and the United States entered the war on April 6. Denounced in the press, Senator La Follette and his family were ostracized for his antiwar views, providing a sobering indication of the treatment Americans who dared to oppose the war against Germany would face.

Two years later on July 10, 1919, Wilson made the same journey down Pennsylvania Avenue to Capitol Hill. This time he rode in brilliant sunshine through cheering crowds and flag-decorated streets. He asked the Senate to ratify a peace treaty that most Americans favored and that he promised would prevent future wars. But Wilson's reception in the Senate was chilly; some even refused to stand when he entered the room, and many others received the address in silence. The Senate ultimately rejected the treaty and Wilson's peace.

Between these two presidential appearances, Americans experienced the horrors of the Great War, confronting and overcoming challenges but also sacrificing some of their national ideals and aspirations. Not only was the war the United States' first major military conflict on foreign soil, but it also changed American life.

Many of the changes, from increased efficiency to Americanization, reflected prewar progressivism, and the war years did promote some reforms. But the war also diverted reform energies into new channels, subordinated generous impulses to attitudes that were more coercive, and strengthened the conservative opposition to reform. The results were often reactionary and contributed to a postwar mood that not only curtailed further reform but also helped defeat the peace treaty upon which so much had been gambled.

# Waging Neutrality

**23.1**    Why were Americans so reluctant to get involved in World War I?

**F** ew Americans were prepared for the Great War that erupted in Europe in August 1914, but fewer still foresaw that their own nation might become involved in it. With near unanimity, they supported neutrality. But American attitudes, decisions, and actions, both public and private, undercut neutrality, and the policies of governments in Berlin, London, and Washington drew the United States into the war.

## The Origins of Conflict

There had been plenty of warning. Since the 1870s, the competing imperial ambitions of the European powers had led to economic rivalries, military expansion, diplomatic maneuvering, and international tensions. A complex system of alliances divided the

**Central Powers** Germany and its World War I allies in Austria, Turkey, and Bulgaria.

**Allies** In World War I, Britain, France, Russia, and other nations fighting against the Central Powers, but not including the United States.

continent into two opposing blocs. In central Europe, the expansionist Germany of Kaiser Wilhelm II allied itself with the multinational Austro-Hungarian Empire. Confronting them, Great Britain and France entered into alliances with tsarist Russia. A succession of crises threatened this precarious balance of power, and in May 1914, an American diplomat reported anxiously, "There is too much hatred, too many jealousies." He predicted "an awful cataclysm."

The cataclysm began a month later. On June 28, a Serbian terrorist assassinated Archduke Franz Ferdinand, the heir to the Austro-Hungarian throne, in Sarajevo. With Germany's support, Austria declared war on Serbia on July 28. Russia then mobilized its army against Austria to aid Serbia, its Slavic client state. To assist Austria, Germany declared war on Russia and then on Russia's ally, France. Hoping for a quick victory, Germany struck at France through neutral Belgium; in response, Britain declared war on Germany on August 4. Soon Turkey and Bulgaria joined Germany and Austria to form the **Central Powers**. The **Allies**—Britain, France, and Russia—were joined by Italy and Japan.

Mass slaughter enveloped Europe as huge armies battled to a stalemate. The British and French faced the Germans along a line of trenches stretching across France and Belgium from the English Channel to Switzerland. Little movement occurred despite great efforts and terrible casualties from artillery, machine guns, and poison gas. In the trenches, soldiers suffered in the cold and mud, surrounded by decaying bodies and human waste, enduring lice, rats, and nightmares, and dying from disease and exhaustion. The belligerents subordinated their economies, politics, and cultures to military demands. The Great War, said one German soldier, had become "the grave of nations."

## American Attitudes

Although the United States had also competed for markets, colonies, and influence, few Americans had expected this calamity. Most believed that the United States had no vital interest in the war and would not become involved. President Wilson issued a proclamation of neutrality and urged Americans to be "neutral in fact as well as in name . . . impartial in thought as well as in action."

However, neither the American people nor their president stayed strictly neutral. German Americans often sympathized with Germany, and many Irish Americans hoped for a British defeat that would free Ireland from British rule. But most Americans sympathized with the Allies. Ethnic, cultural, and economic ties bound most Americans to the British and French. Politically, too, most Americans felt a greater affinity for the democratic Western Allies—tsarist Russia repelled them—than for Germany's more authoritarian government and society. And whereas Britain and the United States had enjoyed a rapprochement since 1895, Germany had repeatedly appeared as a potential rival.

Wilson himself admired Britain's culture and government and distrusted Germany's imperial ambitions. Like other influential Americans, Wilson believed that a German victory would threaten America's economic, political, and perhaps even strategic interests. Secretary of State William Jennings Bryan was genuinely neutral, but most officials favored the Allies. Robert Lansing, counselor of the State Department; Walter Hines Page, the ambassador to England; and Colonel Edward House, Wilson's closest adviser on foreign affairs—all assisted British diplomats, undercut official U.S. protests against British violations of American neutrality, and encouraged Wilson's suspicions of Germany. House and Lansing assured the Allies privately that "we considered their cause our cause."

British propaganda bolstered American sympathies. British writers, artists, and lecturers depicted the Allies as fighting for civilization against a brutal Germany that mutilated nuns and babies. Although German troops, like most other soldiers, did commit outrages, they were not guilty of the systematic barbarity claimed by Allied propagandists. Britain, however, shaped America's view of the conflict. It cut the only

German cable to the United States and censored war news to suit itself. German propaganda directed at American opinion proved so ineffectual that the German ambassador concluded it might as well be abandoned.

Sympathy for the Allies, however, did not mean that Americans favored intervention. Indeed, few Americans doubted that neutrality was the appropriate course and peace the proper goal. The carnage in France solidified their convictions. Wilson was determined to pursue peace as long as his view of national interests allowed.

## The Economy of War

Economic issues soon threatened American neutrality. International law permitted neutral nations to sell or ship war matériel to belligerents, and with the economy mired in a recession when the war began, many Americans looked to war orders to spur economic recovery. But the British navy prevented trade with the Central Powers. Only the Allies could buy American goods. One journalist rejoiced that "war, for Europe, is meaning devastation and death; for America a bumper crop of new millionaires and a hectic hastening of prosperity revival." Other Americans worried that this one-sided war trade undermined genuine neutrality. Congress even considered an embargo on munitions. But few Americans supported the idea.

A second economic issue complicated matters. To finance their war purchases, the Allies borrowed from American bankers. Initially, Secretary of State Bryan persuaded Wilson to prohibit loans to the belligerents as "inconsistent with the true spirit of neutrality." But as the importance of the war orders to both the Allies and the American economy became clear, Wilson ended the ban. By April 1917, American loans to the Allies exceeded $2 billion, nearly a hundred times the amount lent to Germany. These financial ties, like the war trade they underwrote, linked the United States to the Allies and convinced Germany that American neutrality was only a formality.

## The Diplomacy of Neutrality

The same imbalance characterized American diplomacy. Wilson insisted on American neutral rights but acquiesced in British violations of those rights, while sternly refusing to yield on German actions. Wilson argued that while British violations of international law cost Americans property, markets, and time, German violations cost lives.

When the war began, the United States asked belligerents to respect the 1909 **Declaration of London** on neutral rights. Germany agreed to do so; the British refused. Instead, skirting or violating established procedures, Britain blockaded Germany, mined the North Sea, and forced neutral ships into British ports to search their cargoes and confiscate material deemed useful to the German war effort. Wilson branded Britain's blockade illegal and unwarranted, but by October he had conceded many of America's neutral rights in order to avoid conflict with Britain.

The British then prohibited food and other products that Germany had imported during peacetime, thereby interfering further with neutral shipping. Even the British admitted that these steps had no legal justification, but when the Wilson administration finally protested, it undermined its own position by noting that "imperative necessity" might justify a violation of international law. This statement virtually authorized the British to violate American rights. In January 1915, Wilson yielded further by observing that "no very important questions of principle" were involved in the Anglo-American quarrels over ship seizures and that they could be resolved after the war.

**Submarine Warfare.** This policy tied the United States to the British war effort and provoked a German response. With its army stalemated on land and its navy no match for Britain's, Germany decided in February 1915 to use its submarines against Allied shipping in a war zone around the British Isles. Neutral ships risked being sunk by mistake, partly because British ships illegally flew neutral flags. Germany maintained

**Declaration of London**
Statement drafted by an international conference in 1909 to clarify international law and specify the rights of neutral nations.

that the blockade and the acquiescence of neutral countries in British violations of international law made submarine warfare necessary.

In May 1915, a German submarine sank a British passenger liner, the *Lusitania*. It had been carrying arms, and the German embassy had warned Americans against traveling on the ship, but the loss of life—1,198 people, including 128 Americans—caused Americans to condemn Germany. Yet only six of a thousand editors surveyed called for war, and even the combative Theodore Roosevelt estimated that 98 percent of Americans still opposed war. Wilson saw that he had to "carry out the double wish of our people, to maintain a firm front in respect of what we demand of Germany and yet do nothing that might by any possibility involve us in the war."

This was a difficult stance. Wilson demanded that Germany abandon its submarine campaign. His language was so harsh that Bryan resigned, warning that by requiring more of Germany than of Britain, the president violated neutrality and threatened to draw the nation into war. Bryan protested Britain's use of American passengers as shields to protect contraband cargo. "This country cannot be neutral and unneutral at the same time," he declared and proposed prohibiting Americans from traveling on belligerent ships. His proposal gained support in the South and West and was introduced as a resolution in both the Senate and the House in February 1916.

Wilson moved to defeat the resolutions, insisting that they impinged on presidential control of foreign policy and on America's neutral rights. In truth, the resolutions abandoned no vital national interest and offered to prevent another provocative incident. Moreover, neither law nor tradition gave Americans the right to travel safely on belligerent ships. Wilson's assertion of such a right committed him to a policy that could only lead to conflict.

Arguments over submarine warfare climaxed in April 1916. A German submarine torpedoed the French ship *Sussex*, injuring four Americans. Wilson threatened to break diplomatic relations if Germany did not abandon unrestricted submarine warfare against all merchant vessels, enemy as well as neutral. This threat implied war. Germany promised not to sink merchant ships without warning but made its **Sussex Pledge** contingent on the United States' requiring Britain also to adhere to "the rules of international law universally recognized before the war." Wilson's diplomatic victory, then, was hollow. Peace for America would depend on the British adopting a course they had already rejected. Wilson's diplomacy had left the nation's future at the mercy of others.

**Sussex Pledge** Germany's pledge during World War I not to sink merchant ships without warning, on the condition that Britain also observe recognized rules of international laws.

## The Battle over Preparedness

The threat of war sparked a debate over military policy. Theodore Roosevelt and a handful of other politicians, mostly northeastern Republicans convinced that Allied victory was in the national interest, advocated what they called **preparedness**, a program to expand the armed forces and establish universal military training. Conservative business groups also joined the agitation. The National Security League, consisting of eastern bankers and industrialists, combined demands for preparedness with attacks on progressive reforms.

**preparedness** Military buildup in preparation for possible U.S. participation in World War I.

But most Americans, certain that their nation would not join the bloody madness, opposed expensive military preparations. Many supported the peace movement. Leading feminists, such as Jane Addams, Charlotte Perkins Gilman, and Carrie Chapman Catt, formed the Woman's Peace Party in 1915, and other organizations, such as the American League to Limit Armaments, also campaigned against preparedness. Most opponents agreed that military spending would undermine domestic reform and raise taxes while enriching arms merchants and financiers.

Wilson also opposed preparedness initially, but he reversed his position when the submarine crisis with Germany intensified. He also began to champion military expansion lest Republicans accuse him in the 1916 election of neglecting national defense.

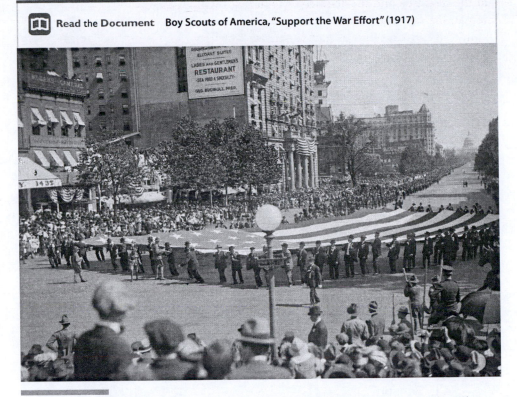

Read the Document    Boy Scouts of America, "Support the War Effort" (1917)

A preparedness parade winds its way down Pennsylvania Avenue in Washington, DC. By 1916, President Wilson, invoking the spirit of patriotism, had given his support to the preparedness program of military expansion.

In early 1916, he made a speaking tour to generate public support for enlarging the armed forces and the navy. Draped in the flag, Wilson marched at the head of a huge preparedness parade in Washington to celebrate the military program.

## The Election of 1916

Wilson's preparedness plans stripped the Republicans of one issue in 1916, and his renewed support of progressive reforms (see Chapter 21) helped to hold Bryan Democrats in line. Wilson continued his balancing act in the campaign itself, at first stressing Americanism and preparedness but then emphasizing peace. The slogan "He Kept Us Out of War" appealed to the popular desire for peace, and the Democratic campaign became one long peace rally.

The Republicans were divided. They had hoped to regain their progressive members after Roosevelt urged the Progressive Party to follow him back into the GOP. But many joined the Democratic camp instead, including several Progressive Party leaders, who endorsed Wilson for having enacted the party's demands of 1912. Roosevelt's frenzied interventionism had alienated many midwestern Republicans opposed to preparedness and cost him any chance of gaining the nomination for himself. Instead, the GOP nominated Charles Evans Hughes, a Supreme Court justice and former New York governor. The platform denounced Wilson's "shifty expedients" in foreign policy and promised "strict and honest neutrality." Unfortunately for Hughes, Roosevelt's attacks on Wilson for not pursuing a war policy persuaded many voters that the GOP was a war party.

The election was the closest in decades (see Map 23.1). When California narrowly went for Wilson, it decided the contest. The results reflected sectional differences, with the South and West voting for Wilson and most of the Northeast and Midwest for Hughes. The desire for peace, all observers concluded, had determined the election.

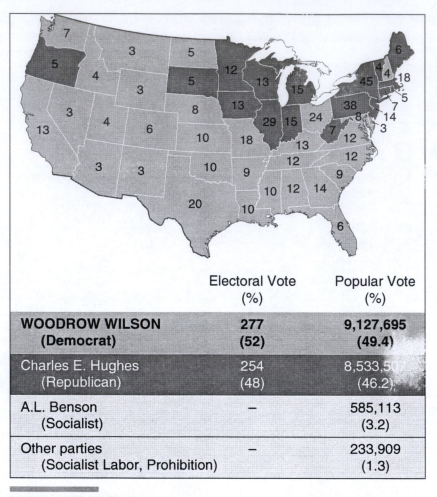

| | Electoral Vote (%) | Popular Vote (%) |
|---|---|---|
| **WOODROW WILSON (Democrat)** | **277 (52)** | **9,127,695 (49.4)** |
| Charles E. Hughes (Republican) | 254 (48) | 8,533,507 (46.2) |
| A.L. Benson (Socialist) | – | 585,113 (3.2) |
| Other parties (Socialist Labor, Prohibition) | – | 233,909 (1.3) |

**MAP 23.1  THE ELECTION OF 1916** Woodrow Wilson won reelection in 1916, despite a reunified Republican Party, by sweeping the South and West on campaign appeals to peace and progressive reform.

## Descent into War

Still, Wilson knew that war loomed, and he made a last effort to avert it. In 1915 and 1916, he had tried to mediate the European conflict, using Colonel House as a secret intermediary. Now he again appealed for an end to hostilities. In January 1917, he sketched out the terms of what he called a "peace without victory." Anything else, he warned, would only lead to another war. The new world order should be based on national equality and **self-determination**, arms reductions, freedom of the seas, and an international organization to ensure peace. It was a distinctly American vision.

Neither the Allies nor the Central Powers were interested. Each side had sacrificed too much to settle for anything short of outright victory. One British leader even denounced Wilson as "the quintessence of a prig" for suggesting that after three years of "this terrible effort," the two sides should accept American principles rather than their own national objectives.

To break the deadlock, Germany resumed unrestricted submarine warfare. German generals believed that even if the United States declared war, it could do little more in the short run to injure Germany than it was already doing. German submarines, they hoped, would end the war by cutting the Allies off from U.S. supplies before the United States could send an army to Europe. On January 31, Germany announced its decision to unleash its submarines in a broad war zone.

**Wilson Commits to War.** Wilson was now virtually committed to a war many Americans opposed. He broke diplomatic relations with Germany and asked Congress to arm American merchant vessels. When the Senate refused, Wilson invoked an antipiracy law of 1819 and armed the ships anyway. Although no American ships had

**self-determination** The right of a people or a nation to decide its own political allegiance or form of government without external influence.

yet been sunk, he also ordered the naval gun crews to fire at submarines on sight. The secretary of the navy warned Wilson that these actions violated international law and were a step toward war; Wilson called his policy "armed neutrality." Huge rallies across America demanded peace.

Several developments soon shifted public opinion. On March 1, Wilson released an intercepted message from the German foreign minister, Arthur Zimmermann, to the German minister in Mexico. It proposed that in the event of war between the United States and Germany, Mexico should ally itself with Germany; in exchange, Mexico would recover its "lost territory in Texas, New Mexico, and Arizona." The Zimmermann note produced a wave of hostility toward Germany and increased support for intervention in the war, especially in the Southwest, which had opposed involvement. When submarines sank four American freighters in mid-March, anti-German feeling broadened.

On April 2, 1917, Wilson delivered his war message, declaring that neutrality was no longer possible, given Germany's submarine "warfare against mankind." To build support for joining a war that most people had long regarded with revulsion and as alien to American interests, Wilson set forth the nation's war goals as simple and noble. The United States would not fight for conquest or domination but for "the ultimate peace of the world and for the liberation of its peoples." Interventionists were delighted with the decision for war but others in Congress opposed any involvement in the war.

After vigorous debate, the Senate passed the war resolution 82 to 6 and the House 373 to 50. On April 6, 1917, the United States officially entered the Great War—what House Democratic leader Claude Kitchin of North Carolina predicted would be "one vast drama of horrors and blood, one boundless stage upon which will play all the evil spirits of earth and hell."

# Waging War in America

**23.2** How did the war effort threaten civil liberties?

Mobilizing for military intervention was a massive undertaking. "It is not an army that we must shape and train for war," announced President Wilson; "it is a Nation." The government reorganized the economy to emphasize centralized management, developed policies to control public opinion and suppress dissent, and transformed the role of government itself.

## Managing the War Economy

To harness the nation's economic power for the war, federal and state governments developed a complex structure of agencies and controls for every sector of the economy, from industry and agriculture to transportation and labor. (See Table 23.1, Major

**TABLE 23.1** MAJOR GOVERNMENT WARTIME AGENCIES

| Agency | Purpose |
| --- | --- |
| War Industries Board | Reorganized industry to maximize wartime production |
| Railroad Administration | Modernized and operated the nation's railroads |
| Food Administration | Increased agricultural production, supervised food distribution and farm labor |
| National War Labor Board | Resolved labor-management disputes, improved labor conditions, and recognized union rights as means to promote production and efficiency |
| Committee on Public Information | Managed propaganda to build public support for the war effort |

Government Wartime Agencies.) Supervised by the Council of National Defense, these agencies shifted resources to war-related enterprises, increased production of goods and services, and improved transportation and distribution.

**Organizing Industry.**   The most important agency was the **War Industries Board (WIB)**, established in July 1917 to set industrial priorities, coordinate military purchasing, and supervise business. Led by financier Bernard Baruch, the WIB exercised unprecedented power over industry by setting prices, allocating scarce materials, and standardizing products and procedures to boost efficiency. Yet Baruch was not an industrial dictator; he aimed at business-government integration. The WIB promoted major business interests, helped suspend antitrust laws, and guaranteed huge corporate profits. Some progressives began to see the dangers, and business leaders the advantages, of government economic intervention.

The Railroad Administration also linked business ambitions to the war economy. Under William McAdoo, it operated the nation's railroads as a unified system to move supplies and troops efficiently. Centralized management eliminated competition, permitted improvements in equipment, and brought great profits to the owners but higher prices to the general public.

**Ensuring Food Supplies.**   Equally effective and far more popular was the Food Administration, headed by Herbert Hoover. Hoover had organized relief supplies for war-torn Belgium and now controlled the production and distribution of food for the United States and its allies. He persuaded millions of Americans to accept meatless and wheatless days, so that the Food Administration could feed military and foreign consumers. Half a million women went door to door to secure food-conservation pledges from housewives. City residents planted victory gardens in parks and vacant lots, and President Wilson even pastured sheep on the White House lawn.

Hoover also worked closely with agricultural processors and distributors, ensuring profits in exchange for cooperation. Farmers profited from the war, too. To encourage production, Hoover established high prices for commodities, and agricultural income rose by 30 percent. State and federal governments provided commercial farmers with sufficient farm labor despite the military draft and competition from high-wage war industries.

**Overseeing Labor Relations.**   The National War Labor Board supervised labor relations. In exchange for labor's cooperation, this agency guaranteed the rights of unions to organize and bargain collectively. With such support, unions sharply increased their membership. The labor board also encouraged improved working conditions, higher wages, and shorter hours. War contracts stipulated an 8-hour day, and by the end of the war, nearly half the nation's workers had achieved the 48-hour week. Wages rose, too, but often only as fast as inflation. These improvements limited labor disputes during the war, and Secretary of War Newton Baker praised labor as "more willing to keep in step than capital." But when such unions as the Industrial Workers of the World did not keep in step, the government suppressed them.

Although these and other government regulatory agencies were dismantled when the war ended, their activities reinforced many long-standing trends in the American economy, from the consolidation of business to the commercialization of agriculture and the organization of labor. They also set a precedent for governmental activism that would prove valuable during the crises of the 1930s and 1940s.

## Women and Minorities: New Opportunities, Old Inequities

**Women and War Work.**   The reorganization of the economy also had significant social consequences, especially for women and African Americans. In response to labor shortages, public officials and private employers exhorted women to join the workforce: "For Every Fighter a Woman Worker," urged one poster. Women now took jobs previously closed to them. More than 100,000 women worked in munitions plants and 40,000 in the steel industry. Women constituted 20 percent or more of all workers making electrical machinery, leather and rubber goods, and food. They operated drills and lathes, controlled cranes in steel mills, and repaired equipment in machine shops. Harriot Stanton Blatch, a suffragist active in the Food Administration, estimated that a million women had replaced men in industry, where "their drudgery is for the first time paid for."

Many working women simply shifted to other jobs, where their existing skills earned better wages and benefits. The reshuffling of jobs among white women opened new vacancies for black women in domestic, clerical, and industrial employment. As black women replaced white women in the garment and textile industries, social reformers spoke of "a new day for the colored woman worker" and African American women themselves celebrated their long-awaited industrial employment. But their optimism was unwarranted and their gains short lived. Racial as well as gender segregation continued to mark employment. Federal efforts to prevent pay inequities and sexual harassment in the workplace were halfhearted and subordinated to the goals of efficiency and productivity. The policies of the government and employers ensured that women would be unable to sustain their wartime advances in the workplace.

**Woman Suffrage and Prohibition.** The war did help women reformers achieve two long-sought objectives: woman suffrage and prohibition. Women's support for the war effort prompted more Americans to support woman suffrage. Congress approved

**Read the Document**  Anna Howard Shaw, Woman's Committee of the Council of National Defense (1917)

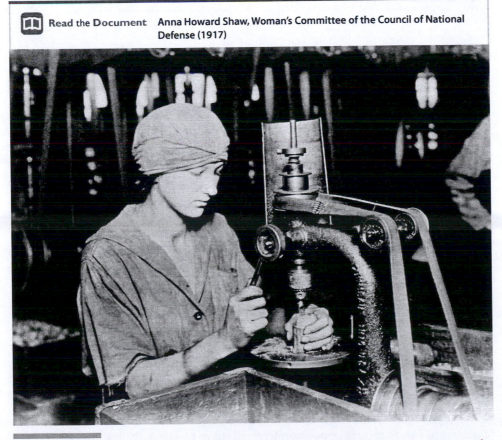

With women's labor crucial for the war effort, both government agencies and private industry recruited women for factory work. Here, a woman countersinks a detonator tube hole in a hand grenade at the Westinghouse Electric & Manufacturing Company in Pennsylvania.

Black women work in a brickyard for wartime construction. Mobilization opened new jobs for women, but racial subordination and segregation persisted. Black women often performed the hardest and least desirable work.

the suffrage amendment, which was ratified in 1920. Convinced that abstaining from alcohol would save grain and make workers and soldiers more efficient, Congress also passed the Prohibition amendment, which was ratified in 1919.

**African Americans and War Work.**    The war also changed the lives of African Americans. The demand for industrial labor caused a huge migration of black people from the rural South, where they had little opportunity, few rights, and no hope. In northern cities, they worked in shipyards, steel mills, and packing houses. Half a million African Americans moved north during the war, doubling and tripling the black populations of Chicago, Detroit, and other industrial cities.

Unfortunately, blacks often encountered the kind of racial discrimination and violence in the North that they had hoped to leave behind in the South. Fearful and resentful whites started race riots in northern cities. In East St. Louis, Illinois, where thousands of black southerners sought defense work, a white mob, in July 1917, murdered at least thirty-nine black people, sparing, as an investigating committee reported, "neither age nor sex in their blind lust for blood."

## Financing the War

To finance the war, the government borrowed money and raised taxes. Business interests favored the first course, but southern and western progressives argued that taxation was more efficient and equitable and would minimize war profiteering. Despite conservative and business opposition to progressive taxation, the tax laws of 1917 and 1918 established a graduated tax structure with higher taxes on large incomes, corporate profits, and wealthy estates. Conservative opposition, however, would frustrate progressives' hopes for permanent tax reforms.

The government raised two-thirds of the war costs by borrowing. Most of the loans came from banks and wealthy investors, but the government also campaigned to sell **Liberty Bonds** to the general public. Celebrities went to schools, churches, and rallies to persuade Americans to buy bonds as their patriotic duty. "Every person who refuses to subscribe," Secretary of the Treasury McAdoo told a California audience, "is a friend of Germany." Using techniques of persuasion and control from advertising and mass entertainment, the Wilson administration thus enlisted the emotions of loyalty, fear, patriotism, and obedience for the war effort.

**Liberty Bonds** Interest-bearing certificates sold by the U.S. government to finance the American World War I effort.

## Conquering Minds

The government also tried to promote a war spirit among the American people by establishing propaganda agencies and enacting legislation to control social attitudes and behavior. This program drew from the restrictive side of progressivism: its impulses toward social control, behavior regulation, and nativism. It also reflected the interests of more conservative forces. The Wilson administration adopted this program of social mobilization because many Americans opposed the war.

"Beat Back the Hun," a poster to induce Americans to buy Liberty Bonds, demonizes the enemy in a raw, emotional appeal. Liberty bond drives raised the immense sum of $23 billion.

**Government Propaganda.**   To rally Americans behind the war effort, Wilson established the **Committee on Public Information (CPI)** under journalist George Creel. Despite its title, the CPI sought to manipulate, not inform, public opinion. Creel described his goal as winning "the fight for the minds of men, for the 'conquest of their convictions.'" The CPI flooded the country with press releases, advertisements, cartoons, and canned editorials. The CPI made newsreels and war movies to capture public attention. It scheduled 75,000 speakers, who delivered a million speeches to 400 million listeners. Its women's division targeted American women in stereotyped emotional terms. It hired artists to design posters, professors to write pamphlets in twenty-three languages, and poets to compose war poems for children.

Other government agencies launched similar campaigns. The Woman's Committee of the Council of National Defense established the Department of Educational Propaganda and Patriotic Education. Carrie Chapman Catt dropped her peace activism to head this bureau, in the hope that the war effort would increase support for woman suffrage. The agency worked to win over women who opposed the war, particularly in the rural Midwest, West, and South. It formed women's speakers' bureaus, developed programs for community meetings at country schools, and distributed millions of pamphlets.

Government propaganda had three themes: national unity, the loathsome character of the enemy, and the war as a grand crusade for liberty and democracy. Obsessed with national unity and conformity, Creel promoted fear, hatred, and prejudice in the name of a triumphant Americanism. Germans were depicted as brutal, even subhuman, rapists and murderers. The campaign suggested that any dissent was unpatriotic, if not treasonous, and dangerous to national survival. This emphasis on unreasoning conformity helped prompt hysterical attacks on German Americans, radicals, and pacifists.

## Suppressing Dissent

The Wilson administration also suppressed dissent, now officially branded disloyalty. For reasons of their own, private interests helped shape a reactionary repression that tarnished the nation's professed idealistic war goals. The campaign also established unfortunate precedents for the future.

**Espionage Act** Law whose vague prohibition against obstructing the nation's war effort was used to crush dissent and criticism during World War I.

**Sedition Act of 1918** Broad law restricting criticism of America's involvement in World War I or the American government, flag, military, taxes, or officials.

Congress rushed to stifle antiwar sentiment. The **Espionage Act** provided heavy fines and up to twenty years in prison for obstructing the war effort, a vague phrase but "omnipotently comprehensive," warned an Idaho senator who opposed the law. In fact, the Espionage Act became a weapon to crush dissent and criticism. Eventually, Congress passed the still more sweeping **Sedition Act of 1918**, which provided severe penalties for speaking or writing against the draft, bond sales, and war production and for criticizing government personnel or policies.

Postmaster General Albert Burleson banned antiwar or radical newspapers and magazines from the mail, suppressing literature so indiscriminately that one observer said he "didn't know socialism from rheumatism." Even more zealous in attacking radicals and presumed subversives was the reactionary attorney general, Thomas Gregory, who made little distinction between traitors and pacifists, war critics, and radicals. Eugene Debs was sentenced to ten years in prison for a "treasonous" speech in which he declared it "extremely dangerous to exercise the right of free speech in a country fighting to make democracy safe in the world." By war's end, a third of the Socialist Party's national leadership was in prison, leaving the party in a shambles.

Gregory also enlisted the help of private vigilantes, including the several hundred thousand members of the reactionary American Protective League, which sought to purge radicals and reformers from the nation's economic and political life. They wiretapped telephones, intercepted private mail, burglarized union offices, broke up German-language newspapers, harassed immigrants, and staged mass raids, seizing thousands of people who they claimed were not doing enough for the war effort.

State and local authorities also suppressed what they saw as antiwar, radical, or pro-German activities. They established 184,000 investigative and enforcement agencies, known as councils of defense or public-safety committees. They encouraged Americans to spy on one another, required people to buy Liberty Bonds, and prohibited teaching German in schools or using the language in religious services and telephone conversations. Indeed, suppression of all things German reached extremes. Germanic names of towns, streets, and people were changed; sauerkraut became liberty cabbage, and the hamburger the liberty sandwich.

Members of the business community exploited the hysteria to promote their own interests at the expense of farmers, workers, and reformers. On the Great Plains from Texas to North Dakota, the business target was the Nonpartisan League, a radical farm group demanding state control or ownership of banks, grain elevators, and flour mills. Although the League supported the war, oversubscribed bond drives, and had George Creel affirm its loyalty, conservatives depicted it as seditious to block its advocacy of political and economic reforms, including the confiscation of large fortunes to pay for the war. Minnesota's public-safety commission condemned members of the Nonpartisan League as traitors and proposed a "firing squad working overtime" to deal with them. Nebraska's council of defense barred League meetings. Public officials and self-styled patriots broke up the League's meetings and whipped and jailed its leaders.

In the West, business interests targeted labor organizations, especially the Industrial Workers of the World. In Arizona, for example, the Phelps-Dodge Company broke a mine strike in 1917 by depicting the Wobbly miners as bent on war-related sabotage. A vigilante mob, armed and paid by the mining company, seized 1,200 strikers, many of them Wobblies and one-third of them Mexican Americans, and herded them into the desert without food or water. Federal investigators found no evidence of sedition among the miners and reported that the company and its thugs had been inspired, not by "patriotism," but by "ordinary strike-breaking motives."

Nonetheless, the government itself assisted the business campaign. It used the army to break loggers' support for the IWW in the Pacific Northwest, and it raided IWW halls across the country in September 1917. The conviction of nearly 200 Wobblies on charges of sedition in three mass trials in Illinois, California, and Kansas crippled the nation's largest industrial union.

In the end, the government was primarily responsible for the war hysteria. It encouraged suspicion and conflict through inflammatory propaganda, repressive laws, and violation of basic civil rights, by supporting extremists who used the war for their own purposes, and by tolerating mob violence against German Americans. This ugly mood would infect the postwar world.

# Waging War and Peace Abroad

**23.3**    What hopes did Wilson have for the Treaty of Versailles?

While mobilizing the home front, the Wilson administration undertook an impressive military effort to help the Allies defeat the Central Powers. Wilson also struggled to secure international acceptance for his plans for a just and permanent peace.

## The War to End All Wars

When the United States entered the war, the Allied position was dire. The losses from three years of trench warfare had sapped military strength and civilian morale. French soldiers mutinied and refused to continue an assault that had cost 120,000 casualties in five days; the German submarine campaign was devastating the British. On the eastern

**Selective Service Act of 1917** The law establishing the military draft for World War I.

front, the Russian army had collapsed, and the Russian government had gradually disintegrated after the overthrow of the tsarist regime.

In May, Congress passed the **Selective Service Act of 1917**, establishing conscription. More than 24 million men eventually registered for the draft, and nearly 3 million entered the army when their numbers were drawn in a national lottery. Almost 2 million more men volunteered, as did more than 13,000 women, who served in the navy and marines. Nearly one-fifth of America's soldiers were foreign-born (Europeans spoke of the "American Foreign Legion"); 367,000 were black. Many Native Americans served with distinction as well; in recognition, Indian veterans were made citizens in 1919, a status extended to all Indians five years later.

Civilians were transformed into soldiers in hastily organized training camps, operated according to progressive principles. Prohibition prevailed in the camps; the poorly educated and largely working-class recruits were taught personal hygiene; worries about sin and inefficiency produced massive campaigns against venereal disease; and immigrants were taught English and American history. Some units were ethnically segregated: At Camp Gordon, Georgia, Italians and Slavs had separate units, with their own officers.

Racial segregation was more rigid, not only in training camps and military units but in assignments as well. The navy assigned black sailors to menial positions, and the army similarly used black soldiers primarily as gravediggers and laborers. But one black combat division was created, and four black regiments fought under French command. France decorated three of these units with its highest citations for valor. White American officers urged the French not to praise black troops, treat black officers as equals, or permit fraternization. But white racism could not diminish the extraordinary record of one of the most famous of the black units in France—the 369th Infantry Regiment, also known as the "Harlem Hellfighters." The 369th spent 191 days in combat and was the first Allied unit to reach the Rhine.

Women were recruited as noncombatant personnel, such as clerks, translators, and switchboard operators, thereby enabling more men to be assigned to combat duty. The navy awarded them equal rank with males performing the same tasks, and they were eligible after the war for veterans' benefits. The army was a different story. Although they served in uniform and under military discipline, women had no formal military status, were ineligible for benefits, and often had their skills and contributions devalued. On the eve of a major battle in France, Merle Egan in the U.S. Army Signal Corps found that some of the men resented taking instructions from a woman. But "when I reminded them that any soldier could carry a gun but the safety of a whole division might depend on the switchboard one of them was operating, I had no more trouble."

**Into Action in France.** The first American troops landed in France in June 1917. The American Expeditionary Force (AEF) was commanded by General John J. Pershing, a career officer, who was forced to send his untrained soldiers across the Atlantic to revive the collapsing morale among the French. Months of training under French direction followed as the Americans learned about trench warfare: using bayonets, grenades, and machine guns and surviving poison-gas attacks. Finally in October, the 1st Division, the Big Red One, moved into the trenches.

Full-scale American intervention began in the late spring of 1918 (see Map 23.2). General Tasker Bliss asked the French chief of staff, "Well, we have come over here to get killed. Where do you want to use us?" In June, the fresh American troops helped the French repulse a German thrust toward Paris at Château-Thierry. Further savage fighting at Belleau Wood blocked the Germans again, prompting a French officer to declare, "You Americans are our hope, our strength, our life." In July, the AEF helped defeat another German advance, at Rheims. The influx of American troops had tipped the balance toward Allied victory. By July 18, the German chancellor later acknowledged, "even the most optimistic among us knew that all was lost. The history of the world was played out in three days."

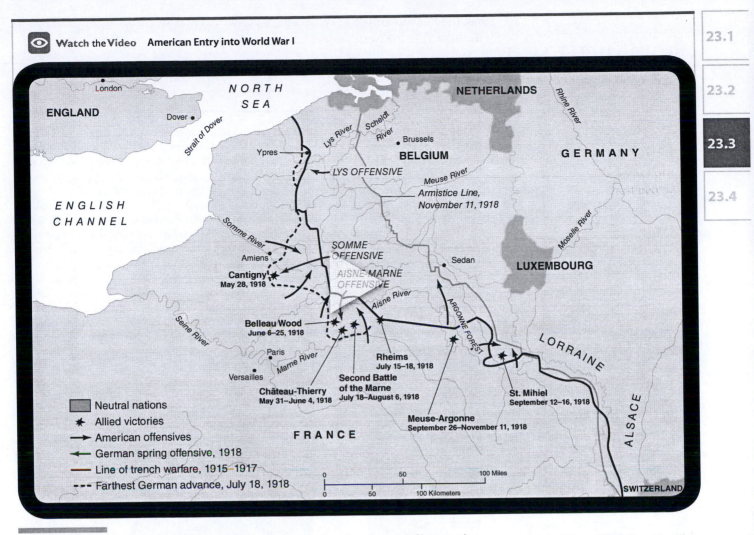

Watch the Video American Entry into World War I

**MAP 23.2 THE WESTERN FRONT, 1918** After three years of trench warfare, the arrival of large numbers of American troops in 1918 enabled the Allies to launch an offensive that drove back the Germans and forced an armistice.

**The Russian Front.** In July, Wilson also agreed to commit 15,000 American troops to intervene in Russia. Russia's provisional government had collapsed when the radical **Bolshevik** faction of the communist movement had seized power in November 1917. Under V. I. Lenin, the Bolsheviks signed an armistice with Germany in early 1918, which freed German troops for the summer offensive in France. The Allied interventions were initially designed to reopen the eastern front and later to help overthrow the Bolshevik government.

Lenin's call for the destruction of capitalism and imperialism alarmed the Allied leaders. One Wilson adviser urged the "eradication" of the Russian government. Soon, American and British troops were fighting Russians in an effort to influence Russia's internal affairs. United States forces remained in Russia even after Germany surrendered in 1918. They did not leave until 1920. These military interventions failed, but they contributed to Russian distrust of the West.

**The Western Front.** The Allies were more successful on the western front. Having stopped the German offensive in July, they launched their own advance. The decisive battle began in late September when an American army over 1 million strong attacked German trenches in the Argonne Forest. Many Americans were still inexperienced; some had been drafted only in July and had spent more time traveling than training. Nevertheless, they advanced steadily, despite attacks with poison gas and heavy artillery.

The battle for the Argonne raged for weeks. A German general reported that his exhausted soldiers faced Americans who "were fresh, eager for fighting, and brave."

**Bolshevik** Member of the Communist movement in Russia that established the Soviet government after the 1917 Russian Revolution.

# From Then to Now
# Women and War

**A**ssessing the problem of preparedness for the war, U.S. Secretary of the Navy Josephus Daniels asked his counsel, "Is there any regulation which specifies that a Navy yeoman be a man?" When the response was no, Daniels directed his subordinates to "enroll women in the naval service as yeomen," adding that "we will have the best clerical assistance the country can provide" and free up men to fight.

Although unable to vote, women clamored for a more active role in the war, and ultimately more than 30,000 women joined the military. The army, however, never formally approved the enlistment of women, and the several hundred women it sent to France as telephone operators were not recognized as veterans until 1978 when they received honorable discharges.

Most women who served in the Great War were nurses; they held no rank and received no benefits but were acknowledged as veterans at war's end. But the Army and Navy Nurse Corps were closed to African American women, who joined the Red Cross in hopes of gaining entry into the military.

The role of women in wartime stirred debate then and now. It was not until the 1990s that women's opportunities in the military changed significantly. By 1994 the military opened up 260,000 new positions for women. Although still prohibited from serving in the infantry or from driving tanks, women took on new responsibilities that increased their risks on the battlefield. But women encountered resistance to their new roles both inside the military and in society as a whole.

The wars in Iraq and Afghanistan rekindled the debate about women in combat. One in every seven soldiers in Iraq was a woman, and more than 140 women were killed in the two wars. Although the public debate continues, in January 2013 the Pentagon, citing numerous studies of women in war, lifted the ban on women in combat.

**Question for Discussion**

- Why has women's role in the military generated so much controversy?

Three women sworn in as Navy Yeomen in Los Angeles in 1917

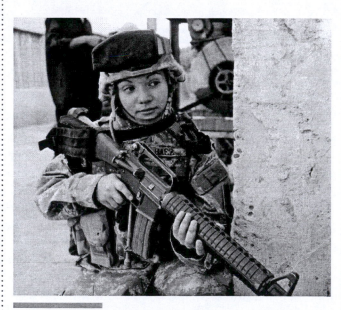

Woman soldier on patrol in Iraq

But he found their sheer numbers most impressive. Eventually, this massive assault overwhelmed the Germans. Despite severe casualties, the AEF had helped the British and French to defeat the enemy. With its allies surrendering, its own army in retreat, and revolution breaking out among the war-weary residents of its major cities, Germany asked for peace. On November 11, 1918, an armistice ended the Great War. More than 115,000 Americans were among the 8 million soldiers and 7 million civilians dead.

American soldiers advancing through smoke and shattered trees of the Argonne Forest in October 1918. The Great War was a conflict of relentless attrition, marked by the horrors of poison gas, artillery bombardment, pandemic disease, and what one American called the "unburied dead."

## The Fourteen Points

The armistice was only a step toward final peace. President Wilson had already enunciated America's war objectives on January 8, 1918, in a speech outlining what became known as the Fourteen Points. In his 1917 war message, Wilson had advocated a more democratic world system, and this new speech spelled out how to achieve it. But Wilson also had a political purpose. The Bolsheviks had published the Allies' secret treaties dividing up the expected economic and territorial spoils of the war. Lenin had called for an immediate peace based on the liberation of all colonies, self-determination for all peoples, and the rejection of annexations and punitive indemnities. Wilson's Fourteen Points reassured the American and Allied peoples that they were fighting for more than imperialist gains and offered an alternative to what he called Lenin's "crude formula" for peace.

Eight of Wilson's points proposed creating new nations, shifting old borders, or ensuring self-determination for peoples previously subject to the Austrian, German, or Russian empire. The point about Russia would haunt Wilson after the Allied interventions there began, for it called on all nations to evacuate Russian territory and permit Russia "an unhampered and unembarrassed opportunity for the independent determination of her own political development" under "institutions of her own choosing." Another five points invoked principles to guide international relations: freedom of the seas, open diplomacy instead of secret treaties, reduction of armaments, free trade, and the fair settlement of colonial claims. Wilson's fourteenth and most important point proposed a league of nations to carry out these ideals and ensure international stability.

Wilson and the German government had these principles in mind when negotiating the armistice. The Allies, however, had never explicitly accepted the Fourteen Points, and framing a final peace treaty would be difficult. While Wilson favored a settlement that would promote international stability and economic expansion, he recognized that the Allies sought "to get everything out of Germany that they can." Indeed, after their human and economic sacrifices, Britain and France wanted tangible compensation, not pious principles.

Convinced of the righteousness of his cause, Wilson decided to attend the peace conference in Paris, although no president had ever gone to Europe while in office. But Wilson weakened his position before he even set sail. First, he urged voters to support Democratic candidates in the November 1918 elections to indicate approval of his peace plan. But the electorate, responding primarily to domestic problems like inflation, gave the Republicans control of both houses of Congress. This meant that any treaty would have to be approved by Senate Republicans angry that Wilson had tried to use war and peace for partisan purposes. Second, Wilson refused to consult with Senate Republicans on plans for the peace conference and failed to name important Republicans to the Paris delegation. It was going to be Wilson's treaty, and Republicans would feel no responsibility to approve it.

## The Paris Peace Conference

The peace conference opened on January 18, 1919. Meeting at the Palace of Versailles, the delegations were dominated by the principal Allied leaders: Wilson of the United States, David Lloyd George of Britain, Georges Clemenceau of France, and Vittorio Orlando of Italy. The Central Powers and Bolshevik Russia were excluded. The treaty would be one-sided except to the extent that Wilson could insist on the liberal terms of the Fourteen Points against French and British intransigence.

For months, the conference debated Wilson's other goals and the Allies' demands for compensation and security. Lloyd George later commented, with reference to the self-righteous Wilson and the assertive Clemenceau, "I think I did as well as might be expected, seated as I was between Jesus Christ and Napoleon Bonaparte." Under protest, Germany signed the **Treaty of Versailles** on June 28, 1919. Its terms were far more severe than Wilson had proposed or Germany had anticipated. Germany had to accept sole responsibility for starting the war, a stipulation that all Germans bitterly resented. It was required to pay huge reparations to the Allies, give up land to France, Poland, Belgium, and Denmark, cede its colonies, limit its army and navy to small self-defense forces, destroy military bases, and promise not to manufacture or purchase armaments.

Wilson gained some acceptance of self-determination. As the German, Austro-Hungarian, Turkish, and Russian empires had collapsed at the end of the war, nationalist groups had proclaimed their independence. On one hand, the peace settlement formally recognized these new nation-states: Poland, Finland, Estonia, Latvia, and Lithuania in eastern Europe and Austria, Hungary, Czechoslovakia, and Yugoslavia in central Europe. On the other hand, France, Italy, Romania, and Japan all annexed territory regardless of the wishes of the inhabitants. Germans were placed under Polish control in Silesia and Czech control in Bohemia. Austria was not allowed to merge with Germany. And the conference sanctioned colonialism by establishing a trusteeship system that enabled France, Britain, and Japan to take over German colonies and Turkish territory.

The Allied leaders endorsed the changes in eastern Europe in part because the new states there were anticommunist and would constitute a barrier against Bolshevism. Communist movements in early 1919 in Germany, Austria, and Hungary alarmed Allied leaders who feared that "the Russian idea was still rising in power,"

**Treaty of Versailles** The treaty ending World War I and creating the League of Nations.

With the defeat of Germany, Americans wanted their soldiers home. Although many returning African American soldiers were denied celebratory homecomings and would face discrimination and hostility, their role in World War I brought fresh confidence and respect to the African American community. Few units stirred the patriotism and pride as did the valiant 369th Infantry Regiment, decorated by the French government for heroism and "gallantry under fire." Here African American friends and families turn out to welcome home the "Men of Bronze," as they were also called.

and they hoped to isolate and weaken Bolshevik Russia. Allied armies were in Russia during the peace conference, and Wilson and the other leaders agreed to provide further aid to fight the Bolsheviks. This hostility to Russia, like the punitive terms for Germany and the concessions to imperial interests, boded ill for a stable and just postwar order.

But Wilson hoped that the final section of the Versailles treaty would resolve the flaws of the agreement by establishing his great international organization to preserve peace: the **League of Nations**. The Covenant, or constitution, of the League was built into the treaty. Its crucial feature, Article Ten, bound the member nations to guarantee each other's independence—a provision that was Wilson's concept of collective security. "At least," he told an aide, "we are saving the Covenant, and that instrument will work wonders, bring the blessing of peace, and then when the war psychosis has abated, it will not be difficult to settle all disputes that baffle us now."

**League of Nations** International organization created by the Versailles Treaty after World War I to ensure world stability.

# ✳ Explore World War I on MyHistoryLab

## HOW DID THE SO-CALLED "WAR TO END ALL WARS" PLAY OUT?

In the first years of the twentieth century, the powers of Europe were entangled in a system of alliances that, in theory, created a balance of power. In practice, the alliance created tensions as nations grew increasingly industrialized and armed. The Balkans provided the spark for this "powder keg," setting in motion the alliance system that caused the initial declarations of war in 1914 between the Central Powers—Germany, Austria-Hungary, the Ottoman Empire, and Bulgaria— and the Allies—France, Great Britain, and Russia. Other countries eventually joined the Allies, including Italy and Japan. Having preferred an isolationist stance on world affairs, the United States was a latecomer to the conflict, joining the Allies in 1917. The war, which introduced new weapons such as poison gas, tanks, and increasingly modern aircraft,

The United States entered World War I in 1917 after it declared war against Germany. This photograph shows an Allied soldier escorting a captured German combatant.

brought incredible devastation for the European powers. The United States was spared much of the toll and emerged out of the war as a new global power.

### HUMAN TOLL OF WORLD WAR I (in millions)

| | Dead | Wounded |
| --- | --- | --- |
| Central Powers | 3.38 | 3.6 |
| Allies | 5.1 | 12.8 |
| Civilians | 13.0 | – |

SOURCE: Ellis, John and Cox, Michael. *The World War I Databook: The Essential Facts and Figures for all the Combatants.* London: Aurum Press, 2001; Urlanis, Boris, *Wars and Population.* Moscow: Progress Publishers, 1971

**KEY QUESTIONS** Use **MyHistoryLab** *Explorer* to **answer** these **questions:**

**Cause ▶▶▶** *How did the European international system set the stage for war?*

Chart the alliances that helped create World War I.

**Consequence ▶▶▶** *How did the battle lines slow the war's course between 1915 and 1917?*

Map the trenches that were key in the failure of both sides to secure easy victory.

**Analysis ▶▶▶** *What were the war's demographic and geopolitcal aftereffects?*

Trace the changes in boundaries in the war's aftermath and the death tolls for the involved countries.

# Waging Peace at Home

**23.4**    What challenges did America face in the aftermath of the war?

W ilson was determined to defeat the opposition to the peace treaty. But many Americans were engaged in their own struggles with the new conditions of a nation suddenly at peace but riven by economic, social, and political conflict. Wilson's battle for the League of Nations would fail tragically. The other conflicts would rage until the election of 1920 restored a normalcy of sorts.

## Battle over the League

Most Americans favored the Versailles treaty. A survey of 1,400 newspapers found fewer than 200 opposed. Thirty-three governors and thirty-two state legislatures endorsed the League of Nations. But when Wilson called for the Senate to accept "the moral leadership . . . and confidence of the world" by ratifying the treaty, he met resistance. Some Republicans wanted to prevent the Democrats from campaigning in 1920 as the party responsible for a victorious war and a glorious peace. But most Republican opponents of the treaty raised serious questions, often reflecting national traditions in foreign relations. Nearly all Democrats favored the treaty, but they were a minority; some Republicans would have to be converted for the treaty to be approved.

Progressive Republican senators, such as Robert La Follette and Hiram Johnson, led one group of opponents. Called the **Irreconcilables**, they opposed participation in the League of Nations, which they saw as designed to perpetuate the power of imperialist countries. Article Ten, they feared, would require the United States to help suppress rebellions in Ireland against British rule or to enforce disputed European borders. Most of the Irreconcilables gave priority to restoring civil liberties and progressive reform at home.

**Irreconcilables** Group of U.S. senators opposed to ratification of the Treaty of Versailles after World War I.

A larger group of opponents had reservations about the treaty's provisions. These **Reservationists** were led by Henry Cabot Lodge, the chair of the Senate Foreign Relations Committee. They regarded Article Ten as eroding congressional authority to declare war. They also fretted that the League might interfere with domestic questions, such as immigration laws.

**Reservationists** Group of U.S. senators opposing approval of the Treaty of Versailles, without significant amendments.

Lodge's opposition was shaped by both partisanship and deep personal hostility. "I never expected to hate anyone in politics with the hatred I feel toward Wilson," Lodge confessed. Wilson reciprocated, and when Lodge proposed reservations or amendments to the treaty, Wilson refused to compromise. He proposed "a direct frontal attack" on his opponents. If they wanted war, he said, he would "give them a belly full." In early September 1919, Wilson set out across the country to win popular support for the League. In three weeks, he traveled 8,000 miles and delivered thirty-seven speeches.

In poor health following a bout with influenza, Wilson collapsed in Pueblo, Colorado. Taken back to Washington, Wilson on October 2 suffered a massive stroke that paralyzed his left side and left him psychologically unstable and temporarily blind. Wilson's physician and his wife, Edith Galt Wilson, kept the nature of his illness secret from the public, Congress, and even the vice president and cabinet. Rumors circulated that Edith Wilson was running the administration, but she was not. Instead, it was immobilized.

By February 1920, Wilson had partially recovered, but he remained suspicious and quarrelsome. Bryan and other Democratic leaders urged him to accept Lodge's reservations to gain ratification of the treaty. Wilson refused. Isolated and inflexible, he ordered Democratic senators to vote with the Irreconcilables against the treaty as amended by Lodge. On March 19, 1920, the Senate killed the treaty.

# Economic Readjustment and Social Conflict

The League was not the only casualty of the struggle to conclude the war. Grave problems shook the United States in 1919 and early 1920. An influenza epidemic had erupted in Europe in 1918 among the massed armies. It now hit the United States, killing perhaps 700,000 Americans, far more than had died in combat. Frightened officials closed public facilities and banned public meetings in futile attempts to stop the contagion.

Meanwhile, the Wilson administration had no plans for an orderly reconversion of the wartime economy, and chaos ensued. The government canceled war contracts and dissolved the regulatory agencies. Noting that "the war spirit of cooperation and sacrifice" had disappeared with the Armistice, Bernard Baruch decided to "turn industry absolutely free" and abolished the War Industries Board as of January 1, 1919. Other agencies followed in such haste that turmoil engulfed the economy.

The government also demobilized the armed forces. With no planning or assistance, veterans were hustled back into civilian life. There they competed for scarce jobs with workers recently discharged from the war industries.

As unemployment mounted, the removal of wartime price controls brought runaway inflation. The cost of food, clothing, and other necessities more than doubled over prewar rates. The return of the soldiers caused a serious housing shortage, and rents skyrocketed. Democratic leaders urged Wilson to devote less time to the League of Nations and more to the cost of living and the tensions it unleashed. Farmers also suffered from economic readjustments. Net farm income declined by 65 percent between 1919 and 1921. Farmers who had borrowed money for machinery and land to expand production for the war effort were left impoverished and embittered.

**Postwar Battles: Gender and Race.** Women also lost their wartime economic advances. Returning soldiers took away their jobs. Male trade unionists insisted that women go back to being housewives. At times, male workers struck to force employers to fire women and barred women from unions in jobs where union membership was required for employment. "During the war they called us heroines," one woman complained, "but they throw us on the scrapheap now." Indeed, state legislatures passed laws prohibiting women from working in many of the occupations they had successfully filled during the war. By 1919, half of the women newly employed in heavy industry during the war were gone; by 1920, women constituted a smaller proportion of the workforce than they had in 1910.

The postwar readjustments also left African Americans disappointed. During the war, they had agreed with W. E. B. Du Bois to "forget our special grievances and close our ranks shoulder to shoulder with our own white fellow citizens." Participation in the war effort, they had hoped, might be rewarded by better treatment thereafter. Now, the meagerness of their reward became clear.

Housing shortages and job competition interacted with racism in 1919 to produce race riots in twenty-six towns and cities, resulting in at least 120 deaths. In Chicago, 38 people were killed and more than 500 injured in a five-day riot that began when white thugs stoned to death a black youth swimming too near "their" beach. White rioters then fired a machine gun from a truck hurtling through black neighborhoods. But black residents fought back, no longer willing, the *Chicago Defender* reported, "to move along the line of least resistance as did their sires." The new militancy reflected both their experiences in the military and in industry and their exposure to propaganda about freedom and democracy.

Racial conflict was part of a postwar battle between Americans hoping to preserve the new social relations fostered by the war effort and those wanting to restore prewar patterns of power and control. In recognition of both the persistence of white racism and the changed attitudes among African Americans, Du Bois revised his prewar stance, affirming, "We return. We return from fighting. We return fighting."

**Fighting for Industrial Democracy.** Even more pervasive discontents roiled as America adjusted to the postwar world. More than 4 million angry workers launched a wave of 3,600 strikes in 1919. They were reacting not only to the soaring cost of living, which undermined the value of their wages, but also to employers' efforts to reassert their authority and destroy the legitimacy labor had won by its participation in the war effort. The abolition of government controls on industry enabled employers not only to raise prices but also to rescind their recognition of unions and reimpose objectionable working conditions. Employers also protected their rising profits by insisting that wages remain fixed. In response, strikers demanded higher wages, better conditions, and recognition of unions and the right of collective bargaining.

The greatest strike involved the American Federation of Labor's attempt to organize steelworkers, who endured dangerous conditions and 12-hour shifts. When the steel companies refused to recognize the union or even discuss issues, 365,000 workers went out on strike in September 1919. Strikers in Pennsylvania pointed out that they had worked "cheerfully, without strikes or trouble of any kind" during the war to "make the world safe for democracy" and that they now sought "industrial democracy." Employers hired thugs to beat the strikers, used strikebreakers to take their jobs, and exploited ethnic and racial divisions. To undercut support for the workers, management portrayed the strikers as disruptive radicals influenced by Bolshevism. After four months, the strike failed.

Employers used the same tactic to defeat striking coal miners, whose wages had fallen behind the cost of living. Refusing to negotiate with the United Mine Workers, coal operators claimed that Russian Bolsheviks had financed the strike to destroy the American economy. Attorney General A. Mitchell Palmer secured an injunction against the strike under the authority of wartime legislation. Because the government no longer controlled coal prices or enforced protective labor rules, miners complained bitterly that the war had ended for corporations but not for workers.

Two municipal strikes in 1919 also alarmed the public when their opponents depicted them as revolutionary attacks on the social order. In Seattle, the Central Labor Council called a general strike to support 35,000 shipyard workers striking for higher wages and shorter hours. When 60,000 more workers from 110 local unions also walked out, the city ground to a halt. The strikers behaved peacefully and protected public health and safety by operating garbage and fire trucks and providing food, water, and electricity. Nevertheless, Seattle's mayor, business leaders, and newspapers attacked them as Bolsheviks and anarchists. Threatened with military intervention, the labor council called off the strike, but not before it had caused a public backlash against unions across the nation.

In Boston, the police commissioner fired police officers for trying to organize a union to improve their inadequate pay. In response, the police went on strike. As in Seattle, Boston newspapers, politicians, and business leaders attributed the strike to Bolshevism, and Wilson denounced the strike as "a crime against civilization." Massachusetts governor Calvin Coolidge mobilized the National Guard and gained nationwide acclaim when he stated, "There is no right to strike against the public safety by anybody, anywhere, anytime." The entire police force was fired; many of their replacements were war veterans.

## The Red Scare

The strikes contributed to an anti-Bolshevik hysteria that swept the country in 1919. The **Red Scare** reflected fears that the Bolshevik revolution in Russia might spread to the United States. Wilson feared that returning African American troops would serve as the "greatest medium in conveying bolshevism to America"; other policymakers targeted aliens, immigrants, and labor activists. Steeped in the antiradical propaganda of the war years, many Americans were also appalled by Russian Bolshevism, described by the *Saturday Evening Post* as a "compound of slaughter, confiscation, anarchy, and universal disorder." But the Red Scare also reflected the willingness of antiunion employers, ambitious politicians, sensational journalists, zealous veterans, and racists to exploit the panic to advance their own purposes.

Fed by misleading reports about Russian Bolshevism and its influence in the United States, the Red Scare reached panic levels by mid-1919. Bombs mailed anonymously to several prominent people on May Day seemed proof enough that a Bolshevik

**Red Scare** Post–World War I anti-Bolshevik hysteria in the United States directed against labor activists, radical dissenters, and some ethnic groups.

conspiracy threatened America. The Justice Department, Congress, and patriotic organizations like the American Legion joined with business groups to suppress radicalism, real and imagined. Wilson and Attorney General Palmer called for more stringent laws and refused to release political prisoners jailed during the war. State governments harassed and arrested hundreds.

Palmer created a new agency, headed by J. Edgar Hoover, to suppress radicals and impose conformity. Its war on radicalism became the chief focus of the Justice Department. As an ambitious and ruthless bureaucrat, Hoover had participated in the government's assault on aliens and radicals during the war. Now he collected files on labor leaders and other "radical agitators" from Senator Robert La Follette to Jane Addams, issued misleading reports on communist influence in labor strikes and race riots, and contacted all major newspapers "to acquaint people like you with the real menace of evil-thinking, which is the foundation of the Red Movement."

In November 1919, Palmer and Hoover began raiding groups suspected of subversion. A month later, they deported 249 alien radicals, including the anarchist Emma Goldman, to Russia. In January 1920, Palmer and Hoover rounded up more than 4,000 suspected radicals in thirty-three cities. Often without warrants, they broke into union halls, club rooms, and private homes, assaulting and arresting everyone in sight. People were jailed without access to lawyers; some were beaten into signing false confessions. The *Washington Post* declared, "There is no time to waste on hairsplitting over infringement of liberty."

((• 📖 **Read the Document**    A. Mitchell Palmer, The Menace of Communism (1920)

At the peak of the Red Scare, few major newspapers questioned the wholesale assault on civil liberties and instead placed fears of Bolshevism above rights of individuals, especially workers, immigrants, and radicals. In this 1919 cartoon, the *Philadelphia Inquirer,* using the American flag as a protective cover, registers its support for the exile of radical immigrants and ideas.

Other Americans began to recoil from the excesses and illegal acts. Support for the Red Scare withered. Palmer's attempt to inflame public emotion backfired. When his predictions of a violent attempt to overthrow the government on May 1, 1920, came to naught, most Americans realized that no menace had ever existed. They agreed with the *Rocky Mountain News*: "We can never get to work if we keep jumping sideways in fear of the bewhiskered Bolshevik." But if the Red Scare faded in mid-1920, the hostility to immigrants, organized labor, and dissent it reflected would endure for a decade.

## The Election of 1920

The Democratic coalition that Wilson had cobbled together on the issues of progressivism and peace came apart after the war. Workers resented the administration's hostility to the postwar strikes. Ethnic groups brutalized by the Americanization of the war years blamed Wilson for the war or condemned his peace settlement. Farmers grumbled about wartime price controls and postwar falling prices. Wartime taxes and the social and economic turmoil of 1919–1920 alienated the middle class. Americans were weary of great crusades and social sacrifices; in the words of Kansas journalist William Allen White, they were "tired of issues, sick at heart of ideals, and weary of being noble." They yearned for what the Republican presidential candidate, Warren Harding of Ohio, called "normalcy."

The Republican ticket in 1920 symbolized the reassurance of simpler times. Harding was a genial politician who devoted more time to golf and poker than to public policy. An Old Guard conservative, he had stayed with the GOP when Theodore Roosevelt led the progressives out in 1912. His running mate, Calvin Coolidge, governor of Massachusetts, owed his nomination to his handling of the Boston police strike.

Wilson called the election of 1920 "a great and solemn referendum" on the League of Nations, but such lofty appeals fell flat. Harding was ambiguous about the League, and the Democratic national platform endorsed it but expressed a willingness to accept amendments or reservations. The Democratic nominees, James Cox, former governor of Ohio, and the young Franklin D. Roosevelt, Wilson's assistant secretary of the navy, favored the League, but it was not a decisive issue in the campaign.

Harding won in a landslide reflecting the nation's dissatisfaction with Wilson and the Democratic Party. Not even his closest backers considered Harding qualified for the White House, but, as Lippmann said, the nation's "public spirit was exhausted" after the war years. The election of 1920 was "the final twitch" of America's "war mind."

## Conclusion

The Great War disrupted the United States and much of the rest of the world. The initial American policy of neutrality yielded to sentimental and substantive links with the Allies and the pressure of German submarine warfare. Despite popular opposition, America joined the conflict when its leaders concluded that national interests demanded it. Using both military and diplomatic power, Woodrow Wilson sought to bring about a more stable and prosperous world order, with an expanded role for the United States. But the Treaty of Versailles only partly fulfilled his hopes, and the Senate refused to ratify the treaty and its League of Nations. The postwar world order would be unstable and dangerous.

Participation in the war, moreover, had changed the U.S. government, economy, and society. Some of these changes, including the centralization of the economy and an expansion of the regulatory role of the federal government, were already under way; some offered opportunities to implement progressive principles or reforms. Woman suffrage and prohibition gained decisive support because of the war spirit. But other consequences of the war betrayed both progressive impulses and the democratic principles the war was allegedly fought to promote. The suppression of civil liberties, manipulation of human emotions, repression of radicals and minorities, and exploitation of national crises by narrow interests helped disillusion the public. The repercussions of the Great War would linger for years, at home and abroad.

**For Suggested Readings go to MyHistoryLab.**

## Chapter Review

### Waging Neutrality

**23.1** Why were Americans so reluctant to get involved in World War I? p. 659

Most Americans regarded war between the Allies and the Central Powers as a European conflict, characterized by slaughter and stalemate. They wanted to avoid war, but President Wilson sympathized with the British and did not stay strictly neutral. American economic ties to the Allies and Germany's resumption of submarine warfare in 1917 led the United States into war.

### Waging War in America

**23.2** How did the war effort threaten civil liberties? p. 665

Wilson mobilized not only the military but also the entire nation and ensured that Americans remained loyal to the war effort; they were instructed to buy Liberty Bonds and plant victory gardens. Government agencies worked to control public opinion, encouraging Americans to spy on each other, and the Espionage and Sedition acts helped curb all dissent and trampled on basic civil rights.

### Waging War and Peace Abroad

**23.3** What hopes did Wilson have for the Treaty of Versailles? p. 671

America's entry into the war led to an Allied victory and an Armistice in November 1918. President Wilson attended the Paris Peace Conference with a vision drawn from his Fourteen Points. But, despite Wilson's plans, the Treaty of Versailles imposed harsh terms on Germany. Wilson hoped that the League of Nations would resolve these flaws and promote peace in the postwar world.

### Waging Peace at Home

**23.4** What challenges did America face in the aftermath of the war? p. 679

Although Wilson lobbied for acceptance of the League of Nations, Republican opposition combined with Wilson's stubbornness to ensure its defeat. Economic and domestic problems, including strikes, racial conflicts, housing shortages, and antiradical activities, challenged the peace on the home front and helped produce both a repressive Red Scare and the election of Republican Warren Harding, who called for "normalcy."

## Timeline

**1914**
**Waging Neutrality**—World War I begins in Europe and President Woodrow Wilson declares U.S. neutrality

`1914`

**1915**
**Waging Neutrality**—Germany begins submarine warfare

`1915`

**1916**
**Waging Neutrality**—Woodrow Wilson is reelected president

`1916`

**1917**
**Waging Neutrality**—The United States declares war on Germany

`1917`

**1918**
**Waging War and Peace Abroad**—Wilson announces his Fourteen Points; Armistice ends World War I

`1918`

**1919**
**Waging War and Peace Abroad**—Paris Peace Conference is held
**Waging Peace at Home**—Red Scare breaks out

`1919`

**1920**
**Waging Peace at Home**—League of Nations is defeated in the U.S. Senate; Warren Harding is elected president

`1920`

# 24 Toward a Modern America: The 1920s

## One American Journey

### Muckraking Journalist Writes about Henry Ford

**H**appy times were here again. American industry, adopting Henry Ford's policy of mass production and low prices, was making it possible for everybody to have his share of everything. The newspapers, the statesmen, the economists, all agreed that American ingenuity had solved the age-old problem of poverty. There could never be another depression....

The war had done something to Henry, it had taught him a new way to deal with his fellow men.... He became more abrupt in his manner, more harsh in his speech. "Gratitude?" he would say. "There's no gratitude in business. Men work for money." From now on he was a business man, and held a tight rein on everything. This industry was his, he had made it himself, and what he wanted of the men he hired was that they should do exactly as he told them....

Every worker had to be strained to the uttermost limit, every one had to be giving the last ounce of energy he had in his carcass.... They were tired when they started in the morning, and when they quit they were grey and staggering with fatigue, they were empty shells out of which the last drop of juice had been squeezed....

*More than a Car*
*Ford*
*A National Institution*

This image celebrates not only the centrality of the automobile but also the mammoth size of the Ford enterprise and Henry Ford's vision of mass production in modern American society.

## LEARNING OBJECTIVES

| 24.1 | 24.2 | 24.3 | 24.4 | 24.5 |
|---|---|---|---|---|
| What contributed to the economic boom of the 1920s? p. 688 | What was the relationship between big business and government in the 1920s? p. 692 | What factors contributed to the growth of America's cities and suburbs in the 1920s? p. 694 | How did new systems of distribution, marketing, and mass communication shape American culture? What forces fueled the cultural divisions in the 1920s? p. 699 | In what ways did Hoover promote the policies of the New Era abroad? What was Hoover's final triumph in the New Era? p. 707 |

 Listen to Chapter 24 on MyHistoryLab

#  Watch the Video Series on MyHistoryLab

Learn about some key topics related to this chapter with the *MyHistoryLab Video Series: Key Topics in U.S. History.*

**1** The 1920s The Roaring Twenties, the Jazz Age, the Lost Generation—these labels describe a decade of rapid change in virtually every facet of American life, from the workplace to the American home. This introductory video surveys the decade that followed World War I in which women won the right to vote, the sale and consumption of alcohol were prohibited, African Americans migrated to the cities of the North in search of a better life, and the culture exploded with new forms of art, literature, and jazz music. Despite the postwar prosperity, however, the decade ended with the stock market crash in 1929, which ushered in the Great Depression.

👁 Watch on MyHistoryLab

Cities and Suburbs Herbert Hoover boasted in the 1928 presidential campaign that Republican policies would bring America to "the final triumph over poverty." This video examines the decade of seemingly endless prosperity that witnessed the growth of cities and suburbs alike. But thanks to mass-produced automobiles, the suburbs grew twice as fast as cities.

Watch on MyHistoryLab 👁 **2**

**3** The New Power of Advertising Much of the consumer culture we have today can be traced back to the revolution in advertising that took place during the 1920s. This video profiles the American consumer and the power of advertising as businesses took advantage of new ways of reaching people. Advertisers used the radio, movies, and billboards to persuade consumers to buy brand-name products that often linked simple consumption with larger issues of personal success and achievement.

👁 Watch on MyHistoryLab

The *Scopes* Trial With the former presidential candidate William Jennings Bryan arguing for the prosecution and the famous defense attorney Clarence Darrow for the high school teacher, John Scopes, the *Scopes* trial pitted fundamentalists and modernists in the contest between the Bible and the science of evolution. This video examines the background, verdict, and aftermath of the court case in the small town of Dayton, Tennessee, that riveted the nation during the summer of 1925.

Watch on MyHistoryLab 👁 **4**

Henry Ford was now getting close to his two million cars a year goal. . . . From the moment the ore was taken out of the ship at the River Rouge plant [in Detroit], through all the processes turning it into steel and shaping it into automobile parts with a hundred-ton press, and putting five thousand parts together into a car which rolled off the assembly line under its own power—all those processes were completed in less than a day and a half!

Some forty-five thousand different machines were now used in the making of Ford cars, in sixty establishments scattered over the United States. . . . Henry Ford was remaking the roads of America, and in the end he would remake the roads of the world—and line them all with filling stations and hot-dog stands of the American pattern.

Upton Sinclair, *The Flivver King: A Story of Ford-America*, Dover Publications, 2012.
Originally published in 1925 by Charles H. Kerr, Publishing, Chicago, IL.

# Personal Journeys Online

- *Chicago Daily Tribune,* "U.S. Rejoices at Historic Flight, President Says Crowns Flying Record, He Tells Lindbergh," 1927. Article conveys the explosive reaction to Lindbergh's unprecedented journey.
- Elsie Johnson McDougald, "The Double Task: The Struggle of Negro Women for Sex and Race Emancipation," 1925. Article attacks racial stereotypes and discusses the diversity among African American women in New York City.

24.1

24.2

24.3

24.4

24.5

**U**pton Sinclair, one of America's most famous muckraking journalists, won his greatest recognition with the 1906 publication of his novel *The Jungle,* which graphically depicted the wretched conditions endured by Chicago's immigrant meatpacking workers. In *The Flivver King,* Sinclair demonstrates his extraordinary ability to weave together the dramatic and historical journey of industrial America, as embodied in the rise of the automobile industry and the revolutionizing vision of Henry Ford, the entrepreneur who captured the American mind and symbolized modern America to the world.

"Machinery," proclaimed Henry Ford, "is the new Messiah." Ford had introduced the assembly line at his automobile factory on the eve of World War I, and by 1925 it was turning out a Model T car every ten seconds. The term "mass production" originated in Henry Ford's 1926 description of the system of flow-production techniques popularly called "Fordism." The system symbolized the nation's booming economy: In the 1920s, Europeans used the word *Fordize* as a synonym for *Americanize.*

The assembly line, however, alienated workers, and even Ford himself conceded that the repetitive operations on the line were "so monotonous that it scarcely seems possible that any man would care to continue long at the same job." Ford first tried to adapt his mostly immigrant workers to these conditions through an Americanization program. His Education Department taught classes in English, sobriety, obedience, and industrial efficiency to the unskilled laborers entering the factory. After the course, they participated in a symbolic pageant: They climbed into a huge "melting pot," 15 feet across and 7 feet deep. After Ford managers stirred the pot with 10-foot ladles, the workers emerged wearing new clothes and waving American flags—new Americans made for the factory. When the labor market became more favorable to management in the early 1920s, Ford abolished the Education Department and relied on discipline to control workers, determined, as Sinclair observed, to keep "a tight rein on everything." To maximize profits and increase efficiency, Ford even prohibited talking, whistling, sitting, or smoking on the job. Wearing fixed expressions—"Fordization of the face"—workers could communicate only without moving their lips in the "Ford whisper." In keeping with the actions of other employers, Ford also joined the assault on labor organization, banning unions altogether and enlisting the aid of spies and informants to guard against their formation.

But even greater control and higher profits did not satisfy Henry Ford, for, like the 1920s itself, he remained conflicted about the progress he championed—the changes he saw and had helped facilitate. Launching a crusade against the new direction America was headed, Ford decided, according to Sinclair, that "what America needed was to be led back to its past." Embracing nativism and Protestantism, Ford, an ardent anti-Semite, targeted Jewish Americans in his diatribes, blaming them for radicalism and labor organization, and he singled out the "International Jew" for allegedly controlling the international financial community.

Henry Ford and Fordism reflected the complexity of the 1920s. Economic growth and technological innovation were paired with social conflict as traditions were destroyed, values were displaced, and new people were incorporated into a society increasingly industrialized, urbanized, and dominated by big business. Industrial production and national wealth soared, buoyed by new techniques and markets for consumer goods. Business values pervaded society, and government promoted business interests.

But not all Americans prospered. Many workers were unemployed, and the wages of still more were stagnant or falling. Farmers endured grim conditions and worse prospects. Social change brought pleasure to some and deep concern to others. City factories like the Ford Works attracted workers from the countryside, increasing urbanization; rapid suburbanization opened other horizons. Leisure activities flourished, and new mass media promoted modern ideas and stylish products. Workers would have to achieve satisfaction through consumption and not production. But such experiences often proved unsettling, and some Americans sought reassurance by imposing their cultural or religious values on everyone around them. The tumultuous decade thus had many unresolved issues, much like the complexity of Henry Ford himself. And Ford so dominated the age that when college students were asked to rank the greatest people of all time, Ford came in third, behind Christ and Napoleon.

# The Economy That Roared

**24.1**    What contributed to the economic boom of the 1920s?

Following a severe postwar depression in 1920 and 1921, the American economy boomed through the remainder of the decade. Gross domestic product soared nearly 40 percent; output per worker-hour, or productivity, rose 72 percent in manufacturing; average per capita income increased by a third. Although the prosperity was not evenly distributed and some sectors of the economy were deeply troubled, most Americans welcomed the industrial expansion and business principles of the New Era.

## Boom Industries

Many factors spurred the economic expansion of the 1920s. The huge wartime and postwar profits provided investment capital that enabled business to mechanize. Mass production spread quickly in American industry; machine-made standardized parts and the assembly line increased efficiency and production. Businesses steadily adopted the scientific management principles of Frederick W. Taylor (see Chapter 21). These highly touted systems, though often involving little more than an assembly-line speedup, also boosted efficiency. The nation more than doubled its capacity to generate electricity during the decade, further bolstering the economy.

The automobile industry drove the economy. Its productivity increased, and sales rose from about 1.9 million vehicles in 1920 to nearly 5 million by 1929, when 26 million vehicles were on the road (see Figure 24.1). The automobile industry employed one of every fourteen manufacturing workers and stimulated other industries, from steel to rubber and glass. It created a huge new market for the petroleum industry and fostered oil drilling in Oklahoma, Texas, and Louisiana. It launched new businesses, from service stations (more than 120,000 by 1929) to garages. It also encouraged the construction industry, a mainstay of the 1920s economy. Large increases in road building and residential housing, prompted by growing automobile ownership and migration to cities and suburbs, provided construction jobs, markets for lumber and other building materials, and profits.

New industries also sprang up. The aviation industry grew rapidly during the 1920s, with government support. The U.S. Post Office subsidized commercial air service by providing air mail contracts to private carriers. Congress then authorized commercial passenger service over the mail routes, with regular traffic opening in 1927 between Boston and New York. By 1930, more than 100 airlines crisscrossed America.

The Great War also stimulated the chemical industry. The government confiscated chemical patents from German firms that had dominated the field and transferred them to U.S. companies like DuPont. With this advantage, DuPont in the 1920s became one

((• 📖 Read the Document    Robert and Helen Lynd, The Automobile Comes to Middletown (1924)

**FIGURE 24.1  REGISTERED MOTOR VEHICLES, 1913–1929** The rapid adoption of automobiles shaped the 1920s, stimulating demand for steel and gasoline, encouraging the use of credit, facilitating urbanization, promoting tourism, and suggesting new cultural horizons.

SOURCE: U.S. Bureau of Public Roads

of the nation's largest industrial firms, a chemical empire producing plastics, finishes, dyes, and organic chemicals. Led by such successes, the chemical industry became a $4 billion giant employing 300,000 workers by 1929.

The new radio and motion picture industries also flourished. Commercial broadcasting began with a single station in 1920. By 1927, there were 732 stations, and Congress created the Federal Radio Commission to prevent wave-band interference. The rationale for this agency, which was reorganized as the Federal Communications Commission (FCC) in 1934, was that the airwaves belong to the American people and not to private interests. Nevertheless, corporations quickly dominated the new industry.

The motion-picture industry became one of the nation's five largest businesses, with 20,000 movie theaters selling 100 million tickets a week. Hollywood studios were huge factories, hiring directors, writers, camera crews, and actors to produce films on an assembly-line basis. While Americans watched Charlie Chaplin showcase his comedic genius in such films as *The Gold Rush* (1925), corporations like Paramount were integrating production with distribution and exhibition to maximize control and profit and eliminate independent producers and theaters. The advent of talking movies later in the decade brought still greater profits and power to the major studios, which alone could afford the increased engineering and production costs.

## Corporate Consolidation

A wave of corporate mergers, rivaling the one at the turn of the century, swept over the 1920s economy. Great corporations swallowed up thousands of small firms. Particularly significant was the spread of **oligopoly**—the control of an entire industry by a few giant firms. The number of automobile manufacturers dropped from 108 to 44, while only three companies—Ford, General Motors, and Chrysler—produced 83 percent of the nation's cars. In the electric light and power industry, nearly 4,000 local utility companies were merged into a dozen holding companies. By 1929, the nation's 200 largest corporations controlled nearly half of all nonbanking corporate wealth.

**oligopoly** An industry, such as steel making or automobile manufacturing, that is controlled by a few large companies.

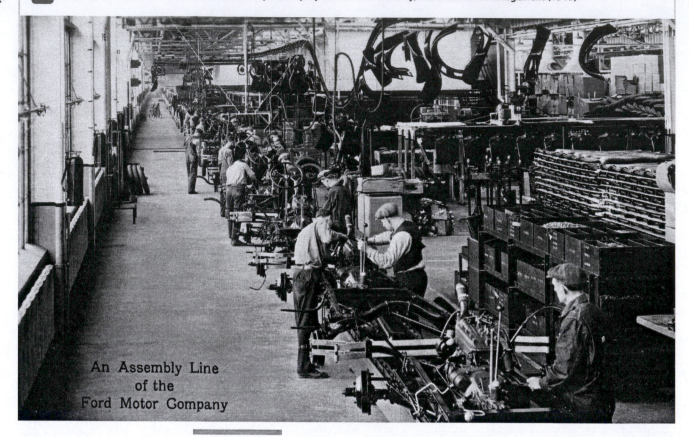

An Assembly Line
of the
Ford Motor Company

Ford Motor Company's assembly line at the River Rouge plant in Detroit. The increasing mechanization of work, linked to managerial and marketing innovations, boosted productivity in the 1920s and brought consumer goods within the reach of far more Americans than before.

Oligopolies also dominated finance and marketing. Big banks extended their control through mergers and by opening branches. By 1929, a mere 1 percent of the nation's banks controlled half its banking resources. In marketing, national chain stores, such as A&P and Woolworth's, displaced local retailers. With 15,000 grocery stores and an elaborate distribution system, A&P could buy and sell goods for less than the corner grocer.

The corporate consolidation of the 1920s provoked little public fear or opposition. Independent retailers campaigned for local zoning regulations and laws to restrict chain stores, but for the most part, Americans accepted the idea that size brought efficiency and productivity.

## Open Shops and Welfare Capitalism

**open shop** Factory or business employing workers whether or not they are union members; in practice, such a business usually refuses to hire union members and follows antiunion policies.

**yellow-dog contracts** Employment agreements binding workers not to join a union.

**welfare capitalism** A paternalistic system of labor relations emphasizing management responsibility for employee well-being.

Business also launched a vigorous assault on labor. In 1921, the National Association of Manufacturers organized an **open-shop** campaign to break union-shop contracts, which required all employees to be union members. Denouncing collective bargaining as un-American, businesses described the open shop, in which union membership was not required and usually prohibited, as the "American plan." They forced workers to sign so-called **yellow-dog contracts** that bound them to reject unions to keep their jobs. Business also used boycotts to force employers into a uniform antiunion front. Bethlehem Steel, for example, refused to sell steel to companies employing union labor. Where unions existed, corporations tried to crush them, using spies or hiring strikebreakers.

Some companies advocated a paternalistic system called **welfare capitalism** as an alternative to unions. Eastman Kodak, General Motors, U.S. Steel, and other firms provided medical services, insurance programs, pension plans, and vacations for their workers and established employee social clubs and sports teams. These policies were designed to undercut labor unions and persuade workers to rely on the corporation. Home-financing plans, for instance, increased workers' dependence on the company, and stock ownership plans inculcated business values among employees. Welfare capitalism, however, covered scarcely 5 percent of the workforce and often benefited only skilled male workers already tied to the company through seniority.

Corporations in the 1920s also promoted company unions, management-sponsored substitutes for labor unions. But company unions were usually forbidden to handle wage and hour issues. Their function was to implement company policies and undermine real unionism. Partly because of these pressures, membership in labor unions fell from 5.1 million in 1920 to 3.6 million in 1929. But unions also contributed to their own decline. Conservative union leaders neglected ethnic and black workers in mass-production industries. Nor did they try to organize women, who were by 1930 nearly one-fourth of all workers. And they failed to respond effectively to other changes in the labor market. The growing numbers of white-collar workers regarded themselves as middle class and beyond the scope of union action.

With increasing mechanization and weak labor unions, workers suffered from job insecurity and stagnant wages. Unemployment reached 12 percent in 1921 and remained a persistent concern of many working-class Americans during the decade. And despite claims to the contrary, hours were long: The average workweek in manufacturing remained more than 50 hours.

The promise of business to pay high wages proved hollow. Real wages (purchasing power) did improve, but most of the improvement came before 1923 and reflected falling prices more than rising wages. After 1923, American wages stabilized. Henry Ford made no general wage hike after 1919, although his workers would have needed an increase of 65 percent to recover the buying power they had enjoyed in 1914. Indeed, in 1928, Ford lowered wage rates. The failure to raise wages when productivity was increasing threatened the nation's long-term prosperity. In short, rising national income largely reflected salaries and dividends, not wages.

Some workers fared worse than others. Unskilled workers, especially southern and eastern Europeans, black migrants from the rural South, and Mexican immigrants, saw their already low wages decline relative to those of skilled workers. Southern workers earned much less than northerners, even in the same industry, and women were paid much less than men even for the same jobs. Overall, the gap between rich and poor widened during the decade. By 1929, fully 71 percent of American families earned less than what the U.S. Bureau of Labor Statistics regarded as necessary for a decent living standard. The maldistribution of income meant that eventually Americans would be unable to purchase the products they made.

Consumer credit, rare before the 1920s, expanded during the decade. Credit offered temporary relief by permitting consumers to buy goods on time. General Motors introduced consumer credit on a national basis to create a mass market for expensive automobiles. By 1927, two-thirds of automobiles were purchased on the installment plan. By 1929, providing consumer credit had become the nation's tenth-largest business. Nevertheless, installment loans did not in the long run raise the purchasing power of an income; they simply added interest charges to the price of products.

## Sick Industries

Despite the general appearance of prosperity, several "sick" industries dragged on the economy. Coal mining, textile and garment manufacturing, and railroads suffered from excess capacity (too many mines and factories), shrinking demand, low returns, and management-labor conflicts. For example, U.S. coal mines had a capacity of a billion tons, but scarcely half of that amount was needed because of increasing use of oil, natural gas, and hydroelectricity. Using company police, strikebreakers, and injunctions, mine operators broke the United Mine Workers and slashed wages by up to one-third. Unemployment in the industry approached 30 percent.

Similarly, the textile industry coped with overcapacity and declining demand by shifting operations from New England to the cheap-labor South, employing girls and young women for 56-hour weeks at 18 cents an hour. Textile companies, aided by local authorities, suppressed strikes in Tennessee and North Carolina. Ella May Wiggins sang of the worries in the mills:

> *How it grieves the heart of a mother,*
> *You every one must know.*
> *For we can't buy for our children,*
> *Our wages are too low.*

SOURCE: Song written by Ellie May (Mae) Wiggins (1900–1929). Unpublished.

Wiggins was murdered by company thugs, leaving behind five small children. The textile industry, despite substandard wages and repressive policies, remained barely profitable.

American agriculture never recovered from the 1921 depression. Agricultural surpluses and shrinking demand forced down prices. Moreover, farmers' wartime expansion left them heavily mortgaged in the 1920s. Small farmers, unable to compete with larger, better-capitalized farmers, suffered most. Many lost their land and became tenants or farm hands. By 1930, only 57 percent of American farmers owned the land they worked, the lowest percentage ever.

Racial discrimination worsened conditions for black and Hispanic tenants, sharecroppers, and farm workers. In the South, African American sharecroppers trapped in grinding poverty endured segregation, disfranchisement, and violence. Mexican immigrants and Hispanic Americans labored as migrant farm workers in the Southwest and California. Exploited by the contract-labor system pervasive in large-scale agriculture, they suffered from poor wages, miserable living conditions, and racism.

# The Business of Government

**24.2**  What was the relationship between big business and government in the 1920s?

The Republican surge in national politics further shaped the economy. In the 1920 election, the Republican slogan was "Less government in business, more business in government." By 1924, Calvin Coolidge, the decade's second Republican president, proclaimed, "This is a business country . . . and it wants a business government." Under such direction, the federal government advanced business interests at the expense of other objectives.

## Republican Ascendancy

Republicans in 1920 had retained control of Congress and put Warren Harding in the White House. Harding was neither capable nor bright, but he had a genial touch that contrasted favorably with Wilson, and he helped shape the modern presidency by giving the president authority over the budget. Recognizing his own limitations, he promised to appoint "the best minds" to his cabinet. Some of his appointees were highly accomplished; and two of them, Secretary of Commerce Herbert Hoover and Secretary of the Treasury Andrew Mellon, shaped economic policy throughout the 1920s.

A self-described progressive dedicated to efficiency, Hoover made the Commerce Department the government's most dynamic office. He cemented its ties with the leading sectors of the economy, expanded its collection and distribution of industrial information, pushed to exploit foreign resources and markets, and encouraged innovation. Hoover's goal was to foster prosperity by making business efficient, responsive, and profitable.

Andrew Mellon had a narrower goal. A wealthy banker and industrialist, he pressed Congress to reduce taxes on businesses and the rich. He argued that lower taxes would enable wealthy individuals and corporations to increase their capital investments, thereby creating new jobs and general prosperity. But Mellon's hope that favoring the rich would cause prosperity to trickle down to the working and middle classes proved ill-founded. Nevertheless, despite the opposition of progressives in Congress, Mellon succeeded in lowering maximum tax rates and eliminating wartime excess-profits taxes in 1921.

The Harding administration promoted business interests in other ways, too. The tariff of 1922 raised import rates to protect industry from foreign competition. High new duties on foreign aluminum, for instance, permitted manufacturers—including Mellon's own Alcoa Aluminum—to raise prices by 40 percent. But high tariffs made it difficult for European nations to earn the dollars to repay their war debts to the United States. High rates also impeded American farm exports and raised consumer prices.

The Harding administration aided the business campaign against unions and curtailed government regulation. By appointing advocates of big business to the Federal Trade Commission and the Federal Reserve Board, among others, Harding made government the collaborator rather than the regulator of business.

Finally, Harding reshaped the Supreme Court into a still more aggressive champion of business. He named the conservative William Howard Taft as chief justice and matched him with three other justices. All were, as one of them proclaimed, sympathetic to business leaders "beset and bedeviled with vexatious statutes, prying commissions, and government intermeddling of all sorts." The Court struck down much of the government economic regulation adopted during the Progressive Era, invalidated restraints on child labor and a minimum wage law for women, and approved restrictions on labor unions.

## Government Corruption

The green light that Harding Republicans extended to private interests led to corruption and scandals. Harding appointed many friends and cronies who saw public service as an opportunity for graft. Attorney General Harry Daugherty's associates in the Justice Department took bribes in exchange for pardons and government jobs. The head of the Veterans Bureau went to prison for cheating disabled veterans of $200 million. Albert Fall, the secretary of the interior, leased petroleum reserves set aside by progressive conservationists to oil companies in exchange for cash, bonds, and cattle for his New Mexico ranch. Exposed for his role in the Teapot Dome scandal, named after a Wyoming oil reserve, Fall became the first cabinet officer in history to go to jail. Daugherty escaped a similar fate by destroying records and invoking the Fifth Amendment.

Harding was appalled by the scandals. "My God, this is a hell of a job!" he told William Allen White. "I have no trouble with my enemies. . . . But my damned friends, . . . they're the ones that keep me walking the floor nights!" Harding died shortly thereafter, probably of a heart attack.

## Coolidge Prosperity

On August 3, 1923, Vice President Calvin Coolidge was sworn in as president by his father while visiting his birthplace in rural Vermont, thereby reaffirming his association with traditional values. This image reassured Americans troubled by the Harding scandals. Coolidge's calm appearance hid a furious temper and a mean spirit. Coolidge supported business with ideological conviction. He opposed the activist presidency of the Progressive Era, cultivating instead a deliberate inactivity calculated to lower expectations of government.

Like Harding, Coolidge installed business supporters in the regulatory agencies. To chair the Federal Trade Commission he appointed an attorney who had condemned the agency as "an instrument of oppression and disturbance and injury instead of help to business." Under this leadership, the FTC described its new goal as "helping business to help itself," which meant approving trade associations and agreements to suppress competition. This attitude, endorsed by the Supreme Court, aided the mergers that occurred after 1925. The *Wall Street Journal* crowed, "Never before, here or anywhere else, has a government been so completely fused with business."

"Coolidge prosperity" determined the 1924 election. The Democrats, hopelessly divided, took 103 ballots to nominate the colorless, conservative Wall Street lawyer John W. Davis. A more interesting opponent for Coolidge was Robert La Follette, nominated by discontented farm and labor organizations that formed a new Progressive Party. La Follette campaigned against "the power of private monopoly over the political and economic life of the American people." The Republicans, backed by immense contributions from business, denounced La Follette as an agent of Bolshevism. The choice, Republicans insisted, was "Coolidge or Chaos." Thus instructed, Americans chose Coolidge, though barely half the electorate bothered to vote.

## The Fate of Reform

But progressive reform was not completely dead. A small group in Congress, led by La Follette and George Norris, attacked Mellon's regressive tax policies and supported measures regulating agricultural processors, protecting workers' rights, and maintaining public ownership of a hydroelectric dam at Muscle Shoals, Alabama, that conservative Republicans wanted to privatize. Yet the reformers' successes were few and often temporary.

The fate of women's groups illustrates the difficulties reformers faced in the 1920s. At first, the adoption of woman suffrage prompted politicians to champion women's reform issues. In 1920, both major parties endorsed many of the goals of the new **League of Women Voters**. Within a year, many states had granted women the right to serve on juries, several enacted equal-pay laws, and Wisconsin adopted an equal-rights law. Congress passed the **Sheppard-Towner Maternity and Infancy Act**, the first federal social-welfare law, in 1921. It provided federal funds for infant and maternity care, precisely the type of protective legislation that the suffragists had described as women's special interest. Women also ran for political office and by 1922 there were fifteen women mayors of small towns throughout the nation.

But thereafter women reformers gained little. As it became clear that women did not vote as a bloc but according to their varying social and economic backgrounds, Congress lost interest in women's issues. In 1929, Congress killed the Sheppard-Towner Act. Nor could reformers gain ratification of a child-labor amendment after the Supreme Court invalidated laws regulating child labor. Conservatives attacked women reformers as "Bolsheviks."

**League of Women Voters** League formed in 1920 advocating for women's rights, among them the right for women to serve on juries and equal-pay laws.

**Sheppard-Towner Maternity and Infancy Act** The first federal social-welfare law, passed in 1921, providing federal funds for infant and maternity care.

# Cities and Suburbs

**24.3** What factors contributed to the growth of America's cities and suburbs in the 1920s?

The 1920 census was the first to report that more Americans lived in urban than in rural areas. The trend toward urbanization accelerated in the 1920s as millions of Americans fled the depressed countryside for the booming cities. This massive population movement interacted with technological innovations to reshape cities, build suburbs, and transform urban life (see Map 24.1).

## Expanding Cities

Urbanization affected every region of the country. In absolute terms, the older industrial cities of the Northeast and upper Midwest grew the most, attracting migrants from the rural South and distressed Appalachia. New York remained the nation's foremost metropolis.

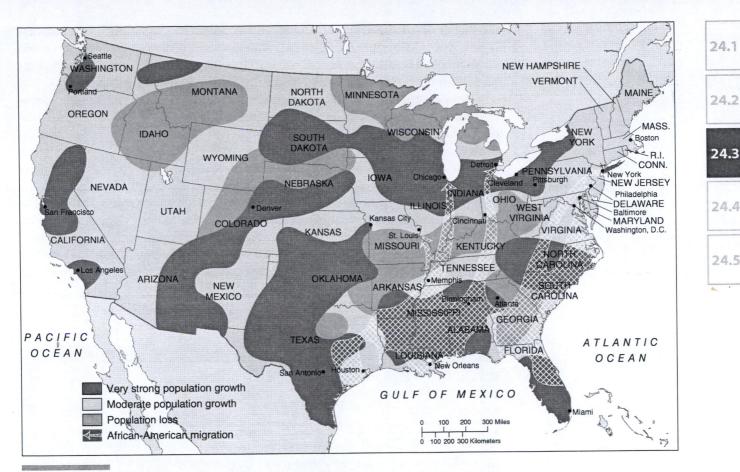

**MAP 24.1 POPULATION SHIFTS, 1920–1930** Rural Americans fled to the cities during the 1920s, escaping a declining agricultural economy to search for new opportunities. African Americans in particular left the rural South for eastern and midwestern cities, but the urban population also jumped in the West and in the South itself.

Rural southerners also headed for southern cities. In fact, the South was the nation's most rapidly urbanizing region. Migrants from the countryside poured into Atlanta, Birmingham, Memphis, and Houston. Little more than jungle before 1914, Miami became the fastest-growing city in the United States during the 1920s—"the Magic City."

In the West, Denver, Portland, and Seattle (each a regional economic hub) and several California cities grew rapidly. Los Angeles grew by 115 percent and by 1930 was the nation's fifth-largest city, with more than 1.2 million people.

The population surge transformed the urban landscape. As land values soared, developers built skyscrapers, giving Cleveland, Kansas City, San Francisco, and many other cities modern skylines. By the end of the decade, American cities had nearly 400 skyscrapers taller than twenty stories.

## The Great Black Migration

A significant feature of the rural-to-urban movement was the **Great Migration** of African Americans from the South. Like other migrants, they were responding chiefly to economic factors. Southern segregation and violence made migration attractive, but job opportunities made it possible. Prosperity created jobs, and with the decline in European immigration, black workers filled the positions previously given to new immigrants. Though generally the lowest-paid and least secure jobs, they were better than sharecropping in the rural South. Black men worked as unskilled or semiskilled laborers; black women became domestics in white homes. The migrants often found adjustment to their new environment difficult. Southern rural black culture clashed with industrial work rhythms and discipline and with urban living. Still, more than 1.5 million African Americans moved to northern cities in the 1920s.

There black ghettos usually developed, more because of prejudice than the wishes of the migrants. Although African Americans, like European immigrants, often wanted to live

**Great Migration** The mass movement of African Americans from the rural South to the urban North, spurred especially by new job opportunities during World War I and the 1920s.

together to sustain their culture, racist restrictions meant that segregation, not congregation, most shaped their urban community. With thousands of newcomers limited to certain neighborhoods, housing shortages developed. High rents and low wages forced black families to share inferior and unsanitary housing that threatened their health and safety.

However, the Great Migration also increased African Americans' racial consciousness, autonomy, and power. In 1928, for instance, black Chicagoans, using the ballot denied to African Americans in the South, elected the first black man to Congress since the turn of the century. Mutual-aid societies and fraternal orders proliferated. Churches were particularly influential. A reporter in 1926 counted 140 black churches in a 150-block area of Harlem.

Another organization also appealed to poor black ghetto dwellers. The Universal Negro Improvement Association (UNIA), organized by Marcus Garvey, a Jamaican immigrant to New York, rejected the NAACP's goal of integration. A black nationalist espousing racial pride, Garvey exhorted black people to migrate to Africa to build a "free, redeemed, and mighty nation." In the meantime, he urged them to support black

**Watch the Video    The Harlem Renaissance**

Zora Neale Hurston, folklorist, anthropologist, and novelist, wrote with wit and verve about the African American South she so closely studied. Part of the dynamic community known as the Harlem Renaissance, Hurston won recognition in 1925 for her short story "Spunk." Her collective work, especially her later novel *Their Eyes Were Watching God*, both reflected and advanced the creative pulse of what one black intellectual regarded as the first opportunity for African Americans to realize "group expression and self-determination."

businesses. UNIA organized many enterprises, including groceries, restaurants, laundries, a printing plant, and the Black Star Steamship Line, intended as a commercial link between the United States, the West Indies, and Africa. UNIA attracted half a million members, the first black mass movement in American history. When Garvey was convicted of mail fraud and deported, however, the movement collapsed.

Racial pride found distinctive expression in the **Harlem Renaissance**, an outpouring of literature, painting, sculpture, and music. Inspired by African American culture and black urban life, writers and artists created works of power and poignancy. Black values replaced traditional stereotypes as African Americans established their own vibrant community. The poetry of Langston Hughes reflected the rhythm and mood of jazz and the blues. And when Hughes declared, "I am a Negro—and beautiful," he demonstrated the pride in a black heritage that defined the movement. Writer Alain Locke wrote of *The New Negro*, celebrating a spirit of creativity that resonated with artists and writers in Harlem. Other leading authors of the Harlem Renaissance who asserted their cultural independence included Claude McKay, who wrote of the black working class in *Home to Harlem* (1928), Zora Neale Hurston, James Weldon Johnson, and Dorothy West.

**Harlem Renaissance** A new African American cultural awareness that flourished in literature, art, and music in the 1920s.

## Barrios

Hispanic migrants also entered the nation's cities in the 1920s, creating their own communities, or barrios. Fifty thousand Puerto Ricans settled in New York, mostly in East ("Spanish") Harlem, where they found low-paying jobs. Far more migrants arrived from Mexico. Although many worked as migrant farm laborers, they often lived in cities in the off-season. Others permanently joined the expanding urban economy in industrial and construction jobs. The barrios, with their own businesses, churches, and cultural organizations, created a sense of permanency.

These communities enabled the newcomers to preserve their cultural values and build social institutions, such as *mutualistas* (mutual-aid societies), that helped them obtain credit, housing, and health care. But the barrios also reflected the hostility that

Increased urbanization meant fewer opportunities for women in rural America, and many Mexican American women preferred factory jobs to laboring in the fields. These young Mexican American women, pictured in 1922, produced baby carriages at a factory in Los Angeles

# ✳ Explore the Immigrants and Migrants in the Early Twentieth Century on MyHistoryLab

## HOW DID MIGRATION AND IMMIGRATION TRENDS SHIFT BETWEEN 1870 AND 1930?

As the 1800s came to a close, internal migration and immigration patterns reoriented in the United States. The flow of settlers to the West shrank as migration from the South to the North increased. Northern cities swelled as rural Southerners left their homes for urban job opportunities. Particularly in the 1910s and 1920s, African

Seen by immigrants aboard ships entering New York City's harbor, the Statue of Liberty continues to be a welcoming symbol of freedom. The colossal bronze was cast in France and erected in 1886 as a joint goodwill project.

Americans fled discrimination in the South in the First Great Migration, moving north—especially to midwestern cities—in search of better opportunities. Moreover, immigrants had played an important role in settling new territories of the United States across the 1800s, but by 1924 increasing nativist sentiment emerging out of fears that political radicals were attempting to infiltrate the country prompted the federal government to issue strict immigration quotas.

### CHANGING POPULATION MOVEMENT PATTERNS

| Direction | 1870 | 1930 |
|---|---|---|
| East to West | 3,300,378 | 2,731,002 |
| South to North | 639,018 | 1,381,500 |

SOURCE: U.S. Census Bureau

## KEY QUESTIONS   Use MyHistoryLab *Explorer* to answer these questions:

**Cause** ▶▶▶ *Why did migration to the West decline?*

Theorize the grounds for this shift.

**Response** ▶▶▶ *For what reasons might people have left the South for the North during this time?*

Conceptualize what "push" and "pull" factors attracted people from the South to the North.

**Consequence** ▶▶▶ *How was growing nativist sentiment reflected in immigration patterns?*

Map the changing immigrant trends around the turn of the twentieth century.

Hispanics encountered in American cities. Los Angeles maintained separate schools for Mexicans, and a social worker reported that "America has repulsed the Mexican immigrant in every step he has taken" toward integration. As new migrants streamed in, conditions in the barrios deteriorated, for few cities provided adequate public services for them. Denver's barrio was described in 1924 as an area "both God and Denver had forgotten," with "no paving, no sidewalks, no sewers."

Some Hispanics fought discrimination. La Orden de Hijos de America ("The Order of the Sons of America"), organized in San Antonio in 1921, campaigned against inequities in schools and the jury system. In 1929, it helped launch the larger League of United Latin American Citizens (LULAC), which would help advance civil rights for all Americans.

## The Road to Suburbia

As fast as the cities mushroomed in the 1920s, the suburbs grew twice as fast. Park Ridge outside Chicago, Inglewood outside Los Angeles, Shaker Heights outside Cleveland, and many others expanded by 400 percent. Some suburbs, such as Highland Park, where Henry Ford built his factory near Detroit, were industrial, but most were havens for the middle and upper classes.

Automobiles created the modern suburb. Nineteenth-century suburbs were small and linear, stretching along the street railway system. The new developments were sprawling and dispersed, for the automobile enabled people to live in formerly remote areas. A single-family house surrounded by a lawn became the social ideal, a pastoral escape from the overcrowded and dangerous city. Many suburbs excluded African Americans, Hispanics, Jews, and working-class people.

Suburbanization and the automobile brought other changes. The government provided federal money to states to build highways, and by the end of the decade, road construction was the largest single item in the national budget. Autos and suburbs also stimulated the growth of new industries. In 1922, J. C. Nichols opened the Country Club Plaza, the first suburban shopping center, in Kansas City; it provided free off-street parking. Department stores and other large retailers began leaving the urban cores for the suburbs, where both parking and more affluent customers were waiting. Drive-in restaurants began with Royce Hailey's Pig Stand in Dallas in 1921. That same year, the first fast-food franchise chain, White Castle, appeared, with its standardized menu and building, serving hamburgers "by the sack" to Americans in record numbers.

# Mass Culture in the Jazz Age

**24.4** How did new systems of distribution, marketing, and mass communication shape American culture? What forces fueled the cultural divisions in the 1920s?

The White Castle chain symbolized a new society and culture. Urbanization and the automobile joined with new systems of distributing, marketing, and communications to mold a mass culture of standardized experiences and interests. Not all Americans participated equally in the new culture, however, and some attacked it.

## Advertising the Consumer Society

Advertising and its focus on increasing consumption shaped the new society. President Coolidge considered advertising "the most potent influence in adopting and changing the habits and modes of life, affecting what we eat, what we wear, and the work and play of the whole nation."

Advertisers exhorted consumers via newspapers, billboards, streetcar signs, junk mail, radio, movies, and even skywriting. They sought to create a single market where everyone, regardless of region and ethnicity, consumed brand-name products. Advertisers attempted to stimulate new wants by ridiculing previous models or tastes as obsolete, acclaiming the convenience of a new brand, or linking the latest fashion with status or sex appeal. The home, in particular, became a focus of consumerism. Middle- and upper-class women purchased mass-produced household appliances, such as electric irons, toasters, vacuum cleaners, washing machines, and refrigerators. Working-class women bought packaged food, ready-made clothing, and other consumer goods to lighten their workload. Advertisers attempted to redefine the housewife's role as primarily that of a consumer, purchasing goods for her family.

A shifting labor market also promoted mass consumption. The increasing number of white-collar workers had more time and money for leisure and consumption. Factory workers, whose jobs often provided little challenge, less satisfaction, and no prospect for advancement, found in consumption not only material rewards but also, thanks to advertisers' claims, some self-respect and fulfillment as stylish and attractive people worthy of attention. Women clerical workers, the fastest-growing occupational group, found in the purchase of clothes and cosmetics a sign of social status and an antidote to workplace monotony.

Under the stimulus of advertising, consumption increasingly displaced the traditional virtues of thrift, prudence, and avoidance of debt. Installment buying became common. By 1928, fully 85 percent of furniture, 80 percent of radios, and 75 percent of washing machines were bought on credit. But with debt rising more than twice as fast as incomes, even aggressive advertising and the extension of credit could not indefinitely prolong the illusion of a healthy economy.

## Leisure and Entertainment

During the 1920s, Americans spent more on recreation and leisure, important features of the new mass society. Millions of people packed into movie theaters whose ornate style symbolized their social importance. In Chicago, the Uptown boasted a 4,000-seat theater, an infirmary, a nursery, and a restaurant; its turreted façade soared eight stories. Inside was a four-story lobby with twin marble staircases, crystal chandeliers, and an orchestra to entertain people waiting to enter. "It is beyond human dreams of loveliness," exclaimed one ad, "achieving that overpowering sense of tremendous size and exquisite beauty."

Movies helped to spread common values and to set national trends in dress, language, and behavior. Studios made films to attract the largest audiences and fit prevailing stereotypes. Cecil B. De Mille titillated audiences while reinforcing conventional standards with religious epics like *The Ten Commandments* (1923) and *The King of Kings* (1927). Set in ancient times, such movies depicted both sinful pleasures and the eventual triumph of moral order. Radio also helped to mold popular culture. The first radio network, the National Broadcasting Company (NBC), was formed in 1926. Soon it was charging $10,000 to broadcast a commercial to a national market. Networks provided standardized entertainment, personalities, and news to Americans across the nation. Radio incorporated listeners into a national society. Rural residents, in particular, welcomed the "talking furniture" for giving them access to the speeches, sermons, and business information available to city dwellers.

The phonograph, another popular source of entertainment, allowed families to listen to music of their choice in their own homes. The phonograph business boomed. Manufacturers turned out more than 2 million phonographs and 100 million records annually. Record companies promoted dance crazes, such as the Charleston, and developed regional markets for country, or "hillbilly," music in the South and West, as well as a "race market" for blues and jazz among the growing urban population, black and white. The popularity of the trumpet player Louis Armstrong and other jazz greats gave the decade its nickname, the **Jazz Age**.

Jazz derived from African American musical traditions. The Great Migration spread it from New Orleans and Kansas City to cities throughout the nation. Indeed, jazz caught the imagination of the world and, according to composer John Alden

**Jazz Age** The 1920s, so called for the popular music of the day as a symbol of the many changes taking place in the mass culture.

Carpenter, it represented "the first art innovation originating in America to be accepted seriously in Europe." Its improvisational and rhythmic characteristics differed sharply from older and more formal music and were often condemned by people who feared that jazz would undermine conventional restraints on behavior. A group in Cincinnati, arguing that the music would implant "jazz emotions" in babies, won an injunction against its performance near hospitals. Henry Ford labeled jazz "musical slush" that encouraged the youth to imitate the "drivel of morons." But the symphony conductor Leopold Stokowski defended jazz as the music of modern America: "Jazz has come to stay because it is an expression of the times, of the breathless, energetic, superactive times in which we are living; it is useless to fight against it."

Professional sports also became more commercialized. Millions of Americans, attracted by the popularity of such celebrities as Babe Ruth of the New York Yankees, crowded into baseball parks to follow major league teams. Ruth treated himself as a commercial commodity, hiring an agent, endorsing Cadillacs and alligator shoes, and defending a salary in 1932 that dwarfed that of President Hoover by declaring, "I had a better year than he did."

Large crowds turned out to watch boxers Jack Dempsey and Gene Tunney pummel each other; those who could not get tickets listened to radio announcers describe each blow. College football attracted frenzied followers among people with no interest in higher education. Universities built huge stadiums—Ohio State's had 64,000 seats. By 1929, the Carnegie Commission noted that the commercialization of college sports had "overshadowed the intellectual life for which the university is assumed to exist."

## The New Morality

The promotion of consumption and immediate gratification weakened traditional self-restraint and fed a desire for fulfillment. The failure of wartime sacrifices to achieve promised glories deepened Americans' growing disenchantment with traditional values. The social dislocations of the war years and growing urbanization accelerated moral and social change. Sexual pleasure became an increasingly open objective. Popularization of Sigmund Freud's ideas weakened prescriptions for sexual restraint; the growing availability of birth-control information enabled women to enjoy sex with less fear of pregnancy; and movie stars like Clara Bow, known as "the It Girl," and Rudolph Valentino flaunted sexuality to mass audiences. Traditionalists worried as divorce rates, cigarette consumption, and hemlines went up while respect for parents, elders, and clergy went down.

Young people seemed to embody the new morality. Rejecting conventional standards, they embraced the era's frenzied dances, bootleg liquor, smoking, more revealing clothing, and sexual experimentation. They welcomed the freedom from parental control that the automobile afforded. The "flapper"—a frivolous young woman with short hair and a skimpy skirt who danced, smoked, and drank in oblivious self-absorption—was a major obsession in countless articles bearing such titles as "These Wild Young People" and "The Uprising of the Young." But the new morality was neither as new nor as widespread as its advocates and critics believed. Signs of change had appeared before the Great War in the popularity of new clothing fashions, social values, and public amusements among working-class and ethnic groups. And if it now became fashionable for the middle class to adopt such attitudes and practices, most Americans still adhered to traditional beliefs and values. Moreover, the new morality offered only a limited freedom. It certainly did not promote social equality for women, who remained subject to traditional double standards, with marriage and divorce laws, property rights, and employment opportunities biased against them.

## The Searching Twenties

Many writers rejected what they considered the materialism, conformity, and provincialism of mass culture. Their criticism made the postwar decade one of the most creative periods in American literature. The brutality and hypocrisy of the war stimulated the critics' disillusionment and alienation. What Gertrude Stein called the Lost Generation considered, in the words of F. Scott Fitzgerald, "all Gods dead, all wars fought, all faiths in man shaken." Ernest Hemingway, wounded as a Red Cross volunteer during the war, rejected idealism in his novel *A Farewell to Arms* (1929), declaring that he no longer saw any meaning in "the words sacred, glorious, and sacrifice."

Novelists also turned their attention to American society. In *The Great Gatsby* (1925), Fitzgerald traced the self-deceptions of the wealthy. Sinclair Lewis ridiculed middle-class society and its narrow business culture in *Babbitt* (1922), whose title character provided a new word applied to the smug and shallow. In 1930, Lewis became the first American to win the Nobel Prize in literature.

Other writers condemned the mediocrity and intolerance of mass society. The critic Harold Stearns edited *Civilization in the United States* (1922), a book of essays. Its depiction of a repressive society sunk in hypocrisy, conformity, and materialism prompted his departure for Paris, where he lived, like Hemingway and Fitzgerald, as an expatriate, alienated from America. H. L. Mencken made his *American Mercury* the leading magazine of cultural dissenters. Conventional and conservative himself, Mencken heaped vitriol on the "puritans," "peasants," and "prehensile morons" he saw everywhere in American life.

When President Coolidge declined an invitation to exhibit American paintings in Paris by declaring that there were none, he seemed to confirm for the critics the boorishness of American society. But many of the critics were as self-absorbed as their targets. When the old progressive muckraker Upton Sinclair complained that he found nothing "constructive" in Mencken's voluminous writings, Mencken was delighted. "Uplift," he retorted, "has damn nigh ruined the country." Fitzgerald claimed to have "no interest in politics at all." Such attitudes dovetailed with the society they condemned.

## Culture Wars

Despite the blossoming of mass culture and society in the 1920s, conflicts divided social groups. Some of these struggles involved reactions against the new currents in American life, including technological and scientific innovations, urban growth, and materialism. But movements to restrict immigration, enforce Prohibition, prohibit the teaching of evolution, and even sustain the Ku Klux Klan did not have simple origins, motives, or consequences. The forces underlying the culture wars of the 1920s would surface repeatedly in the future. (See Table 24.1, Issues in the Culture Wars of the 1920s.)

((• 📖 **Read the Document**   Margaret Sanger, Family Planning (1926)

**TABLE 24.1** ISSUES IN THE CULTURE WARS OF THE 1920s

| Issue | Proponent View | Opponent View |
|---|---|---|
| The new morality | Promotes greater freedom and opportunities for fulfillment | Promotes moral collapse |
| Evolutionism | A scientific advance linked to notions of progress | A threat to religious belief |
| Jazz | Modern and vital | Unsettling, irregular, vulgar, and primitive |
| Immigration | A source of national strength from ethnic and racial diversity | A threat to the status and authority of old-stock white Protestants |
| Great Migration | A chance for African Americans to find new economic opportunities and gain autonomy and pride | A threat to traditional white privilege, control, and status |
| Prohibition | Promotes social and family stability and reduces crime | Restricts liberty and increases crime |
| Fundamentalism | An admirable adherence to traditional religious faith and biblical injunctions | A superstitious creed given to intolerant interference in social and political affairs |
| Ku Klux Klan | An organization promoting community responsibility, patriotism, and traditional social, moral, and religious values | A group of religious and racial bigots given to violent vigilantism and fostering moral and public corruption |
| Mass culture | Increases popular participation in national culture; provides entertainment | Promotes conformity, materialism, mediocrity, spectacle, and relaxation |
| Consumerism | Promotes material progress and higher living standards | Promotes waste, sterility, and self-indulgence |

## Nativism and Immigration Restriction

For years, many Americans, from racists to reformers, had campaigned to restrict immigration. In 1917, Congress required immigrants to pass a literacy test. But renewed immigration after the war revived the anti-immigration movement, and the propaganda of the war and the Red Scare years generated public support for more restriction. Depicting immigrants as radicals, racial inferiors, religious subversives, or criminals, nativists clamored for congressional action. The arrests of two Italian-born anarchists, Nicola Sacco and Bartolomeo Vanzetti, in May 1920, fueled the controversy over radicalism and immigration. Charged with armed robbery and murder, they proclaimed their innocence and insisted that they were on trial solely for their political beliefs. Convicted in 1921, they were executed in 1927. Opponents of the verdict saw the trial and execution as a result of public hysteria, but defenders, like evangelist Billy Sunday, championed it as a vindication of American justice.

The passage of the Emergency Quota Act in 1921 responded to popular concerns by reducing immigration by about two-thirds and establishing quotas for nationalities on the basis of their numbers in the United States in 1910. Restrictionists, however, demanded more stringent action, especially against the largely Catholic and Jewish immigrants from southern and eastern Europe. Coolidge himself urged that America "be kept American," by which he meant white, Anglo-Saxon, and Protestant.

Congress adopted this racist rationale in the **National Origins Act of 1924**, which proclaimed its objective to be the maintenance of the "racial preponderance" of "the basic strain of our population." This law restricted immigration quotas to 2 percent of the foreign-born population of each nationality as recorded in the 1890 census, which was taken before the mass immigration from southern and eastern Europe. Another provision, effective in 1929, restricted total annual immigration to 150,000, with quotas that nearly eliminated southern and eastern Europeans. The law also completely excluded Japanese immigrants.

Other actions targeted Japanese residents in America. California, Oregon, Washington, Arizona, and other western states prohibited them from owning or leasing land, and in 1922, the Supreme Court ruled that, as nonwhites, they could never become naturalized citizens. Dispirited by the prejudice of the decade, Japanese residents hoped for fulfillment through their children, the *Nisei*, who were American citizens by birth.

Ironically, the Philippines, as a U.S. territory, was not subject to the National Origins Act, and Filipino immigration increased ninefold during the 1920s. Most Filipino newcomers became farm laborers, especially in California, or worked in Alaskan fisheries. Similarly, because the law did not apply to immigrants from the Western Hemisphere, Mexican immigration also grew. Nativists lobbied to exclude Mexicans, but agribusiness interests in the Southwest blocked any restrictions on low-cost migrant labor.

## The Ku Klux Klan

Nativism was also reflected in the popularity of the revived Ku Klux Klan, the goal of which, according to its leader, was to protect "the interest of those whose forefathers established the nation." Founded in Georgia in 1915 and modeled on its Reconstruction predecessor, the new Klan was a national, not only a southern, movement and claimed several million members by the mid-1920s. Admitting only native-born white Protestants, the Klan embodied the fears of a traditional culture threatened by social change. Ironically, its rapid spread owed much to modern business and promotional techniques as hundreds of professional recruiters raked in hefty commissions selling Klan memberships to those hoping to defend their way of life.

In part, the Klan was a fraternal order, providing entertainment, assistance, and community for its members. Its picnics, parades, charity drives, and other social and family-oriented activities—perhaps a half million women joined the Women of the Ku Klux Klan—sharply distinguished the organization from both the small, secretive Klan of the nineteenth century and the still smaller, extremist Klan of the later twentieth century. Regarding themselves as reformers, Klan members supported immigration restriction and Prohibition.

**National Origins Act of 1924** Law sharply restricting immigration on the basis of immigrants' national origins and discriminating against southern and eastern Europeans and Asians.

***Nisei*** United States citizens born of immigrant Japanese parents.

But the Klan also exploited racial, ethnic, and religious prejudices and campaigned against many social groups and what it called "alien creeds." It attacked African Americans in the South, Mexicans in Texas, Japanese in California, and Catholics and Jews everywhere. A twisted religious impulse ran through much of the Klan's organization and activities. It hired itinerant Protestant ministers to spread its message, erected altars and flaming crosses at its meetings, and sang Klan lyrics to the tunes of well-known hymns. The Klan also resorted to violence. In 1921, for example, a Methodist minister who belonged to the Klan murdered a Catholic priest on his own doorstep, and other Klansmen burned down Catholic churches. The leader of the Oregon Klan insisted that "the only way to cure a Catholic is to kill him."

To the Klan, Catholics and Jews symbolized not merely subversive religions but also the ethnic diversity and swelling urban population that challenged traditional Protestant culture. To protect that culture, the Klan attempted to censor or disrupt "indecent" entertainment, assaulted those it accused of adultery, and terrorized doctors who performed abortions.

While the Klan's appeal seemed rooted in the declining countryside, it also attracted urban residents. Chicago had the largest Klan organization in the nation, with 50,000 members, and Houston, Dallas, Portland, Indianapolis, Denver, and the satellite communities ringing Los Angeles were also Klan strongholds. Urban Klansmen were largely lower or lower middle class, many recently arrived from the country and retaining its attitudes; others were long-term urban residents who feared being marginalized by social changes, especially by competition from immigrants and new ideas.

The Klan also ventured into politics, with some success. But eventually it encountered resistance. In the North, Catholic workers disrupted Klan parades. In the South, too, Klan excesses provoked a backlash. After the Klan in Dallas flogged sixty-eight people in a "whipping meadow" along the Trinity River in 1922, respect turned to outrage. Newspapers demanded that the Klan disband, district attorneys began to prosecute Klan thugs,

**Read the Document**    Hiram Evans, "The Klan's Fight for Americanism" (1926)

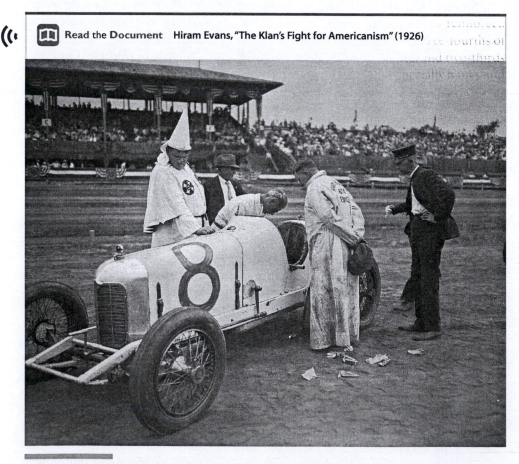

To entertain families and friends, the KKK held "Klan Day at the Races," pictured here at Denver's Overland Park Race Track.

and in 1924 Klan candidates were defeated by a ticket headed by Miriam "Ma" Ferguson, whose gubernatorial campaign called for anti-Klan laws and for the loss of tax exemptions for churches used for Klan meetings. Elsewhere the Klan was stung by revelations of criminal behavior and corruption by Klan leaders, who had been making fortunes pocketing membership fees and selling regalia to followers. The Klan crusade to purify society had bred corruption and conflict everywhere. By 1930, the Klan had nearly collapsed.

## Prohibition and Crime

Like the Klan, Prohibition both reflected and provoked social tensions in the 1920s. Reformers had long believed that prohibiting the sale of alcohol would improve social conditions, reduce crime and family instability, increase economic efficiency, and purify politics. They rejoiced in 1920 when the Eighteenth Amendment, prohibiting the manufacture, sale, or transportation of alcoholic beverages, took effect. Congress then passed the **Volstead Act**, which defined the forbidden liquors and established the Prohibition Bureau to enforce the law. But many social groups, especially in urban ethnic communities, opposed Prohibition, and the government could not enforce the law where public opinion did not endorse it.

Evasion was easy. By permitting alcohol for medicinal, sacramental, and industrial purposes, the Volstead Act gave doctors, priests, and druggists a huge loophole through which to satisfy their friends' needs. City dwellers made "bathtub gin," and rural people distilled "moonshine." Scofflaws frequented the speakeasies that replaced saloons or bought liquor from bootleggers and rumrunners, who imported it from Canada, Cuba, or Mexico. The limited resources of the Prohibition Bureau often allowed bootleggers to operate openly.

The ethics and business methods of bootleggers soon shocked Americans, however. The huge profits encouraged organized crime, which had previously concentrated on gambling and prostitution, to develop elaborate liquor-distribution networks. Operating outside the law, crime "families" used violence to enforce contracts, suppress competition, and attack rivals. In Chicago, Al Capone's army of nearly a thousand gangsters killed hundreds. Using the profits from bootlegging and new tools like the automobile and the submachine gun, organized crime corrupted city governments and police forces.

Gradually, even many "drys"—people who had initially favored Prohibition—dropped their support, horrified by the boost the amendment gave organized crime and worried about the general disrespect for law that it promoted. A 1926 poll found that four-fifths of Americans wanted to repeal or modify Prohibition. Yet it remained in force because it was entangled in party politics and social conflict. Many rural Protestant Americans saw Prohibition as a symbolic cultural issue. As the comedian Will Rogers said, "Mississippi will vote dry and drink wet as long as it can stagger to the polls." Prohibition represented the ability of rural Protestants to control the newcomers in the expanding cities. Democrats called for repeal in their 1928 and 1932 platforms, and in 1933, thirty-six states ratified an amendment repealing what Herbert Hoover had called a "noble experiment."

**Volstead Act** The 1920 law defining the liquor forbidden under the Eighteenth Amendment and giving enforcement responsibilities to the Prohibition Bureau of the Department of the Treasury.

## Old-Time Religion and the Scopes Trial

Religion provided another fulcrum for traditionalists attempting to stem cultural change. Protestant fundamentalism, which emphasized the infallibility of the Bible, including the creation story, emerged at the turn of the century as a conservative reaction to religious modernism and the social changes brought by the mass immigration of Catholics and Jews, the growing influence of science and technology, and the secularization of public education. But the fundamentalist crusade to reshape America became formidable only in the 1920s. Evangelists like Billy Sunday and Aimee Semple McPherson attracted thousands to their revivals across America. Striking and dramatic, McPherson conducted massive faith-healing ceremonies as she promoted her "Foursquare Gospel." In 1923, she opened the Angelus Temple in Los Angeles—a white domed building large enough for 5,000 of her followers. A charismatic orator, McPherson embraced Hollywood theatrics to stir her crowds and raise vast sums of money. She crisscrossed the nation in her "Gospel Car," promising salvation for all those who despaired over cultural change and modernizing trends.

Fundamentalist groups, colleges, and publications sprang up throughout the nation, especially in the South. The anti-Catholic sentiment exploited by the Klan was but one consequence of fundamentalism's insistence on strict biblical Christianity. A second was the assault on Darwin's theory of evolution, which contradicted literal interpretations of biblical creation. Fundamentalist legislators tried to prevent the teaching of evolution in public schools in at least twenty states. In 1923, Oklahoma banned textbooks based on Darwinian theory, and Florida's legislature denounced teaching evolution as "subversive." In 1925, Tennessee forbade teaching any idea contrary to the biblical account of human origins.

Social or political conservatism, however, was not an inherent part of old-time religion. The most prominent antievolution politician, William Jennings Bryan, continued to campaign for political, social, and economic reforms. Never endorsing the Klan, he served on the American Committee on the Rights of Religious Minorities and condemned anti-Semitism and anti-Catholicism. Bryan feared that Darwinism promoted political and economic conservatism. The survival of the fittest, he complained, elevated force and brutality, ignored spiritual values and democracy, and discouraged altruism and reform. How could a person fight for social justice "unless he believes in the triumph of right"?

The controversy over evolution came to a head when the American Civil Liberties Union (ACLU) responded to Tennessee's violation of the constitutional separation of church and state by offering to defend any teacher who tested the antievolution law. John Scopes, a high school biology teacher in Dayton, Tennessee, did so and was arrested. The Scopes trial attracted national attention after Bryan agreed to assist the

Evangelist Aimee Semple McPherson delivering her "Foursquare Gospel" that offered all sinners salvation.

prosecution, and Clarence Darrow, a famous Chicago lawyer and prominent atheist, volunteered to defend Scopes.

Millions of Americans tuned their radios to hear the first trial ever broadcast. The judge, a fundamentalist, sat under a sign urging people to "Read Your Bible Daily." He ruled that scientists could not testify in support of evolution: Because they were not present at the creation, their testimony would be "hearsay." But he did allow Darrow to put Bryan on the stand as an expert on the Bible. Bryan insisted on the literal truth of every story in the Bible, allowing Darrow to ridicule his ideas and force him to concede that some biblical passages had to be construed symbolically. Though the local jury took only eight minutes to convict Scopes, fundamentalists suffered public ridicule from reporters, including H. L. Mencken, who sneered at the "hillbillies" and "yokels" of Dayton.

But fundamentalism was hardly destroyed, and antievolutionists continued their campaign. New organizations, such as the Bryan Bible League, lobbied for state laws and an antievolution amendment to the Constitution. Three more states forbade teaching evolution, but by 1929 the movement had faltered. Even so, fundamentalism retained religious influence and would again challenge science and modernism in American life.

# Herbert Hoover and the New Era

 **24.5** In what ways did Hoover promote the policies of the New Era abroad? What was Hoover's final triumph in the New Era?

A broad and at home, Americans in the 1920s sought peace and economic order. Rejection of the Treaty of Versailles and the League of Nations did not foreshadow isolationism. Indeed, in the 1920s, the United States became more deeply involved in international matters than ever before in peacetime. This involvement both produced important successes and sowed the seeds for serious future problems.

## War Debts and Economic Expansion

The United States was the world's dominant economic power in the 1920s, changed by the Great War from a debtor to a creditor nation. The loans the United States had made to its allies during the war troubled the nation's relations with Europe throughout the decade. American insistence on repayment angered Europeans, who saw the money as a U.S. contribution to the joint war effort against Germany. Moreover, high American tariffs blocked Europeans from exporting goods to the United States and earning dollars to repay their debts. Eventually, the United States readjusted the terms for repayment, and American bankers extended large loans to Germany, which used the money to pay reparations to Britain and France, whose governments then used the same money to repay the United States. This unstable system depended on a continuous flow of money from the United States.

America's global economic role expanded in other ways as well. Exports, especially of manufactured goods, soared; by 1929, the United States was the world's largest exporter, responsible for one-sixth of all exports. American investment abroad more than doubled between 1919 and 1930. To expand their markets and avoid foreign tariffs, many U.S. companies became **multinational corporations**, establishing branches or subsidiaries abroad. Ford built assembly plants in England, Japan, Turkey, and Canada. International Telephone and Telegraph owned two dozen factories in Europe and employed more overseas workers than any other U.S. corporation.

Other companies gained control of foreign supply sources. American oil companies invested in foreign oil fields, especially in Latin America, where they controlled more than half of Venezuelan production. The United Fruit Company developed such huge operations in Central America that it often dominated national economies. In Costa Rica, the company had a larger budget than the national government.

**multinational corporations** Firms with direct investments, branches, factories, and offices in a number of countries.

Europeans and Latin Americans alike worried about this economic invasion; even Secretary of Commerce Herbert Hoover expressed concerns. Multinationals, he warned, might eventually take markets from American manufacturers and jobs from American workers. Business leaders, however, dismissed such reservations.

Hoover's concerns, moreover, did not prevent him from promoting economic expansion abroad. The government worked to open doors for American businesses in foreign countries, helping them to secure access to trade, investment opportunities, and raw materials. Hoover's Bureau of Foreign Commerce opened fifty offices around the world to boost American business. Hoover also pressed the British to give U.S. corporations access to rubber production in the British colony of Malaya. Secretary of State Charles Evans Hughes negotiated access to Iraqi oil fields for U.S. oil companies. The government also authorized bankers and manufacturers to form combinations, exempt from antitrust laws, to exploit foreign markets.

## Rejecting War

Although government officials cooperated with business leaders to promote American strategic and economic interests, they had little desire to use force abroad. Popular reaction against the Great War, strengthened by a strong peace movement, constrained policymakers. Having repudiated collective security as embodied in the League of Nations, the United States nonetheless sought to minimize international conflict and promote its national security. In particular, the State Department sought to restrict the buildup of armaments among nations.

At the invitation of President Harding, delegations from nine nations met in Washington at the Washington Naval Conference in 1921 to discuss disarmament. The conference drafted a treaty to reduce battleship tonnage and suspend the building of new ships for a decade. The terms virtually froze the existing balance of naval power, with the first rank assigned to Britain and the United States, followed by Japan and then France and Italy. Japan and the United States also agreed not to fortify their possessions in the Pacific any further and to respect the Open Door in East Asia. Public opinion welcomed the treaty; the U.S. Senate ratified it with only one dissenting vote, and the 1924 Republican platform hailed it as "the greatest peace document ever drawn."

The United States made a more dramatic gesture in 1928, when it helped draft the **Kellogg-Briand Pact**. Signed by sixty-four nations, the treaty renounced aggression and outlawed war. Without provisions for enforcement, however, it was little more than symbolic. The Senate reserved the right of self-defense, repudiated any responsibility for enforcing the treaty, and maintained U.S. claims under the Monroe Doctrine.

**Kellogg-Briand Pact** A 1928 international treaty that denounced aggression and war but lacked provisions for enforcement.

## Managing the Hemisphere

Senate insistence on the authority of the Monroe Doctrine reflected the U.S. claim to a predominant role in Latin America. The United States continued to dominate the hemisphere to promote its own interests. It exerted its influence through investments, control of the Panama Canal, invocation of the Monroe Doctrine, and, when necessary, military intervention.

In response to American public opinion, the peace movement, and Latin American nationalism, the United States retreated from the extreme gunboat diplomacy of the Progressive Era, withdrawing troops from the Dominican Republic and Nicaragua. Secretary of State Hughes assured Latin Americans that "we covet no territory; we seek no conquest; the liberty we cherish for ourselves we desire for others; and we accept no rights for ourselves that we do not accord to others." But Haiti remained under U.S. occupation throughout the decade, American troops stayed in Cuba and Panama, and the United States directed the financial policies of other Latin American countries. Moreover, it sent the marines into Honduras in 1924 and back to Nicaragua in 1926. Such interventions could establish only temporary stability while provoking further Latin American hostility. "We are hated and despised," said one American

# From Then to Now
# The Culture Wars

C ultural conflict raged through American society in the 1920s. Nativists demanded immigration restrictions; the Ku Klux Klan played on fears of racial, ethnic, and religious minorities; prohibitionists grappled with the minions of Demon Rum; and Protestant fundamentalists campaigned to prohibit the teaching of evolution in public schools. Beginning in the 1960s, fueled as before by challenges to traditional values and beliefs—African American demands for civil rights, opposition to the Vietnam War, the women's rights movement and women's growing presence in the workplace, a new wave of immigration (dominated this time by Asians and Latin Americans), the gay rights movement—cultural conflict flared again and continues to burn.

The central battleground of today's culture wars, however, is women's rights, and especially abortion rights. Ever since the Supreme Court ruled in *Roe v. Wade* in 1973 that women had a right to an abortion, opponents have sought to curtail or abolish that right in the name of family values. Antiabortion protests became increasingly violent in the 1980s and 1990s. Although the Supreme Court has upheld *Roe v. Wade* and laws restraining demonstrations at abortion clinics, it has also upheld state laws imposing limits on abortion rights. In 2007, moreover, the Supreme Court reversed its earlier ruling by banning late-term abortions and specifically excluding a woman's health as

a factor for consideration. The presidential campaign of 2012 further underscored the saliency of abortion rights as America's conservatives championed the Republican platform calling for a "human life amendment"—a constitutional ban on all abortions. Moreover, eight states have passed legislation requiring women to undergo ultrasound screenings before having abortions. Advocates of women's rights and reproductive freedom continue to denounce these efforts as a "war on women," especially women's expanded role in society.

Gay rights is another battleground in the culture wars. Religious conservatives, again in the name of family values, have sought to counter efforts to extend civil rights protections to gays and lesbians. Same-sex marriage has produced a volatile struggle, igniting public debate and provoking protest and legal challenges.

According to one popular analysis, the antagonists in today's culture wars are, on one side, those who find authority in religious traditions and, on the other, those who find authority in society and human reason. The war is not over, and cultural conflict, motivated by deeply rooted convictions, is likely to remain a persistent undercurrent in American life.

**Question for Discussion**

- What do these cultural conflicts reveal about American society?

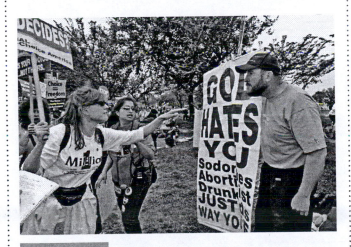

Pro-choice and antiabortion protesters square off at the pro-choice "March for Women's Lives" in the Washington, DC, Mall in April 2004.

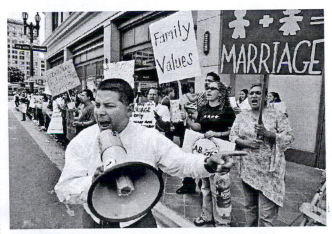

Denouncing the Massachusetts ruling legalizing same-sex marriage, chanting protesters in California invoke "family values" to reaffirm their belief in heterosexual-only unions.

businessman in Nicaragua. "This feeling has been created by employing American marines to hunt down and kill Nicaraguans in their own country."

Latin American resentment led to a resolution at the 1928 Inter-America Conference denying the right of any nation "to intervene in the internal affairs of another." The U.S. delegation rejected the measure, but the anger of Latin Americans prompted the Hoover administration to rescind support for the Roosevelt Corollary (see Chapter 22), and J. Reuben Clark, chief legal officer of the State Department, drafted the Clark Memorandum. Not published until 1930, this document stated that the Roosevelt Corollary was not a legitimate extension of the Monroe Doctrine and thereby helped prepare the way for the so-called Good Neighbor Policy toward Latin America. Still, the United States did not pledge nonintervention and retained the means, both military and economic, to dominate the hemisphere.

## Hoover and the Final Triumph of the New Era

As the national economy steamed ahead in 1928, the Republicans chose as their presidential candidate Herbert Hoover, a man who symbolized the policies of prosperity and the New Era. Hoover was not a politician—he had never been elected to office—but a successful administrator who championed rational and efficient economic development. A cooperative government, he believed, should promote business interests and encourage corporations to form trade associations to ensure stability and profitability. It should not regulate economic activities. Hoover's stiff managerial image was softened by his humanitarian record and his roots in rural Iowa.

The Democrats, by contrast, chose a candidate who evoked the cultural conflicts of the 1920s. Alfred E. Smith, a four-term governor of New York, was a Catholic, an opponent of Prohibition, and a Tammany politician tied to the immigrant constituency of New York City. His nomination plunged the nation into the cultural strife that had divided the Democrats in 1924. Rural fundamentalism, anti-Catholicism, Prohibition,

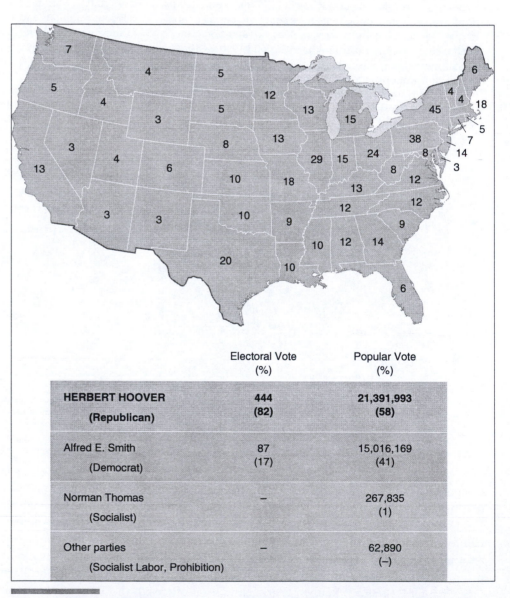

|  | Electoral Vote (%) | Popular Vote (%) |
|---|---|---|
| **HERBERT HOOVER** (Republican) | **444** **(82)** | **21,391,993** **(58)** |
| Alfred E. Smith (Democrat) | 87 (17) | 15,016,169 (41) |
| Norman Thomas (Socialist) | – | 267,835 (1) |
| Other parties (Socialist Labor, Prohibition) | – | 62,890 (–) |

**MAP 24.2  THE ELECTION OF 1928** The cultural conflicts of the 1920s shaped the 1928 election. Al Smith carried the largest cities, but Herbert Hoover swept most of the rest of the nation, even attracting much of the usually Democratic South.

and nativism were crucial factors in the campaign. The fundamentalist assault was unrelenting. Billy Sunday attacked Smith and the Democrats as "the forces of hell," and a Baptist minister in Oklahoma City warned his congregation, "If you vote for Al Smith, you're voting against Christ and you'll all be damned."

But Hoover was, in certain ways, the more progressive candidate. Sympathetic to labor, sensitive to women's issues, hostile to racial segregation, and favorable to the League of Nations, Hoover had always distanced himself from what he called "the reactionary group in the Republican party." By contrast, despite supporting factory reform and state welfare legislation to benefit his urban working-class constituents, Smith was as parochial as his most rural adversaries. He responded to a question about the needs of the states west of the Mississippi by asking, "What states *are* west of the Mississippi?"

Although many Americans voted against Smith because of his social background, the same characteristics attracted others. Millions of urban and ethnic voters, previously Republican or politically uninvolved, voted for Smith and laid the basis for the new Democratic coalition that would emerge in the 1930s. In 1928, however, with the nation still enjoying the economic prosperity so closely associated with Hoover and the Republicans, the Democrats were routed (see Map 24.2).

In his campaign, Hoover boasted that Republican policies could bring America to "the final triumph over poverty." But 1928 would be the Republicans' final triumph for a long time. The vaunted prosperity of the 1920s was ending, and the country faced a future dark with poverty.

## Conclusion

The New Era of the 1920s changed America. Technological and managerial innovations produced giant leaps in productivity, new patterns of labor, a growing concentration of corporate power, and high corporate profits. Government policies, from protective tariffs and regressive taxation to the relaxation of regulatory laws, reflected and reinforced the triumphs of the business elite over traditional cautions and concerns.

The decade's economic developments, in turn, stimulated social change, drawing millions of Americans from the countryside to the cities, creating an urban nation, and fostering a new ethic of materialism, consumerism, and leisure and a new mass culture based on the automobile, radio, the movies, and advertising. This social transformation swept up many Americans but left others unsettled by the erosion of traditional practices and values. Henry Ford, who as Upton Sinclair observed, remade the "roads of America," was also disturbed by America's new direction and reflected the ambivalence others shared about modern society. The concerns of many traditionalists often found expression in campaigns for Prohibition and against immigration, the revival of the Ku Klux Klan, and the rise of religious fundamentalism. Intellectuals denounced the materialism and conformity they saw in the new social order and fashioned new artistic and literary trends.

But the impact of the decade's trends was uneven. Mechanization increased the productivity of some workers but cost others their jobs; people poured into the cities while others left for the suburbs; Prohibition, intended to stabilize society, instead produced conflict, crime, and corruption; government policies advanced some economic interests but injured others. Even the notion of a "mass" culture obscured the degree to which millions of Americans were left out of the New Era. With no disposable income and little access to electricity, rural Americans scarcely participated in the joys of consumerism; racial and ethnic minorities were often isolated in ghettos and barrios; and many workers faced declining opportunities. Most ominous was the uneven prosperity undergirding the New Era, and this unequal distribution of wealth and income made the economy unstable and vulnerable to a disastrous collapse.

**For Suggested Readings go to MyHistoryLab.**

# Chapter Review

## The Economy That Roared

**24.1** What contributed to the economic boom of the 1920s? p. 688

The automobile drove the economy's growth and stimulated other industries, creating new products and jobs. The radio, motion-picture, and chemical industries became economic giants. Corporate mergers resulted in oligopolies, but Americans were reassured by claims of increased efficiency and productivity. Still, not all Americans or industries benefited from the uneven prosperity of the 1920s.

## The Business of Government

**24.2** What was the relationship between big business and government in the 1920s? p. 692

The Republican ascendancy in national politics shaped the economy by promoting business interests at home and abroad. The curtailment of government regulation and the placement of business leaders in regulatory agencies advanced the growth of big business and ensured that even the Supreme Court became a champion of business. Reformers challenged the pro-business actions of government but without much success.

## Cities and Suburbs

**24.3** What factors contributed to the growth of America's cities and suburbs in the 1920s? p. 694

By 1920 more Americans lived in urban than rural areas. Millions of American fled the depressed rural areas for urban opportunity, including the Great Migration of blacks to the North and Hispanic migrants to barrios. Cities boomed as skyscrapers transformed skylines, but suburbs grew even faster. Automobiles created these modern suburbs, and the construction of highways altered America's landscape.

## Mass Culture in the Jazz Age

**24.4** How did new systems of distribution, marketing, and mass communication shape American culture? What forces fueled the cultural divisions in the 1920s? p. 699

Urbanization and the automobile joined with new forms of advertising to mold a mass culture of consumerism, where brand names and buying on credit shaped the economy. New forms of leisure and entertainment transformed American society and gave the decade its nickname: the Jazz Age. But these same developments provoked social divisions—culture wars—between traditionalists and the proponents of modern changes.

## Herbert Hoover and the New Era

**24.5** In what ways did Hoover promote the policies of the New Era abroad? What was Hoover's final triumph in the New Era? p. 707

In foreign affairs, Hoover endorsed the same cooperative principles between business and government that shaped his domestic policies. He helped businesses secure new trading and investment opportunities and open international offices to boost American business abroad. Hoover symbolized the prosperity of the era and predicted in his 1928 election the elimination of poverty—a prediction that would dissolve in the coming depression.

# Timeline

**1915**
**Mass Culture in the Jazz Age**—Ku Klux Klan is founded anew

1915

**1920**
**Cities and Suburbs**—Urban population exceeds rural population for the first time

1920

**The Business of Government**—Warren Harding is elected president
**Mass Culture in the Jazz Age**—Prohibition takes effect

**1921**
**The Business of Government**—Sheppard-Towner Maternity and Infancy Act is passed

1921

**1923**
**The Business of Government**—Harding dies; Calvin Coolidge becomes president

1923

**1924**
**Mass Culture in the Jazz Age**—National Origins Act sharply curtails immigration
**The Business of Government**—Coolidge is elected president

1924

**1925**
**Mass Culture in the Jazz Age**—Scopes trial is held in Dayton, Tennessee

1925

**1928**
**Herbert Hoover and the New Era**—Kellogg-Briand Pact is signed; Herbert Hoover is elected president

1928

# 25 The Great Depression and the New Deal 1929–1939

## One American Journey

### President Roosevelt Delivers Fireside Chat over Radio

**We are bringing order out of the old** chaos with a greater certainty of labor at a reasonable wage and of more business at a fair profit. These governmental and industrial developments hold promise of new achievements for the nation.

Our first problem was, of course, the banking situation because, as you know, the banks had collapsed. Some banks could not be saved but the great majority of them, either through their own resources or with government aid, have been restored to complete public confidence. This has given safety to millions of depositors in these banks.

The second step we have taken in the restoration of normal business enterprise has been to clean up thoroughly unwholesome conditions in the field of investment. . . . The country now enjoys the safety of bank savings under the new banking laws, the careful checking of new securities under the Securities Act and the curtailment of rank stock speculation through the Securities Exchange Act. I sincerely hope that as a result people will be discouraged in unhappy efforts to get rich quick by speculating in securities. The average person almost always loses. Only a very small minority of the people of this country believe in gambling as a substitute for the very old philosophy of Benjamin Franklin that the way to wealth is through work.

Extraordinarily popular, President Franklin D. Roosevelt reached out to ordinary Americans in his political campaigns and use of the radio in his "fireside chats," promising a "new deal" that would provide the "greatest good for the greatest number of citizens."

## LEARNING OBJECTIVES

**25.1** What triggered the Great Depression? p. 715

**25.2** How did Herbert Hoover respond to the depression; why did his policies fail? p. 722

**25.3** What were the goals of the early New Deal? p. 725

**25.4** How did the major accomplishments of the Second New Deal affect America's social and economic life? p. 730

**25.5** Why did the New Deal lose momentum after 1936? p. 741

**25.6** How did Roosevelt respond to the rise of fascism in Europe? p. 742

Listen to Chapter 25 on MyHistoryLab

25.1

25.2

25.3

25.4

25.5

25.6

# ◉ Watch the Video Series on MyHistoryLab

Learn about some key topics related to this chapter with the *MyHistoryLab Video Series: Key Topics in U. S. History.*

**1** **The Great Depression and the Promise of the New Deal: 1929–1940** This video surveys the key events of the Great Depression of the 1930s, which was the most severe economic challenge the United States faced in the first 200 years of its history. On the heels of the 1929 stock market crash, a three-year spate of bank failures further weakened the nation's financial system while the Dust Bowl plunged the middle of the country into an agricultural crisis.

◉ Watch on MyHistoryLab

**The Great Depression** This video probes deeper into the hardships facing the nation during the 1930s. In the 1920s, the United States, despite growing inequalities in wealth, avoided the general malaise that had afflicted the international economy following the conclusion of World War I. However, with the stock market crash of 1929, the "Roaring 20s" gave way to an economic depression that quickly spread across the United States and led to widespread unemployment. **2**

Watch on MyHistoryLab ◉

**3** **The President Takes on the Depression** This video explains how President Herbert Hoover's response to the nation's economic woes differed from Franklin Delano Roosevelt's "New Deal" for America. After being sworn in as the new president in 1933, FDR brought renewed hope to a country that sorely needed it.

◉ Watch on MyHistoryLab

**The New Deal** President Roosevelt set out immediately to address an ailing nation. This video chronicles FDR's presidency from its first 100 days, which saw the implementation of New Deal programs, such as the Civilian Conservation Corps (CCC) and the Tennessee Valley Authority (TVA). But the early New Deal did not end the depression, and in 1935, Roosevelt undertook several important economic and social reforms, including the passage of the Social Security Act. Those reforms helped produce his landslide victory in 1936.

Watch on MyHistoryLab ◉

Those, fortunately few in number, who are frightened by boldness and cowed by the necessity for making decisions, complain that all we have done is unnecessary and subject to great risks. Now that these people are coming out of their storm cellars, they forget that there ever was a storm.

[But] nearly all Americans are sensible and calm people. We do not get greatly excited nor is our peace of mind disturbed, whether we be businessmen or workers or farmers, by awesome pronouncements concerning the unconstitutionality of some of our measures of recovery and relief and reform. We are not frightened by reactionary lawyers or political editors. All these cries have been heard before.

I still believe in ideals. I am not for a return to that definition of Liberty under which for many years a free people were being gradually regimented into the service of the privileged few. I prefer and I am sure you prefer that broader definition of Liberty under which we are moving forward to greater freedom, to greater security for the average man than he has ever known before in the history of America.

Franklin D. Roosevelt Presidential Library. Excerpted from President Franklin D. Roosevelt's radio address entitled "On Moving Forward to Greater Freedom and Greater Security," September 30, 1934.

## Personal Journeys Online

- Letter from Eleanor Roosevelt to Walter White, 1936. Roosevelt writes against lynching.
- Paul Taylor, "Again the Covered Wagon," *Survey Graphic*, July 1935. Article on the migration of "Okies" to California during the Dust Bowl.

25.1

25.2

25.3

25.4

25.5

25.6

**A**s President Franklin D. Roosevelt acknowledges in this 1934 radio address, the U.S. economy had utterly collapsed. Men, women, children everywhere saw their families and dreams shattered, watched their life savings vanish in faulty banks, and felt the sting of humiliation as they stood in bread lines or begged for clothes or food scraps. The winter of 1932–1933 had been particularly cruel: Unemployment soared and stories of malnutrition and outright starvation made headlines in newspapers throughout the nation.

The election of Franklin D. Roosevelt in 1932 had, however, lifted the spirits and hopes of jobless Americans throughout the nation. They enthusiastically responded to his "new deal for the American people" and particularly embraced his use of the radio to address the nation. In these "fireside chats," the president offered reassurance about the economic crisis, compassionately explaining his decisions and policies, as he did in this 1934 address. And he promised a brighter future, charting a new journey, he predicted, that would restore confidence among despairing Americans and provide greater economic security for the nation's citizens. "Among our objectives," Roosevelt insisted, "I place the security of the men, women, and children of the Nation first."

The leadership of Franklin and Eleanor Roosevelt and the programs of the **New Deal** connected Americans to the White House as never before. To be sure, FDR's bold rhetoric occasionally outdistanced his legislative agenda, and certain programs hardly worked against what he termed the "privileged few." Moreover, his policies often failed to challenge the racism and sexism that precluded a new deal for all Americans. Still, the unprecedented federal activism of the 1930s effectively restored confidence to many Americans and permanently transformed the nation's responsibility for the welfare of its citizens.

**New Deal** The economic and political policies of the Roosevelt administration in the 1930s.

# Hard Times in Hooverville

**25.1** | What triggered the Great Depression?

**T**he prosperity of the 1920s ended in a stock market crash that revealed the flaws honeycombing the economy. As the nation slid into a catastrophic depression, factories closed, employment and incomes tumbled, and millions lost their homes, hopes, and dignity. Some protested and took direct action; others looked to the government for relief.

## Crash!

The buoyant prosperity of the New Era, more apparent than real by the summer of 1929, collapsed in October, when the stock market crashed. During the preceding two years, the market had hit record highs, stimulated by optimism, easy credit, and speculators' manipulations. But after peaking in September, it suffered several sharp checks, and on October 29, "Black Tuesday," panicked investors dumped their stocks, wiping out the previous year's gains in one day. Confidence in the economy disappeared, and the slide continued for months, and then years. The market hit bottom in July 1932. By then, the stock of U.S. Steel had plunged from $262 to $22, Montgomery Ward from

25.1

**Great Depression** The nation's worst economic crisis, extending throughout the 1930s, producing unprecedented bank failures, unemployment, and industrial and agricultural collapse and prompting an expanded role for the federal government.

25.2

25.3

25.4

25.5

25.6

$138 to $4. Much of the paper wealth of America had evaporated, and the nation sank into the **Great Depression**.

The Wall Street crash marked the beginning of the depression, but it did not cause it. The depression stemmed from weaknesses in the New Era economy. Most damaging was the unequal distribution of wealth and income. Workers' wages and farmers' incomes had fallen far behind industrial productivity and corporate profits; by 1929, the richest 0.1 percent of American families had as much total income as the bottom 42 percent (see Figure 25.1). With more than half the nation's people living at or below the subsistence level, there was not enough purchasing power to maintain the economy.

A second factor was that oligopolies dominated American industries. By 1929, the 200 largest corporations (out of 400,000) controlled half the corporate wealth. Their power led to "administered prices," prices kept artificially high and rigid rather than determined by supply and demand. Because it did not respond to purchasing power, this system not only helped bring on economic collapse but also dimmed prospects for recovery.

Weaknesses in specific industries had further unbalanced the economy. Agriculture suffered from overproduction, declining prices, and heavy debt; so did the

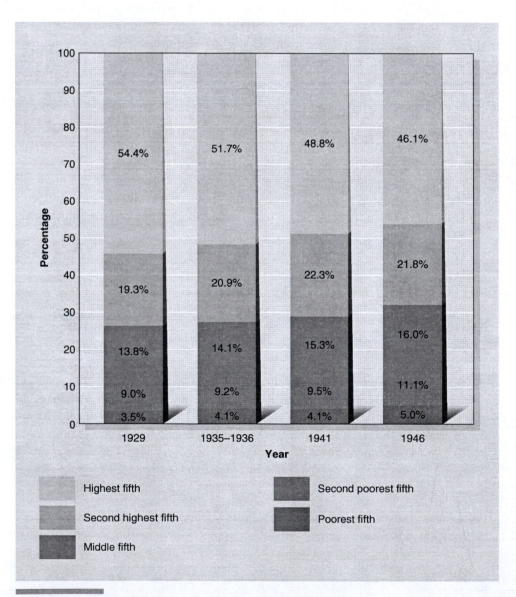

**FIGURE 25.1  DISTRIBUTION OF INCOME IN THE UNITED STATES, 1929–1946** An unequal distribution of income contributed to the Great Depression by limiting purchasing power. Only slight changes occurred until after World War II, but other factors gradually stabilized the national economy.

SOURCE: U.S. Bureau of the Census.

coal and textile industries. These difficulties left the economy dependent on a few industries for expansion and employment, and these industries could not carry the burden. Banking presented other problems. Poorly managed and regulated, banks had contributed to the instability of prosperity; they now threatened to spread the panic and depression.

International economic difficulties spurred the depression as well. Shut out from U.S. markets by high tariffs, Europeans had depended on American investments to manage their debts and reparation payments from the Great War. The stock market crash dried up the flow of American dollars to Europe, causing financial panics and industrial collapse and making the Great Depression global. In turn, European nations curtailed their imports of American goods and defaulted on their debts, further debilitating the U.S. economy.

Government policies also bore some responsibility for the crash and depression. Failure to enforce antitrust laws had encouraged oligopolies and high prices; failure to regulate banking and the stock market had permitted financial recklessness and irresponsible speculation. Reducing tax rates on the wealthy had also encouraged speculation and contributed to the maldistribution of income. Opposition to labor unions and collective bargaining helped keep workers' wages and purchasing power low. The absence of an effective agricultural policy and the high tariffs that inhibited foreign trade and reduced markets for agricultural products hurt farmers. In short, the same governmental policies that shaped the booming 1920s economy also led to economic disaster.

State and local fiscal policies also pointed to economic problems for the 1930s. The expansion of public education and road construction led to higher property taxes throughout the nation, and although per capita tax collection at the federal level actually declined between 1920 and 1929, the tax burden in states and cities increased dramatically. Indeed, state and local taxes rose faster than personal incomes in the 1920s. The real estate industry reported a decline as early as 1926, and homeowners steadily protested their higher property taxes. But the crash did more than expose the weaknesses of the economy. Business lost confidence and refused to make investments that might have brought recovery. Instead, banks called in loans and restricted credit, and depositors tried to withdraw their savings, which were uninsured. The demand for cash caused banks to fail, dragging the economy down further. And the Federal Reserve Board prolonged the depression by restricting the money supply.

## The Depression Spreads

By early 1930, the effects of financial contraction were painfully evident. Factories shut down or cut back, and industrial production plummeted. By 1932, one-fourth of the labor force was out of work (see Figure 25.2), and the wages of those Americans lucky enough to work fell sharply. Personal income dropped by more than half between 1929 and 1932. Moreover, the depression began to feed on itself in a vicious circle: Shrinking wages and employment cut into purchasing power, causing businesses to slash production again and lay off workers, thereby further reducing purchasing power.

The depression particularly battered farmers. Commodity prices fell by 55 percent between 1929 and 1932, stifling farm income. Unable to pay their mortgages, many farm families lost their homes and fields. The dispossessed roamed the byways, highways, and railways of a troubled country.

Urban families were also evicted when they could not pay their rent. Some moved in with relatives; others lived in **Hoovervilles**—the name reflects the bitterness directed at the president—shacks where people shivered, suffered, and starved. Oklahoma City's vast Hooverville covered 100 square miles.

Soup kitchens became standard features of the urban landscape, with lines of the hungry stretching for blocks. But charities and local communities could not meet the massive needs, and neither the states nor the federal government had welfare or unemployment compensation programs.

**Hooverville** Shantytown, sarcastically named after President Hoover, in which unemployed and homeless people lived in makeshift shacks, tents, and boxes. Hoovervilles cropped up in many cities in 1930 and 1931.

25.1

25.2

25.3

25.4

25.5

25.6

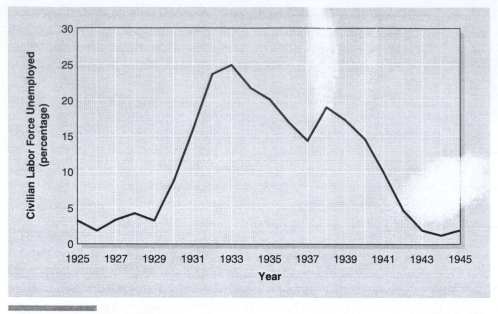

**FIGURE 25.2 UNEMPLOYMENT, 1925–1945** Unemployment soared in the early 1930s, spreading distress and overwhelming charities and local relief agencies. Federal programs improved conditions, but only America's entry into World War II really ended the problem.

SOURCE: U.S. Bureau of the Census.

## "Women's Jobs" and "Men's Jobs"

The depression affected wage-earning women in complex ways. Although they suffered 20 percent unemployment by 1932, women were less likely than men to be fired. Gender segregation had concentrated women in low-paid service, sales, and clerical jobs that were less vulnerable than the heavy industries where men predominated. But while traditional attitudes somewhat insulated working women, they also reinforced opposition to female employment, especially that of married women. Three-fourths of the nation's school systems refused to hire married women as teachers, and one-fourth dismissed female teachers who married. Many private employers, especially banks and insurance companies, also fired married women.

Firing women, however, rarely produced jobs for men, because few men sought positions in fields dominated by women. Men did displace women as teachers, social workers, and librarians, but firing women simply aggravated the suffering of families. Disapproval of female employment implied that women did not deserve equal opportunities and stiffened the opposition to opening "men's jobs" to women when women were desperate for work. Despite such hostility, the proportion of married women in the workforce increased in the 1930s as women took jobs to help their families survive, and about one-third of working married women provided the sole support for their families.

## Families in the Depression

"I have watched fear grip the people in our neighborhood around Hull House," wrote Jane Addams as the depression deepened in 1931. Divorce declined because it was expensive, but desertion increased, and people postponed marriage. Birthrates fell. Husbands and fathers, the traditional breadwinners, were often humiliated and despondent when laid off from work. Unemployed men, sociologists reported, "lost much of their sense of time and dawdled helplessly and dully about the streets," dreading to return home.

Women's responsibilities, by contrast, often grew. The number of female-headed households increased sharply. Not only did some women become wage earners, but their traditional role as homemakers also gained new significance. To make ends meet,

25.1

25.2

25.3

25.4

25.5

25.6

# ✳ Explore the Great Depression on MyHistoryLab

## HOW BAD WAS THE GREAT DEPRESSION?

Although alternating boom and bust cycles have proven an integral part of modern capitalism, the economic hard times that prevailed throughout the 1930s stand out as an exceptional case. Never before, and never since, have environmental, political, and economic factors combined to create so deep and so prolonged an economic catastrophe as that which Americans experienced during the era of the Great Depression. In the accompanying graph, notice the extremely high rates of unemployment that American workers endured during the 1930s compared to other, more moderate, spikes in unemployment that occurred during other periods of economic distress.

Breadlines like this one were a common sight during the Great Depression.

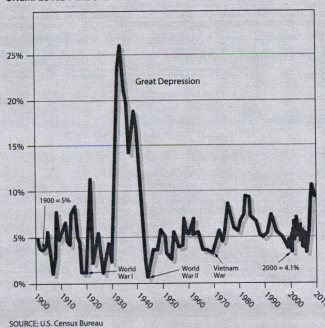

UNEMPLOYED PERSONS AS A PERCENTAGE OF THE CIVILIAN LABOR FORCE

Great Depression

1900 = 5%

World War I

World War II

Vietnam War

2000 = 4.1%

SOURCE: U.S. Census Bureau

**KEY QUESTIONS**    Use **MyHistoryLab** *Explorer* **to answer** these **questions:**

**Cause ▶▶▶** *How did financial sector instability contribute to the Great Depression?*

Map the spread of bank failures in the United States from 1928–1933.

**Consequence ▶▶▶** *Where did the depression hit the hardest?*

Map the differences in regional economic impacts over time.

**Choices ▶▶▶** *How did geographic mobility help Americans facing economic hardship?*

Map the migration of Americans into and out of different regions of the country during the depression.

719

25.1

25.2

25.3

25.4

25.5

25.6

Homeless Americans gathered in squalid Hoovervilles like this one in Seattle and struggled to survive.

many women sewed their own clothing and raised and canned vegetables, reversing the trend toward consumerism. Some also took on extra work at home. In San Antonio, one in every ten families had boarders, and in Alabama, housewives took in laundry at 10 cents for a week's wash load.

The depression also affected children. Some parents sacrificed their own well-being to protect their children. But children felt the tension and fear, and many went without food. In New York City, 139 people, most of them children, died of starvation and malnutrition in 1933. Boys and girls stayed home from school and church because they lacked shoes or clothing. As hope faded, family conflicts increased. The California Unemployment Commission concluded that the depression had left the American family "morally shattered. There is no security, no foothold, no future."

## "Last Hired, First Fired"

The depression particularly harmed racial minorities. With fewer resources and opportunities, they were less able than other groups to absorb the economic pain. African Americans were caught in a double bind, reported a sociologist at Howard University in 1932: They were "the last to be hired and the first to be fired." Black unemployment rates were more than twice the white rate, reflecting increased job competition and persistent racism.

25.1

25.2

25.3

25.4

25.5

25.6

Racism also limited the assistance African Americans received. Religious and charitable organizations often refused to care for black people. Local and state governments set higher relief eligibility requirements for blacks than for whites and provided them with less aid. Out of work for longer periods of time and without even modest relief assistance, African Americans were forced to crowd together in already cramped apartments, while still paying exorbitant rents to white landlords. An African American social worker described the despair and poverty of Harlem's residents: "Packed in damp, rat-ridden dungeons, they existed in squalor not too different from that of Arkansas sharecroppers." The Urban League affirmed, "At no time in the history of the Negro since slavery has his economic and social outlook seemed so discouraging."

Hispanic Americans also suffered. As mostly unskilled workers, they faced increasing competition for decreasing jobs paying declining wages. They were displaced even in the California agricultural labor force, which they had dominated. By the mid-1930s, they made up only a tenth of the state's migratory labor force, which increasingly consisted of white people who had fled the South and the Great Plains. Other jobs were lost when Arizona, California, and Texas barred Mexicans from public works and highway construction jobs. Vigilantes threatened employers who hired Mexicans rather than white Americans.

Economic woes and racism drove nearly half a million Mexican immigrants and their American-born children from the United States. Local authorities in the Southwest, with the blessing of the Department of Labor, urged all Mexicans, regardless of their citizenship status, to return to Mexico and free up jobs and relief assistance for white Americans. To intimidate Mexican residents, the U.S. Immigration Service conducted several raids, rounding up people and demanding immediate proof of citizenship.

## Protest

Bewildered and discouraged, most Americans reacted to the crisis without protest. Influenced by traditional individualism, many blamed themselves for their plight. But others did act, especially to protect their families. Protests ranged from small desperate gestures like stealing food and coal to more dramatic deeds. In Louisiana, women seized a train to call attention to the needs of their families; in New Jersey, in the "bloodless battle of Pleasantville," 100 women held the city council hostage to demand assistance.

The Great Depression made more desperate the plight of Mexican Americans; they faced discrimination and feared deportation. As migrant laborers, they also struggled with the forces of nature as they traveled from field to field in search of work. Here a young woman picks carrots in rural Texas in 1939.

25.1

25.2

25.3

25.4

25.5

25.6

Communists, socialists, and other radicals organized more formal protests. Communists led the jobless into "unemployment councils" that staged hunger marches, demonstrated for relief, and blocked evictions. Socialists built similar organizations, including the People's Unemployment League in Baltimore, which had 12,000 members. Groups of this kind provided protection and assistance. However, local officials often suppressed their protests. In 1932, police fired on the Detroit Unemployment Council as it marched to demand food and jobs, killing four marchers and wounding many more.

Rural protests also broke out. Again, communists organized some of them, as in Alabama, where the Croppers' and Farm Workers' Union mobilized black agricultural laborers in 1931 to demand better treatment. In the Midwest, the Farmers' Holiday Association, organized among family farmers in 1932, stopped the shipment of produce to urban markets, hoping to drive up prices. A guerrilla war broke out as farmers blocked roads and halted freight trains, dumped milk in ditches, and fought bloody battles with deputy sheriffs. Midwestern farmers also tried to prevent foreclosure of their farms. In Nebraska, a Farmers' Holiday leader warned that if the state did not halt foreclosures, "200,000 of us are coming to Lincoln and we'll tear that new State Capitol Building to pieces."

# Herbert Hoover and the Depression

**25.2** How did Herbert Hoover respond to the depression; why did his policies fail?

The Great Depression challenged the optimism, policies, and philosophy that Herbert Hoover had carried into the White House in 1929. The president took unprecedented steps to resolve the crisis but shrank back from the interventionist policies activists urged. His failures, personal as well as political and economic, led to his repudiation and to a major shift in government policies.

## The Failure of Voluntarism

Hoover fought economic depression more vigorously than any previous president, but he believed that voluntary private relief was preferable to federal intervention. The role of the national government, he thought, was to advise and encourage the voluntary efforts of private organizations, individual industries, or local communities.

Hoover obtained pledges from business leaders to maintain employment and wage levels. But most corporations soon repudiated these pledges, slashed wages, and laid off workers. Hoover himself complained, "You know, the only trouble with capitalism is capitalists; they're too damn greedy." Still, he rejected government action.

Hoover also depended on voluntary efforts to relieve the misery caused by massive unemployment. He created the President's Organization for Unemployment Relief to help raise private funds for voluntary relief agencies. Charities and local authorities, he believed, should help the unemployed; direct federal relief would expand government power and undermine the recipients' character. He vetoed congressional attempts to aid the unemployed.

The depression rendered Hoover's beliefs meaningless. Private programs to aid the unemployed scarcely existed. Only a few unions, such as the Amalgamated Clothing Workers, had unemployment funds, and these were soon spent. Company plans for unemployment compensation covered less than 1 percent of workers, revealing the charade of the welfare capitalism of the 1920s. Private charitable groups like the Salvation Army, church associations, and ethnic societies quickly exhausted their resources. Nor could local governments cope, and their efforts declined as the depression deepened. By 1932, more than 100 cities made no relief appropriations at all.

25.1
25.2
25.3
25.4
25.5
25.6

Hands in their pockets, hungry men stand numbly in one of New York City's 82 breadlines. Said one observer: "The wretched men, many without overcoats or decent shoes, usually began to line up soon after six o'clock, in good weather or bad, rain or snow."

Only eight state governments provided even token assistance. Constitutional restrictions on taxes and indebtedness stopped some from responding to the relief crisis. Others lacked the will.

As the depression worsened, Hoover adopted more activist policies. He persuaded Congress to cut taxes to boost consumers' buying power, and he increased the public works budget. The Federal Farm Board lent money to cooperatives and spent millions trying to stabilize crop prices. Unable to control production, however, the board conceded failure by late 1931. More successful was the Reconstruction Finance Corporation (RFC). Established in January 1932, the RFC lent federal funds to banks, insurance companies, and railroads so that their recovery could "trickle down" to ordinary Americans. Hoover still opposed direct aid to the general public, although he finally allowed the RFC to lend small amounts to state and local governments for unemployment relief.

Far more action was necessary, but Hoover remained committed to voluntarism and a balanced budget. Hoover's ideological limitations infuriated Americans who saw him as indifferent to their suffering and a reactionary protector of privileged business interests—an image his political opponents encouraged.

## Repudiating Hoover: The 1932 Election

Hoover's treatment of the **Bonus Army** symbolized his unpopularity and set the stage for the 1932 election. In 1932, unemployed veterans of World War I gathered in Washington, demanding payment of service bonuses not due until 1945. Hoover

**Bonus Army** A group of unemployed veterans who demonstrated in Washington for the payment of service bonuses, only to be dispersed violently by the U.S. Army in 1932.

25.1

25.2

25.3

25.4

25.5

25.6

Bonus Marchers battling police in Washington, DC, in 1932. Police and military assaults on these homeless veterans infuriated Americans and prompted Democratic presidential nominee Franklin D. Roosevelt to declare, "Well, this will elect me."

refused to meet with them, and Congress rejected their plan. But 10,000 veterans erected a shantytown at the edge of Washington and camped in vacant public buildings. Hoover decided to evict the veterans, but General Douglas MacArthur exceeded his cautious orders and on July 28 led cavalry, infantry, and tanks against the ragged Bonus Marchers. The troops cleared the buildings and assaulted the shantytown, dispersing the veterans and their families and setting their camp on fire.

This assault provoked widespread outrage. The administration tried to brand the Bonus Marchers as communists and criminals, but subsequent investigations refuted such claims. The incident confirmed Hoover's public image as harsh and insensitive.

In the summer of 1932, with no prospects for victory, Republicans renominated Hoover. Confident Democrats selected Governor Franklin D. Roosevelt of New York, who promised "a new deal for the American people." FDR had prepared for the presidency, but in 1921, he contracted polio, which paralyzed him from the waist down. His struggle with this ordeal gave him greater maturity, compassion, and determination and his continued involvement in politics owed much to his wife, Eleanor, a social reformer and Democratic activist.

The 1932 campaign gave scant indication of what Roosevelt's New Deal might involve. The Democratic platform differed little from that of the Republicans, and Roosevelt spoke in vague or general terms. Still, observers found clues in Roosevelt's record in New York, where he had created the first state system of unemployment relief and supported social welfare and conservation. More important was his outgoing personality, which radiated warmth and hope in contrast to Hoover's gloom.

25.1

25.2

25.3

25.4

25.5

25.6

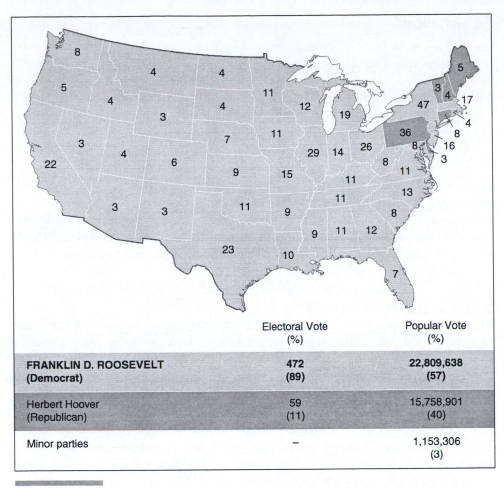

| | Electoral Vote (%) | Popular Vote (%) |
|---|---|---|
| **FRANKLIN D. ROOSEVELT (Democrat)** | **472 (89)** | **22,809,638 (57)** |
| Herbert Hoover (Republican) | 59 (11) | 15,758,901 (40) |
| Minor parties | – | 1,153,306 (3) |

**MAP 25.1  THE ELECTION OF 1932** In the midst of the Great Depression, only the most rock-ribbed Republican states failed to turn to Franklin D. Roosevelt and the Democrats for relief. The election of 1932 was a landslide.

FDR carried every state south and west of Pennsylvania (see Map 25.1). It was the worst rout of a Republican candidate ever (except in 1912, when the party had split). Yet Hoover would remain president for four more months, as the Constitution then required. And in those four months, the depression worsened, spreading misery throughout America. The final blow came in February 1933, when panic struck the banking system. Nearly 6,000 banks had already failed, robbing 9 million depositors of their savings. Desperate Americans rushed to withdraw their funds from the remaining banks, pushing them to the brink. With the federal government under Hoover immobilized, state governments shut the banks to prevent their failure. By March, an eerie silence had descended on the nation.

# Launching the New Deal

**25.3**  What were the goals of the early New Deal?

n the midst of this national anxiety, Franklin D. Roosevelt pushed forward an unprecedented program to resolve the crises of a collapsing financial system, crippling unemployment, and agricultural and industrial breakdown and to promote reform. The early New Deal achieved successes and attracted support, but it also had limitations and generated criticism that suggested the need for still greater innovations.

25.1

25.2

25.3

25.4

25.5

25.6

**fireside chats** Speeches broadcast nationally over the radio in which President Franklin Roosevelt explained complex issues and programs in plain language, as though his listeners were gathered around the fireside with him.

**Federal Deposit Insurance Corporation (FDIC)** Government agency that guarantees bank deposits, thereby protecting both depositors and banks.

**Securities and Exchange Commission (SEC)** Federal agency with authority to regulate trading practices in stocks and bonds.

## Action Now!

On March 4, 1933, Franklin Delano Roosevelt became president and immediately reassured the American people. He insisted that "the only thing we have to fear is fear itself" and he promised "action, and action now!" Summoning Congress, Roosevelt pressed forward on a broad front. In the first three months of his administration, the famous Hundred Days of the New Deal, the Democratic Congress passed many important laws. (See Table 25.1, Major Laws of the Hundred Days.)

Roosevelt's program reflected a mix of ideas, some from FDR himself, and some from a diverse group of advisers, including academic experts dubbed the "brain trust," politicians, and social workers. It also incorporated principles from the progressive movement, precedents from the Great War mobilization, and even plans from the Hoover administration. Above all, the New Deal was a practical response to the depression. FDR had set its tone in his campaign when he declared, "The country needs, and, unless I mistake its temper, the country demands bold, persistent experimentation. . . . Above all, try something."

FDR first addressed the banking crisis. On March 5, he proclaimed a national bank holiday, closing all remaining banks. Congress then passed his Emergency Banking Act, a conservative measure that extended government assistance to sound banks and reorganized weak ones. Prompt government action, coupled with a reassuring **fireside chat** over the radio by the president, restored popular confidence in the banks. When they reopened on March 13, deposits exceeded withdrawals. In June, Congress created the **Federal Deposit Insurance Corporation (FDIC)** to guarantee bank deposits up to $2,500.

The financial industry was also reformed. The Glass-Steagall Act separated investment and commercial banking to curtail risky speculation. The Securities Act reformed the sale of stocks to prevent the insider abuses that had characterized Wall Street, and in 1934 the **Securities and Exchange Commission (SEC)** was created to regulate the stock market. Two other financial measures in 1933 created the Home Owners Loan Corporation and the Farm Credit Administration, which enabled millions to refinance their mortgages.

### TABLE 25.1 MAJOR LAWS OF THE HUNDRED DAYS

| Law | Objective |
|---|---|
| Emergency Banking Act | Stabilized the private banking system |
| Agricultural Adjustment Act | Established a farm recovery program based on production controls and price supports |
| Emergency Farm Mortgage Act | Provided for the refinancing of farm mortgages |
| National Industrial Recovery Act | Established a national recovery program and authorized a public works program |
| Federal Emergency Relief Act | Established a national system of relief |
| Home Owners Loan Act | Protected homeowners from mortgage foreclosure by refinancing home loans |
| Glass-Steagall Act | Separated commercial and investment banking and guaranteed bank deposits |
| Tennessee Valley Authority Act | Established the TVA and provided for the planned development of the Tennessee River Valley |
| Civilian Conservation Corps Act | Established the CCC to provide work relief on reforestation and conservation projects |
| Farm Credit Act | Expanded agricultural credits and established the Farm Credit Administration |
| Securities Act | Required full disclosure from stock exchanges |
| Wagner-Peyser Act | Created a U.S. Employment Service and encouraged states to create local public employment offices |

## Creating Jobs

Roosevelt also provided relief for the unemployed. The Federal Emergency Relief Administration (FERA) furnished funds to state and local agencies. Harry Hopkins, who had headed Roosevelt's relief program in New York, became its director and one of the New Deal's most important members. FERA spent over $3 billion before it ended in 1935, and by then Hopkins and FDR had developed new programs that provided work rather than just cash. Work relief, they believed, preserved both the skills and the morale of recipients. In the winter of 1933–1934, Hopkins spent nearly $1 billion to create jobs for 4 million men and women through the Civil Works Administration (CWA). The CWA hired laborers to build roads and airports, teachers to staff rural schools, and singers and artists to give public performances. The Public Works Administration (PWA) provided work relief on useful projects to stimulate the economy through public expenditures. Directed by Harold Ickes, the PWA spent billions from 1933 to 1939 to build schools, hospitals, courthouses, dams, and bridges.

One of FDR's personal ideas, the Civilian Conservation Corps (CCC), combined work relief with conservation. Launched in 1933, the CCC employed 2.5 million young men to work on reforestation and flood-control projects, build roads and bridges in national forests and parks, restore Civil War battlefields, and fight forest fires. The men lived in isolated camps and earned $30 a month, $25 of which had to be sent home. One of the most popular New Deal agencies, the CCC lasted until 1942.

## Helping Some Farmers

Besides providing relief, the New Deal promoted economic recovery. In May 1933, Congress established the Agricultural Adjustment Administration (AAA) to combat the depression in agriculture caused by crop surpluses and low prices. The AAA subsidized farmers who agreed to restrict production. The objective was to boost farm prices to parity, a level that would restore farmers' purchasing power to what it had been in 1914.

Agricultural conditions improved. Farm prices rose from 52 percent of parity in 1932 to 88 percent in 1935, and gross farm income rose by 50 percent. Not until 1941, however, would income exceed the level of 1929, a poor year for farmers. Moreover, some of the decreased production and increased prices stemmed from devastating droughts and dust storms on the Great Plains. The AAA itself harmed poor farmers while aiding larger commercial growers. As southern planters restricted their acreage, they dismissed tenants and sharecroppers, and with AAA payments, they bought new farm machinery, reducing their need for farm labor.

## The Flight of the Blue Eagle

The New Deal attempted to revive U.S. industry with the National Industrial Recovery Act (NIRA), which created the National Recovery Administration (NRA). The NRA sought to halt the slide in prices, wages, and employment by suspending antitrust laws and authorizing industrial and trade associations to draft codes setting production quotas, price policies, wages and working conditions, and other business practices. The codes promoted the interests of business generally and big business in particular, but Section 7a of the NIRA guaranteed workers the rights to organize unions and bargain collectively—a provision that John L. Lewis of the United Mine Workers called an Emancipation Proclamation for labor.

Hugh Johnson became director of the NRA. He persuaded business leaders to cooperate in drafting codes and the public to patronize participating companies. The NRA Blue Eagle insignia and its slogan "We Do Our Part" covered workplaces, storefronts, and billboards. Blue Eagle parades marched down the nation's main streets and climaxed in a massive demonstration in New York City.

25.1

25.2

25.3

25.4

25.5

25.6

25.1
25.2
25.3
25.4
25.5
25.6

A coal miner greeting Franklin D. Roosevelt in West Virginia in 1932. Roosevelt's promise of a New Deal revived hope among millions of Americans trapped in hard times.

Support for the NRA waned, however. Corporate leaders used it to advance their own goals and to discriminate against small producers, consumers, and labor. Businesses also violated the labor rights specified in Section 7a. Defiant employers rejected collective bargaining and even used violence to smother unions. The NRA did little to enforce Section 7a. Workers felt betrayed. Roosevelt tried to reorganize the NRA, but the act remained controversial until the Supreme Court declared it unconstitutional in 1935.

## Critics Right and Left

The early New Deal did not end the depression. Recovery was fitful and uneven; millions of Americans remained unemployed. Nevertheless, the New Deal's efforts to grapple with problems, its successes in reducing suffering and fear, and Roosevelt's own skills carried the Democratic Party to victory in the 1934 elections. But New Deal policies also provoked criticism, from both those convinced that too little had been achieved and those alarmed that too much had been attempted.

Despite the early New Deal's pro-business character, conservatives complained that the expansion of government activity and its regulatory role weakened the autonomy of American business. They also condemned the efforts to aid nonbusiness groups as socialistic, particularly the "excessive" spending on unemployment relief and the "instigation" of labor organizing. These critics attracted little popular support, however, and their selfishness antagonized Roosevelt.

More realistic criticism came from the left. In 1932, FDR had campaigned for "the forgotten man at the bottom of the economic pyramid," and some radicals argued that the early New Deal had forgotten the forgotten man. Communists and socialists focused public attention on the poor, especially in the countryside. In California, communists organized Mexican, Filipino, and Japanese farm workers into the Cannery and Agricultural Workers Union; in Arkansas and Tennessee, socialists in 1934 helped organize sharecroppers into the Southern Tenant Farmers Union, protesting the "Raw Deal" they had received from the AAA. Both unions encountered violent reprisals. Growers killed three picketers in California's San Joaquin Valley; in Arkansas, landlords shot union organizers and led vigilante raids on sharecroppers' shacks. This terrorism, however, created sympathy for farmworkers.

Increased labor militancy in 1934 pressed Roosevelt. The number of workers participating in strikes leaped from 325,000 in 1932 (about the annual average since 1925) to 1.5 million in 1934. From dockworkers in Seattle and copper miners in Butte to streetcar drivers in Milwaukee and shoemakers in Boston, workers demanded their rights. Textile workers launched the largest single strike in the nation's history, shutting down the industry in twenty states.

Rebuffing FDR's pleas for fair treatment, employers moved to crush the strikes, often using complaisant police and private strikebreakers. In Minneapolis, police shot sixty-seven teamsters, almost all in the back, as they fled an ambush arranged by employers; in Toledo, company police and National Guardsmen attacked autoworkers with tear gas, bayonets, and rifle fire; and in the textile strike, police killed six picketers in South Carolina. Against such powerful opponents, workers needed help to achieve their rights. Harry Hopkins and other New Dealers realized that labor's demands could not be ignored.

Four prominent individuals mobilized popular discontent to demand government action to assist groups neglected by the New Deal. Representative William Lemke of North Dakota, an agrarian radical leader of the Nonpartisan League, called attention to rural distress and rejected the New Deal's limited response to farmers crushed by the depression. In his own state, nearly two-thirds of the farmers had lost their land through foreclosures.

Francis Townsend, a California physician, proposed to aid the nation's elderly, many of whom were destitute. The Townsend Plan called for a government pension to every American over the age of 60, provided that the recipient retired from work and spent the entire pension. This scheme promised to extend relief to the elderly, open jobs for the unemployed, and stimulate economic recovery.

Father Charles Coughlin, a Catholic priest in the Detroit suburb of Royal Oak, threatened to mobilize another large constituency against the limitations of the early New Deal. Thirty million Americans listened eagerly to his weekly radio broadcasts, which mixed religion with anti-Semitism and demands for social justice and financial reform. Coughlin initially welcomed the New Deal as "Christ's Deal." But after concluding that FDR's policies favored "the virile viciousness of business and finance," Coughlin organized the National Union for Social Justice to lobby for his goals. With support among lower-middle-class, heavily Catholic, urban ethnic groups, Coughlin posed a real challenge to Roosevelt's Democratic Party.

Roosevelt found Senator Huey P. Long of Louisiana still more worrisome. Alternately charming and autocratic, Long had modernized his state with taxation and educational reforms and an extensive public works program after his election as governor in 1928. Moving to the Senate and eyeing the White House, Long proposed more comprehensive social welfare policies than the New Deal had envisaged. In 1934, he organized the Share-Our-Wealth Society. His plan to end poverty and unemployment called for confiscatory taxes on the rich to provide every family with a decent income, health coverage, education, and old-age pensions. Long's appeal was enormous. Within months, his organization claimed more than 27,000 clubs and 7 million members.

25.1

25.2

25.3

25.4

25.5

25.6

25.1

25.2

25.3

**25.4**

25.5

25.6

These dissident movements raised complex issues and simple fears. They built on concerns about the New Deal, both demanding government assistance and fretting about government intrusion. Their programs were often ill-defined or impractical—Townsend's plan would cost more than half the national income; and some of the leaders, like Coughlin and Long, approached demagoguery. Nevertheless, their popularity warned Roosevelt that government action was needed to satisfy reform demands and ensure his reelection in 1936.

## Consolidating the New Deal

**25.4** How did the major accomplishments of the Second New Deal affect America's social and economic life?

Responding to the persistence of the depression and political pressures, Roosevelt in 1935 undertook economic and social reforms that some observers have called the Second New Deal. The new measures shifted government action more toward reform even as they still addressed relief and recovery. Nor did FDR's interest in reform simply reflect cynical politics. He had championed progressive measures in the past, and many of his advisers had deep roots in reform movements.

**⊙ Watch the Video** Dorothea Lange and *Migrant Mother*

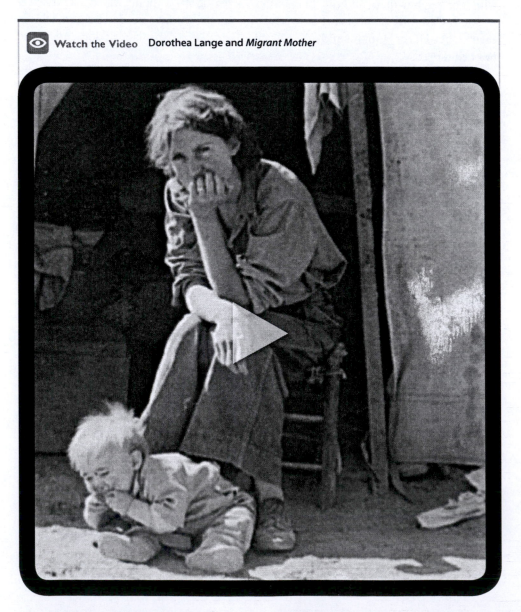

The New Deal enabled photographers and artists to take to the road to capture images of the nation's dispossessed. This photograph by Dorothea Lange of an 18-year-old mother and her child in a migrant labor camp in 1937 illustrates both despair and detachment and conveys the grinding poverty of the Great Depression.

After the 1934 elections gave the president an even more Democratic Congress, Harry Hopkins exulted: "Boys—this is our hour. We've got to get everything we want—a works program, social security, wages and hours, everything—now or never."

## Weeding Out and Lifting Up

"In spite of our efforts and in spite of our talk," Roosevelt told the new Congress in 1935, "we have not weeded out the overprivileged and we have not effectively lifted up the underprivileged." To do so, he developed "must" legislation. One of the new laws protected labor's rights to organize and bargain collectively. The Wagner National Labor Relations Act, dubbed "Labor's Magna Carta," guaranteed workers the right to organize unions and prohibited employers from adopting unfair labor practices, such as firing union activists and forming company unions. The law also set up the National Labor Relations Board (NLRB) to enforce these provisions, protect workers from coercion, and supervise union elections.

**Social Security.** Of greater long-range importance was the Social Security Act. Other industrial nations had established national social insurance systems much earlier, but only the Great Depression moved the United States to accept the idea that the federal government should protect the poor and unemployed. Even so, the law was a compromise, framed by a nonpartisan committee of business, labor, and public representatives and then weakened by congressional conservatives. It provided unemployment compensation, old-age pensions, and aid for dependent mothers and children and the blind.

The conservative nature of the law appeared in its stingy benefit payments, its lack of health insurance, and its exclusion of more than one-fourth of all workers, including many in desperate need of protection, such as farm laborers and domestic servants. Moreover, unlike in other nations, the old-age pensions were financed through a regressive payroll tax on both employees and employers rather than through general tax revenues. Thus the new system was more like a compulsory insurance program.

Despite its weaknesses, the Social Security Act was one of the most important laws in American history and it provided, as Roosevelt pointed out, "at least some measure of protection to the average citizen and to his family against the loss of a job and against poverty-ridden old age." Moreover, by establishing federal responsibility for social welfare, it inaugurated a welfare system that subsequent generations would expand.

**Money, Tax, and Land Reform.** Another reform measure, the Banking Act of 1935, increased the authority of the Federal Reserve Board over the nation's currency and credit system and decreased the power of the private bankers whose irresponsible behavior had contributed to the depression and the appeal of Father Coughlin. The Revenue Act of 1935, passed after Roosevelt assailed the "unjust concentration of wealth and economic power," provided for graduated income taxes and increased estate and corporate taxes. Opponents called it the Soak the Rich Tax, but with its many loopholes it was scarcely that, and it was certainly not a redistributive measure such as Huey Long had proposed. Nevertheless, it set a precedent for progressive taxation and attracted popular support.

The Second New Deal also responded belatedly to the environmental catastrophe that had turned much of the Great Plains from Texas to the Dakotas into a Dust Bowl (see Map 25.2). Since World War I, farmers had stripped marginal land of its native grasses to plant wheat. When drought and high winds hit the plains in 1932, crops failed, and nothing was left to hold the soil. Dust storms blew away millions of tons of topsoil, despoiling the land and darkening the sky a thousand miles away. Families abandoned their farms in droves. Many of these poor "Okies" headed for California, their plight captured in John Steinbeck's novel *The Grapes of Wrath* (1939).

In 1935, Roosevelt established the Resettlement Administration to focus on land reform and help poor farmers. Under Rexford Tugwell, this agency initiated soil

25.1

25.2

25.3

25.4

25.5

25.6

25.1

25.2

25.3

**25.4**

25.5

25.6

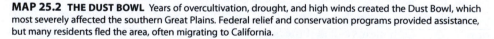

**Watch the Video** *The Plough That Broke the Plains* (1934)

Severe wind erosion, 1935–1936

Severe wind erosion, 1938

Severe wind erosion, 1940

Most severe wind erosion, 1935–1938

**MAP 25.2 THE DUST BOWL** Years of overcultivation, drought, and high winds created the Dust Bowl, which most severely affected the southern Great Plains. Federal relief and conservation programs provided assistance, but many residents fled the area, often migrating to California.

erosion projects and attempted to resettle impoverished farmers on better land, but the problem exceeded its resources. Congress moved to save the land, if not its people, by creating the Soil Conservation Service in 1935.

## Expanding Relief

If reform gained priority in the Second New Deal, relief remained critical. With millions still unemployed, Roosevelt pushed through Congress in 1935 the Emergency Relief Appropriation Act, authorizing $5 billion—at the time the largest single appropriation in American history—for emergency public employment. Roosevelt created the Works Progress Administration (WPA) under Hopkins, who set up work relief programs to assist the unemployed and boost the economy. Before its end in 1943, the WPA gave jobs to 9 million people (more than a fifth of the labor force) and spent

# From Then to Now
# Social Security

25.1

25.2

25.3

**25.4**

25.5

25.6

N o politician will "ever scrap my social security program." So predicted FDR when he signed the Social Security Act in 1935. He based his confidence on the provisions in the act that linked benefits to payroll deductions. Because workers contributed to the program, they would feel a "right to collect their pensions and unemployment benefits." But Roosevelt could not have imagined just how successful the Social Security program would become as time went on. It now assists more than 50 million Americans, and, over the next two decades, nearly 80 million Americans will be eligible for benefits. The nation's first "baby boomer," Kathleen Casey-Kirschling, who was born one second after midnight on January 1, 1946, filed to receive Social Security payments that began in January 2008. And many baby boomers have followed her.

But the successful expansion of the program has also called its future into question. Critics of the program may not propose "scrapping" Social Security, but they do advocate a major overhaul. In part, their opposition stems from a backlash against "big government" that emerged in the 1960s and ultimately found its champion in Republican President Ronald Reagan, who declared, "Government is not the solution to

Americans eagerly embraced the Social Security program in the 1930s, proudly displaying their Social Security cards and even having their numbers tattooed on their bodies.

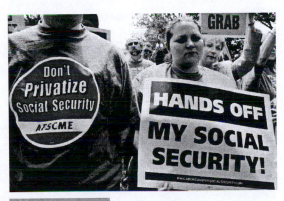

President George W. Bush's campaign to reform Social Security stirred angry protest throughout America.

our problems; government is the problem." Citing long-term concerns about the program's solvency, these critics call for privatizing the system, enabling contributors to invest their Social Security accounts in the stock market, for example.

Former president George W. Bush made revamping Social Security the centerpiece of his 2005 State of the Union Address and launched a sixty-day nationwide tour to drum up support for Social Security reform. But the American people overwhelmingly rejected his plans for privatization, and the subsequent collapse of Wall Street further stiffened their resolve. The election in 2008 of Democratic President Barack Obama—an opponent of privatization—reassured many Americans of continued federal support for what they regard as the "most successful program in our country's history." Questions about the future of Social Security and privatization, however, reemerged in the presidential campaign of 2012, and once again the public reaction against changing the program was swift and strong.

**Question for Discussion**

- Why does the vast majority of Americans continue to support Social Security despite the critics of "big government"?

nearly $12 billion. Three-fourths of its expenditures went on construction projects that could employ manual labor: The WPA built 125,000 schools, post offices, and hospitals; 8,000 parks; nearly 100,000 bridges; and enough roads and sewer systems to circle the earth thirty times. The WPA laid much of the basic infrastructure on which the nation still relies.

The WPA also developed work projects for unemployed writers, artists, musicians, and actors. "Why not?" said FDR. "They are human beings. They have to live." WPA programs allowed people to use their talents while surviving the depression, increased popular access to cultural performances, and established a precedent for federal support of the arts.

The National Youth Administration (NYA), another WPA agency, gave part-time jobs to students, enabling 2 million high school and college students to stay in school, learn skills, and do productive work. At Duke University, law student Richard M. Nixon earned 35 cents an hour doing research in the library. Lyndon Johnson, a Texas NYA official, believed that "if the Roosevelt administration had never done another thing, it would have been justified by the work of this great institution for salvaging youth."

## The Roosevelt Coalition and the Election of 1936

The 1936 election gave Americans an opportunity to judge FDR and the New Deal. Conservatives alarmed at the expansion of government, business people angered by regulation and labor legislation, and wealthy Americans furious with tax reform decried the New Deal. But they were a minority. Even the presidential candidate they supported, Republican Governor Alf Landon of Kansas, endorsed much of the New Deal, criticizing merely the inefficiency and cost of some of its programs.

The programs and politicians of the New Deal had created an invincible coalition behind Roosevelt. Despite ambivalence about large-scale government intervention, the New Deal's agricultural programs reinforced the traditional Democratic allegiance of white southerners while attracting many western farmers. Labor legislation clinched the active support of the nation's workers. Middle-class voters, whose homes had been saved and whose hopes had been raised, also joined the Roosevelt coalition.

So did urban ethnic groups, who had benefited from welfare programs and appreciated the unprecedented recognition Roosevelt's administration gave them. FDR named the first Italian American to the federal judiciary, for example, and appointed five times as many Catholics and Jews to government positions as the three Republican presidents had during the 1920s. African Americans voted overwhelmingly Democratic for the

 **Read the Document**  Franklin D. Roosevelt, Fireside Chat (September 6, 1936)

Eleanor Roosevelt campaigns with FDR. A visible activist for social and economic reform, she was also politically important in building the powerful Roosevelt coalition. "Previously," said the journalist Ruby Black, "a President's wife acted as if she didn't know that a political party existed."

25.1
25.2
25.3
25.4
25.5
25.6

first time. Women, too, were an important part of the Roosevelt coalition, and Eleanor often attracted their support as much as Franklin did.

This political realignment produced a landslide. Roosevelt polled 61 percent of the popular vote and the largest electoral vote margin ever recorded, 523 to 8. Democrats also won huge majorities in Congress. Roosevelt's political coalition reflected a mandate for himself and the New Deal; it would enable the Democrats to dominate national elections for three decades.

The landslide of 1936 revealed the impact of the New Deal on Americans. Industrial workers mobilized to secure their rights, women and minorities gained increased, if still limited, opportunities to participate in American society, and southerners and westerners benefited from government programs they turned to their own advantage. Government programs changed daily life, and ordinary people often helped shape the new policies.

25.1

25.2

25.3

25.4

25.5

25.6

## Labor on the March

The labor revival in the 1930s reflected both workers' determination and government support. Workers wanted to improve their wages and benefits as well as to gain union recognition and union contracts that would allow them to limit arbitrary managerial authority and achieve some control over the workplace. This larger goal provoked opposition from employers and their allies and required workers to organize, strike, and become politically active. Their achievement was remarkable.

The Second New Deal helped. By guaranteeing labor's rights to organize and bargain collectively, the Wagner Act sparked a wave of labor activism. But if the government ultimately protected union rights, the unions themselves had to form locals, recruit members, and demonstrate influence in the workplace.

At first, those tasks overwhelmed the American Federation of Labor (AFL). Its reliance on craft-based unions and reluctance to organize immigrant, black, and women workers left it unprepared for the rush of industrial workers seeking unionization. More progressive labor leaders saw that industry-wide unions were more appropriate for unskilled workers in mass-production industries. Forming the Committee for Industrial Organization (CIO) within the AFL, they campaigned to unionize workers in the steel, auto, and rubber industries, all notoriously hostile to unions. AFL leaders insisted that the CIO disband and then in 1937 expelled its unions. The militants reorganized as the separate **Congress of Industrial Organizations**. (In 1955, the two groups merged as the AFL-CIO.)

The split roused the AFL to increase its own organizing activities, but it was primarily the new CIO that put labor on the march. It inspired workers previously neglected by organized labor. The CIO's interracial union campaign in the Birmingham steel mills, said one organizer, was "like a second coming of Christ" for black workers, who welcomed the union as a chance for social recognition as well as economic opportunity. The CIO also employed new and aggressive tactics, particularly the sit-down strike, in which workers, rather than picketing outside the factory, simply sat inside the plant, thereby blocking both production and the use of strikebreakers.

The CIO won major victories despite bitter opposition from industry and its allies. The issue was not wages but labor's right to organize and bargain with management. Sit-down strikes paralyzed General Motors (GM) in 1937 after it refused to recognize the United Auto Workers (UAW). GM tried to force the strikers out of its Flint, Michigan plants by turning off the heat, using police and tear gas, threatening strikers' families, and obtaining court orders to clear the plant by military force. But the governor refused to order National Guardsmen to attack, and the strikers held out, aided by the Women's Emergency Brigade, working-class women who picketed the building, heckled the police, and smuggled food to the strikers. After six weeks, GM signed a contract with the UAW. Chrysler soon followed suit. Ford refused to recognize the union until 1941, often violently disrupting organizing efforts.

**Congress of Industrial Organizations (CIO)** An alliance of industrial unions that spurred the 1930s organizational drive among the mass-production industries.

25.1

25.2

25.3

25.4

25.5

25.6

Steel companies also used violence against unionization. In the Memorial Day Massacre in Chicago in 1937, police guarding a plant of the Republic Steel Company fired on strikers and their families, killing ten people as they tried to flee. A Senate investigation found that Republic and other companies had hired private police to attack workers seeking to unionize, stockpiled weapons and tear gas, and corrupted officials. Federal court orders finally forced the companies to bargain collectively.

New Deal labor legislation, government investigations and court orders, and the federal refusal to use force against strikes helped the labor movement secure basic rights for American workers. Union membership leaped from under 3 million in 1932 to 9 million by 1939, and workers won higher wages, better working conditions, and more economic democracy.

## Women and the New Deal

New Deal relief programs had a mixed impact on working women. Formal government policy required equal consideration for women and men, but local officials so flouted this requirement that Eleanor Roosevelt urged Harry Hopkins to "impress on state administrators that the women's programs are as important as the men's. They are so apt to forget us!" Women on relief were restricted to women's work—more than half worked on sewing projects, regardless of their skills—and were paid scarcely half of what men received. WPA training programs also reinforced traditional ideas about women's work; black women, for example, were trained to be maids, dishwashers, and cooks. Although women constituted nearly one-fourth of the labor force, they obtained only 19 percent of the jobs created by the WPA, 12 percent of those created by the FERA, and 7 percent of those created by the CWA. The CCC excluded women altogether. Still, relief agencies provided crucial assistance to women during the depression.

Other New Deal programs also had mixed benefits for women. Despite demands by the League of Women Voters and the Women's Trade Union League for "equal pay for equal work and equal opportunity for equal ability regardless of sex," many NRA codes mandated lower wage scales for women than for men, which officials justified as reflecting long-established customs. But by raising minimum wages, the NRA brought relatively greater improvement to women, who were concentrated in the lowest-paid occupations, than to male workers. The Social Security Act did not cover domestic servants, waitresses, or women who worked in the home, but it did help mothers with dependent children.

Still more significant, the Social Security Act reflected and reinforced prevailing notions about proper roles for men and women. The system was based on the idea that men should be wage earners and women should stay at home as wives and mothers. Accordingly, if a woman worked outside the home and her husband was eligible for benefits, she would not receive her own retirement pension. And if a woman had no husband but had children, welfare authorities would remove her from work-relief jobs regardless of whether she wanted to continue to work, and would give her assistance from the Aid to Dependent Children (ADC) program, which was also created under the Social Security Act. These new programs, then, while providing much-needed assistance, also institutionalized a modern welfare system that segregated men and women in separate spheres and reaffirmed the then popular belief that the success of the family depended on that separation.

Women also gained political influence under the New Deal, although Molly Dewson, the director of the Women's Division of the Democratic Party, exaggerated when she exclaimed, "The change from women's status in government before Roosevelt is unbelievable." Dewson herself exercised considerable political power and helped to shape the party's campaigns. Around Dewson revolved a network of women, linked by friendships and experiences in the National Consumers' League, Women's Trade Union League, and other progressive reform organizations. Appointed to many positions in the Roosevelt administration, they helped develop and implement New

Deal social legislation. Secretary of Labor Frances Perkins was the first woman cabinet member and a key member of the network; other women were in the Treasury Department, the Children's Bureau, and relief and cultural programs.

Eleanor Roosevelt was their leader. Described by a Washington reporter as "a cabinet member without portfolio," she roared across the social and political landscape of the 1930s, pushing for women's rights, demanding reforms, traveling across the country, writing newspaper columns and speaking on the radio, developing plans to help unemployed miners in West Virginia and abolish slums in Washington, and lobbying both Congress and her husband. FDR used her as his eyes and ears and sometimes his conscience. He rebuffed her critics with a jaunty, "Well, that is my wife; I can't do anything about her." Indeed, Eleanor Roosevelt had become not merely the most prominent first lady in history but a force in her own right and a symbol of the growing importance of women in public life.

## Minorities and the New Deal

Despite the move of African Americans into the Democratic Party, the New Deal's record on racial issues was limited. Although Roosevelt deplored racial abuses, he never pushed for civil rights legislation, fearing to antagonize southern congressional Democrats whose support he needed. For similar reasons, many New Deal programs discriminated against African Americans. And racist officials discriminated in allocating federal relief. Atlanta, for instance, provided average monthly relief checks of $32.66 to whites but only $19.29 to blacks.

Nonetheless, disproportionately poor and unemployed African Americans did benefit from the New Deal's welfare and economic programs. W. E. B. Du Bois asserted that "large numbers of colored people in the United States would have starved to death if it had not been for the Roosevelt policies," adding that the New Deal served to sharpen their sense of the value of citizenship by making clear the "direct connection between politics and industry, between government and work, [and] between voting and wages." And key New Dealers campaigned against racial discrimination. Eleanor Roosevelt prodded FDR to appoint black officials, wrote articles supporting racial equality, and flouted segregationist laws. Attacked by white racists, she was popular in the black community. Harry Hopkins and Harold Ickes also promoted equal rights. As black votes in northern cities became important, pragmatic New Dealers also began to pay attention to black needs.

African Americans themselves pressed for reforms. Civil rights groups protested discriminatory policies, including the unequal wage scales in the NRA codes and the CCC's limited enrollment of black youth. African Americans demonstrated against racial discrimination in hiring and their exclusion from federally financed construction projects.

In response, FDR took more interest in black economic and social problems. He prohibited discrimination in the WPA in 1935, and the NYA adopted enlightened racial policies. Roosevelt also appointed blacks to important positions, including the first black federal judge. Many of these officials began meeting regularly at the home of Mary McLeod Bethune of the National Council of Negro Women. Dubbed the Black Cabinet, they worked with civil rights organizations, fought discrimination in government, influenced patronage, and stimulated black interest in politics.

The New Deal improved economic and social conditions for many African Americans. Black illiteracy dropped because of federal education projects, and the number of black college students and graduates more than doubled, in part because the NYA provided student aid to black colleges. New Deal relief and public health programs reduced black infant mortality rates and raised life expectancy rates. Conditions for black people continued to lag behind those for white people, and discrimination persisted, but the black switch to the Roosevelt coalition reflected the New Deal's benefits.

Native Americans also benefited from the New Deal. The depression had imposed further misery on a group already suffering from poverty, wretched health conditions,

25.1

25.2

25.3

25.4

25.5

25.6

25.1

25.2

25.3

25.4

25.5

25.6

and the nation's lowest educational level. Many New Deal programs had limited applicability to Indians, but the CCC appealed to their interests and skills. Appointed commissioner of the Bureau of Indian Affairs in 1933, John Collier promoted conservation work among Native Americans, calling the CCC a "creative force" for Indian communities. Ultimately, more than 80,000 Native Americans received training in agriculture, forestry, and animal husbandry, along with basic academic subjects. CCC projects, together with those undertaken by the PWA and the WPA, built schools, hospitals, roads, and irrigation systems on reservations. New Deal officials also refocused government Indian policy, which had undermined tribal authority and promoted assimilation by reducing Indian landholding and attacking Indian culture. Collier prohibited interference with Native American religious or cultural life, directed the Bureau to employ more Native Americans, and prevented Indian schools from suppressing native languages and traditions.

Collier also persuaded Congress to pass the Indian Reorganization Act of 1934, often called the Indians' New Deal. The act guaranteed religious freedom, reestablished tribal self-government, and halted the sale of tribal lands. It also provided funds to expand Indian landholdings, support Indian students, and establish tribal businesses. But social and economic problems persisted on the isolated reservations, and white missionaries and business interests attacked Collier's reforms as atheistic and communistic. And not all Native Americans supported Collier's reforms,

With an appointment in the National Youth Administration, the educator Mary McLeod Bethune was the highest-ranking African American woman in the Roosevelt administration. She advised FDR on all racial matters and envisioned "dozens of Negro women coming after me, filling positions of trust and strategic importance."

asserting that he, too, stereotyped Indians and their culture, and labeling his efforts as "back-to-the-blanket" policies designed to make Native American cultures historical commodities.

Hispanic Americans received less assistance from the New Deal. Relief programs aided many Hispanics in California and the Southwest but ignored those who were not citizens. Moreover, local administrators often discriminated against Hispanics, especially by providing higher relief payments to Anglos. Finally, by excluding agricultural workers, neither the Social Security Act nor the Wagner Act gave Mexican Americans much protection or hope. Farm workers remained largely unorganized, exploited, and at the mercy of agribusinesses.

## The New Deal: North, South, East, and West

"We are going to make a country," President Roosevelt declared, "in which no one is left out." And with that statement, along with his belief that the federal government must take the lead in building a new "economic constitutional order," FDR ensured that his New Deal programs and policies fanned out throughout the nation.

**The New Deal in the South.** The New Deal's agricultural program boosted farm prices and income more in the South than any other region. By controlling cotton production, it also promoted diversification; its subsidies financed mechanization. The resulting modernization helped replace an archaic sharecropping system with an emergent agribusiness. The rural poor were displaced, but the South's agricultural economy advanced.

The New Deal also improved southern cities. FERA and WPA built urban sewer systems, airports, bridges, roads, and harbor facilities. Whereas northern cities had already constructed such facilities themselves—and were still paying off the debts these had incurred—the federal government largely paid for such modernization in the South, giving its cities an economic advantage.

Federal grants were supposed to be awarded to states in proportion to their own expenditures, but although southern politicians welcomed New Deal funds, they refused to contribute their share of the costs. Nationally, the federal proportion of FERA expenditures was 62 percent; in the South, it was usually 90 percent and never lower than 73 percent.

Federal money enabled southern communities to balance their budgets, preach fiscal orthodoxy, and maintain traditional claims of limited government. Federal officials complained about the South's "parasitic" behavior in accepting aid but not responsibility, and even southerners acknowledged the hypocrisy of the region's invocation of state's rights. "We recognize state boundaries when called on to give," noted the *Houston Press*, "but forget them when Uncle Sam is doing the giving."

The federal government had a particularly powerful impact on the South with the **Tennessee Valley Authority (TVA)**, launched in 1933 (see Map 25.3). Coordinating activities across seven states, the TVA built dams to control floods and generate hydroelectric power, produced fertilizer, fostered agricultural and forestry development, encouraged conservation, improved navigation, and modernized school and health systems. Private utility companies denounced the TVA as socialistic, but most southerners supported it. Its major drawback was environmental damage that only became apparent later. Over a vast area of the South, it provided electricity for the first time.

The New Deal further expanded access to electricity by establishing the Rural Electrification Administration (REA) in 1935. Private companies had refused to extend power lines into the countryside because it was not profitable, consigning 90 percent of the nation's farms to drudgery and darkness. The REA revolutionized farm life by sponsoring rural nonprofit electric cooperatives. By 1941, 35 percent of American farms had electricity; by 1950, 78 percent.

**Tennessee Valley Authority (TVA)** Federal regional planning agency established to promote conservation, produce electric power, and encourage economic development in seven southern states.

25.1
25.2
25.3
25.4
25.5
25.6

25.1

25.2

25.3

25.4

25.5

25.6

📖 **Read the Document**   Tennessee Valley Authority Act (1933)

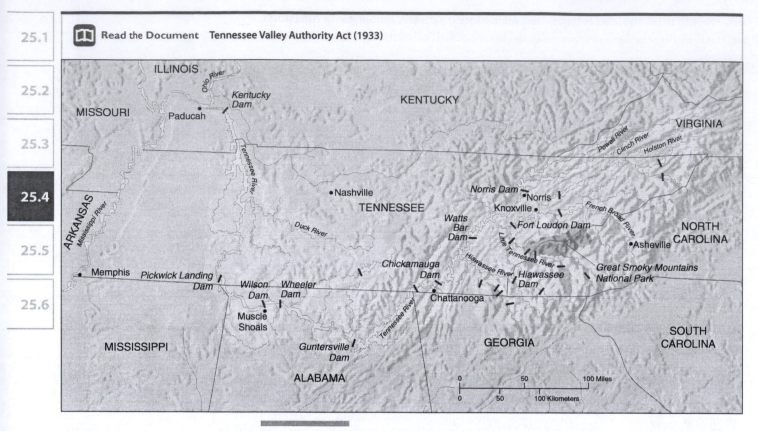

**MAP 25.3   THE TENNESSEE VALLEY AUTHORITY**  By building dams and hydroelectric power plants, the TVA controlled flooding and soil erosion and generated electricity that did much to modernize a large region of the Upper South.

**The New Deal in the West.**  The New Deal also changed the West. Westerners received the most federal money per capita in welfare, relief projects, and loans. Like southerners, they accepted federal aid and clamored for more.

The Bureau of Reclamation, established in 1902, emerged as one of the most important government agencies in the West. It built huge dams to control the western river systems and promote large-scale development. By furnishing capital and expertise, the government subsidized and stimulated western economic development, particularly the growth of agribusiness.

Westerners welcomed such assistance but rarely shared the federal goals of rational resource management. Instead, they often wanted to continue to exploit the land and resented federal supervision as colonial control. In practice, however, the government worked in partnership with the West's agribusinesses and timber and petroleum industries.

## The New Deal and Public Activism

Despite Hoover's fear that government responsibility would discourage local initiative, the 1930s witnessed an upsurge in activism. New Deal programs, in fact, often encouraged or empowered groups to shape public policy. Moreover, because the administration worried about centralization, some federal agencies fostered what New Dealers called "grassroots democracy." The AAA set up committees that ultimately included more than 100,000 people to implement agricultural policy and held referendums on crop controls; local advisory committees guided the federal management of the West's public grasslands and mandated cooperation with associations of livestock raisers.

At times, local administration of national programs enabled groups to exploit federal policy for their own advantage. Wealthy planters shaped AAA practices at the expense of poor tenant farmers; local control of TVA projects excluded black people. But federal programs often allowed previously unrepresented groups to contest traditionally dominant interests. Often seeing greater opportunities for participation and influence in federal programs than in city and state governments, community groups campaigned to expand federal authority. In short, depression conditions and New Deal programs actually increased citizen involvement in public affairs.

# Ebbing of the New Deal

**25.5**    Why did the New Deal lose momentum after 1936?

After his victory in 1936, Roosevelt committed himself to further reforms. "I see one-third of a nation ill-housed, ill-clad, ill-nourished," he declared in his second inaugural address. "The test of our progress is not whether we add more to the abundance of those who have much; it is whether we provide enough for those who have too little." But determined opponents, continuing economic problems, and the president's own missteps blocked his reforms and deadlocked the New Deal.

## Challenging the Court

Roosevelt regarded the Supreme Court as his most dangerous opponent. During his first term, the Court had declared several important measures unconstitutional. Indeed, most of the justices were elderly conservatives, appointed by Republicans and unsympathetic to an activist federal government. It seemed that the Court would also strike down the Second New Deal.

Emboldened by the 1936 landslide, Roosevelt decided to restructure the federal judiciary. In early 1937, he proposed legislation authorizing the president to name a new justice for each one serving past the age of 70. Additional justices, he said, would increase judicial efficiency. But his real goal was to appoint new justices more sympathetic to the New Deal.

His Court plan led to a divisive struggle. The proposal was perfectly legal: Congress had the authority, which it had used repeatedly, to change the number of justices on the Court. But Republicans and conservative Democrats attacked the plan as a scheme to "pack" the Court and subvert the separation of powers among the three branches of government. Some conservatives called the president a dictator, but even many liberals expressed reservations about the plan or FDR's lack of candor in proposing it.

The Court itself undercut support for FDR's proposal by upholding the Social Security and Wagner acts and minimum-wage legislation. Moreover, the retirement of a conservative justice allowed Roosevelt to name a sympathetic successor. Congress rejected Roosevelt's plan.

Roosevelt's challenge to the Court hurt the New Deal. It worried the public, split the Democratic Party, and revived conservatives. Opponents promptly attacked other New Deal policies, from support for unions to progressive taxation. Henceforth, a conservative coalition of Republicans and southern Democrats in Congress blocked FDR's reforms.

## More Hard Times

A sharp recession, beginning in August 1937, added to Roosevelt's problems. The New Deal's deficit spending had reflected his desire to alleviate suffering, not a conviction that it would stimulate economic recovery. As the economy improved in 1936, Roosevelt decided to cut federal expenditures and balance the budget. But private investment and employment remained stagnant, and the economy plunged, producing what Republicans dubbed the "Roosevelt recession."

In 1938, Roosevelt reluctantly increased spending. New appropriations for the PWA and other government programs revived the faltering economy, but neither FDR

25.1

25.2

25.3

25.4

**25.5**

25.6

25.1

25.2

25.3

25.4

25.5

**25.6**

nor Congress would spend what was necessary to end the depression. Only the vast expenditures for World War II would bring full recovery.

## Political Stalemate

The recession interrupted the momentum of the New Deal and strengthened its opponents. In late 1937, their leaders in Congress issued a "conservative manifesto" decrying New Deal fiscal, labor, and regulatory policies. Holding seniority in a Congress malapportioned in their favor, they blocked most of Roosevelt's reforms. In 1938, Congress rejected tax reforms and reduced corporate taxes.

Congress also heavily amended the few measures that passed but those acts were not insignificant. The National Housing Act of 1937 created the United States Housing Authority, made public housing a permanent federal program, provided rent subsidies to low-income families, and financed slum clearance. The Fair Labor Standards Act of 1938 established the first national minimum wage and a 40-hour workweek for all workers engaged in interstate commerce, and it set strict limitations on child labor.

To protect the New Deal, Roosevelt turned again to the public, with whom he remained immensely popular. In the 1938 Democratic primaries, he campaigned against the New Deal's conservative opponents. But FDR could not transfer his personal popularity to the political newcomers he supported. What his foes attacked as a purge failed. Roosevelt lost further political leverage when the Republicans gained seventy-five seats in the House and seven in the Senate and thirteen governorships.

The 1938 elections did not repudiate the New Deal, for the Democrats retained majorities in both houses of Congress. But the Republican revival and the survival of the conservative southern Democrats guaranteed that the New Deal had gone as far as it ever would. With Roosevelt in the White House and his opponents controlling Congress, the New Deal ended in political stalemate.

# Good Neighbors and Hostile Forces

**25.6** How did Roosevelt respond to the rise of fascism in Europe?

Even before FDR's conservative opponents derailed the New Deal, the president felt their impact in the area of foreign policy. Isolationists in Congress counseled against any U.S. involvement in world affairs and appealed to the growing national disillusionment with America's participation in the Great War to support their position. Moreover, Roosevelt himself, although not an isolationist, believed that the gravity of the nation's economic depression warranted a primary focus on domestic recovery and, in the early years of his presidency, took few international initiatives.

The actions he did take related directly to salvaging America's desperate economy. As the depression worsened in 1933, American businesses searched for new markets throughout the world, and key business leaders informed FDR that they would welcome the opportunity to expand trade to the Soviet Union. Moscow was also eager to renew ties to the United States, and President Roosevelt extended formal recognition of the Soviet Union in November 1933.

Enhancing trade opportunities and rescuing the economy from the damage wrought by high tariffs figured prominently in Roosevelt's policies in the Western Hemisphere. In large measure, Roosevelt merely extended the Good Neighbor policy begun by his predecessor. But the Great Depression strained U.S. and Latin American relations, sending economic shock waves throughout Central and South America and, in several instances, helping propel to power ruthless dictators who ruled with iron fists and U.S. support.

## Neutrality and Fascism

Outside the hemisphere, during his first term as president, Roosevelt generally followed the policy of avoiding involvement in Europe's political, economic, and social problems. But the aggressive actions of Adolf Hitler in Germany ultimately led Roosevelt to a different position, and in the latter part of the decade, he faced the task of educating the American public, still resentful of U.S. participation in World War I, about the fascist danger that was spreading in Europe.

Hitler came to power in 1933, shortly before FDR entered the White House, and he pledged to restore German pride and nationalism in the aftermath of the Versailles Treaty. As the leader of the National Socialist Workers Party, or Nazis, Hitler established a **fascist government**—a one-party dictatorship closely aligned with corporate interests, committed to a "biological world evolution," and determined to establish a new empire, the Third Reich. He vowed to eliminate Bolshevik radicalism and purify the German "race" through the elimination of those he deemed undesirable, especially targeting Jews, the group Hitler blamed for most, if not all, of Germany's ills.

Others aided the spread of fascism. Italian leader Benito Mussolini, who had assumed power in 1922 and envisaged emulating the power and prestige of the Roman Empire, brutally attacked Ethiopia in 1935. The following year, a young fascist military officer, Francisco Franco, led an uprising in Spain and, with the assistance of Italy and Germany, successfully ousted the Spanish Republic and its loyalist supporters by 1939 to create an authoritarian government. Meanwhile, Hitler implemented

**fascist government** Subscribing to a philosophy of governmental dictatorship that merges the interests of the state, armed forces, and big business; associated with the dictatorship of Italian leader Benito Mussolini between 1922 and 1943 and also often applied to Nazi Germany.

25.1
25.2
25.3
25.4
25.5
**25.6**

On November 9, 1938, Nazi Germany launched an attack on Jews, destroying their businesses and burning their synagogues. This street scene in Berlin shows the shattered windows of Jewish businesses. Nazi leader Joseph Goebbels recorded the event, known as *Kristallnacht*, in his diary: "Yesterday: Berlin. There, all proceeded fantastically. One fire after another. It is good that way.... 100 dead. But no German property damaged."

25.1

25.2

25.3

25.4

25.5

25.6

his plan of conquest: He remilitarized the Rhineland in 1936, and in 1938 he annexed Austria.

The aggressive actions of Germany and Italy failed to eclipse U.S. fears of becoming involved in another European war. Congress passed Neutrality Acts designed to continue America's trade with its world partners but prohibit the president from taking sides in the mounting European crisis.

**Appeasement and More Neutrality.** After annexing Austria, Hitler pushed again in 1938 when he demanded the Sudetenland from Czechoslovakia. The French and the British refused to stand up to Hitler, following instead a policy of appeasement. Meeting in Munich in September 1938, the leaders of England and France abandoned their security obligations to the Czechs, yielding the Sudetenland to Hitler in exchange for a weak promise of no more annexations.

In America, too, the sentiment was for peace at all costs. Isolationism compounded by anti-Semitism and by the divisions between the leaders of the American Jewish community combined to ensure that the United States would not become a haven for Jews suffering under Nazi brutality. News of Nazi atrocities against Austrian Jews in 1938 shocked the American press, and Hitler's violent pogrom, known as *Kristallnacht* ("Night of the Broken Glass"), conducted against Jews throughout Germany in November 1938, added fresh proof of Nazi cruelty. Although the United States recalled its ambassador from Berlin to protest the pogrom (in response, Germany recalled its ambassador from Washington), it did not alter its restrictive immigration-quota system to provide refuge for German Jews.

As Europe edged closer to war, the relationship between the United States and Japan became more strained. Japan resented U.S. economic interests in East Asia and was offended by the policy of excluding Japanese immigrants. The United States regarded Japan's desires for empire as threatening but also needed Japan as a trading partner, especially in the economically depressed 1930s. Consequently, in September 1931, when Japan seized Manchuria, the United States did little more than denounce the action. Again in 1937, after Japanese troops attacked Chinese forces north of Beijing and outright war began between Japan and China, the United States merely condemned the action. That same year, President Roosevelt denounced "the epidemic of world lawlessness," indicting the aggressiveness of Italy, Germany, and Japan and calling for a "quarantine" of aggressors, but he continued his policy of refusing to risk war with Japan.

## Edging toward Involvement

After the Munich agreement, President Roosevelt moved away from domestic reform toward preparedness for war, fearful that conflict in Europe was unavoidable and determined to revise the neutrality laws. In his State of the Union address in January 1939, FDR explained that America's neutrality laws might "actually give aid to an aggressor and deny it to the victim." By the fall of that year, he had won support for eliminating the prohibition on arms sales and adding armaments to the list of cash-and-carry items—a revision that would enable the United States to provide important assistance to Britain and France in the winter of 1939–1940. Hitler's defiance of the Munich agreement in Czechoslovakia, overrunning Prague by March 1939, merely anticipated his next move toward Poland and also convinced the British and the French that war was imminent.

# Conclusion

The Great Depression and the New Deal mark a major divide in American history. The depression cast doubt on the traditional practices, policies, and attitudes that underlay not only the nation's economy but also its social and political institutions and relationships. The New Deal brought only partial economic recovery. However, its economic policies, from banking and securities regulation to unemployment compensation, farm price supports, and minimum wages, created barriers against another depression. The gradual adoption of compensatory spending policies expanded the government's role in the economy. Responding to the failures of private organizations and state and local governments, the federal government assumed the obligation to provide social welfare.

Roosevelt also expanded the role of the presidency. As his White House took the initiative for defining public policy, drafting legislation, lobbying Congress, and communicating with the nation, it became the model for all subsequent presidents. Not only was the president's power increased, but Roosevelt made the federal government, rather than state or local governments, the focus of public interest and expectations.

Roosevelt and the New Deal also revitalized the Democratic Party, drawing minorities, industrial workers, and previously uninvolved citizens into a coalition with white southerners. The tensions in so broad-based a coalition sometimes prevented effective public policies, but the coalition made the Democrats the dominant national party.

By the end of the 1930s, as international relations deteriorated, FDR was already considering a shift, as he later said, from Dr. New Deal to Dr. Win-the-War. Reluctant to move beyond public opinion that did not want war and limited by neutrality legislation, FDR cautiously led the nation toward war—this time against an enemy far more threatening than the Great Depression. Ironically, only then would President Roosevelt end the depression that had ravaged the nation for nearly a decade.

**For Suggested Readings go to MyHistoryLab.**

25.1

25.2

25.3

25.4

25.5

25.6

# Chapter Review

## Hard Times in Hooverville

 **25.1** What triggered the Great Depression? p. 715

Systemic weaknesses in the economy produced a devastating collapse that challenged the very fabric of America and made the depression global. Risky speculation on Wall Street and among bankers, weaknesses in agriculture, coal, and textiles, along with a staggering disparity in wealth and faulty fiscal policies, fueled the decline.

## Herbert Hoover and the Depression

**25.2** How did Herbert Hoover respond to the depression; why did his policies fail? p. 722

A champion of private initiative, President Hoover refused to yield from his belief that voluntary efforts could and should relieve the misery of mass unemployment. The scope of the depression, however, exhausted the resources of private charities and local governments.

## Launching the New Deal

**25.3** What were the goals of the early New Deal? p. 725

When FDR took office, he promised action and his first 100 days illustrated his determination to "try something." He tackled the banking crisis, reviving banks and restoring confidence; he provided relief to the unemployed; he addressed the agricultural crisis; and he attempted to revive industry by regulating prices and wages along with allowing workers the right to organize.

## Consolidating the New Deal

**25.4** How did the major accomplishments of the Second New Deal affect America's social and economic life? p. 730

By reaching out to new constituencies, the Second New Deal brought greater economic security to many Americans. The Social Security Act, despite its limitations, helped the elderly and the jobless. Labor won the right to unionize and the jobless found work with the WPA. Americans responded by voting for FDR in 1936.

## Ebbing of the New Deal

**25.5** Why did the New Deal lose momentum after 1936? p. 741

After his 1936 victory, FDR attempted to expand both the New Deal and the Supreme Court—the latter move alienated friends and foes alike. His decision to reduce spending in 1937 contributed to a downturn his critics called the "Roosevelt recession." Capitalizing on FDR's mistakes, congressional conservatives stalled new legislation, effectively ending the New Deal by 1938.

## Good Neighbors and Hostile Forces

**25.6** How did Roosevelt respond to the rise of fascism in Europe? p. 742

Although FDR worried about Hitler and the rise of Nazism, he reluctantly challenged the isolationist sentiments of many Americans. He denounced the aggressor nations in 1937 and moved toward military preparedness in the United States. To aid the British and French, he won revisions in the neutrality legislation and continued to educate the American public about the fascist menace.

# Timeline

**1929**
Hoover—Stock market crashes

**1932**
Hoover—Bonus Army routed in Washington, DC

New Deal—Franklin D. Roosevelt elected president

**1933**
Hostile Forces—Adolf Hitler comes to power in Germany

New Deal—Many New Deal laws passed during FDR's first 100 days

**1934**
New Deal—Securities and Exchange Commission (SEC) established

**1935**
New Deal—Social Security Act establishes a federal social insurance system

**1935**
New Deal—Works Progress Administration (WPA) created

**1936**
New Deal—Roosevelt reelected president

American Life—Sit-down strike begins

**1937**
New Deal—"Roosevelt recession" begins

**1938**
American Life—Congress of Industrial Organizations (CIO) founded

**1938**
Hostile Forces—Kristallnacht, violent pogrom against Jews, occurs in Germany

# 26 World War II
## 1939–1945

## One American Journey

Eyewitness Account by Atomic Scientist Enrico Fermi

*December, 1942*

**T**he scene [under the stadium] at The University of Chicago would have been confusing to an outsider, if he could have eluded the security guards and gained admittance. He would have seen only what appeared to be a crude pile of black bricks and wooden timbers. . . .

We gathered on a balcony about 10 feet above the floor of the large room in which the structure had been erected. Beneath us was a young scientist, George Weil, whose duty it was to handle the last control rod that was holding the reaction in check. . . .

Finally, it was time . . . . Slowly, Weil started to withdraw the main control rod. On the balcony, we watched the indicators which measured the neutron count and told us how rapidly the disintegration of the uranium atoms under their neutron bombardment was proceeding.

At 11:35 A.M., the counters were clicking rapidly. Then, with a loud clap, the automatic control rods slammed home. The safety point had been set too low.

At 2:30, Weil pulled out the control rod in a series of measured adjustments. Shortly after, the intensity shown by the indicators began to rise at a slow but ever-increasing rate. At this moment we knew that the self-sustaining [nuclear] reaction was under way.

The event was not spectacular, no fuses burned, no lights flashed.

## LEARNING OBJECTIVES

| 26.1 (( | 26.2 (( | 26.3 (( | 26.4 (( | 26.5 (( |
|---|---|---|---|---|
| Why were most Americans reluctant to get involved in World War II? p. 749 | How did the Allies fare in 1941 and 1942? p. 755 | What steps did the U.S. government take to organize the economy for war? p. 759 | How did the war affect the everyday lives of Americans? p. 765 | How did the Allies win the war? p. 770 |

The United States fought Germany and Japan as part of an alliance known as the United Nations. This government poster shows the flags of the many nations advancing together, the Stars and Stripes, the Union Jack of Great Britain, and the hammer and sickle of the Soviet Union in the most prominent positions.

From *The American Journey*, Seventh Edition. Goldfield, Abbott, Anderson, Argersinger, Argersinger and Barney Copyright © 2014 by Pearson Education, Inc. All rights reserved.

# 👁 Watch the Video Series on MyHistoryLab

Learn about some key topics related to this chapter with the *MyHistoryLab Video Series: Key Topics in U.S. History.*

**1** **World War II: 1939–1945** This introductory video examines why the United States, as well as its enemies and allies, fought another world war. During World War II, and under the leadership of Franklin Delano Roosevelt, the United States became a true superpower and helped to establish the United Nations to secure the peace rather than retreat once more into isolationism.

👁 Watch on MyHistoryLab

**Origins of World War II** This video looks at the causes of World War II, especially its roots in the previous world war and the Great Depression. Although technically neutral after the conflict broke out in 1939, the United States once more favored Great Britain. Its opposition to the expansion of the empire of Japan led to war with Japan and its Axis partners Germany and Italy following the Japanese attack on Pearl Harbor in December 1941.

Watch on MyHistoryLab 👁 **2**

**3** **Japanese American Internment** The attack on Pearl Harbor and the declaration of war led political and military leaders on the West Coast to call for internment of all persons of Japanese ancestry and Japanese American citizens (*Nisei*) because they were seen as potential traitors as well as a fifth column for carrying out acts of espionage. This video discusses how the federal government rounded up more than 100,000 individuals and placed them in internment camps for the duration of the war.

👁 Watch on MyHistoryLab

**The End of the War** This video describes the last phase of World War II, which saw the United States, the Soviet Union, and Britain overcome the last-ditch resistance of Germany, the liberation of the Nazi concentration camps, and the first use of atomic weapons at Hiroshima and Nagasaki that forced the end of the war. The background to the postwar peace is also examined, for the ideological differences of the United States and its ally the Soviet Union resulted in the Cold War that followed the Allied victory.

Watch on MyHistoryLab 👁 **4**

But to us it meant that release of atomic energy on a large scale would be only a matter of time.

U.S. Department of Energy

## Personal Journeys Online

- Patricia Cain Koehler, *Oregon Historical Quarterly* (Fall 1990). Helping to build aircraft carriers during World War II.
- Leon Overstreet in S. L. Sanger, *Working on the Bomb: An Oral History of World War II Hanford* (1995). A construction worker remembers the Manhattan Project.
- Bill Mauldin, in Studs Terkel, *The Good War* (1985). The famous cartoonist explains the origins of his characters Willie and Joe, the typical World War II GIs.

**E**nrico Fermi was describing the first controlled nuclear chain reaction—the critical experiment from which atomic weapons and atomic power would soon develop. Fermi had emigrated to escape the growing political repression of Fascist Italy. In 1942, after the United States joined the ongoing global conflict of World War II,

Fermi was put in charge of nuclear fission research at the University of Chicago and played a leading role in efforts to develop an atomic bomb. The following year found Fermi, other atomic scientists, and their families at Los Alamos, a science city that the government built hurriedly on a high plateau in northern New Mexico, where isolation was supposed to ensure secrecy and help the United States win the race with Nazi Germany to develop atomic weapons.

The Fermis were not the only family to give Los Alamos a multinational flavor. Enrico's wife, Laura Fermi, remembered that it was "all one big family and all one big accent. . . . Everybody in science was there, both from the United States and from almost all European countries." Absent were scientists from the Soviet Union, which was bearing the worst of the fighting against Germany but was carefully excluded from the secret of the atomic bomb.

The internationalism of Los Alamos mirrored the larger war effort. Japan's attack on Pearl Harbor in December 1941 thrust the United States into a war that spanned the globe. America's allies against Japan in the Pacific and East Asia included Great Britain, Australia, and China. In Europe, its allies against Nazi Germany and Fascist Italy included Great Britain, the Soviet Union, and more than twenty other nations. The scientists racing to perfect the atomic bomb knew that victory was far from certain. Germany and Japan had piled one conquest on another since the late 1930s, and they continued to seize new territories in 1942. Allied defeat in a few key battles could have resulted in a standoff or an Axis victory. A new weapon might end the war more quickly or make the difference between victory and defeat.

The war's domestic impacts were as profound as its international consequences. The race to build an atomic bomb was only one part of a vast effort to harness the resources of the United States to the war effort. The war highlighted racial inequalities, gave women new opportunities, and fostered growth in the South and West. By devastating the nation's commercial rivals, compelling workers to retrain and factories to modernize, World War II left the United States dominant in the world economy. It also increased the size and scope of the federal government and built an alliance among the armed forces, big business, and science that helped shape postwar America.

# The Dilemmas of Neutrality

**26.1** Why were most Americans reluctant to get involved in World War II?

Americans in the 1930s wanted no part of another overseas war by a wide margin. Despite two years of German victories and a decade of Japanese aggression against China, opinion polls in the fall of 1941 showed that a majority of voters still hoped to avoid war. President Roosevelt's challenge was to lead the United States toward rearmament and support for Great Britain and China without alarming a reluctant public.

## The Roots of War

The roots of World War II can be found in the aftereffects of World War I. The peace settlement created a set of small new nations in eastern Europe that were vulnerable to aggression by their much larger neighbors, Germany and the Soviet Union (more formally, the Union of Soviet Socialist Republics, or USSR). Italy and Japan thought that the Treaty of Versailles had not recognized their stature as world powers. Many Germans were convinced that Germany had been betrayed rather than defeated in 1918. In the 1930s, economic crisis undermined an already shaky political order. Economic hardship and political instability fueled the rise of right-wing dictatorships that offered

👁 **Watch the Video**  Hitler and Roosevelt

The raspy-voiced Adolf Hitler had a remarkable ability to stir the German people. He and his inner circle made skillful use of propaganda, exploiting German resentment over the country's defeat in World War I with carefully staged mass rallies.

**Greater East Asia Co-Prosperity Sphere** Japanese goal of an East Asian economy controlled by Japan and serving the needs of Japanese industry.

territorial expansion by military conquest as the way to redress old rivalries, dominate trade, and gain access to raw materials.

Japanese internal propaganda in the 1930s stressed the need to rebuild Japan's greatness. Japanese nationalists believed that the United States, Britain, and France had treated Japan unfairly after World War I, despite its participation against Germany. They believed that Japan should expel the French, British, Dutch, and Americans from Asia and create a **Greater East Asia Co-Prosperity Sphere**, in which Japan gave the orders and other Asian peoples complied. Seizing the Chinese province of Manchuria to expand an East Asian empire that already included Korea and Taiwan emboldened Japan's military in 1931. A full-scale invasion of China followed in 1937. Japan took many of the key cities and killed tens of thousands of civilians in the "rape of Nanking," but failed to dislodge the government of Jiang Jieshi (Chiang Kai-shek) and settled into a war of attrition.

Italian aggression embroiled Africa and the Mediterranean. The Fascist dictator Benito Mussolini had sent arms and troops to aid General Francisco Franco's right-wing rebels in Spain. The three-year civil war, which ended with Franco's victory in 1939, became a bloody testing ground for new German military tactics and German and Italian ambitions against democratic Europe.

In Germany, Adolf Hitler mixed the desire to reassert national pride and power after the defeat of World War I with an ideology of racial hatred. Coming to power by constitutional means in 1933, Hitler quickly consolidated his grip by destroying opposition parties, and made himself the German Führer, or absolute leader. Proclaiming the start of a 1000-year Reich ("empire"), he combined the historic German interest in eastward expansion with a long tradition of racialist thought about German superiority.

Special targets of Nazi hatred were the Jews, who were prominent in German business and professional life but soon faced persecution aimed at driving them from the country. In 1935, the Nuremberg Laws denied civil rights to Jews and the campaign against them intensified. On November 9, 1938, in vicious attacks across Germany that became known as *Kristallnacht* ("Night of the Broken Glass"), Nazi thugs rounded up, beat, and murdered Jews; smashed property; and burned synagogues. The Nazi government began expropriating Jewish property and excluded Jews from most employment.

Germany and Italy formed the Rome-Berlin Axis in October 1936 and the Tripartite Pact with Japan in 1940, leading to the term **Axis Powers** to describe the aggressor nations. Political dissidents in all three nations had already been suppressed. Hitler's Germany was the most repressive. The Nazi concentration camp began as a device for political terrorism, where socialists and other dissidents and "antisocials"—homosexuals and beggars—could be separated from "pure" Germans and made to disappear into "night and fog." Soon the systematic discrimination and concentration camps would evolve into massive forced-labor camps and then into hellish extermination camps.

**Axis Powers** The opponents of the United States and its allies in World War II. The Rome-Berlin Axis was formed between Germany and Italy in 1936 and included Japan after 1940.

## Hitler's War in Europe

After annexing Austria through a coup and seizing and slicing up Czechoslovakia, Germany demonstrated the worthlessness of the Munich agreement by invading Poland on September 1, 1939. Britain and France, Poland's allies, declared war on Germany but could not stop the German war machine. Western journalists covering the three-week conquest of Poland coined the term *blitzkrieg*, or "lightning war," to describe the German tactics. Armored divisions with tanks and motorized infantry punched holes in defensive positions and raced forward 30 or 40 miles per day.

Hitler's greatest advantage was the ability to attack when and where he chose. From September 1939 to October 1941, Germany marched from victory to victory (see Map 26.1). Striking from a central position against scattered enemies, Hitler chose the targets and timing of each new front: eastward to smash Poland in September 1939; northward to conquer Denmark and Norway in April and May 1940; westward to defeat the Netherlands, Belgium, and France in May and June 1940, an attack that Italy also joined; southward into the Balkans, enlisting Hungary, Romania, and Bulgaria as allies and conquering Yugoslavia and Greece in April and May 1941. Hitler also launched the Battle of Britain in the second half of 1940. German planes bombarded Britain mercilessly, in an unsuccessful effort to pound the British into submission.

Hitler gambled once too often in June 1941. Having failed to knock Britain out of the war, he invaded the Soviet Union. The attack caught the Red Army off guard. Germany and the Soviet Union had signed a nonaggression pact in 1939, and the Soviets had helped to dismember Poland. Hitler hoped that smashing the Soviet Union and seizing its vast resources would make Germany invincible. From June until December 1941, more than 4 million Germans with Italian, Hungarian, and Romanian allies pushed through Belarus, Ukraine, and western Russia. Before desperate Soviet counterattacks and a bitter winter stopped the German columns, they had reached the outskirts of Moscow and expected to finish the job in the spring.

*blitzkrieg* German war tactic in World War II ("lightning war") involving the concentration of air and armored firepower to punch and exploit holes in opposing defensive lines.

## Trying to Keep Out

Americans who opposed intervention in the European conflict were sometimes called isolationists, but they considered themselves realists who remembered the lessons of World War I. Strong sentiment against intervention shaped public debate and limited President Roosevelt's ability to help Britain and its allies.

Much of the emotional appeal of neutrality came from disillusionment with the American crusade in World War I, which had failed to make the world safe for democracy. Many opponents of intervention wanted the United States to protect its traditional spheres of interest in Latin America and the Pacific.

**MAP 26.1  AXIS EUROPE, 1941, ON THE EVE OF HITLER'S INVASION OF THE SOVIET UNION**
After almost two years of war, the Axis Powers controlled most of Europe, from the Atlantic Ocean to the Soviet border, through annexation, military conquest, and alliances. Failure to force Britain to make peace caused Hitler to look eastward in 1941 to attempt the conquest of the Soviet Union.

Noninterventionists spanned the political spectrum from left-leaning labor unions to conservative business tycoons like Henry Ford. The country's ethnic variety also complicated U.S. responses. Nazi aggression ravaged the homelands of Americans of Polish, Czech, Greek, and Norwegian ancestry. More than 5 million German Americans remembered the anti-German sentiment of World War I, while many of the 4.6 million Italian Americans admired Mussolini. Any move to intervene in Europe had to take these different views into account, meaning that Roosevelt had to move slowly and carefully in his effort to align the United States on the side of Britain.

## Edging toward Intervention

Still, Roosevelt's appeals to democratic values gained support in 1939 and 1940. Radio broadcasts from England describing London under German bombing heightened the sense of imperiled freedom. The importance of open markets also bolstered interventionism. United States business leaders had little doubt that Axis victories would bring economic instability and require crushing defense budgets to protect Fortress America.

Because 85 percent of the American people agreed that the nation should fight only if it was directly attacked, Roosevelt had to chip away at neutrality, educating, arguing, and taking one step at a time. The first step came in October 1939, when Congress reluctantly allowed arms sales to belligerent nations on a "cash-and-carry" basis. In control of the Atlantic, France and Britain were the only expected customers.

Isolationism and anti-Semitism help to explain why the United States accepted only a few thousand Jewish refugees. American law strictly limited the numbers of Europeans who could enter the United States, and Congress in 1939 declined to authorize the entry outside the quotas of 20,000 Jewish children. Bureaucrats at the State Department blocked entry to "undesirables," such as left-wing opponents of Hitler, and were unsympathetic to Jewish refugees. The consequences of these restrictions would prove tragic later in the war, as the Nazis began systematic genocide of European Jews.

**The Collapse of France and U.S. Rearmament.**   Despite the efforts of noninterventionists, in 1940 the United States edged closer to involvement in the war. In May, the Roosevelt administration established the National Defense Advisory Commission and the Council of National Defense. The sudden defeat of France, which had survived four years of German attacks in World War I, made the new war seem far more serious. The United States no longer had the option of standing on the sidelines while European nations fought to a standstill. In the summer of 1940, Congress voted to expand the army to 2 million men, build 19,000 new warplanes, and add 150 ships to the navy. Lawmakers approved the nation's first peacetime draft in September, requiring 16.5 million men between the ages of 21 and 35 to register for military service.

In the same month, the United States concluded a destroyer deal with Britain. The British were desperate for small, maneuverable warships to guard imports of food and war materials against German submarines. The Americans had long wanted additional air and naval bases to guard the approaches to North America. Roosevelt met both needs by trading fifty old destroyers for the use of bases on British territories in the Caribbean, Bermuda, and Newfoundland.

**The Election of 1940.**   In the presidential election of 1940, foreign policy was secondary. Wendell Willkie, the Republican nominee, unlike many in his party, shared Roosevelt's belief in the importance of aid to Britain. The big campaign issue was therefore whether FDR's unprecedented try for a third term represented arrogance or a legitimate concern for continuity in a time of peril. The election was tighter than in 1932 or 1936, but Roosevelt received 55 percent of the vote. The president pledged that no Americans would fight in a foreign war. But if the United States were attacked, he said privately, the war would no longer be "foreign."

## The Brink of War

After the election, FDR and his advisers edged the United States toward stronger support of Britain and put pressure on Japan. In January 1941, Roosevelt proposed the lend-lease program, which allowed Britain to "borrow" military equipment for the duration of the war. Behind the scheme was Britain's inability to pay for American goods. "Well, boys," their ambassador explained to a group of reporters, "Britain's broke."

The **Lend-Lease Act** triggered intense political debate. The Committee to Defend America by Aiding the Allies argued the administration's position. In opposition, the strongly isolationist America First Committee claimed that lend-lease would allow the president to declare anything a "defense article." Their spokesperson, Charles Lindbergh, protested that the United States should not surrender weapons that it might need to defend itself. Congress finally passed the measure in March 1941, authorizing the president to lease, lend, or otherwise dispose of arms and other equipment to any country whose defense was considered vital to the security of the United States. The program proved invaluable in aiding Great Britain.

**Lend-Lease Act** Program begun in 1941 through which the United States transferred military equipment to Britain and other World War II allies.

**Atlantic Charter** Statement of common principles and war aims developed by President Franklin Roosevelt and British Prime Minister Winston Churchill at a meeting in August 1941.

Roosevelt soon began an undeclared war in the North Atlantic, instructing the navy to report sightings of German submarines to the British. In September, the U.S. destroyer *Greer* clashed with a German submarine. Portraying the incident as German aggression, Roosevelt proclaimed a "shoot on sight" policy for German subs and ordered American ships to escort British convoys to within 400 miles of Britain. In reply, German submarines torpedoed the destroyer *Kearny* on October 17 and sank the destroyer *Reuben James,* with the loss of more than 100 lives, on October 30. The United States was now approaching outright naval war with Germany.

**The Atlantic Charter.** With U.S. ships on a war footing in the North Atlantic, Roosevelt and the British prime minister, Winston Churchill, met secretly off Newfoundland in August 1941, to map out military strategy and postwar goals. They agreed that the defeat of Germany was their first priority, and Japan was secondary. Their joint proclamation, known as the **Atlantic Charter**, provided both a political umbrella and moral justification for American involvement in the war. Echoing Woodrow Wilson, Roosevelt insisted on a commitment to oppose territorial conquest, support self-government, promote freedom of the seas, and create a system of economic collaboration. Churchill signed to keep Roosevelt happy, but the document papered over differences between U.S. and British expectations about the future of world trade and European colonial possessions.

Some historians think that Roosevelt hoped the United States could support Britain short of war. Others believe that he accepted the inevitability of war but hesitated to outpace public opinion. In this second interpretation, FDR wanted to eliminate Hitler without going to war if possible, with war if necessary. "I am waiting to be pushed into the situation," he told his secretary of the treasury.

**Events in the Pacific.** The final shove came not in the Atlantic but in the Pacific, where Japan and the United States had sharply differing worldviews. The United States favored open international trade that benefited its economy and fit with policies going back to Theodore Roosevelt and Woodrow Wilson. Japanese leaders saw a future in which their nation was destined to lead East Asia. In 1940, as part of its rearmament program, the United States decided to build a "two-ocean navy." This decision antagonized Japan, prodding it toward a war that most U.S. leaders hoped to postpone or avoid. Through massive investment and national sacrifice, Japan had achieved roughly 70 percent of U.S. naval strength by late 1941. However, America's buildup promised to reduce the ratio to only 30 percent by 1944. Furthermore, the United States was restricting Japan's vital imports of steel, iron ore, and aluminum in an effort to curb its military aggression. In July 1941, after Japan occupied French Indochina, Roosevelt froze Japanese assets in the United States, blocked shipments of petroleum products, and began to build up U.S. forces in the Philippines. These actions caused Japan's rulers to consider war against the United States while Japan still had a petroleum reserve. Both militarily and economically, it looked in Tokyo as if 1942 was Japan's last chance to achieve permanent dominance in East Asia.

Japanese war planners never seriously considered a full-scale invasion of the United States or expected a decisive victory. They hoped that attacks on American Pacific bases would shock the United States into letting Japan have its way in Asia or at least win time to create impenetrable defenses in the central Pacific.

## December 7, 1941

On December 7, 1941, the Japanese navy launched a surprise attack on American bases in Hawaii. The Japanese fleet sailed a 4,000-mile loop through the empty North Pacific, avoiding merchant shipping and American patrols. Before dawn on December 7, 1941, six Japanese aircraft carriers launched 351 planes in two bombing strikes against Pearl Harbor. Because the United States had cracked the Japanese codes, it knew by November that Japanese military action was imminent but expected the blow to come in Southeast Asia, not Hawaii.

When the smoke cleared, Americans counted their losses: eight battleships, eleven other warships, and nearly all military aircraft damaged or destroyed, and 2,403 people killed. They could also count their good fortune. Dockyards, drydocks, and oil storage tanks remained intact because the Japanese admiral had refused to order a third attack. And the American aircraft carriers, at sea on patrol, were unharmed. They proved far more important than battleships as the war developed. Within hours, the Japanese attacked U.S. bases at Guam, Wake Island, and in the Philippines.

Speaking to Congress the following day, Roosevelt proclaimed December 7, 1941, "a date which will live in infamy." He asked for and got a declaration of war against Japan. Hitler and Mussolini declared war on the United States on December 11, supporting their Tripartite Pact ally.

On January 1, 1942, the United States, Britain, the Soviet Union, and twenty-three other nations subscribed to the principles of the Atlantic Charter and pledged not to negotiate a separate peace.

# Holding the Line

**26.2** How did the Allies fare in 1941 and 1942?

Japan's armies quickly conquered most of Southeast Asia; its navy forced the United States onto the defensive in the central Pacific. As it turned out, Japan's conquests reached their limit after six months, but in early 1942, this was far from clear. At the same time, in Europe, Allied fortunes went from bad to worse. Again, no one knew that German and Italian gains would peak at midyear. Decisive turning points did not come until November 1942, a year after the United States entered the war, and not until the middle of 1943 could the **Allies**—the United States, Britain, the Soviet Union, China, and other nations at war with Germany, Japan, and Italy—begin with confidence to plan for victory.

## Stopping Germany

In December 1941, the United States plunged into a truly global war that was being fought on six distinct fronts (see Map 26.2). In North Africa, the British were battling Italian and German armies that were trying to seize the Suez Canal, a critical transportation link to Asia. Along the 1,000-mile **Eastern Front**, Soviet armies held defensive positions as German forces, pushing deeply into Soviet territory, reached the outskirts of Moscow and Leningrad (now St. Petersburg). In the North Atlantic, German submarines stalked merchant ships carrying supplies to Britain. In China, Japan controlled the most productive provinces but could not crush Chinese resistance. In Southeast Asia, Japanese troops attacked the Philippines, the Dutch East Indies (now Indonesia), New Guinea, Malaya, and Burma. In the central Pacific, the Japanese fleet confronted the U.S. Navy. With the nation facing danger across both the Atlantic and Pacific oceans, Roosevelt helped Americans understand the global nature of the conflict by calling it the "second world war."

Despite the popular desire for revenge against Japan, the Allies had already decided to defeat Germany first. The reasoning was simple: Germany was far stronger than Japan. Defeat of Japan would not ensure the defeat of Germany, especially if it crushed the Soviet Union or starved Britain into submission. By contrast, a strategy that helped the Soviets and British survive and then destroyed German military power would doom Japan.

**The Eastern Front and the Battle of Stalingrad.** The Eastern Front held the key to Allied hopes. In 1941, Germany had seized control of 45 percent of the Soviet population, 47 percent of its grain production, and more than 60 percent of its coal,

**Allies** In World War I, Britain, France, Russia, and other belligerent nations fighting against the Central Powers but not including the United States, which insisted upon being merely an associated nation. In World War II, the Allies fighting the Axis Powers included the United States as well as the Soviet Union, Great Britain, France, China, and other nations.

**Eastern Front** The area of military operations in World War II located east of Germany in eastern Europe and the Soviet Union.

**MAP 26.2  A GLOBAL WAR** World War II was truly a global war. As this map indicates, fighting engulfed both sides of the Eurasian continent and spread into the Atlantic, Pacific, and Indian oceans. The United States was the only major belligerent nation that was insulated from the battle fronts by two oceans.

steel, and aluminum industries. Hitler next sought to destroy the Soviet capacity to wage war, targeting southern Russia, an area rich in grain and oil. The German thrust in 1942 was also designed to eliminate the British from the Middle East.

The turning point of the war in Europe came at Stalingrad (present-day Volgograd), an industrial center on the western bank of the Volga River. After initially aiming at the city, German armies turned south toward the Russian oil fields, leaving a dangerous strongpoint on their flank. In September and October 1942, German, Italian, and Romanian soldiers fought their way house by house into the city. At night, the Soviets ferried their wounded across the Volga and brought in ammunition. For both Hitler and Stalin, the city became a test of will that outweighed even its substantial military importance.

The Red Army delivered a counterstroke on November 18 that cut off 290,000 Axis soldiers. Airlifts kept the Germans fighting for more than two additional months, but they surrendered in February 1943. This was the first German mass capitulation, and it came at immense human cost to both sides. The Soviet army suffered more deaths in this battle than the United States did in the entire war.

Behind the victory was an extraordinary revival of the Soviet capacity to make war. In the desperate months of 1941, the Soviets dismantled nearly 3,000 factories and rebuilt them far to the east of the German advance in the midst of Siberian winter. As many as 25 million workers and their families followed the factories eastward. By the time the two armies clashed at Stalingrad, the Soviets were producing four times as many tanks and warplanes as the Germans, portending the outcome of the battles to come.

## The Survival of Britain

After the failure of German air attacks in 1940, the British struggled to save their empire and supply themselves with food and raw materials. In World War I, German submarines (known as U-boats, from *Unterseeboot*) had nearly isolated Great Britain. In 1940 and 1941, they tried again. Through the end of 1941, German "tonnage warfare" sank British, Allied, and neutral merchant vessels faster than they could be replaced.

**The Battle of the Atlantic.** The British fought back in what came to be known as the **Battle of the Atlantic**. Between 1939 and 1944, planning and rationing cut Britain's need for imports in half. At sea, the British organized protected convoys. Merchant ships sailing alone were defenseless against submarines. Grouping them with armed escorts "hardened" the targets and made them more difficult to find in the wide ocean.

**Battle of the Atlantic** The long struggle between German submarines and the British and U.S. navies in the North Atlantic from 1940 to 1943.

Nevertheless, German submarines dominated the Atlantic in 1942, sinking 144 ships in June alone. U-boats operated as far as the Caribbean and the Carolinas, where the dangers of Cape Hatteras forced coastal shipping out to sea. The balance shifted only when Allied aircraft began to track submarines with radar, spot them with searchlights as they maneuvered to the surface, and attack them with depth charges. New sonar systems allowed escort ships to measure submarines' direction, speed, and depth. By the spring of 1943, American shipyards were launching ships faster than the Germans could sink them. Within a few months, Germany was losing two U-boats for every cargo vessel it destroyed and the Allies had effectively won the Battle of the Atlantic.

**North Africa.** British ground fighting in 1942 centered in North Africa, where the British operated out of Egypt and the Italians and Germans from the Italian colony of Libya. By October 1942, Field Marshal Erwin Rommel's German and Italian forces were within striking distance of the Suez Canal. At El Alamein, however, General Bernard Montgomery forced the enemy to retreat in early November and lifted the danger to the Middle East.

## Retreat and Stabilization in the Pacific

Reports from eastern Asia after Pearl Harbor were appalling. The Japanese attack on the Philippines (see Map 26.3) had been another tactical surprise that destroyed most American air power on the ground and isolated U.S. forces. In February, a numerically inferior Japanese force seized British Singapore, until then considered an anchor of Allied strength. In a three-month siege, Japan overwhelmed Filipino and U.S. defensive positions on the Bataan Peninsula outside Manila; thousands of their captives died of maltreatment on their way to prisoner-of-war camps in what is remembered as the Bataan Death March. On May 6, the last American bastion, the island fortress of

**MAP 26.3 WORLD WAR II IN THE PACIFIC, FROM PEARL HARBOR TO MIDWAY** The first six months after the Japanese attack on Pearl Harbor brought a string of Japanese victories and conquests in the Pacific, the islands southeast of Asia, and the British colonies of Malaya and Burma. Japan's advance was halted by a standoff battle in the Coral Sea, a decisive U.S. naval victory at Midway, and the length and vulnerability of Japanese supply lines to the most distant conquests.

Corregidor in Manila Bay, surrendered. The Japanese fleet was virtually undamaged at the end of April, and the Japanese army was triumphant in conquest of European and American territories in Southeast Asia.

**The Battles of the Coral Sea and Midway.** The first check to Japanese expansion came on May 7–8, 1942, in the Battle of the Coral Sea, where U.S. aircraft carriers halted a Japanese thrust toward Australia and confirmed that the U.S. Navy could fight effectively. In June, the Japanese struck at the island of Midway, 1,500 miles northwest of Honolulu. Their goal was to destroy American carrier forces. Having cracked Japanese radio codes, U.S. forces were aware of the plan and refused the bait. On the morning of June 4, the Japanese and American carrier fleets faced off across 175 miles of ocean, each sending planes to search out the other. United States Navy dive bombers found the Japanese fleet and sank or crippled three aircraft carriers in five minutes; another damaged Japanese carrier sank later in the day. The Battle of Midway ended Japanese efforts to expand in the Pacific.

# Mobilizing for Victory

**26.3** What steps did the U.S. government take to organize the economy for war?

War changed the lives of most Americans. Millions of men and women served in the armed forces, and millions more worked in defense factories. In order to keep track of this staggering level of activity, the number of civilian employees of the federal government quadrupled to 3.8 million, a much greater increase than during the New Deal. The breadth of involvement in the war effort gave Americans a common purpose that softened the divisions of region, class, and national origin while calling attention to continuing inequalities of race.

## Organizing the Economy

The need to fight a global war brought a huge expansion of the federal government. Congress authorized the president to reorganize existing government departments and create new agencies. The War Manpower Commission allocated workers among vital industries and the military. The War Production Board invested $17 billion for new factories and managed $181 billion in war-supply contracts, favoring existing corporations because they had experience in large-scale production.

Children in the East Harlem neighborhood of New York clean and flatten tin cans as their contribution to the war effort early in 1942. Thousands of other children participated in similar scrap metal drives around the nation.

The Office of Price Administration (OPA) fought inflation with price controls and rationing that began with tires, sugar, and coffee and eventually included meat, butter, gasoline, and shoes. "Use it up, wear it out, make it do or do without" was the OPA's slogan. Consumers used ration cards and ration stamps to obtain scarce products. With gasoline scarce, horse-drawn delivery wagons made a comeback.

By slowing price increases, the OPA helped convince Americans to buy the war bonds that financed half the war spending. Americans also felt the bite of the first pay-roll deductions for income taxes as the government secured a steady flow of revenues and soaked up some of the high wages that would have pushed inflation. In total, the federal budget in 1945 was $98 billion, eleven times as large as in 1939, and the national debt had increased more than sixfold.

Industry had reluctantly begun to convert from consumer goods to defense production in 1940 and 1941. Existing factories retooled to make war equipment, and huge new facilities turned out thousands of planes and ships. Baltimore, Atlanta, Fort Worth, Los Angeles, and Seattle became centers for aircraft production. New Orleans, Portland, Oregon, and the San Francisco Bay area were shipbuilding centers.

The United States applied mass-production technology to aircraft production at a time when Japan was building warplanes one at a time and Germany in small batches. The most spectacular example was the new Ford plant at Willow Run, Michigan, designed to adapt assembly-line approaches to manufacturing B-24 bombers. Where the typical automobile had 15,000 parts, a B-24 had 1,550,000. The assembly line itself was more than a mile long, starting with four separate tracks that gradually merged into one. By 1943, the plant was delivering ten planes a day. American aircraft workers were twice as productive as their German counterparts and four times more productive than Japanese.

Most defense contracts went to such established industrial states as Michigan, New York, and Ohio, but the relative impact was greatest in the South and West, where the war marked the takeoff of what Americans would later call the Sunbelt. Millions of Americans moved back and forth across the country to war jobs. Washington, DC, teemed with staff officers, stenographers, and other office workers who helped to coordinate the war effort. Local leaders in cities from Charlotte to Fort Worth to Phoenix saw the war as an economic opportunity and campaigned for defense factories and military bases.

The output of America's war industries was staggering (see Figure 26.1). One historian estimates that 40 percent of the world's military production was coming from the United States by 1944. Surging farm income pulled agriculture out of its long slump. Organized labor offered a no-strike pledge for the duration, assuring that no one could accuse unions of undermining the war effort but limiting the economic gains of some workers and dampening the militancy of the CIO. Nevertheless, overall per capita income doubled, and the poorest quarter of Americans made up some of the ground lost during the Great Depression.

## The Enlistment of Science

The war reached into scientific laboratories as well as shops and factories. At the center of the scientific enterprise was Vannevar Bush, former dean at the Massachusetts Institute of Technology (MIT). As head of the newly established Office of Scientific Research and Development, Bush guided spending to develop new drugs such as antibiotics, blood-transfusion procedures, weapons systems, radar, sonar, and dozens of other military technologies. The scale of research and development dwarfed previous scientific work and set the pattern of massive postwar federal support for science.

The most costly scientific effort was the development of radar, or radio detection and ranging devices. Building on British research on microwaves, the United States put $3 billion into the Radiation Laboratory at MIT. Increasingly compact and sophisticated radar systems helped to defeat the German and Japanese navies and to give the Allies control of the air over Europe. Radar research and engineering laid the basis for microwave technology, transistors, and integrated circuits after the war.

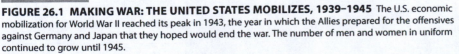

**FIGURE 26.1  MAKING WAR: THE UNITED STATES MOBILIZES, 1939–1945** The U.S. economic mobilization for World War II reached its peak in 1943, the year in which the Allies prepared for the offensives against Germany and Japan that they hoped would end the war. The number of men and women in uniform continued to grow until 1945.

SOURCE: United States Government, Military Records for World War II

In the summer of 1945, *Time* magazine planned a cover story on radar as the weapon that won the war. However, the *Time* story was upstaged by the atomic bomb, the product of the war's other great scientific effort. As early as 1939, Albert Einstein had written to FDR about the possibility of such a weapon and the danger of falling

**Manhattan Project** The effort, using the code name Manhattan Engineer District, to develop an atomic bomb under the management of the U.S. Army Corps of Engineers during World War II.

behind the Germans. In late 1941, Roosevelt established the **Manhattan Project**. By December 2, 1942, scientists proved that it was possible to create and control a sustained nuclear reaction.

The Manhattan Project moved from theory to practice in 1943. The physicist J. Robert Oppenheimer directed the young scientists at Los Alamos in designing a nuclear-fission bomb. The Manhattan Project ushered in the age of atomic energy. Plutonium from Hanford fueled the first bomb tested at the Trinity site in New Mexico on July 16, 1945. The explosion astonished even the physicists; Oppenheimer quoted from Hindu scriptures in trying to comprehend the results: "Now I am become Death, destroyer of worlds."

## Men and Women in the Military

World War II required a more than thirtyfold expansion of the U.S. armed forces from their 1939 level of 334,000 soldiers, sailors, and Marines. By 1945, 8.3 million men and women were on active duty in the army and army air forces and 3.4 million in the navy and Marine Corps, totals exceeded only by the Soviet Union. In total, some 350,000

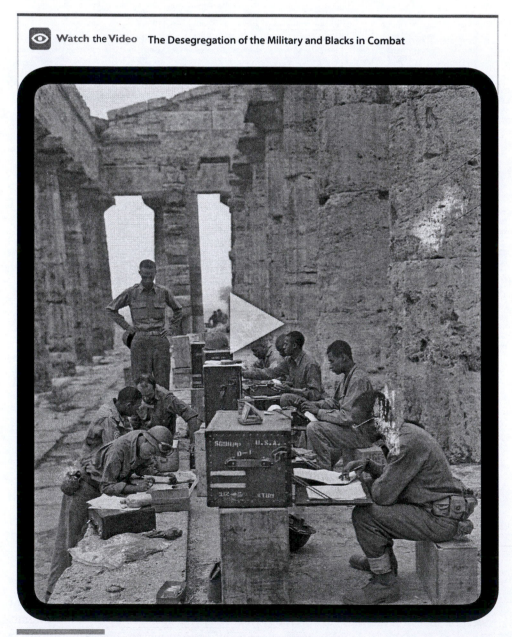

**Watch the Video   The Desegregation of the Military and Blacks in Combat**

African Americans served in the military in large numbers during World War II. Here a signals company has set up operations in the ruins of an ancient temple in southern Italy.

# From Then to Now
# Military Draft or Volunteer Military

A s war ravaged Europe and East Asia, the United States instituted the nation's first peacetime military draft in 1940. With a brief suspension in 1947–1948, the Selective Service System assumed an omnipresent role in the lives of young men for a third of a century.

This changed on July 1, 1973, when Congress allowed draft authority to expire, leaving the United States to depend on volunteers to staff its armed services. Under the political pressures of the Vietnam War and heeding arguments in favor of free choice, President Richard Nixon put his weight behind recommendations to end the draft, and members of both parties were happy to go along. Energetic military recruiters replaced local draft boards as the points of contact between young Americans and the military.

The result, at best, has been a highly trained, motivated, and professional military that has offered particular opportunities to women and African Americans. Members of the military are now older and more likely to be married than in the 1950s and 1960s. The contemporary armed forces have similarities to a mature industry in which investments in sophisticated equipment make it possible to function effectively with fewer workers—although the small size of the regular armed forces has meant greater use of the National Guard and Reserves and repeated deployments during the long wars in Afghanistan and Iraq. A volunteer military also means that a smaller proportion of the American population has direct experience of military life, either directly or through a family member. As World War II drew to a close in 1945, one out of every twelve Americans was on active duty. At the height of the Cold War in the mid-1950s, the figure was roughly one out of fifty. In recent years it has been one in two hundred.

**Question for Discussion**

- What difference does it make for national politics that active military personnel now make up a smaller share of the American population than at any time since the 1930s?

Blues singer Huddie Ledbetter, better known as Leadbelly, was one of tens of millions of American men who registered with draft boards during World War II.

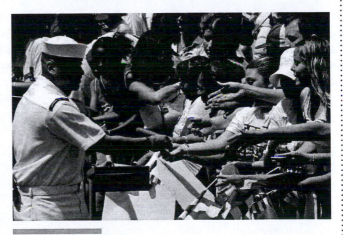

An all-volunteer armed forces requires constant public relations and recruiting efforts.

women and more than 16 million men served in the armed forces; 292,000 died in battle, 100,000 survived prisoner-of-war camps, and 671,000 returned wounded.

**Native Americans in the Military.** Twenty-five thousand American Indians served in the armed forces. Most were in racially integrated units, and Harvey Natcheez, of the Ute tribe, was the first American to reach the center of conquered Berlin. Because the Navajo were one of the few tribes that had not been studied by German anthropologists, the Army Signal Corps decided that their language would be unknown to the Axis armies. Roughly 400 members of the tribe were "code-talkers" who served in Marine radio combat-communication teams in the Pacific theater, transmitting vital information in Navajo.

**African Americans in the Military.** Approximately 1 million African Americans served in the armed forces during World War II. African American leaders had pressed for a provision in the Selective Service Act to bar discrimination "against any person on account of race or color." But as it had since the Civil War, the army organized black soldiers in segregated units and often assigned them to the menial jobs, such as construction work, and excluded them from combat until manpower shortages forced changes in policy.

The average black soldier encountered discrimination on and off the base. Towns adjacent to army posts were sometimes open to white soldiers but off limits to blacks. At some southern bases, German prisoners of war watched movies from the first rows along with white GIs while African American soldiers watched from the back. Military courts were quick to judge and harshly punish black GIs. It took racially based riots at army bases in North Carolina and Georgia to open up equal (although segregated) access to base recreation facilities.

Despite the obstacles, all-black units, such as the 761st Tank Battalion and the 99th Pursuit Squadron, earned distinguished records. Hundreds of African Americans trained as airmen at a segregated Tuskegee, Alabama, base. More broadly, the war experience helped to invigorate postwar efforts to achieve equal rights, as had also been true after World War I.

**Women in the Military.** The nation had a different—but also mixed—reaction to the women who joined the armed forces as army and navy nurses and as members of the WACS (Women's Army Corps), WAVES (Navy), SPARS (Coast Guard), and Marine Corps Women's Reserve. The armed services tried not to change established gender roles. Military officials told Congress that women in uniform could free men for combat. Many of the women hammered at typewriters, worked switchboards, inventoried supplies. Others, however, worked close to combat zones as photographers, code analysts, weather forecasters, radio operators, and nurses. WAC officers battled the tendency of the popular press to call females in the service "girls" rather than "women" or "soldiers" yet emphasized that military service promoted "poise and charm."

World War II opened new professional opportunities for women, as suggested in the 1943 recruiting poster for the Navy's WAVES (Women Accepted for Voluntary Emergency Service) showing an aviation control tower operator—a role that women quickly dominated at stateside naval air stations.

# The Home Front

**26.4** How did the war affect the everyday lives of Americans?

The war inexorably penetrated everyday life. Residents in war-production cities had to cope with throngs of new workers. Especially in 1941 and 1942, many were unattached males—young men waiting for their draft call and older men without their families. Military and defense officials worried about sexually transmitted diseases and pressured cities to shut down their vice districts. At the same time, college officials scrambled to fill their classrooms, especially after the draft age dropped to 18 in 1942. Many colleges and universities responded to federal requests with special training programs for future officers and engineering and technical training for military personnel.

## Families in Wartime

Many Americans put their lives on fast forward. Men and women often decided to beat the clock with instant matrimony. Couples who had postponed marriage because of the depression could afford to marry as the economy picked up. War intensified casual romances and heightened the appeal of marriage as an anchor in troubled times. Altogether, the war years brought 1.2 million "extra" marriages, compared to the rate for the period 1920–1939.

The war's impact on families was gradual. The draft started with single men, then called up married men without children, and finally tapped fathers in 1943. Left at home were millions of "service wives," whose compensation from the government was $50 per month.

The war had mixed effects on children. "Latchkey children" of working mothers often had to fend for themselves, but middle-class kids whose mothers stayed home could treat the war as an interminable scout project, with salvage drives and campaigns to sell war bonds. In the rural Midwest, children picked milkweed pods to stuff life jackets; in coastal communities, they participated in blackout drills. Seattle high schools set aside one class period a day for the High School Victory Corps, training boys as messengers for air-raid wardens, while girls knitted sweaters and learned first aid.

## Women in the Workforce

As draft calls took men off the assembly line, women changed the composition of the industrial workforce. The war gave them new job opportunities that were embodied in the image of Rosie the Riveter. Women made up one-quarter of West Coast shipyard workers and nearly half of Dallas and Seattle aircraft workers. Most women in the shipyards were clerks and general helpers. The acute shortage of welders and other skilled workers, however, opened thousands of lucrative journeyman positions to them. Aircraft companies, which compounded the labor shortage by stubborn "whites only" hiring, developed new power tools and production techniques to accommodate the smaller average size of women workers, increasing efficiency for everyone on the production line.

By July 1944, 19 million women held paid jobs, up 6 million in four years. Women typed and filed in offices, but they also wrote propaganda for the Office of War Information and analyzed intelligence data for the office of Strategic Service. Women's share of manufacturing jobs rose from 22 to 33 percent, many of them as W.O.W.s or Woman Ordnance Workers. Mirroring the sequence in which the military draft took men, employers recruited single women before turning to married women in 1943 and 1944. The federal government funded daycare programs that served 600,000 children. Some women worked out of patriotism. Many others, however, needed to support their families and already had years of experience in the workforce. As one of the workers

((• 📖 Read the Document   Virginia Snow Wilkinson, "From Housewife to Shipfitter," *Harper's* (1943)

As millions of men entered the armed forces, millions of women went to work. By 1943, federal agencies were actively recruiting women workers. Those who took production-line jobs received the greatest attention, like this worker at the Lockheed Aircraft Corporation plant in Burbank, California, which produced thousands of P-38 "Lightning" fighter planes.

recalled of herself and a friend, "We both had to work, we both had children, so we became welders, and if I might say so, damn good ones."

Americans did not know how to respond to the growing numbers of working women. The country needed their labor, but many worried that their employment would undermine families. Employment recruitment posters showed strong, handsome women with rolled-up sleeves and wrenches in hand, but *Life* magazine reassured readers that women in factories could retain their sex appeal. Men and women commonly assumed that women would want to return to the home after victory.

## Ethnic Minorities in the War Effort

Mexican American workers made special contributions to the war effort. As defense factories and the military absorbed workers, western farms and railroads faced an acute shortage of workers. In the 1930s, western states had tried to deport Mexican nationals who were competing for scarce jobs. In 1942, however, the United States and Mexico negotiated the *bracero* program, under which the Mexican government recruited workers to come to the United States on six- to twelve-month contracts. More than 200,000 Mexicans worked on U.S. farms under the program, and more than 100,000 worked for western railroads. Although *bracero* workers still faced discrimination, the U.S. government tried to improve working conditions because it wanted to keep public opinion in Latin America favorable to the Allied cause.

The war was a powerful force for the assimilation of Native Americans. Forty thousand moved to off-reservation jobs; they were a key labor force for military supply depots throughout the West. The average cash income of Indian households tripled during the war. Many stayed in cities at its end. The experience of the war accelerated the fight for full civil rights. Congress had made Indians citizens in 1924, in part to recognize their contributions in World War I, but several states continued to deny them the vote. Activists organized the National Congress of American Indians in 1944 and began the efforts that led the U.S. Supreme Court in 1948 to require states to grant voting rights.

African Americans, too, found economic advancement through war jobs. Early in the mobilization, labor leader A. Philip Randolph of the Brotherhood of Sleeping Car Porters worked with Walter White of the NAACP to plan a "Negro March on Washington" to protest racial discrimination by the federal government. To head off a major embarrassment, Roosevelt issued Executive Order 8802 in June 1941, barring racial discrimination in defense contracts and creating the **Fair Employment Practices Committee (FEPC)**; the order coined a phrase that reverberated powerfully through the coming decades: "No discrimination on grounds of race, color, creed, or national origin."

The FEPC's small staff resolved fewer than half of the employment-discrimination complaints, and white resistance to black coworkers remained strong. In Mobile, New Orleans, and Jacksonville, agreements between shipyards and segregated unions blocked skilled black workers from high-wage jobs. Nevertheless, African American membership in labor unions doubled, and wartime prosperity raised the average black income from 41 percent of the white average in 1939 to 61 percent by 1950, particularly because labor shortages raised farm wages.

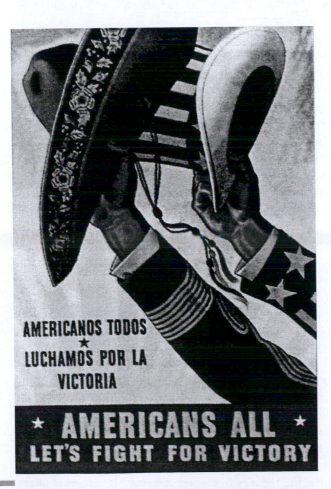

**Fair Employment Practices Committee (FEPC)** Federal agency established in 1941 to curb racial discrimination in war production jobs and government employment.

The government worked hard to encourage Hispanics to support the war effort, both for their direct contributions and to maintain good relations with Mexico and other Latin American nations.

Outside the workplace, African American women found that many voluntary service groups were racially segregated. In response, they formed the Women's Army for National Defense. They did their part by selling war bonds, helping with civil defense, and organizing USO clubs for black soldiers.

Many African Americans saw themselves as engaged in a "Double V" effort for victory against tyranny abroad and victory over racism at home. Economic gains helped. So did the fact that many were able to vote for the first time, either because they had moved to northern states where voting was not racially limited or because they were servicemen serving overseas. The economic and political changes helped to build a base for the civil rights movement that gained momentum in the postwar decades.

## Clashing Cultures

As men and women migrated in search of work, they also crossed or collided with traditional boundaries of religion, region, and race. Some of the most troublesome conflicts arose as African American migration out of the South accelerated in the early 1940s. Many of the migrants headed for well-established black neighborhoods in northern cities. Others created new African American neighborhoods in western cities. White southerners and black northerners with different ideas of racial etiquette found themselves side by side in West Coast shipyards. In the Midwest, black migrants from the South and white migrants from Appalachia crowded into cities such as Cincinnati and Chicago, competing for the same high-wage jobs and scarce apartments.

Tensions between black and white residents exploded in at least fifty cities in 1943 alone. New York's Harlem neighborhood erupted in a riot after rumors of attacks on black servicemen. In Detroit, the issue was the boundary between white and black territory. In June 1943, an argument over the use of Detroit's Belle Isle Park set off three days of violence: twenty-five black people and nine white people died in the most serious racial riot of the war.

Tensions were simultaneously rising between Mexican Americans and Anglos. As the Mexican community in Los Angeles swelled to an estimated 400,000, newspapers published anti-Mexican articles. On June 6, 1943, off-duty sailors and soldiers attacked Latinos on downtown streets and invaded Mexican American neighborhoods. The main targets were so-called *pachucos*—young Chicanos who wore flamboyant "zoot suits" with long, wide-shouldered jackets and pleated, narrow-cuffed trousers, whom the rioters considered delinquents or draft dodgers. The attacks dragged on for a week of sporadic violence against blacks and Filipinos as well as Latinos. The assaults were poignantly ironic because 750,000 Mexican Americans served in the armed forces and were the most decorated group relative to their numbers.

## Internment of Japanese Americans

On February 19, 1942, President Roosevelt authorized the secretary of war to define restricted areas and remove civilian residents who were threats to national security. The primary targets were 112,000 Japanese Americans in California and parts of Washington, Oregon, and Arizona. Japanese immigrants and their children in the western states had experienced forty years of hostility because of racial prejudice, fear of the growing power of Japan, and jealousy of their business success. The outbreak of war triggered anti-Japanese hysteria and gave officials an excuse to take action against enemy aliens (immigrants who retained Japanese citizenship) and their American-born children. As the general commanding on the West Coast put it, "A Jap is a Jap. It makes no difference whether he is an American citizen or not."

In the months after Pearl Harbor, some Japanese from the West Coast managed to move to other parts of the country, but most were unable to leave because of families and businesses. At the end of April 1942, Japanese in the coastal states were given a week to organize their affairs and report to assembly centers at fairgrounds and armories, where they were housed before being moved again to internment camps in isolated

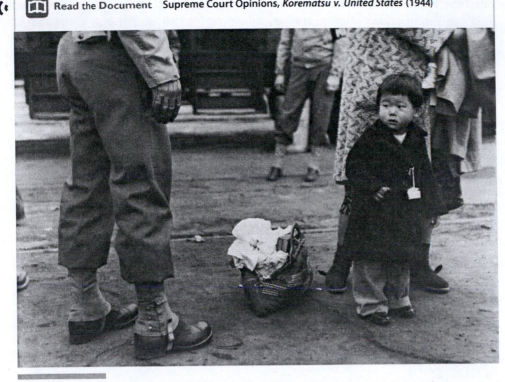

((● 📖 **Read the Document**   Supreme Court Opinions, *Korematsu v. United States* (1944)

26.1

26.2

26.3

**26.4**

26.5

In 1942, the federal government moved Japanese Americans living in four western states to isolated internment camps. This family in Los Angeles is waiting for the first step in that journey.

locations in the western interior. Here, they were housed in tarpaper barracks, hemmed in by barbed-wire, and guarded by military police. The victims reacted to the hardship and stress of their forced journeys in different ways. Several thousand second-generation Japanese Americans renounced their citizenship in disgust. But many others demonstrated their loyalty by cooperating with the authorities, finding sponsors who would help them move to other parts of the country, or joining the 442nd Regimental Combat Team, the most decorated American unit in the European war.

Although the U.S. Supreme Court sanctioned the removals in *Korematsu v. United States* (1944), the nation officially recognized its liability for lost property with the Japanese Claims Act of 1948. The nation acknowledged its broader moral responsibility in 1988, when Congress approved redress payments to each of the 60,000 surviving evacuees.

The internment of West Coast Japanese contrasted with the treatment of Japanese Americans by the military government of Hawaii, whose long history as a multiethnic society made residents less inclined to look for a racial scapegoat. Fewer than 1 percent of Hawaii's Japanese American population of 160,000 were interned, although they and other residents were under the authority of military law until 1944. The treatment of mainland Japanese Americans also contrasted with the situation of German Americans and Italian Americans. The government interned approximately 11,000 German nationals and German Americans who were explicitly seen as individual threats. Until November 1942, it imposed curfews and travel restrictions on Italians and Italian Americans on the West Coast, but it interned fewer than 2,000. Both numbers were tiny fractions of the total populations.

## The End of the New Deal

Roosevelt's New Deal ran out of steam in 1938. The war had reinvigorated his political fortunes by focusing national energies on foreign policy, over which presidents have the greatest power. After the 1942 election left Congress in the hands of Republicans and conservative southern Democrats, lawmakers ignored proposals that war emergency housing be used to improve the nation's permanent housing stock, abolished the National Resources Planning Board, curtailed rural electrification, and crippled the Farm Security Administration. Roosevelt himself declared, at a 1943 press conference, that "Dr. Win-the-War" had replaced "Dr. New Deal."

The presidential election of 1944 raised few new issues of substance. The Republicans nominated Governor Thomas Dewey of New York, who had made his reputation as a crime-fighting district attorney. The Democrats renominated Roosevelt. Missouri Senator Harry S. Truman, a tough investigator of American military preparedness, replaced liberal New Dealer Henry Wallace as Roosevelt's running mate. The move appeased southern Democrats and moved the ticket toward the political center.

The most important issue was a fourth term for Roosevelt. Supporters argued that the nation could not afford to change leaders in the middle of a war, but Dewey's vigor and relative youth (he was twenty years younger than FDR) pointed up the president's failing health. Voters gave Roosevelt 432 electoral votes to 99, but the narrowing gap in the popular vote—54 percent for Roosevelt and 46 percent for Dewey—made the Republicans eager for 1948.

# War and Peace

**26.5**  How did the Allies win the war?

I n January 1943, the U.S. War Department completed the world's largest office building, the Pentagon. The building housed 23,000 workers along 17.5 miles of corridors. The building provided the space in which military planners could coordinate the tasks of raising and equipping the armed forces that would strike directly at Germany and Japan. Indeed, while Congress was chipping away at federal programs, the war effort was massively expanding the government presence in American life. The gray walls of the Pentagon symbolized a U.S. government that was outgrowing its prewar roots.

## Turning the Tide in Europe

The unanswered military question of 1942 and 1943 was when the United States and Britain would open a second front against Germany by attacking across the English Channel. United States leaders wanted to justify massive mobilization with a war-winning campaign and to strike across Europe to occupy the heart of Germany. Stalin needed a full-scale invasion of western Europe to divert German forces from the Eastern Front, where Soviet troops were inflicting 90 percent of German battle casualties.

The Allies spent 1943 hammering out war aims and strategies. Meeting in Casablanca in January 1943, Roosevelt and Churchill demanded the unconditional surrender of Italy, Germany, and Japan. The phrase meant that there would be no deals that kept the enemy governments or leaders in power and was an effort to avoid the mistake of ending World War I with Germany intact. Ten months later, the Allied leaders huddled again. At Tehran, the United States and Britain promised to invade France within six months. "We leave here," said the three leaders, "friends in fact, in spirit, in purpose."

The superficial harmony barely survived the end of the war. The Soviets had shouldered the brunt of the war for nearly two and a half years, suffering millions of casualties and seeing their nation devastated. Stalin and his generals scoffed at the small scale of early U.S. efforts. Roosevelt's ideal of self-determination for all peoples, embodied in the Atlantic Charter, seemed naïve to Churchill, who wanted the major powers to carve out realistic spheres of influence in Europe. Stalin wanted control of eastern Europe to protect the Soviet Union against future invasions and assumed that realistic statesmen would understand.

**The Campaign in North Africa.** The United States entered the ground war against Germany and Italy with Operation TORCH. Soon after the British victory at El Alamein, British and American troops under General Dwight Eisenhower landed in French Morocco and Algeria on November 8, 1942, against little opposition (see Map 26.4). These were territories that the Germans had left under a puppet French government after the French military collapse in 1940. German troops that remained in North Africa taught U.S. forces hard lessons in tactics and leadership, but their stubborn resistance ended in May 1943, leaving all of Africa in Allied hands.

**The Invasion of Italy.** The central Mediterranean remained the focus of U.S. and British action for the next year, despite the fact that the hard-pressed Soviets were

**MAP 26.4  WORLD WAR II IN EUROPE, 1942–1945** Nazi Germany had to defend its conquests on three fronts. Around the Mediterranean, American and British forces pushed the Germans out of Africa and southern Italy, while guerrillas in Yugoslavia pinned down many German troops. On the Eastern Front, Soviet armies advanced hundreds of miles to drive the German army out of the Soviet Union and eastern Europe. In June 1944, U.S. and British landings opened the Western Front in northern France for a decisive strike at the heart of Germany.

desperate for their allies to attack the heart of German power in northern Europe. However, the British feared military disaster from a premature landing in across the English Channel and proposed strikes in southern Europe, which Churchill inaccurately called the "soft underbelly" of Hitler's empire. United States Army chief of staff George Marshall and President Roosevelt agreed to invade Italy in 1943, in part so that U.S. troops could participate in the ground fighting in Europe. Allied forces overran Sicily in July and August, but the Italian mainland proved more difficult. When Sicily fell, the Italian king and army forced Mussolini from power and began to negotiate peace with Britain and America (but not the Soviet Union). In September, the Allies announced an armistice with Italy, and Eisenhower's troops landed south of Naples on September 9. Germany responded by occupying the rest of Italy.

Just as American military planners had feared, the Italian campaign soaked up Allied resources. The mountainous Italian Peninsula was one long series of defensive positions, and the Allies repeatedly bogged down. Week after week, the experience of GIs on the line was the same: "You wake up in the mud and your cigarettes are all wet and you have an ache in your joints and a rattle in your chest." The Allies only managed to gain control of two-thirds of Italy before German resistance crumbled in the final weeks of the war.

**Soviet Advances and the Battle of Kursk.** Meanwhile, the Soviets recruited, rearmed, and upgraded new armies, despite enormous losses. They learned to outfight the Germans in tank warfare and rebuilt munitions factories beyond German reach. They also made good use of 17.5 million tons of U.S. lend-lease assistance. As Soviet soldiers recaptured western Russia and Ukraine, they marched in 13 million pairs of American-made boots and ate U.S. rations. They traveled in 78,000 jeeps and 350,000 Studebaker, Ford, and Dodge trucks. "Just imagine how we could have advanced from Stalingrad to Berlin without [lend-lease vehicles]," future Soviet premier Nikita Khrushchev later commented.

The climactic battle of the German-Soviet war erupted on July 5, 1943. The Germans sent 2,760 tanks against the Kursk salient, a huge wedge that the Red Army had pushed into their lines. In 1941 and 1942, such a massive attack would have forced the Soviets to retreat, but now Soviet generals had prepared a defense in depth with 19,000 artillery pieces and 3,400 tanks of their own. With more than 2 million men actively engaged for more than two weeks, Kursk was the largest pitched battle of the war. It marked the end of the last great German offensive, leaving Germany capable of a fighting retreat but too weak to have any hope of winning the war and expecting an American and British attack across the English Channel.

## Operation OVERLORD

**D-Day** June 6, 1944, the day of the first paratroop drops and amphibious landings on the coast of Normandy, France, in the first stage of Operation OVERLORD during World War II.

On **D-Day**—June 6, 1944—American, British, and Canadian forces landed on the coast of Normandy in northwestern France. The landings were the largest amphibious operation ever staged. Six divisions went ashore from hundreds of attack transports carrying 4,000 landing craft, as vividly dramatized in the film *Saving Private Ryan*. Dozens of warships and 12,000 aircraft provided support. One British and two American airborne divisions dropped behind German positions. When the sun set on the "longest day," the Allies had a tenuous toehold in France. Americans had been waiting for the news. In Montgomery, Alabama, flags appeared along the streets and traffic halted at 5:00 P.M. for buglers from nearby bases and the high school to sound the "call to the colors." At 6:00 P.M. all movie projectors were stopped to allow time for prayer.

The landing finally satisfied Soviet demands for a more balanced war effort, but the next few weeks brought limited success. The Allies secured their beachheads and poured more than a million men and hundreds of thousands of vehicles ashore in the first six weeks. Although the Germans had concentrated forces farther north where they expected the attack, German defenders kept the Allies pinned for weeks along a narrow coastal strip. **Operation OVERLORD**, the code name for the entire campaign

**Operation OVERLORD** United States and British invasion of France in June 1944 during World War II.

across northern France, met renewed success in late July and August. United States troops improved their fighting skills through "experience, sheer bloody experience." They finally broke through the German lines around the town of St.-Lô and then drew a ring around the Germans that slowly closed on the town of Falaise. The Germans lost a quarter of a million troops.

The German command chose to regroup closer to Germany rather than fight in France. The Allies liberated Paris on August 25; Free French forces (units that had never surrendered to the Nazis) led the entry. The drive toward Germany was the largest U.S. operation of the war. The only impediments appeared to be winter weather and pushing forward enough supplies for the rapidly advancing armies.

The story was similar on the Eastern Front, where the Soviets relentlessly battered one section of the German lines after another. By the end of 1944, the Red Army had entered the Balkans and reached central Poland. The Soviets had suffered as many as 24 million military and civilian deaths and sustained by far the heaviest burden in turning back Nazi tyranny (see Table 26.1).

## Victory and Tragedy in Europe

In the last months of 1944, massive air strikes finally began to reduce German war production, which had actually increased during 1943 and much of 1944. The Americans flew daylight raids from air bases in Britain with heavily armed B-17s ("Flying Fortresses") and B-24s, ("Liberators") to destroy factories with precision bombing. On August 17, 1943, however, Germans shot down or damaged 19 percent of the bombers that attacked the aircraft factories of Regensburg and the ball-bearing factories of Schweinfurt. The Americans had to seek easier targets.

Gradually, however, the balance shifted and the air war grew into a true second front. P-51 escort fighters helped B-17s overfly Germany in relative safety after mid-1944. Thousand-bomber raids on railroads and oil facilities began to cripple the German economy. The raids forced Germany to devote 2.5 million workers to air defense and damage repair and to divert fighter planes from the front lines. The air raids cut German military production by one-third through 1944, destroyed the transportation system, and left Germany a set of isolated regions living off stockpiles of food and raw materials.

TABLE 26.1  MILITARY AND CIVILIAN DEATHS IN WORLD WAR II

| | |
|---|---|
| Soviet Union | 24 million |
| China | 10 to 20 million |
| Germany and Austria | 6 to 7 million |
| Poland | 5.8 million |
| Indonesia | 3.4 million |
| Japan | 2.7 million |
| India | 1 to 2 million |
| Yugoslavia | |
| French Indochina (Vietnam, Laos, Cambodia) | |
| France | .5 to 1 million |
| Greece | |
| Hungary | |
| Philippines | |
| Romania | |
| Czechoslovakia | .3 to .5 million |
| Great Britain | |
| Italy | |
| Korea | |
| Lithuania | |
| The Netherlands | |
| United States | |

**The Battle of the Bulge and the Collapse of Germany.**   Even as the air bombardment intensified, Hitler struck a last blow. Stripping the Eastern Front of armored units, he launched twenty-five divisions against thinly held U.S. positions in the Ardennes Forest of Belgium on December 16, 1944. He hoped to split U.S. and British forces by capturing the Belgian port of Antwerp. The attack surprised the Americans, and taking advantage of snow and fog that grounded Allied aircraft, the Germans drove a 50-mile bulge into U.S. lines. Although the Americans took substantial casualties, the German thrust literally ran out of gas beyond the town of Bastogne. The Battle of the Bulge never seriously threatened the outcome of the war, but pushing the Germans back through the snow-filled forest gave GIs a taste of the conditions that marked the war in the Soviet Union.

One of the war's most controversial actions came in February 1945, when British and American bombers attacked the historic city of Dresden. The raid triggered a firestorm that killed 25,000 people, many of them civilian refugees displaced by the Soviet advance. Because the Soviet army was less than a hundred miles from Berlin but the Western Allies had yet to cross the Rhine, critics have seen the raid as a purely political gesture by the British and Americans against a nonmilitary target. However, Dresden did have suburban factories producing for the military, and the city was a junction of major rail and telephone lines whose disruption created another obstacle to Germany's last-ditch resistance.

The Nazi empire collapsed in the spring of 1945. American and British divisions crossed the Rhine in March and enveloped Germany's industrial core. The Soviets drove through eastern Germany toward Berlin. On April 25, American and Soviet troops met on the Elbe River. Hitler committed suicide on April 30 in his concrete bunker deep under devastated Berlin, which surrendered to the Soviets on May 2. The Nazi state formally capitulated on May 8.

**The Holocaust.**   The defeat of Germany revealed appalling evidence of the evil at the heart of the Nazi ideology of racial superiority. After occupying Poland in 1939, the Nazis had transformed concentration camps into forced-labor camps, where overwork, starvation, and disease killed hundreds of thousands of Jews, Gypsies, Poles, Russians, and others the Nazis classed as subhuman. As many as 7 million labor conscripts from eastern and western Europe provided forced labor in fields, factories, mines, and repair crews, often dying on the job from overwork and starvation.

The "final solution" to what Hitler thought of as the "Jewish problem" went far beyond slave labor. The German army in 1941 had gained practice with death by slaughtering hundreds of thousands of Jews and other civilians as it swept across Russia. In the fall of that year, Hitler decided on the total elimination of Europe's Jews. The elite SS, Hitler's personal army within the Nazi Party, in 1942 set out to do his bidding. At Auschwitz, Treblinka, and several other death camps, the SS organized the efficient extermination of up to 6 million Jews and 1 million Poles, Gypsies, and others who failed to fit the Nazi vision of the German master race. Prisoners arrived by forced marches and cattle trains. Those who were not worked or starved to death were herded into gas chambers and then incinerated in huge crematoriums.

The evidence of genocide—systematic racial murder—is irrefutable. Allied officials had begun to hear reports of mass murder midway through the war, but memories of the inaccurate propaganda about German atrocities in World War I made many skeptical. Moreover, the camps were located in the heart of German-controlled territory, areas that Allied armies did not reach until 1945. At Dachau in southwestern Germany, American forces found 10,000 bodies and 32,000 prisoners near death through starvation. Soviet troops who overran the camps in Poland found even more appalling sights—gas chambers as big as barns, huge ovens, the dead stacked like firewood. For more than half a century, the genocide that we now call the **Holocaust** has given the world its most vivid images of inhumanity.

**Holocaust** The systematic murder of millions of European Jews and others deemed undesirable by Nazi Germany.

**Read the Document**   Rudolf Hoess, The Holocaust: Memoirs from the Commandant of Auschwitz (1940s)

The Nazi regime sent slave laborers too weak to continue working on its V-2 rocket project to the Nordhausen concentration camp to die of starvation. When U.S. troops liberated the camp in April 1945, they found more than 3,000 corpses.

## The Pacific War

In the Pacific, as in Europe, the United States used 1943 to probe enemy conquests and to build better submarines, bigger aircraft carriers, and superior planes. Washington divided responsibilities in the Pacific theater. General Douglas MacArthur operated in the islands that stretched between Australia and the Philippines. Admiral Chester Nimitz commanded in the central Pacific. The Allies planned to isolate Japan from its southern conquests. The British moved from India to retake Burma. The Americans advanced along the islands of the southern Pacific to retake the Philippines. With Japan's army still tied down in China, the Americans then planned to bomb Japan into submission.

Racial hatred animated both sides in the Pacific war and fueled a "war without mercy." Americans often characterized Japanese soldiers as vermin. Political cartoons showed Japanese as monkeys or rats, and some Marines had "Rodent Exterminator" stenciled on their helmets. In turn, the Japanese depicted themselves as the "leading race" with the duty to rule the rest of Asia. Japan treated Chinese, Filipinos, and other conquered peoples with contempt and brutality, and the record of Japanese atrocities is substantial. Japanese viewed Americans as racial mongrels and called them demons. Each side expected the worst of the other and frequently lived up to expectations.

The Pacific campaigns of 1944 are often called **island hopping**. Planes from American carriers controlled the air, allowing the navy and land forces to isolate and capture the most strategically located Japanese-held islands while bypassing the rest.

MacArthur used a version of the bypass strategy in the Solomon Islands and New Guinea, leapfrogging past Japanese strong points. The invasion of the Philippines repeated the approach by landing on Leyte, in the middle of the island chain. The Philippine campaign also destroyed the last offensive capacity of the Japanese fleet. In the Battle of Leyte Gulf, the U.S. Navy sank four Japanese battleships, four carriers, and ten cruisers. The Japanese home islands were left with no defensive screen against an expected invasion.

**island hopping**  In the Pacific Theater during World War II, the strategy in which U.S. forces seized selected Japanese-held islands while bypassing and isolating other islands held by Japan.

# ✳ Explore World War II in the Pacific on MyHistoryLab

## WHAT WERE U.S. INTERESTS IN THE PACIFIC THEATER OF WORLD WAR II?

As the United States built its overseas colonies in the Pacific during the decades prior to World War II, Japanese leaders, who were trying to build a colonial empire for their own country, felt threatened. Industrialization and a growing population in Japan meant that the country needed more resources than the home islands could provide. Following the example of European colonial powers, Japan began its own course of expansion during the late 1800s. Soon the empire of Japan acquired Korea, China, and islands in the Pacific as tributary colonies. Imperial competition with the United States prompted a surprise attack on the American naval base at Pearl Harbor on December 7, 1941, bringing the United States into World War II. Initially the Japanese enjoyed military success across the Pacific, but soon the United States began to push the Japanese forces back toward the home islands. Both before and during the course of the war, the Japanese committed a number of atrocities, both against military foes and civilians. In the United States, the American government removed more than 100,000 Japanese Americans and Japanese resident aliens to relocation centers in the West. Japan finally surrendered in August 1945 after the cites of Hiroshima and Nagasaki were nearly destroyed by the first atomic bombs used in combat and dropped by U.S. warplanes.

This aerial photograph shows the mushroom cloud over the Japanese city of Nagasaki on August 9, 1945, following the detonation of the second atomic bomb that, with the bombing of Hiroshima, led to Japan's surrender and the end of World War II.

### SELECTED MAJOR U.S. PACIFIC THEATER EVENTS

| Year | Event | Victor |
|------|-------|--------|
| 1941 | Attack on Pearl Harbor | Japan |
| 1942 | Battle of Bataan | Japan |
| 1942 | Battle of Midway | U.S. |
| 1942 | Battle of Guadalcanal | U.S./Allies |
| 1944 | Battle of Leyte | U.S./Allies |
| 1945 | Battle of Iwo Jima | U.S. |
| 1945 | Battle of Okinawa | U.S./Allies |
| 1945 | Hiroshima: First Atomic Bombing | |
| 1945 | Nagasaki: Second Atomic Bombing | |

**KEY QUESTIONS**    Use **MyHistoryLab** *Explorer* to **answer** these **questions:**

**Analysis** ▶▶▶ *How did the Japanese military initially succeed across the Pacific in the war?*

Map the progress of early Japanese victories.

**Response** ▶▶▶ *What atrocities did Japanese armed forces commit to various groups?*

Understand these offenses.

**Consequence** ▶▶▶ *How did the U.S. government violate the civil rights of its own people during the war?*

See the unfolding of the Japanese evacuation program.

During 1943 and 1944, the United States also savaged the Japanese economy. Submarines choked off food, oil, and raw materials bound for Japan and island bases. By 1945, imports to Japan were one-eighth of the 1940 level. Heavy bombing of Japan began in early 1944, using the new long-range B-29. Japan's dense wooden cities were more vulnerable than their German counterparts, and Japanese air defenses were much weaker. A fire-bomb raid on Tokyo on the night of March 9, 1945, killed 124,000 people and left 1 million homeless; it was perhaps the single biggest mass killing of all time. Overall, conventional bombing destroyed 42 percent of Japan's industrial capacity. By the time the United States captured the islands of Iwo Jima and Okinawa in fierce fighting (April–June 1945) and neared the Japanese home islands, Japan's position was hopeless.

## Searching for Peace

At the beginning of 1945, the Allies sensed victory. Conferring from February 4 to 11 in the Ukrainian town of Yalta, Roosevelt, Stalin, and Churchill planned for the postwar world. The most important American goal was to enlist the Soviet Union in finishing off the Pacific war. Americans hoped that a Soviet attack on Manchuria would tie down enough Japanese troops to reduce U.S. casualties in invading Japan. Stalin repeated his intent to declare war on Japan within three months of victory in Europe, in return for a free hand in Manchuria.

In Europe, the Allies had decided in 1944 to divide Germany and Austria into French, British, American, and Soviet occupation zones and to share control of Berlin. The Red Army already controlled Bulgaria, Romania, and Hungary, countries that had helped the Germans; Soviet officials were installing sympathetic regimes there. Soviet armies also controlled Poland. The most that Roosevelt could coax from Stalin was a vague pledge to allow participation of non-communists in coalition governments in eastern Europe. Stalin also agreed to join a new international organization, the United Nations (UN), whose foundations were laid at a conference in San Francisco in the spring of 1945. The new organization was intended to correct the mistakes of World War I, when the United States had stayed aloof from the League of Nations and had relied on international treaties without mechanisms of enforcement. American leaders wanted the UN to provide a framework through which the United States could coordinate collective security against potential aggressors while retaining its own military strength as the primary means to preserve the peace.

Conservative critics later charged that the Western Powers "gave away" eastern Europe at the **Yalta Conference**. In fact, the Soviet Union gained little that it did not already control. In East Asia as well, the Soviets could seize the territories the agreement granted them. Roosevelt may have overestimated his ability to charm Stalin, but the Yalta agreements were realistic diplomacy that could not undo the results of four years of fighting by the Soviet army.

**Truman and Potsdam.** On April 12, two months after Yalta, Roosevelt died of a cerebral hemorrhage. Harry Truman, the new president, was a shrewd politician, but his experience was limited; Roosevelt had not even told him about the Manhattan Project. Deeply distrustful of the Soviets, Truman first ventured into personal international diplomacy in July 1945 at a British-Soviet-American conference at Potsdam, near Berlin. Most of the sessions debated the future of Germany. The leaders endorsed the expulsion of ethnic Germans from eastern Europe and moved the borders of Poland 100 miles west into historically German territory.

Truman also made it clear that the United States expected to dominate the occupation of Japan. Its goal was to democratize the Japanese political system and reintroduce Japan into the international community, a policy that succeeded. The **Potsdam Declaration** on July 26 summarized U.S. policy and gave Japan an opening for surrender. However, the declaration failed to guarantee that Emperor Hirohito would not be tried as a war criminal. The Japanese response was so cautious that Americans read it as rejection.

**Yalta Conference** Meeting of U.S. president Franklin Roosevelt, British prime minister Winston Churchill, and Soviet premier Joseph Stalin held in February 1945 to plan the final stages of World War II and postwar arrangements.

**Potsdam Declaration** Statement issued by the United States during a meeting of U.S. president Harry Truman, British prime minister Winston Churchill, and Soviet premier Joseph Stalin held at Potsdam, near Berlin, in July 1945 to plan the defeat of Japan and the future of Eastern Europe and Germany. In it, the United States declared its intention to democratize the Japanese political system and reintroduce Japan into the international community and gave Japan an opening for surrender.

### TABLE 26.2  THE DECISION TO USE THE ATOMIC BOMB

| Americans have long argued about whether the use of atomic bombs on the Japanese cities of Hiroshima and Nagasaki was necessary to end the war. Several factors probably influenced President Truman's decision to use the new weapon. | |
| --- | --- |
| Military necessity | After the war, Truman argued that the use of atomic bombs was necessary to avoid an invasion of Japan that would have cost hundreds of thousands of lives. Military planners expected Japanese soldiers to put up the same kind of suicidal resistance in defense of the home islands as they had to American landings in the Philippines, Iwo Jima, and Okinawa. More recently, historians have argued that the Japanese military was near collapse and an invasion would have met far less resistance than feared. |
| Atomic diplomacy | Some historians believe that Truman used atomic weapons to overawe the Soviet Union and induce it to move cautiously in expanding its influence in Europe and East Asia. Truman and his advisers were certainly aware of how the bomb might influence the Soviet leadership. |
| Domestic politics | President Roosevelt and his chief military advisers had spent billions on the secret atomic bomb project without the full knowledge of Congress or the American public. The managers of the Manhattan Project may have believed that only proof of its military value would quiet critics and justify the huge cost. |
| Momentum of war | The United States and Britain had already adopted wholesale destruction of German and Japanese cities as a military tactic. Use of the atomic bomb looked like a variation on fire bombing, not the start of a new era of potential mass destruction. In this context, some historians argue, President Truman's choice was natural and expected. |

**The Atomic Bomb.**   Secretary of State James Byrnes now urged Truman to use the new atomic bomb, tested just weeks earlier. Japan's ferocious defense of Okinawa had confirmed American fears that the Japanese would fight to the death. Thousands of suicide missions by kamikaze pilots who tried to crash their planes into U.S. warships seemed additional proof of Japanese fanaticism. Prominent Americans were wondering if unconditional surrender was worth another six or nine months of bitter fighting. In contrast, using the bomb to end the conflict quickly would ensure that the United States could occupy Japan without Soviet participation, and the bomb might intimidate Stalin. (See Table 26.2.) In short, a decision not to use atomic weapons was never a serious alternative in the summer of 1945.

In early August, the United States dropped two of the three available nuclear bombs on Japan. On August 6, at Hiroshima, the first bomb killed at least 80,000 people and poisoned thousands more with radiation. A second bomb, three days later at Nagasaki, took another 40,000 lives. Japan ceased hostilities on August 14 and surrendered formally on September 2. The world has wondered ever since whether the United States might have defeated Japan without resorting to atomic bombs, but recent research shows that the bombs were the shock that allowed the emperor and peace advocates to overcome military leaders who wanted to fight to the death.

## How the Allies Won

The Allies won with economic capacity, technology, and military skill. The ability to outproduce the enemy made victory certain in 1944 and 1945, but it was the ability to outthink and outmaneuver the Axis Powers that staved off defeat in 1942 and 1943.

In the spring of 1942, an unbroken series of conquests had given the Axis Powers control of roughly one-third of the world's production of industrial raw materials, up from only 5 percent in 1939. But while Germany and Japan struggled to turn these resources into military strength, the Soviet Union accomplished wonders in relocating and rebuilding its manufacturing capacity after the disasters of 1941. The United States, meanwhile, rearmed with astonishing swiftness, accomplishing in one year what Germany had thought would take three. By 1944, the United States was outproducing all of its enemies combined; over the course of the war, it manufactured two-thirds of all the war materials used by the Allies.

The United States and the Soviet Union not only built more planes and tanks than the Axis nations, but they also built better ones. The Soviets developed and mass-produced the T-34, the world's most effective tank. American aircraft designers soon jumped ahead of the Germans. The United States and Britain gained the lead in communication systems, radar, code-breaking capability, and, of course, atomic weapons. Even behind the lines the Allies had the technical advantage. The U.S. and British forces that invaded France were fully motorized, and Soviet forces increasingly so, while the German army still depended on horses to draw supply wagons and artillery.

The Allies learned hard lessons from defeat and figured out how to outfight the Axis. Hitler's generals outsmarted the Soviet military in 1941, Japan outmaneuvered the British and Americans in the first months of the Pacific war, and the German navy came close to squeezing the life from Great Britain in 1942. In 1943 and 1944, the tables were turned. The Russians reexamined every detail of their military procedures and devised new tactics that kept the vast German armies off guard and on the defensive. New ways to fight U-boats in the Atlantic devastated the German submarine service and staved off defeat. Americans in the Pacific utilized the full capacity of aircraft carriers, while Japanese admirals still dreamed of confrontations between lines of battleships.

Finally, the Allies had the appeal of democracy and freedom. The Axis nations were clearly the aggressors. Germany and Japan made bitter enemies by exploiting and abusing the people of the countries they conquered, from Yugoslavia and France to Malaya and the Philippines, and incited local resistance movements. The Allies were certainly not perfect, but they fought for the ideals of political independence and were welcomed as liberators as they pushed back the Axis armies.

## Conclusion

The United States ended the war as the world's overwhelming economic power. It had put only 12 percent of its population in uniform, less than any other major combatant. For every American who died, twenty Germans and dozens of Soviets perished. Having suffered almost no direct destruction, the United States was able to dictate a postwar economic trading system that favored its interests.

Nevertheless, the insecurities of the war years influenced the United States for decades. A nation's current leaders are often shaped by its last war. Churchill had directed strategy, and Hitler, Mussolini, and Truman had all fought in World War I and carried its memories into World War II. The lessons of World War II would similarly influence the thinking of presidents from Dwight D. Eisenhower in the 1950s to George H. W. Bush in the 1990s. Even though the United States ended 1945 with the world's mightiest navy, biggest air force, and only atomic bomb, memories of the instability that had followed World War I made its leaders nervous about the shape of world politics.

One result in the postwar era was conflict between the United States and the Soviet Union, whose only common ground had been a shared enemy. After Germany's defeat, their wartime alliance gave way to hostility and confrontation in the Cold War. At home, international tensions fed the pressure for social and political conformity. The desire to enjoy the fruits of victory after years of economic depression and sacrifice made the postwar generation sensitive to perceived threats to steady jobs and stable families. For the next generation, the unresolved business of World War II would haunt American life.

**For Suggested Readings go to MyHistoryLab.**

# Chapter Review

## The Dilemmas of Neutrality

**26.1** Why were most Americans reluctant to get involved in World War II? p. 749

The United States entered the global war in Europe and Asia with great reluctance because of bitter memories of World War I and a desire to build up fortress America. Nevertheless, events abroad pushed the nation toward rearmament, aid to Britain short of war, and pressure on Japan that led to that nation's decision to go to war.

## Holding the Line

**26.2** How did the Allies fare in 1941 and 1942? p. 755

The year 1941 was a year of victories for Germany and Japan, followed by a year in which the United States Britain, and their allies struggled to stem the tide of aggression. The result was a truly worldwide war with fronts in the Atlantic and Pacific oceans, North Africa, Russia, China, and Southeast Asia.

## Mobilizing for Victory

**26.3** What steps did the U.S. government take to organize the economy for war? p. 759

The war effort required the United States to mobilize millions of men and women in the armed forces and to redirect the nation's huge industrial capacity to war production that eventually eclipsed the output of other nations. America's edge in scientific research proved another key element in victory.

## The Home Front

**26.4** How did the war affect the everyday lives of Americans? p. 765

The war effort penetrated every aspect of American life. It disrupted families but opened new opportunities for women. It was a step forward for civil rights but also triggered racial conflict. Perhaps most importantly in the long run, it reshuffled millions of Americans and began to erode barriers of regional isolation, race, ethnicity, and social class.

## War and Peace

**26.5** How did the Allies win the war? p. 770

By 1944–1945, the Allies had developed superior tactics and weapons. With the Soviet Union bearing the greatest burden, the Allies slowly but inexorably pushed German armies out of their conquests and into Germany itself. In the Pacific, the United States destroyed Japanese naval power and devastated Japanese cities. But German and Japanese surrender opened the door to new tensions that would soon lead to the Cold War.

# Timeline

**1938**
Neutrality—Munich agreement between Germany, Britain, and France

**1939**
Neutrality—Germany invades Poland; Great Britain and France declare war on Germany

**1940**
Neutrality—The United States begins to draft men into the armed forces

**1941**
Neutrality—Germany invades the Soviet Union
Holding the Line—Japan attacks U.S. military bases in Hawaii and the Philippines

**1942**
Holding the Line—Naval battles in the Coral Sea and off the island of Midway blunt Japanese expansion; Soviet forces encircle a German army at Stalingrad

**1944**
War and Peace—Allied forces land in Normandy; the U.S. Navy destroys Japanese sea power in the battles of the Philippine Sea and Leyte Gulf

**1945**
War and Peace—Roosevelt, Stalin, and Churchill meet at Yalta to plan the postwar world; Franklin Roosevelt dies; Harry S. Truman becomes president

War and Peace—The United Nations is organized at an international meeting in San Francisco; Japan surrenders after the detonation of atomic bombs over Hiroshima and Nagasaki

# 27 The Cold War at Home and Abroad
## 1946–1952

## One American Journey

### Reminiscence by Postwar Suburbanite

**Veterans wake up!** Your dream home is here.

Dreaming of the good life? Beautiful Lakewood is more than owning a home. . . . It is a new and better way of living.

Advertisements like these for the new Los Angeles County community of Lakewood in 1950 aimed at families hungry for a place of their own after the privations of World War II. "Owning your own home . . . to have a place of our own was very, very special," remembered Jackie Rynerson.

The ads tried to make it sound easy, showing a young boy saying: We just bought a slick two-bedroom home for $43 a month and NO DOWN PAYMENT because Pop's a veteran! Even so, June Tweedy recalled that it was still a big step to

As international tensions rose with the onset of the Cold War, Americans wondered how to prepare for a possible nuclear war. Many families stocked extra food and water and bought a battery-powered radio, but few actually installed backyard bomb shelters like the one being tested by this family in a Long Island suburb.

## LEARNING OBJECTIVES

| 27.1 | 27.2 | 27.3 | 27.4 | 27.5 |
|---|---|---|---|---|
| What was the catalyst for the economic boom that began in 1947? p. 783 | How was Harry Truman able to win the 1948 presidential election? p. 788 | What were the origins of the Cold War? p. 793 | How did the Korean War shape American domestic politics? p. 798 | Why did fear of Communism escalate in the years following World War II? p. 804 |

 Listen to Chapter 27 on MyHistoryLab

From *The American Journey*, Seventh Edition. Goldfield, Abbott, Anderson, Argersinger, Argersinger and Barney Copyright © 2014 by Pearson Education, Inc.

##  Watch the Video Series on MyHistoryLab

Learn about some key topics related to this chapter with the *MyHistoryLab Video Series: Key Topics in U.S. History.*

**1** **The Cold War: 1945–1953** Although the United States and the Soviet Union were allies during World War II, their mutual mistrust still existed, lurking in the background. With the end of the war and the Soviet Union's development of an atomic bomb, the two superpowers—one representing capitalism and the other world communism—vied for economic, political, and military influence around the globe. This video provides an introduction to the Cold War that dominated this period, in which the combatants fought each indirectly, even on the battlefields of the Korean War.

Watch on **MyHistoryLab**

**Origins of the Cold War** This video explores the tensions that existed between the Soviet Union and its allies—the United States, England, and France—before and after World War II. Of special significance is the Yalta Conference that mapped out "spheres of influence" that evolved into the NATO alliance and the Warsaw Pact. The video also looks at the new post-colonial nations of Africa and Asia and at the formation of the United Nations to keep the peace in a world soon to be overrun with nuclear weapons. **2**

Watch on **MyHistoryLab**

**3** **Truman Doctrine and the Marshall Plan** The Truman Doctrine and the Marshall Plan expanded the influence of the United States as this video demonstrates. The Truman Doctrine, inspired by communist insurgency in Greece and Soviet pressure on Turkey, declared that the United States would provide economic and military aid to support nations in remaining free. The Marshall Plan, part of that policy, provided money, investment, food, and other resources to rebuild much of war-torn Western Europe and keep its people from electing communist governments subservient to the Soviet Union.

Watch on **MyHistoryLab**

**The Korean War** This video explores the Korean War, in which the United States and the United Nations under its influence, attempted to halt communist North Korea's invasion of South Korea in 1950. Called a "police action," the Korea War legitimized the UN's role as a peacekeeper and proved that the United States would risk going to war to contain communism. For this reason, the Korean War in many ways anticipated the conflict in Vietnam. **4**

Watch on **MyHistoryLab**

become a suburban homeowner. "When you put your little check down for your down payment, it was like signing away your life. It seemed like a lot in those days."

From *The Lakewood Story: History, Tradition, Values* Copyright © 2004.
Reprinted by permission.

## Personal Journeys Online

- "This Is How I Keep House," *McCall's*, April 1949. The routine of a typical Levittown housewife.
- Eric Hodgins, *Mr. Blandings Builds His Dream House* (1946). A fictional New York advertising agent buys a house in the far edge of suburbia.
- Atlanta Housing Council, "Proposed Areas for Expansions of Negro Housing in Atlanta, Georgia." Papers of the Atlanta Urban League, Atlanta University Center, Atlanta, Georgia. Reprinted in Andrew Wiese and Becky Nicolaides, *The Suburb Reader* (2006). Atlanta Housing Council suggests ways to continue residential segregation in a growing city.

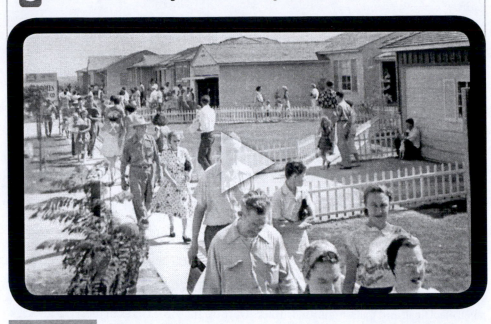

Watch the Video   Creating Domestic Bliss During the Cold War

In the years after World War II, builders found it hard to keep up with the demand for new homes. When this street of model homes opened in Lakewood, California, in 1950, as many as 20,000 people inspected the houses in a single weekend.

**L**akewood's new families were moving into one of the most successful of the giant subdivisions that blossomed in the postwar decade. Like Levittown, New York, in the same years, it attracted a flood of buyers desperate for a home of their own. On the first day of sales on Palm Sunday, 1950, 25,000 people lined up in front of the sales office, and 7,200 houses sold in the first ten months, most before they were actually built.

The size of the Lakewood crowds indicated the severity of the housing shortage after World War II and the intense desire of Americans to return to normal life. After years of hardship, Americans longed for economic opportunity. Even President Truman replaced the model gun on his White House desk with a model plow. Lakewooders were part of the first wave in the suburbanization of postwar America. Over the next decades, the families who made the journey from city neighborhoods to thousands of new subdivisions would start the baby boom and rekindle the economy with their purchases of automobiles, appliances, and televisions.

This compelling desire to enjoy the promise of American life after years of sacrifice helps explain why Americans reacted so fiercely to new challenges and threats. They watched as congressional conservatives and President Truman fought over the fate of New Deal programs. More worrisome was the confrontation with the Soviet Union that was soon being called the **Cold War.** Triggered by the Soviet Union's imposition of communist regimes throughout Eastern Europe, the Cold War grew into a global contest in which the United States tried to counter Soviet influence around the world.

**Cold War** The political and economic confrontation between the Soviet Union and the United States that dominated world affairs from 1946 to 1989.

## Launching the Great Boom

**27.1**   What was the catalyst for the economic boom that began in 1947?

**W**hen World War II ended, Americans feared that demobilization would bring a rerun of the inflation and unemployment that had followed World War I. Indeed, in the first eighteen months of peace, rising prices, strife between labor and management, and shortages of everything from meat to automobiles confirmed their anxiety. But in fact, 1947 and 1948 ushered in an economic expansion that lasted for a quarter century. The resulting prosperity would finance a military buildup and an activist foreign policy. It also supported continuity in domestic politics from the late 1940s to the mid-1960s.

## Reconversion Chaos

Japan's sudden surrender took the United States by surprise. The Pentagon, already scaling back defense spending, canceled $15 billion in war contracts in the first two days after the Japanese surrender. Public pressure demanded that the military release the nation's 12 million service personnel as rapidly as possible. GIs in Europe and the South Pacific waited impatiently for their turn on slow, crowded troop ships. Even at the rate of 25,000 discharges a day, it took a year to get all of them back to civilian life.

Veterans came home to shortages of food and consumer goods. High demand and short supply meant inflationary pressure, checked temporarily by continuing the Office of Price Administration until October 1946. Meanwhile, producers, consumers, and retailers scrambled to evade price restrictions and scarcities.

A wave of strikes made it hard to retool factories for civilian products. Inflation squeezed factory workers, who had accepted wage controls during the war effort. Since 1941, prices had risen twice as fast as base wages. In the fall of 1945, more and more workers went on strike to redress the balance; the strikes interrupted the output of products from canned soup to copper wire. By January 1946, some 1.3 million auto, steel, electrical, and packinghouse workers were off the job. Strikes in these basic industries shut other factories down for lack of supplies. Presidential committees crafted settlements that allowed steel and auto workers to make up ground lost during the war, but they also allowed corporations to pass on higher costs to consumers.

## Economic Policy

The economic turmoil of 1946 set the stage for two major and contradictory efforts to deal more systematically with peacetime economic readjustment. The Employment Act of 1946 and the Taft-Hartley Act of 1947 represented liberal and conservative approaches to the peacetime economy.

The Employment Act was an effort by congressional liberals to ward off economic crisis by fine-tuning government taxation and spending. It started as a proposal for a full-employment bill that would ensure everyone's "right to a useful and remunerative job." Watered down in the face of business opposition, it still defined economic growth and high employment as national goals. It also established the **Council of Economic Advisers** to assist the president. Even this weak legislation, putting the federal government at the center of economic planning, would have been unthinkable a generation earlier.

In the short term, the Employment Act aimed at a problem that did not materialize. Economists had predicted that the combination of returning veterans and workers idled by canceled defense work would bring depression-level unemployment of 8 to 10 million. In fact, more than 2 million women provided some slack by leaving the labor force outright. Federal agencies hastened their departure by publishing pamphlets asking men the pointed question, "Do you want your wife to work after the war?" In addition, a savings pool of $140 billion in bank accounts and war bonds created a huge demand for consumer goods and workers to produce them. Total employment rose rather than fell with the end of the war, and unemployment in 1946–1948 stayed below 4 percent.

From the other end of the political spectrum, the **Taft-Hartley Act** climaxed a ten-year effort by conservatives to reverse the gains made by organized labor in the 1930s. The act passed in 1947 because of anger about continuing strikes. In April 1946, a forty-day coal strike hampered industrial production. The coal settlement was only days old when the nation faced an even more crippling walkout by railroad workers. Truman asked for the unprecedented power to draft strikers into the army; the threat undercut the union and led to a quick and dramatic settlement.

In November 1946, Republicans capitalized on the problems of reconversion chaos, labor unrest, and dissatisfaction with Truman to win control of Congress for the first time since the 1920s. They used their new power to adopt Taft-Hartley, which

**Council of Economic Advisers** Board of three professional economists established in 1946 to advise the president on economic policy.

**Taft-Hartley Act** Federal legislation of 1947 that substantially limited the tools available to labor unions in labor-management disputes.

was a serious counterattack by big business against large unions. It outlawed several union tools as "unfair labor practices." It barred the closed shop (the requirement that all workers hired in a given company or plant be union members) and blocked secondary boycotts (strikes against suppliers or customers of a targeted business). The federal government could postpone a strike by imposing a cooling-off period, which gave companies time to stockpile their products. Officers of national unions had to swear that they were not Communists or Communist sympathizers, even though corporate executives had no similar obligation.

## The GI Bill

Another landmark law for the postwar era passed Congress without controversy. The Servicemen's Readjustment Act of 1944 was designed to ease veterans back into the civilian mainstream. Popularly known as the **GI Bill of Rights**, it was one of the federal government's most successful public assistance programs. Rather than pay cash bonuses to veterans, as after previous wars, Congress tied benefits to specific public goals. The GI Bill guaranteed loans of up to $2,000 for buying a house or farm or starting a business, a substantial sum at a time when a new house cost $6,000. The program allowed millions of veterans to attend college with money for tuition and books plus monthly stipends.

The GI Bill democratized American higher education by making college degrees accessible to men with working-class backgrounds. It brought far more students into higher education than could otherwise have enrolled. In the peak year of 1947, veterans made up half of all college students. Veterans helped convert the college degree, once available primarily to the socially privileged, into a basic business and professional credential. However, many colleges and universities were not open to African Americans. Moreover, the GI tide unfortunately crowded women out of classrooms. Women's share of bachelor's degrees dropped from 40 percent in 1940 to 25 percent in 1950.

## Assembly-Line Neighborhoods

Americans faced a housing shortage after the war. In 1947, fully 3 million married couples were unable to set up their own households. Most doubled up with relatives while they waited for the construction industry to respond. Hunger for housing was fierce. Eager buyers lined up for hours and paid admission fees to tour model homes or to put their names in drawings for the opportunity to buy.

**GI Bill of Rights** Legislation in June 1944 that eased the return of veterans into American society by providing educational and employment benefits.

With the flood of veterans seeking college degrees after World War II, universities had to improvise to find adequate housing. On this Rhode Island campus, war surplus Quonset huts made do as housing for married students.

**Levittown** Any of three large suburban housing developments built in New York, Pennsylvania, and New Jersey in the late 1940s and 1950s.

The solution started with the federal government and its Veterans Administration (VA) mortgage program. By guaranteeing repayment, the VA allowed veterans to get home-purchase loans from private lenders without a down payment. Neither the VA program nor the New Deal–era Federal Housing Administration (FHA) mortgage insurance program, however, could do any good unless there were houses to buy. Eyeing the mass market created by the federal programs, innovative private builders devised their own solution. In 1947, William Levitt, a New York builder who had developed defense housing projects, built 2,000 houses for veterans on suburban Long Island. His basic house had 800 square feet of living space in two bedrooms, living room, kitchen, and bath, a 60-by-100-foot lot, and an unfinished attic waiting for the weekend handyman. It was only one-third the size of the typical new house fifty years later, but it gave new families a place to start. There were 6,000 **Levittown** houses by the end of 1948 and more than 17,000 by 1951.

From 1946 through 1950, the federal government backed $20 billion in VA and FHA loans, approximately 40 percent of all home-mortgage debt. Housing starts neared 2 million in the peak year of 1950. By the end of the 1940s, 55 percent of American households owned their homes. The figure continued to climb until the 1980s, broadening access to the dream of financial security for many families. In the 1960s the combined population of suburban areas would pass the populations of large central cities and of smaller towns and rural areas, where population actually declined. By the twenty-first century, a majority of all Americans would be suburbanites.

**Isolation and Discrimination.**   Unfortunately, the suburban solution to the housing shortage came with costs. The vast new housing tracts tended to isolate women and children from traditional community life. Moreover, they were of little benefit to African Americans. As the migration of black workers and their families to northern and western cities continued after the war, discrimination excluded them from new housing. Federal housing agencies and private industry worsened the problem by **redlining** older neighborhoods, which involved withholding home-purchase loans and insurance coverage from inner-city areas that were deemed too risky as investments. Thus, public and private actions kept African Americans in deteriorating inner-city ghettos.

**redlining** Restricting mortgage credit and insurance for properties in neighborhoods defined as being high risk.

## Steps toward Civil Rights

The urgent need for decent housing helped to motivate African Americans to demand full rights as citizens. The wartime experience of fighting for freedom abroad while suffering discrimination at home steeled a new generation of black leaders to close the gap between America's ideal of equality and its performance. As had also been true after World War I, some white Americans held the opposite view, hoping to reaffirm racial segregation. A wave of racist violence surged across the South after the war; special targets were black veterans who tried to register to vote. However, many white Americans felt uneasy about the contradiction between a crusade for freedom abroad and racial discrimination at home.

In this era of rapid change and racial tension, the Truman administration recognized the importance of upholding civil rights for all Americans. Caught between pressure from black leaders and the fear of alienating southern Democrats, the president in 1946 appointed the Committee on Civil Rights, whose report developed an agenda for racial justice that would take two decades to put into effect. The National Association for the Advancement of Colored People (NAACP) had already begun a campaign of antisegregation lawsuits, which the Justice Department now began to support. The administration ordered federal housing agencies to modify their racially restrictive policies and prohibited racial discrimination in federal employment. Federal committees began to push for desegregation of private facilities in the symbolically important city of Washington, DC. In an important decision in the case of *Shelley v. Kraemer* (1948), the Supreme Court held that clauses in real estate deeds that forbid selling or renting to minorities could not be enforced in the courts.

The president also ordered "equality of treatment and opportunity" in the armed services in July 1948. The army in particular dragged its feet, hoping to limit black enlistees to 10 percent of the total. Manpower needs and the record of integrated units in the war in Korea from 1950 to 1953 persuaded the reluctant generals. Over the next generation, African Americans would find the military an important avenue for career opportunities.

Changes in national policy were important for ending racial discrimination, but far more Americans were interested in lowering racial barriers in professional team sports. Americans had applauded individual black champions, such as boxer Joe Louis and sprinter Jesse Owens, but team sports required their members to travel, practice, and play together. The center of attention was Jack Roosevelt ("Jackie") Robinson, a gifted African American athlete, who opened the 1947 baseball season as a member of the Brooklyn Dodgers. Robinson broke the color line that had reserved the modern major leagues for white players. His ability to endure taunting and hostility and still excel on the ballfield opened the door for other African Americans and Latinos.

## Consumer Boom and Baby Boom

The housing boom was a product of both pent-up demand and a postwar "family boom." Americans celebrated the end of the war with weddings; the marriage rate in 1946 surpassed even its wartime high. Many women who left the labor force opted for marriage, and at increasingly younger ages. By 1950, the median age at which women married would be just over 20 years—lower than at any previous time in the twentieth century.

New marriages jumpstarted the "baby boom," as did already married couples who decided to catch up after postponing childbearing during the war. In the early 1940s, an average of 2.9 million children per year were born in the United States; in 1946–1950, the average was 3.6 million. Those 3.5 million "extra" babies needed diapers, swing sets, lunch boxes, bicycles, and schoolrooms (see Figure 27.1).

Fast-growing families also needed to stock up on household goods. Out of an average household income of roughly $4,000 in 1946 and 1947, a family of four had $300 to $400 a year for furnishings and appliances. A couple who studied *Consumer Reports* might equip its new suburban kitchen with a Dripolator coffee maker for

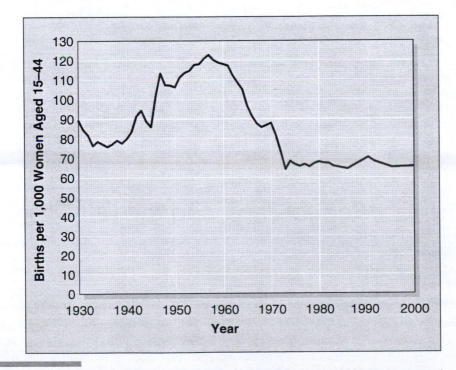

**FIGURE 27.1 THE POSTWAR BABY BOOM: THE U.S. BIRTHRATE, 1930–2000** The baby boom after World War II was the product of high marriage rates and closely spaced children. The generation of Americans born between 1945 and 1960 has strongly affected American society and politics as its members went to school and college, entered the workforce, started their own families, and now have begun to plan for retirement in the twenty-first century. SOURCE: U.S. Census Bureau.

Advertisements for the new consumer wonder television emphasized TV viewing as a wholesome activity for which families gathered around tiny screens set in large consoles that dominated living rooms. This 1950s ad also suggests the central role that TV would play in defining the roles of mothers to the baby boom generation.

$2.45 and a Mirro-Matic pressure cooker for $12.95. The thrifty family could get along with a Motorola table radio in brown plastic for under $30; for $100, it could have a massive radio-phonograph combination in a 4-foot console as the centerpiece of a well-equipped living room.

# Truman, Republicans, and the Fair Deal

**27.2**   How was Harry Truman able to win the 1948 presidential election?

From new radios to new homes to new jobs, the economic gains of the postwar years propelled Americans toward the political center. After fifteen years of economic crisis and world war, they wanted to enjoy prosperity. William Levitt tried to humorously capture the American satisfaction with the fruits of free enterprise when he said in 1948 that "no man who owns his house and lot can be a Communist; he has too much to do."

Recognizing this attitude, Harry Truman and his political advisers tried to define policies acceptable to moderate Republicans as well as to Democrats. This meant

# From Then to Now
# The Automobile Industry

In 1950, U.S. automakers sold a record 6.7 million passenger cars and 1.3 million trucks and buses. Americans were playing catch-up after World War II had diverted auto factories into war production—and they were buying American. Only 21,000 vehicles were imported in 1950, or just one of every 400 new vehicles. General Motors alone had nearly half of the American auto market with its range of brands for every bank account, from Chevrolet to Pontiac, Oldsmobile, Buick, and finally Cadillac.

The world was also buying American. In total, 75 percent of the world's new cars rolled off U.S. assembly lines. Major U.S. automakers were expanding branch plants overseas and building up subsidiary brands in Europe and Australia.

Six decades later, the American automobile industry looked vastly different. In 2008, the United States had dropped to third place in world automobile production, behind Japan and China. Its output was scarcely larger than in 1950 and amounted to less than 12 percent of world production.

Of the "big three" automakers, only Ford had survived without massive change. Chrysler had been acquired by the German auto giant Daimler from 1998 to 2007. In June 2009, after large infusions of federal aid failed to stem its cash flow problems, the company reorganized with the Italian automaker Fiat as 20 percent owner, the United States and Canadian governments as 10 percent owners, and the rest owned by the United Auto Workers health care trust.

General Motors also went through bankruptcy in July 2009, despite massive infusions of cash under both the Bush and Obama administrations. The company shed its overseas brands (Saab, Opel) and several domestic makes (Pontiac, Saturn, Hummer). Chevrolet, Buick, Cadillac, and GMC were sold to a new General Motors Company in which the U.S. government held a majority share and the Canadian government, UAW, and bondholders the rest. What changed?

Advertisement for 1950 Studebaker.

Closed GM plant in Flint, Michigan, one of many automobile factories shut down by troubled automobile companies starting in the 1980s.

Foreign competition broke Detroit's near monopoly. European companies, especially Volkswagen, successfully tapped the U.S. market in the 1960s, followed by Japanese and Korean companies. Countries like China and Brazil created their own automobile.

United States automakers grew inflexible. In successful established industries, corporate managers and labor unions both have an interest in keeping things as they are. GM in particular was unable to follow through on successful initiatives like the Saturn.

The energy crunch of 2008 also hurt. When gasoline prices skyrocketed in the midst of an economic recession and customers began to demand fuel-efficient cars, U.S. automakers were locked into a market strategy that emphasized SUVs and pickups. It took the crisis of 2009 to shock companies like GM into drastic changes that returned them to profitability.

Even more basic, however, is the reality that Americans have enough cars. Every adult American can now sit behind a steering wheel of a passenger car or truck at the same time and still leave 20 million vehicles sitting idle in driveways and parking lots.

We will need to keep producing and buying new trucks and cars to replace ones that wear out and swap older, inefficient vehicles for ones that use less fuel per mile. However, the market is essentially saturated. Cars are in the same category as refrigerators and land-line telephones. After a century, Americans are no longer adopting them as new technologies. We're simply maintaining the status quo until something better comes along.

**Question for Discussion**

- Has the restructuring of the American automobile industry been the result of bad business decisions or fundamental changes in the world economy?

creating a bipartisan coalition to block Soviet influence in Western Europe and defending the core of the New Deal's social and economic agenda at home.

This political package is known as the strategy of the "vital center," after the title of a 1949 book by Arthur Schlesinger, Jr. The book linked anti-communism in foreign policy with efforts to enact inclusive social and economic policies to extend freedom abroad and at home. The vital center reflected the political reality of the Cold War years, when Democrats had to prove that they were tough on communism before they could enact domestic reforms. The approach defined the heart of the Democratic Party for twenty years and found full expression in the administrations of John Kennedy (1961–1963) and Lyndon Johnson (1963–1969).

## Truman's Opposition

Truman had unexpected luck in his campaign for a full term as president in 1948. Besides the Republicans, he faced new fringe parties on the far right and far left that allowed him to position himself in the moderate center.

Truman's opponents represented the left-leaning American Progressive Party, the **Dixiecrats** (officially the States' Rights Democrats), and the Republicans.

**Dixiecrats** Southern Democrats who broke from the party in 1948 over the issue of civil rights and ran a presidential ticket as the States' Rights Democrats.

Harry Truman greets supporters and railroad workers in Pittsburgh at the start of an eighteen-state campaign tour in June 1948. Truman's grassroots campaign and down-home style helped him pull out an unexpected victory in November 1948.

The Progressive candidate was Henry Wallace, who had been FDR's vice president from 1941 to 1945, before being dumped in favor of Truman; more recently, he had been Truman's secretary of commerce. The Dixiecrat candidate, Governor Strom Thurmond of South Carolina, had bolted the Democratic Party over civil rights. The most serious challenger was Republican Thomas Dewey, who had run against Roosevelt in 1944. Wallace cast himself as the prophet for "the century of the common man." After Truman fired him from the cabinet in 1946 for advocating a conciliatory stance toward the Soviet Union, Wallace continued to denounce U.S. foreign policy. Enthusiastic college crowds raised his sights from "scaring the Democratic Party left-ward" to running for president.

Wallace argued that the United States was forcing the Cold War on the Soviet Union and undermining American ideals by diverting attention from poverty and racism at home. He wanted to repeal the draft and destroy atomic weapons. His arguments had merit, for the United States was becoming a militarized society, but Wallace struck most voters as a kook, and he made skepticism about the Cold War increasingly vulnerable to right-wing attack.

At the other political extreme were the southerners who walked out when the 1948 Democratic National Convention called for full civil rights for African Americans. The raucous convention debate previewed the politics of the 1960s and the deep divisions within the Democratic Party that would lead to Republican gains in the South a generation later. Mayor Hubert Humphrey of Minneapolis challenged the Democratic Party "to get out of the shadow of states' rights and walk forthrightly into the bright sunshine of human rights."

Tom Dewey, Truman's real opponent, had a high opinion of himself. He had been an effective governor of New York and represented the moderate eastern establishment within the Republican Party. Fortunately for Truman, Dewey lacked the common touch. Smooth on the outside, he alienated people who should have been his closest supporters. He was a bit of a snob and was an arrogant campaigner, refusing to interrupt his morning schedule to talk to voters.

Dewey was also saddled with the results of the Republican-controlled "do-nothing" 80th Congress (1947–1948). Truman used confrontation with Congress to rally voters who had supported the New Deal. He introduced legislation that he knew would be ignored, and he used his veto even when he knew Congress would override it. All the while he was building a list of campaign issues by demonstrating that the Republicans were obstructionists. Vote for me, Truman argued, to protect the New Deal, or vote Republican to bring back the days of Herbert Hoover.

## Whistle-Stopping across America

The 1948 presidential campaign mixed old and new. For the last time, a major candidate crisscrossed the nation by rail and made hundreds of speeches from the rear platforms of trains. For the first time, national television broadcast the two party conventions, although the primitive cameras showed the handful of viewers little more than talking heads.

Truman ran on both character and issues. He was a widely read and intelligent man who cultivated the image of a backslapper. "I'll mow 'em down . . . and I'll give 'em hell," he told his vice presidential running mate. Crowds across the country greeted him with "Give 'em hell, Harry!" He covered 31,700 miles in his campaign train and gave ten speeches a day. Republicans belittled the small towns and cities he visited, calling them "whistle stops." Democrats made the term a badge of pride for places like Laramie, Wyoming, and Pocatello, Idaho.

Truman brought the campaign home to average Americans. He tied Dewey to inflation, housing shortages, and fears about the future of Social Security (an issue that Democrats would continue to use into the next century). In industrial cities, he hammered at the Taft-Hartley Act. In the West, he pointed out that Democratic

| | Electoral Vote (%) | Popular Vote (%) |
|---|---|---|
| **HARRY S. TRUMAN** **(Democrat)** | **303** **(57)** | **24,105,812** **(49.5)** |
| Thomas E. Dewey (Republican) | 189 (36) | 21,970,065 (45.1) |
| Strom Thurmond (States' Rights) | 39 (7) | 1,169,063 (2.4) |
| Henry A. Wallace (Progressive) | – | 1,157,172 (2.4) |
| Other candidates (Socialist, Prohibition, Socialist Labor, Socialist Workers) | – | 272,713 (.6) |

**MAP 27.1  THE ELECTION OF 1948**  Harry Truman won a narrow victory in the presidential election of 1948 by holding many of the traditionally Democratic states of the South and West and winning key industrial states in the Midwest. His success depended on the coalition of rural and urban interests that Franklin Roosevelt had pulled together in the 1930s.

administrations had built dams and helped to turn natural resources into jobs. He called the Republicans the party of privilege and arrogance. The Democrats, he said, offered opportunity for farmers, factory workers, and small business owners.

Truman got a huge boost from Dewey's unwillingness to fight. Going into the fall with a big lead in the public opinion polls, Dewey sought to avoid mistakes. The results astounded the poll takers, who had stopped sampling opinion in mid-October just as a swing to Truman gathered strength. Wallace and Thurmond each took just under 1.2 million votes. Dewey received nearly 22 million popular votes and 189 electoral votes, but Truman won more than 24 million popular votes and 303 electoral votes (see Map 27.1).

Truman and the Democrats benefited from voters who hoped to retain the gains of the New Deal. They also drew in new voters who came of age with the experiences of World War II and strong government fresh in their minds, leading them to identify with the political party that seemed most willing to use government to maintain postwar prosperity.

## Truman's Fair Deal

Truman hoped to build on the gains of the New Deal. In his State of the Union address in January 1949, he called for a Fair Deal for all Americans. He promised to extend the

New Deal and ensure "greater economic opportunity for the mass of the people." Over the next four years, however, conservative Republicans and southern Democrats forced Congress to choose carefully, accepting proposals that expanded existing programs but rejecting new departures.

With the Housing Act of 1949, the federal government reaffirmed its concern about families who had been priced out of the private market. Passed with the backing of conservative Senator Robert Taft, "Mr. Republican" to his admirers, the act provided money for local housing agencies to buy, clear, and resell land for housing. The intent was to clear "substandard and blighted areas" and replace them with affordable modern apartments. The program never worked as intended because of scanty appropriations, poor design of the replacement housing, and local decisions that concentrated public housing in segregated minority neighborhoods, but it established the goal of decent housing for all Americans.

In 1950, Congress revitalized the weak Social Security program. Benefits went up by an average of 80 percent, and 10.5 million additional people received old-age and survivors' insurance. Most of the new coverage went to rural and small-town people, thus consolidating the broad support that has made it politically difficult to change Social Security ever since, even in the face of projected shortages in the twenty-first century.

Congress rejected other Fair Deal proposals that would remain on the national agenda for decades. A Senate filibuster killed a permanent Fair Employment Practices Commission to fight racial discrimination in hiring, halting progress toward civil rights. The medical establishment blocked a proposal for national health insurance as "socialistic," leaving the issue to be revisited in the 1960s with the passage of Medicare and Medicaid, in the 1990s with Bill Clinton's failed proposals for health care reform, and in 2010 with the Obama administration's successful fight to greatly expand health insurance coverage. The overall message from Truman's second term was clear: Americans liked what the New Deal had given them but were hesitant about new initiatives.

# Confronting the Soviet Union

**27.3**    What were the origins of the Cold War?

The backdrop to political battles at home were rapidly escalating tensions with the Soviet Union. In 1945, the United States and the Soviet Union were allies, victorious against Germany and planning the defeat of Japan. By 1947, they were engaged in a diplomatic and economic confrontation and soon came close to war over the city of Berlin. The business tycoon and presidential adviser Bernard Baruch characterized the conflict in April 1947 as a "cold war," and newspaper columnist Walter Lippmann quickly popularized the term.

Over the next forty years, the United States and the Soviet Union contested for economic, political, and military influence around the globe. The heart of Soviet policy was to control Eastern Europe as a buffer zone against Germany. The centerpiece of American policy was to link the United States, Western Europe, and Japan into an alliance of overwhelming economic power. For the United States, the Cold War was simultaneously an effort to promote democracy in Europe, maintain a favorable military position in relation to the Soviet Union, and preserve its leadership of the world economy.

Each side in the Cold War thought the worst of the other. Behind the conflicts were Soviet insecurity about an aggressive West and American fear of Communist expansionism. Americans and Soviets frequently interpreted each other's actions in the most threatening terms, turning miscalculations and misunderstandings into crises. A U.S. public that had suffered through nearly two decades of economic depression and war reacted to international problems with frustration and anger. The emotional burdens of the Cold War warped and narrowed a generation of American political life around the requirements of anti-Communism.

## The End of the Grand Alliance

The Yalta Conference of February 1945 had recognized military realities by marking out rough spheres of influence. The Soviet defeat of Germany on the Eastern Front had made the Soviet Union the only military power in Eastern Europe. The American and British attacks through Italy and France had made the Western allies dominant in Western Europe and the Mediterranean. The Soviets, Americans, British, and French shared control of defeated Germany, each with its own occupation zone and its own sector of Berlin, the former German capital located inside the Soviet zone. The Western allies had the better of the bargain. Defeated Italy and Japan, whose reconstruction was firmly in Western hands, had far greater economic potential than Soviet-controlled Bulgaria, Romania, or Hungary, and the western occupation zones in West Germany held more people and industrial potential than the Russian zone in East Germany.

As the victorious powers tried to put their broad agreements into operation, they argued bitterly about Germany and Eastern Europe. Was the Soviet Union to dominate Eastern Europe as its protective buffer, or was the region to be open to Western economic and political influence? For Poland, Truman and his advisers claimed that Yalta had assumed open elections on the American model. The Soviet Union claimed that Yalta had ensured that any Polish government would be friendly to Soviet interests and acted to guarantee that this would be so.

The United States put economic pressure on the Soviet Union but also tried to involve it in new international organizations. The Senate approved American membership in the newly organized United Nations (UN) with only two opposing votes, a sharp contrast to its rejection of the League of Nations in 1920. Cities all over the United States vied to be chosen for the UN headquarters. Unlikely candidates like Rapid City, South Dakota, and Sault Saint Marie, Michigan, competed with more likely candidates like Boston and San Francisco. Philadelphia almost took the prize until a last-minute donation of land by the Rockefeller family sealed the deal for the east side of Manhattan.

The Washington-based **International Monetary Fund (IMF)** and the **World Bank** were designed to revive international trade. The IMF stabilized national currencies against the short-term pressures of international trade. The World Bank drew on the resources of member nations to make economic development loans to governments for such projects as new dams or agricultural modernization. These organizations ensured that the reviving world economy would revolve around the industrial and technological power of the United States, and they continue to dictate the economic policy of many developing nations into the twenty-first century.

In 1946, the United States presented a plan in the United Nations to control atomic energy. Bernard Baruch suggested that an international agency should oversee all uranium production and research on atomic explosives. The Baruch plan emphasized enforcement and inspections that would have opened the Soviet nuclear effort to American interference, an unacceptable prospect for a nation trying to catch up with the United States by building its own atomic bombs. On-site inspection would remain a problem in arms-control in the twenty-first century in relation to the nuclear programs of Iran and North Korea.

While UN delegates debated the future of atomic energy, American leaders were becoming convinced of Soviet aggressiveness. In February 1946, George Kennan, a senior American diplomat in Moscow, sent a "long telegram" to the State Department that depicted a Soviet Union driven by expansionist Communist ideology. The British encouraged the same tough stand. Lacking the strength to shape Europe on its own, Great Britain repeatedly nudged the United States to block Soviet influence. Speaking at Westminster College in Missouri in March 1946, Winston Churchill warned that the

**International Monetary Fund (IMF)** International organization established in 1945 to assist nations in maintaining stable currencies.

**World Bank** Officially the International Bank for Reconstruction and Development, an international organization established in 1845 that assists governments around the world in economic development efforts.

Soviet Union had dropped an "iron curtain" across the middle of Europe and urged a firm Western response.

Churchill's speech matched the mood in official Washington. Truman's foreign-policy advisers shared the belief in an aggressive Soviet Union, and the president himself saw the world as a series of either-or choices. Added to military apprehension were worries about political and economic competition. Communist parties in war-ravaged Europe and Japan were exploiting discontent. In Asia and Africa, the allegiance of nationalists who were fighting for independence from European powers remained in doubt. America's leaders worried that much of the Eastern Hemisphere might fall under Soviet control, and they walked an uneasy line between supporting European allies and recognizing the importance of self-determination for all peoples.

Were Truman and his advisers right about Soviet intentions? The evidence is mixed. In their determination to avoid another Munich, Truman and his foreign-policy circle ignored examples of Soviet caution and conciliation. The Soviets withdrew troops from Manchuria in northern China and acquiesced in America's control of defeated Japan. They allowed a neutral but democratic government in Finland and technically free elections in Hungary and Czechoslovakia (although it was clear that Communists would do well there). They demobilized much of their huge army and reduced their forces in Eastern Europe.

However, the Soviet regime also acted to justify American fears. The Soviet Union could not resist exerting influence in the Middle East. It pressured Turkey to give it partial control of the exit from the Black Sea. It retained troops in northern Iran until warned out by the United States. The Soviets were ruthless in support of Communist control in Eastern Europe in 1946 and 1947; they aided a Communist takeover in Bulgaria, backed a coup in Romania, and undermined the last non-Communist political opposition in Poland. United States policymakers read these Soviet actions as a rerun of Nazi aggression and determined not to let a new totalitarian threat undermine Western power.

## The Truman Doctrine and the Marshall Plan

Whatever restraint the Soviet Union showed was too late or too little. Early in 1947, Truman acted decisively. The British could no longer afford to back the Greek government that was fighting a civil war against Communists, and U.S. officials feared that a Communist takeover in Greece would threaten the stability of Italy, France, and the Middle East. Truman coupled his case for intervention in Greece with an appeal for aid to neighboring Turkey, which lived under the shadow of the Soviet Union. On March 12, he told Congress that the United States faced a "fateful hour" and requested $400 million to fight Communism in Greece and Turkey and secure the free world. Congress agreed, and the United States became the dominant power in the eastern Mediterranean.

Framing the specific request was a sweeping declaration that became known as the **Truman Doctrine**. The president pledged to use U.S. economic power to help free nations everywhere resist internal subversion or aggression. "It must be the policy of the United States," he said, "to support free peoples who are resisting attempted subjugation by armed minorities or by outside pressures. . . . I believe that our help should be primarily through economic and financial aid, which is essential to economic stability and orderly political processes."

Meanwhile, Europe was sliding toward chaos. Germany was close to famine after the bitter winter of 1946–1947. Western European nations were bankrupt and unable to import raw materials for their factories. Overstressed medical systems could no longer control tuberculosis and other diseases. Communist parties had gained in Italy, France, and Germany.

The U.S. government responded with unprecedented economic aid. Secretary of State George C. Marshall announced the European Recovery Plan on June 5, 1947. What the press quickly dubbed the **Marshall Plan** committed the United States to help rebuild Europe. The United States invited Soviet and Eastern European participation, but under

**Truman Doctrine** President Harry Truman's statement in 1947 that the United States should assist other nations that were facing external pressure or internal revolution; an important step in the escalation of the Cold War.

**Marshall Plan** The European Recovery Program (1948–51), which provided U.S. economic assistance to European nations; named for Secretary of State George Marshall.

795

terms that would have reduced Moscow's control over its satellite economies. The Soviets refused, fearing that the United States wanted to undermine its influence, and instead organized their Eastern European satellites in their own association for Mutual Economic Assistance, or Comecon, in 1949. In Western Europe, the Marshall Plan was a success. Aid totaled $13.5 billion over four years. It met many of Europe's economic needs and quieted class conflict. The Marshall Plan expanded American influence through cooperative efforts. Because Europeans spent much of the aid on U.S. goods and machinery, and because economic recovery promised markets for U.S. products, business and labor both supported it. In effect, the Marshall Plan created an "empire by invitation," in which Americans and Europeans jointly planned Europe's recovery.

United States policy in Japan followed the pattern set in Europe. As supreme commander of the Allied Powers, General Douglas MacArthur acted as Japan's postwar dictator. He tried to change the values of the old war-prone Japan through social reform, democratization, and demilitarization. At the end of 1947, however, the United States decided that democracy and pacifism could go too far. Policymakers were fearful of economic collapse and political chaos, just as in Europe. The "reverse course" in occupation policy aimed to make Japan an economic magnet for other nations in East Asia, pulling them toward the American orbit and away from the Soviet Union.

## Soviet Reactions

The bold American moves in the first half of 1947 put the Soviet Union on the defensive. In response, Soviet leaders orchestrated strenuous opposition to the Marshall Plan by French and Italian Communists. East of the Iron Curtain, Hungarian Communists expelled other political parties from a coalition government. Bulgarian Communists shot opposition leaders. Romania, Bulgaria, and Hungary signed defense pacts with the Soviet Union.

In early 1948, the Soviets targeted Czechoslovakia. For three years, a neutral coalition government had balanced trade with the West with a foreign policy friendly to the Soviet Union. In February 1948, while Russian forces assembled on the Czech border, local Communists took advantage of political bumbling on the governing coalition. Taking control through a technically legal process, they pushed aside Czechoslovakia's democratic leadership and turned the nation into a dictatorship and Soviet satellite within a week.

The climax of the Soviet reaction came in divided Berlin, located 110 miles inside the Soviet Union's East German occupation zone. The city was divided into four sectors: one controlled by the Soviets and the others by the United States, Britain, and France. On June 4, 1948, Soviet troops blockaded surface traffic into Berlin, cutting off the U.S., British, and French sectors. The immediate Soviet aim was to block Western plans to merge their three German occupation zones into an independent federal republic (West Germany). Rather than abandon 2.5 million Berliners or shoot their way through, the Western nations responded to the **Berlin blockade** by airlifting supplies to the city. Stalin decided not to intercept the flights. After eleven months, the Soviets abandoned the blockade, making the Berlin airlift a triumph of American resolve.

## American Rearmament

The coup in Czechoslovakia and the Berlin blockade shocked American leaders and backfired on the Soviets. The economic assistance strategy of 1947 now looked inadequate. Congress responded in 1948 by reinstating the military draft and increasing defense spending. Much of the money bought new warplanes, as thrifty congressmen decided that air power was the easiest way for the United States to project its military power abroad.

The United States had already begun to modernize and centralize its national security apparatus, creating the institutions that would run foreign policy in the second half of the century. The National Security Act of July 1947 created the **Central Intelligence Agency (CIA)** and the **National Security Council (NSC)**. The CIA handled intelligence gathering and covert operations. The NSC assembled top diplomatic and

**Berlin blockade** A 300-day Soviet blockade of land access to U.S., British, and French occupation zones in Berlin, 1948–1949.

**Central Intelligence Agency (CIA)** Agency that coordinates the gathering and evaluation of military and economic information on other nations, established in 1947.

**National Security Council (NSC)** The formal policymaking body for national defense and foreign relations, created in 1947 and consisting of the president, the secretary of defense, the secretary of state, and others appointed by the president.

((• 📖 Read the Document   Harry S. Truman, The Truman Doctrine (1947)

27.1

27.2

27.3

27.4

27.5

Berlin was still a devastated city in 1948. When the Soviet Union closed off ground access to the British, French, and American occupation zones, the city became a symbol of the West's Cold War resolve. Allied aircraft lifted in food, fuel, and other essentials for West Berliners for nearly a year until the Soviets ended the blockade.

military advisers in one committee. In 1949, legislation also created the Department of Defense to oversee the army, navy, and air force (independent from the army since 1947). The civilian secretary of defense soon began to exercise influence on foreign policy equal to that of the secretary of state. The new post of chairman of the Joint Chiefs of Staff was supposed to coordinate the rival branches of the military.

In April 1949, ten European nations, the United States, and Canada signed the North Atlantic Treaty as a mutual defense pact. American commitments to the **North Atlantic Treaty Organization (NATO)** included military aid and the deployment of U.S. troops in Western Europe. NATO was the insurance policy that Western Europeans required to accept the economic and military revival of West Germany, which was necessary for a strong Europe. After 1955, its counterpart would be the **Warsaw Pact** for mutual defense among the Soviet Union and its European satellites (see Map 27.2).

Two years later, the United States signed similar but less comprehensive agreements in the western Pacific: the ANZUS Pact with Australia and New Zealand and a new treaty with the Philippines. The alliances reassured Pacific allies that were nervously watching the United States negotiate a unilateral peace treaty with Japan (ignoring the Soviet Union). The United States overcame opposition from nations Japan had attacked in World War II by promising to assist their defense and maintaining military bases in Japan. Taken together, peacetime rearmament and mutual defense pacts amounted to a revolution in American foreign policy.

**North Atlantic Treaty Organization (NATO)** Military alliance of the United States, Canada, and European nations created in 1949 to protect Europe against possible Soviet aggression.

**Warsaw Pact** Military alliance of the Soviet Union and Communist nations of Eastern Europe from 1955 to 1989.

((• 📖 Read the Document   Winston Churchill, "Iron Curtain" Speech (March 5, 1946)

**MAP 27.2  COLD WAR IN EUROPE**  In the late 1940s and 1950s, the Cold War split Europe into rigidly divided Western and Eastern blocs. Members of NATO allied with the United States to oppose Soviet expansion. The Soviet Union directed the military and foreign policies of members of the Warsaw Pact.

# Cold War and Hot War

 **27.4**   How did the Korean War shape American domestic politics?

The first phase of the Cold War reached a crisis in the autumn of 1949. Two key events seemed to tilt the world balance against the United States and its allies. In September, Truman announced that the Soviet Union had tested its own atomic bomb. A month later, the Communists under Mao Zedong (Mao Tse-tung) took power in China. The following summer, civil war in Korea sucked the United States into a fierce war with Communist North Korea and China.

## The Nuclear Shadow

Experts in Washington had known that the Soviets were working on an A-bomb, but the news dismayed the average citizen. As newspapers and magazines scared their

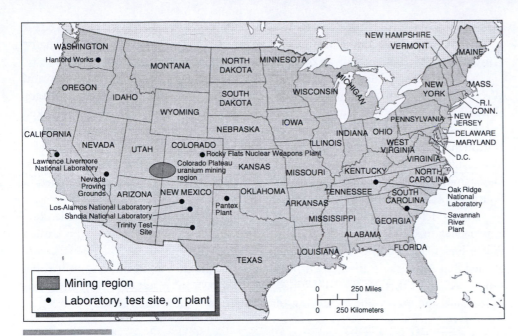

**MAP 27.3  THE LANDSCAPE OF NUCLEAR WEAPONS** The development and production of nuclear weapons were concentrated in the West and South. The World War II sites of Hanford, Los Alamos, and Oak Ridge remained active after the war. Workers at Savannah River, Rocky Flats, and Pantex produced nuclear materials. Scientists and engineers at Lawrence-Livermore and Sandia laboratories designed and assembled weapons that were tested at the Nevada Proving Grounds. Prospectors with Geiger counters swarmed over the canyons of southwestern Colorado and southeastern Utah in a uranium-mining rush in the early 1950s.

readers with artists' renditions of the effects of an atomic bomb on New York or Chicago, the shock tilted U.S. nuclear policy toward military uses. In 1946, advocates of civilian control had won a small victory when Congress established the Atomic Energy Commission (AEC). The AEC tried to balance research on atomic power with continued testing of new weapons. Now Truman told the AEC to double the output of fissionable uranium and plutonium for "conventional" nuclear weapons.

A more momentous decision soon followed. Truman decided in January 1950 to authorize work on the "super" bomb—the thermonuclear fusion weapon that would become the hydrogen bomb (H-bomb). The first hydrogen bomb test came in the South Pacific in November 1952. Releasing 100 times the energy of the Hiroshima bomb, the detonation tore a mile-long chasm in the ocean floor. Great Britain became the third nuclear power in the same year. The Soviet Union tested its own hydrogen bomb only nine months after the United States.

The nuclear arms race and the gnawing fear of nuclear war multiplied the apprehensions of the Cold War. Under the guidance of the Federal Civil Defense Administration, Americans learned that they should always keep a battery-powered radio and tune to 640 or 1240 on the AM dial for emergency information when they heard air raid sirens. Schoolchildren learned to hide under their desks when they saw the blinding flash of a nuclear detonation.

More insidiously, nuclear weapons development generated new environmental and health problems. Soldiers were exposed to posttest radiation with minimal protection. Nuclear tests in the South Pacific dusted fishing boats with radioactivity and forced islanders to abandon contaminated homes. Las Vegas promoted tests in southern Nevada as tourist attractions, but radioactive fallout contaminated large sections of the West and increased cancer rates among "downwinders" in Utah. Weapons production and atomic experiments contaminated vast tracts in Nevada, Washington, and Colorado and left huge environmental costs for later generations (see Map 27.3).

## The Cold War in Asia

Communist victory in China's civil war was as predictable as the Soviet nuclear bomb but no less controversial. The collapse of Jiang Jieshi's Nationalist regime was nearly inevitable, given its corruption and narrow support. Nevertheless, Americans looked for a scapegoat when Jiang's anti-Communist government and remnants of the Nationalist army fled to the island of Taiwan off China's southern coast.

Advocates for Jiang, mostly conservative Republicans from the Midwest and West, were certain that Truman's administration had done too little. "China asked for a sword," complained one senator, "and we gave her a dull paring knife." Critics looked for scapegoats. Foreign Service officers who had honestly analyzed the weakness of the Nationalists were accused of Communist sympathies and hounded from their jobs. The results were tragedy for those unfairly branded as traitors and damage to the State Department, a weakness that would haunt the United States as it became entangled in Southeast Asia in the 1950s and 1960s.

Mao's victory expanded a deep fissure between the "Europe first" and "Asia first" approaches to U.S. foreign policy. Both during and after World War II, the United States had made Europe its first priority. Strong voices, however, had persistently argued that America's future lay with China, Japan, and the Pacific nations. Influential senators claimed that the "loss of China" was the disastrous result of putting the needs of England and France above the long-term interests of the United States.

## NSC-68 and Aggressive Containment

**National Security Council Paper 68 (NSC-68)** Policy statement that committed the United States to a military approach to the Cold War.

The turmoil of 1949 led to a comprehensive statement of American strategic goals. In April 1950, the State Department prepared a sweeping report known as **National Security Council Paper 68 (NSC-68)**. The document described a world divided between the forces of "slavery" and "freedom" and assumed that the Soviet Union was actively aggressive, motivated by greed for territory and a "fanatic faith" in Communism. To defend civilization itself, said the experts, the United States should use as much force as needed to resist Communist expansion anywhere and everywhere.

**containment** The policy of resisting further expansion of the Soviet bloc through diplomacy and, if necessary, military action, developed in 1947–1948.

The authors of NSC-68 thought in terms of military solutions. In the original **containment** policy, Truman and his advisers had hoped to contain the Soviets by diplomacy and by integrating the economies of Europe and Japan with that of the United States. Now that the Soviets had the atomic bomb, however, the American atomic shield might be neutralized. Instead, NSC-68 argued that the United States needed to press friendly nations to rearm and make its former enemies into military allies. It also argued that the nation needed expensive conventional forces to defend Europe on the ground and to react to crises as a "world policeman." NSC-68 thus advocated nearly open-ended increases in the defense budget (which, in fact, tripled between 1950 and 1954).

The thinking behind the report led the United States to approach the Cold War as a military competition and to view political changes in Africa and Asia as parts of a Soviet plan. The need for a flexible military response became the centerpiece of a U.S. policy of active intervention that led eventually to the jungles of Vietnam in the 1960s. And the report's implied strategy of bankrupting the Communists through competitive defense spending helped destroy the Soviet Union at the end of the 1980s.

## War in Korea, 1950–1953

The success of Mao and the Chinese Communists forced the Truman administration to define national interests in eastern Asia and the western Pacific. Most important was Japan, still a potential industrial power despite its devastating defeat. The United States had denied the Soviet Union any part in the occupation of Japan in 1945 and had shaped a more democratic nation that would be a friendly trading partner. Protected by American armed forces, Japan would be part of a crescent of offshore strong points that included Alaska, Okinawa, the Philippines, Australia, and New Zealand.

Two questions remained at the start of 1950 (and were still troublesome in the twenty-first century). One was the future of Taiwan and the remnants of Jiang's regime. Some American policymakers wanted to defend Jiang against the Communists. Others assumed that his tattered forces would collapse and allow Mao to complete the

United Nation forces in Korea fought the weather as well as Communist North Koreans and Chinese. Baking summer heat alternated with fierce winters. Snow and cold were a major help to the Chinese when they surprised U.S. forces in November 1950 and drove American troops such as these southward.

Communist takeover of Chinese territory. The other question was Korea, whose own civil war would soon bring the world to the brink of World War III.

The Korean Peninsula is the closest point on the Asian mainland to Japan. With three powerful neighbors—China, Russia, and Japan—Korea had always had to fight for its independence. From 1910 to 1945, it was an oppressed colony of the Japanese Empire. As World War II ended, Soviet troops moved down the peninsula from the north and American forces landed in the south, creating a situation similar to that in Germany. The 38th parallel, which Russians and Americans set as the dividing line between their zones of occupation, became a de facto border. The United States in 1948 recognized an independent South Korea, with its capital at Seoul, under a conservative government led by Syngman Rhee. Rhee's support came from large landowners and from a police force trained by the Japanese before 1945. The Soviets recognized a separate North Korea, whose Communist leader, Kim Il Sung, advocated radical social and political change. Both leaders saw the 38th parallel as a temporary barrier and hoped to unify all Koreans under their own rule. Each crushed political dissent and tried to undermine the other with economic pressure and commando raids.

As early as 1947, the United States had decided that Korea was not essential to American military strategy. Planners assumed that U.S. air power in Japan could neutralize unfriendly forces on the Korean Peninsula. In January 1950, Secretary of State Dean Acheson carefully excluded Korea from the primary "defensive perimeter" of the United States but kept open the possibility of international guarantees for Korean security.

# ✳ Explore the Korean War on MyHistoryLab

## WHY DID CONFLICT COME TO THE KOREAN PENINSULA?

After the defeat of Germany and Japan in World War II, many Americans feared a new foe: communism and its spread. The Korean Peninsula, which had been controlled by the Japanese Empire, was divided in two occupation areas after the war, with the Soviet Union controlling the north and the United States in the south. Though allies in World War II, relations between the United States and the Soviet Union chilled as Americans worried that the Soviets were trying to spread communism across the globe. The Soviet Union set up a communist government in its zone of Korea while the United States worked for a market-friendly administration in the south. Soon hostilities broke out on the peninsula in June 1950 as the North launched a surprise attack on the South. What followed was a war over ideology that ended in a stalemate three years later.

U.S. F-86 Sabre fighter jets like this one saw much action against the comparable MiG 15s used by China during the Korean War.

## CIVILIAN DEATHS IN THE KOREAN WAR

TOTAL DEATHS: 2.8 MILLION

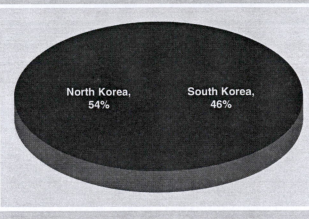

North Korea, 54%    South Korea, 46%

---

**KEY QUESTIONS**    Use **MyHistoryLab** *Explorer* to **answer** these **questions:**

**Response ▶▶▶** *How was communism portrayed in the United States during this time?*

Consider the public response to this ideology and to the Korean War.

**Analysis ▶▶▶** *How did the two sides fare in the war as it unfolded?*

Map troop movements and advancements on the Korean Peninsula.

**Cause ▶▶▶** *Why did the warring parties get involved in the conflict?*

Understand the rationale for the involvement of various players.

On June 25, 1950, North Korea, helped by Soviet equipment and Chinese training, attacked South Korea. The invasion began the **Korean War,** which lasted until 1953. Truman and Acheson believed that Moscow lay behind the invasion. In fact, Kim originated the invasion plan because he seemed to be losing the civil war in the south, and he spent a year persuading Stalin to agree to it. Stalin hoped that the conquest of South Korea would force Japan to sign a favorable treaty with the Soviet Union.

American leaders thought that the explosion of a hot war after five years of world tension demanded a military response. As the South Korean army collapsed, Truman committed American ground troops from Japan on June 30. The United States also had the good fortune of securing an endorsement from the United Nations. Because the Soviet Union was temporarily boycotting the UN, it could not use its veto when the Security Council asked UN members to help South Korea. The Korean conflict remained officially a UN action. Although U.S. generals ran the show, twenty-one other nations committed military resources in a true multinational coalition.

**Korean War** War between North Korea and South Korea (1950–1953) in which the People's Republic of China fought on the side of North Korea and the United States and other nations fought on the side of South Korea under the auspices of the United Nations.

## The Politics of War

Fortunes in the first year of the Korean conflict seesawed three times. The first U.S. combat troops were outnumbered, outgunned, and unable to stop the North Koreans. By early August, Americans clung to a narrow toehold around the port of Pusan on the tip of the Korean Peninsula. As reinforcements arrived, however, General Douglas MacArthur transformed the war with a daring amphibious counterattack at Inchon, 150 miles behind North Korean lines. The overextended North Korean army collapsed and fled north.

The temptation to push across the 38th parallel and unify the peninsula under Syngman Rhee was irresistible. MacArthur and Washington officials disregarded warnings by China that it would enter the war if the United States tried to reunite Korea by force. United States and South Korean troops rolled north, drawing closer and closer to the boundary between North Korea and China.

Chinese forces attacked MacArthur's command in late October but then disappeared. MacArthur dismissed the attacks as a token gesture. In fact, they were a final warning. On November 26, the Chinese struck the American columns with 300,000 troops who had gone undetected by American aviation. Their assault drove the UN forces into a two-month retreat that again abandoned Seoul.

Despite his glaring mistake, MacArthur remained in command until he publicly contradicted national policy. In March 1951, with the UN forces again pushing north, Truman prepared to offer a cease-fire that would have preserved the separate nations of South and North Korea. MacArthur tried to preempt the president by demanding that China admit defeat or suffer the consequences. He then published a direct attack on the administration's policy of limiting the Asian war to ensure the security of Europe. President Truman had no choice. To protect civilian control of the armed forces, he relieved MacArthur of his command on April 11, 1951. In Korea itself, U.S. and South Korean forces stabilized a strong defensive line that cut diagonally across the 38th parallel. Here the conflict settled into trench warfare. What had started as a civil war was now an international conflict between the two sides in the larger Cold War. The war's only glamour was in the air, where the arrival of new F-86 Sabrejets in 1952 allowed American pilots to clear the skies of Chinese aviators in Russian-made MiG-15s.

Stabilization of the Korean front ushered in two years of truce negotiations beginning in July 1951, for none of the key actors wanted a wider war. The Chinese were careful to keep their warplanes north of the ground combat zone. The Russians stayed out of the war. The United States learned a painful lesson in 1950 and was willing to accept a divided Korea.

Negotiations stalled over thousands of Chinese prisoners of war who might not want to return to China. The political decision to turn free choice for POWs into a symbol of resistance to Communism left Truman's administration bogged down in a grinding war. Nearly half of the 140,000 U.S. casualties came after the truce talks started. The war was a decisive factor behind the Republican victory in the November 1952 elections and dragged on until June 1953, when an armistice returned the peninsula roughly to its prewar political division, a situation that endured into the twenty-first century.

The blindly ambitious attack into North Korea was a great failure of intelligence and strategic leadership. Nearly everyone in Washington shared the blame. Civilian leaders could not resist the desire to roll back Communism. Truman hoped for a striking victory before the 1950 congressional elections. The Joint Chiefs of Staff failed to effectively challenge a general with MacArthur's heroic reputation. MacArthur himself allowed ambition and wishful thinking to jeopardize his army.

**Consequences of the Korean War.**   The war in Korea was a preview of Vietnam fifteen years later. American leaders propped up an undemocratic regime to defend democracy. Both North Koreans and South Koreans engaged in savage political reprisals as the battlefront shifted back and forth. American soldiers found it hard to distinguish between allied and enemy Koreans. American emphasis on massive firepower led U.S. forces to demolish entire villages to kill single snipers. The air force tried to break North Korean resistance by pouring bombs on cities, power stations, factories, and dams; General Curtis Le May estimated that the bombings killed a million Koreans.

The Korean War had global consequences. It helped to legitimize the United Nations and set a precedent for its peacekeeping role in places like the Middle East. In Washington, it confirmed the ideas underlying NSC-68. Two days after the North Korean invasion, President Truman ordered the Seventh Fleet to interpose between mainland China and the Nationalist Chinese on Taiwan, a decision that guaranteed twenty years of hostility between the United States and China. In the same month, the United States began to aid France's struggle to retain control over its Southeast Asian colony of Indochina, which included Laos, Cambodia, and Vietnam. It did so even as it encouraged European nations to grant independence to other colonies farther from China.

In Europe, the United States now pushed to rearm West Germany as part of a militarized NATO and sent troops to Europe as a permanent defense force. Rearmament also stimulated German economic recovery and bound West Germany to the political and economic institutions of the North Atlantic nations. In 1952, the European Coal and Steel Community marked an important step toward economic cooperation that would evolve into the European Union by the end of the century. Dwight Eisenhower, who had led the Western allies in the invasion of France and Germany, became the new NATO commander in April 1951; his appointment symbolized the American commitment to Western Europe.

# The Second Red Scare

 **27.5**   Why did fear of Communism escalate in the years following World War II?

The "second Red Scare" was an assault on civil liberties that stretched from the mid-1940s to the mid-1950s. Political conflicts over domestic policy and fears of the deepening Cold War both fueled worries about Soviet spying and subversion. The outbreak of war in Korea added to the perfect storm of fears about the loyalty of fellow Americans. The result dwarfed the Red Scare of 1919–1920. Legitimate concerns about espionage mixed with suspicions that Communist sympathizers in high places were helping Stalin and Mao. The scare was also a weapon that the conservative wing of the Republican Party used against the men and women who had built Roosevelt's New Deal. (See Table 27.1.)

((• 📖 **Read the Document**    Ronald Reagan, Testimony Before the House Un-American Activities Committee (1947)

TABLE 27.1  THE SECOND RED SCARE

| Type of Anti-Communist Effort | Key Tools | Results |
|---|---|---|
| Employee loyalty programs | Executive orders by Truman and Eisenhower U.S. attorney general's list of subversive organizations | Thousands of federal and state workers fired, careers damaged |
| Congressional investigations | HUAC McCarran Committee Army-McCarthy hearings | Employee blacklists, investigation of writers and intellectuals, Hollywood Ten |
| Criminal prosecutions | Trials for espionage and conspiracy to advocate violent overthrow of the U.S. government | Convictions of Communist Party leaders (1949), Alger Hiss (1950), and Rosenbergs (1951) |
| Restrictions on Communist Party | Internal Security Act (1950) Communist Control Act (1954) | Marginalization of far left in labor unions and politics |

Efforts to root out suspected subversives operated on three tracks. National and state governments established loyalty programs to identify and fire suspect employees. The courts punished members of suspect organizations. Congressional and state legislative investigations followed the whims of committee chairs. Anti-Communist crusaders often relied on dubious evidence and eagerly believed the worst. They also threatened basic civil liberties.

## The Communist Party and the Loyalty Program

The Communist Party in the United States was in rapid decline as a political factor after World War II. Many intellectuals had left the party over the Nazi-Soviet Pact in 1939. The Congress of Industrial Organizations (CIO) and United Auto Workers unions froze Communists out of leadership positions, bringing industrial unions into the American mainstream. President Truman responded to the Republican landslide in 1946 with Executive Order 9835 in March 1947, initiating a loyalty program for federal employees. Truman may have been trying to head off more drastic action by Congress. Nevertheless, Order 9835 was a blunt instrument. It authorized the attorney general to prepare a list of "totalitarian, Fascist, Communist, or subversive" organizations and made membership or even "sympathetic association" with such groups grounds for dismissal. The loyalty program applied to approximately 8 million Americans working for the federal government or defense contractors; similar state laws affected another 5 million.

Federal employees worked under a cloud of fear. Would the cooperative store they had once patronized or the protest group they had joined in college suddenly appear on the attorney general's list? Would someone complain that they had disloyal books on their shelves? Loyalty boards asked about religion, racial equality, and a taste for foreign films. They also tried to identify homosexuals, who were thought to be targets for blackmail by foreign agents. The loyalty program resulted in 1,210 firings and 6,000 resignations under Truman and comparable numbers during Dwight Eisenhower's first term from 1953 to 1956.

## Naming Names to Congress

Congress was even busier than the executive branch. The congressional hunt for subversives had its roots in 1938, when Congressman Martin Dies, a Texas Democrat, created the Special Committee on Un-American Activities. Originally intended to ferret out pro-fascists, the Dies Committee evolved into the permanent **House Committee on Un-American Activities (HUAC)** in 1945. It investigated "un-American propaganda" that attacked constitutional government.

**House Un-American Activities Committee** Congressional committee (1938–1975) that investigated suspected Nazi and Communist sympathizers.

One of HUAC's juiciest targets was Hollywood, whose reputation for loose morals, foreign-born directors, Jewish producers, and left-leaning writers aroused the suspicions of many congressmen. HUAC sought to make sure that no un-American messages were being peddled through America's most popular entertainment.

When the hearings opened in October 1947, studio executives Jack Warner of Warner Brothers and Louis B. Mayer of MGM assured HUAC of their anti-Communism. So did the popular actors Gary Cooper and Ronald Reagan. By contrast, eight screenwriters and two directors—the so-called Hollywood Ten—refused to discuss their past political associations, citing the free-speech protections of the First Amendment to the Constitution. HUAC countered with citations for contempt of Congress. The First Amendment defense failed when it reached the Supreme Court, and the Ten went to jail in 1950. Other actors, writers, and directors found themselves on the Hollywood blacklist, banned from jobs where they might insert Communist propaganda into American movies.

At the start of 1951, the new Senate Internal Security Subcommittee went into action. The McCarran Committee, named for the Nevada senator who chaired it, targeted diplomats, labor union leaders, professors, and school teachers. Both committees turned their investigations into rituals. The real point was not to force personal confessions from witnesses but to badger them into identifying friends and associates who might have been involved in suspect activities.

State legislatures imitated Congress by searching for "Reducators" among college faculty in such states as Oklahoma, Washington, and California. College presidents frequently fired faculty who took the Fifth Amendment. Harvard apparently used its influence to stay out of the newspapers, cutting a deal in which the FBI fed it information about suspect faculty, whom the university quietly fired. More common was the experience of the economics professor fired from the University of Kansas City after testifying before the McCarran Committee. He found it hard to keep any job once his name had been in the papers. A local dairy fired him because it thought its customers might be uneasy having a radical handle their milk bottles.

## Subversion Trials

In 1948, the Justice Department indicted the leaders of the American Communist Party under the Alien Registration Act of 1940. Eleven men and women were convicted in 1949 of conspiring to advocate the violent overthrow of the U. S. government through their speech and publications.

The case of Alger Hiss soon followed. In 1948, a former Communist, Whittaker Chambers, named Hiss as a Communist with whom he had associated in the 1930s. Hiss, who had held important posts in the State Department, first denied knowing Chambers but then admitted to having known him under another name. He continued to deny any involvement with Communists and sued Chambers for slander. As proof, Chambers revealed microfilms that he had hidden inside a pumpkin on his Maryland farm, and Congressman Richard Nixon quickly announced the discovery. Tests seemed to show that the "pumpkin papers" were State Department documents that had been copied on a typewriter Hiss had once owned. With the new evidence, the Justice Department indicted Hiss for perjury—lying under oath. A first perjury trial ended in deadlock, but a second jury convicted Hiss in January 1950.

Hiss was a potent symbol as well as a possible spy. To his opponents, Hiss stood for every wrong turn the nation had taken since 1932. In contrast, his supporters found a virtue in every trait his enemies hated, from his refined taste to his education at Johns Hopkins University and Harvard Law School. Many supporters believed that he had been framed. However, Soviet records and American intelligence intercepts that became public in the 1990s confirm that he did indeed spy for the Soviets from the mid-1930s through 1945.

The case of Julius and Ethel Rosenberg represented a similar test of belief. In 1950, the British arrested nuclear physicist Klaus Fuchs, who confessed to passing atomic secrets to the Soviets when he worked at Los Alamos in 1944 and 1945. The "Fuchs spy ring" soon implicated the Rosenbergs, New York radicals of strong beliefs but limited sophistication. Convicted in 1951 on the vague charge of conspiring to commit espionage, they were sent to the electric chair in 1953 after refusing to buy a reprieve by naming other spies.

As with Alger Hiss, the government had a plausible but not airtight case. After their trial, the Rosenbergs became a cause for international protest. Their small children became pawns and trophies in political demonstrations. There is now no doubt that Julius Rosenberg was an important part of a successful Soviet spy ring that passed atomic secrets to the Soviets, but Ethel Rosenberg's involvement was limited. In the words of FBI director J. Edgar Hoover, the government charged her "as a lever" to pressure her husband into naming his confederates. More broadly, Hiss and Rosenberg were only the most prominent of more than a hundred Americans who were Soviet agents and spies, many of whom escaped detection and punishment.

## Senator McCarthy on Stage

The best-remembered participant in the second Red Scare was Senator Joseph McCarthy of Wisconsin. Crude, sly, and ambitious, McCarthy had ridden to victory in the Republican landslide of 1946. He burst into national prominence on February 9, 1950. In a rambling speech in Wheeling, West Virginia, he latched on to the issue of Communist subversion. Although no transcript of the speech survives, he supposedly stated, "I have here in my hand a list of 205 that were known to the Secretary of State as being members of the Communist Party and who, nevertheless, are still working and shaping the policy of the State Department." In the following days, the 205 Communists changed quickly to 57, to 81, to 10, to 116. McCarthy's rise to fame climaxed with an incoherent six-hour speech to the Senate. Over the next several years, his speeches were aimed at moving targets, full of multiple untruths. He threw out so many accusations, true or false, that the facts could never catch up.

The Senate disregarded McCarthy, but the public heard only the accusations, not the lack of evidence. Senators treated McCarthy as a crude outsider in their exclusive club, but voters in 1950 turned against his most prominent opponents. Liberal politicians ran for cover; conservatives were happy for McCarthy to attract media attention away from HUAC and the McCarran Committee. In 1951, McCarthy even called George Marshall, then serving as secretary of defense, an agent of Communism. The idea was ludicrous. Marshall was one of the most upright Americans of his generation, the architect of victory in World War II, and a key contributor to the stabilization of Europe. Nevertheless, McCarthy was so popular that the Republicans featured him at their 1952 convention and their presidential candidate, Dwight Eisenhower, conspicuously failed to defend Marshall, who had been chiefly responsible for Eisenhower's fast-track career.

McCarthy's personal crudeness made him a media star but eventually undermined him. Given control of the Senate Committee on Government Operations in 1953, he investigated dozens of agencies from the Government Printing Office to the Army Signal Corps. Early in 1954, he investigated an army dentist with a supposedly subversive background. The back-and-forth confrontation led to two months of televised hearings. The cameras brought political debates into living rooms and put McCarthy's bullying style on trial. "Have you no decency?" asked the army's lawyer, Joseph Welch, at one point.

The end came quickly. McCarthy's "favorable" rating in the polls plummeted. The U.S. Senate finally voted 67 to 22 in December 1954 to condemn McCarthy for conduct "unbecoming a Member of the Senate." When he died in 1957, he had been repudiated by the Senate and ignored by the media that had built him up.

Senator Joe McCarthy used press releases and carefully managed congressional committee hearings to attack suspected Communists, although he had almost no hard information. At the Army-McCarthy hearings in June 1954, he clashed with attorney Joseph Welch. Here Welch listens as McCarthy points to Oregon on a map that supposedly showed Communist Party organization in the United States.

## Understanding McCarthyism

**McCarthyism** Anti-communist attitudes and actions associated with Senator Joe McCarthy in the early 1950s, including smear tactics and innuendo.

The antisubversive campaign that everyone now calls **McCarthyism**, however, died a slower death. It had actually originated with the Truman administration, and laws such as the Internal Security Act (1950) and the Immigration and Nationality Act (1952), remained as tools of political control during the Eisenhower administration. HUAC continued to mount investigations as late as the 1960s.

In retrospect, at least four factors made Americans afraid of Communist subversion. One was the legitimate concern about atomic spies. The Soviet Union had developed an extensive espionage network in the early 1940s. More than a few U.S. officials passed on secret information, some of it dangerous to national security. A second was an undercurrent of anti-Semitism and nativism, for many labor organizers and Communist Party members (like the Rosenbergs) had Jewish and Eastern European backgrounds. Third was southern and western resentment of the nation's Ivy League elite. Fourth, and most prevalent, was a widespread fear that the world was spinning out of control. Many people sought easy explanations for global tensions. It was basically reassuring if Soviet and Chinese Communist successes were the result of American traitors rather than of Communist strengths.

Partisan politics mobilized the fears and resentments into a political force. From 1946 through 1952, the conservative wing of the Republican Party used the Red Scare to attack New Dealers and liberal Democrats. HUAC, the McCarran Committee, and McCarthy were all tools for bringing down the men and women who had been moving the United States toward a more active government at home and abroad. The Republican elite used McCarthy until they won control of the presidency and Congress in 1952, and then abandoned him.

The broader goal of the second Red Scare was conformity of thought. Many of the professors and bureaucrats targeted for investigation had indeed been Communists or interested in Communism, usually in the 1930s and early 1940s. Most saw it as a way to increase social justice, and they sometimes excused the failures of Communism in the Soviet Union. Unlike the handful of real spies, however, they were targeted not for actions but for ideas. The investigations and loyalty programs were efforts to ensure that Americans kept any left-wing ideas to themselves.

## Conclusion

Despite the turmoil and injustice of the second Red Scare and deep worries about nuclear war, the United States emerged from the Truman years remarkably prosperous. It was also more secure from international threats than many nervous Americans appreciated. The years from 1946 to 1952 set the themes for a generation that believed that the United States could do whatever it set its mind to: end poverty, land an astronaut on the moon, thwart Communist revolutions in other countries. There was a direct line from Harry Truman's 1947 declaration that the United States would defend freedom around the world to John Kennedy's 1961 promise that the nation would bear any burden necessary to protect free nations from Communism. As the world moved slowly toward greater stability in the 1950s, Americans were ready for a decade of confidence.

**For Suggested Readings go to MyHistoryLab.**

# Chapter Review

## Launching the Great Boom

**27.1** What was the catalyst for the economic boom that began in 1947? p. 783

Americans approached the conversion from wartime to peacetime with fear of a renewed economic depression. Instead, the pent-up demand for housing and consumer goods and the beginnings of the "baby boom" soon fed a new surge of economic growth, although labor-management relations remained contentious.

## Truman, Republicans, and the Fair Deal

**27.2** How was Harry Truman able to win the 1948 presidential election? p. 788

President Truman surprised political experts and confounded Republicans by winning reelection in 1948 against a divided opposition. His administration was able to protect the programs of the New Deal but not to pass major new initiatives.

## Confronting the Soviet Union

 **27.3** What were the origins of the Cold War? p. 793

The wartime alliance among the United States, Britain, and the Soviet Union came apart in 1946 and 1947 because of differing interests and expectations for the future of Europe and the Middle East. The United States cemented ties with Western Europe through the Marshall Plan and NATO while the Soviet Union took similar steps in Eastern Europe. By the end of the decade, a politically divided world had settled into forty years of Cold War.

## Cold War and Hot War

 **27.4** How did the Korean War shape American domestic politics? p. 798

The focus of the Cold War shifted to Asia in 1949, with Communist victory in China, and in 1950, with the outbreak of war in Korea. The armed confrontation of the Korean War ushered in a massive expansion of American military capacity and presence around the world.

## The Second Red Scare

**27.5** Why did fear of Communism escalate in the years following World War II? p. 804

The deepening Cold War, fears of Soviet nuclear weapons, and bitter political divisions at home fueled fears of internal subversion in the late 1940s and 1950s. The danger of Soviet espionage was real, but efforts to ensure loyalty reached beyond what was necessary for national security.

# Timeline

**1946**
**The Great Boom—** Employment Act creates Council of Economic Advisers
**The Soviet Union—** Winston Churchill delivers his "iron curtain" speech

**1947**
**The Soviet Union—** Truman Doctrine is announced; Marshall Plan begins providing economic aid to Europe
**The Great Boom—** Taft-Hartley Act rolls back gains of organized labor

**1948**
**The Soviet Union—** Berlin airlift overcomes Soviet blockade

**1949**
**The Soviet Union—** North Atlantic Treaty Organization is formed

**1950**
**Second Red Scare—** Senator Joseph McCarthy begins his Red hunt
**Cold War and Hot War—** NSC-68 is drafted and accepted as U.S. policy; Korean War begins

**1951**
**Second Red Scare—** Julius and Ethel Rosenberg are convicted of conspiring to commit espionage

**1952**
**Cold War and Hot War—** United States tests the hydrogen bomb

# 28 The Confident Years 1953–1964

## One American Journey

### Oral History with Little Rock Student

**T**he first day I was able to enter Central High School [in Little Rock, Arkansas, September 23, 1957], what I felt inside was terrible, wrenching, awful fear. On the car radio I could hear that there was a mob. I knew what a mob meant and I knew that the sounds that came from the crowd were very angry. So we entered the side of the building, very, very fast. Even as we entered there were people running after us, people tripping other people. There has never been in my life any stark terror or any fear akin to that. I'd only been in the school a couple of hours and by that time it was apparent that the mob was just overrunning the school. Policemen were throwing down their badges and the mob was getting past the wooden sawhorses because the police would no longer fight their own in order to protect us. So we were all called into the principal's office, and there was great fear that we would not get out of this building. . . . Even the adults, the school officials, were panicked, feeling like there was no protection. . . . [A] gentleman, who I believed to be the police chief, said . . . "I'll get them out." And we were taken to the basement of this

On August 28, 1963, Rev. Martin Luther King, Jr. delivered his famous "I Have a Dream" speech to the March on Washington for Jobs and Freedom. The address was a climactic moment in the civil rights movement, encapsulating the optimism of decades of struggle, but the March on Washington also papered over emerging divisions that would become apparent later in the 1960s.

## LEARNING OBJECTIVES

| 28.1 | 28.2 | 28.3 | 28.4 | 28.5 |
|---|---|---|---|---|
| How did the "Decade of Affluence" alter social and religious life in America? p. 813 | What impact did Dwight Eisenhower's foreign policy have on U.S. relations with the Soviet Union? p. 822 | What was John F. Kennedy's approach to dealing with the Soviet Union? p. 827 | What was the significance of *Brown v. Board of Education of Topeka?* p. 832 | How did Lyndon B. Johnson continue the domestic agenda inherited from the Kennedy administration? In what ways did he depart from it? p. 839 |

((• Listen to Chapter 28 on MyHistoryLab

From *The American Journey*, Seventh Edition. Goldfield, Abbott, Anderson, Argersinger, Argersinger and Barney.

#  Watch the Video Series on MyHistoryLab

Learn about some key topics related to this chapter with the *MyHistoryLab Video Series: Key Topics in U.S. History.*

**1**  **The Affluent Society: 1953–1960**  Americans in the 1950s faced a changing society, workplace, economy, and popular culture following the end of the Korean War, overshadowed by the ever-present threat of nuclear annihilation. This video surveys many issues and groups, from labor unions to women, who, in the domestic sphere of the growing American suburbs, were seen by advertisers as key decision makers regarding the goods and services that comprised the so-called "Affluent Society."

Watch on MyHistoryLab

**The Suburban Ideal**  This video profiles the young veterans of World War II and the Korean War whose desire to start a family and own a home led to the "baby boom" of the 1950s and the explosive growth of American suburbs. Not all Americans, however, saw the consumerism, careerism, and conformity as a positive development, given the cultural achievements of the Beat Generation and the rise of rock-and-roll with its inherent message of rebellion.  **2**

Watch on MyHistoryLab

**3**  **The Age of Ike**  The administration of President Dwight Eisenhower adopted a very confrontational position in relation to communism around the globe, as this video demonstrates. While the Departments of State and Defense as well as the Central Intelligence Agency carried out the "policy of containment" on a global scale, Eisenhower saw, however, that protecting the United States from communism entailed reliance on a "military-industrial complex"—an interdependence of government, American industry, and the U.S. military—that endangered the very nature of the American republic.

Watch on MyHistoryLab

**The Civil Rights Movement**  The Supreme Court decision of *Brown v. Board of Education* (1954) became the first key event in the civil rights movement. This video looks at the impact and enforcement of that decision, and then discusses the efforts of Martin Luther King, Jr. and many others to overturn the Jim Crow laws of the South, using legal and nonviolent strategies such as the Montgomery (Alabama) bus boycott, to pave the way for the Civil Rights Act of 1964.  **4**

Watch on MyHistoryLab

place. And we were put into two cars, grayish blue Fords. And the man instructed the drivers, he said, "Once you start driving, do not stop." And he told us to put our heads down. This guy revved up his engine and he came up out of the bowels of this building, and as he came up, I could just see hands reaching across this car, I could hear the yelling, I could see guns, and he was told not to stop. "If you hit somebody, you keep rolling, 'cause the kids are dead." And he did just that, and he didn't hit anybody, but he certainly was forceful and aggressive in the way he exited this driveway, because people tried to stop him and he didn't stop. He dropped me off at home. And I remember saying, "Thank you for the ride," and I should've said, "Thank you for my life."

Melba Patillo Beals, in Henry Hampton and Steve Frayer, eds., *Voices of Freedom: An Oral History of the Civil Rights Movement from the 1950s through the 1980s.* Published by Bantam, 1990. Copyrighted by Blackside Inc.

## Personal Journeys Online

**M**elba Pattillo was one of the nine African American students who entered previously all-white Central High in the fall of 1957. Her enrollment in the high school, where she managed to last through a year of harassment and hostility, was a symbolic step in the journey toward greater racial equality in U.S. society. School integration in Little Rock implemented the U.S. Supreme Court decision in the case of *Brown v. Board of Education* in 1954, which declared that racially segregated schools violated the mandate that all citizens receive equal protection of the law. The violence with which some white residents of Little Rock responded, and the courage of the students, marked one of the key episodes in the long campaign for equal civil rights.

The struggle for full civil rights for all Americans was rooted in national ideals, but it was also shaped by the continuing tensions of the Cold War. President Dwight Eisenhower acted against his own inclinations and sent federal troops to keep the peace in Little Rock in part because he worried about public opinion in other nations. As the United States and the Soviet Union maneuvered for influence in Africa and Asia, domestic events sometimes loomed large in foreign relations.

Despite challenges at home and abroad, Americans were fundamentally confident during the decade after the Korean War. They expected corporations to use scientific research to craft new products for eager customers and medical researchers to conquer diseases. When the Soviet Union challenged U.S. preeminence and launched the first artificial space satellite in 1957, Americans responded with shock followed by redoubled efforts to regain what they considered their rightful world leadership in science and technology.

# A Decade of Affluence

**28.1** How did the "Decade of Affluence" alter social and religious life in America?

**A**mericans in the 1950s believed in the basic strength of the United States. Television's *General Electric Theater* was third in the ratings in 1956–1957. Every week its host, Ronald Reagan, a popular Hollywood lead from the late 1930s, stated, "At General Electric, progress is our most important product." It made sense to his viewers. Large, technologically sophisticated corporations were introducing new marvels: orlon sweaters and Saran Wrap, long-playing records and Polaroid cameras. As long as the United States defended free enterprise, Reagan told audiences on national speaking tours, the sky was the limit.

## What's Good for General Motors

Dwight Eisenhower presided over the prosperity of the 1950s. Both Democrats and Republicans had courted him as a presidential candidate in 1948. Four years later, he picked the Republicans because he wanted to make sure that the party remained committed to NATO and collective security in Europe rather than retreat into isolationism. He easily defeated the Democratic candidate, Adlai Stevenson, the moderately liberal governor of Illinois.

**Eisenhower and the Politics of the Middle.** Over the next eight years, Eisenhower claimed the political middle for Republicans. Satisfied with postwar America, Eisenhower accepted much of the New Deal but saw little need for further reform. In a 1959 poll, liberals considered him a fellow liberal and conservatives thought him a conservative. Eisenhower's first secretary of defense, "Engine Charlie" Wilson, had headed General Motors. At his Senate confirmation hearing, he proclaimed, "For years, I thought what was good for the country was good for General Motors and vice versa." Wilson's statement captured a central theme of the 1950s. Not since the 1920s had Americans been so excited about the benefits of big business.

**The New Prosperity.** The economy in the 1950s gave Americans much to like. Between 1950 and 1964, output grew by a solid 3.2 percent per year. American workers in the 1950s had more disposable income than ever before. Their productivity, or output per worker, increased steadily. Average compensation per hour of work rose faster than consumer prices in nine of eleven years from 1953 to 1964. Rising productivity made it easy for corporations to share gains with large labor unions. The steel and auto industries set the pace with contracts that gave their workers a middle-class way of life. In turn, labor leaders lost interest in making radical changes in American society. In 1955, the older and politically more conservative American Federation of Labor (AFL) absorbed the younger Congress of Industrial Organizations (CIO). The new AFL-CIO positioned itself as a partner in prosperity and foe of communism at home and abroad. It was a quiet consensus that seemed to benefit everyone—workers who could afford new consumer goods and corporations that could sell to them. The United States increasingly became a "consumer's republic" that defined mass consumption as the solution to social and economic problems.

For members of minority groups with regular industrial and government jobs, the 1950s could also be economically rewarding. Detroit, Dayton, Oakland, and other industrial cities offered them factory jobs at wages that could support a family. Black people worked through the Urban League, the National Association of Colored Women, and other race-oriented groups to secure fair-employment laws and jobs with large corporations. Many Puerto Rican migrants to New York found steady work in the Brooklyn Navy Yard. Mexican American families in San Antonio benefited from maintenance jobs at the city's military bases. Steady employment allowed black people and Latinos to build strong community institutions and vibrant neighborhood business districts.

However, there were never enough family-wage jobs for all of the African American and Latino workers who continued to move to northern and western cities. Many Mexican Americans were still migrant farm laborers and workers in nonunionized sweatshops. Minority workers were usually the first to suffer from the erosion of some industrial jobs and the shift of other jobs to new suburban factories that were isolated from minority neighborhoods. Black unemployment crept upward to twice the white rate, laying the seeds of frustration that would burst forth in the 1960s.

Native Americans faced equally daunting prospects. To cut costs and accelerate assimilation, Congress pushed the policy of termination between 1954 and 1962. The government sold tribal land and assets, distributed the proceeds among tribal members, and terminated its treaty relationship with the tribe. Applied to such tribes as the Klamaths in Oregon and the Menominees in Wisconsin, termination gave thousands of Indians one-time cash payments but cut them adrift from the security of tribal organizations. The Bureau of Indian Affairs encouraged Indians to move to large cities, but jobs were often unavailable. The new urban populations would nourish growing militancy among Native Americans in the 1960s and 1970s.

## Reshaping Urban America

If Eisenhower's administration opted for the status quo on many issues, it nevertheless reshaped U.S. cities around an agenda of economic development. In 1954, Congress transformed the public housing program into urban renewal. Cities used federal funds to replace low-rent businesses and run-down housing on the fringes of their downtowns with new hospitals, civic centers, sports arenas, office towers, and luxury apartments. Urban renewal temporarily revitalized older cities in the Northeast and Midwest that were already feeling the competition of the fast-growing South and West.

Only a decade later, the same cities would be urban crisis spots, in part because of accumulating social costs from urban renewal. The bulldozers often leveled minority neighborhoods in the name of downtown expansion. Urban renewal displaced Puerto Ricans in New York, African Americans in Atlanta and Norfolk, and Mexican Americans in Denver. In Los Angeles, Dodger Stadium replaced a lively Latino community.

The Eisenhower administration also revolutionized American transportation. By the early 1950s, Americans were fed up with roads designed for Model A Fords: They wanted to enjoy their new V-8 engines and the 50 million new cars sold between 1946 and 1955. The solution was the **Federal Highway Act of 1956**, creating a national system of 41,000 miles of interstate and defense highways. The legislation wrapped a program to build 41,000 miles of freeways in the language of the Cold War. The roads would be wide and strong enough for trucks hauling military hardware; they were also supposed to make it easy to evacuate cities in case of a Soviet attack.

Although the first interstate opened in Kansas in 1956, most of the mileage came into use in the 1960s and 1970s. Interstates halved the time of city-to-city travel. They were good for General Motors, the steel industry, and the concrete industry, requiring the construction equivalent of sixty Panama Canals. The highways promoted long-distance trucking at the expense of railroads. They also wiped out hundreds of homes per mile when they plunged through large cities. As with urban renewal, the bulldozers most often plowed through African American or Latino neighborhoods, where land was cheap and white politicians could ignore protests. Some cities, such as Miami, used the highways as barriers between white and black neighborhoods.

Interstates accelerated suburbanization. The beltways or perimeter highways that began to ring most large cities made it easier and more profitable to develop new subdivisions and factory sites than to reinvest in city centers. Federal grants for sewers and other basic facilities further cut suburban costs. Continuing the pattern of the late 1940s, suburban growth added a million new single-family houses per year.

## Comfort on Credit

Prosperity transformed spending habits. The 1930s had taught Americans to avoid debt. The 1950s taught them to buy on credit. Families financed their new houses with 90 percent Federal Housing Administration (FHA) mortgages and 100 percent Veterans Administration (VA) mortgages. They filled the rooms by signing installment contracts at furniture and appliance stores and charging the drapes and carpeting on department store credit cards. The value of consumer debt, excluding home mortgages, tripled from 1952 to 1964.

New forms of marketing facilitated credit-based consumerism. The first large-scale suburban shopping center was Northgate in Seattle, which assembled all the elements of the full-grown mall—small stores facing an interior corridor between anchor department stores and surrounded by parking. By the end of the decade, developers were building malls with 1 million square feet of shopping floor. At the start of the 1970s, the universal credit card (Visa, MasterCard) made shopping even easier.

Surrounding the new malls were the servants and symbols of America's car culture. Where cities of the early twentieth century had been built around public transportation—streetcars and subways—those of the 1950s depended on private automobiles. Interstate highways sucked retail business from small-town main streets to interchanges on the edge of town. Nationally franchised motels and fast-food restaurants sprang up along suburban shopping strips, pioneered by Holiday Inn (1952) and McDonald's (nationally franchised in 1955). By shopping along highways rather than downtown, suburban whites also opted to minimize contact with people of other races.

**Federal Highway Act of 1956** Measure that provided federal funding to build a nationwide system of interstate and defense highways.

Americans in the 1950s increasingly enjoyed the incomes and paid vacation time that allowed them to consider the exciting possibilities of air travel. This advertisement for Delta Airlines appeared in 1958.

The spread of automobiles contributed to increased leisure travel. More workers had two-week vacations and time to take to their families on the road. Between 1954 and 1963, the number of visits to National Parks doubled to more than 100 million and visits to National Forests nearly tripled. On television from 1956 to 1963, variety show hostess Dinah Shore tied the nation's best-selling car to the appeal of vacationing as she belted out the jingle "Drive your Chevrolet through the USA, America's the greatest land of all."

## The New Fifties Family

Family life in the Eisenhower years departed from historic patterns. Prosperity allowed children to finish school and young adults to marry right after high school. Young women faced strong social pressure to pursue husbands rather than careers. In a decade when the popular press worried about "latent homosexuality," single men were suspect. The proportion of single adults reached its twentieth-century low in 1960. At all social levels, young people married quickly and had an average of three children spaced closely together, adding to the number of baby boomers whose needs would influence American society into the twenty-first century. Strong families, said experts, defended against communism by teaching American values.

**The Impact of Television.**   Television was made to order for the family-centered fifties. By 1960, fully 87 percent of households had sets (see Figure 28.1). Popular entertainment earlier had been a communal activity; people saw movies as part of a group, cheered baseball teams as part of a crowd. Television was watched in the privacy of the home.

Experts hoped that 90-minute dramas would elevate popular taste, but morning talk shows, quiz shows, and puppet shows like *Howdy Doody* were common in the

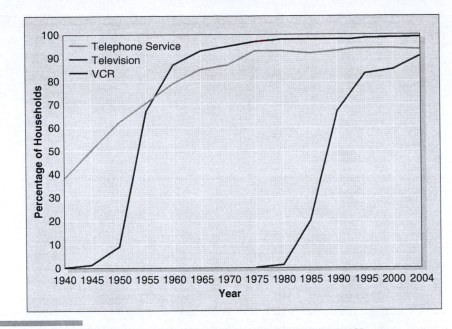

**FIGURE 28.1  HOUSEHOLDS WITH TELEPHONES, TELEVISIONS, AND VCRs**  American life in the twentieth century was transformed by a sequence of electronic consumer goods, from telephones to laptop computers. Entertainment items (televisions and videocassette recorders) spread even more rapidly among consumers than did the home telephone.

SOURCE: *Statistical Abstract of the United States.*

early days because they were cheap to produce. Variety hours recycled old vaudeville formats. Soap operas, 15-minute newscasts, and Saturday morning adventure shows were adapted straight from radio.

Situation comedies were the most successful programs. Viewers liked continuing characters who resolved everyday problems in half an hour. A few shows dealt with characters outside the middle-class mainstream, such as the bus driver and sewer worker played by Jackie Gleason and Art Carney on *The Jackie Gleason Show* and *The Honeymooners* (1952–1957). Most successful shows depicted the ideal of family togetherness. The families on *The Adventures of Ozzie and Harriet* (1952–1966), *Father Knows Best* (1954–1962), and *Leave It to Beaver* (1957–1962) were white, polite, and happy. The Nelsons, Andersons, and Cleavers bore northern European names and lived in single-family houses with friendly neighbors. Thousands of school-aged baby boomers wondered why their families didn't have good times like the families on the picture tube.

**Stay-at-Home Moms and Working Women.**  The 1950s extended the stay-at-home trend of the postwar years. Women gave up some of their earlier educational gains. Their share of new college degrees and professional jobs fell. Despite millions of new electrical appliances, the time spent on housework increased. Magazines proclaimed that proper families maintained distinct roles for dad and mom, and mom was urged to find fulfillment in a well-scrubbed house and children.

In fact, far from allowing women to stay home as housewives, family prosperity in the 1950s often depended on their earnings. The number of employed women reached new highs. By 1960, nearly 35 percent of all women held jobs, including 7.5 million mothers with children under 17 (see Figure 28.2). The pressures of young marriages, large families, and economic needs interacted to erode some of the assumptions behind the idealized family and laid the groundwork for dramatic social changes in the 1960s and 1970s.

## Inventing Teenagers

Teenagers in the 1950s joined adults as consumers of movies, clothes, and automobiles. Advertisers tapped and expanded the growing youth market by promoting a distinct

Read the Document *Ladies' Home Journal*, "Young Mother" (1956)

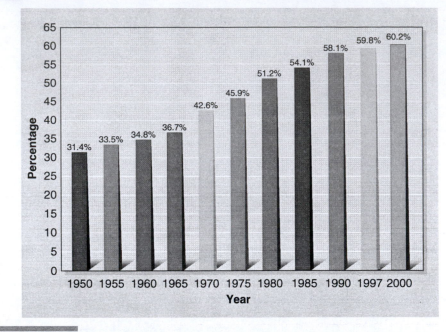

**FIGURE 28.2 WORKING WOMEN AS A PERCENTAGE OF ALL WOMEN, 1950–2000** The proportion of American women who are part of the labor force (working or looking for work) has increased steadily since 1950, with the fastest increase between 1965 and 1985.

SOURCE: U.S. Department of Labor

"youth culture," an idea that became omnipresent in the 1960s and 1970s. Many cities matched their high schools to the social status of their students: college-prep curricula for middle-class neighborhoods, vocational and technical schools for future factory workers, and separate schools or tracks for African Americans and Latinos. In effect, the schools trained some children to be doctors and officers and others to be mechanics and enlisted men.

All teenagers shared rock-and-roll, a new music of the mid-1950s that adapted black urban rhythm-and-blues for a white mass market. Rhythm-and-blues was the hard-edged and electrified offspring of traditional blues and gospel music. In turn, rock music augmented its black roots by drawing vitality from poor white southerners familiar with country-and-western music (Buddy Holly, Elvis Presley), Hispanics (Richie Valens), and, in the 1960s, the British working class (the Beatles). Record producers played up the association between rock music and youthful rebellion.

Technological changes helped rock split off from adult pop music. Portable phonographs and 45-rpm records let kids listen to rock-and-roll in their own rooms. Car radios and transistor radios (first marketed around 1956) let disc jockeys reach teenagers outside the home. The result was separate music for young listeners and separate advertising for teenage consumers, the roots of the teenage mall culture of the next generation.

The raucous sounds and rebellious lyrics of early rock-and-roll gave adult authorities even more reason to emphasize social conformity. Schools, churches, and elected officials responded with dress codes, campaigns against sinful comic books, and worry about juvenile delinquency. Young people responded by crowding movie theaters for *Rebel Without a Cause* (1955), in which James Dean played an anguished teenager in stifling suburbia. Outside the realm of mass entertainment, the Beats were coming together in San Francisco, where novelists like Jack Kerouac, poets like Gary Snyder, artists, and musicians drifted in and out of the City Lights bookstore. They attracted national attention in 1955 when Allen Ginsberg first chanted his poem "Howl," with its blistering attack on stifling materialism.

In his first years as a star, Elvis Presley brought new energy to the world of popular music.

## Turning to Religion

Leaders from Dwight Eisenhower to FBI Director J. Edgar Hoover advocated church-going as an antidote for communism. Regular church attendance grew from 48 percent of the population in 1940 to 63 percent in 1960. Moviegoers flocked to biblical epics: *The Robe* (1953), *The Ten Commandments* (1956), and *Ben Hur* (1959). *Newsweek* talked about the "vast resurgence of Protestantism," and *Time* claimed that "everybody knows that church life is booming in the U.S."

The situation was more complex. Growing church membership looked impressive at first, but the total barely kept pace with population growth. In some ways, the so-called return to religion was new. Congress created new connections between religion and government when it added "under God" to the Pledge of Allegiance in 1954 and required currency to bear the phrase "In God We Trust" in 1955.

Another strand in the religious revival was found in the revitalized evangelical and fundamentalist churches. During the 1950s, the theologically and socially conservative Southern Baptists passed the Methodists as the largest Protestant denomination. The evangelist Billy Graham continued the grand American tradition of the mass revival meeting. In auditoriums and stadiums, he preached personal salvation in words that everyone could understand. Graham was a pioneer in the resurgence of evangelical Christianity that gradually shifted the tone of American religious life by stressing an individual approach to belief and social issues.

Other important changes to come in American religion had their roots in the 1950s and early 1960s. Boundaries between many Protestant denominations blurred as church leaders emphasized national unity, paving the way for the ecumenical movement and denominational mergers. Supreme Court decisions sowed the seeds for later political activism among evangelical Christians. In *Engel v. Vitale* (1962), the Court ruled that public schools could not require children to start the school day with group prayer. *Abington Township v. Schempp* (1963) prohibited devotional Bible reading in the schools. Such decisions alarmed many evangelicals; within two decades, school prayer would be a central issue in national politics.

## The Gospel of Prosperity

For scholars and journalists who had grown up during the Great Depression, the prosperity of the 1950s was a big story. William H. Whyte, Jr., searched American corporations for the changing character of the United States in *The Organization Man* (1956). In *The Affluent Society* (1958), economist John Kenneth Galbraith predicted that the challenge of the future would be to ensure the fair distribution of national wealth.

At times in these years, production and consumption outweighed democracy in the American message to the world. Officially, Americans argued that abundance

((• 📖 **Read the Document**    Richard M. Nixon and Nikita S. Khrushchev, The Kitchen Debate (1959)

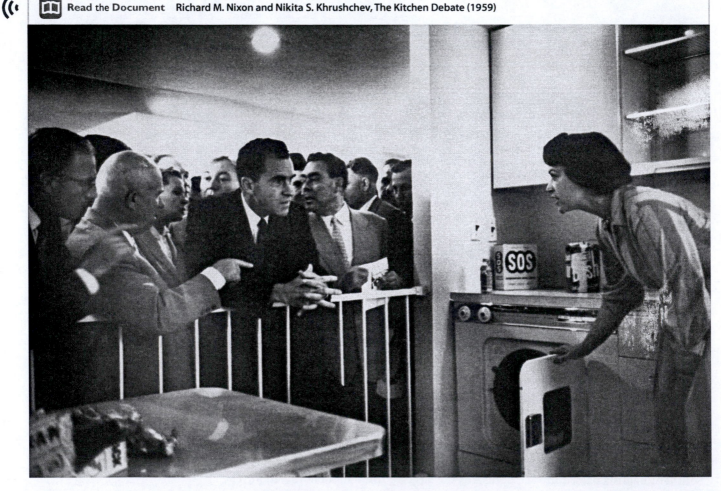

The U.S. exhibit at a technology exposition in Moscow in 1959 displayed a wide range of American consumer goods, from soft-drink dispensers to sewing machines. It included a complete six-room ranch house with an up-to-date kitchen where, in a famous encounter dubbed the "kitchen debate," Vice President Richard Nixon and Soviet Communist Party Chairman Nikita Khrushchev disputed the merits of capitalism and communism.

was a natural by-product of a free society. In fact, it was easy to present prosperity as a goal in itself, as Vice President Richard Nixon did when he represented the United States at a technology exposition in Moscow in 1959. The U.S. exhibit included twenty-one models of automobiles and a complete six-room ranch house. In its "miracle kitchen," Nixon engaged Soviet Communist Party chairman Nikita Khrushchev in a carefully planned "kitchen debate." The vice president claimed that the "most important thing" for Americans was "the right to choose": "We have so many different manufacturers and many different kinds of washing machines so that the housewives have a choice."

Khrushchev heard a similar message when he visited the United States in September 1959. His itinerary started with a helicopter ride over rush-hour Washington to show the ubiquity of individually owned automobiles. He went to a farm in Coon Rapids, Iowa, a machine shop in Pittsburgh, and Hollywood movie studios. Although Khrushchev never believed that ordinary workers had miracle kitchens, he returned to Moscow knowing that America meant "business."

## The Underside of Affluence

The most basic criticism of the ideology of prosperity was the simplest—that affluence concealed vast inequalities. Michael Harrington had worked among the poor before writing *The Other America* (1962). He reminded Americans about the "underdeveloped nation" of 40 to 50 million poor people who had missed the last two decades of prosperity. The poor were old people living on stale bread in bug-infested hotels. They were white families in the valleys of Appalachia, African Americans in city ghettos, and Hispanic migrant workers whose children went for months without a glass of milk.

If Harrington found problems at the bottom of U.S. society, C. Wright Mills found dangers in the way that the Cold War distorted American society at the top. *The Power Elite* (1956) described an interlocking alliance of big government, big business, and the military. The losers in a permanent war economy, said Mills, were economic and political democracy. His ideas would reverberate in the 1960s during the Vietnam War.

Other critics targeted the alienating effects of consumerism and the conformity of homogeneous suburbs, coining terms like "slurb" and writing books like *The Crack in the Picture Window* (1957) and *The Split Level Trap* (1961). Although much of the antisuburban rhetoric was based on intellectual snobbery rather than research, it represented significant dissent from the praise of affluence.

There was far greater substance to the increasing dissatisfaction among women, who faced conflicting images of the perfect woman in the media. On one side was the comforting icon of Betty Crocker, the fictional spokeswoman for General Mills who made housework and cooking look easy. On the other side were sultry sexpots like Marilyn Monroe and the centerfold women of *Playboy* magazine, which first appeared in 1953. Women wondered how to be both Betty and Marilyn.

Women also faced practical problems and legal limitations. In nearly every state, a husband had the right to unilaterally change the family's legal residence. Sexual harassment was legal—and scarcely recognized as an issue. Employers could fire women for getting married or pregnant.

In 1963, Betty Friedan's book *The Feminine Mystique* recognized that thousands of middle-class housewives were seething behind their picture windows. It followed numerous articles in *McCall's, Redbook,* and the *Ladies' Home Journal* about the unhappiness of college-educated women who were expected to find total satisfaction in kids and cooking. Friedan repackaged the message of the women's magazines along with the results of a survey of her Smith College classmates, who were then entering their forties. What Friedan called "the problem that has no name" was a sense of personal emptiness. The ideas were not original, but her background as a journalist helped her craft a book that flew off the shelves and packed an emotional wallop. Many women later recalled that "something clicked" when they read it.

# Facing Off with the Soviet Union

 **28.2** What impact did Dwight Eisenhower's foreign policy have on U.S. relations with the Soviet Union?

Americans got a reassuring new face in the White House in 1953, but not new policies toward the world. As had been true since 1946, the nation's leaders weighed every foreign policy decision for its effect on the Cold War. The United States pushed ahead in an arms race with the Soviet Union, stood guard on the borders of China and the Soviet empire, and judged political changes in Latin America, Africa, and Asia for their effect on the global balance of power.

## Why We Liked Ike

In the late twentieth century, few leaders were able to master both domestic policy and foreign affairs. Some presidents, such as Lyndon Johnson, were more adept at social problems than diplomacy. By contrast, Richard Nixon and George H. W. Bush were more interested in the world outside the United States.

Dwight Eisenhower was also a "foreign-policy president." As a general, he had understood that military power should serve political ends. He had helped to hold together the alliance that defeated Nazi Germany and built NATO into an effective force in 1951–1952. He then sought the Republican nomination, he said, to ensure that the United States would keep its international commitments. He sealed his victory in 1952 by emphasizing his foreign-policy expertise, telling a campaign audience that "to bring the Korean war to an early and honorable end . . . requires a personal trip to Korea. I shall make that trip . . . I shall go to Korea."

What makes Eisenhower's administration hard to appreciate is that many of its accomplishments were things that did not happen. Eisenhower refused to dismantle the social programs of the New Deal. He exerted American political and military power around the globe but avoided war. Preferring to work behind the scenes, he knew how to delegate authority and keep disagreements private.

In his "hidden-hand" presidency, Eisenhower sometimes masked his intelligence. It helped his political agenda if Americans thought of him as a smiling grandfather. He was the first president to have televised news conferences and knew how to manipulate them. The "Ike" whose face smiled from "I Like Ike" campaign buttons and who gave rambling, incoherent answers at White House press conferences knew exactly what he was doing—controlling information and keeping the opposition guessing. When his press secretary advised him to duck questions at one press conference, Ike replied, "Don't worry, I'll just confuse them." He was easily reelected in 1956, when Americans saw no reason to abandon competent leadership.

## A Balance of Terror

**massive retaliation** Popular name for the military doctrine adopted in the 1950s, whereby the United States promised to respond to any attack on itself or its allies with massive force, including nuclear weapons.

The backdrop for U.S. foreign policy was the growing capacity for mutual nuclear annihilation. The rivalry between the United States and the Soviet Union was played out within a framework of deterrence, the knowledge that each side could launch a devastating nuclear attack. The old balance of power had become a balance of terror.

The Eisenhower administration's doctrine of **massive retaliation** took advantage of America's superior technology while economizing on military spending. Eisenhower and his advisers worried that matching the land armies of China and the Soviet Union would inflate the role of the federal government in American society (see Figure 28.3). Eisenhower compared uncontrolled military spending to crucifying humankind on a "cross of iron." "Every gun that is fired," he warned, "every warship launched, every rocket fired signifies . . . a theft from those who hunger and are not fed, those who are cold and not clothed." The administration concentrated military spending where the nation already had the greatest advantage—on atomic weapons.

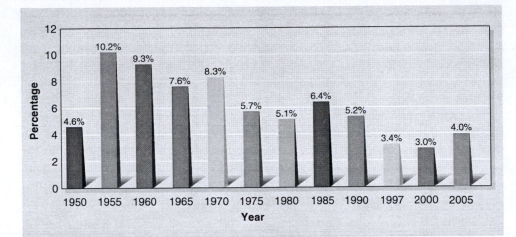

**FIGURE 28.3 DEFENSE SPENDING AS A PERCENTAGE OF GROSS DOMESTIC PRODUCT, 1950–2005** Defense spending has been an important force for economic development and innovation. The impact of the defense budget on the domestic economy was greatest in the mid-1950s, at the height of the Cold War. Lesser peaks came during the Vietnam War in the late 1960s and the Reagan administration defense buildup in the early 1980s.

SOURCE: *Statistical Abstract of the United States.*

In response to any serious attack, the United States would direct maximum force against the homeland of the aggressor. Secretary of State Dulles called for "a maximum deterrent at a bearable cost." Reporters translated the policy as "more bang for the buck."

The massive-retaliation doctrine treated nuclear weapons as ordinary or even respectable. It put European and American cities on the front line in the defense of Germany, for it meant that the United States would react to a Soviet conventional attack on NATO by dropping nuclear bombs on the Soviet Union, which would presumably retaliate in kind. The National Security Council in 1953 made reliance on "massive retaliatory damage" by nuclear weapons official policy.

The doctrine grew even more fearful as the Soviet Union developed its own hydrogen bombs. The chairman of the Atomic Energy Commission terrified the American people by mentioning casually that the Soviets could now obliterate New York City. Dozens of nuclear weapons tests in the late 1950s made the atomic threat immediate.

The Soviet Union added to the worries about atomic war by launching the world's first artificial satellite. On the first Sunday of October 1957, Americans discovered that *Sputnik*—Russian for "satellite"—was orbiting the earth. The Soviets soon lifted a dog into orbit while U.S. rockets fizzled on the pad. Soviet propagandists claimed that their technological "first" showed the superiority of Soviet Communism, and Americans wondered if the United States had lost its edge. Schools beefed up science courses and began to introduce the "new math," Congress passed the National Defense Education Act to expand college and postgraduate education, and the new **National Aeronautics and Space Administration (NASA)** took over the satellite program in 1958.

The crisis was more apparent than real. Eisenhower had rejected the use of available military rockets for the U.S. space program in favor of developing new launch vehicles, and he overlooked the symbolic impact of *Sputnik*. He thus built himself into a political box, for the combination of Soviet rocketry and nuclear capacity created fear that the Soviet Union was building hundreds of intercontinental ballistic missiles (ICBMs) to overwhelm American air defenses. Although there was no "missile gap," Eisenhower was unwilling to reveal secret information that might have allayed anxiety.

**National Aeronautics and Space Administration (NASA)** Federal agency created in 1958 to manage American space flights and exploration.

## The American Approach to the Cold War

Someone who heard only the campaign speeches in 1952 might have expected sharp foreign-policy changes under Eisenhower, but there was more continuity than change.

John Foster Dulles, Eisenhower's secretary of state, had attacked the Democrats as defeatists and appeasers. He demanded that the United States liberate Eastern Europe from Soviet control and encourage Jiang Jieshi to attack Communist China. In 1956, Dulles proudly claimed that tough-minded diplomacy had repeatedly brought the United States to the verge of war: "We walked to the brink and looked it in the face. We took strong action."

In fact, Eisenhower viewed the Cold War in the same terms as Truman. He worried about the "sullen weight of Russia" pushing against smaller nations and saw a world caught between the incompatible values of freedom and communism, but caution replaced campaign rhetoric about "rolling back" Communist regimes. Around the periphery of the Communist nations, from eastern Asia to the Middle East to Europe, the United States accepted the existing sphere of Communist influence but attempted to block its growth.

The U.S. worldview assumed both the right and the need to intervene in the affairs of other nations, especially countries in Latin America, Asia, and Africa. Policymakers saw these nations as markets for U.S. products and sources of vital raw materials. If Communist governments could not be rolled back in Eastern Europe, the CIA could still undermine anti-American governments in the third world. The Soviets themselves took advantage of local revolutions even when they did not instigate them; in doing so they confirmed Washington's belief that the developing world was a game board on which the superpowers carried on their rivalry by proxy.

Along with economic motivations and military concerns, religious belief played an important role in shaping the Cold War. When national leaders decried "godless communism," they were voicing a widely shared concern rather than mouthing a slogan. Roman Catholic leaders and laypeople worried about the restricted freedom of religious practice in Eastern Europe. Members of the nation's political elite often had ties or sympathy with missionary work in China, making them deeply suspicious of the new communist regime. At the top, strong religious convictions influenced the way that Harry Truman, Dwight Eisenhower, and John Foster Dulles viewed the confrontation with China and the Soviet Union in moral as well as practical terms.

## U.S. Alliances and the Third World

Since the time of George Washington's Farewell Address, the United States had avoided what Thomas Jefferson called "entangling alliances" with other nations, and it entered foreign wars only with great reluctance in 1917 and 1941.

Under the pressures of the Cold War, however, the United States initiated and constructed a series of mutual defense pacts with dozens of other nations in an effort to prevent the expansion of communism from the Soviet Union and China. First and most important was the North Atlantic Treaty Organization (NATO), which bound the United States and Canada to the mutual defense of Western Europe in 1949. Quick to follow were alliances with Japan in 1951, with Australia and New Zealand in 1952 (the ANZUS pact), and with South Korea in 1953. The next year the United States, Britain, and France tried to imitate NATO with the **Southeast Asia Treaty Organization (SEATO)** that included Thailand, the Philippines, and Pakistan (which then included what is now Bangladesh). The Central Treaty Organization (CENTO) came in 1955 with Pakistan, Iran, Iraq, Turkey, the United States, and Britain.

As a counter to both the western alliances and the Warsaw Pact of the communist bloc, Indonesia's president Sukarno in 1955 hosted a meeting of Asian and African nations that wanted to remain uncommitted. The nations that attended the meeting at Bandung, Indonesia, called for a "third way" that did not require aligning themselves with either side in the Cold War. In 1961, President Tito of Yugoslavia hosted the first official Non-Aligned Movement Summit, where the key figures were Tito, Sukarno, Prime Minister Nehru of India, President Nasser of Egypt, and President Nkrumah of Ghana. The nonaligned nations were termed the "Third World" in contrast to the First World of the United States and its alliances and the Second World of communist nations.

**Southeast Asia Treaty Organization (SEATO)** Mutual defense alliance signed in 1954 by the United States, Britain, France, Thailand, Pakistan, the Philippines, Australia, and New Zealand.

Among the U.S. alliances, SEATO and CENTO dissolved in the 1970s, but NATO remains a keystone of American foreign policy.

## Containment in Action

Twice during Eisenhower's first term, the CIA subverted democratically elected governments that seemed to threaten U.S. interests. In Iran, which had nationalized British and U.S. oil companies in an effort to break the hold of Western corporations, the CIA in 1953 backed a coup that toppled the government and helped the young shah, as the reigning monarch was called, to gain control. The shah then cooperated with the United States, but his increasingly repressive regime would lead to his overthrow in 1979 and deep Iranian resentment of the United States. In Guatemala, the leftist government was threatening the United Fruit Company. When the Guatemalans accepted weapons from the Communist bloc in 1954, the CIA imposed a regime friendly to U.S. business (see Map 28.1).

**MAP 28.1  U.S. INTERVENTION AROUND THE CARIBBEAN SINCE 1954** The United States has long kept a careful eye on the politics of neighboring nations to the south. In the second half of the twentieth century, the United States frequently used military assistance or force to influence or intervene in Caribbean and Central American nations. The purpose has usually been to counter or undermine left-leaning governments; some interventions, as in Haiti, have been intended to stabilize democratic regimes.

For most Americans in 1953, democracy in Iran was far less important than ending the war in Korea and stabilizing relations with China. Eisenhower declined to escalate the Korean War by blockading China and sending more U.S. ground forces. Instead, he positioned atomic bombs on Okinawa, only 400 miles from China. The nuclear threat, along with the continued cost of the war on both sides, brought the Chinese to a truce that left Korea divided into two nations.

Halfway around the world, there was a new crisis when three U.S. friends—France, Britain, and Israel—ganged up on Egypt. France was angry at Egyptian support for revolutionaries in French Algeria. Britain was even angrier at Egypt's nationalization of the British-dominated Suez Canal. And Israel wanted to weaken its most powerful Arab enemy. On October 29, 1956, Israel attacked Egypt. A week later, British and French forces attempted to seize the canal.

Although the United States had been the first nation to recognize Israel in 1948, the relationship was much less close than it would become. The United States forced a quick cease-fire, partly to maintain its standing with oil-producing Arab nations. Because Egypt blocked the canal with sunken ships, the war left Britain and France dependent on American oil that Eisenhower would not provide until they left Egypt. Resolution of the crisis involved one of the first uses of peacekeeping troops under the United Nations flag.

In Europe, Eisenhower accepted the status quo because conflicts there could result in nuclear war. In 1956, challenges to Communist rule arose in East Germany, Poland, and Hungary and threatened to break up the Soviet empire. The Soviets replaced liberal Communists in East Germany while accepting a more liberal leader in Poland. In Hungary, however, reformers took the fatal step of proposing to quit the Warsaw Pact. At exactly the same time that war was raging in the Middle East, open warfare broke out in Hungary on November 4 when the Soviet army rolled across the border to preserve the Soviet empire. Hungarian freedom fighters in Budapest used rocks and firebombs against Soviet tanks for several days, while pleading in vain for Western aid. NATO would not risk war with the Soviet Union. Tens of thousands of Hungarians died, and 200,000 fled when the Soviets crushed the resistance.

## Global Standoff

The Soviet Union, China, and the United States and its allies were all groping in the dark in the 1950s and 1960s. In one international crisis after another, each player misinterpreted the other's motivations and diplomatic signals. Now that documents from both sides of the Cold War are becoming available, historians realize what dangerously different meanings the two sides gave to their confrontations between 1953 and 1964.

A good example is the U-2 spy plane affair of 1960, which derailed progress toward nuclear disarmament. The Kremlin was deeply worried that West Germany and China might acquire nuclear bombs. Washington wanted to reduce military budgets and nuclear fallout. Both countries voluntarily suspended nuclear tests in 1958 and prepared for a June 1960 summit meeting in Paris, where Eisenhower intended to negotiate a test ban treaty. But on May 1, 1960, Soviet air defenses shot down an American U-2 aircraft over the heart of Russia and captured the pilot, Francis Gary Powers. The frail-looking black plane was a CIA operation. Designed to soar above the range of Soviet anti-aircraft missiles, U-2s had assured American officials that there was no missile gap.

When Moscow trumpeted the news of the plane's downing, Eisenhower took personal responsibility in hopes that Khrushchev would accept the U-2 as an unpleasant reality of international espionage. Unfortunately, the planes meant something very different to the Soviets, touching their festering sense of inferiority. They had stopped protesting the flights in 1957, because they saw complaints as demeaning. The Americans thought their silence signaled acceptance. Khrushchev had staked his future on good relations with the United States; when Eisenhower refused to apologize in Paris, Khrushchev stalked out. Disarmament was set back for years because the two sides had such different understandings of the same events.

The most important aspect of Eisenhower's foreign policy was continuity. Despite militant rhetoric, the administration pursued containment as defined under Truman. The Cold War consensus, however, prevented the United States from seeing the nations of the developing world on their own terms. By viewing every independence movement and social revolution as part of the competition with Soviet or Chinese Communism, U.S. leaders created unnecessary problems. In the end, Eisenhower left troublesome and unresolved issues—upheaval in Latin America, civil war in Vietnam, tension in Germany, the nuclear arms race—for his successor, John Kennedy, who wanted to confront the Communist Bloc even more vigorously.

# John F. Kennedy and the Cold War

**28.3**    What was John F. Kennedy's approach to dealing with the Soviet Union?

John Kennedy was a man of contradictions. A Democrat who promised to get the country moving again, he presided over policies whose direction was set under Eisenhower. Despite stirring rhetoric about leading the nation toward a **New Frontier** of scientific and social progress, he recorded his greatest failures and successes in the continuing Cold War.

**New Frontier**  John F. Kennedy's domestic and foreign policy initiatives, designed to reinvigorate a sense of national purpose and energy.

## The Kennedy Mystique

Kennedy won the presidency over Richard Nixon in a cliff-hanging election that was more about personality and style than about substance (see Map 28.2). Both candidates were determined not to yield another inch to Soviet or Chinese Communism. The charming and eloquent Kennedy was a well-publicized hero from World War II who tempered ruthless ambition with respect for public service. His forthright campaigning allayed voter concern about his Roman Catholicism. Nixon started off the frontrunner. He had wider experience and was a shrewd tactician, but he was also self-righteous and awkward. Eisenhower had wanted to drop Nixon as vice president in 1956 and gave him only lukewarm support in 1960—when a reporter asked Eisenhower to cite important decisions to which Nixon had contributed, Ike replied, "Give me a week and I might think of one."

Television was crucial to the outcome. The campaign featured the first televised presidential debates. In the first session, Nixon actually gave better replies, but his nervousness and a bad makeup job turned off millions of viewers, who admired Kennedy's energy. Nixon never overcame the setback. The race was tight to the end, with tiny margins in crucial states giving Kennedy the victory. His televised inauguration was the perfect setting for an impassioned plea for national unity: "My fellow Americans," he challenged, "ask not what your country can do for you—ask what you can do for your country."

Kennedy brought dash to the White House. His beautiful and refined wife, Jackie, made sure to seat artists and writers next to diplomats and businessmen at White House dinners. Kennedy's staff and large family played touch football, not golf. No president had shown such verve since Teddy Roosevelt. People began to talk about Kennedy's "charisma," his ability to lead by sheer force of personality. In fact, the image of a fit, vigorous man concealed the reality that he was battling severe physical ailments that demanded constant medical attention and often left him with debilitating pain.

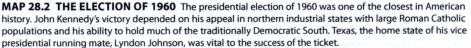

| | Electoral Vote (%) | Popular Vote (%) |
|---|---|---|
| **JOHN F. KENNEDY** (Democrat) | **303** **(56)** | **34,226,731** **(49.9)** |
| Richard M. Nixon (Republican) | 219 (41) | 34,108,157 (49.7) |
| Other | 15 (3) | 197,029 (.4) |

Note: Fifteen electors voted for Harry Byrd, although he had not been an active candidate. Minor party candidates took a tiny percentage of the popular vote.

**MAP 28.2 THE ELECTION OF 1960** The presidential election of 1960 was one of the closest in American history. John Kennedy's victory depended on his appeal in northern industrial states with large Roman Catholic populations and his ability to hold much of the traditionally Democratic South. Texas, the home state of his vice presidential running mate, Lyndon Johnson, was vital to the success of the ticket.

Behind the glamorous façade, Kennedy remained a puzzle. One day, he could propose the Peace Corps; another day, he could approve plots to assassinate Fidel Castro. Visitors who expected a shallow glad-hander were astonished to meet a sharp, hardworking man who was eager to learn about the world. One savvy diplomat commented, "I have never heard of a president who wanted to know so much."

## Kennedy's Mistakes

Kennedy and Khrushchev perpetuated similar problems. Talking tough to satisfy their more militant countrymen, they repeatedly pushed each other into a corner, continuing the problems of mutual misunderstanding that had marked the 1950s. When Khrushchev promised, in January 1961, to support "wars of national liberation," he was really fending off Chinese criticism. But Kennedy overreacted in his first State of the Union address by asking for more military spending.

Three months later, Kennedy fed Soviet fears of American aggressiveness by sponsoring an invasion of Cuba. At the start of 1959, Fidel Castro had toppled the corrupt dictator Fulgencio Batista, who had made Havana infamous for Mafia-run gambling and prostitution. Castro then nationalized American investments, and thousands of Cubans fled to the United States.

When 1,400 anti-Castro Cubans landed at Cuba's **Bay of Pigs** on April 17, 1961, they were following a plan prepared by the Eisenhower administration. The CIA had

**Bay of Pigs** Site in Cuba of an unsuccessful landing by 1,400 anti-Castro Cuban refugees in April 1961.

trained and armed the invaders and convinced Kennedy that the landing would trigger spontaneous uprisings. But when Kennedy refused to commit U.S. armed forces to support them, Cuban forces captured the attackers.

Kennedy followed the Bay of Pigs debacle with a hasty and ill-thought-out summit meeting with Khrushchev in Vienna in June. Poorly prepared and nearly incapacitated by agonizing back pain, Kennedy made little headway. Coming after Kennedy's refusal to salvage the Bay of Pigs by military intervention, the meeting left the Soviets with the impression that the president was weak and dangerously erratic.

To exploit Kennedy's perceived vulnerability, the Soviet Union renewed tension over Berlin, deep within East Germany. The divided city served as an escape route for hundreds of thousands of East Germans. Khrushchev now threatened to transfer the Soviet sector in Berlin to East Germany, which had no treaty obligations to France, Britain, or the United States. If the West had to deal directly with East Germany for access to Berlin, it would have to recognize a permanently divided Germany. Kennedy sounded the alarm: He doubled draft calls, called up reservists, and warned families to build fallout shelters. Rather than confront the United States directly, however, the Soviets and East Germans, on August 13, 1961, built a wall around the western sectors of Berlin while leaving the access route to West Germany open. The **Berlin Wall** thus isolated East Germany without challenging the Western allies in West Berlin itself. In private, Kennedy accepted the wall as a clever way to stabilize a dangerous situation: "A wall," he said, "is a hell of a lot better than a war." Tensions remained high for months as the two sides tested each other's resolve. However, Berlin remained a point of East-West tension until East German Communism collapsed in 1989 and Berliners tore down the hated wall.

**Berlin Wall** Wall erected by East Germany in 1961 that isolated West Berlin from the surrounding areas in Communist-controlled East Berlin and East Germany.

## Getting into Vietnam

United States involvement in Vietnam, located in Southeast Asia on the southern border of China, dated to 1949–1950. After World War II ended, France had fought to maintain its colonial rule there against rebels who combined Communist ideology with fervor for national independence under the leadership of Ho Chi Minh. Although the United States supported independence of most other European colonies, the triumph of Mao Zedong in China and the Korean War caused policymakers to see Vietnam as another Cold War conflict (see Map 28.3). The United States picked up three-quarters of the costs. Nevertheless, the French military position collapsed in 1954 after Vietnamese forces overran the French stronghold at Dien Bien Phu. The French had enough, and President Eisenhower was unwilling to join another Asian war. A Geneva peace conference "temporarily" divided Vietnam into a Communist north and a non-Communist south and scheduled elections for a single Vietnamese government.

The United States then replaced France as the supporter of the pro-Western Vietnamese in the south. Washington's client was Ngo Dinh Diem, an anti-Communist from South Vietnam's Roman Catholic elite. United States officials encouraged Diem to put off the elections and backed his efforts to construct an independent South Vietnam. Ho meanwhile consolidated the northern half as a communist state that claimed to be the legitimate government for all Vietnam. Another indirect consequence of the Vienna summit was the growing U.S. entanglement in South Vietnam, where Kennedy saw a chance to take a firm stand and reassert America's commitment to containment. Diem controlled the cities with the help of a large army and a Vietnamese elite that had worked with the French, but Communist insurgents known as the **Viet Cong** were gaining strength in the countryside. The United States stepped up its supply of weapons and sent advisers, including members of one of Kennedy's military innovations, the Army Special Forces Group (Green Berets).

**Viet Cong** Communist rebels in South Vietnam who fought the pro-American government established in South Vietnam in 1954.

United States aid did not work. Despite overoptimistic reports and the help of 16,000 U.S. troops, Diem's government by 1963 was losing the loyalty—the "hearts and minds"—of many South Vietnamese. North Vietnamese support for the Viet Cong

**MAP 28.3 SEATO AND OTHER EAST ASIAN COUNTRIES WITH TIES TO THE UNITED STATES**
In East Asia and the western Pacific, the United States in the 1950s constructed a series of alliances to resist Soviet and Chinese Communist influence.

canceled the effect of U.S. assistance. Diem courted a second civil war by violently crushing opposition from Vietnamese Buddhists. Kennedy's administration tacitly approved a coup on November 1 that killed Diem and his brother and installed an ineffective military junta.

## Missile Crisis: A Line Drawn in the Waves

The escalating tensions of 1961 in Southeast Asia, the Caribbean, and Germany were a prelude to the crisis that came closest to triggering a nuclear war. On October 15, reconnaissance photos revealed Soviets at work on launching sites in Cuba from which nuclear missiles could hit the United States. Top officials spent five exhausting and increasingly desperate days sorting through the options. A full-scale invasion of Cuba was not feasible on short notice, and "surgical" air strikes were technically impossible. Either sort of military operation would kill hundreds of Soviet personnel and force Moscow to react. Secretary of Defense Robert McNamara suggested demanding removal of the missiles and declaring a naval "quarantine" against the arrival of further offensive weapons. A blockade would buy time for diplomacy.

Kennedy imposed the blockade on Monday, October 22 that raised the specter of nuclear war. Americans would have been even more afraid had they known that some of the missiles were operational and that Soviets in Cuba were authorized to use them in self-defense. While Khrushchev hesitated, Soviet ships circled outside the quarantine line. On Friday, Khrushchev offered to withdraw the missiles in return for a U.S. pledge not to invade Cuba. On Saturday, a second communication nearly dashed this hopeful opening by raising a new complaint about U.S. missiles on the territory of NATO allies. The letter was the result of pressure by Kremlin hard-liners and Khrushchev's own wavering. Kennedy decided to accept the first letter and ignore the second. The United States pledged not to invade Cuba and secretly promised to remove obsolete Jupiter missiles from Turkey. Khrushchev accepted these terms on Sunday, October 28.

Why did Khrushchev risk the Cuban gamble? One reason was to protect Castro as a symbol of Soviet commitment to anti-Western regimes in the developing world. Kennedy had tried to preempt Castroism in 1961 by launching the **Alliance for Progress**, an economic-development program for Latin America that tied aid to social reform. However, the United States had also orchestrated the Bay of Pigs invasion and funded a CIA campaign to sabotage Cuba. High U.S. officials were not contemplating a full-scale invasion, but Castro and Khrushchev had reason to fear the worst.

Khrushchev also hoped to redress the strategic balance. As Kennedy discovered on taking office, the United States actually led the world in the deployment of strategic missiles. Intermediate-range rockets gave the Soviet Union a nuclear club over Western Europe, but in October 1962, the Soviet Union had fewer than 50 ICBMs to aim at the United States and China. The United States was creating a defensive triad of 1,000 land-based Minuteman missiles, 500 long-range bombers, and 600 Polaris missiles on nuclear submarines targeted on the Soviet Union. The strategic imbalance had sustained NATO during the Berlin confrontation, but 40 launchers in Cuba with two warheads each would have doubled the Soviet capacity to strike at the United States.

Soviet missiles in Cuba thus flouted the Monroe Doctrine and posed a real military threat. Kennedy and Khrushchev had also backed each other into untenable positions. In September, Kennedy had warned that the United States could not tolerate Soviet offensive weapons in Cuba, never dreaming that they were already there. Had Khrushchev acted openly (as the United States had done when it placed missiles in Turkey), the United States would have been hard-pressed to object under international law. By acting in secret and breaking previous promises, the Soviets outsmarted themselves.

In the end, both sides were cautious. Khrushchev backed down rather than fight. Kennedy fended off hawkish advisers who wanted to destroy Castro. The world had trembled, but neither nation wanted war over "the missiles of October."

## Science and Foreign Affairs

The two superpowers competed through science as well as diplomacy. When Kennedy took office, the United States was still playing catch-up in space technology. A Russian, Yuri Gagarin, was the first human to orbit the earth, on April 12, 1961. American John Glenn did not match Gagarin's feat until February 1962. Kennedy committed the United States to placing a U.S. astronaut on the moon by 1970. The decision narrowed a multifaceted scientific and military program to a massive engineering project that favored the economic capacity of the United States (see Table 28.1).

The Soviet Union and the United States were also fencing about nuclear weapons testing. After the three-year moratorium, both resumed tests in 1961–1962. Renewed testing let the Russians show off huge hydrogen bombs with yields of 20 and 30 megatons—roughly 1,000 times the power of the bombs. Both nations worked on

**Alliance for Progress** Program of economic aid to Latin America during the Kennedy administration.

TABLE 28.1 THE UNITED STATES AND THE SPACE RACE

| Year | Event |
|------|-------|
| 1957 | Soviets launch *Sputnik*, the first artificial satellite. |
| 1961 | Soviet cosmonaut Yuri Gagarin is the first human to orbit the earth. |
| | John Kennedy commits the United States to land a man on the moon by 1970. |
| 1962 | John Glenn is the first American to orbit the earth. |
| 1969 | Neil Armstrong and Buzz Aldrin walk on the moon. |
| 1972 | Americans walk on the moon for the last time. |
| 1973 | Temporary orbiting space station Skylab in operation. |
| 1975 | U.S. *Apollo* and Soviet *Soyuz* spacecraft rendezvous and dock in orbit. |
| 1981 | First U.S. space shuttle is launched. |
| 1986 | *Challenger* crew dies in space shuttle explosion. |
| 1990 | Hubble Space Telescope is launched into orbit. |
| 2000 | U.S. and Russian crew begins living aboard International Space Station. |
| 2011 | Last space shuttle flight. |

multiple-targetable warheads, antiballistic missiles, and other innovations that might destabilize the balance of terror.

After the missile crisis showed his toughness, however, Kennedy had enough political maneuvering room to respond to pressure from liberal Democrats and groups like Women Strike for Peace and the Committee for a Sane Nuclear Policy by giving priority to disarmament. In July 1963, the United States, Britain, and the Soviet Union signed the **Limited Test Ban Treaty**, which outlawed nuclear testing in the atmosphere, in outer space, and under water, although not underground. France and China, the other nuclear powers, refused to sign, and the treaty did not halt weapons development, but it was the most positive achievement of Kennedy's foreign policy and a step toward later disarmament treaties.

**Limited Test Ban Treaty** Treaty, signed by the United States, Britain, and the Soviet Union, outlawing nuclear testing in the atmosphere, in outer space, and under water.

# Righteousness Like a Mighty Stream: The Struggle for Civil Rights

**28.4**   What was the significance of *Brown v. Board of Education of Topeka?*

Supreme Court decisions are based on abstract principles, but they involve real people. One was Linda Brown of Topeka, Kansas, a third-grader whose parents were fed up with sending her past an all-white public school to attend an all-black school a mile away. The Browns volunteered to help the NAACP challenge Topeka's school segregation by trying to enroll Linda in their neighborhood school, beginning a legal case that reached the Supreme Court. On May 17, 1954, the Court decided **Brown v. Board of Education of Topeka**, opening a new civil rights era. Led by the persuasive power of the new chief justice, Earl Warren, the Court unanimously reversed the 1896 case of *Plessy v. Ferguson* by ruling that sending black children to "separate but equal" schools denied them equal treatment under the Constitution.

**Brown v. Board of Education of Topeka** Supreme Court decision in 1954 that declared that "separate but equal" schools for children of different races violated the Constitution.

## Getting to the Supreme Court

The *Brown* decision climaxed a twenty-five-year campaign to reenlist the federal courts on the side of equal rights. (See Table 28.2, Civil Rights: The Struggle for

TABLE 28.2  CIVIL RIGHTS: THE STRUGGLE FOR RACIAL EQUALITY

| Area of Concern | Key Actions | Results |
|---|---|---|
| Public school integration | Federal court cases | *Mendez v. Westminster* (1946)<br>*Brown v. Board of Education of Topeka* (1954)<br>Enforcement by presidential action, Little Rock (1957)<br>Follow-up court decisions, including mandatory busing programs in 1970s |
| Equal access to public facilities | Montgomery bus boycott (1955)<br>Lunch counter sit-ins (1960)<br>Freedom rides (1961)<br>Birmingham demonstrations (1963)<br>March on Washington (1963) | Civil Rights Act of 1964 |
| Equitable voter registration | Voter registration drives, including Mississippi Summer Project (1964) | *Smith v. Allwright* (1944)<br>Voting Rights Act of 1965<br>Voting Rights Act Amendments and Extension 1975 |
| | Demonstrations and marches, including Selma to Montgomery march (1965) | |

Racial Equality.) The work began in the 1930s when Charles Hamilton Houston, from Howard University's law school, trained a corps of civil rights lawyers. Working on behalf of the NAACP, he hoped to erode *Plessy* by suits focused on interstate travel and professional graduate schools (the least defensible segregated institutions, because states seldom provided alternatives). In 1938, Houston's student Thurgood Marshall, a future Supreme Court justice, took over the NAACP job. He and other NAACP lawyers such as Constance Baker Motley risked personal danger crisscrossing the South to file civil rights lawsuits wherever a local case emerged. In 1949, Motley was the first black lawyer to argue a case in a Mississippi courtroom since Reconstruction.

Efforts in the 1940s and early 1950s, often fueled by the experience of World War II soldiers, had important successes. In *Smith v. Allwright* (1944), the Supreme Court invalidated the all-white primary, leading to increased black voter registration in many southern communities. With new political power, and often with the cooperation of relatively progressive white leaders, blacks fought for specific improvements, such as equal pay for teachers or the hiring of black police officers.

The *Brown* case combined lawsuits from Delaware, Virginia, South Carolina, the District of Columbia, and Kansas. In each instance, students and families braved community pressure to demand equal access to a basic public service. Chief Justice Earl Warren brought a divided Court to unanimous agreement. Viewing public education as central for the equal opportunity that lay at the heart of American values, the Court weighed the consequences of segregated school systems and concluded that separate meant unequal.

*Brown* also built on efforts by Mexican Americans in the Southwest. After World War II, Latino organizations such as the League of United Latin American Citizens battled job discrimination and ethnic segregation. In 1946, Mexican American parents sued five California school districts that systematically placed their children in separate schools. In the resulting case of *Mendez v. Westminster*, federal courts prohibited segregation of Mexican American children in California schools as a violation of the equal protection clause of the Fourteenth Amendment. Eight years later, the Supreme Court forbade Texas to exclude Mexican Americans from juries. These cases provided precedents for the Court's decision in *Brown* and subsequent civil rights cases.

## Deliberate Speed

Racial segregation by law was largely a southern problem, the legacy of Jim Crow laws (see Chapter 17). The civil rights movement therefore focused first on the South, allowing Americans elsewhere to think of racial injustice as a regional issue.

Few southern communities desegregated schools voluntarily, for to do so undermined the entrenched principle of a dual society. Their reluctance was bolstered in 1955 when the Supreme Court allowed segregated states to carry out the 1954 decision "with all deliberate speed" rather than immediately.

The following year, 101 southern congressmen and senators issued the **Southern Manifesto**, which asserted that the Court decision was unconstitutional. President Eisenhower privately deplored the desegregation decision, which violated his sense of states' rights and upset Republican attempts to gain southern votes. At the same time, many in Washington knew that racial discrimination offered, in the worlds of Dean Acheson, "the most effective kind of ammunition" for Soviet propaganda.

Eisenhower's distaste for racial integration left the Justice Department on the sidelines. Courageous parents and students had to knock on schoolhouse doors, often carrying court orders. Responses varied: School districts in border states, such as Maryland, Kentucky, and Oklahoma, desegregated relatively peacefully; farther south, African American children often met taunts and violence.

The first crisis came in Little Rock, Arkansas, in September 1957. The city school board admitted nine African Americans, including Melba Pattillo, to Central High, while segregationist groups, such as the White Citizens Council, stirred up white fears. Claiming he feared violence, Governor Orval Faubus surrounded Central High with the National Guard and turned the new students away. Under intense national pressure, Faubus withdrew the Guard. The black students entered the school, but a mob forced the police to sneak them out after two hours. Fuming at the governor's defiance of federal authority, Eisenhower reluctantly nationalized the National Guard and sent in the 101st Airborne Division to keep order. Eight of the students endured a year of harassment in the hallways of Central.

Virginians in 1958–1959 tried avoidance rather than confrontation. Massive resistance was a state policy that required local school districts to close rather than accept black students. When court orders to admit nineteen black students triggered the shutdown of four high schools and three junior highs in Norfolk, white parents tried to compensate with private academies and tutoring, but it was soon apparent that a modern community could not dismantle public education.

Change came slowly to state universities. Border states desegregated colleges and professional schools with few incidents. However, the University of Alabama admitted Autherine Lucy under court order in 1956 but expelled her before she could attend classes. In 1962, James Meredith tried to enter the University of Mississippi, igniting a riot that the state refused to control. Because the governor directly defied the federal courts and broke promises to the administration, President Kennedy sent in the army. A year later, Governor George Wallace of Alabama grabbed headlines by "standing in the schoolhouse door" to prevent integration of the University of Alabama, gaining a national prominence that culminated in a third-party candidacy for president in 1968.

The breakthrough in school integration did not come until the end of the 1960s, when the courts rejected further delays, and federal authorities threatened to cut off education funds. As late as 1968, only 6 percent of African American children in the South attended integrated schools. By 1973, the figure was 90 percent. Attention thereafter shifted to northern communities, whose schools were segregated, not by law, but by the divisions between white and black neighborhoods and between white suburbs and multiracial central cities, a situation known as de facto segregation.

Elizabeth Eckford, one of the first black students to attend Central High in Little Rock, Arkansas, in 1957, enters the school amid taunts from white students and bystanders.

## Public Accommodations

The civil rights movement also sought to integrate public accommodations. Most southern states separated the races in bus terminals and movie theaters. They required black riders to take rear seats on buses. They labeled separate restrooms and drinking fountains for "colored" users. Hotels denied rooms to black people, and restaurants refused them service.

The struggle to end segregated facilities started in Montgomery, Alabama. On December 1, 1955, Rosa Parks refused to give up her bus seat to a white passenger and was arrested. Parks was part of a network of civil rights activists who wanted to challenge segregated buses and was the secretary of the Montgomery NAACP. As news of her action spread, the community institutions that enriched southern black life went into action. The Women's Political Council, a group of college-trained black women, initiated a mass boycott of the privately owned bus company. Martin Luther King, Jr., a 26-year-old pastor, led the boycott. He galvanized a mass meeting with a speech that quoted the biblical prophet Amos: "We are determined here in Montgomery to work and fight until justice runs down like water, and righteousness like a mighty stream."

Montgomery's African Americans organized their boycott in the face of white outrage. A car pool substituted for the buses despite police harassment. As the boycott

# ✳ Explore the Civil Rights Movement on MyHistoryLab

## HOW DID CONDITIONS FOR AFRICAN AMERICANS BEGIN TO CHANGE IN THE MID-1900s?

Laws in the South known as "Jim Crow laws"—regulations that banned African Americans and whites from, for example, marrying, dining, going to school, or socializing together—ensured racial discrimination. In the North, segregation undergirded the social structure. However, African American leaders started to make advancements in their fight for equality in the 1950s and 1960s. Civil rights activists protested across the South, making national headlines. In the industrial cities of the North and West, large numbers of African Americans arrived in the Second Great Migration between 1940 and 1970 as they sought better opportunities than the South afforded them. From these cities, many also began to speak out for an end to racism.

Holding a poster against racial bias in Mississippi are four NAACP leaders (l. to r.), Henry L. Moon, Roy Wilkins, Herbert Hill, and Thurgood Marshall.

### SHIFTS IN AFRICAN AMERICAN POPULATION IN SELECTED COUNTIES, 1940–1950

| County | Change in Persons | Percent Change |
|---|---|---|
| Columbia County, Georgia | −1,108 | −20 |
| Cook County, Illinois | +226,822 | +60 |
| Los Angeles County, California | +142,672 | +94 |
| Quitman County, Mississippi | −2,416 | −9 |
| Wayne County, Michigan | +172,122 | +70 |

SOURCE: *1950 Census, Historic GIS Data: Slavery, Citizenship, & Civil Rights,* Teaching American History Project, www.upa.pdx.edu/IMS/currentprojects/TAHv3/Slave_Citizen_GIS.html.

## KEY QUESTIONS    Use MyHistoryLab *Explorer* to answer these questions:

**Cause ▶▶▶** *What challenges did African Americans face during the era of segregation?*

Use socioeconomic patterns to consider discrimination.

**Comparison ▶▶▶** *In what parts of southern cities did African Americans live?*

Map segregation in selected urban centers.

**Consequence ▶▶▶** *What was the demographic impact of the Second Great Migration?*

Consider the results of this move to the urban North and West.

survived months of pressure, the national media began to pay attention. After nearly a year, the Supreme Court agreed that the bus segregation law was unconstitutional. Victory in Montgomery depended on steadfast participation from all segments of the city's African American community. Success also revealed the discrepancy between white attitudes in the Deep South and national opinion. For white southerners, segregation was a local concern best defined as a legal or constitutional matter. For other Americans, it was increasingly an issue of the South's deviation from national moral norms.

The Montgomery boycott won a local victory and made King famous, but it did not propel immediate change. King formed the **Southern Christian Leadership Conference (SCLC)** and sparred with the NAACP about community-based versus court-based civil rights tactics, but four African American college students in Greensboro, North Carolina, started the next phase of the struggle. On February 1, 1960, they put on jackets and ties and sat down at the segregated lunch counter in Woolworth's, waiting through the day without being served. Their patient courage brought more demonstrators; within two days, eighty-five students packed the store. The tactic had been used successfully in Wichita eighteen months earlier, but Greensboro caught national attention. Nonviolent sit-ins spread throughout the South.

In such comparatively sophisticated border cities as Nashville, Tennessee, sit-ins integrated lunch counters. Elsewhere, they precipitated white violence and mass arrests. Like soldiers on a battlefield, nervous participants in sit-ins and demonstrations drew strength from one another. "If you don't have courage," said one young woman in Albany, Georgia, "you can borrow it." King welcomed nonviolent confrontation. SCLC leader Ella Baker, one of the movement's most important figures, helped the students form a new organization, the **Student Nonviolent Coordinating Committee (SNCC)**.

The year 1961 brought "freedom rides" to test the segregation of interstate bus terminals, which were supposed to be integrated under federal law. The idea came from James Farmer of the **Congress of Racial Equality (CORE)**, who copied a little-remembered 1947 Journey of Reconciliation that had tested the integration of interstate trains. Two buses carrying black and white passengers met only minor problems in Virginia, the Carolinas, and Georgia, but Alabamians burned one of the buses and attacked the riders in Birmingham, where they beat demonstrators senseless and clubbed a Justice Department observer. The riders traveled into Mississippi under National Guard protection but were arrested at the Jackson bus terminal. The rides, which continued through the summer, proved that African Americans were in charge of their own civil rights revolution.

## The March on Washington, 1963

John Kennedy was a tepid supporter of the civil rights movement and entered office with no civil rights agenda. He appointed segregationist judges to mollify southern congressmen and would have preferred that African Americans stop disturbing the fragile Democratic Party coalition.

In the face of the slow federal response, the SCLC concentrated for 1963 on rigidly segregated Birmingham. April began with sit-ins and marches that aimed to integrate lunch counters, restrooms, and stores and secure open hiring for some clerical jobs. Birmingham's commissioner of public safety, Bull Connor, used fire hoses to blast demonstrators against buildings and roll children down the streets. When demonstrators fought back, his men chased them with dogs. Continued marches brought the arrest of hundreds of children. King's "Letter from Birmingham City Jail" stated the case for protest: "We have not made a single gain in civil rights without determined legal and nonviolent pressure. . . . Freedom is never voluntarily given by the oppressor; it must be demanded by the oppressed."

The Birmingham demonstrations were inconclusive. White leaders accepted minimal demands on May 10 but delayed enforcing them. Antiblack violence

**Southern Christian Leadership Conference (SCLC)** Black civil rights organization founded in 1957 by Martin Luther King, Jr. and other clergy.

**Student Nonviolent Coordinating Committee (SNCC)** Black civil rights organization founded in 1960 and drawing heavily on younger activists and college students.

**Congress of Racial Equality (CORE)** Civil rights group formed in 1942 and committed to nonviolent civil disobedience.

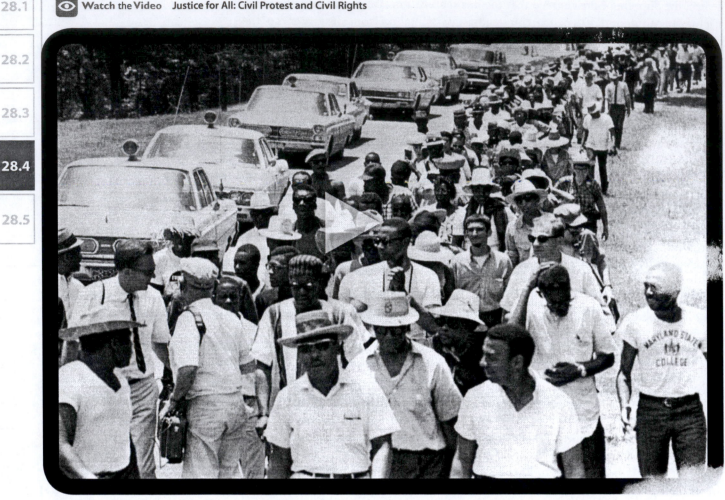

The civil rights movement involved huge rallies like the March on Washington, but it also required hundreds of smaller actions like this 1963 march led by Martin Luther King, Jr. in Yalobusha County in northern Mississippi.

continued, including a bomb that killed four children in a Birmingham church. Meanwhile, the events in Alabama had forced President Kennedy to board the freedom train with an eloquent June 11 speech and to send a civil rights bill to Congress. "Are we to say . . . that this is the land of the free, except for Negroes, that we have no second-class citizens, except Negroes . . .? Now the time has come for the nation to fulfill its promise."

On August 28, 1963, a rally in Washington transformed African American civil rights into a national cause. A quarter of a million people, black and white, marched to the Lincoln Memorial. The day gave Martin Luther King, Jr. a national pulpit. His call for progress toward Christian and American goals had immense appeal. Television cut away from afternoon programs for his "I Have a Dream" speech.

The March on Washington drew on activism in the North as well as the South. African Americans in northern states and cities did not face the legal segregation of the South, but they had unequal access to jobs and housing because of private discrimination. They fought back with demands for fair housing and fair employment laws, sometimes with success and sometimes triggering white backlash. A New York law against employment discrimination, for example, was one of the factors that had pushed the Brooklyn Dodgers to sign Jackie Robinson. Only two months before the gathering at the national capital, 125,000 people had participated in a Walk to Freedom in Detroit.

The March on Washington demonstrated the mass appeal of civil rights and its identification with national values. It also papered over growing tensions within the civil rights movement. In the mid-1960s a growing militancy split the civil rights effort and moved younger African Americans, as well as Latinos and Native Americans, to emphasize their own distinct identities within American society.

## Religious Belief and Civil Rights

Although *Brown* and other civil rights court decisions drew on the secular Constitution, much of the success of the southern civil rights movement came from grassroots Christianity. A century earlier, the abolitionist crusade had drawn much of its power from evangelistic revival movements. Now in the 1950s and 1960s, black southerners drew on prophetic Christianity to forge and act on a vision of a just society. Religious conviction and solidarity provided courage in the face of opposition.

At the same time, most white Christians understood that segregation contradicted the message of the Bible. The two largest religious groups in the South, the Presbyterian Church of the United States and the Southern Baptist Convention, took public stands in favor of desegregation in the mid-1950s. Revival leader Billy Graham shared a pulpit with Martin Luther King, Jr. in 1957 and insisted against local laws that his revival services be integrated. The opponents of civil rights thus lacked the moral support of the South's most fundamental cultural institutions.

In this context, it was no accident that black churches were organizing centers for civil rights work. King named his organization the Southern Christian Leadership Conference with clear intent and purpose.

# "Let Us Continue"

**28.5** How did Lyndon B. Johnson continue the domestic agenda inherited from the Kennedy administration? In what ways did he depart from it?

The two years that followed King's speech mingled despair and accomplishment. The optimism of the March on Washington shattered with the assassination of John Kennedy in November 1963. In 1964 and 1965, however, President Lyndon Johnson pushed through Kennedy's legislative agenda and much more in a burst of government activism unmatched since the 1930s. Federal legislation brought victory to the first phase of the civil rights revolution, launched the **War on Poverty**, expanded health insurance and aid to education, and opened an era of environmental protection.

**War on Poverty** Set of programs introduced by Lyndon Johnson between 1963 and 1966 designed to break the cycle of poverty by providing funds for job training, community development, nutrition, and supplementary education.

## Dallas, 1963

In November 1963, President Kennedy visited Texas to raise money and patch up feuds among Texas Democrats. On November 22, the president's motorcade took him near the Texas School Book Depository building in Dallas, where Lee Harvey Oswald had stationed himself at a window on the sixth floor. When Kennedy's open car swung into the sights of his rifle, Oswald fired three shots that wounded Texas governor John Connally and killed the president. Vice President Lyndon Johnson took the oath of office as president on Air Force One while the blood-spattered Jacqueline Kennedy looked on. Two days later, as Oswald was being led from one jail cell to another, Jack Ruby, a Texas nightclub owner, killed him with a handgun in full view of TV cameras. Despite voluminous conspiracy theories and weaknesses in the report of an investigating commission chaired by Chief Justice Earl Warren, the hard evidence clearly shows that Oswald was a frustrated misfit who acted alone.

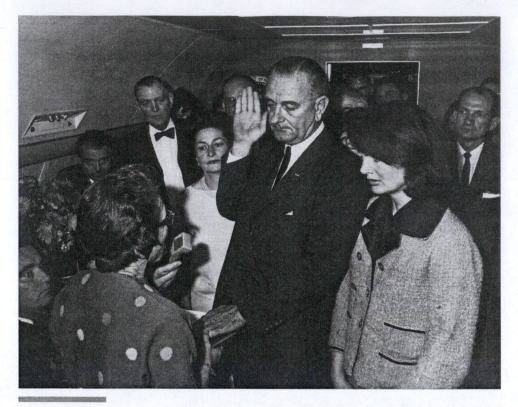

Lyndon Johnson takes the oath of office aboard Air Force One on the ground in Dallas as the widowed Jacqueline Kennedy looks on.

## War on Poverty

Five days after the assassination, Lyndon Johnson claimed Kennedy's progressive aura for his new administration. "Let us continue," he told the nation, promising to implement Kennedy's policies. In fact, Johnson was vastly different from Kennedy. He was a professional politician who had reached the top through Texas politics and congressional infighting. As Senate majority leader during the 1950s, he had built a web of political obligations and friendships. Johnson's upbringing in rural Texas shaped a man who was ambitious, ruthless, and often personally crude, but also deeply committed to social equity. He had entered public life with the New Deal in the 1930s and believed in its principles. Johnson, not Kennedy, was the true heir of Franklin Roosevelt.

Johnson inherited a domestic agenda that the Kennedy administration had defined but not enacted. Kennedy's New Frontier had met the same fate as Truman's Fair Deal. Initiatives in education, medical insurance, tax reform, and urban affairs had stalled or been gutted by conservatives in Congress.

Kennedy's farthest-reaching initiative was rooted in the acknowledgment that poverty was a persistent U.S. problem. Michael Harrington's study *The Other America* became an unexpected best seller. As poverty captured public attention, Kennedy's economic advisers devised a community-action program that emphasized education and job training, a national service corps, and a youth conservation corps. They prepared proposals to submit to Congress in 1964 that focused on social programs intended to alter behaviors that were thought to be passed from generation to generation, thus following the American tendency to attribute poverty to the personal failings of the poor.

Johnson made Kennedy's antipoverty package his own. Adopting Cold War rhetoric, he declared "unconditional war on poverty." The core of Johnson's program was the **Office of Economic Opportunity (OEO)**. Established under the direction of Kennedy's brother-in-law R. Sargent Shriver, the OEO operated the Job Corps

**Office of Economic Opportunity (OEO)** Federal agency that coordinated many programs of the War on Poverty between 1964 and 1975.

for school dropouts, the Head Start program to prepare poor children for school, and VISTA (Volunteers in Service to America), a domestic Peace Corps. OEO's biggest effort went to more than community-action agencies that provided health and educational services. Despite flaws, the War on Poverty improved life for millions of Americans.

## Civil Rights, 1964–1965

Johnson's passionate commitment to economic betterment accompanied a commitment to civil rights. In Johnson's view, segregation not only deprived African Americans of access to opportunity but also distracted white southerners from their own poverty and underdevelopment.

One solution was the **Civil Rights Act of 1964**. The law prohibited segregation in public accommodations, such as hotels, restaurants, theaters, and parks, and outlawed employment discrimination on federally assisted projects. It also created the Equal Employment Opportunity Commission (EEOC) and included gender in the list of categories protected against discrimination, a provision whose consequences were scarcely suspected in 1964.

Even as Congress was debating civil rights legislation, **Freedom Summer** moved political power to the top of the civil rights agenda. Organized by the SNCC, the Mississippi Summer Freedom Project was a voter-registration drive that sent white and black volunteers to the small towns and back roads of Mississippi. The target was a political system that used rigged literacy tests and intimidation to keep black southerners from voting. In Mississippi in 1964, only 7 percent of eligible black citizens were registered voters. Local black activists had laid the groundwork for a registration effort with years of courageous effort through the NAACP and voter leagues. Now an increasingly militant SNCC took the lead. Freedom Summer gained 1,600 new voters and taught 2,000 children in SNCC-run Freedom Schools at the cost of beatings, bombings, church arson, and the murder of three project workers.

Another outgrowth of the SNCC effort was the Mississippi Freedom Democratic Party (MFDP), a biracial coalition that bypassed Mississippi's all-white Democratic Party, followed state party rules, and sent its own delegates to the 1964 Democratic convention. To preserve party harmony, President Johnson refused to expel the "regular" Mississippi Democrats and offered instead to seat two MFDP delegates and enforce party rules for 1968. The MFDP walked out, seething with anger. Fannie Lou Hamer, an MFDP delegate who had already suffered in the struggle for voting rights, remembered, "We learned the hard way that even though we had all the law and all the righteousness on our side—that white man is not going to give up his power to us. We have to build our own power."

Freedom Summer and political realities both focused national attention on voter registration. Lyndon Johnson and Martin Luther King, Jr. agreed on the need for federal voting legislation when King visited the president in December 1964 after winning the Nobel Peace Prize. For King, power at the ballot box would help black southerners to take control of their own communities. For Johnson, voting reform would fulfill the promise of American democracy. It would also benefit the Democratic Party by replacing with black voters the white southerners who were drifting toward the anti-integration Republicans.

The target for King and the SCLC was Dallas County, Alabama, where only 2 percent of eligible black residents were registered, compared with 70 percent of white residents. Peaceful demonstrations started in January 1965. By early February, jails in the county seat of Selma held 2,600 black people whose offense was marching to the courthouse to demand the vote. The campaign climaxed with a march from Selma to the state capital of Montgomery. SNCC leader John Lewis remembered, "I don't know what we expected. I think maybe we thought we'd be arrested and jailed, or maybe they wouldn't do anything to us. I had a little knapsack on my shoulder with an apple,

**Civil Rights Act of 1964** Federal legislation that outlawed discrimination in public accommodations and employment on the basis of race, skin color, sex, religion, or national origin.

**Freedom Summer** Voter-registration effort in rural Mississippi organized by black and white civil rights workers in 1964.

a toothbrush, toothpaste, and two books in it: a history of America and a book by [Christian theologian] Thomas Merton."

On Sunday, March 7, 500 marchers crossed the bridge over the Alabama River, to meet a sea of state troopers. The troopers gave them two minutes to disperse and then attacked on foot and horseback "as if they were mowing a big field." The attack drove the demonstrators back in bloody confusion while television cameras rolled.

As violence continued, Johnson addressed a joint session of Congress to demand action on voting rights. "Our mission is at once the oldest and the most basic of this country: to right wrong, to do justice, to serve man." He ended with the refrain of the civil rights movement: "We shall overcome." The **Voting Rights Act** that he signed on August 6, 1965, outlawed literacy tests and provided for federal voting registrars in states where registration or turnout in 1964 was less than 50 percent of the eligible population. It applied initially in seven southern states. Black registration in these states jumped from 27 percent to 55 percent within the first year. In 1975, Congress extended coverage to Hispanic voters in the Southwest. The act required new moderation from white leaders, who had to satisfy black voters, and it opened the way for black and Latino candidates to win positions at every level of state and local government. By opening the political process to previously excluded citizens, the Voting Rights Act was as revolutionary and far-reaching as the Nineteenth Amendment, which guaranteed women the right to vote, and the Labor Relations Act of 1935, which recognized labor unions as the equals of corporations.

## War, Peace, and the Landslide of 1964

Lyndon Johnson was the peace candidate in 1964. Johnson had maintained Kennedy's commitment to South Vietnam. On the advice of such Kennedy holdovers as Defense Secretary Robert McNamara, he stepped up commando raids and naval shelling of North Vietnam, on the assumption that North Vietnam controlled the Viet Cong. On August 2, North Vietnamese torpedo boats attacked the U.S. destroyer *Maddox* in the Gulf of Tonkin while it was eavesdropping on North Vietnamese military signals. Two days later, the *Maddox* and the *C. Turner Joy* reported another torpedo attack (probably false sonar readings). Johnson ordered a bombing raid in reprisal and asked Congress to authorize "all necessary measures" to protect U.S. forces and stop further aggression. Congress passed the **Gulf of Tonkin Resolution** with only two nay votes, effectively authorizing the president to wage undeclared war.

Johnson's militancy paled beside that of his Republican opponent. Senator Barry Goldwater of Arizona represented the new right wing of the Republican Party, which was drawing strength from the South and West. Goldwater wanted minimal government interference in free enterprise and aggressive confrontation with Communist nations. Campaign literature accurately described him as "a choice, not an echo." He declared that "extremism in the defense of liberty is no vice," raising visions of vigilantes and mobs. Goldwater's campaign made Johnson look moderate.

The election was a landslide. Johnson's 61 percent of the popular vote was the greatest margin recorded in a presidential election. Democrats racked up two-to-one majorities in Congress. For the first time in decades, liberal Democrats could enact their domestic program without begging votes from conservative southerners or Republicans, and Johnson could achieve his goal of a **Great Society** based on freedom and opportunity for all (see Table 28.3).

The result was a series of measures that Johnson pushed through Congress before the Vietnam War eroded his political standing and distracted national attention. The National Endowment for the Arts and the National Endowment for the Humanities seemed uncontroversial at the time but would later become the focus of liberal and conservative struggles over the character of American life. The Wilderness Act (1964), which preserved 9.1 million acres from development, would prove another political battlefield in the face of economic pressures in the next century.

---

**Voting Rights Act** Legislation in 1965 that overturned a variety of practices by which states systematically denied voter registration to minorities.

**Gulf of Tonkin Resolution** Request to Congress from President Lyndon Johnson in response to North Vietnamese torpedo boat attacks in which he sought authorization for "all necessary measures" to protect American forces and stop further aggression.

**Great Society** Theme of Lyndon Johnson's administration, focusing on poverty, education, and civil rights.

## TABLE 28.3  GREAT SOCIETY LEGISLATION AND PROGRAMS

| | |
|---|---|
| Health Care | Medicare (1965)<br>Medicaid (1965) |
| Education | Head Start (1965/1966)<br>Upward Bound (1965)<br>Elementary and Secondary Education Act (1965)<br>Higher Education Act (1965)<br>Teacher Corps (1965–1981) |
| Transportation | Department of Transportation (1966)<br>National Highway Traffic Safety Administration (1966/1970) |
| Consumer Protection | Fair Packing and Labeling Act (1966) |
| Employment and Antipoverty | Office of Economic Opportunity (1964–1981)<br>Job Corps (1964)<br>VISTA [Americorps] (1964)<br>Community Action Program (1964)<br>Model Cities (1966–1974) |

The goal of increasing opportunity for all Americans stirred the president most deeply. The Elementary and Secondary Education Act was the first general federal aid program for public schools, allocating $1.3 billion for textbooks and special education. The Higher Education Act funded low-interest student loans and university research facilities. The Medical Care Act created **Medicare**, federally funded health insurance for the elderly, and **Medicaid**, which helped states offer medical care to the poor.

It is sometimes said that the United States declared war on poverty and lost. In fact, the nation came closer to winning the war on poverty than it did the war in Vietnam. New or expanded social insurance and income-support programs, such as Medicare, Medicaid, Social Security, and food stamps, cut the proportion of poor people from 22 percent of the American population in 1960 to 13 percent in 1970 (see Figure 28.4). Infant mortality dropped by a third because of improved nutrition and better access to health care for mothers and children. Taken together, the political results of the 1964 landslide moved the United States much closer to the vision of an end to poverty and racial injustice.

**Medicare** Basic medical insurance for the elderly, financed through the federal government; program created in 1965.

**Medicaid** Supplementary medical insurance for the poor, financed through the federal government; program created in 1965.

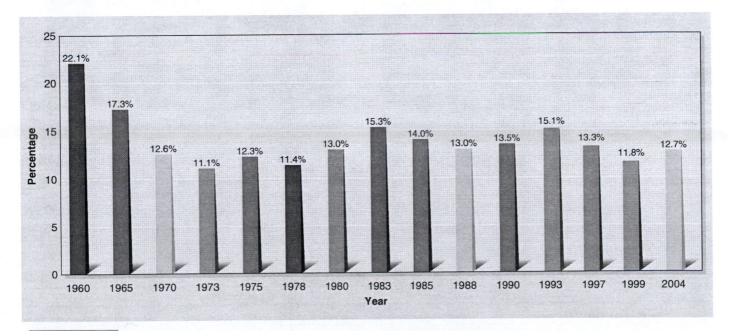

**FIGURE 28.4 POVERTY RATE, 1960–2004** With the improvement of federal health insurance, assistance for the elderly, and antipoverty programs, the proportion of Americans living in poverty dropped dramatically in the later 1960s. It began to inch upward again in the 1980s, when the priorities of the federal government shifted.

SOURCE: *Statistical Abstract of the United States.*

## From Then to Now
# Medical Research on Polio and AIDS

W hen Dr. Jonas Salk announced an effective vaccine for polio on April 12, 1955, the United States gained a new hero whose personal story had taken him from an immigrant neighborhood in Brooklyn to a pinnacle of medical science. In the confident mid-1950s, the polio vaccine seemed another proof of America's ability to improve the world.

Fear of polio haunted American families after World War II. Most Americans knew at least one child who hobbled through life on crutches and metal leg braces. Hospitals filled with new cases every summer—58,000 in 1952 alone. Many children clung to life inside iron lungs, metal cylinders that pumped air in and out of a hole in the throat.

Salk's announcement was welcome news. A generation later, President Ronald Reagan would list the polio vaccine with the steam engine and the silicon chip as one of the great modern discoveries.

Scientists first identified a new disease pattern, acquired immune deficiency syndrome (AIDS), in 1981. The name described the symptoms resulting from the human immunodeficiency virus (HIV), which destroys the body's ability to resist disease. Worldwide, the HIV death toll was 2.9 million by 2006, and nearly 40 million people were living with HIV.

HIV/AIDS triggers many of the same intense emotions as polio. It strikes people in their prime and gradually wastes their strength. At the same time, HIV/AIDS remains as daunting scientifically as it has been politically volatile. In 2002, the federal budget allocated $2.8 billion for HIV/AIDS research and another $10 billion for prevention and treatment programs in the United States and other nations, amounts vastly greater than the funds spent fighting polio. If Salk's success confirmed American confidence in the 1950s, the global struggle against HIV and AIDS mirrors the complexity of the twenty-first century.

**Question for Discussion**

- How has the scale and funding for medical and scientific research changed since the 1950s?

Invented in 1927, the iron lung was a respirator that sustained life for thousands of polio victims whose breathing was paralyzed by the disease.

Polio was eradicated in Europe and the Americas, but it continued to ravage Africa into the twenty-first century.

## Conclusion

The era commonly remembered as the 1950s stretched from 1953 to 1964. United States foreign policy involved vigilant anti-communism and the confidence to intervene in trouble spots around the globe. At home, the Supreme Court's *Brown* decision introduced a decade-long civil rights revolution that reached its emotional peak with the March on Washington and its political climax with the Civil Rights Act (1964) and

Voting Rights Act (1965). However, many patterns of personal behavior and social relations remained unchanged. Women faced similar expectations from the early fifties to the early sixties. Churches showed more continuity than change.

In retrospect, it is remarkable how widely and deeply the Cold War shaped U.S. society. Fundamental social institutions, such as marriage and religion, got extra credit for their contributions to anti-communism. The nation's long tradition of home-grown radicalism was virtually silent in the face of the Cold War consensus. Even economically meritorious programs like more money for science and better roads were accepted more easily if linked to national defense.

**For Suggested Readings go to MyHistoryLab.**

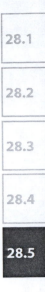

# Chapter Review

## A Decade of Affluence

**28.1** How did the "Decade of Affluence" alter social and religious life in America? p. 813

In the decade after the Korean War, Americans enjoyed widespread prosperity symbolized by suburban houses and new cars pouring off Detroit assembly lines. While social commentators struggled to understand the success story, corporations courted Americans as consumers through television and popular music, franchised businesses, and shopping malls.

## Facing Off with the Soviet Union

**28.2** What impact did Dwight Eisenhower's foreign policy have on U.S. relations with the Soviet Union? p. 822

The Cold War, with its shadow of possible nuclear annihilation, largely controlled the ways in which the United States related to the world. American leaders judged foreign policy decisions and the actions of other nations for their effects on the balance of power between the United States and the Soviet Union.

## John F. Kennedy and the Cold War

**28.3** What was John F. Kennedy's approach to dealing with the Soviet Union? p. 827

The Cold War reached its most dangerous point in the early 1960s with U.S.-Soviet confrontations over Berlin and Cuba, escaping nuclear war by the narrowest of margins.

## Righteousness Like a Mighty Stream: The Struggle for Civil Rights

**28.4** What was the significance of *Brown v. Board of Education of Topeka?* p. 832

Building on work in earlier decades, the civil rights movement of 1953–1964 transformed race relations in the realms of education, public accommodations, and political rights. At the same time, it left unsolved problems of racial equity in both the South and North.

## "Let Us Continue"

**28.5** How did Lyndon B. Johnson continue the domestic agenda inherited from the Kennedy administration? In what ways did he depart from it? p. 839

Lyndon Johnson used his immense political skills to advance the cause of economic opportunity for all Americans. The programs of the Great Society left a permanent and positive mark on American society in fields such as health care, employment, and civil rights.

# Timeline

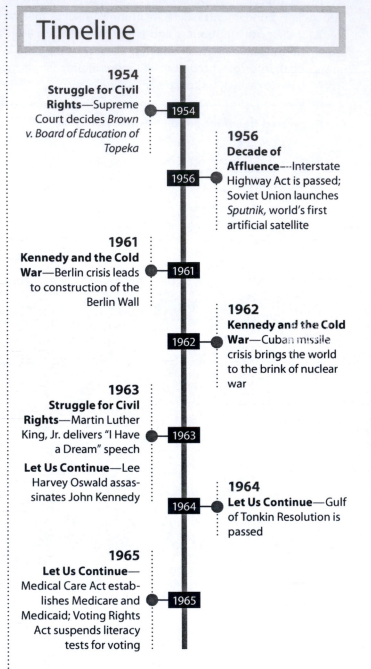

**1954**
**Struggle for Civil Rights**—Supreme Court decides *Brown v. Board of Education of Topeka*

1954

**1956**
**Decade of Affluence**—Interstate Highway Act is passed; Soviet Union launches *Sputnik,* world's first artificial satellite

1956

**1961**
**Kennedy and the Cold War**—Berlin crisis leads to construction of the Berlin Wall

1961

**1962**
**Kennedy and the Cold War**—Cuban missile crisis brings the world to the brink of nuclear war

1962

**1963**
**Struggle for Civil Rights**—Martin Luther King, Jr. delivers "I Have a Dream" speech
**Let Us Continue**—Lee Harvey Oswald assassinates John Kennedy

1963

**1964**
**Let Us Continue**—Gulf of Tonkin Resolution is passed

1964

**1965**
**Let Us Continue**—Medical Care Act establishes Medicare and Medicaid; Voting Rights Act suspends literacy tests for voting

1965

# 29 Shaken to the Roots 1965–1980

## One American Journey

Interview with Labor Activist
Dolores Huerta

**T**he strike [against California grape growers] broke out in September of 1965. . . . The whole boycott is a nonviolent tool. It's an economic sanction, so to speak, but it's a way that people can participate. One thing about nonviolence is that it opens the doors for everyone to participate, the women, the children. And women being involved on the picket lines made it easier for the men then to accept nonviolence. . . . I consider nonviolence to be a very strong spiritual force because it's almost like an energy that goes out and touches people.

Most of them [the farm workers] were either first generation Mexican-Americans or recent immigrants. To get them to accept the whole philosophy that you can create a movement with nonviolence was not easy. It was not easy. To get them to understand that—and this you could see happening in people, that they would become transformed. They would actually become stronger through practicing nonviolence.

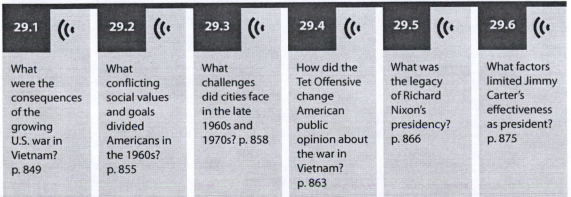

Cesar Chavez and Dolores Huerta (right) leading a meeting during the United Farm Workers five-year-long strike against Delano, California grape growers.

## LEARNING OBJECTIVES

| 29.1 | 29.2 | 29.3 | 29.4 | 29.5 | 29.6 |
|---|---|---|---|---|---|
| What were the consequences of the growing U.S. war in Vietnam? p. 849 | What conflicting social values and goals divided Americans in the 1960s? p. 855 | What challenges did cities face in the late 1960s and 1970s? p. 858 | How did the Tet Offensive change American public opinion about the war in Vietnam? p. 863 | What was the legacy of Richard Nixon's presidency? p. 866 | What factors limited Jimmy Carter's effectiveness as president? p. 875 |

Listen to Chapter 29 on MyHistoryLab

29.1

29.2

29.3

29.4

29.5

29.6

# 👁 Watch the Video Series on MyHistoryLab

Learn about some key topics related to this chapter with the *MyHistoryLab Video Series: Key Topics in U.S. History.*

**1** **From a Great Society to a Conservative One: 1969–1980** The liberalism of the 1960s gave way to the more conservative politics of the 1970s and 1980s. This video assesses the election of Richard M. Nixon in 1968, which signaled a political shift away from the Great Society programs of the 1960s to a more conservative social agenda. Foreign policy, especially under President Ronald Reagan in the 1980s, moved away from the détente of the 1970s to a more confrontational agenda with the Soviet Union. Although the movement politics of the 1960s made strides, especially for women's rights and gay rights in terms of awareness (the Stonewall uprising), they also engendered further resistance to the issues.

👁 Watch on MyHistoryLab

**Watergate** The Watergate scandal resulted in the resignation of President Richard M. Nixon and led to a growing distrust of the federal government. This video examines Watergate from its origins in the presidential election of 1972 (the burglary of Democratic National Committee headquarters) through the Nixon administration's cover-up of the crime, and the congressional hearings that finally forced Nixon to step aside or face impeachment in 1974. **2**

Watch on MyHistoryLab 👁

**3** **The Women's Movement** This video surveys the women's movement during the 1970s and 1980s, when the right for a woman to have an abortion was ensured by the Supreme Court decision of *Roe v. Wade* and the Equal Rights Amendment to the U.S. Constitution was considered and nearly ratified. While women continued to make gains in the workforce and in higher education (Title IX), the Stop ERA movement as well as a strong anti-feminist backlash strengthened the hand of conservative Republicans in the 1980s.

👁 Watch on MyHistoryLab

**Jimmy Carter** Taking advantage of the post-Watergate mood of the nation in 1976, Jimmy Carter positioned himself as an outsider to beat Gerald Ford. This video profiles Carter and describes his early success and his commitment of human rights around the world. It also discusses the stagnant economy and the foreign policy disaster of the Iranian hostage crisis, both of which contributed to his loss to Ronald Reagan in 1980. **4**

Watch on MyHistoryLab

I gave a speech [at Northern Illinois University] and this one young man came up to me afterwards and he said, "My mother works in the fields. She's an onion picker." He says, "and I was always ashamed of my mother until today." … We have to get farm workers the same types of benefits, the same type of wages, the respect that they deserve because they do the most sacred work of all. They feed our nation every day.

Dolores Huerta, interview with Vincent Harding at The Veterans of Hope Project, www.veteransofhope.org/show.php?vid=51&tid=46&sid=77. Reprinted by permission.

## Personal Journeys Online

29.1

29.2

29.3

29.4

29.5

29.6

**F**rom the early 1960s, Dolores Huerta was a coworker with Cesar Chavez in organizing the United Farm Workers (UFW) union. Her personal journey took her from her birthplace in the state of New Mexico, to Stockton, California, where she grew up in a multiracial neighborhood, and then to every corner of the United States as a spokesperson for the UFW. In this interview, she reflected on the power of nonviolent approaches such as the national boycott of table grapes that was the UFW's most successful tactic.

Her story speaks not only to the importance of grassroots action and to the role of churches as sources of social change, but also to the depth of economic and cultural divisions within the United States in the later 1960s and 1970s. At the same time that groups like the UFW worked to build social movements across ethnic differences, many minority Americans responded to slow progress toward racial equality by advocating separation rather than integration, helping to plunge the nation's cities into crisis, while other Americans began to draw back from some of the objectives of racial integration. The failure to win an easy victory in Vietnam eroded the nation's confidence and fueled bitter divisions about the nation's goals. Stalemate in Southeast Asia, political changes in third-world countries, and an oil supply crisis in the 1970s challenged U.S. influence in the world. Political scandals, summarized as "Watergate," undercut faith in government. Fifteen years of turmoil forced a grudging recognition of the limits to American military power, economic capacity, governmental prerogatives, and even the ideal of a single American dream.

# Deeper into Vietnam

**29.1**    What were the consequences of the growing U.S. war in Vietnam?

**P**leiku is a town in Vietnam 240 miles north of Saigon (now Ho Chi Minh City). In 1965, Pleiku was the site of a South Vietnamese army headquarters and U.S. military base. At 2:00 A.M. on February 7, Viet Cong attacked the U.S. base, killing eight Americans and wounding a hundred. President Johnson ordered retaliatory airstrikes. A month later, Johnson ordered a full-scale air offensive code-named ROLLING THUNDER.

The official reason for the bombing was to pressure North Vietnam to negotiate an end to the war. In the back of President Johnson's mind were the need to prove his toughness and the mistaken assumption that China was aggressively backing North Vietnam.

29.1

29.2

29.3

29.4

29.5

29.6

The air strikes pushed the United States over the line from propping up the South Vietnamese government to leading the war effort. A president who desperately wanted a way out of Southeast Asia kept adding U.S. forces. Eventually, the war in Vietnam would distract the United States from the goals of the Great Society and drive Johnson from office. It hovered like a shadow over the next two presidents, set back progress toward global stability, and divided the American people.

## Escalation

Lyndon Johnson faced limited options in Vietnam. The pervasive American determination to contain communism and Kennedy's previous commitments there hemmed Johnson in. Advisers persuaded him that controlled military escalation—a middle course between withdrawal and all-out war—could secure Vietnam. They failed to understand the extent of popular opposition to the official government in Saigon and the willingness of North Vietnam to sacrifice to achieve national unity.

ROLLING THUNDER put the United States on the up escalator to war. Because an air campaign required ground troops to protect bases in South Vietnam, U.S. Marines landed on March 8. More bombs, a pause, an offer of massive U.S. aid—nothing brought North Vietnam to the negotiating table. Meanwhile, defeat loomed. Johnson dribbled in new forces and expanded their mission from base security to combat. On July 28, he finally gave Westmoreland doubled draft calls and an increase in U.S. combat troops from 75,000 to 275,000 by 1966 (see Figure 29.1).

Johnson's decision turned a South Vietnamese war into a U.S. war. Secretary of Defense McNamara was clear about the change: "We have relied on South Vietnam to carry the brunt. Now we would be responsible for a satisfactory military outcome." At the end of 1967, U.S. forces in South Vietnam totaled 485,000.

**search and destroy** U.S. military tactic in South Vietnam, using small detachments to locate enemy units and then massive air, artillery, and ground forces to destroy them.

The U.S. strategy on the ground was **search and destroy**. As conceived by Westmoreland, sophisticated surveillance and heavily armed patrols were used to locate enemy detachments, which could then be destroyed by air strikes, artillery, and reinforcements carried in by helicopter. The approach made sense when the opposition consisted of North Vietnamese troops and large Viet Cong units.

However, most opponents were not North Vietnamese divisions but South Vietnamese guerrillas, meaning that the Westmoreland strategy was flawed. The Viet Cong forced the United States to make repeated sweeps through farms and villages. The enemy was difficult for Americans to recognize among farmers and workers, making South Vietnamese society itself the target. The U.S. penchant for massive firepower killed thousands of Vietnamese and made millions refugees. Because the South Vietnamese government was unable to secure areas after American sweeps, the Viet Cong often reappeared after the Americans had crashed through a district.

The U.S. air war also had limited results. Pilots dropped a vast tonnage of bombs on the Ho Chi Minh Trail, a network of supply routes from North Vietnam to South Vietnam through the mountains of neighboring Laos. Despite the bombing, thousands of workers converted rough paths into roads that were repaired as soon as they were damaged. The air assault on North Vietnam itself remained "diplomatic," intended to force North Vietnam to stop intervening in the South Vietnamese civil war. Since North Vietnam's leadership considered North and South to be one country, the American goal was unacceptable. Despite the massive influx of American troops and firepower, the war was not winnable under conditions that the United States could accept. The United States wanted to engage in a limited war with a specific political goal of shoring up an independent South Vietnamese government. The Viet Cong and North Vietnam, in contrast, were fighting a total war of revolution and national liberation that continued struggles since the 1940s. There was no way for the United States to overcome this commitment without a level of mobilization or risk that would have been impossible to sell to the American people.

29.1

29.2

29.3

29.4

29.5

29.6

Read the Document James B. Stockdale, *A Vietnam Experience: Ten Years of Reflection* (1982)

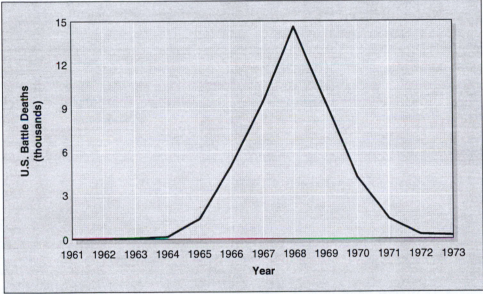

**FIGURE 29.1 THE UNITED STATES IN VIETNAM** American involvement in Vietnam grew slowly during the Kennedy administration from 1961 to 1963, expanded rapidly under Lyndon Johnson from 1964 to 1968, and fell just as rapidly under Richard Nixon from 1969 to 1973. The Nixon Doctrine tried to substitute American weapons and equipment for American military personnel but failed to prevent a North Vietnamese victory in 1975 after U.S. withdrawal.

SOURCE: *Statistical Abstract of the United States.*

## Fighting in 'Nam

The Vietnam War reached deep into American society. The number of military personnel on active duty in Vietnam at any one time peaked at 543,000 in August 1969 before the United States began slowly to disengage. Over the course of the war, roughly 2,700,000 men and women served in Vietnam itself and another 700,000 in support roles elsewhere in Southeast Asia. One out of every sixty Americans directly experienced the war.

Front-line troops, with the mobility provided by helicopters and aircraft, averaged more days of direct combat than had veterans of World War II. With 47,000 combat deaths and 211,000 total casualties, the Vietnam War was the nation's third most deadly after the two world wars. Casualties among North Vietnamese and South Vietnamese soldiers and civilians were far higher.

29.1

29.2

29.3

29.4

29.5

29.6

Particularly in the early years of the conflict, military service deepened the nation's racial divide. In 1965, when African Americans made up 11 percent of the nation's population, 24 percent of the soldiers who died in Vietnam were black. This disparity forced the Defense Department to revise combat assignments and eliminate the racial difference in the later years of the war.

Disaffection among soldiers mounted as the war dragged on. Racial tensions sapped morale on the front lines. Troops sometimes lost discipline and hunkered down, waiting for their tours of duty to end. Soldiers "fragged" (killed) several hundred of their own gung-ho or incompetent officers, and the high command had to adapt its code of justice to keep an army on the job. At the same time, drug use was far less extreme than popular myth would have it. Taken together, recreational drug use, mostly behind the front lines, was not much different than in other wars—although marijuana now challenged traditional alcohol.

## From Dissent to Confrontation

At home, protest against the war quickly followed the commitment of U.S. combat forces. In the 1950s, dissenters on the left had been too intimidated by McCarthyism to protest overcommitment to the Cold War. Now a coalition of experienced antiwar workers and new college activists openly challenged the Cold Warriors. The first national antiwar march took place in Washington on April 17, 1965. Twenty-five thousand people picketed the White House, assembled at the Washington Monument for speeches by Senator Ernest Gruening of Alaska (one of the two dissenting votes on the Gulf of Tonkin Resolution) and African American leaders, and walked up the Mall to the Capitol.

Many opponents were "realists" who argued that the war was a mistake. Foreign policy expert Hans Morgenthau fully supported anti-Soviet containment in Europe but argued that the United States had no vital interests in Vietnam. Senator J. William

**Read the Document**    Martin Luther King, Jr., "Conscience and the Vietnam War" (1967)

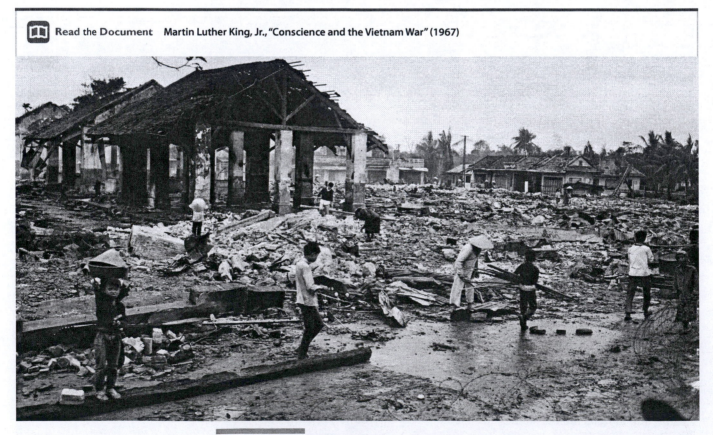

The city of Hue suffered severe damage in the Tet Offensive and its aftermath. Here refugees return to the rubble of bombed-out houses.

Fulbright published *The Arrogance of Power* in 1967, a book arguing that even the United States needed to recognize limits on its political and military power.

Martin Luther King, Jr. offered one of the strongest condemnations of the war in a speech at New York's Riverside Church on April 4, 1967. He stepped beyond the specifics of civil rights to decry the diversion of resources from domestic programs to the military, the impacts of the war on the people of Vietnam, and what he saw as the poisonous effects of warfare on the soul of America. The speech was a deeply Christian argument for policies of negotiation and reconciliation in place of war.

In 1966 and 1967, antiwar activity changed from respectful protest to direct confrontations with what protesters called the war machine. The tone of the debate became nasty as protesters chanted "Hey, hey, LBJ! How many kids did you kill today?" Much of the anger was directed at the military draft administered by the **Selective Service System**. As the name implies, Selective Service supposedly picked the young men who could best serve the nation as soldiers and deferred induction of those with vital skills. As the war expanded, the administration tried to hold the allegiance of the middle class by finding ways to exempt their sons from service in Vietnam. Full-time college enrollment was good for a deferment; so was the right medical diagnosis from the right doctor. As a result, draftees and enlistees tended to be small-town and working-class youth. They were also young. The average GI in World War II had been in his mid-twenties; the typical soldier in Vietnam was 19 or 20. Women who served as military nurses tended to come from the same small-town and working-class backgrounds where patriotism was unquestioned.

Draft resistance provided a direct avenue for protest against the war. Some young men burned the small paper cards that indicated their selective service classification, causing Congress to enact steep penalties for the act. Several thousand moved to Canada, to spend a decade or more in exile. Thousands of others described their religious and ethical opposition to war in applications for conscientious-objector classification. Much smaller numbers went to jail for refusing to cooperate in any way with the Selective Service System. And a handful of activists, including the Catholic priests Daniel Berrigan and Philip Berrigan, directly disrupted its operations by invading draft-board offices and trying to burn files or douse them with animal blood.

29.1

29.2

29.3

29.4

29.5

29.6

**Selective Service System** Federal agency that coordinated military conscription before and during the Vietnam War.

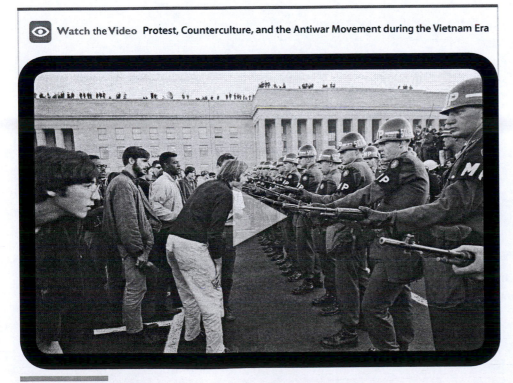

👁 **Watch the Video** Protest, Counterculture, and the Antiwar Movement during the Vietnam Era

In October 1967, 100,000 people marched on the Pentagon to protest the war in Vietnam.

29.1

29.2

29.3

29.4

29.5

29.6

# ✳ Explore the Vietnam War on MyHistoryLab

## WHAT DID THE WAR IN VIETNAM MEAN FOR THE UNITED STATES?

Between 1955 and 1975, a civil war raged across Vietnam between a communist government in the north and a weak democracy-dictatorship in the south. In the context of the Cold War, the United States supported the South Vietnamese government, hoping to stop the spread of communism. By the early 1960s, the American government began increasing its troop presence in Vietnam and in 1965 sent its first combat units. American military intervention in Vietnam and into the neighboring countries of Southeast Asia grew. As casualties mounted and little in the way of military progress was made, the intervention became increasingly unpopular at home, and antiwar protests spread. Some 58,000 American servicemen and women died before the United States withdrew in 1975. Soon after, the South Vietnamese government fell as the country was united under a single communist government.

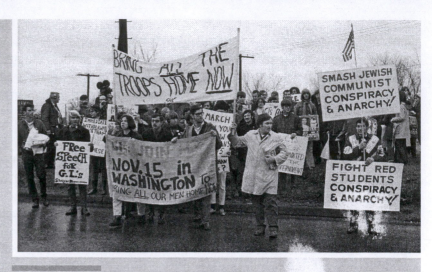

These antiwar marchers, protesting U.S. involvement in Southeast Asia are met by a lone counter-protester at Fort Devens in Ayer, Massachusetts, in 1970.

### AMERICAN ARMED FORCES DEATHS IN VIETNAM

| Year | Deaths | Year | Deaths |
|------|--------|------|--------|
| 1956–1959 | 4 | 1968 | 16,899 |
| 1960 | 5 | 1969 | 11,780 |
| 1961 | 16 | 1970 | 6,173 |
| 1962 | 53 | 1971 | 2,414 |
| 1963 | 122 | 1972 | 759 |
| 1964 | 216 | 1973 | 68 |
| 1965 | 1,928 | 1974 | 1 |
| 1966 | 6,350 | 1975 | 62 |
| 1967 | 11,363 | | |

SOURCE: *Statistical Information about Fatal Casualties of the Vietnam War National Archives,* National Archives, http://www.archives.gov/research/military/vietnam-war/casualty-statistics. html#home.

**KEY QUESTIONS** Use **MyHistoryLab** *Explorer* to answer these **questions:**

**Cause** ▶▶▶ *What geographic challenges did American forces face in Vietnam?*

Map features that hindered the U.S. military effort.

**Response** ▶▶▶ *What was the significance of various U.S. military operations in Vietnam, especially the Tet Offensive?*

Explore the unfolding of the war.

**Consequence** ▶▶▶ *What relationships may have existed between war deaths and other socioeconomic factors in an area?*

Chart potential correlations and consider underlying reasons.

# New Voices

29.1

**29.2**

29.3

29.4

29.5

29.6

**29.2**   What conflicting social values and goals divided Americans in the 1960s?

In 1968, supporters of the U.S. role in Vietnam had plunked down $22 million at the box office to watch an aging John Wayne in *The Green Berets*. The year before, however, they had already spent five times that much ($104 million) on the 1967 sensation *The Graduate*. Where Wayne had played a traditional hero, Dustin Hoffman's character Benjamin Braddock resonated with a new generation who were increasingly disillusioned with a nation whose values as well as economy were symbolized by the artificiality of plastic. Two years later, *Easy Rider* (1969) also doubled the *Green Beret* box office with its story of two drug-using dropouts whose motorcycle trip across the continent represented the pace of social change.

## New Left and Community Activism

The antiwar movement was part of a growing grassroots activism that took much of its tone from the university-based **Students for a Democratic Society (SDS)**. The group was important for its ideas, not its size. Its Port Huron Statement, adopted in 1962, called for grassroots action and participatory democracy. Building on the ideas of such 1950s dissenters as C. Wright Mills, SDS wanted to counter the trends that seemed to be turning Americans into tiny cogs in the machinery of big government, corporations, and universities. SDS thought of itself as a "New Left" that was free from the doctrinal squabbles that hampered the old left of the 1930s and 1940s.

Many of the original SDS leaders were also participants in the civil rights movement. The same was true of Mario Savio, founder of the **Free Speech Movement (FSM)** at the University of California at Berkeley in 1964. Savio hoped to build a multi-issue "community of protest" around the idea of "a free university in a free society." FSM protests climaxed with a December sit-in that led to 773 arrests and stirred protest on other campuses.

What SDS wanted to do with its grassroots organizing resembled the federal community-action programs associated with the war on poverty. The **Model Cities Program** (1966) invited residents of poor neighborhoods to write their own plans for using federal funds to improve local housing, education, health services, and job opportunities. Model Cities assemblies challenged the racial bias in programs like urban renewal and helped train community leaders.

In the 1970s and 1980s, when SDS was long gone and the Model Cities Program was fading, the lessons of grassroots reform would still be visible in alternative organizations and political movements that strengthened democracy from the bottom up. Activists staffed food cooperatives, free clinics, women's health groups, and drug-counseling centers across the country. Community-based organization was a key element in self-help efforts by African Americans, Asian Americans, and Latinos.

## Youth Culture and Counterculture

The popular context for the serious work of the New Left was the growing youth culture and **counterculture**. Millions of young people in the second half of the 1960s expressed their alienation from American society by sampling drugs or chasing the rainbow of a youth culture. The middle-aged and middle class ignored the differences and dubbed the rebellious young "hippies."

The youth culture took advantage of the nation's prosperity. It was consumerism in a tie-dyed T-shirt. A high point was the 1969 Woodstock rock festival in New York State. But Woodstock was an excursion, not a life-altering commitment. Members of the Woodstock Generation were consumers in a distinct market niche, dressing but not living like social reformers or revolutionaries.

**Students for a Democratic Society (SDS)** The leading student organization of the New Left of the early and mid-1960s.

**Free Speech Movement (FSM)** Student movement at the University of California, Berkeley, formed in 1964 to protest limitations on political activities on campus.

**Model Cities Program** Effort to target federal funds to upgrade public services and economic opportunity in specifically defined urban neighborhoods between 1966 and 1974.

**counterculture** Various alternatives to mainstream values and behaviors that became popular in the 1960s, including experimentation with psychedelic drugs, communal living, a return to the land, Asian religions, and experimental art.

29.1

29.2

29.3

29.4

29.5

29.6

Within the youth culture was a smaller and more intense counterculture that added Eastern religion, social radicalism, and evangelistic belief in the drug LSD. The Harvard professor Timothy Leary and the writer Aldous Huxley claimed that hallucinogenic or psychedelic drugs, such as mescaline and LSD, would swing open the "doors of perception." San Francisco's Haight-Ashbury district became a national mecca for hippies in 1967's "Summer of Love," and hippie districts sprang up around university campuses across the country.

The cultural rebels of the late 1950s and early 1960s had been trying to combine personal freedom with new social arrangements. Many hippies were more interested in altering their minds with drugs than with politics or poetry. Serious exploration of societal alternatives was left for the minority who devoted themselves to the political work of the New Left, communal living, women's liberation, and other movements.

## Communes

Out of the half-secular, half-spiritual vision of the counterculture came people who not only dropped out of mainstream institutions but also tried to drop into miniature societies built on new principles. Thousands of Americans in the late 1960s and 1970s formed "intentional communities" or "communes." Their members usually tried to combine individual freedom and spontaneity with cooperative living. Upper New England, the Southwest, and the northern Pacific coast were commune country. Rural communes usually located on marginal land too poor to support commercial farming; members pored over *The Whole Earth Catalog* (1968) to figure out how to live on the land.

Communes were artificial families that often suffered from the same inequality between men and women that would fuel the feminist revolt. They were emotional hothouses that often collapsed because their members had incompatible goals.

However, a number of communes were serious endeavors. Some tried to follow spiritual leadings from Christianity or Buddhism. Thousands of smaller and less conspicuous urban communes whose members occupied large old houses pursued experiments in socialism, environmentalism, or feminism. Such efforts helped to spread the ideas of organic farming, cooperative land ownership, and low-consumption environmentalism that would move into the mainstream.

## Grassroots Conservatism

Very different religious values helped to shape grassroots conservatism that paralleled liberal community activism with very different goals. Among the most fertile seedbeds for conservatism were new communities in Orange County, the San Fernando Valley, and other booming areas in Southern California. These suburbs were heavily dependent on the defense industry and heavily populated by migrants from the South who were evangelical Southern Baptists, Nazarenes, or Pentacostals. In the context of the Cold War, many of these residents emphasized militant preparedness and patriotism, individual rights, and personal morality. At the extreme, men sometimes joined the John Birch Society, which thought that even Dwight Eisenhower had dangerous communist tendencies. Meanwhile, women talked around kitchen tables and organized to support conservative political candidates and win school board elections to make sure that instruction was not too radical.

Conservatives also built lasting institutions. For example, the Campus Crusade for Christ, founded at UCLA in 1951, expanded rapidly in the 1960s from headquarters in San Bernadino. The grassroots conservatives would throw their all into Barry Goldwater's unsuccessful campaign for president in 1964, and they would help make Ronald Reagan governor of California in 1966.

Another conservative strand came from the urban working class in older cities, who had begun to move toward the political right as early as the 1950s. Urban renewal sometimes destroyed their neighborhoods to benefit economic elites. At the same time, growing black populations looking for affordable housing raised fears of unwanted neighborhood change. In response, many white urbanites framed local resistance to neighborhood integration in the form of protecting property rights. The same theme appeared in suburban communities in cities like Atlanta, where the rhetoric and tools of property rights and individualism helped to preserve neighborhood racial segregation.

These several elements represented different parts of the so-called "silent majority" that Republicans began to court in the 1970s and which helped to put Ronald Reagan in the White House in 1981.

29.1

29.2

29.3

29.4

29.5

29.6

## The Feminist Critique

At the other end of the political spectrum from the conservative women of Orange County were feminists who expanded on Betty Friedan's ideas from the early 1960s. The growing dissatisfaction of many women with their domestic roles (not to mention their often secondary positions in communes and radical organizations) helped set the stage for a revived feminism that was another result of the ferment of the 1960s. Important steps in this revival included the Presidential Commission on the Status of Women in 1961, the addition of gender as one of the categories protected by the Civil Rights Act of 1964 (see Chapter 28), and the creation of the National Organization for Women (NOW) in 1966.

Mainstream feminism targeted unequal opportunity in the job market. Newspapers in the early 1960s segregated help-wanted ads by sex, listing "Girl Friday" jobs in one column and professional work in another. College-educated baby boomers encountered "glass ceilings" and job discrimination, in which companies hired less qualified men who "needed the job" rather than more qualified women who supposedly did not. Throughout the mid-1960s and 1970s, activists battled to open job categories to women, who battled for equal pay for everyone with equal qualifications and responsibilities.

Changes in sexual behavior paralleled efforts to equalize treatment in the workplace. More reliable methods of contraception, especially birth-control pills introduced in the early 1960s, gave women greater control over childbearing. In some ways a replay of ideas from the 1920s, a new sexual revolution eroded the double standard that expected chastity of women but tolerated promiscuity among men. One consequence was a singles culture that accepted sexual activity between unmarried men and women.

More radical versions of the feminist message came from women who had joined the civil rights and antiwar movements only to find themselves working the copy machine and the coffeemaker while men plotted strategy. Radicals caught the attention of the national media with a demonstration against the 1968 Miss America pageant. Protesters crowned a sheep as Miss America and encouraged women to make a statement by tossing their bras and makeup in the trash.

Women's liberation took off as a social and political movement in 1970 and 1971. Within a few years, millions of women had recognized events and patterns in their lives as discrimination based on gender. The feminist movement, and specific policy measures related to it, put equal rights and the fight against sexism (a word no one knew before 1965) on the national agenda and gradually changed how Americans thought about the relationships between men and women. Feminists focused attention on rape as a crime of violence and called attention to the burdens the legal system placed on rape victims. In the 1980s and 1990s, they also challenged sexual harassment in the workplace, gradually refining the boundaries between acceptable and unacceptable behavior.

## Coming Out

The new militancy among gay men and lesbians drew on several of the social changes of the late 1960s and 1970s. Willingness to acknowledge and talk about nonstandard sexual behavior was part of a change in public values. Tactics of political pressure came from the antiwar and civil rights movements.

29.1

29.2

29.3

29.4

29.5

29.6

Gay activism spread from big cities to small communities, from the coasts to Middle America. New York police had long harassed gay bars and their customers. When police raided Manhattan's Stonewall Inn in June 1969, however, patrons fought back in a weekend of disorder. The **Stonewall Rebellion** was a catalyst for homosexuals to assert themselves as a political force. San Francisco also became a center of gay life.

With New Yorkers and San Franciscans as examples, more and more gay men and lesbians "came out," or went public about their sexual orientation. They published newspapers, organized churches, and lobbied politicians for protection of basic civil rights such as equal access to employment, housing, and public accommodations. They staged "gay pride" days and marches. In 1974, the American Psychiatric Association eliminated homosexuality from its official list of mental disorders.

# Cities Under Stress

**29.3** What challenges did cities face in the late 1960s and 1970s?

I n the confident years after World War II, big cities had an upbeat image. By the 1970s, however, slums and squalid back streets dominated popular imagery. Movies and television reinforced the message that cities had become places of random and frequent violence.

## Diagnosing an Urban Crisis

The nation entered the 1960s with the assumption that urban problems were growing pains. Exploding metropolitan areas needed money for streets, schools, and sewers. Politicians viewed the difficulties of central cities as by-products of exuberant suburban growth, which left outmoded downtowns in need of physical redevelopment.

Central cities had a special burden in caring for the domestic poor, however. Baltimore, for example, had 27 percent of the Maryland population in 1970 but 66 percent of the state's welfare recipients. Impoverished and often fragmented families needed schools to serve as social-work agencies as well as educational institutions. Poor people with no other access to health care treated city hospital emergency rooms as the family doctor.

Many urban problems were associated with the "second ghettos" created by the migration of 2.5 million African Americans from southern farms to northern and western cities in the 1950s and 1960s. By 1970, one-third of all African Americans lived in the twelve largest cities, crowding into ghetto neighborhoods dating from World War II.

At the end of their journeys, postwar black migrants found systems of race relations that limited their access to decent housing, the best schools, and many unionized jobs. Many families arrived just in time to face the consequences of industrial layoffs and plant closures in the 1970s and 1980s. Already unneeded in the South because of the mechanization of agriculture, the migrants found themselves equally unwanted in the industrial North, caught in decaying neighborhoods and victimized by crime.

Central cities faced additional financial problems unrelated to poverty and race. Many of their roads, bridges, fire stations, and water mains were 50 to 100 years old by the 1960s and 1970s, and they were wearing out. Decay of urban utility and transportation systems was a by-product of market forces and public policy. Private developers often borrowed money saved through northeastern bank accounts, insurance policies, and pension funds to finance new construction in sunbelt suburbs. The defense budget pumped tax dollars from the old industrial cities into the South and West.

## Conflict in the Streets

African Americans and Hispanics who rioted in city streets in the mid-1960s were fed up with the lack of job opportunities, with substandard housing, and with crime.

29.1

29.2

**29.3**

29.4

29.5

29.6

Prominent black writers, such as James Baldwin in *The Fire Next Time* (1963), had warned of the mounting anger. Suddenly the fires were real. Riots in Rochester, Harlem, and Brooklyn in July 1964 opened four years of racial violence. Before they subsided, the riots had scarred most big cities and killed 200 people, most of them African Americans.

The explosion of the Watts neighborhood in Los Angeles fixed the danger of racial unrest in the public mind. Trouble started on August 11, 1965, when a white highway-patrol officer arrested a young African American for drunken driving. Loud complaints drew a crowd, and the arrival of Los Angeles police turned the bystanders into an angry mob that attacked passing cars. The primary targets were symbols of white authority and businesses with reputations for exploiting their customers, a conclusion reached by the National Advisory Commission on Civil Disorders. Rioting, looting, and arson spread through Watts for two days until the National Guard cordoned off the trouble spots and occupied the neighborhood on August 14 and 15.

After Watts, Americans expected "long hot summers" and got them. Scores of cities suffered riots in 1966, including a riot by Puerto Ricans in Chicago that protested the same problems blacks faced. The following year, the worst violence was in Newark, New Jersey, and in Detroit, where forty-three deaths and blocks of blazing buildings stunned television viewers.

Few politicians wanted to admit that African Americans and Hispanics had serious grievances. Their impulse was to blame riffraff and outside agitators. This theory was wrong. Almost all participants were neighborhood residents. Except that they were younger, they were representative of the African American population, and their violence came from the frustration of rising expectations. Despite the political gains of the civil rights movement, unemployment remained high, and the police still treated all blacks as potential criminals. The urban riots were political actions to force the problems of African Americans onto the national agenda.

## Minority Self-Determination

Minority separatism and demands for self-determination tapped the same anger that fueled the urban riots. Drawing on a long heritage of militancy (such as armed resistance during racial riots), activists challenged the central goal of the civil rights movement, which sought full integration and participation in American life. The phrase **Black Power**, popularized by SNCC leader Stokely Carmichael, summed up the new alternative.

**Expressions of Black Power.**   Black Power translated many ways—control of one's own community through the voting machine, celebration of the African American heritage, creation of a parallel society that shunned white institutions. Its intellectual roots reached back to Marcus Garvey and included admiration for anticolonial nationalism in Africa and Asia. At the personal level, it was a synonym for black pride. In the political realm, it pointed toward the successful campaigns of Richard Hatcher in Gary, Indiana, and Carl Stokes in Cleveland, the first African Americans elected mayors of large northern cities.

Black Power also meant increased interest in the **Nation of Islam**, or Black Muslims, who combined a version of Islam with radical separatism. They called for self-discipline, support of black institutions and businesses, and total rejection of whites. The Nation of Islam appealed to blacks who saw no future in integration. It was strongest in northern cities, such as Chicago, where it offered an alternative to the life of the ghetto streets.

In the early 1960s, Malcolm X emerged as a leading Black Muslim. Growing up as Malcolm Little, he was a streetwise criminal until he converted to the Nation of Islam in prison. After his release, Malcolm preached that blacks should stop letting whites set the terms by which they judged their appearance, communities, and accomplishments. He emphasized the African cultural heritage and economic self-help and proclaimed

**Black Power** Philosophy emerging after 1965 that real economic and political gains for African Americans could come only through self-help, self-determination, and organizing for direct political influence.

**Nation of Islam** Religious movement among black Americans that emphasizes self-sufficiency, self-help, and separation from white society.

29.1

29.2

29.3

29.4

29.5

29.6

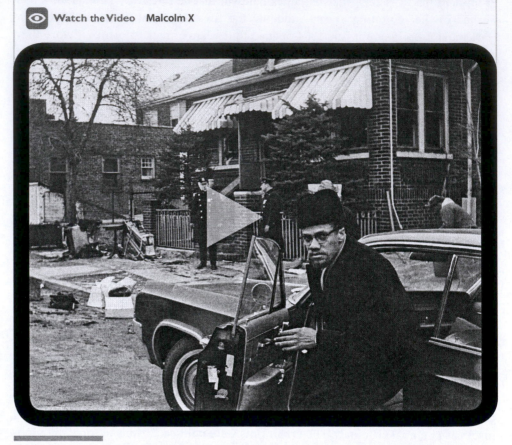

Watch the Video   Malcolm X

Malcolm X arrives home in New York after his house was bombed on February 14, 1965. He would be assassinated a week later.

himself an extremist for black rights. In the last year of his life, however, he returned from a pilgrimage to Mecca willing to consider limited acceptance of whites. Rivals within the movement assassinated him in February 1965, but his ideas lived on in *The Autobiography of Malcolm X.*

**Black Panthers** Political and social movement among black Americans, founded in Oakland, California, in 1966 and emphasizing black economic and political power.

The **Black Panthers** pursued similar goals. Bobby Seale and Huey Newton grew up in the Oakland, California, area and met as college students. They saw African American ghettos as internal colonies in need of self-determination and created the Panthers in 1966. The Panthers asserted their equality by shadowing police patrols to prevent mistreatment of African Americans and carried weapons into the California State Legislature in May 1967 to protest gun control. The Panthers also promoted community-based self-help efforts, such as a free-breakfast program for school children and medical clinics, and ran political candidates. In contrast to the rioters in Watts, the Panthers had a political program, if not the ability to carry it through. Panther chapters imploded when they attracted thugs and shakedown artists as well as visionaries. Nevertheless, the Panthers survived as a political party into the 1970s. Former Panther Bobby Rush entered Congress in 1992.

**Hispanic Activism in the Southwest.**   Latinos in the Southwest developed their own Brown Power movement in the late 1960s. Led by Reies López Tijerina, Hispanics in rural New Mexico demanded the return of lands that had been lost to Anglo Americans despite the guarantees of the Treaty of Guadalupe Hidalgo in 1848. Mexican Americans in the 1970s organized for political power in southern Texas communities where they were a majority.

The best-known Hispanic activism combined social protest with the crusading spirit of earlier labor union organizing campaigns. Cesar Chavez organized the multiracial United Farm Workers (UFW) among Mexican American agricultural workers in California in 1965. Chavez was committed both to nonviolent action for social justice

29.1

29.2

29.3

29.4

29.5

29.6

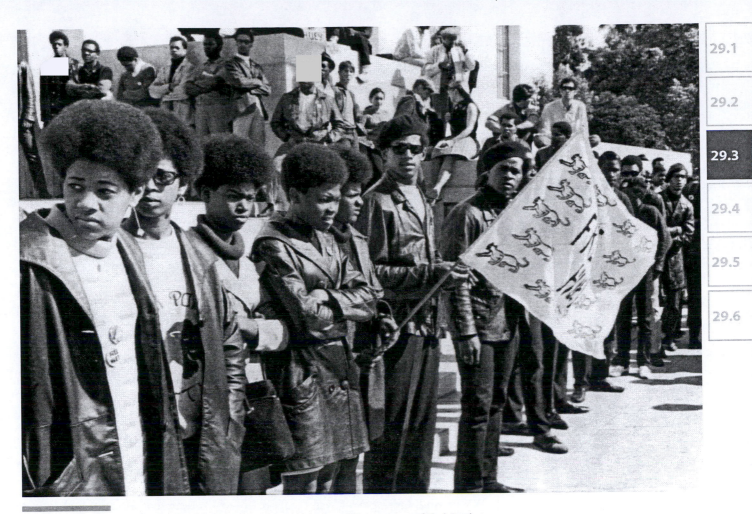

Showing the deep rift between many black and white Americans in the late 1960s, supporters of Black Panther Huey Newton stand outside the Alameda County courthouse in Oakland, California, where Newton was on trial for voluntary manslaughter following a confrontation with police.

and to the labor movement. UFW demands included better wages and safer working conditions, such as less exposure to pesticides. Because farm workers were not covered by the National Labor Relations Act of 1935, the issue was whether farm owners would recognize the union as a bargaining agent and sign a contract. Chavez supplemented work stoppages with national boycotts against table grapes, lettuce, and certain brands of wine, making *la huelga* ("the strike") into *la causa* for urban liberals.

Latino political activism had strong appeal for young people. Ten thousand young Chicanos stormed out of Los Angeles high schools in March 1968 to protest poor education and racist teachers. Some students organized as Brown Berets to demand more relevant education and fairer police treatment. Many rejected assimilation in favor of community self-determination and began to talk about *la raza* ("the people"), whose language and heritage descended from centuries of Mexican history. "Chicano" itself was a slang term with insulting overtones that was now adopted as a badge of pride and cultural identity.

**Native Americans Assert Their Identity.**  Native Americans also fought both for equal access to American society and to preserve cultural traditions through tribal institutions. Like efforts to secure rights and opportunities for African Americans and Latinos, the "Red Power" movement had deep roots in efforts to reverse the termination policy of the 1950s and to secure economic improvements for reservations. Indians in cities like Los Angeles and Portland came together across tribal lines to develop social and cultural services.

One result of this political work came in 1968, when Congress restored the authority of tribal law on reservations. Three years later, the Alaska Native Claims Settlement

29.1
29.2
29.3
29.4
29.5
29.6

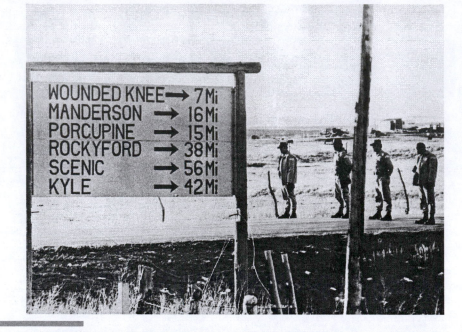

Armed confrontation between militant Indians and state and federal law enforcement at Wounded Knee, South Dakota, in 1973 recalled the decades of warfare between plains tribes and the U.S. Army in the previous century.

Act granted native Alaskans 44 million acres and $963 million to settle claims for their ancestral lands. Legally sophisticated tribes sued for compensation and enforcement of treaty provisions, such as fishing rights in the Pacific Northwest. Larger tribes established their own colleges, such as Navajo Community College (1969) and Oglala Lakota College (1971).

A second development was media-oriented protests that asserted Red Power. One of the earliest was a series of "fish-ins" in which Indians from Washington State, helped by the multitribal National Indian Youth Council, exercised treaty-based fishing rights in defiance of state regulations. Native American students gained national attention by seizing the abandoned Alcatraz Island for a cultural and educational center (1969–1971). Indians in Minneapolis created the **American Indian Movement (AIM)** in 1968 to increase economic opportunity and stop police mistreatment. AIM participated in the cross-country Broken Treaties Caravan, which climaxed by occupying the Bureau of Indian Affairs in Washington in 1972. AIM also allied with Sioux traditionalists on the Pine Ridge Reservation in South Dakota against the tribe's elected government. In 1973, they took over the village of Wounded Knee, where the U.S. Army in 1890 had massacred 300 Indians. They held out for seventy days before leaving peacefully.

## Suburban Independence: The Outer City

In the mid-1960s, the United States became a suburban nation. The 1970 census found more people living in the suburban counties of metropolitan areas (37 percent) than in central cities (31 percent) or in small towns and rural areas (31 percent). Just after World War II, most new suburbs had been bedroom communities that depended on the jobs, services, and shopping of central cities. By the late 1960s, suburbs were evolving into "outer cities," whose inhabitants had little need for the old central city.

**Suburban Economic Growth and Political Influence.** Suburbs captured most new jobs, leaving the urban poor with few opportunities for employment. In the fifteen largest metropolitan areas, the number of central city jobs fell by 800,000 in the 1960s, while the number of suburban jobs rose by 3.2 million. Suburbs also gained a growing share of public facilities intended to serve the entire metropolitan area. As pioneered in California, community colleges served the suburban children of the baby boom.

**American Indian Movement (AIM)** Group of Native American political activists who used confrontations with the federal government to publicize their case for Indian rights.

Suburban political power grew along with economic clout. In 1962, the Supreme Court handed down a landmark decision in the case of **Baker v. Carr**. Overturning laws that treated counties or other political subdivisions as the units to be represented in state legislatures, *Baker* required that legislative seats be apportioned on the basis of population. The principle of "one person, one vote" broke the stranglehold of rural counties on state governments, but the big beneficiaries were not older cities, but fast-growing suburbs. By 1975, suburbanites held the largest block of seats in the House of Representatives. Reapportionment in 1982, based on the 1980 census, produced a House that was even more heavily suburban.

**School Busing Controversies.**  School integration controversies in the 1970s reinforced a tendency for suburbanites to separate themselves from city problems. In *Swann v. Charlotte-Mecklenburg Board of Education* (1971), the U.S. Supreme Court held that crosstown busing was an acceptable solution to the de facto segregation that resulted from residential patterns within a single school district. When school officials around the country failed to achieve racial balance, federal judges ordered their own busing plans. Although integration through busing occurred peacefully in dozens of cities, many white people resented the practice. Working-class students who depended on public schools found themselves on the front lines of integration, while many middle-class families switched to private education. For many Americans, the image of busing for racial integration was fixed in 1975, when white citizens in Boston reacted with violence against black students who were bused to largely white high schools in the South Boston and Charlestown neighborhoods. The goal of equal opportunity clashed with equally strong values of neighborhood, community, and ethnic solidarity.

Because the Supreme Court also ruled that busing programs normally stopped at school-district boundaries, suburbs with independent districts escaped school integration. One result was to make busing self-defeating, for it led white families to move out of the integrating school district. Others placed their children in private academies, as happened frequently in the South. The political separation of suburbs from city thus allowed white suburbanites to think of themselves as defending local control rather than privilege.

**Baker v. Carr** U.S. Supreme Court decision in 1962 that allowed federal courts to review the appointment of state legislative districts and established the principle that such districts should have roughly equal populations ("one person, one vote").

**Swann v. Charlotte-Mecklenburg Board of Education** U.S. Supreme Court decision in 1971 that upheld cross-city busing to achieve the racial integration of public schools.

# The Year of the Gun, 1968

**29.4**  How did the Tet Offensive change American public opinion about the war in Vietnam?

Some years are turning points that force society to reconsider its basic assumptions. In 1914, the violence of World War I undermined Europe's belief in progress. In 1933, Americans had to rethink the role of government. In 1968, mainstream Americans increasingly turned against the war in Vietnam; student protest and youth counterculture turned ugly; and political consensus shattered.

## The Tet Offensive

At the end of 1967, U.S. officials were overconfidently predicting victory. Then, on January 30, 1968, at the beginning of Tet, the Vietnamese New Year, the Viet Cong attacked thirty-six of forty-four provincial capitals and the national capital, Saigon. They hit the U.S. embassy and reached the runways of Tan Son Nhut air base. If the United States was winning, the Tet Offensive should not have been possible.

As a military effort, the attacks failed. United States and South Vietnamese troops repulsed the attacks and cleared the cities. But the offensive was a psychological blow that convinced the American public that the war was quicksand. Television coverage of the Tet battles made the bad publicity worse. At least until Tet, the commentary from

29.1

29.2

29.3

29.4

29.5

29.6

network news anchors had supported the U.S. effort, but the pictures undermined civilian morale. A handful of images stayed in people's memories—a Buddhist monk burning himself to death in protest; a child with flesh peeled off by napalm; a South Vietnamese official executing a captive on the streets of Saigon.

In the wake of the Tet crisis, General Westmoreland's request for 200,000 more troops forced a political and military reevaluation. Clark Clifford, a dedicated Cold Warrior, was the new secretary of defense. Now he had second thoughts. Twenty "wise men"—the big names of the Cold War—told the president that the war was unwinnable on terms acceptable to America's allies and to many Americans. By devouring resources and souring relations with other nations, it endangered rather than enhanced American security. The best option, the wise men told LBJ, was disengagement. (See Table 29.1, Why Were We in South Vietnam?)

## LBJ's Exit

The president was already in political trouble. After other prominent Democrats held back, Minnesota's liberal senator Eugene McCarthy had decided to challenge Johnson in the presidential primaries. Because he controlled the party organizations in two-thirds of the states, Johnson did not need the primary states for renomination and ignored the first primary in New Hampshire. McCarthy won a startling 42 percent of the popular vote and twenty of twenty-four delegates in the New Hampshire primary. The vote was a protest against Johnson's Vietnam policy rather than a clear mandate for peace. Nevertheless, the vote proved that the political middle would no longer hold.

By showing Johnson's vulnerability, New Hampshire also drew Robert Kennedy into the race. The younger brother of JFK, Kennedy could be arrogant and abrasive,

TABLE 29.1  WHY WERE WE IN SOUTH VIETNAM?

| U.S. leaders offered a number of justifications for U.S. military involvement in Vietnam. Here are some of the key arguments, with points that supported or questioned the explanation. | | |
|---|---|---|
| To Prop Up a Domino: | Communist success in South Vietnam would undermine pro-American regimes in adjacent nations, which would topple like a row of dominoes. | |
| | Pro | The firm U.S. stand contributed to an anti-Communist coup in Indonesia in 1965 and encouraged pro-American interests in Thailand and the Philippines. |
| | Con | Detailed knowledge of each nation in Southeast Asia shows that their own histories and internal issues were far more important in determining their futures than was U.S. action in Vietnam. |
| To Contain China: | China's Communist regime wanted to expand its control throughout Asia. | |
| | Pro | The People's Republic of China was hostile to the United States, as shown in the Korean War, and had a long history of trying to control Vietnam. |
| | Con | North Vietnam had closer ties to the Soviet Union than to China and played the two Communist nations against each other to preserve its independence from China. |
| To Defeat Aggression: | South Vietnam was an independent nation threatened by invasion. | |
| | Pro | The major military threat to South Vietnam after 1965 came from the growing presence of the North Vietnamese army, and U.S. military intervention was necessary to counter that invasion. |
| | Con | The conflict in South Vietnam originated as a civil war within South Vietnam. Moreover, South and North Vietnam were a single nation, artificially divided in 1954, so that North Vietnam was trying to reunify rather than invade South Vietnam. |
| To Protect Democracy: | South Vietnam was a democratic nation that deserved U.S. support. | |
| | Pro | South Vietnam had an emerging middle class and an opportunity to develop democratic institutions. |
| | Con | South Vietnam was never a true democracy, ruled first by civilian dictator Ngo Dinh Diem and then a series of military strongmen. |

but was more successful than other mainstream politicians in touching the hearts of Hispanic and African American voters.

Facing political challenges and an unraveling war, on March 31, 1968, Johnson announced a halt to most bombing of North Vietnam, opening the door for peace negotiations that formally began in May 1969. He then astounded the country by withdrawing from the presidential race. It was a statesmanlike act by a man who had been consumed by a war he did not want, had never understood, and could not end.

## Red Spring

Turmoil also came to Columbia University in New York City in April 1968. Its African American students and its SDS chapter had several grievances. One was the university's cooperation with the Pentagon-funded Institute for Defense Analysis. Another was its plan to build a gymnasium on park land that might better serve the residents of Harlem. Students occupied university buildings, including the library and the president's office, for a week until police evicted them. A student strike and additional clashes with the authorities lasted until June.

The "battle of Morningside Heights" (the location of Columbia) generated banner headlines in the United States, but it was tame when compared to Europe. During the same "Red Spring," revolts by angry university students and workers created upheaval on both sides of the Iron Curtain. Examples of rebellion traveled back and forth across the Atlantic in news stories and television clips, connecting the unrest as a global phenomenon.

Students rioted in Italy and Berlin over rigid university systems, the Vietnam War, and the power of multinational corporations. Workers and students protested against the Franco regime in Spain. In Paris, student demonstrations against the Vietnam War turned into attacks on the university system and the French government. Students fought police in the Paris streets in the first days of May and radical industrial workers called a general strike. The government nearly toppled before the disturbance subsided.

Grassroots rebellion also shook the Soviet grip on Eastern Europe. Alexander Dubcek, the new leader of the Czech Communist Party, brought together students and the middle class around reforms that caused people to talk about the "Prague Spring"—a blossoming of democracy inside the Soviet bloc. Here the changes went too far. As Czechs pressed for more and more political freedom, the Soviet Union feared losing control of one of its satellites. On August 21, 500,000 troops from the Soviet Union and other Warsaw Pact nations rolled across the border and forced Czechoslovakia back into line.

## Violence and Politics: King, Kennedy, and Chicago

Johnson's dramatic withdrawal was followed by the violent disruption of U.S. politics through assassination and riot. On April 4, 1968, an ex-convict, James Earl Ray, shot and killed Martin Luther King, Jr. as he stood on the balcony of a Memphis motel. King was in Memphis to support striking city workers, an example of his increasing emphasis on economic justice and equality as well as civil rights. King's death was the product of pure racial hatred, and it triggered a climactic round of violence in black ghettos. Fires devastated the West Side of Chicago and downtown Washington, DC. The army guarded the steps of the Capitol, ready to protect Congress from its fellow citizens.

The shock of King's death was still fresh when another political assassination stunned the nation. On June 5, Robert Kennedy won California's primary election. He was still behind Vice President Hubert Humphrey in the delegate count but coming on strong. As Kennedy walked out of the ballroom at his headquarters in the Ambassador Hotel in Los Angeles, a Jordanian immigrant named Sirhan Sirhan put a bullet in his brain for reasons unknown.

Kennedy's death ensured the Democratic nomination for Humphrey, a liberal who had loyally supported Johnson's war policy. After his nomination, Humphrey faced the Republican Richard Nixon and the Independent George Wallace. Nixon positioned

29.1

29.2

29.3

29.4

29.5

29.6

29.1

29.2

29.3

29.4

29.5

29.6

himself as the candidate of the political middle. Wallace appealed to southern whites and working-class northerners who feared black militancy and hated "the ivory-tower folks with pointy heads."

Both got great help from the Democratic Convention, held in Chicago on August 26–29. While Democrats feuded among themselves, Chicago Mayor Richard Daley and his police department monitored antiwar protesters. The National Mobilization Committee to End the War in Vietnam drew from the New Left and from older peace activists—sober and committed people who had fought against nuclear weapons in the 1950s and the Vietnam War throughout the 1960s. They wanted to embarrass the Johnson-Humphrey administration by marching to the convention hall on nomination night. Mixed in were the Yippies, an informal group who planned to attract young people to Chicago with the promise of street theater, media events, and confrontation that would puncture the pretensions of the power structure.

The volatile mix was ready for a spark. On August 28, the same night that Democratic delegates were nominating Humphrey, tensions exploded in a police riot. Protesters and Yippies had congregated in Grant Park, across Michigan Avenue from downtown hotels. Police waded into the crowds with clubs and tear gas. Young people fought back with rocks and bottles. Television caught the hours of violence that ended when the National Guard separated police from demonstrators. For Humphrey, the convention was a catastrophe, alienating liberal Democrats and associating Democrats with disorder in the public mind.

The election was closer than Humphrey had any right to hope (see Map 29.1). Nixon appealed to the white middle class and claimed that he had a secret plan to end the war. He also used increasing fears about crime and street violence as a "wedge issue" to split worried white voters from the Democrats. Election day gave Wallace 13.5 percent of the popular vote, Humphrey 42.7 percent of the popular vote and 191 electoral votes, and Nixon 43.4 percent of the popular vote and 301 electoral votes.

The Wallace candidacy was a glimpse of the future. The national media saw Wallace in terms of bigotry and a backlash against civil rights, getting only part of the story. Many of Wallace's northern backers were unhappy with both parties. Liberal on economic issues but conservative on family and social issues, many of these working-class voters evolved into "Reagan Democrats" by the 1980s.

# Nixon, Watergate, and the Crisis of the Early 1970s

**29.5** What was the legacy of Richard Nixon's presidency?

Richard Nixon's painful public presence and dishonesty have tended to obscure his administration's accomplishments. He reduced tensions in the Cold War. He reluctantly upgraded civil rights enforcement, set goals for minority hiring by federal contractors, and presided over impressive environmental legislation.

## Getting Out of Vietnam, 1969–1975

After 1968, things got worse in Southeast Asia before they got better. Nixon had no secret plan to end the war. Opposition intensified with the revelation that U.S. soldiers in March 1968 had slaughtered hundreds of men, women, and children in the South Vietnamese village of My Lai after failing to find any Viet Cong. This crime accentuated the dehumanizing power of war and showed how far the United States was straying from its ideals. Protests at home culminated in 1969 with the Vietnam Moratorium on October 15, when 2 million protesters joined rallies across the country.

29.1

29.2

29.3

29.4

**29.5**

29.6

| | Electoral Vote (%) | Popular Vote (%) |
|---|---|---|
| **RICHARD M. NIXON** (Republican) | **301** **(56)** | **31,785,480** **(43.4)** |
| Hubert H. Humphrey (Democrat) | 191 (36) | 31,275,165 (42.7) |
| George C. Wallace (American Independent) | 46 (8) | 9,906,473 (13.5) |
| Other candidates | – | 221,134 (.3) |
| (Dick Gregory, Socialist Labor; Fred Halstead and Paul Boutelle, Socialist Workers; Eugene McCarthy, Peace and Freedom; E. Harold Munn and Rolland E. Fisher, Prohibition) | | |

**MAP 29.1 THE ELECTION OF 1968** Richard Nixon won the presidency with the help of George Wallace, the American Independent Party candidate. Wallace won several southern states, offering an alternative to white southerners unhappy with the Democratic Party but not yet prepared to vote Republican. He also drew northern working-class votes away from Hubert Humphrey and thus helped Nixon to take several midwestern states.

Nixon and Vice President Spiro Agnew responded by trying to isolate the antiwar opposition, but Nixon also reduced the role of U.S. ground forces. He claimed that his policies represented "the great silent majority of my fellow Americans." The administration arranged for a "spontaneous" attack by construction workers on antiwar protesters in New York. The hard-hat counterattack was a cynically manipulated symbol, but Nixon and Agnew tapped genuine anger about failure in Asia and rapid change in U.S. society.

**"Vietnamization" and the Secret War against Cambodia.** Nixon's secretary of defense, Melvin Laird, responded to the antiwar sentiment with "Vietnamization," withdrawing U.S. troops as fast as possible without undermining the South Vietnamese government. In July 1969, the president announced the **Nixon Doctrine**. The United States would help other countries fight their wars with weapons and money but not with soldiers.

**Nixon Doctrine** President Nixon's new American policy (1969) toward Asia in which the United States would honor treaty commitments but would gradually disengage and expect Asian nations to handle military defense on their own.

29.1

29.2

29.3

29.4

29.5

29.6

The policy substituted machines for men. Americans rearmed and enlarged the South Vietnamese army and surreptitiously bombed Communist bases in neutral Cambodia.

The secret war against Cambodia culminated on April 30, 1970, with an invasion aimed at smashing Viet Cong and North Vietnamese bases to allow time to rebuild the South Vietnamese army. Americans who had hoped that the war was fading away were outraged. Students shut down hundreds of colleges. At Kent State University in Ohio, the National Guard was called in to maintain order. Taunts, tossed bottles, and the recent record of violence put them on edge. On May 4, one unit fired on a group of young people and killed four of them. At Jackson State University in Mississippi, two students were killed when troops fired on their dormitory.

**Stalemate and Cease-Fire.** The Cambodian "incursion" extended the military stalemate in Vietnam to U.S. policy. Beginning in December 1969, a new lottery system for determining the order of draft calls by birthdate let two-thirds of young men know they would not be drafted. In December 1970, Congress repealed the Gulf of Tonkin Resolution and prohibited the use of U.S. ground troops outside South Vietnam. Cambodia, however, was already devastated. The U.S. invasion had destabilized its government and opened the way for the bloodthirsty Khmer Rouge, who killed millions of Cambodians in the name of a working-class revolution. Vietnamization continued; only 90,000 U.S. ground troops were still in Vietnam by early 1972. A final air offensive in December smashed Hanoi into rubble and helped to force four and a half years of peace talks to a conclusion.

The cease-fire began on January 27, 1973. It confirmed U.S. withdrawal from Vietnam. North Vietnamese and Viet Cong forces would remain in control of the territory they occupied in South Vietnam, but they were not to be reinforced or substantially reequipped. The United States promised not to increase its military aid to South Vietnam. There were no solid guarantees for the South Vietnamese government. Immediately after coming to terms with North Vietnam, Nixon suspended the draft in favor of an all-volunteer military.

In 1975, South Vietnam collapsed. Only the U.S. presence had kept its political and religious factions together. For the first two years after the Paris agreement, North Vietnam quietly rebuilt its military capacity. In the spring of 1975, it opened an offensive, and South Vietnamese resistance evaporated.

## Nixon and the Wider World

To his credit, Richard Nixon took U.S. foreign policy in new directions even while he was struggling to escape from Vietnam and Cambodia. Like Dwight Eisenhower before him, Nixon's reputation as an anti-Communist allowed him to improve relations with China and the Soviet Union. Indeed, he hoped to distract the American people from frustration in Southeast Asia with accomplishments elsewhere.

One of the first triumphs was a legacy from previous administrations. On July 20, 1969, Buzz Aldrin and Neil Armstrong completed the longest journey anyone had yet taken. Their successful landing on the moon climaxed a five-day trip across the quarter million miles separating the earth from the moon. Their *Apollo 11* expedition combined science and Cold War politics. The American flag that they planted on the lunar surface represented victory in one phase of the space race between the United States and the Soviet Union. The National Aeronautics and Space Administration had been working since 1961 to meet John F. Kennedy's goal of a manned trip to the moon before the end of the decade.

Closer to home, Nixon and Henry Kissinger, his national security adviser (and later secretary of state), shared what they considered a realistic view of foreign affairs. For both men, foreign policy was not about crusades or moral stands. It was about the balance of world economic and military power. With the United States weakened by the Vietnam War and the Soviets worried by the rise of China, the time was ripe to move toward a new balance among the three nations.

29.1

29.2

29.3

29.4

29.5

29.6

Richard Nixon and Secretary of State William Rogers on the Great Wall during Nixon's historic visit to China.

Since 1950, the United States had acted as if China did not exist, insisting that the Nationalist regime in Taiwan was the legitimate Chinese government. But the People's Republic of China was increasingly isolated within the Communist world. In 1969, it almost went to war with the Soviet Union. Nixon was eager to take advantage of Chinese-Soviet tension. Secret talks led to an easing of the American trade embargo in April 1971. Kissinger then arranged for Nixon's startling visit to Mao Zedong in Beijing in February 1972.

Playing the "China card" helped to improve relations with the Soviet Union. The Soviets needed increased trade with the United States and a counterweight to China; the United States was looking for help in getting out of Vietnam; and both countries wanted to limit nuclear armaments. Protracted negotiations led to the **Strategic Arms Limitation Treaty (SALT)** that Nixon signed in Moscow in May 1972. The agreement blocked the creation of extensive ABM systems but failed to limit bombers, cruise missiles, or multiple independently targeted warheads on single missiles.

Diplomats used the French word ***détente*** to describe the new U.S. relations with China and the Soviet Union. *Détente* means an easing of tensions, not friendship or alliance. It facilitated travel between the United States and China. It allowed U.S. farmers to sell wheat to the Soviets. More broadly, *détente* implied that the United States and China recognized mutual interests in Asia and that the United States acknowledged the Soviet Union as an equal in world affairs. *Détente* made the world safer.

**Strategic Arms Limitation Treaty (SALT)** Treaty signed in 1972 by the United States and the Soviet Union to slow the nuclear arms race.

***détente*** (French for "easing of tension") Used to describe the new U.S. relations with China and the Soviet Union in 1972.

## Courting Middle America

Nixon designed domestic policy to help him win reelection. His goal was to solidify his "Middle American" support. The strategy targeted the growing populations of the South and the suburbs, as well as blue-collar voters who were ready to abandon the Democrats for law-and-order Republicans.

The Nixon White House preferred to ignore troubled big cities. Instead, Nixon tilted federal assistance to the suburbs. The centerpiece of his **New Federalism** was General Revenue Sharing (1972), which passed federal funds directly to local governments with no limits on use. By 1980, it had transferred more than $18 billion to the states and more than $36 billion to local governments. Revenue sharing was a suburban-aid program. Its no-strings grants supplemented the general funds of every full-service government, whether a city of 2 million or a suburban town of 500.

Nixon hoped to move cautiously in enforcing school desegregation, but a task force led by Secretary of Labor George Shultz crafted an approach that allowed substantial desegregation. In this instance, as elsewhere with his domestic policies, Nixon

**New Federalism** President Richard Nixon's policy to shift responsibilities of government programs from the federal level to the states.

29.1

29.2

29.3

29.4

29.5

29.6

was inflammatory in speeches but moderate in action, increasing the funding of federal civil rights agencies.

## Oil, OPEC, and Stagflation

One of the most troublesome domestic issues was inflation. The cost of living began to outpace wages in the late 1960s. Economists saw the situation as a classic example of "demand-pull" inflation, in which too many dollars from government and consumer spending were chasing too few goods and services. One of the causes was LBJ's decision to fight in Vietnam without tax increases until 1968. An income tax cut in 1969, supported by both parties, made the situation worse. Inflation eroded the value of savings and pensions. It also made U.S. goods too expensive for foreign buyers and generated a trade deficit that placed pressures on the international value of the dollar.

The U.S. economy took another hit from inflation in 1973–1974. This time it was "cost-push" inflation, in which a price increase for one key product raises the cost of producing other items. The main cause was the sharp increase in the price of energy, an input to every product and service. Angry at U.S. support for Israel in the Arab-Israeli War of October 1973, Arab nations imposed an embargo on oil exports that lasted from October 1973 to March 1974. The shortages eased when the embargo ended, but the **Organization of Petroleum Exporting Countries (OPEC)** had challenged the ability of the industrial nations to dictate world economic policy.

While Nixon searched for short-term political advantage, underlying problems of the U.S. economy went untreated. After thirty years at the top, the United States could no longer dominate the world economy by itself. The newly found power of OPEC was obvious. Just as important was the surging industrial capacity of Germany and Japan, which now had economies as modern as the United States. Declining rates of investment in industrial capacity seemed to put the United States in danger of following the British road to economic obsolescence and second-level status. Indeed, a new term entered the popular vocabulary in 1971: *Stagflation* was the painful combination of stagnant economic growth, high unemployment, and inflation that matched no one's economic theory but everyone's daily experience.

**Organization of Petroleum Exporting Countries (OPEC)** Cartel of oil-producing nations in Asia, Africa, and Latin America that gained substantial power over the world economy in the mid- to late 1970s by controlling the production and price of oil.

## Americans as Environmentalists

In the turbulent 1970s, Americans found one issue they could agree on. In the 1970s, resource conservation grew into a multifaceted environmental movement that spanned both political parties.

After the booming 1950s, Americans had started to pay attention to "pollution," a catchall for the damage that advanced technologies and industrial production did to natural systems. Rachel Carson's *Silent Spring* in 1962 pushed pollution onto the national agenda. Carson, a well-regarded science writer, described the side effects of DDT and other pesticides on animal life, imagining spring without birds. Her book resonated with many suburbanites, who realized that urban sprawl was providing housing and shopping centers at the cost of bulldozed forests and farms, polluted streams, and smog-choked skies.

Environmentalism gained strength among Americans in 1970. On April 22, 10,000 schools and 20 million other people took part in Earth Day, an occasion first conceived by Wisconsin senator Gaylord Nelson. Earth Day gained a grassroots following in towns and cities across the country. New York closed Fifth Avenue to automobiles for the day. Companies touted their environmental credentials. The event helped to transform the technical field of pollution control into a broadly based movement.

The American establishment had been looking for a safe and respectable crusade to divert the idealism and discontent of the 1960s. Now the mainstream media and a savvy president discovered the ravaged planet. An expedient pro-environmental stance might attract some of the antiwar constituency. Nixon had already signed the

29.1

29.2

29.3

29.4

29.5

29.6

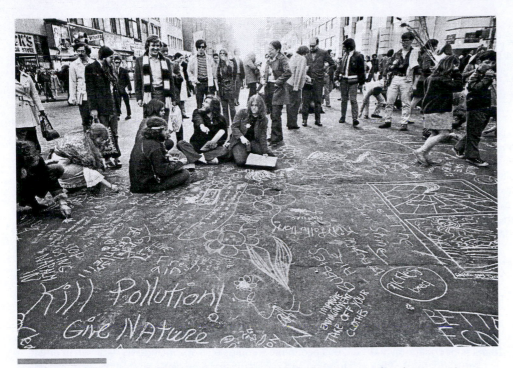

Earth Day brought out Americans from small-town Main Streets to these busy streets of Manhattan, tapping idealism frustrated by the ongoing challenges of civil rights and the seemingly endless war in Southeast Asia.

National Environmental Policy Act on January 1, 1970, and later in the year created the **Environmental Protection Agency (EPA)** to enforce environmental laws. The rest of the Nixon administration brought legislation on clean air, clear water, pesticides, hazardous chemicals, and endangered species (see Table 29.2, The Environmental Decades) that made environmental management and protection part of governmental routine. The Carter years brought more attention to environmental cleanup with the Superfund program and the set-aside of huge tracts of land in Alaska for national parks and wildlife refuges.

**Environmental Protection Agency (EPA)** Federal agency created in 1970 to oversee environmental monitoring and cleanup programs.

((•  📖 **Read** the **Document**   Rachel Carson, *Silent Spring* (1962)

TABLE 29.2  THE ENVIRONMENTAL DECADES

| Administration | Focus of Concern | Legislation |
|---|---|---|
| Johnson | Wilderness and wildlife | Wilderness Act (1964) |
| | | National Wildlife Refuge System (1966) |
| | | Wild and Scenic Rivers Act (1968) |
| Nixon | Pollution control and endangered environments | National Environmental Policy Act (1969) |
| | | Environmental Protection Agency (1970) |
| | | Clean Air Act (1970) |
| | | Occupational Safety and Health Act (1970) |
| | | Water Pollution Control Act (1972) |
| | | Pesticide Control Act (1972) |
| | | Coastal Zone Management Act (1972) |
| | | Endangered Species Act (1973) |
| Ford | Energy and hazardous materials | Toxic Substances Control Act (1976) |
| | | Resource Conservation and Recovery Act (1976) |
| Carter | Energy and hazardous materials | Energy Policy and Conservation Act (1978) |
| | | Comprehensive Emergency Response, Compensation, and Liability Act (Superfund) (1980) |
| | Parks and wilderness | Alaska National Interest Lands Conservation Act (1980) |

29.1

29.2

29.3

29.4

29.5

29.6

## From Then to Now
# Energy Worries

A fter a generation of postwar prosperity, the United States in the 1970s consumed more energy per person than any other nation. The OPEC oil embargo of 1973–1974 hit home in daily life. Gasoline and heating oil became scarce and expensive. Long lines at gas pumps and hurried rationing systems (such as allowing half the nation to fill their gas tanks on odd-numbered days and the other half on even-numbered days) panicked Americans whose daily journeys to work and school depended on automobiles.

One response was to change personal habits. Americans switched off lights, turned down thermostats, and put on sweaters. Congress required states to enforce a fuel-saving highway speed limit of 55 miles per hour to get federal highway funds and enacted the first fuel economy standards for automobiles. The fuel efficiency of the average new car doubled from 14 miles per gallon in 1973 to 28 miles per gallon by the late 1980s, and more efficient imports captured a third of the U.S. car market by 1980.

A parallel response was to experiment with new energy sources. Oil companies tried to squeeze more petroleum out of abandoned wells and searched for new oil fields in the northern Rockies. Huge strip mining operations tackled coal deposits in isolated areas like Wyoming that had previously been too far from markets. Homeowners put solar panels on their roofs to heat water. The federal government funneled money into energy research as scientists experimented with wind power and solar generation of electricity.

The pressure on oil supplies eased in the 1980s and 1990s. Even as petroleum imports passed domestic production in 1996, many Americans forgot about energy policy until the new century brought new crises—first rolling electrical blackouts in California, then surging gasoline prices in 2006 and 2007 and again in following years. The responses would be similar—changes in personal choices like interest in hybrid automobiles, stronger federal standards for fuel efficiency, and a boom in alternative energy sources like biofuels and wind power. The 2009 economic stimulus package included $70 billion in direct funding and tax credits for renewable energy projects and energy efficiency investment.

**Question for Discussion**

- What are differences and similarities in the causes of energy price increases between the 1970s and recent years?

Wind-power generators near San Diego, among the many wind farms that began to cover windy hillsides across the American West in the new century.

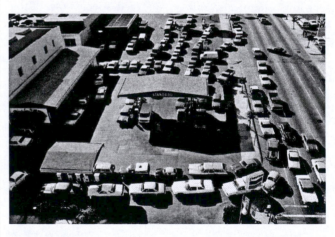

Motorists line up for scarce supplies of gasoline in 1979, when political upheaval in Iran created the second energy crisis and gasoline shortage of the 1970s.

As Americans became more aware of human-caused environmental hazards, they realized that minority and low-income communities had more than their share of problems. Landfills and waste disposal sites were frequently located near minority neighborhoods. In Buffalo, white working-class residents near the Love Canal industrial site discovered in 1978 that an entire neighborhood was built on land contaminated by decades of chemical dumping. Activists sought to understand the health effects and force compensation, paving the way for the Superfund cleanup legislation.

# From Dirty Tricks to Watergate

The **Watergate** crisis pivoted on Richard Nixon's character. Despite his solid political standing, Nixon saw enemies everywhere and overestimated their strength. Subordinates learned during his first administration that the president would condone dishonest actions—"dirty tricks"—if they stood to improve his political position. In 1972 and 1973, dirty tricks grew from a scandal into a constitutional crisis when Nixon abused the power of his office to cover up wrongdoing and hinder criminal investigations.

The chain of events that undermined Nixon's presidency started with the **Pentagon Papers**. In his last year as secretary of defense, Robert McNamara had commissioned a report on the U.S. road to Vietnam. The documents showed that the country's leaders had planned to expand the war even while they claimed to be looking for a way out. In June 1971, one of the contributors to the report, Daniel Ellsberg, leaked it to the *New York Times*. Its publication infuriated Nixon.

In response, the White House compiled a list of journalists and politicians who opposed Nixon. As one White House staffer, John Dean, put it, the president's men could then "use the available federal machinery [Internal Revenue Service, FBI] to screw our political enemies." Nixon set up a special investigations unit in the White House. Two former CIA employees, E. Howard Hunt and G. Gordon Liddy, became the chief "plumbers," as the group was known because its job was to prevent leaks of information.

Early in 1972, Hunt went to work for CREEP—the Committee to Re-Elect the President—while Liddy took another position on the presidential staff. CREEP was already hatching plans to undermine Democrats with rumors and pranks. Then, on June 17, 1972, five inept burglars hired with CREEP funds were caught breaking into the Democratic National Committee office in Washington's Watergate apartment building. The people involved knew that an investigation would lead back to the White House. Nixon felt too insecure to ride out what would probably have been a small scandal. Instead, he initiated a cover-up. On June 23, he ordered his assistant H. R. Haldeman to warn the FBI off the case with the excuse that national security was involved. Nixon compounded this obstruction of justice by arranging a $400,000 bribe to keep the burglars quiet.

The cover-up worked in the short run. As mid-level officials from the Justice Department pursued their investigation, the public lost interest in what looked more like slapstick than a serious crime. Nixon's opponent in the 1972 election was South Dakota senator George McGovern, an impassioned opponent of the Vietnam War. McGovern was honest, intelligent, and well to the left of center on such issues as the defense budget and legalization of marijuana. He did not appeal to the white southerners and blue-collar northerners whom Nixon and Agnew were luring from the Democrats. An assassination attempt that took George Wallace out of national politics also helped Nixon win in a landslide.

The cover-up began to come apart with the trial of the Watergate burglars in January 1973. Federal Judge John Sirica used the threat of heavy sentences to pressure one burglar into a statement that implied that higher-ups had been involved. Meanwhile, the *Washington Post* was linking Nixon's people to dirty tricks and illegal campaign contributions. White House Counsel John Dean, who coordinated much of the effort, reported to Nixon in March that the scandal and cover-up had become a "cancer on the presidency." Nixon was aware of many of the actions that his subordinates had undertaken. He now began to coach people on what they should tell investigators, claimed his staff had lied to him, and tried to set up Dean to take the fall.

In the late spring and early summer, attention shifted to the televised hearings of the Senate's Select Committee on Presidential Campaign Activities. Its chair was Sam Ervin of North Carolina, whose down-home style masked a clever mind. The real questions, it became obvious, were what the president knew and when he knew it. It seemed to be John Dean's word against Richard Nixon's.

**Watergate** A complex scandal involving attempts to cover up illegal actions taken by administration officials and leading to the resignation of President Richard Nixon in 1974.

**Pentagon Papers** Classified Defense Department documents on the history of the U.S. involvement in Vietnam, prepared in 1968 and leaked to the press in 1971.

29.1

29.2

29.3

29.4

29.5

29.6

29.1

29.2

29.3

29.4

29.5

29.6

A bombshell turned the scandal into a constitutional crisis when the committee learned that Nixon had made tape recordings of his White House conversations. Both the Senate and the Watergate special prosecutor, Archibald Cox, subpoenaed the tapes. Nixon refused to give them up, citing executive privilege and the separation of powers. In late October, after he failed to cut a satisfactory deal, he fired his attorney general and the special prosecutor. This "Saturday-night massacre" caused a storm of protest, and many Americans thought that it proved that Nixon had something to hide. In April 1974, he finally released edited transcripts of the tapes, with foul language deleted and key passages missing; he claimed that his secretary had accidentally erased crucial material. Finally, on July 24, 1974, the U.S. Supreme Court ruled unanimously that Nixon had to deliver sixty-four tapes to the new special prosecutor.

Opposition to the president now spanned the political spectrum from Barry Goldwater to liberal Democrats, and Congress began impeachment proceedings. Republicans joined Democrats in voting three articles of impeachment: for hindering the criminal investigation of the Watergate break-in, for abusing the power of the presidency by using federal agencies to deprive citizens of their rights, and for ignoring the committee's subpoena for the tapes. Before the full House could vote on the articles of impeachment and send them to the Senate for trial, Nixon delivered the tapes. One of them contained the "smoking gun," direct evidence that Nixon had participated in the cover-up on June 23, 1972, and had been lying ever since. On August 8, he announced his resignation, effective the following day.

Watergate was two separate but related stories. On one level, it was about individuals who deceived or manipulated the American people. Nixon and his cronies wanted to win too badly to play by the rules and repeatedly broke the law. Nixon paid for his overreaching ambition with the end of his political career; more than twenty others paid with jail terms. On another level, the crisis was a lesson about the Constitution. The separation of powers allowed Congress and the courts to rein in a president who had spun out of control. The Ervin Committee hearings in 1973 and the House Judiciary Committee proceedings in 1974 were rituals to assure Americans that the system still worked. Nevertheless, the sequence of political events from 1968 to 1974 disillusioned many citizens.

## The Ford Footnote

Gerald Ford was Nixon's appointee to replace Spiro Agnew, who had resigned and pleaded no contest to charges of bribery and income tax evasion in 1973 as Watergate was gathering steam. Ford was competent but unimaginative. His first major act was his most controversial—the pardon of Nixon for "any and all crimes" committed while president. Since Nixon had not yet been indicted, the pardon saved him from future prosecution.

Ford's administration presided over the collapse of South Vietnam in 1975, but elsewhere in the world, *détente* continued. United States diplomats joined the Soviet Union and thirty other European nations in the capital of Finland to sign the **Helsinki Accords**. The agreements called for increased commerce between the Eastern and Western blocs and for human rights guarantees. They also legitimized the national boundaries that had been set in Eastern Europe in 1945.

In 1976, Ford's Democratic opponent was a political enigma. James Earl Carter, Jr., had been a navy officer, a farmer, and the governor of Georgia. He was one of several new-style politicians who transformed southern politics in the 1970s. Carter and the others left race-baiting behind to talk like modern New Dealers, emphasizing that whites and blacks both needed better schools and economic growth. He appealed to Democrats as someone who could reassemble LBJ's political coalition and return the South to the Democratic Party. In his successful campaign, Carter presented himself as an alternative to party hacks and Washington insiders (see Map 29.2).

**Helsinki Accords** Agreement in 1975 among NATO and Warsaw Pact members that recognized European national boundaries as set after World War II and included guarantees of human rights.

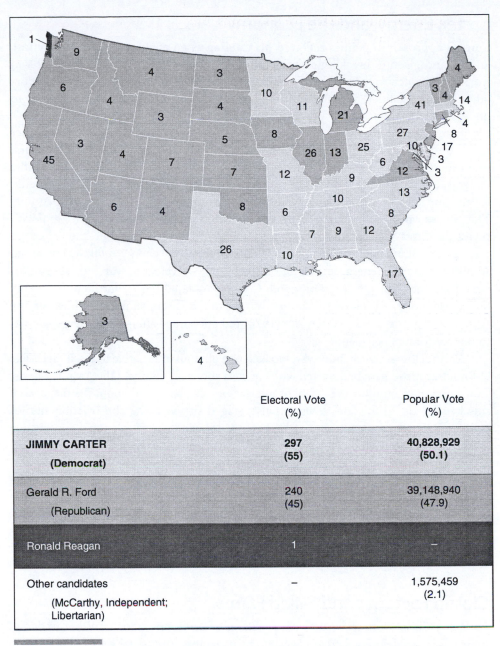

| | Electoral Vote (%) | Popular Vote (%) |
|---|---|---|
| **JIMMY CARTER** (Democrat) | **297** (55) | **40,828,929** (50.1) |
| Gerald R. Ford (Republican) | 240 (45) | 39,148,940 (47.9) |
| Ronald Reagan | 1 | – |
| Other candidates (McCarthy, Independent; Libertarian) | – | 1,575,459 (2.1) |

**MAP 29.2  THE ELECTION OF 1976** Georgian Jimmy Carter ran in 1976 as an outsider to Washington politics. He capitalized on a reputation as a progressive governor and on the Watergate scandal, which had damaged the Republican Party.

29.1
29.2
29.3
29.4
29.5
29.6

# Jimmy Carter: Idealism and Frustration in the White House

**29.6**   What factors limited Jimmy Carter's effectiveness as president?

Jimmy Carter took office with little room to maneuver. Watergate bequeathed him a powerful and self-satisfied Congress and a combative press. OPEC oil producers, Islamic fundamentalists, and Soviet generals followed their own agendas. The American people themselves were fractionalized and quarrelsome, uneasy with the new advocacy of equality for women, uncertain as a nation whether they shared the same values and goals.

29.1

29.2

29.3

29.4

29.5

29.6

## Carter, Energy, and the Economy

Carter's approach to politics reflected his training as an engineer. He was analytical, logical, and given to breaking a problem into its component parts. He was better at working with details than at defining broad goals. He failed to understand the importance of personalities, was uncomfortable with compromise, and did not seem to understand the basic rules of Washington politics.

The biggest domestic problem remained the economy, which slid into another recession in 1978. Another jump in oil prices helped make 1979 and 1980 the worst years for inflation in the postwar era. Interest rates surged past 20 percent as the Federal Reserve tried to reduce inflation by squeezing business and consumer credit. Carter himself was a fiscal conservative whose impulse was to cut federal spending. This course worsened unemployment and alienated liberal Democrats, who wanted to revive the Great Society.

Carter simultaneously proposed a comprehensive energy policy. He asked Americans to make energy conservation the moral equivalent of war—to accept individual sacrifices for the common good. Congress created the Department of Energy but refused to raise taxes on oil and natural gas to reduce consumption. However, the Energy Policy and Conservation Act (1978) did encourage alternative energy sources to replace foreign petroleum.

Antinuclear activism, however, blocked one obvious alternative to fossil fuels. The antinuclear movement had started with concern about the ability of the Atomic Energy Commission to monitor the safety of nuclear-power plants and about the disposal of spent fuel rods. In the late 1970s, activists staged sit-ins at the construction sites of nuclear plants. A near-meltdown at the Three Mile Island nuclear plant in Pennsylvania in March 1979 stalemated efforts to expand nuclear-power capacity.

When the OPEC price hikes undermined the inflation-fighting effort in the summer of 1979, Carter told the nation that a "moral and spiritual crisis" demanded a rebirth of the American spirit. The public did not know whether he had preached a sermon or given them marching orders. A cabinet reshuffle a few days later was supposed to show that he was firmly in charge. Instead, the media painted the president as inconsistent and incompetent.

## Closed Factories and Failed Farms

Ford and Carter both faced massive problems of economic transition that undercut their efforts to devise effective government programs. Industrial decay stalked such "gritty cities" as Allentown, Pennsylvania; Trenton, New Jersey; and Gary, Indiana. Communities whose workers had made products in high volume for a mass market found that technological revolutions made them obsolete. Critics renamed the old manufacturing region of the Northeast and Middle West the Rustbelt in honor of its abandoned factories. Stories of **deindustrialization** were similar in small cities like Springfield, Ohio, and large cities like Cleveland. As high-paying jobs in unionized industries disappeared, sagging income undermined small businesses and neighborhoods. Falling tax revenue brought Cleveland to the verge of bankruptcy in 1978; bankers forced public service cuts and tax increases, which meant further job losses.

Plant closures were only one facet of business efforts to increase productivity by substituting machinery for employees. Between 1947 and 1977, American steelmakers doubled output while cutting their workforce from 600,000 to 400,000. High interest rates and a strong dollar made U.S. exports too expensive and foreign imports cheap, forcing American manufacturers to cut costs or perish.

Parallel to the decline of heavy industry was the continuing transformation of American agriculture from small family enterprises to corporate agribusinesses. Agriculture was a national success story in the aggregate, but one accompanied by many human and environmental costs. The early 1970s brought an unexpected boom in farming. Crop failures and food shortages around the world in 1972 and 1973 expanded

**deindustrialization** The process of economic change involving the disappearance of outmoded industries and the transfer of factories to new low-wage locations, with devastating effects in the Northeast and Midwest, especially in the 1970s and 1980s.

markets and pushed up prices for U.S. farm products. For a few years, agriculture looked like the best way for the United States to offset the high cost of imported oil. But the boom was over by the 1980s, when global commodity prices slumped. Farmers found themselves with debts they could not cover.

The boom of the 1970s was thus a brief interruption in the long-term transformation of U.S. agriculture. The number of farms slid from 4 million in 1960 to 2.4 million in 1980 and 1.9 million in 2000. Many farmers sold out willingly, glad to escape from drudgery and financial insecurity. Others could not compete in an agricultural system that favored large-scale production by demanding large amounts of capital for equipment and fertilizer. By the 1990s, the 600,000 largest farms and ranches were responsible for 94 percent of total U.S. farm production, and fewer than 2 percent of American workers made their living from farming.

## Building a Cooperative World

Despite troubles on the home front, Carter's first two years brought foreign policy successes that reflected a new vision of a multilateral world. As a relative newcomer to international politics, Carter was willing to work with African, Asian, and Latin American nations on a basis of mutual respect. Carter appointed Andrew Young—an African American from Georgia with long experience in the civil rights movement—as ambassador to the United Nations, where he worked effectively to build bridges to third-world nations. Carter convinced the Senate in 1978 to approve treaties to transfer control of the Panama Canal to Panama by 2000, removing a sore point in relations with Latin America.

Carter's moral convictions were responsible for a new concern with human rights around the globe. He criticized the Soviet Union for prohibiting free speech and denying its citizens the right to emigrate, angering Soviet leaders, who did not expect the human rights clauses of the Helsinki Accords to be taken seriously. Carter was also willing to criticize some (but not all) American allies. He withheld economic aid from South Africa, Guatemala, Chile, and Nicaragua, which had long records of human rights abuses.

Carter had several successes. He completed the Nixon initiative by normalizing diplomatic relations with China. He also risked his reputation and credibility in September 1978 to bring Egyptian President Anwar al-Sadat and Israeli Prime Minister Menachem Begin together at Camp David, the presidential retreat. He refused to admit failure and dissuaded the two leaders from walking out. A formal treaty known popularly as the **Camp David Agreement** was signed in Washington on March 26, 1979. The pact normalized relations between Israel and its most powerful neighbor and led to Israel's withdrawal from the Sinai Peninsula.

**Camp David Agreement**
Agreement to reduce points of conflict between Israel and Egypt, hammered out in 1977 with the help of U.S. President Jimmy Carter.

## New Crises Abroad

In the last two years of Carter's administration, the Cold War sprang back to life around the globe and smothered the promise of a new foreign policy. The Soviets ignored the human rights provisions of the Helsinki Accords. Soviet advisers or Cuban troops intervened in African civil wars. At home, Cold Warriors who had never accepted *détente* found it easier to attack Carter than Nixon.

**The Failure of Salt II.**    Carter inherited negotiations for SALT II—a strategic arms-limitation treaty that would have reduced both the U.S. and Soviet nuclear arsenals—from the Ford administration. SALT II met stiff resistance in the Senate. Opponents claimed it would create a "window of vulnerability" in the 1980s that would invite the Soviets to launch a nuclear first strike. Carter tried to counter criticism by stepping up defense spending, starting a buildup that would accelerate under Ronald Reagan.

Hopes for SALT II vanished on December 24, 1979, when Soviet troops entered Afghanistan, a technically neutral Muslim nation on the southern border of the

29.1
29.2
29.3
29.4
29.5
29.6

29.1

29.2

29.3

29.4

29.5

29.6

Soviet Union. A pro-Soviet government had fallen into factional strife, while tribes-people, unhappy with modernization, were mounting increasing resistance. One of the factions invited intervention by the Soviets, who quickly installed a client government. The situation resembled the U.S. involvement in South Vietnam. Similar, too, was the inability of Soviet forces to suppress the Afghan guerrillas, who had American weapons and controlled the mountains. In the end, it took the Soviets a decade to find a way out.

**The Iranian Hostage Crisis.** The final blow to Carter's foreign policy came in Iran. Since 1953, the United States had strongly backed Iran's monarch, Shah Reza Pahlevi. The shah modernized Iran's economy, but his secret police jailed and tortured political opponents. United States aid and oil revenues helped him build a large army, but the Iranian middle class despised his authoritarianism, and Muslim fundamentalists opposed the westernizing influence of modernization. A revolution toppled the shah at the start of 1979.

The upheaval installed a nominally democratic government, but the Ayatollah Ruhollah Khomeini, a Muslim cleric who hated the United States, exercised real power. Throughout 1979, Iran grew increasingly anti-American. After the United States allowed the exiled shah to seek medical treatment in New York, a mob stormed the U.S. embassy in Tehran on November 4, 1979, and took more than sixty Americans hostage. They demanded that Carter surrender the shah. The administration tried economic pressure and diplomacy, but Khomeini had no desire for accommodation. When Iran announced in April 1980 that the hostages would remain in the hands of the militants rather than be transferred to the government, Carter ordered an airborne rescue. Even a perfectly managed effort would have been difficult. The hostages were held in the heart of a city of 4 million hostile Iranians, hundreds of miles from the nearest aircraft carrier and thousands of miles from U.S. bases. Hampered by lack of

The Iran hostage crisis reflected intense anti-American feelings in Iran and provoked an equally bitter anti-Iranian reaction in the United States. Fifty-two of the more than sixty U.S. embassy employees first seized were held for 444 days, giving the United States a painful lesson about the limits on its ability to influence events around the world.

coordination among the military services, the attempt turned into a fiasco that added to the national embarrassment and a feeling of powerlessness. The United States and Iran finally reached agreement on the eve of the 1980 election. The hostages gained their freedom after 444 days, at the moment Ronald Reagan took office as the new president.

The hostage crisis consumed Jimmy Carter the way that Vietnam had consumed Lyndon Johnson. It gripped the public and stalemated other issues. Carter's tragedy was that "his" Iranian crisis was the fruit of policies hatched by the Eisenhower administration and pursued by every president since then, all of whom had overlooked the shah's despotic government because of his firm anti-communism.

After thirty years in which the United States had viewed the entire world as a Cold War battlefield, Carter was willing to accept the developing world on its own terms. His human rights efforts showed that evangelical religious convictions could be tied to progressive aims. He wanted to avoid supporting oppressive regimes, but the past was too burdensome. Iranian rage at past policies of the sort Carter hoped to change destroyed his ability to direct a new course. After he left office, his continuing work for peace and humanitarian efforts would earn him the Nobel Peace Prize in 2002.

## Conclusion

In the mid-1970s, Americans encountered real limits to national capacity. From 1945 to 1973, they had enjoyed remarkable prosperity. That ended in 1974. Long lines at gas stations showed that prosperity was fragile. Cities and regions felt the costs of obsolete industries. Environmental damage caused many Americans to reconsider the goal of economic expansion.

The nation also had to recognize that it could not run the world. American withdrawal from Vietnam in 1973 and the collapse of the South Vietnamese government in 1975 were defeats; the United States ended up with little to show for a long and painful war. SALT I stabilized the arms race, but it also recognized that the Soviet Union was an equal.

These challenges came amid deep economic and social changes in the United States. The ways Americans made their livings and the range of opportunities they faced were in flux. Farm laborers had better working conditions but auto workers had fewer jobs. The nation finished the 1970s more egalitarian than it had been in the early 1960s but also more divided. More citizens had the opportunity to advance economically and to seek political power, but there were deepening fissures between social liberals and cultural conservatives, rich and poor, whites and blacks. In 1961, John Kennedy had called on his fellow citizens to "bear any burden, pay any price" to defend freedom. By 1980, the nation had neither the economic capacity to pay any price nor the unity to agree on what burdens it should bear.

**For Suggested Readings go to MyHistoryLab.**

29.1

29.2

29.3

29.4

29.5

29.6

## Chapter Review

### Deeper into Vietnam

**29.1** What were the consequences of the growing U.S. war in Vietnam? p. 849

In the second half of the 1960s, military commitments in Vietnam and reactions at home were an all-consuming issue that fundamentally reshaped U.S. society and politics.

### New Voices

**29.2** What conflicting social values and goals divided Americans in the 1960s? p. 855

After the relative consensus of the 1950s, Americans in the 1960s and 1970s listened to new ideas from both the political left and right. At the same time, young people, women, and sexual minorities demanded recognition as equal citizens.

### Cities under Stress

**29.3** What challenges did cities face in the late 1960s and 1970s? p. 858

American cities underwent multiple crises in the later 1960s and 1970s that ranged from racially motivated riots to severe economic stress. The result was to shift the balance of economic and political power from older cities to suburbs and simultaneously to begin to empower minority voters.

### The Year of the Gun, 1968

**29.4** How did the Tet Offensive change American public opinion about the war in Vietnam? p. 863

The year 1968 brought turmoil at home and abroad. Both the Vietnam War and the antiwar movement reached crisis points that turned U.S. politics upside down. Revolts against the postwar political establishment spanned both sides of the Atlantic and both sides of the Iron Curtain.

### Nixon, Watergate, and the Crisis of the Early 1970s

**29.5** What was the legacy of Richard Nixon's presidency? p. 866

Despite substantial accomplishments in environmental policy, civil rights, and foreign affairs, Richard Nixon is remembered for the Watergate scandal that arose from his reelection campaign.

### Jimmy Carter: Idealism and Frustration in the White House

**29.6** What factors limited Jimmy Carter's effectiveness as president? p. 875

Americans faced serious challenges to both economic prosperity and global political influence in the last years of the 1970s, undercutting the ability of President Jimmy Carter to pursue new initiatives and leaving many Americans unhappy with the situation of their nation.

## Timeline

**1965** Cities Under Stress—Residents of Watts neighborhood in Los Angeles riot

**1968** Year of the Gun—Viet Cong launches Tet Offensive

**1969** Nixon and the Crisis of the 1970s—Neil Armstrong and Buzz Aldrin walk on the moon

**1972** Nixon and the Crisis of the 1970s—Nixon visits China

**1973** Nixon and the Crisis of the 1970s—United States moves to all-volunteer armed forces

**1974** Nixon and the Crisis of the 1970s—Nixon resigns as president, is succeeded by Gerald Ford

**1975** Nixon and the Crisis of the 1970s—Communists triumph in South Vietnam

**1978** Jimmy Carter, Idealism and Frustration—Carter brings the leaders of Egypt and Israel to Camp David for successful peace talks

**1979** Jimmy Carter, Idealism and Frustration—Iranian militants take U.S. embassy hostages

**1980** Jimmy Carter, Idealism and Frustration—Soviet troops enter Afghanistan

# 30 The Reagan Revolution and a Changing World 1981–1992

## One American Journey

Interview with a Refugee
from Cambodia

**W**hen I became an American citizen a few months ago, it was very emotional for me. I was happy that I could be part of my new country. I do feel loyalty to the United States. I think of myself as both Cambodian and an American citizen. I cannot forget where I came from.

My maiden name was Thann Meng Vann. When I became an American citizen, I took an American name, Celia, and my husband's family name, Noup, because I hope that he will some day return. I lost contact with him when our country was falling in April 1975. The outpost he commanded was surrounded by Khmer Rouge. I have never found out what happened to him after he was captured. Sometimes I have seen him in my dreams, but he never talks to me.

## LEARNING OBJECTIVES

| 30.1 | 30.2 | 30.3 | 30.4 |
|------|------|------|------|
| What was revolutionary about Ronald Reagan's presidency? p. 884 | How and why did the Cold War come to an end? p. 896 | How did growth in the Sunbelt shape national politics in the 1980s and 1990s? p. 905 | What key social and cultural issues divided Americans in the 1980s and 1990s? p. 909 |

The tangle of freeways that frame downtown Houston reflect the nation's dependence on automobiles and the continued shift of population and economic activity to the Sunbelt region of the South and West.

  **Listen to Chapter 30 on MyHistoryLab**

# ⊙ Watch the Video Series on MyHistoryLab

Learn about some key topics related to this chapter with the *MyHistoryLab Video Series: Key Topics in U.S. History.*

**1** Ending the Cold War: 1980–1991 To distance itself from the Carter administration and portray the United States as a resurgent power, President Ronald Reagan's administration adopted an aggressive anti-communist stance, primarily directed at the Soviet Union. This video provides an overview of the Cold War's renewed intensity and how the United States helped to bring about the collapse of Soviet Union and the communist regimes of its Warsaw Pact neighbors, as well as such policy initiatives and debacles as Star Wars, the arming of the Afghan rebels, and the Iran-Contra affair.

⊙ Watch on MyHistoryLab

**The Comeback of the Cold Warriors** This video surveys the Reagan administration's worldview, especially in regard to communism at home and abroad, and its lack of emphasis on diplomacy. The discussion covers Iran-Contra (the funding of anti-Communist forces in Latin America) and the support of the tribal rebels against the Soviet Union and its allied regime in Afghanistan as well as the Strategic Defense Initiative (SDI), euphemistically known as Star Wars. **2**

Watch on MyHistoryLab ⊙

**3** Republican America This video examines the domestic and economic policies of the Reagan administration. The 1980s saw both benefits and setbacks with the institution of supply-side, or "trickle-down," economics, largely gained through tax breaks for corporations and wealthy individuals and deregulation. The 1980s also saw Americans become increasingly conservative as social-issue politics, as well as groups such as the Moral Majority, took a leading role.

 Watch on MyHistoryLab

**The Cold War: Where Did the Enemy Go?** When Mikhail Gorbachev's *perestroika* and *glasnost* policies failed in reforming the economy and society of the Soviet Union, the quick collapse of the Soviet Union and the end of other Communist governments in Eastern Europe caught the United States by surprise. This video explores the end of the Cold War and the controversial part played by the Reagan administration's policies as well as other contributory factors, such as the Solidarity movement in Poland. **4**

Watch on MyHistoryLab

The first time I dreamed about my husband was in a hut where the Khmer Rouge had ordered my family to stay after our city, Phnom Penh, was evacuated. In the dream, I saw him in our bedroom in Phnom Penh. He looked very sad. I woke up in the middle of the night. I shouted. I cried out loud.

The next day, the Communists sent an old person to talk with me, to tell me that they heard me in the night. They warned me not to do that any more. For four years they tried to kill me. They tried every trick in the book to catch me breaking their rules.

Now, in my dreams at night, people speak in the Cambodian language. But I never dream about Cambodia. No more. My dreams always take place in a house with my daughters that is unknown to me. It is always the same house, on a streetcorner, three stories high.

On weekdays, I live in the house that my daughter Mealy and her husband rent; it is only five minutes from my shop. On weekends, I live with my daughter Monie and her husband in Torrance. I share the cost of food for the households. Sometimes I buy groceries. And I pay some rent for both Parika and me. I try to help my children as much as I can. I can't take it all with me. [Laughs]

I have four grandchildren, all babies—two years, one year, and a few months. The only time I have for them is on weekends, when my daughters are working at my shop. I babysit the kids while I do bookkeeping. I enjoy their company.

We've been here seven years now. My children still think like Cambodians, but their way of acting is American.

From Celia Noup in Al Santoli, *New Americans: An Oral History*
(1988 Random House, Inc.) © 1988 Reprinted by permission of the author.

## Personal Journeys Online

- Jubilee Lau, "Chinese and Proud of It," 1996. From Hong Kong to Idaho in the 1980s.
- Richard Rodriguez, *Hunger of Memory*, 1982. Learning English in an immigrant household.
- Ana Cabellero, 1980s. Mexican American Generations in El Paso. Interview in Al Santoli, *New Americans*, 1988.

**C**elia Noup taught school for twenty years in Cambodia, which borders on South Vietnam. In 1975, after a long civil war, the Communist Khmer Rouge insurgents took over Cambodia's capital, Phnom Penh, and forced its inhabitants into the countryside to work in the fields. Four years later, Noup managed to make her way to a refugee camp in neighboring Thailand and then to the United States. Here she joined hundreds of thousands of other refugees who arrived in the later 1970s and 1980s from war-devastated nations such as Cambodia, Vietnam, Laos, Ethiopia, and Afghanistan. Within a decade, she was working from 5:00 A.M. to 7:00 P.M. in her own donut shop near the Los Angeles airport and worrying about helping her children buy houses.

Celia Noup's journey shows some of the ways that new waves of immigration from Asia, Latin America, and Africa have changed the United States over the last generation. Immigrants fueled economic growth in the 1980s and 1990s with their labor and their drive to succeed in business. They revitalized older neighborhoods in cities from coast to coast and changed the ethnic mix of major cities. And they created new racial tensions that found their way into national political debates about immigration and into open conflict in places such as Miami and Los Angeles.

Noup's story is also a reminder of the drawn-out consequences of the U.S. involvement in Vietnam and the long shadow of the Cold War. The Cambodian civil war was fueled by reactions to the Vietnamese war and the U.S. invasion of Cambodia in 1969. American refugee policy was humanitarian but also political, opening the door to people fleeing Communist regimes but holding it shut against refugees from right-wing dictatorships. In Washington, foreign policy decisions in the 1980s started with the desire of a new administration to reaffirm American toughness after failures in Vietnam and ended with the astonishing evaporation of the Cold War.

By the end of Ronald Reagan's presidency (1981–1989), new rules governed domestic affairs as well as international relations. In the 1980s Americans decided to reverse the growth of federal government responsibilities that had marked both Republican and Democratic administrations since the 1930s. By the 1990s, the center of U.S. politics had shifted substantially to the right.

The backdrop to the political changes was massive readjustments in the American economy that began in the 1970s with the decline of heavy industry and then continued to shift employment from factory jobs to service jobs. The ideology of unregulated markets celebrated economic success and made "yuppies," or young urban professionals, the center of media attention, but behind the lifestyle stories was troubling reality: a widening gap between the rich and poor. The result by 1992 was a nation that was much more secure in the world than it had been in 1980, but also more divided against itself.

# Reagan's Domestic Revolution

**30.1** What was revolutionary about Ronald Reagan's presidency?

Political change began in 1980, when Ronald Reagan and his running mate, George H. W. Bush, rode American discontent to a decisive victory in the presidential election (see Map 30.1). Building on a conservative critique of American policies and developing issues that Jimmy Carter had placed on the national agenda, Reagan presided over revolutionary changes in U.S. government and policies. The consequences of his two terms included an altered role for government,

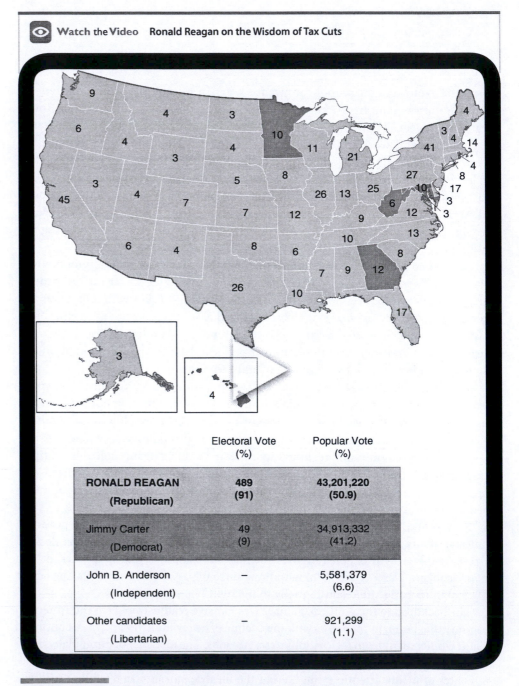

**Watch the Video    Ronald Reagan on the Wisdom of Tax Cuts**

|  | Electoral Vote (%) | Popular Vote (%) |
| --- | --- | --- |
| **RONALD REAGAN** (Republican) | **489 (91)** | **43,201,220 (50.9)** |
| Jimmy Carter (Democrat) | 49 (9) | 34,913,332 (41.2) |
| John B. Anderson (Independent) | – | 5,581,379 (6.6) |
| Other candidates (Libertarian) | – | 921,299 (1.1) |

**MAP 30.1  THE ELECTION OF 1980** Ronald Reagan won in a landslide in 1980. Independent candidate John Anderson took more votes from Jimmy Carter than from Reagan, but Reagan's personal magnetism was a powerful political force. His victory confirmed the shift of the South to the Republican Party.

powerful but selective economic growth, and a shift of domestic politics away from bread-and-butter issues toward moral or lifestyle concerns.

## Reagan's Majority

Ronald Reagan reinvented himself several times on his unusual journey to the White House. A product of small-town Illinois, he succeeded in Hollywood in the late 1930s as a romantic lead actor while adopting the liberal politics common at the time. After World War II, he moved rapidly to the political right as a spokesman for big business. He entered politics with a rousing conservative speech at the 1964 Republican convention and then accepted the invitation of wealthy California Republicans to run for governor in 1966, serving two terms in that office.

Some of Reagan's most articulate support came from anti-Communist stalwarts of both parties, who feared that the United States was losing influence in the world. Despite Jimmy Carter's tough actions in 1979 and 1980 and increased defense spending, such conservatives had not trusted him to do enough. Soviet military buildup, charged the critics, was creating a "window of vulnerability," a dangerous period when the Soviet Union might threaten the United States with a first strike by nuclear weapons.

Other Reagan voters directed their anger at government bureaucracies. Wealthy entrepreneurs from the fast-growing South and West believed that Nixon-era federal offices, such as the Environmental Protection Agency and the Occupational Safety and Health Administration, were choking their businesses in red tape. Many of these critics had amassed new fortunes in oil, real estate, and retailing and hated the taxes that funded social programs.

Christian conservatives worried that social activists were using the federal courts to alter traditional values. Jimmy Carter, a member of the Southern Baptist church, had won a clear majority among white evangelical voters in 1976, but Reagan's contrasting position on school prayer and abortion gave him the edge in 1980 and made him the overwhelming preference of conservative Christian voters in 1984.

In many ways, the two groups were mismatched. Christian moralists had little in common with the high-rolling hedonists and Hollywood tycoons with whom Reagan rubbed shoulders. But they shared a deep distrust of the federal establishment.

Foreign policy activists and opponents of big government would have been unable to elect Reagan without disaffected blue-collar and middle-class voters who deserted the Democrats. Reagan's campaign hammered on the question "Are you better off than you were four years ago?" Democrats faced a special dilemma with the deepening tension between working-class white voters and black voters, a division that had roots in the expansion of African American populations and neighborhoods in cities like Detroit and Chicago during the 1950s and 1960s. Democrats needed both groups to win but found white blue-collar voters deeply alienated by affirmative action and busing for school integration.

A further Democratic challenge was Ronald Reagan's personal appeal. The new president won over many Americans by surviving a 1981 assassination attempt in fine spirits. Reagan's popularity compounded the Democrats' inability to excite younger voters. The mid-1980s consistently showed that roughly two-thirds of people in their twenties and early thirties were choosing the Republicans as the party of energy and new ideas, leaving the Democrats to the middle-aged and elderly.

In the election of 1984, Democrats sealed their fate by nominating Walter Mondale, who had been vice president under Carter. Mondale was earnest, honest, and dull. Reagan ran on the theme "It's Morning in America," with the message that a new age of pride and prosperity had begun. Mondale assumed that Americans cared enough about the exploding federal deficit that Reagan's defense spending had produced to accept an across-the-board tax increase. With the economy growing and inflation now in check, most voters did not want Mondale to remind them of long-range financial realities, and Reagan won reelection with 98 percent of the electoral votes. His election confirmed that the American public found conservative ideas increasingly attractive.

# Conservative Worldviews

Reagan's approach to public policy drew on neoconservative intellectuals who offered a coherent critique of the New Deal–New Frontier approach to U.S. government. Some of the leading figures were journalists and academics who had embraced the ideas of the "vital center" a generation earlier (see Chapter 27). Now they feared that the anti-war movement had undermined the anti-Communist stance and that social changes were corrupting mainstream values.

**Downsizing the Great Society.** Worries about big government permeated the critique of domestic policy. Edward Banfield's radical ideas about the failures of the Great Society set the tone of the neoconservative analysis. In *The Unheavenly City* (1968), he questioned the basic idea of public solutions for social problems. He argued that inequality is based on human character and rooted in the basic structure of society; government action can only solve problems that require better engineering, such as pollution control, better highways, or the delivery of explosives to military targets. Government's job, said Banfield, was to preserve public order, not to right wrongs or encourage unrealistic expectations.

Other conservative writers elaborated Banfield's ideas. Charles Murray's 1984 book, *Losing Ground,* tried to do for neoconservative domestic policy what Michael Harrington's *The Other America* had done for liberal policy. Murray argued that welfare assistance hurt more than it helped, by discouraging individual efforts at self-improvement. The blame for continued poverty, he said, must lie in the welfare programs themselves. Murray's book distorts the evidence and makes flawed arguments, but it had a major impact on political debates.

**Free-Market Utopians.** Another strand of conservative argument came from free-market utopians. After years of stagflation, Americans were eager to read in media like the *Wall Street Journal* that unleashing free markets would trigger renewed prosperity.

The common themes of the conservative critique were simple: Free markets work better than government programs; government intervention does more harm than good; government assistance saps the initiative of the poor. In 1964, three-quarters of Americans had trusted Washington "to do what is right." By 1980, three-quarters were convinced that the federal government wasted tax money. **Neoconservatives** offered the details to support Reagan's own summary: "Government is not the solution to our problems; government is the problem." The cumulative effect was to trash the word "liberal" and convince many Americans that labor unions and minorities were "special interests" but that oil tycoons, defense contractors, and other members of Reagan's coalition were not.

The conservative cause found support in new "think tanks" and political lobbying organizations, established because many conservatives were convinced that university faculty members were hopelessly liberal. The result was to shift the terms of political discussion substantially in a conservative direction between 1975 and 1990.

**Conservative Political Savvy.** Conservatives promoted their ideology with new political tactics. Wealthy businesspeople funded alternative organizations, such as the Manhattan Institute, the Heritage Foundation, and the American Enterprise Institute, where conservative analysts could develop policy proposals and opinion pieces for newspapers. Targeted mailings raised funds and mobilized voters with emotional appeals while bypassing the mass media, with their supposed preference for mainstream or liberal policies. Conservative organizers also knew how to use radio call-in shows to spread their message. Such appeals contrasted with the Democrats' reliance on more traditional ways to get out the vote through personal contacts and labor unions. Through the 1980s, Democrats repeatedly found themselves blindsided by creative Republican campaign tactics.

**neoconservatives** A group of intellectuals who revived and updated conservative political ideas in the 1980s.

# Reaganomics: Deficits and Deregulation

The heart of the 1980s revolution was the **Economic Recovery and Tax Act of 1981 (ERTA)**, which reduced personal income tax rates by 25 percent over three years. The explicit goal was to stimulate business activity by lowering taxes overall and slashing rates for the rich. Cutting the government's total income by $747 billion over five years, ERTA meant less money for federal programs and more money in the hands of consumers and investors to stimulate economic growth.

Reagan's first budget director, David Stockman, later revealed a second goal. ERTA would lock in deficits by "pulling the revenue plug." Because defense spending and Social Security were untouchable, Congress would find it impossible to create and fund new programs without cutting old ones. If Americans still wanted social programs, they could enact them at the local or state level, but Washington would no longer pay.

The second part of the economic agenda was to free capitalists from government regulations, in the hope of increasing business innovation and efficiency. The **deregulation** revolution built on a head start from the 1970s. A federal antitrust case had split the unified Bell System of AT&T and its subsidiaries into seven regional telephone companies and opened long-distance service to competition. Congress also deregulated air travel in 1978, resulting in cheaper and more frequent air service for major hubs and poorer and more expensive service for small cities.

**Environmental Regulation and Federal Lands.** Corporate America used the Reagan administration to attack environmental legislation as "strangulation by regulation." Reagan's new budgets sliced funding for the Environmental Protection Agency. Vice President Bush headed the White House Task Force on Regulatory Relief, which

**Economic Recovery and Tax Act of 1981 (ERTA)** A major revision of the federal income tax system.

**deregulation** Reduction or removal of government regulations and encouragement of direct competition in many important industries and economic sectors.

Older American cities in the 1980s continued to feel the effects of deindustrialization as old manufacturing facilities, such as this factory in Gary, Indiana, closed or relocated production to the Sunbelt or to other countries.

**Sagebrush Rebellion** Political movement in the western states in the early 1980s that called for easing of regulations on the economic issue of federal lands and the transfer of some or all of those lands to state ownership.

delayed or blocked regulations on hazardous wastes, automobile emissions, and exposure of workers to chemicals on the job.

Most attention, however, went to the controversial appointment of a Colorado lawyer, James Watt, as secretary of the interior. The federal government owns 30 percent of the land in the United States, with more than nine-tenths of those holdings in the western states. As a result, issues of resource conservation and development are vitally important in western politics. Watt was therefore sympathetic to a western movement known as the **Sagebrush Rebellion**, which wanted the vast federal land holdings in the West transferred to the states for less environmental protection and more rapid economic use. Federal resource agencies sold trees to timber companies at a loss to the Treasury, expanded offshore oil drilling, and expedited exploration for minerals.

**Deregulation of Banking.** The early 1980s also transformed American financial markets. Savings and loans had traditionally been conservative financial institutions that funneled individual savings into safe home mortgages. Under new rules, they began to compete for deposits by offering high interest rates and reinvesting the money in much riskier commercial real estate. By 1990, the result was a financial crisis in which bad loans destroyed hundreds of S&Ls, especially in the Southwest. American taxpayers were left to bail out depositors to the tune of hundreds of billions of dollars to prevent a collapse of the nation's financial and credit system—a preview of the even vaster financial crisis of 2008.

With the deregulation of financial markets, corporate consolidations and mergers flourished. Corporate raiders raised money with "junk bonds"—high-interest, high-risk securities—and snapped up profitable and cash-rich companies that could be milked of profits and assets. The merger mania channeled capital into paper transactions rather than investments in new equipment and products. Another effect was to damage the economies of small and middle-sized communities by transferring control of local companies to outside managers.

In the short term, the national economy boomed in the mid-1980s. Deregulated credit, tax cuts, and massive deficit spending on defense fueled exuberant growth. The decade as a whole brought nearly 20 million new jobs, especially for professional and managerial workers, office support staff, salespeople, and workers providing personal services. Inflation dipped to 3 percent per year. The stock market mirrored the overall prosperity; the Dow Jones average of blue-chip industrial stock prices more than tripled from August 1982 to August 1987.

## Crisis for Organized Labor

The flip side of the economic boom was another round in the Republican offensive against labor unions. Reagan set the tone when he fired more than 11,000 members of the Professional Air Traffic Controllers Organization for violating a no-strike clause in their hiring agreements. He claimed to be enforcing the letter of the law, but the message to organized labor was clear. For many years, corporations had hesitated to hire permanent replacements for striking workers. With Reagan's example, large companies, such as Hormel and Phelps-Dodge, chose that option, undercutting the strike as an effective union strategy.

**Decline of Union Membership and Blue-Collar Jobs.** Organized labor counted a million fewer members at the end of Reagan's administration in 1989 than in 1964, even though the number of employed Americans had nearly doubled. As union membership declined and unions struggled to cope with the changing economy, corporations seized the opportunity to demand wage rollbacks and concessions on working conditions as trade-offs for continued employment, squeezing workers in one plant and then using the settlement to pressure another. Workers in the 1970s and

The working-class family depicted on the television show *Roseanne* offered viewers a glimpse of the problems facing many Americans in an era of economic change marked by deindustrialization and the rise of service jobs.

1980s faced the threat that employers might move a factory to a new site elsewhere in the United States or overseas. Or a company might sell out to a new owner, who could close a plant and reopen without a union contract.

Another cause for shrinking union membership was the overall decline of blue-collar jobs, from 36 percent of the American workforce in 1960 to roughly 25 percent at the end of the 1990s. Unionization of white-collar workers made up only part of the loss from manufacturing. Unions were most successful in recruiting government workers, such as police officers, teachers, and bus drivers. By the late 1980s, the American Federation of State, County, and Municipal Employees had twice the membership of the United Steel Workers. In the private sector, however, many white-collar jobs were in small firms that were difficult to organize.

**Impact of Economic Restructuring.**    In the 1950s and 1960s, increasing productivity, expanding markets for U.S. goods, and strong labor unions had made it possible for factory workers to enter the middle class. In an era of deindustrialization, however, companies replaced blue-collar workers with machinery or shifted production to nonunion plants. The corporate merger mania of the 1980s added to instability when takeover specialists loaded old companies with new debt, triggering efforts to cut labor costs, sell off plants, or raid pension funds for cash to pay the interest. Manufacturing

# ✱ Explore the Reagan Revolution on MyHistoryLab

## HOW DID THE "REAGAN REVOLUTION" OF THE 1980s SHAPE AMERICAN POLITICS?

In the presidential election of 1980, Republican Ronald Reagan won a landslide victory over Jimmy Carter. Economic stagnation and foreign policy difficulties had marked the previous years, while Reagan promised smaller government at home and stronger government abroad. In 1984, Reagan won an even more impressive victory over Democratic candidate Walter Mondale. One reason for these landslide victories was that a group of traditionally Democratic voters—white, socially conservative, blue-collar workers—changed party affiliation during the Reagan years and voted Republican.

Reagan's supply-side economic policy, which included limited government deregulation and tax breaks for middle-class and wealthy Americans, brought economic prosperity, but did not change the duress many suffered as other market forces saw the country move from an industrial to a service economy. Abroad, the Cold War began to end during

Taking advantage of a troubled economy and national mood, former California governor and actor Ronald Reagan won the elections of 1980 and 1984 for the Republican Party based on the "Bringing America Back" message.

Reagan's second administration with the weakening of the Soviet Union and the erosion of communist control in its Warsaw Pact allies.

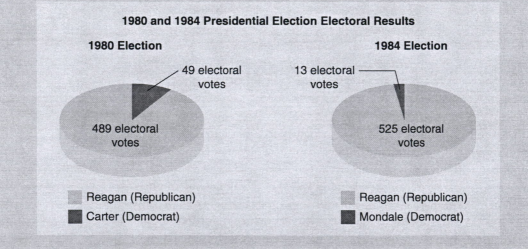

**1980 and 1984 Presidential Election Electoral Results**

**1980 Election**

49 electoral votes

489 electoral votes

■ Reagan (Republican)
■ Carter (Democrat)

**1984 Election**

13 electoral votes

525 electoral votes

■ Reagan (Republican)
■ Mondale (Democrat)

**KEY QUESTIONS**   Use **MyHistoryLab** *Explorer* **to answer** these **questions:**

**Cause ▶▶▶** *How did support for Republican and Democratic presidential candidates change in the elections from 1976–1988?*

Chart these trends to consider their causation.

**Analysis ▶▶▶** *Where did the incidence of poverty stay high?*

Map the regions where economic difficulties remained prevalent.

**Response ▶▶▶** *How did the Soviet Union's collapse redraw the map of Europe and Central Asia?*

Explore the unfolding of the end of the Cold War.

employment in the 1980s declined by nearly 2 million jobs, with the expansion of high-tech manufacturing concealing much higher losses in traditional industries.

## An Acquisitive Society

The new prosperity fueled lavish living by the wealthy and a fascination with the "lifestyles of the rich and famous." Prime-time soap operas flourished, bringing to the small screen stories of intrigue among the rich folks. With a few exceptions, even the "middle class" in television sitcoms enjoyed lives available only to the top 20 percent of Americans.

The national media in the early 1980s discovered yuppies, or young urban professionals, who were both a marketing category and a symbol of social change. These upwardly mobile professionals supposedly defined themselves by elitist consumerism. Middle-line retailers like Sears had clothed Americans for decades and furnished their homes. With the help of catalog shopping, status-seeking consumers now flocked to such upscale retailers as Neiman-Marcus and Bloomingdale's.

Far richer than even such atypical yuppies were wheeler-dealers who made themselves into media stars of finance capitalism. The autobiography of Lee Iacocca, who had helped revive the fortunes of the Chrysler Corporation, was a best seller in 1984, portraying the corporate executive as hero. *Forbes* magazine began to publish an annual list of the nation's 400 richest people. Long before his television show, real estate developer Donald Trump made himself a celebrity with a well-publicized personal life and a stream of projects crowned with his name: office tower, hotel, casino. In his best-selling novel *The Bonfire of the Vanities* (1987), Tom Wolfe depicted a New York where the art dealers and stockbrokers of glitzy Manhattan meet the poor of the devastated South Bronx only through an automobile accident, to their mutual incomprehension and ruin. Meanwhile, in the real New York, the incomes of people in the lower third of the economic ladder declined during the 1980s, while those of the top tenth rose by 40 percent.

New movements in popular music reacted to the acquisitive 1980s. Punk rock pared rock-and-roll to its basics, lashing out at the emptiness of the 1970s disco sound. Punk music influenced grunge bands such as Nirvana, which expressed alienation from consumerism. Hip-hop originated among African Americans and Latinos in New York, soon adding the angry and often violent lyrics of rap. Rap during the 1980s was about personal power and sex, but it also dealt with social inequities and deprivation and tapped some of the same anger and frustration that had motivated Black Power advocates in the 1960s.

## Mass Media and Fragmented Culture

On June 1, 1980, Cable News Network (CNN) gave television viewers their first chance to watch news coverage 24 hours a day. Soon executives in Zurich, college students in Nairobi, and farmers in Omaha were all tuning in to the version of world events pulled together in CNN's Atlanta headquarters. CNN made a global reputation with live reporting on the pro-democracy protests of Chinese students in Beijing in 1989. When American bombs began to fall on Baghdad in January 1991, White House officials watched CNN to find out how their war was going.

CNN and the rest of cable television reflected both the fragmentation of American society in the 1980s and 1990s and the increasing dependence on instant communication. As late as 1980, ordinary Americans had few choices for learning about their nation and world: virtually identical newscasts on NBC, CBS, and ABC and similar stories in *Time* and *Newsweek* helped to create a common understanding. Fifteen years later, they had learned to surf through dozens of cable channels in search of specialized programs and were beginning to explore the amazing variety of the World Wide Web (see Chapter 31). Hundreds of magazines for niche markets had replaced the general-circulation periodicals of the postwar generation. Vast quantities of information were

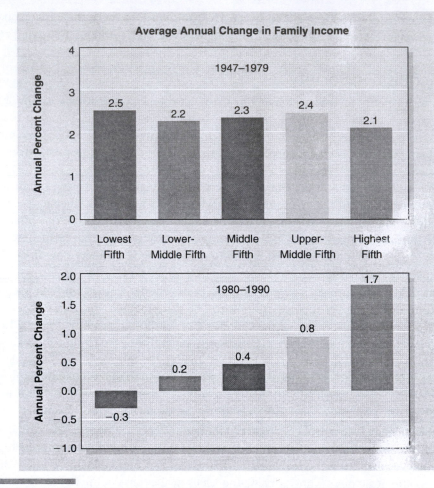

**FIGURE 30.1  CHANGES IN REAL FAMILY INCOME, 1947–1979 AND 1980–1990** In the 1980s, the poor got poorer, the middle class made slight gains, and the most affluent 20 percent of the Ameri.... .... .... very well. Tax changes that helped well-off households were one factor. Another factor was the er........ .... ....... wage jobs in manufacturing.

SOURCE: U.S. Census Bureau

more easily available, but much of it was packaged for a subdivided marketplace of specialized consumers.

## Poverty amid Prosperity

Federal tax and budget changes had different effects on the rich and poor (see Figure 30.1). Those in the top fifth increased their share of after-tax income relative to everyone else during the 1980s, and the richest 1 percent saw their share of all privately held wealth grow from 31 percent to 37 percent. The 1981 tax cuts also came with sharp increases in the Social Security tax, which hit lower-income workers the hardest. The tax changes meant that the average annual income of households in the bottom 20 percent *declined* and that many actually paid higher taxes.

Cities and their residents absorbed approximately two-thirds of the cuts in the 1981–1982 federal budget. Provisions for accelerated depreciation (tax write-offs) of factories and equipment in the 1981 tax act encouraged the abandonment of center-city factories in favor of new facilities in the suburbs. One result was a growing jobs-housing mismatch. There were often plenty of jobs in the suburbs, but the poorer people who most needed the jobs were marooned in city slums and dependent on public transit that seldom served suburban employers.

Federal tax and spending policies in the 1980s decreased the security of middle-class families. As the economy continued to struggle through deindustrialization, average wage rates fell in the 1980s when measured in real purchasing power. The squeeze put pressure on traditional family patterns and pushed into the workforce women who might otherwise have stayed home. Many Americans no longer expected to surpass their parents' standard of living.

**Corporate Downsizing and White-Collar Jobs.** Lower-paying office jobs fell under the same sorts of pressure as factory jobs with the increasing reliance of banks, telephone companies, and credit card companies on automation. Increasing numbers of clerical and office workers in organizations of all sorts, from corporations to universities, were "temps" who shifted from job to job. The shift toward temporary and part-time workers not only kept wages low but also allowed less spending on health insurance and other benefits.

The chill of corporate downsizing hit white-collar families most heavily toward the end of the 1980s. Big business consolidations delivered improved profits by squeezing the ranks of middle managers as well as assembly-line workers. With fewer workers to supervise and with new technologies to collect and distribute information, companies could complete their cost cutting by trimming administrators.

**Increase in the Poverty Rate.** At the lower end of the economic ladder, the proportion of Americans living in poverty increased. After declining steadily from 1960 to a low of 11 percent in 1973, the poverty rate climbed back to the 13 to 15 percent range. Although the economy in the 1980s created lots of new jobs, half of them paid less than poverty-level wages. Conservative critics began to talk about an underclass of Americans permanently outside the mainstream economy because of poor education, drug abuse, or sheer laziness. In fact, talk of an underclass was a way to avoid confronting the realities of limited economic opportunity. Most of the nation's millions of poor people lived in households with employed adults. In 1992, fully 18 percent of all full-time jobs did not pay enough to lift a family of four out of poverty, a jump of 50 percent over the proportion of underpaid jobs in 1981. One of the biggest barriers to better employment was not a disinterest in work, but rather the isolation of many job seekers in poverty neighborhoods without access to suburban jobs or the informal social networks that are the best way to find good employment.

**The Wage Gap and the Feminization of Poverty.** Nor could most women, even those working full-time, expect to earn as much as men. In the 1960s and 1970s, the average working woman earned just 60 percent of the earnings of the average man (see Table 30.1). Only part of the wage gap could be explained by measurable factors, such

TABLE 30.1 WOMEN'S ANNUAL EARNINGS AS A PERCENT OF MEN'S EARNINGS (FULL-TIME WORKERS)

| | |
|---|---|
| 1955 | 64 percent |
| 1960 | 61 percent |
| 1965 | 60 percent |
| 1970 | 59 percent |
| 1975 | 59 percent |
| 1980 | 60 percent |
| 1985 | 65 percent |
| 1990 | 72 percent |
| 1995 | 72 percent |
| 2000 | 74 percent |
| 2005 | 77 percent |
| 2010 | 77 percent |

U.S. Census data show the median earnings of women who worked full-time and year-round, compared to those of men, rising gradually but still lagging those of men.

SOURCE: Ariane Hegewisch and Angela Edwards. Fact Sheet #C350/The Gender Wage Gap: 2011, page 2. Copyright © 2012. Reprinted by permission of the Institute for Women's Policy Research.

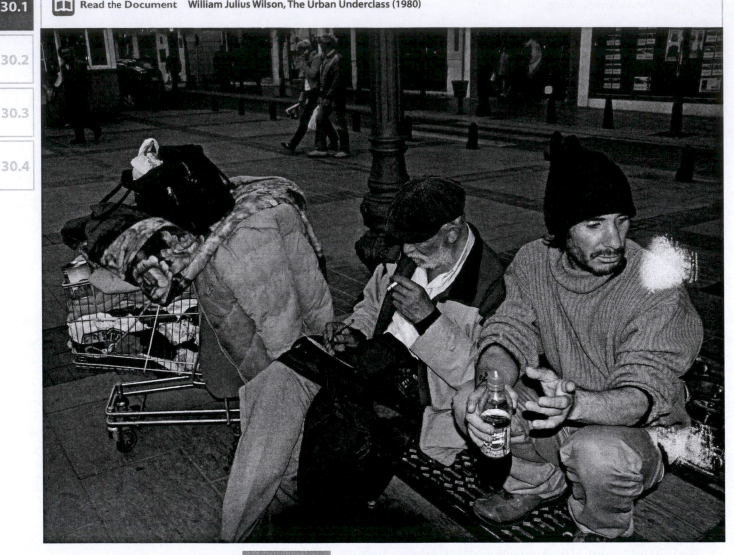

Estimates of the number of homeless in the late 1980s ranged from 300,000 to 3 million, depending on the definition of homelessness and the political goals of the estimator.

as education or experience. The gap narrowed in the 1980s and 1990s, with women's earnings rising to 72 percent of men's by 1990 and reaching 77 percent by 2010. About half of the change was the result of bad news—the decline of earnings among men as high-wage factory jobs disappeared. The other half was the positive result of better-educated, younger women finding better jobs. Indeed, women earned 57 percent of the four-year college degrees awarded in 2002 (up from 38 percent in 1960) and 47 percent of first professional degrees (up from 3 percent).

Nevertheless, the low earning capacity of women with limited educations meant that women were far more likely than men to be poor. Women constituted nearly two-thirds of poor adults at the end of the 1980s. Only 6 percent of married-couple households were below poverty level, but 32 percent of households headed by a woman without a husband present were poor. The feminization of poverty and American reliance on private support for child rearing also meant that children had a higher chance of living in poverty than adults and that poor American children were worse off than their peers in other advanced nations.

**Homelessness in America.**    Falling below even the working poor were growing numbers of homeless Americans. Large cities have always had transient laborers, derelict alcoholics, and voluntarily homeless hobos. In the 1980s, several factors made homelessness more visible and pressing. A new approach to the treatment of the mentally ill reduced the population of mental hospitals from 540,000 in 1960 to only 140,000 in 1980. Deinstitutionalized patients were supposed to receive community-based treatment, but many ended up on the streets and in overnight shelters. New forms of self-destructive drug abuse, such as crack addiction, joined alcoholism. A boom in downtown real estate destroyed old skid row districts with their bars, missions, and dollar-a-night hotels.

These factors tripled the number of permanently homeless people during the early and middle 1980s, from 200,000 to somewhere between 500,000 and 700,000. Twice or three times that many may have been homeless for part of a given year. For every person in a shelter on a given night, two people were sleeping on sidewalks, in parks, in cars, and in abandoned buildings.

## Consolidating the Revolution: George H. W. Bush

In 1988, George Herbert Walker Bush, Reagan's vice president for eight years, won the presidential election with 56 percent of the popular vote and forty out of fifty states. Bush's view of national and world politics reflected a background in which personal connections counted. He was raised as part of the New England elite, built an oil business in Texas, and then held a series of high-level federal appointments.

Michael Dukakis, the Democratic nominee in 1988, was a dry-as-dust, by-the-numbers manager who offered the American people "competence." The Bush campaign director, Lee Atwater, looked for hot-button issues that could fit onto a three-by-five card. He found that Dukakis as governor of Massachusetts had vetoed a bill requiring school children to recite the Pledge of Allegiance (arguing correctly that it would be overturned in the courts). Even more damaging, Massachusetts officials had allowed

After a jury acquitted the police officers involved in the beating of motorist Rodney King in April 1992, much of Los Angeles erupted in rioting that left smoldering buildings and revealed deep racial and economic tensions.

30.1

**30.2**

30.3

30.4

a murderer named Willie Horton a weekend furlough from prison, during which he committed a brutal rape. Pro-Bush advertisements tapped into real worries among the voters—fear of crime, racial tension (Horton was black), eroding social values.

The ads locked Bush into a rhetorical war on crime and drugs that was his major domestic policy. Americans had good cause to be worried about public safety, but most were generally unaware that the likelihood of becoming the target of a violent crime had leveled off and would continue to fall in the 1990s or that crime was far worse in minority communities than elsewhere, in part due to gang- and drug-related activities. Bush tripled the federal drug control budget and stepped up efforts to stop the flow of illegal drugs across the border. Longer sentences and mandatory jail time meant that half of federal prison inmates in 1990 were in for drug crimes.

George Bush believed that Americans wanted government to leave them alone. He ignored a flood of new ideas from entrepreneurial conservatives, such as Department of Housing and Urban Development (HUD) Secretary Jack Kemp. The major legislation from his administration was a transportation bill that shifted federal priorities from highway building toward mass transit and the **Americans with Disabilities Act** (1990) to prevent discrimination against people with physical handicaps.

The same attitude produced weak economic policies. The national debt had amounted to 50 percent of personal savings in 1980 but swelled to 125 percent by 1990. The massive budget deficits of the 1980s combined with growing trade deficits to turn the United States from an international creditor to a debtor nation. After pledging no new taxes in his campaign, Bush backed into a tax increase in 1990. A strong leader might have justified the taxes to the nation, but voters found it hard to forget the president's waffling and attempts to downplay the importance of his decision.

The most conspicuous domestic event of the Bush administration—the "Rodney King riot" of April 1992 in Los Angeles—was a reminder of the nation's inattention to the problems of race and poverty. Rodney King was a black motorist who had been savagely clubbed and kicked by police officers while being arrested after a car chase on March 3, 1991. A nearby resident captured the beating on videotape from his apartment. Early the next year, the four officers stood trial for unjustified use of force before a suburban jury. The televised trial and the unexpected verdict of not guilty on April 29 stirred deep anger that escalated into four days of rioting.

The disorder revealed multiple tensions among ethnic groups and was far more complex than the Watts outbreak of 1965 (see Chapter 29). African Americans from south-central Los Angeles participated, but so did Central American and Mexican immigrants in adjacent districts, who accounted for about one-third of the 12,000 arrests. The disorder spread south to Long Beach and north to the edge of upscale neighborhoods in Westwood and Beverly Hills. Rioters assaulted the downtown police headquarters and city hall. As in 1965, some targets were white passers-by and symbols of white authority. But members of competing minority groups were also victims as angry black people targeted hundreds of Korean-owned and Vietnamese-owned shops as symbols of economic discrimination. Four days of disorder left fifty-eight people dead, mostly African Americans and Latinos.

**Americans with Disabilities Act**
Legislation in 1992 that banned discrimination against physically handicapped persons in employment, transportation, and public accommodations.

## The Climax of the Cold War

 **30.2**    How and why did the Cold War come to an end?

Ronald Reagan entered office determined to reassert U.S. leadership in world affairs and not to lose the Cold War. He considered the Soviet Union not a coequal nation with legitimate world interests but an "evil empire," like something from the *Star Wars* movies. After the era of *détente*, global tensions had started to mount in the late 1970s. They were soon higher than they had been since the

896

1960s. But by the end of Reagan's two terms, unexpected changes were rapidly bringing the Cold War to an end, and George H. W. Bush faced a radically new set of foreign policy issues.

## Confronting the Soviet Union

Who renewed the Cold War after Nixon's diplomacy of *détente* and Carter's early efforts at negotiation? The Soviets had pursued military expansion in the 1970s, triggering the fear that they might stage a nuclear Pearl Harbor. The Soviet Union in 1980 was supporting Marxist regimes in civil wars in Angola, Ethiopia, Nicaragua, and especially Afghanistan, where its 1980 intervention led to a decade of costly and futile military occupation. Were these actions parts of a careful plan? Or did they result from the Cold War inertia of a rudderless nation that reacted to situations one at a time? Given the aging Soviet leadership and the economic weaknesses revealed in the late 1980s, it makes more sense to see the Soviets as muddling along rather than executing a well-planned global strategy.

On the American side, Reagan's readiness to confront "the focus of evil in the modern world" reflected the views of many conservative supporters that the Soviet Union was a monolithic and ideologically motivated foe bent on world conquest. In hindsight, some Reaganites claim that the administration's foreign policy and massive increases in defense spending were part of a deliberate and coordinated scheme to check a Soviet offensive and bankrupt the Soviet Union by pushing it into a new arms race. It is just as likely, however, that the administration's defense and foreign policy initiatives were a set of discrete but effective decisions.

The Reagan administration reemphasized central Europe as the focus of superpower rivalry, just as it had been in the 1950s and early 1960s. To counter improved Soviet armaments, the United States began to place cruise missiles and mid-range Pershing II missiles in Europe in 1983. NATO governments approved the action, but it frightened millions of their citizens, especially when officials in Washington began to talk about the possibility of a winnable nuclear war in National Security Directive D-13 (1981). All that Americans needed for survival, said one administration official, were "enough shovels" to dig fallout shelters.

Escalation of the nuclear arms race reinvigorated the antiwar and antinuclear movement in the United States as well as Europe. Drawing on the experience of the antiwar movement, the nuclear-freeze campaign caught the imagination of many Americans in 1981 and 1982. It sought to halt the manufacture and deployment of new atomic weapons by the great powers. Nearly a million people turned out for a nuclear-freeze rally in New York in 1982. Hundreds of local communities endorsed the freeze or took the symbolic step of declaring themselves nuclear-free zones.

In response, Reagan announced the **Strategic Defense Initiative (SDI)**, or Star Wars program, in 1983. SDI was to deploy new defenses that could intercept and destroy ballistic missiles as they rose from the ground and arced through space, although all of the proposed technologies were untested and some only existed in the imagination. Few scientists thought that SDI could work. Many arms control experts thought that defensive systems were dangerous and destabilizing, because strong defenses suggested that a nation might be willing to risk a nuclear exchange. Nevertheless, President Reagan found SDI appealing, for it offered a way around the balance of terror.

**Strategic Defense Initiative (SDI)** President Reagan's program, announced in 1983, to defend the United States against nuclear missile attack with untested weapons systems and sophisticated technologies.

## Risky Business: Foreign Policy Adventures

The same administration that sometimes seemed reckless in its grand strategy also took risks to assert U.S. influence in global trouble spots to block or roll back Soviet influence. Reagan asserted America's right to intervene anywhere in the world to support local groups fighting against Marxist governments. The assumption underlying this assertion, which later became known as the **Reagan Doctrine**, was that Soviet-influenced

**Reagan Doctrine** The policy assumption that Soviet-influenced governments in Asia, Africa, and Latin America needed to be eliminated if the United States was to win the Cold War.

governments in Asia, Africa, and Latin America needed to be eliminated if the United States was to win the Cold War.

Nevertheless, Reagan kept the United States out of a major war and backed off in the face of serious trouble. Foreign interventions were designed to achieve symbolic victories rather than change the global balance of power. The exception was the Caribbean and Central America, the "backyard" where the United States had always claimed an overriding interest and where left-wing action infuriated Reagan's conservative supporters.

**Intervention and Covert Activities in Central America.** The Reagan administration attributed political turmoil in Central America to Soviet influence and to arms and agitators from Soviet-backed Cuba. Between 1980 and 1983, the United States sent more military aid to conservative governments and groups in Central America than it had during the previous thirty years. Indeed, Central America became the focus of a secret foreign policy operated by the Central Intelligence Agency (CIA) and then by National Security Council (NSC) staff, since Congress was not convinced of the danger. The CIA and the NSC engaged not just in espionage but in direct covert operations. The chief target was Nicaragua, the Central American country where leftist Sandinista rebels had overthrown the Somoza dictatorship in 1979. In the early 1980s, Reagan approved CIA plans to arm and organize approximately 10,500 so-called Contras, from the remnants of Somoza's national guard. From bases in Honduras, the Contras harassed the Sandinistas with sabotage and raids. Reagan called the Contras "freedom fighters," listened to stories of their exploits, and hunched over maps to follow their operations in detail. Meanwhile, Americans with different views aided refugees from the war zones of Central America through the church-based sanctuary movement ("sanctuary" could imply both legal economic assistance and direct defiance of efforts to deport refugees).

The Reagan administration bent the law to support its covert effort to overthrow the Sandinista regime. An unsympathetic Congress blocked U.S. funding for the Contras. In response, CIA director William Casey directed Lieutenant Colonel Oliver North of the National Security Council staff to illegally organize aid from private donors. The arms pipeline operated until a supply plane was shot down in 1986. The Contras failed as a military effort, but the civil war and international pressure persuaded the Sandinistas to allow free elections that led to a democratic, centrist government.

**The War against Drugs.** The American war against drugs was simultaneously shaping U.S. policy in the Caribbean and straining relations with Latin America. As president, George H. W. Bush parlayed the war on drugs into war on Panama during his first year in office, extending the American tradition of ousting uncooperative governments around the Caribbean. General Manuel Noriega, the Panamanian strongman, had once been on the CIA payroll. He had since turned to international drug sales in defiance of U.S. antismuggling efforts. On December 20, 1989, American troops invaded Panama, hunted down Noriega, and brought him back to stand trial in the United States on drug-trafficking charges. A handful of Americans and thousands of Panamanians died, many of them civilians caught in the cross-fire.

**Intervention in the Middle East.** If the results of intervention in Nicaraugua and Panama were mixed, intervention in the Middle East was a failure. In 1982, Israel invaded Lebanon, a small nation to its north, to clear Palestinian guerrillas from its borders and set up a friendly Lebanese government. The Israeli army bogged down in a civil war between Christian Arabs and Muslims. Reagan sent U.S. Marines to preserve the semblance of a Lebanese state and provide a face-saving exit for Israel. In October 1983, a terrorist car bomb killed 241 Marines in their barracks. The remainder were soon gone, confirming the Syrian observation that Americans were "short of breath" when it came to Middle East politics. The debacle in Lebanon undermined U.S.-backed peace initiatives in the Middle East.

**The Iran-Contra Affair.** Even less effective were the Reagan administration's secret efforts to sell weapons to Iran in return for Iranian help in securing the release of Americans held hostage by pro-Iranian Islamic radicals in Lebanon. The United States in 1985 joined Israel in selling 500 antitank missiles to Iran, and then embroiled in a long, bitter war with Iraq. The deal followed stern public pronouncements that the United States would never negotiate with terrorists and considered Iran's religious leaders to be backers of international terrorism. It also violated the official trade embargo against Iran, which had been in place since the U.S. embassy seizure in 1979. In May 1986, National Security adviser Robert McFarlane flew to Iran for more arms-for-hostages talks, carrying a chocolate cake and a Bible autographed by Reagan to present to the Iranian leader Ayatollah Khomeini. When the deals came to light in 1986 and congressional hearings were held in the summer of 1987, Americans were startled to learn that Colonel North had funneled millions of dollars from the arms sales to the Nicaraguan Contras in a double evasion of the law.

As had been true with Watergate, the Iran-Contra affair was a two-sided scandal. First was the blatant misjudgment of operating a secret, bumbling, and unlawful foreign policy that depended on international arms dealers and ousted Nicaraguan military officers. Second was a concerted effort to cover up the illegal and unconstitutional actions. North shredded relevant documents and lied to Congress. In his final report in 1994, Special Prosecutor Lawrence Walsh found that President Reagan and Vice President Bush were aware of much of what had gone on and had participated in efforts to withhold information and mislead Congress.

**U.S. Policy in Asia.** American policy in Asia was a refreshing contrast with practices in Central America and the Middle East. In the Philippines, American diplomats helped push corrupt president Ferdinand Marcos out and opened the way for a popular uprising to put Corazon Aquino in office. Secretary of State George Shultz made sure that the United States supported popular democracy while reassuring the Philippine military. In South Korea, the United States similarly helped ease out an unpopular dictator by firmly supporting democratic elections that brought in a more popular but still pro-American government.

## Embracing *Perestroika*

The thaw in the Cold War started in Moscow as Soviet leaders sought to salvage a system under severe economic stress. Mikhail Gorbachev, part of a new generation of Soviet leaders, became general secretary of the Communist Party in 1985, when the Soviet Union was trapped in the sixth year of its failed attempt to control Afghanistan. Gorbachev was the picture of vigor compared to his three elderly predecessors. A master of public relations who charmed Western Europe's leaders and public, he was also a modernizer in a long Russian tradition that stretched back to Tsar Peter the Great in the eighteenth century. Gorbachev startled Soviet citizens by urging **glasnost**, or political openness, with free discussion of issues and relaxation of controls on the press. He followed by setting the goal of **perestroika**, or restructuring of the painfully bureaucratic Soviet economy that was falling behind capitalist nations. His hope was that market-oriented reforms would help the Soviet Union keep up with the United States.

Gorbachev decided that he needed to reduce the crushing burden of Soviet defense spending if the Soviet Union was to have any chance of modernizing. During Reagan's second term, the Soviets offered one concession after another in a drive for arms control, and the president had the vision (or audacity) to embrace the new Soviet position. He cast off decades of belief in the dangers of Soviet Communism and had the political courage to take Gorbachev seriously. One of his reasons for SDI had been his belief that the abolition of nuclear weapons was better than fine-tuning the balance of terror. Now he was willing to forget his own rhetoric. He frightened his own staff when he met with Gorbachev in the summer of 1986 and accepted the principle of deep cuts in strategic forces, although they could not then agree on specifics.

**glasnost** Russian for "openness," applied to Mikhail Gorbachev's encouragement of new ideas and easing of political repression in the Soviet Union.

**perestroika** Russian for "restructuring," applied to Mikhail Gorbachev's efforts to make the Soviet economic and political systems more modern, flexible, and innovative.

📖 **Read the Document** Mikhail Gorbachev, The Need for Economic Reform (1987)

Mikhail Gorbachev, holding the child, hosted a summit meeting with President Reagan in Moscow in May 1988. Their smiles ignored the lack of progress toward disarmament beyond the Intermediate-Range Nuclear Forces (INF) Treaty of the previous year.

**Intermediate-Range Nuclear Forces (INF) Treaty** Disarmament agreement between the United States and the Soviet Union under which an entire class of missiles would be removed and destroyed and on-site inspections would be permitted for verification.

In the end, Reagan negotiated the **Intermediate-Range Nuclear Forces (INF) Treaty** over the strong objections of the CIA and the Defense Department. INF was the first true nuclear disarmament treaty. (See Table 30.2, Controlling Nuclear Weapons: Four Decades of Effort.) Previous agreements had only slowed the growth of nuclear weapons; they were "speed limits" for the arms race. The new pact matched Soviet SS-20s with U.S. cruise missiles as an entire class of weapons that would be destroyed, with on-site inspections for verification.

## Crisis and Democracy in Eastern Europe

Reagan's successor, President George Bush, a believer in personal diplomacy, based much of his foreign policy on his changing attitudes toward Mikhail Gorbachev. He

## TABLE 30.2 CONTROLLING NUCLEAR WEAPONS: FOUR DECADES OF EFFORT

| | | |
|---|---|---|
| Limiting the testing of nuclear weapons | Limited Test Ban Treaty (1963) | Banned nuclear testing in the atmosphere, ocean, and outer space. |
| | Comprehensive Test Ban Treaty (1996) | Banned all nuclear tests, including underground tests. Rejected by U.S. Senate in 1999. |
| Halting the spread of nuclear weapons | Nuclear Non-Proliferation Treaty (1968) | Pledged 5 recognized nuclear nations (United States, Soviet Union, Britain, France, China) to pursue disarmament in good faith, and 140 other nations not to acquire nuclear weapons. |
| | Strategic Arms Limitation Treaty (SALT I, 1972) | Limited the number of nuclear-armed missiles and bombers maintained by the United States and Soviet Union. Closely associated with U.S.-Soviet agreement to limit deployment of antiballistic missile systems to one site each. |
| | Strategic Arms Limitation Treaty (SALT II, 1979) | Further limited the number of nuclear-armed missiles and bombers. Not ratified but followed by Carter and Reagan administrations. |
| Reducing the number of nuclear weapons | Intermediate-Range Nuclear Forces (INF) Treaty (1987) | Required the United States to eliminate 846 nuclear-armed cruise missiles, and the Soviet Union to eliminate 1,846 SS-20 missiles. |
| | Strategic Arms Reduction Treaty (START I, 1991) | By July 1999, led to reductions of approximately 2,750 nuclear warheads by the United States and 3,725 warheads by the nations of the former Soviet Union. Expired December 2009. |
| | Strategic Arms Reduction Treaty (START II, 1993) | Set further cuts in nuclear arsenals. Ratified by Russia in April 2000. Russia withdrew in 2002 after the United States abandoned the Anti-Ballistic Missile Treaty. |
| | Strategic Offensive Reductions (2002) | Russia and the United States each agreed to deploy no more than 1,700–2,200 strategic nuclear warheads. |
| | New START (2010) | Russia and the United States agreed to reduce deployed strategic warheads to 1,550 each. |

SOURCE: Arms Control Association.

started lukewarm, talking tough to please the Republican right wing. Bush feared that Gorbachev, by instituting reforms that challenged the entrenched Communist Party leaders, was being imprudent: one of the worst things he could say about another leader. Before 1989 was over, however, the president had decided that Gorbachev was okay. For the next two years, the United States pushed the pro-democratic transformation of Eastern Europe while being careful not to gloat in public or damage Gorbachev's position at home.

**The End of Communist Regimes in Eastern Europe.**   The people of Eastern Europe overcame both U.S. and Soviet caution. Gorbachev had urged his Eastern European allies to emulate *perestroika* to free their economies from stifling controls. Instead of careful economic liberalization, the Warsaw Pact system collapsed. Poland held free elections in June 1989, Hungary adopted a democratic constitution in October, and pro-democracy demonstrations then forced out Communist leaders in other Eastern European countries. When East Germans began to flee westward through Hungary, the East German regime bowed to mounting pressure and opened the Berlin Wall on November 9. By the end of 1989, there were new democratic or non-Communist governments in Czechoslovakia, Romania, Bulgaria, and East Germany. These largely peaceful revolutions destroyed the military and economic agreements that had harnessed the satellites to the Soviet economy (the Warsaw Pact and COMECON). The Soviet Union swallowed hard, accepted the loss of its satellites, and slowly withdrew its army from Eastern Europe.

**German Reunification and the Dissolution of the Soviet Union.**   Events in Europe left German reunification as a point of possible conflict. Soviet policy since 1945 had sought to prevent the reemergence of a strong, united Germany that might again threaten its neighbors. West Germany removed one obstacle when it reassured Poland

## From Then to Now
# The Berlin Wall

O n November 9, 1989, the Communist government of East Germany opened the gates in the wall that had surrounded West Berlin since 1961. The action and the spontaneous celebration that followed marked the symbolic end of the Cold War and the literal crumbling of the Iron Curtain—the physical and legal barriers that had divided the Communist nations of Eastern Europe from the nations of the West.

The special status of Berlin as an island within East Germany under the joint control of the United States, Britain, France, and the Soviet Union had allowed East Germans and other Eastern Europeans to move freely into the western sectors through the 1950s. Once there, they could sometimes find their way to the West. By 1961, the drain of millions of educated and ambitious East Germans was undermining that nation's economy.

The response of the German Democratic Republic—East Germany—was to suddenly and unilaterally close all of the border crossings on August 13, 1961, after which they hastily installed barbed wire with permanent barricades. Families suddenly found themselves divided and businesses were cut off from customers. The action directly violated postwar agreements and challenged the United States, but it also defused a problem that had been pushing the United States and the Soviet Union close to a war that neither wanted. As a provocation short of war, the Wall symbolized the standoff of the Cold War in Europe.

The East Germans repeatedly rebuilt and strengthened the Wall, eventually with 12-foot-high concrete modules. They also cleared a "death strip" on their side to prevent escapes. The Wall ran through the heart of the city, most conspicuously cutting across the historic Brandenburg square in its very center. It also looped around the suburbs of West Berlin for a total of 87 miles. The barrier was not absolute. Westerners could enter East Berlin through checkpoints with proper visas, and slowly relaxing regulations allowed East Germans to make temporary visits to West Berlin. West Berliners decorated their side of the tall concrete slab with political slogans, graffiti, and art.

The Wall was the most visible and potent representation of the Iron Curtain. President John Kennedy visited Berlin in 1963 and reaffirmed American support for West Berlin by declaring "Ich bin ein Berliner." Twenty years later, President Ronald Reagan famously stood before the Wall and called on the Soviet Union and East Germany to dismantle the barrier: "Mr. Gorbachev, tear down this wall!"

As the isolation of Eastern Europe eroded in 1989, the Wall became obsolete. In the summer and fall, tens of thousands of East Germans traveled to the West via Hungary and Czechoslovakia, which had already loosened their border controls. On November 9, the East German government bowed to the inevitable and opened the border crossings. Thousands of jubilant East Berliners poured past the border guards and the Wall was effectively breached. It would be several more months before all limitations on free movement disappeared and authorities began to systematically dismantle it, but the fall of the Berlin Wall remains a potent reminder of the challenges of journeys to freedom.

**Question for Discussion**

- How has the Berlin Wall functioned as a symbol of American engagement with the world?

U.S. Army forces in place at Checkpoint Charlie, a guarded access point between East Berlin and West Berlin, at the time of the Cold War confrontation of 1961 that came close to war.

Germans celebrate the opening of the Berlin Wall and free movement between East Berlin and West Berlin.

and Russia that Germany would seek no changes in the boundaries drawn after World War II. By July 1990, the United States and the Soviet Union had agreed that a reunited Germany would belong to NATO. The decision satisfied France and Britain that a stronger Germany would still be under the influence of the Western allies. In October, the two Germanies completed their political unification, although it would be years before their mismatched economies functioned as one. Reunification was the last step in the diplomatic legacy of World War II.

The final act in the transformation of the Soviet Union began with a failed coup against Mikhail Gorbachev in August 1991. The Soviet Union had held free elections in 1989. Now Gorbachev scheduled a vote on a new constitution that would decrease the power of the central government. Old-line Communist bureaucrats who feared the change arrested Gorbachev in his vacation house and tried to take over the government apparatus in Moscow. Boris Yeltsin, president of the Russian Republic, organized the resistance. Muscovites flocked to support Yeltsin and defied tank crews in front of the Russian Parliament building. Within three days, the plotters themselves were under arrest.

The coup hastened the fragmentation of the Soviet Union. Before the month was out, the Soviet Parliament banned the Communist Party. Gorbachev soon resigned. Previously suppressed nationalist feelings caused all fifteen component republics of the Soviet Union to declare their independence. The superpower Union of Soviet Socialist Republics ceased to exist. Russia remained the largest and strongest of the new states, followed by Ukraine and Kazakhstan.

The end of the Cold War leaves the historical assessment of the last half century of U.S. foreign policy open to debate. Some scholars see the demise of the Soviet empire as ultimate justification for forty years of Cold War. Dissenters argue the opposite—that the collapse of European Communism shows that American leaders had magnified its threat (see Table 30.3).

## The Persian Gulf War

The uncertainty of international power after the Cold War and the new freedom for the United States to act without worrying about Russian reactions set the stage for war in the Persian Gulf region. On August 2, 1990, President Saddam Hussein of Iraq seized

### TABLE 30.3 WHY DID THE COLD WAR END?

Commentators have offered a number of explanations for the rapid failure of the Soviet Union and the collapse of Soviet power at the end of the 1980s. All of these factors made contributions to the complex unraveling of the Cold War.

| | |
|---|---|
| Economic exhaustion | The United States in the late 1970s embarked on a great modernization and expansion of its military forces. The Soviet Union exhausted its economy and revealed its technical backwardness by trying to keep pace. Gorbachev's policy of *perestroika* was an attempt to reduce the bureaucratic inertia of the economy. |
| Failure of leadership | The Soviet Union in the 1970s and early 1980s was governed by unimaginative bureaucrats. A closed elite that thought only of preserving their privileges and authority could not adapt to a changing world. The policy of *glasnost* was an effort to encourage new ideas. |
| Intervention in Afghanistan | The disastrous intervention in Afghanistan revealed the limits of Soviet military power. It alienated the large Muslim population of the Soviet Union and brought disillusionment with the incompetence of Soviet leaders. |
| Triumph of democratic ideas | As political discussion became more free, the appeal of democratic ideas took on its own momentum, especially in Eastern European satellite nations such as East Germany, Czechoslovakia, and Poland. |
| Power of nationalism | The collapse of the Soviet empire was triggered by the resurgence of national sentiments throughout the Soviet empire. National sentiments fueled the breakaway of the Eastern European satellite nations such as Hungary, Romania, and Poland. Nationalism also broke up the Soviet Union itself as fourteen smaller socialist republics declared independence from the Russian-dominated Union. |

the small neighboring oil-rich country of Kuwait. The quick conquest gave Iraq control of 20 percent of the world's oil production and reserves. President Bush demanded unconditional withdrawal, enlisted European and Arab allies in an anti-Iraq coalition, and persuaded Saudi Arabia to accept substantial U.S. forces to protect it against Iraqi invasion. Within weeks, the Saudis were host to tens of thousands of U.S. soldiers and hundreds of aircraft.

The background for Iraq's invasion was a simmering dispute over border oil fields and islands in the Persian Gulf. Iraq was a dictatorship that had just emerged from an immensely costly eight-year war with Iran. Saddam Hussein had depended on help from the United States and Arab nations in this war, but Iraq was now economically exhausted. Kuwait was a small, rich nation whose ruling dynasty enjoyed few friends but plenty of oil royalties. The U.S. State Department had signaled earlier in 1990 that it might support some concessions by Kuwait in its dispute with Iraq. Having been favored in the past by the United States, Saddam Hussein read the signal as an open invitation to do what he wanted.

The Iraqis gave Bush a golden opportunity to assert America's world influence. The Bush administration was concerned that Iraq might target oil-rich Saudi Arabia. The importance of Middle East oil helped to enlist France and Britain as military allies and to secure billions of dollars from Germany and Japan. Iraq had antagonized nearly all its neighbors. The collapse of Soviet power and Gorbachev's interest in cooperating with the United States meant that the Soviets would not interfere with U.S. plans.

Bush and his advisers offered a series of justifications for U.S. actions. First, and most basic, were the desire to punish armed aggression and the presumed need to protect Iraq's other neighbors. In fact, there was scant evidence of Iraqi preparations against Saudi Arabia. The buildup of U.S. air power plus effective economic sanctions would have accomplished both protection and punishment. Sanctions and diplomatic pressure might also have brought withdrawal from most or all of Kuwait. However, additional American objectives—to destroy Iraq's capacity to create nuclear weapons and to topple Saddam's regime—would require direct military action.

Bush probably decided on war in October, eventually increasing the number of American troops in Saudi Arabia to 580,000. The United States stepped up diplomatic pressure by securing a series of increasingly tough United Nations resolutions that culminated in November 1990 with Security Council Resolution 678, authorizing "all necessary means" to liberate Kuwait. The president convinced Congress to agree to military action under the umbrella of the UN. The United States ignored compromise plans floated by France and last-minute concessions from Iraq.

War began one day after the UN's January 15 deadline for Iraqi withdrawal from Kuwait. **Operation Desert Storm** opened with massive air attacks on command centers, transportation facilities, and Iraqi forward positions. The air war destroyed 40 to 50 percent of Iraqi tanks and artillery by late February. The attacks also seriously hurt Iraqi civilians by disrupting utilities and food supplies.

The forty-day rain of bombs was the prelude to a ground attack (see Map 30.2). On February 24, 1991, these forces swept into Iraq in a great arc. Americans, Saudis, Syrians, and Egyptians advanced directly to liberate Kuwait. A cease-fire came 100 hours after the start of the ground war. The **Persian Gulf War** cost allied forces only 240 deaths in action, compared to perhaps 100,000 for the Iraqis.

Bush directed Desert Storm with the "Vietnam syndrome" in mind, believing that Americans were willing to accept war only if it involved overwhelming U.S. force and ended quickly. The United States hoped to replace Saddam Hussein without disrupting Iraqi society. Instead, the 100-hour war incited armed rebellions against Saddam in southern Iraq by Shiites, a group within the Muslim religion whose adherents comprise a majority in Iraq, and in the north by the ethnically distinct Kurds. Because Bush and his advisers were unwilling to get embroiled in a civil war or commit the United States to occupy all of Iraq, they stood by while Saddam crushed the uprisings. In one sense, the United States won the war but not the peace. Saddam Hussein became a hero to many in the Islamic world simply by surviving.

**Operation Desert Storm** Code name for the successful offensive against Iraq by the United States and its allies in the Persian Gulf War (1991).

**Persian Gulf War** War (1991) between Iraq and a U.S.-led coalition that followed Iraq's invasion of Kuwait and resulted in the expulsion of Iraqi forces from that country.

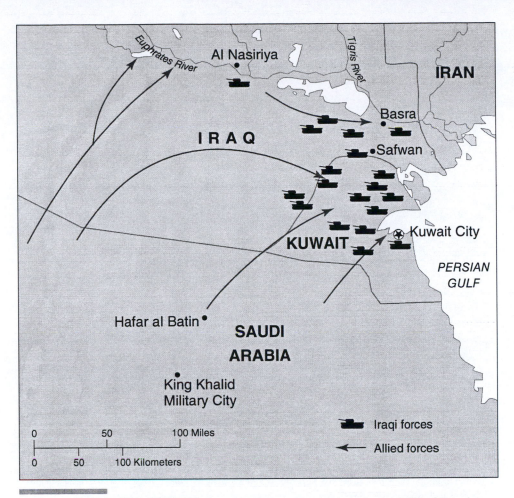

**MAP 30.2  THE PERSIAN GULF WAR** Ground operations against Iraq in the Persian Gulf War followed six weeks of aerial bombardment. The ground attack, which met quick success, was a multinational effort by the United States, Britain, France, Saudi Arabia, and other Arab nations. The war freed Kuwait from Iraqi occupation but stopped before forcing a change in Iraq's government.

# Growth in the Sunbelt

**30.3**  How did growth in the Sunbelt shape national politics in the 1980s and 1990s?

The rise in military and defense spending from the late 1970s through the early 1990s, including for the Persian Gulf War, was one of the most powerful sources of growth in the **Sunbelt**, the southern and western regions of the United States. Americans had discovered this "new" region in the 1970s. Kevin Phillips's book *The Emerging Republican Majority* (1969) first popularized the term "Sunbelt." People and economic activity had been flowing southward and westward since World War II, shifting the balance of power away from the Northeast. Sections of the South and West, historically controlled from the northeastern industrial core, had developed as independent centers of economic change and often conservative politics to go along with booming economies.

The rise of the Sunbelt, which is anchored by Florida, Texas, and California, reflected the leading economic trends of the 1970s and 1980s, including military spending, immigration from Asia and Latin America, and recreation and retirement spending. Corporations liked the business climate of the South, which had weak labor laws, low taxes, and generally low costs of living and doing business.

New factories dotted the southern landscape, often in smaller towns rather than cities. General Motors closed factories in Flint, Michigan, but invested in a new Saturn

**Sunbelt** The states of the American South and Southwest.

905

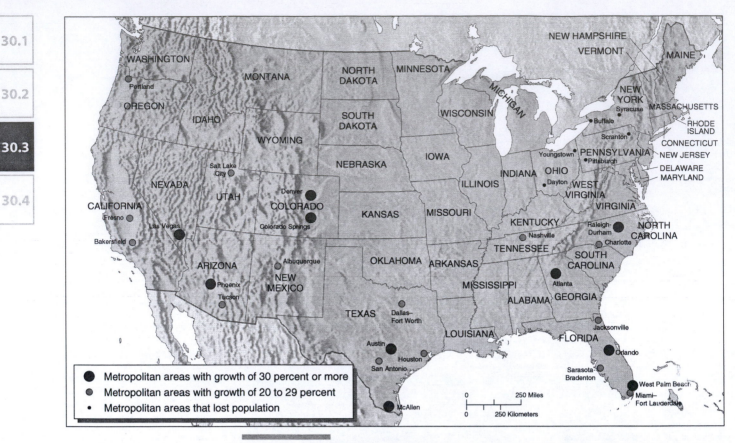

**MAP 30.3 FAST-GROWING AND SHRINKING METROPOLITAN AREAS, 1990–2000** In the 1990s, boom cities were found in the Southeast, the Southwest, and on the West Coast. In contrast, the large metropolitan areas that lost population were all in Ohio, New York, or Pennsylvania, the areas hardest hit by the decline of jobs in established manufacturing industries.

plant in Spring Hill, Tennessee. In contrast to troubled industrial cities in the Northeast and Midwest, cities like Orlando, Charlotte, Atlanta, Dallas, and Phoenix enjoyed headlong prosperity. Houston, with sprawling growth, business spinoffs from NASA, and purring air conditioners, epitomized the booming metropolitan areas of the South and West (see Map 30.3).

## The Defense Economy

The Vietnam buildup and reinvestment in the military during the Carter (1977–1981) and Reagan (1981–1989) administrations fueled Sunbelt growth. During the forty years from the Korean conflict to the Persian Gulf War, the United States made itself the mightiest military power ever known. Military bases and defense contractors remolded the economic landscape, as mild winters and clear skies for training and operations helped the South and West attract more than 75 percent of military payrolls.

Big cities and small depended on defense spending. Southern California thrived on more than 500,000 jobs in the aircraft industry. A thousand miles away, visitors to Colorado Springs could drive past sprawling Fort Carson and visit the new Air Force Academy, opened in 1958. Sunk deep from view was the North American Air Defense Command headquarters beneath Cheyenne Mountain west of the city.

Defense spending underwrote the expansion of American science and technology. Nearly one-third of all engineers worked on military projects. Large universities, such as MIT, the University of Michigan, the California Institute of Technology, and Stanford, were leading defense contractors. The modern electronics business started in New York, Boston, and the San Francisco Bay area with research and development for military uses, such as guided-missile controls. California's Silicon Valley grew with military sales long before it turned to consumer markets. The space component of the aerospace industry was equally reliant on the defense economy, with NASA spending justified by competition with the Soviet Union. NASA's centers were scattered across the South: launch facilities at the Kennedy Space Center in Cape Canaveral, Florida; research labs at Huntsville, Alabama; and Houston's Manned Spacecraft Center as the control center for space exploration.

## Americans from around the World

Few Americans anticipated the effects of the **Immigration and Nationality Act of 1965**, which transformed the ethnic mix of the United States (see Table 30.4) and helped to stimulate the Sunbelt boom. The new law initiated a change in the composition of the American people by abolishing the national quota system in effect since 1924. Quotas had favored immigrants from Western Europe and limited those from other parts of the world. The old law's racial bias contradicted the self-proclaimed role of the United States as a defender of freedom, and immigration reform was part of the propaganda battle of the Cold War. The new law gave preference to family reunification and welcomed immigrants from all nations equally. The United States also accepted refugees from Communism outside the annual limits.

**Immigration and Nationality Act of 1965** Federal legislation that replaced the national quota system for immigration with overall limits of 170,000 immigrants per year from the Eastern Hemisphere and 120,000 per year from the Western Hemisphere.

Immigration reform opened the doors to Mediterranean Europe, Latin America, and Asia. Legal migration to the United States surged from 1.1 million in 1960–1964 to nearly 4 million for 1990–1994. Nonlegal immigrants may have doubled the total number of newcomers in the 1970s and early 1980s. Not since World War I had the United States absorbed so many new residents.

Immigration changed the nation's ethnic mix. Members of officially defined ethnic and racial minorities accounted for 25 percent of Americans in 1990 and 30 percent in 2000. Roughly 28 million Americans had been born in other countries according to the 2000 census, or 10.4 percent of the population. This was lower than the high of 14.7 percent in 1910 but a great increase from the low of 4.7 percent in 1970. One-third of the foreign-born were from Latin America and one-fourth were from Asia.

The largest single group of new Americans came from Mexico. The long border facilitated easy movement from south to north. Especially in the border states of Texas, New Mexico, Arizona, and California, permanent immigrants mingled with tourists, family members on visits, temporary workers, and other workers without legal permission to enter the United States. Mexican Americans were the largest minority group in many southwestern and western states in the later twentieth century.

The East Coast especially welcomed migrants from the West Indies and Central America. Many Puerto Ricans, who hold U.S. citizenship, came to Philadelphia and New York in the 1950s and 1960s. Other countries sending large numbers of immigrants included Haiti, the Dominican Republic, Guatemala, Honduras, Nicaragua, El Salvador, and Jamaica. Cuban refugees from Castro's regime concentrated in Miami and in major cities such as Chicago and New York.

**Read the Document** Cecelia Rosa Avila, Third Generation Mexican American (1988)

TABLE 30.4 MAJOR RACIAL AND ETHNIC MINORITIES IN THE UNITED STATES

| | 1960 Population (in millions) | Percentage of Total | 2000 Population (in millions) | Percentage of Total |
|---|---|---|---|---|
| American Indians | 0.5 | 0.3 | 2.5 | 0.9 |
| Asians and Pacific Islanders | 1.1 | 0.6 | 10.6 | 3.7 |
| African Americans | 18.9 | 10.5 | 34.7 | 12.3 |
| Hispanics | not available | | 35.3 | 12.5 |

Another great immigration occurred eastward across the Pacific. Chinese, Filipinos, Koreans, Samoans, and other Asians and Pacific Islanders constituted only 6 percent of newcomers to the United States in 1965 but nearly half of all arrivals in 1990. The number of ethnic Chinese in the United States jumped from a quarter of a million in 1965 to 1.65 million in 1990. Immigrants from Taiwan, Hong Kong, and the People's Republic created new Chinatowns in Houston and San Diego and crowded into the historic Chinatowns of New York and San Francisco.

The most publicized Asian immigrants were refugees from Indochina after the Communist victory in 1975. The first arrivals tended to be highly educated professionals who had worked with the Americans. Another 750,000 Vietnamese, Laotians, and Cambodians arrived after 1976 by way of refugee camps in Thailand, as did Celia Noup. Most settled on the West Coast.

In addition to Southeast Asians, political conflicts and upheavals sent other waves of immigrants to the United States. Many Iranians fled the religious regime that took power in their country in the late 1970s, at the same time that Ethiopians were fleeing a nation shattered by drought, civil war, and doctrinaire Marxism. To escape repression in the Soviet Union, Jews and conservative Christians came to the United States in the 1980s, and the collapse of Communism in the Soviet Union opened the door for more Russians, Ukrainians, Romanians, and other Eastern Europeans.

Recent immigrants found both economic possibilities and problems. On the negative side, legal and illegal immigration added to the number of nonunion workers. By one estimate, two-thirds of the workers in the Los Angeles garment trade were undocumented immigrants. Most worked for small, nonunion firms in basements and storefronts, without health insurance or pensions. But a positive contrast was the abundance of opportunities for talent and ambition in the expanding economy of the mid-1980s and 1990s. The 130,000 Vietnamese immigrants of 1975 had an average income above the national average by 2000. Asians and Pacific Islanders by 2000 constituted 22 percent of the students in California's public universities. Like earlier European immigrants, many newcomers opened groceries, restaurants, and other businesses that served their own group before expanding into larger markets.

## Old Gateways and New

The new immigration from Asia, Latin America, and the Caribbean had its most striking effects in coastal and border cities. New York again became a great mixing bowl of the U.S. population. By 1990, some 28 percent of the population of New York City was foreign-born, compared to 42 percent at the height of European immigration in 1910.

Just as important was the transformation of southern and western cities into gateways for immigrants from Latin America and Asia. Los Angeles emerged as "the new Ellis Island" that rivaled New York's historic role in receiving immigrants. The sprawling neighborhoods of East Los Angeles make up the second-largest Mexican city in the world. New ethnic communities appeared in Los Angeles suburbs: Iranians in Beverly Hills, Chinese in Monterey Park, Japanese in Gardena, Thais in Hollywood, Samoans in Carson, Cambodians in Lakewood. One hundred languages are spoken among students entering Los Angeles schools.

New York, Chicago, and Los Angeles are world cities as well as immigrant destinations. Like London and Tokyo, they are capitals of world trade and finance, with international banks and headquarters of multinational corporations. They have the country's greatest concentrations of international lawyers, accounting firms, and business consultants. The deregulation of international finance and the explosive spread of instant electronic communication in the 1980s confirmed their importance as global decision centers (see Table 30.5).

Similar factors have turned Miami into an economic capital of the Caribbean. A quarter million Cuban businessmen, white-collar workers, and their families moved to the United States between 1959 and 1962 to escape Castro's socialist government. By the late 1970s Cubans owned about one-third of the area's retail stores and many

TABLE 30.5  GLOBAL CITIES

| Ranked by Population in 2005 (population in millions) | | Ranked as Economic Decision Centers |
| --- | --- | --- |
| Tokyo, Japan | 35.7 | 1. London |
| **New York** | 19.0 | 2. **New York** |
| Cuidad de Mexico | 19.0 | 3. Hong Kong |
| Mumbai, India | 19.0 | 4. Paris |
| Sao Paulo, Brazil | 18.8 | 5. Tokyo |
| Delhi, India | 15.9 | 6. Singapore |
| Shanghai, China | 15.0 | 7. **Chicago** |
| Kolkata, India | 14.8 | 8. Milan |
| Dhaka, Bangladesh | 13.5 | 9. **Los Angeles** |
| Buenos Aires, Argentina | 12.8 | 10. Toronto |
| **Los Angeles** | 12.5 | 11. Madrid |
| Karachi, Pakistan | 12.1 | 12. Amsterdam |

SOURCES: UN Department of Economic and Social Affairs/Population Division, *World Urbanization Prospects: The 2007 Revision*; Peter J. Taylor and Robert Lang, "U.S. Cities in the 'World City Network,'" The Brookings Institution, February 2005.

of its other businesses. Their success in business made Miami a major Latino market and helped to attract millions of Latin American tourists and shoppers. Access to the Caribbean and South America also made Miami an international banking and commercial center with hundreds of offices for corporations engaged in U.S.–Latin American trade.

Cross-border communities in the Southwest, such as El Paso, Texas, and Juarez, Mexico, or San Diego, California, and Tijuana, Mexico, became "Siamese twins joined at the cash register." Employees with work permits commuted from Mexico to the United States. American popular culture flowed southward. Bargain hunters and tourists passed in both directions.

Both nations promoted the cross-border economy. The Mexican government in the mid-1960s began to encourage a "platform economy" by allowing companies on the Mexican side of the border to import components and inputs duty-free as long as 80 percent of the items were re-exported and 90 percent of the workers were Mexicans. The intent was to encourage U.S. corporations to locate assembly plants south of the border. Such *maquila* industries were able to employ lower-wage workers and avoid strict antipollution laws (leading to serious threats to public health on both sides of the border). From the Gulf of Mexico to the Pacific Ocean, 1,800 *maquiladora* plants employed roughly half a million workers. North of the border, U.S. factories supplied components under laws that meshed with the Mexican regulations.

# Values in Collision

**30.4**  What key social and cultural issues divided Americans in the 1980s and 1990s?

In 1988, two very different religious leaders sought a presidential nomination. Pat Robertson's campaign for the Republican nomination tapped deep discontent with the changes in American society since the 1960s. A television evangelist, Robertson used the mailing list from his *700 Club* program to mobilize conservative Christians and push the Republican Party farther to the right on family and social issues. Jesse Jackson, a civil rights leader and minister from Chicago, mounted a grassroots campaign with the opposite goal of moving the Democratic Party to the left on social and economic policy. Drawing on his experience in the black civil rights movement, he assembled a "Rainbow Coalition" that included labor unionists, feminists, and others whom Robertson's followers feared. Both Jackson and Robertson used their powerful personalities and religious convictions to inspire support from local churches and churchgoers.

In diagnosing social ills, Robertson pointed to the problems of individual indulgence, while Jackson pointed to racism and economic inequality. Their sharp divergence expressed differences in basic values that divided Americans in the 1980s and beyond. In substantial measure, the conflicts were rooted in the social and cultural changes of the 1960s and 1970s that had altered traditional institutions. Changes in roles and expectations among women and new openness about gay and lesbian sexuality were particularly powerful in dividing U.S. churches and politics.

## Women's Rights and Public Policy

The women's liberation movement of the 1960s achieved important gains when Congress wrote many of its goals into law in the early 1970s. Title IX of the Educational Amendments (1972) to the Civil Rights Act prohibited discrimination by sex in any educational program receiving federal aid. The legislation expanded athletic opportunities for women and slowly equalized the balance of women and men in faculty positions. In the same year, Congress sent the Equal Rights Amendment (ERA) to the states for ratification. The amendment read, "Equal rights under the law shall not be denied or abridged by the United States or by any state on account of sex." More than twenty states ratified in the first few months. As conservatives who wanted to preserve traditional family patterns rallied strong opposition, however, the ERA faced increasingly tough battles in state legislatures and stalled, three states short, until the time limit for ratification expired in 1982.

**Abortion Rights and Conservative Reaction.**   In January 1973, the U.S. Supreme Court expanded the debate about women's rights with the case of ***Roe v. Wade***. Voting 7 to 2, the Court struck down state laws forbidding abortion in the first three months of pregnancy and set guidelines for abortion during the remaining months. Drawing on the earlier decision of *Griswold v. Connecticut,* which dealt with birth control, the Court held that the Fourteenth Amendment includes a right to privacy that blocks states from interfering with a woman's right to terminate a pregnancy. The Supreme Court later upheld congressional limitations on the use of federal funds for abortion in *Webster v. Reproductive Health Services* (1989) and allowed some state restrictions in *Planned Parenthood v. Casey* (1992). Nevertheless, the *Roe* decision remained in place.

These changes came in the context of increasingly sharp conflict over the feminist agenda. Both the ERA and *Roe* stirred impassioned support and equally passionate opposition that pushed the two major political parties in opposite directions. Behind the rhetoric were male fears of increased job competition during a time of economic contraction and concern about changing families. Also fueling the debate was a deep split between the mainstream feminist view of women as fully equal individuals and the contrary conservative belief that women had a special role as anchors of families, an updating of the nineteenth-century idea of separate spheres. The debate about abortion drew on the same issue of women's relationship to families but added strong religious voices, particularly the formal opposition of the Roman Catholic Church to abortion. The arguments tapped such deep emotion that the two sides could not even agree on a common language, juxtaposing a right to life against rights to privacy and freedom of choice.

**Women in the Workforce.**   The most sweeping change in the lives of American women did not come from federal legislation or court cases, but from the growing likelihood that a woman would work outside the home. In 1960, some 32 percent of married women were in the labor force; forty years later, 61 percent were working or looking for work (along with 69 percent of single women). Federal and state governments

*Roe v. Wade* U.S. Supreme Court decision in 1973 that disallowed state laws prohibiting abortion during the first three months (trimester) of pregnancy and established guidelines for abortion in the second and third trimesters.

slowly responded to the changing demands of work and family with new policies, such as a federal childcare tax credit.

An important reason for the increase in working women from 29 million in 1970 to 66 million in 2000 was the broad shift from manufacturing to service jobs, reducing demand for factory workers and manual laborers and increasing the need for such "women's jobs" as data-entry clerks, reservation agents, and nurses. Indeed, the U.S. economy still divides job categories by sex. There was some movement toward gender-neutral hiring in the 1970s because of legal changes and the pressures of the women's movement. Women's share of lawyers more than quadrupled, of economists more than tripled, and of police detectives more than doubled. Nevertheless, job types were more segregated by sex than by race in the 1990s.

## AIDS and Gay Activism

After the increasing openness about sexual orientation in the 1970s, the character of life in gay communities took an abrupt turn in the 1980s when a new worldwide epidemic emerged. Scientists identified a new disease pattern, **acquired immunodeficiency syndrome (AIDS)**, in 1981. The name described the symptoms resulting from infection by the human immunodeficiency virus (HIV), which destroys the body's ability to resist disease. HIV is transferred through blood and semen. In the 1980s, the most frequent American victims were gay men and intravenous drug users.

A decade later, it was clear that HIV/AIDS was a national and even global problem. By the end of 2005, AIDS had been responsible for 550,000 deaths in the United States, and transmission to heterosexual women was increasing. The U.S. Centers for Disease Control and Prevention estimated roughly 40,000 new cases of HIV infection per year at the beginning of the twenty-first century, bringing the total of infected Americans to around 1.2 million. Once a problem of big cities, HIV infection had spread to every American community and had helped to change American attitudes about the process of dying through the spread of hospices for the care of the terminally ill. Meanwhile, the toll of AIDS deaths in other parts of the world, particularly eastern Africa, dwarfed that in the United States and made it a world health crisis. (See From Then to Now, Chapter 28.)

By the 1990s, Americans were accustomed to open discussion of gay sexuality, if not always accepting of its reality. Television stars and other entertainers could "come out" and retain their popularity. So could politicians in certain districts. On the issue of gays in the military, however, Congress and the Pentagon were more cautious, accepting a policy that made engaging in homosexual acts, though not sexual orientation itself, grounds for discharge.

## Churches in Change

Americans picture mining frontiers as rip-roaring places, where a handful of women hold the fort while the men work hard, drink deep, and carry on. Modern Grand Junction, Colorado, however, was far less exciting. Efforts to develop the oil-shale resources of western Colorado pushed the population of Grand Junction from 60,000 to 80,000 in the 1980s. Hopes were high and money was easy, but there was also a boom in religion. Newcomers to Grand Junction searched for family stability and a sense of community by joining established congregations and organizing new churches. The telephone book in 1985 listed twenty-eight mainline Protestant and Catholic churches, twenty-four Baptist churches (reflecting the Oklahoma and Texas roots of many oil workers), five more liberal churches, and more than fifty Pentecostal, Bible, and evangelical churches. Nearly a dozen Christian schools supplemented the public schools.

Religion is prominent in daily lives, institutions, and public policy debates throughout the United States. Americans take their search for spiritual grounding much more seriously than do citizens of other industrial nations (see Map 30.4 on page 913). Roughly half of privately organized social activity (such as charity work) is

**acquired immunodeficiency syndrome (AIDS)** A complex of deadly pathologies resulting from infection with the human immunodeficiency virus (HIV).

The AIDS Quilt, displayed in Washington in October 1992, combined individual memorials to AIDS victims into a powerful communal statement. The quilt project reminded Americans that AIDS had penetrated every American community.

church related. In the mid-1970s, 56 percent of Americans said that religion was "very important" to them, compared to only 27 percent of Europeans. Moreover, religious belief is an important source of political convictions and a basis for political action.

As Grand Junction also suggests, mainline Protestant denominations that traditionally defined the center of American belief struggled after 1970. The United Methodist Church, the Presbyterian Church U.S.A., the United Church of Christ, and the Episcopal Church battled internally over the morality of U.S. foreign policy, the role of women in the ministry, and the reception of gay and lesbian members. They were strengthened by an ecumenical impulse that united denominational branches divided by ethnicity or regionalism. However, they gradually lost their position among American churches, in part because liberal Protestantism has historically been strongest in the slow-growing Northeast and Midwest.

By contrast, evangelical Protestant churches have benefited from the direct appeal of their message and from strong roots in the booming Sunbelt. Members of evangelical

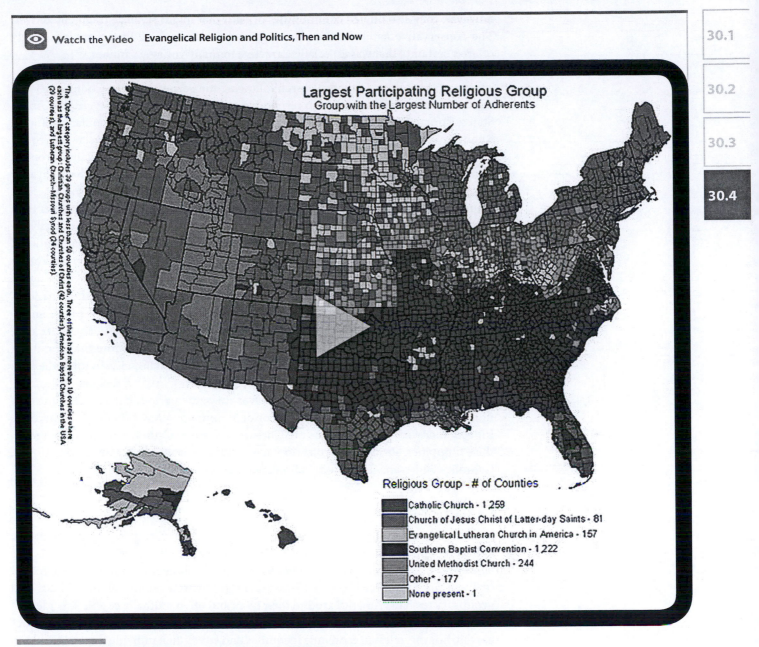

**MAP 30.4 RELIGIOUS GEOGRAPHY OF THE UNITED STATES** Differences in dominant religious groups in the United States reflect the history of immigration (Lutherans in the upper Midwest, Roman Catholics in the Northeast and Southwest), internal migration (the concentration of Mormons in and near Utah), and cultural differences between North and South.

SOURCE: Adapted from D.E. Jones, S. Doty, C. Grammich, J.E. Horsch, R. Housseal, M. Lynn, J.P. Marcum, K.M. Sanchagrin, and R.H. Taylor, *Religious Congregations and Membership in the United States 2000: An Enumeration by Region, State and County Based on Data Reported for 149 Religious Bodies*, p. 562. Copyright © 2000 Glenmary Research Center, Nashville, TN.

churches (25 percent of white Americans) now outnumber the members of mainline Protestant churches (20 percent). Major evangelical denominations include Baptists, the Church of the Nazarene, and the Assemblies of God. Fundamentalists, defined by a belief in the literal truth of the Bible, are a subset of evangelicals. So are 8 to 10 million Pentecostals and charismatics, who accept "gifts of the spirit," such as healing by faith and speaking in tongues.

Outsiders knew evangelical Christianity through "televangelists" such as Oral Roberts and Pat Robertson. Spending on religious television programming rose from $50 million to $600 million by 1980. The "electronic church" built on the radio preaching and professional revivalism of the 1950s. By the 1970s it reached 20 percent of American households.

Evangelical churches emphasized religion as an individual experience focused on personal salvation. Unlike many of the secular and psychological avenues to fulfillment, however, they also offered communities of faith that might stabilize fragmented lives. The conservative nature of their theology and social teaching in a changing society offered certainty that was especially attractive to many younger families.

Another important change in national religious life was the continuing Americanization of the Roman Catholic Church following the Second Vatican Council in 1965, in which church leaders sought to respond to postwar industrial society. In the United States, Roman Catholicism moved toward the center, helped by the popularity of John Kennedy and by worldly success that made Catholics the economic peers of Protestants. Even as the tight connection between Catholicism and membership in European immigrant communities gradually faded, Asian and Latino immigrants brought new vigor to many parishes, and many inner-city churches became centers for social action. Church practice lost some of its distinctiveness; celebrating Mass in English rather than Latin was an important move toward modernization, but it also sparked a conservative countereffort to preserve the traditional liturgy. Traditional and nontraditional Catholics also disagreed about whether priests should be allowed to marry and other adaptations to American culture.

The new globalization of American society simultaneously increased the nation's religious diversity and confirmed the dominant position of Christianity. Many immigrants from Asia and Africa came with their native religious beliefs. There are now hundreds of Hindu temples and thousands of Buddhist centers. More than a million Muslims now worship in mosques that are found in every major city. In total, the proportion of Americans who identify themselves with non-Christian religions grew from 3 percent in 1990 to 4 percent in 2001. Over the same period, however, the proportion identifying with a Christian group or denomination grew from 86 to 87 percent. Indeed, many recent immigrants are Christians: Roman Catholics from Vietnam and the Philippines, Protestants from Korea, evangelicals from the former Soviet Union, Catholics and evangelicals from Latin America.

## Culture Wars

In the 1950s and 1960s, Americans argued most often over foreign policy, racial justice, and the economy. Since the 1980s and 1990s, they also have quarreled over beliefs and values, especially as the patterns of family life have become more varied. In the course of these quarrels, religious belief has heavily influenced politics as individuals and groups try to shape America around their own, and often mutually conflicting, ideas of the godly society. Americans who are undogmatic in religion are often liberal in politics as well, hoping to lessen economic inequities and strengthen individual social freedom. Likewise, religious and political conservatism tend to go together.

The division on social issues is related to theological differences within Protestantism. The "conservative" emphasis on personal salvation and the literal truth of the Bible expresses itself in a desire to restore "traditional" social patterns. Conservatives worry that social disorder occurs when people follow personal impulses and pleasures. In contrast, the "liberal" or "modern" emphasis on the universality of the Christian message restates the Social Gospel with its call to build the Kingdom of God through social justice and may recognize divergent pathways toward truth. Liberals worry that greed in the unregulated marketplace creates disorder and injustice.

The cultural conflict also transcends the historic three-way division of Americans among Protestants, Catholics, and Jews. Instead, the conservative-liberal division now cuts through each group. For example, Catholic reformers, liberal Protestants, and Reform Jews may find agreement on issues of cultural values despite theologies that are worlds apart. The same may be true of conservative Catholics, fundamentalist Protestants, and Orthodox Jews.

Conservatives initiated the culture wars, trying to stabilize what they feared was an American society spinning out of control because of lack of self-discipline and sexual indulgence. In fact, the evidence on the sexual revolution is mixed. Growing numbers of teenagers reported being sexually active in the 1970s, but the rate of increase tapered off in the 1980s. The divorce rate began to drop after 1980 and births to teenagers after 1990. Sexual advice and self-help books proliferated, with such titles as *Open Marriage* (1972) and *The Joy of Sex* (1972), but most adults remained staid and monogamous, according to data from 1994. Perhaps the logical extension of reading about sex in the 1970s was an astonishing eagerness to talk about sex in the 1990s, a decade when soap-opera story lines and talk shows covered everything from family violence to exotic sexual tastes.

The explosion of explicit attention to sexual behavior set the stage for religiously rooted battles over two sets of issues. One cluster revolved around so-called family values, questioning the morality of access to abortion, the acceptability of homosexuality, and the roles and rights of women. A second set of concerns focused on the supposed role of public schools in undermining morality through sex education, unrestricted reading matter, nonbiblical science, and the absence of prayer. The Supreme Court decisions in 1962 and 1963 that prohibited vocal prayer and devotional Bible reading in public schools were targets for many. Opinion polls show clear differences among religious denominations on such issues as censorship of library books, acceptability of racially segregated neighborhoods, freedom of choice in terminating pregnancy, and homosexuality.

A culturally conservative issue with great popular appeal in the early 1990s was an effort to prevent states and localities from protecting homosexuals against discrimination. Under the slogan "No special rights," antigay measures passed in Cincinnati, Colorado, and communities in Oregon in 1993 and 1994, only to have the Supreme Court overturn the Colorado law in *Romer v. Evans* (1996). It is important to note that public support for lesbian and gay civil rights varied among issues, with strong support for equal employment opportunity and much less for making marriage available to same-sex couples, although these attitudes changed substantially in the twenty-first century. Support also varied based on whether the issues were framed in terms of specified rights for gays or in terms of the right of everyone to be free from government interference with personal decisions, such as living arrangements and sexual choices.

## Conclusion

Americans entered the 1980s searching for stability after energy crises and deinsustrialization at home and the Tehran hostage crisis overseas. Traditional values seemed under siege. Ronald Reagan's presidential campaign played to these insecurities by promising to revitalize the older ways of life and restore the United States to its former influence.

Taken as a whole, the years from 1981 through 1992 redirected the course of American life. The astonishing collapse of the Soviet Union ended forty years of Cold War. New political leadership in Washington reversed the fifty-year expansion of federal government programs to deal with economic and social inequities. Prosperity alternated with recessions that shifted the balance between regions. The stock market rode a roller coaster, familiar corporate names vanished, and inequality increased after narrowing for a generation.

At the same time, every revolution has its precursors. The Reagan-Bush years extended changes that began in the 1970s, particularly the conservative economic policies and military buildup of the troubled Carter administration. In retrospect, the growing weakness of the Soviet Union should also have been apparent in the same decade, had not the United States been blinded by its fear of Communist power. Intervention in the Persian Gulf amplified U.S. policies that had been in place since the CIA intervened in Iran in 1953. The outbreak of violence in Los Angeles after the Rodney King verdict showed that race relations remained tense, complicated by the growing numbers of Latinos and immigrants from Asia who competed with African Americans for economic advancement.

**For Suggested Readings go to MyHistoryLab.**

# Chapter Review

## Reagan's Domestic Revolution

**30.1** What was revolutionary about Ronald Reagan's presidency? p. 884

Ronald Reagan's two presidential administrations led to fundamental changes in the political and economic balance in the United States. The nation reemphasized the use of deregulated markets rather than government to meet national needs, with a paradoxical result of economic growth and increasing inequality.

## The Climax of the Cold War

**30.2** How and why did the Cold War come to an end? p. 896

After escalating Cold War tensions in the early 1980s, communist regimes in the Soviet Union and Eastern Europe imploded at the end of the decade under the pressures of economic inefficiency and grassroots dissatisfaction. These developments, largely the result of internal forces, left the United States with unrivaled world influence.

## Growth in the Sunbelt

**30.3** How did growth in the Sunbelt shape national politics in the 1980s and 1990s? p. 905

Fundamental changes were unavoidably transforming American society by the 1980s. The South and West were growing at the expense of the old industrial core. At the same time, immigrants from Asia and Latin America were changing the nation's ethnic mix and the definition of "typical" American.

## Values in Collision

**30.4** What key social and cultural issues divided Americans in the 1980s and 1990s? p. 909

The pace of social change left Americans deeply conflicted over the proper roles for women, the acceptance of gays and lesbians, the acceptable boundaries of artistic expression, religious values, and the future of organized religion.

# Timeline

**1980**
**Reagan's Domestic Revolution**—Ronald Reagan is elected president

1980

**1981**
**Values in Collision**—AIDS is recognized as a new disease

1981

**1985**
**Climax of the Cold War**—Mikhail Gorbachev initiates economic and political reforms in the Soviet Union

1985

**1989**
**Climax of the Cold War**—Communist regimes in Eastern Europe collapse; Germans tear down Berlin Wall

1989

**1990**
**Climax of the Cold War**—Iraq invades Kuwait, and United States sends forces to the Persian Gulf
**Reagan's Domestic Revolution**—Americans with Disabilities Act is adopted

1990

**1991**
**Climax of the Cold War**—Soviet Union dissolves into independent nations

1991

**1992**
**Reagan's Domestic Revolution**—Acquittal of officers accused of beating Rodney King triggers Los Angeles riots

1992

# 31 Complacency, Crisis, and Global Reengagement 1993–2012

## One American Journey

Personal Account by Hurricane
Katrina Survivor

**W**hen Katrina came and **left**, we started clapping.... I looked out the window and I said, "Lord, look at this here. We got to roll up our sleeves and start cleaning up."... I had this little storm tracker radio.... I'm listening, and I'm looking at our automobile, and it was being submerged every minute that went by. I'm saying, "Something is wrong, because this water should be receding, but it's coming in faster."... I heard the man on the radio say, "If you're held up anywhere in New Orleans, you need to try your best to make it to the

Survivors of Hurricane Katrina struggle to reach temporary safety at the Louisiana Superdome in New Orleans on August 30, 2005. An estimated 15,000 to 20,000 people took refuge there from the storm and subsequent flooding before evacuation to Houston and other cities.

## LEARNING OBJECTIVES

| 31.1 | 31.2 | 31.3 | 31.4 | 31.5 | 31.6 |
|---|---|---|---|---|---|
| How did Bill Clinton try to capture the political center? p. 919 | What role did new information technologies play in the economic boom of the 1990s? p. 927 | What gains did women and minorities make in national politics in the 1990s? p. 932 | What were the key goals of George W. Bush's presidency? p. 939 | How did the terrorist attacks of September 11, 2001, change foreign policy for the following decade? p. 942 | How did the government and the American people respond to the repeated domestic crises and economic challenges of the twenty-first century? p. 947 |

**Listen to Chapter 31 on MyHistoryLab**

From *The American Journey*, Seventh Edition. Goldfield, Abbott, Anderson, Argersinger, Argersinger and Barney Copyright © 2014 by Pearson Education, Inc. All rights reserved.

31.1

31.2

31.3

31.4

31.5

31.6

# ⊙ Watch the Video Series on MyHistoryLab

Learn about some key topics related to this chapter with the *MyHistoryLab Video Series: Key Topics in U.S. History.*

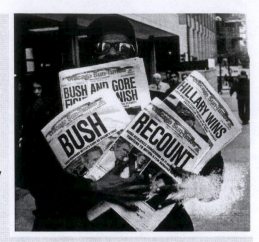

**1** **1990s and the New Century** The decade that closed the twentieth century and introduced the new millennium can best be described in two words—*dynamic* and *diverse*. Not only were Americans interconnected globally, but President Clinton also committed the United States, the lone superpower, to the role of world peacekeeper as China became our chief trading partner and rival, with its imports that filled American stores. During the 1990s, the Internet and World Wide Web came of age, as did the personal computer. This video also discusses the information technology revolution, which created instant dot.com millionaires, and the uncertain economy that was rocked by scandals such as Enron at the end of the decade.

 Watch on MyHistoryLab

**The Clinton Years** The election of President Bill Clinton in 1992 seemed improbable given that the incumbent had carried out the successful First Iraq War and had overseen the collapse of Communism in Europe. However, even with a strong showing by a third-party candidate, Clinton won the election and took the Democratic Party into a more centrist economic position while at the same time championing legislation meant to improve the lives of women and families. These and other highlights are discussed in this video, including Clinton's sexual misconduct while in office, which led to an investigation by a special prosecutor and resulted in his impeachment in the House of Representatives.

Watch on MyHistoryLab ⊙ **2**

**3** **The Election of 2000** The highly controversial 2000 presidential election saw the Supreme Court intervene in the electoral process, thus securing the electoral college victory for George W. Bush, in spite of Al Gore's winning of a majority of the popular vote. This video relates how the electoral controversy surrounding voting in the state of Florida eventually led to a month-long recount effort that ended with Bush getting Florida's electoral votes.

⊙ Watch on MyHistoryLab

**Politics in the New Millennium** The terrorist attacks on the twin towers of New York's World Trade Center and the Pentagon in Washington, DC, on September 11, 2001, established the focus of American foreign and domestic policy for the next decade. This video examines the administration of George W. Bush, which used the attacks to justify wars in both Afghanistan and Iraq, as well as to pass sweeping new security legislation, such as the PATRIOT Act and the Homeland Security Act. It also analyzes the election in 2008 of the first black president, Barack Obama. **4**

Watch on MyHistoryLab ⊙

Superdome or convention center, because the levees have been breached and we can't stop the water."

The Superdome was about half a mile away . . . we had a few light things like a toothbrush and your driver's license. So we had to walk through the water to about our waist. At the time there was just a lot of stuff from the automobiles like gas, oil, and stuff like that in the water. We saw some dead bodies as we were walking. . . . We left about 10:00, and we got there about 11:00 or 12:00.

We thought we was going to a shelter, but it was more of a prison. Outside the Superdome, we was searched by the military. . . . Soon as we got in there, I knew something wasn't right. . . . There wasn't no effort to try and get us out, but they constantly was bringing more people into the Superdome.

31.1

31.2

31.3

31.4

31.5

31.6

You could count the white people in the rest of the Superdome on one hand. I say 99 percent was black and poor. I know everybody else feels like we weren't in a major city in America, our country.

Kevin Owens, in D'Ann R. Penner and Keith C. Ferdinand, *Overcoming Katrina:*
*African American Voices from the Crescent City and Beyond. Copyright © 2008*
Palgrave Macmillan. Reprinted by permission.

## Personal Journeys Online

- Anthony Fernandez III, "Remembering the Oklahoma City Bombing," 2007. A search and rescue worker describes the background of the picture on page 925.
- Dawn Shurmaitis, 2001. Volunteering in the aftermath of the September 11, 2001, attack.
- John McNamara, 2002. A New York firefighter describes the day of the World Trade Center attack.

**K**evin Owens was among the tens of thousands of New Orleans residents who were flooded out of their homes in August 2005 when levees failed in the aftermath of Hurricane Katrina. Like many others, his first Katrina journey took him and his family to temporary safety in the Louisiana Superdome, where overcrowding and lack of food and sanitation meant days of misery. His second Katrina journey came when federal officials evacuated Superdome refugees to Texas, and his third when he and his family left Texas for a job in Birmingham, Alabama. He had returned to New Orleans to assess the damage to his house and told his interviewer that he would like to be part of the rebuilding process. He felt in the meanwhile "like I've been robbed of everything I love." As of 2009, the city's population was still down 130,000 or 30 percent from the pre-Katrina total.

The disaster of Hurricane Katrina struck many Americans as proof that the nation was in trouble. Following the terrorist attacks of September 11, 2001, and the war in Iraq where the United States seemed unable to consolidate its early victories, the inadequate emergency response in New Orleans showed deep problems as home. The events in these first years of the twenty-first century ended a decade of prosperity at home and complacency about the place of the United States in the world. For most of the 1990s, prosperity had allowed politics to focus on social issues, such as health care and education, as well as on bitterly partisan but often superficial battles over personalities and presidential behavior. However, the 9-11 terrorists had attacked buildings that were symbols of the nation's economic and military power, and Katrina devastated a well-loved city that represented good times to many Americans. In the new century, Americans struggled to cope with deeply partisan politics, to cope with a fast-changing and troubled economy, and to understand their changing place in the world.

# Politics of the Center

**31.1** How did Bill Clinton try to capture the political center?

**I**n the race for president in 1992, the "war room" was the decision center where Bill Clinton and his staff planned tactics and countered Republican attacks. On the wall was a sign with a simple message: "It's the economy, stupid." The short sentence was a reminder that victory lay in emphasizing everyday problems that George H. W. Bush had neglected. Clinton promised economic leadership and attention to everyday problems. He promised to reduce government bureaucracy and the deficit, touted the value of stable families, and talked about health care and welfare reform. His message revealed an insight into the character of the United States in the 1990s. What mattered

31.1

31.2

31.3

31.4

31.5

31.6

most were down-to-earth issues, not the distant problems of foreign policy, which seemed to have little urgency after the end of the Cold War.

Bill Clinton's election, first term, and reelection in 1996 showed the attraction of pragmatic policies and the political center in a two-party system.

## The Election of 1992: A New Generation

The mid-1990s brought a new generation into the political arena. The members of "Generation X" came of voting age with deep worries about the foreclosing of opportunities. They worried that previous administrations had ignored growing economic divisions and let the competitive position of the United States deteriorate. The range of suggested solutions differed widely—individual moral reform, a stronger labor movement, leaner competition in world markets—but the generational concern was clear.

This generational change made 1992 one of the most volatile national elections in decades. A baby boomer and successful governor of Arkansas who was not widely known nationally, Democrat Bill Clinton decided that George H. W. Bush was vulnerable when more senior Democrats opted to pass on the contest. His campaign for the nomination overcame accusations of womanizing and his use of a student deferment to avoid military service in Vietnam. Clinton made sure that the Democrats fielded a

President Bill Clinton was a great campaigner with a natural touch with the public. Here he takes up a borrowed saxophone at a White House celebration for the fortieth anniversary of the Newport Jazz Festival.

31.1

31.2

31.3

31.4

31.5

31.6

full baby boomer (and southern) ticket by choosing as his running mate the equally youthful Tennessean Albert Gore, Jr.

Bush, the last politician of the World War II generation to gain the White House, won renomination by beating back the arch-conservative Patrick Buchanan. The Republican National Convention in Houston showed how important cultural issues had become to the Republican Party. The party platform conformed to the beliefs of the Christian right. Buchanan delivered a startling speech that called for right-thinking Americans to crusade against unbelievers. Buchanan's divisive comments were a reminder of the multiple ways that religious belief was reshaping U.S. politics.

The wild card was the Texas billionaire Ross Perot, whose independent campaign started with an appearance on a television talk show. Perot loved flip charts, distanced himself from professional politicians, and claimed to talk sense to the American people. He also tried to occupy the political center. In May, Perot outscored both Bush and Clinton in opinion polls, but his behavior became increasingly erratic. He withdrew from the race and then reentered after floating stories that he was the target of dark conspiracies.

Bush campaigned as a foreign policy expert. He expected voters to reward him for the end of the Cold War, but he ignored anxieties about the nation's direction at

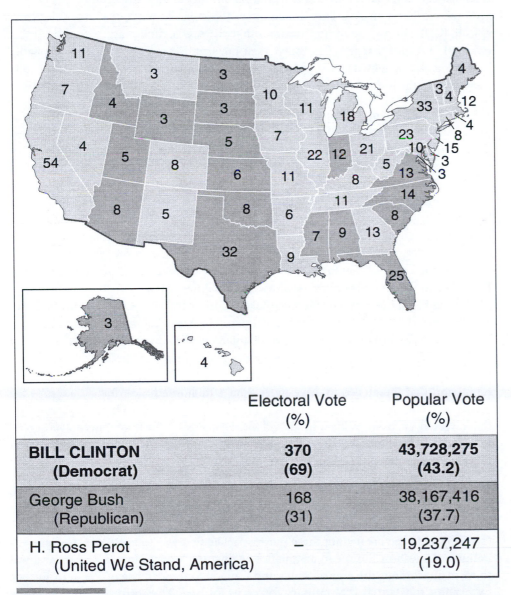

| | Electoral Vote (%) | Popular Vote (%) |
|---|---|---|
| **BILL CLINTON** (Democrat) | **370** **(69)** | **43,728,275** **(43.2)** |
| George Bush (Republican) | 168 (31) | 38,167,416 (37.7) |
| H. Ross Perot (United We Stand, America) | – | 19,237,247 (19.0) |

**MAP 31.1  THE ELECTION OF 1992** Bill Clinton defeated George H. W. Bush in 1992 by reviving the Democratic Party in the industrial Northeast and enlisting new Democratic voters in the western states, where he appealed both to Hispanic immigrants and to people associated with fast-growing, high-tech industries. He won reelection in 1996 with the same pattern of support. However, the coalition was an unstable combination of "Old Democrats," associated with older industries and labor unions, and "New Democrats," favoring economic change, free trade, and globalization.

31.1

31.2

31.3

31.4

31.5

31.6

home. His popularity had surged immediately after the Persian Gulf War, only to fall as the country became mired in a recession. In fact, voters in November 1992 ranked the economy first as an issue, the federal budget deficit second, health care third, and foreign policy eighth. Clinton hammered away at economic concerns, appealing to swing voters, such as suburban independents and blue-collar Reagan Democrats. He presented himself as the leader of new, pragmatic, and livelier Democrats.

Election day gave the Clinton-Gore ticket 43 percent of the popular vote, Bush 38 percent, and Perot 19 percent. Clinton held the Democratic core of northern and midwestern industrial states and loosened the Republican hold on the South and West (see Map 31.1). Millions who voted for Perot were casting a protest vote for "none of the above" and against "politics as usual" rather than hoping for an actual Perot victory. Clinton ran best among voters over 65, who remembered FDR and Harry Truman, and voters under 30.

## Policing the World

Although Clinton was much more interested in domestic policies, he inherited a confused expectation that the United States could use its military and economic power to keep the world on an even keel and counter ethnic hatred without incurring serious risks to itself. During the administration's first years, U.S. diplomats helped broker an Israel-PLO accord that gave Palestinians self-government in Gaza and the West Bank. The world also benefited from a gradual reduction of nuclear arsenals and from a 1996 treaty to ban the testing of nuclear weapons.

**Bosnia and Kosovo.** Clinton reluctantly committed the United States to a multinational effort to end the bloody civil war in ethnically and religiously divided Bosnia in 1995. In the early 1990s, the former Communist nation of Yugoslavia, in southeastern Europe, fragmented into five independent nations: Slovenia, Macedonia, Croatia, Bosnia, and Yugoslavia (the name retained by the predominantly Serbian nation with its capital at Belgrade). Bosnia, divided both ethnically and religiously between Christians and Muslims, erupted in bitter civil war. Christian Serbs, supported by Belgrade, engaged in massacres and deportations of Muslim Bosnians with the goal of creating "ethnically clean" Serbian districts. Too late to stop most bloodshed, NATO troops after 1995 enforced a brittle peace accord and a division of territory into Bosnian and Serb sectors under a shaky federated government.

The U.S. military revisited the same part of Europe in 1999, when the United States and Britain led NATO's intervention in Kosovo. The overwhelming majority of people in this Yugoslav province were ethnic Albanians who had chafed under the control of the Serb-controlled Yugoslav government. When a Kosovar independence movement began a rebellion, Yugoslav president Slobodan Milosevic responded with brutal repression that threatened to drive more than 1 million ethnic Albanians out of the province. To protect the Kosovars, NATO in March 1999 began a bombing campaign that targeted Yugoslav military bases and forces in Kosovo. In June, Yugoslavia agreed to withdraw its troops and make way for a multinational NATO peacekeeping force, marking a measured success for U.S. policy.

**The Reinvention of NATO.** To satisfy Russia, the peacekeeping force that entered Kosovo in June was technically a U.S. operation, but it was a reinvented NATO that negotiated with Yugoslavia. Fifty years earlier, the North Atlantic Treaty Organization (NATO) had been created for three purposes. The first was to unite non-Communist nations of Western Europe in an alliance against the Soviet Union. The second was to formally commit the United States and Canada to the defense of Western Europe by placing substantial U.S. military forces in Europe. The third was to establish a framework that would make the rearmament of West Germany acceptable to other European nations. For the next forty years—until the collapse of Eastern European communism—NATO coordinated Western European defense planning and remained a foundation stone of U.S. foreign policy.

The new NATO was a product of the new Europe of the 1990s. A key step was expansion into the former Soviet sphere in Eastern Europe. In 1999, NATO formally admitted Poland, Hungary, and the Czech Republic over the objections of Russia. Three years later, NATO agreed to give Russia a formal role in discussions about a number of its policy decisions, further eroding the barriers of the Cold War, and it added another nine nations of Eastern Europe in 2004 and 2009.

## Clinton's Neoliberalism

Domestic policy attracted Clinton's greatest interest, and his first term can be divided into two parts. In 1993–1994, he worked with a slim Democratic majority in Congress to modernize the U.S. economy, taking advantage of an economic upturn that lasted for most of the decade. In 1995 and 1996, however, he faced solid Republican majorities, the result of an unanticipated Republican tide in the November 1994 elections.

The heart of Clinton's agenda was an effort to make the U.S. economy more equitable domestically and more competitive internationally. These goals marked Clinton as a **neoliberal** who envisioned a partnership between a leaner government and a dynamic private sector. Steps to "reinvent" government cut federal employment below Reagan administration levels. A new tax bill reversed some of the inequities of the 1980s by increasing taxes on the wealthiest 1.2 percent of households. In early 1993, Clinton pushed through the Family and Medical Leave Act, which provided up to 12 weeks of unpaid leave for workers with newborns or family emergencies and had been vetoed twice by George H. W. Bush.

Clinton's biggest setback was the failure of comprehensive health care legislation. The goals seemed simple at first: containment of health care costs and extension of basic medical insurance from 83 percent of Americans under age 65 to 100 percent. In the abstract, voters agreed that something needed to be done. However, the plan that emerged from a health care task force headed by the president's wife, Hillary Rodham Clinton, ran to 1,342 pages of complex regulations, with something for everyone to dislike. Senior citizens worried about limits on Medicare spending. Insurance companies did not want more regulations. Businesses did not want the costs of insuring their workers. Taxpayers liked the idea of wider medical insurance coverage but not the idea of paying for it through higher taxes or rationing of medical services. Thus the reform effort went nowhere.

**neoliberal** Advocate or participant in the effort to reshape the Democratic Party for the 1990s around a policy emphasizing economic growth and competitiveness in the world economy.

## Contract with America and the Election of 1996

Conservative political ideology and personal animosity against both Bill and Hillary Clinton were both part of the background for an extraordinary off-year election in 1994, in which voters defeated dozens of incumbents and gave Republicans control of Congress. For most of 1995, the new speaker of the House, Newt Gingrich of Georgia, dominated political headlines as he pushed the **Contract with America**, the official Republican campaign platform for the 1994 elections, which called for a revolutionary reduction in federal responsibilities.

Clinton laid low and let the new Congress attack environmental protections, propose cuts in federal benefits for the elderly, and try to slice the capital gains tax to help the rich. As Congress and the president battled over the budget, congressional Republicans refused to authorize interim spending and forced the federal government to shut down for more than three weeks between November 1995 and January 1996. Gingrich was the clear loser in public opinion, both for the shutdowns and for his ideas. Democrats painted Gingrich and his congressional allies as a radical fringe who wanted to gut Medicare and Medicaid, undermine education, punish legal immigrants, and sell off national parks—core values and programs that most Americans wanted to protect.

After the budget confrontations, 1996 brought a series of measures to reward work—a centrist position acceptable to most Americans. The minimum wage increased.

**Contract with America** Platform proposing a sweeping reduction in the role and activities of the federal government on which many Republican candidates ran for Congress in 1994.

31.1

31.2

31.3

31.4

31.5

31.6

**Temporary Assistance for Needy Families (TANF)** Federal program tying benefits to work requirements and time limits; created in 1996 to replace earlier welfare programs to aid families and children.

Congress made pension programs easier for employers to create and made health insurance portable when workers changed jobs. After tough negotiations, Clinton signed bipartisan legislation to "end welfare as we know it." **Temporary Assistance for Needy Families (TANF)** replaced Aid to Families with Dependent Children (AFDC). TANF had strict requirements that aid recipients be seeking work or be enrolled in schooling, and it set a time limit on assistance. By 2001, the number of public assistance recipients had declined 58 percent from its 1994 high, but there were doubts that many of the former recipients had found jobs adequate to support their families. In perspective, TANF signaled a basic shift in attitudes toward families. The assistance programs in the 1930s had been designed to keep mothers home with their children. The new law assumed that they should be at work, perhaps reflecting the fact that most middle-class women now expected to be in the workforce.

Clinton's reelection in 1996 was a virtual replay of 1992. His opponent, Robert Dole, represented the World War II generation of politicians. Because the nation was prosperous and at peace, and because Clinton had claimed the political center and sounded like Dwight Eisenhower, the results were never in doubt. Clinton became the first Democratic president to be elected to a second term since Franklin Roosevelt. The Clinton-Gore ticket took 70 percent of the electoral votes and 49 percent of the popular vote (versus 41 percent for Dole and 9 percent for a recycled Ross Perot).

The election confirmed that voters liked the pragmatic center. They were cautious about the radical free-market advocates on the extreme right, showing little interest in having Republicans actually put the Contract with America into practice. They were equally unimpressed by liberal advocates of extensive entitlements on the European model. What voters wanted was to continue the reduction of the federal role in domestic affairs that had begun in the 1980s without damaging social insurance programs.

## The Dangers of Everyday Life

Part of the background for the sometimes vicious politics of mid-decade was a sense of individual insecurity and fear of violence that coexisted with an economy that was booming in some sectors but still leaving many Americans behind.

**Random Violence and Domestic Terrorism.**  One after another, headlines and news flashes in the 1990s proclaimed terrifying random acts of violence. The greatest losses of life came in Waco, Texas, and in Oklahoma City. On April 19, 1993, federal agents raided the fortified compound of the Branch Davidian cult outside Waco after a 51-day siege. The raid triggered a fire, probably set from inside, that killed more than 80 people. On the second anniversary of the Waco raid, Timothy McVeigh packed a rented truck with explosive materials and detonated it in front of the federal office building in downtown Oklahoma City, presumably as revenge against what he considered an oppressive government. The blast collapsed the entire front of the nine-story building and killed 169 people. In April 1999, two high school students in Littleton, Colorado, took rifles and pipe bombs into Columbine High School to kill 12 classmates, a teacher, and themselves; schools in Arkansas and Oregon experienced similar terror from gun-wielding students.

**Crime and the War on Drugs.**  Conservatives, including many gun-ownership advocates, put their faith in strict law enforcement as the best route to public security. The 1990s saw numerous states adopt "three-strike" measures that drastically increased penalties for individuals convicted of a third crime. One result was an explosive growth of the prison industry, diverting state money from education and health care. Mandatory minimum sentencing caused Louisiana's prison population to grow by 50 percent between 1994 and 2001. Mississippi legislation that severely restricted the possibility of parole caused an even greater jump in the state's prison population from 10,700 in 1994 to 37,700 in 2001. The number of people serving sentences of a year or

📖 **Read the Document**  *U.S. v. Timothy James McVeigh,* Sentencing (August 14, 1997)

31.1

31.2

31.3

31.4

31.5

31.6

Search and rescue worker Anthony Fernandez and rescue dog Aspen pause during the search through the ruins of the Oklahoma City federal building after its bombing by domestic terrorists in 1995.

longer in state and federal prisons grew from 316,000 in 1980 to 740,000 in 1990 and 1,422,000 in 2004, with another 714,000 being held for shorter periods in local jails. By 2007, more than one in every hundred adults was behind bars.

The war on drugs, begun in the 1980s, was the biggest contributor to the prison boom. As the drug war dragged on through the 1990s, the federal government poured billions of dollars into efforts to stop illegal drugs from crossing the Mexican border or from landing by boat or airplane. The United States intervened in South American nations that produced cocaine, particularly Peru and Colombia, aiding local military efforts to uproot crops and battle drug lords. Meanwhile, aggressive enforcement of

31.1

31.2

31.3

31.4

31.5

31.6

domestic laws against drug possession or sales filled U.S. prison cells. The antidrug campaign fell most heavily on minorities.

In fact, crime fell steadily for a decade after reaching a peak in the early 1990s, a trend that would continue in the twenty-first century. The rate of violent crime as reported by the FBI (murder, rape, robbery, aggravated assault) fell by 46 percent from 1993 to 2010, including a 49 percent drop in the number of murders. The rate of major property crimes (burglary, larceny-theft, and motor vehicle theft) fell by 38 percent over the same period. Easing fears combined with escalating costs to cause some states to rethink the reliance on prison terms. California voters adopted a measure that provided for treatment rather than prison for many drug offenders. States began to legalize certain types of marijuana use. Other states, ranging from Mississippi to Connecticut to North Dakota, softened some of their sentencing laws. The number of adults in jails and prisons would actually decrease from 2008 to 2009, the first such drop in the thirty years for which data were available.

## Morality and Partisanship

If the economy was the fundamental news of the later 1990s, Bill Clinton's personal life was the hot news. In 1998 and 1999, the United States was riveted by revelations about the president's sex life, doubts about his integrity, and debates about his fitness for high office. Years of rumors, innuendos, and lawsuits culminated in 1999 in the nation's second presidential impeachment trial. To his enemies, Clinton's behavior seemed one more example of disregard for law and morality, while his supporters found the entire issue to be distracting partisan politics.

President Clinton's problems began in 1994 with the appointment of a special prosecutor to investigate possible fraud in the **Whitewater** development, an Arkansas land promotion in which Bill and Hillary Clinton had invested in the 1980s. The probe by Kenneth Starr, the independent counsel, however, expanded into a wide-ranging investigation that encompassed the firing of the White House travel-office staff early in 1993, the suicide of White House aide Vincent Foster, and the sexual behavior of the president. Meanwhile, Paula Jones had brought a lawsuit claiming sexual harassment by then-governor Clinton while she was a state worker in Arkansas. The investigation of Whitewater brought convictions of several friends and former associates of the Clintons, but no evidence pointing decisively at either Bill or Hillary Clinton.

The legal landscape changed in January 1998, with allegations about an affair between the president and Monica Lewinsky, a former White House intern. Lewinsky admitted to the relationship privately and then to Starr's staff after the president had denied it in a sworn deposition for the Paula Jones case. This opened Clinton to charges of perjury and obstruction of justice. Although a federal judge dismissed Jones's suit in April, the continued unfolding of the Lewinsky affair treated the nation to a barrage of personal details about Bill Clinton, revealing flaws in Clinton's character and his willingness to shade the truth.

In the fall of 1998, the Republican leaders who controlled Congress decided that Clinton's statements and misstatements justified initiating the process of impeachment. In December, the majority on the House Judiciary Committee recommended four articles of impeachment, or specific charges against the president, to the House of Representatives. By a partisan vote, the full House approved two of the charges and forwarded them to the Senate. The formal trial of the charges by the Senate began in January 1999 and ended on February 12. Moderate Republicans joined Democrats, ensuring that the Senate would fall far short of the two-thirds majority required for conviction and removal from office (see Table 31.1).

Why did congressional Republicans pursue impeachment to the bitter end? It was clear by the end of 1998 that a majority of Americans strongly disapproved of Clinton's conduct but did not think that his personal behavior merited removal from office. (See Table 31.1, Presidential Impeachment.) The 1998 election, which reduced the Republican majority in the House and resulted in the resignation of Newt Gingrich,

**Whitewater** A failed Arkansas land development for which Bill and Hillary Clinton were accused of fraud but not indicted because of lack of evidence.

## TABLE 31.1 PRESIDENTIAL IMPEACHMENT

| Andrew Johnson, 1868 | Charges | Failure to comply with Tenure of Office Act requiring congressional approval to fire cabinet members |
| --- | --- | --- |
| | Political Lineup | Radical Republicans against Johnson; Democrats and moderate Republicans for him |
| | Actions | Tried and acquitted by Senate |
| | Underlying Issues | Johnson's opposition to Republican plans for reconstruction of southern states after the Civil War |
| Richard Nixon, 1974 | Charges | Obstruction of justice in Watergate investigation, abuse of power of federal agencies for political purposes, refusal to recognize congressional subpoena |
| | Political Lineup | Democrats and many Republicans against Nixon |
| | Actions | Charges approved by House committee; Nixon resigned before action by the full House of Representatives |
| | Underlying Issues | Nixon's construction of a secret government and his efforts to undermine integrity of national elections |
| Bill Clinton, 1999 | Charges | Perjury and obstruction of justice in the investigation of sexual-misconduct allegations by Paula Jones |
| | Political Lineup | Conservative Republicans against Clinton; Democrats and some moderate Republicans for him |
| | Actions | Tried and acquitted by Senate |
| | Underlying Issues | Republican frustration with Clinton's ability to block their agenda; deep concern about Clinton's character and moral fitness for presidency |

confirmed the opinion polls. At the same time, 25 to 30 percent of Americans remained convinced that Clinton was a disgrace whose presence in the White House demeaned the nation. In other words, although anti-Clinton people were a powerful force within the Republican Party and impeachment was certainly motivated by politics, it was also another battle in America's continuing culture wars.

# A New Economy?

What role did new information technologies play in the economic boom of the 1990s?

Within months of the impeachment trial, Americans had a new worry. In the closing months of 1999, many people stocked up on canned food and kerosene, powdered milk, ammunition, and cash. They were preparing to survive, not foreign invasion or natural disaster, but rather the possible collapse of the global computer network. Europeans called the problem the "millennium bug," while Americans referred to it as the "Y2K" problem (for Year 2000). Early programs had used only two digits for years in dates because memory space was precious, leading to fears that old programs would treat 2000 as 1900 or choke in electronic confusion. In fact, almost nothing happened.

From a larger perspective, the Y2K worries illustrate how much the American economy had changed in the preceding decade, and how mysterious the changes seemed. More than ever, the U.S. economy was a global economy; and, unlike any time in the past, it depended on electronic computing to manage and transmit vast quantities of data. The impact of the electronic revolution was still being absorbed into the structures and routines of everyday life as Americans put Y2K behind them and looked to a new century.

31.1
31.2
31.3
31.4
31.5
31.6

31.1

31.2

31.3

31.4

31.5

31.6

**Internet** The system of interconnected computers and servers that allows the exchange of e-mail, posting of websites, and other means of instant communication.

## The Prosperous 1990s

From 1992 through 2000, Americans enjoyed nine years of continuous economic expansion. Unemployment dropped from 7.2 percent in 1992 to 4.0 percent at the start of 2000 as American businesses created more than 12 million new jobs. Key states like California rebounded from economic recession with new growth driven by high-tech industries, entertainment, and foreign trade. The stock market soared during the 1990s; rising demand for shares in established blue-chip companies and new **Internet** firms swelled the value of individual portfolios, retirement accounts, and pension funds. The rate of home ownership rose after declining for fifteen years. Prosperity also trickled down to Americans at the bottom of the economic ladder. The proportion of Americans in poverty dropped to 12 percent in 1999, and the gap between rich and poor began to narrow (slightly) for the first time in two decades.

The economic boom was great news for the federal budget. Tight spending and rising personal income turned perennial deficits into surpluses for 1998, 1999, and 2000. Reduced borrowing by the U.S. Treasury resulted in low interest rates, which further fueled corporate expansion and consumer spending. In 1997, Clinton signed a deficit-reduction bill that seemed to promise fiscal stability.

Behind the statistics were substantial gains in the efficiency of the U.S. economy. International rivals, especially Japan, experienced severe economic slumps in the mid-1990s. In the United States, in contrast, by the end of the decade the productivity of manufacturing workers was increasing more than 4 percent per year, the highest rate in a generation. Part of the gain was the payoff from the painful business restructuring and downsizing of the 1970s and 1980s. Another cause was improvements in efficiency from the full incorporation of personal computers and electronic communication into everyday life and business practice.

To many observers, the growth of the 1990s looked like the beginning of a new wave of sustained economic expansion like earlier waves triggered by technological innovation. Until then, such waves had followed 50-year cycles that began with a 30-year period of rapid expansion followed by two decades of consolidation and slow growth. From 1945 to 1974, for example, the automobile and aerospace industries helped Europe, Japan, and the United States enjoy an era of sustained growth that was followed by two decades of painful economic readjustment and problems. In the later 1990s, fast-growing information-based industries such as electronic communications, software, biotechnology, and medicine seemed to be jump-starting another era of prosperity. However, many individual technology companies failed in 2001 and 2002. The dotcom bust dragged down the stock market for several years, and the real estate bubble that followed diverted investment from productive uses, leaving the United States weaker, rather than stronger, in relation to rising nations like China.

## The Service Economy

At the beginning of the twenty-first century, the United States was an economy of services. As fewer Americans drove tractors and toiled on assembly lines, more became service workers. The service sector includes everyone not directly involved in producing and processing physical products. Service workers range from lawyers to hair stylists, from police officers who write traffic tickets to theater employees who sell movie tickets. In 1965, services already accounted for more than half of American jobs. By the end of the 1990s, their share rose to close to 75 percent.

Service work varies greatly. At the bottom of the scale are minimum-wage jobs held mostly by women, immigrants, and the young, such as cleaning people, childcare workers, hospital orderlies, and fast-food workers. These positions offer little in terms of advancement, job security, or benefits. In contrast, many of the best new jobs are in information industries. Teaching, research, advertising, mass communications, and professional consulting depend on producing and manipulating information. All of these fields have grown. They add to national wealth by creating and applying new ideas rather than by supplying standardized products and services.

31.1

**31.2**

31.3

31.4

31.5

31.6

The information economy flourishes in large cities with libraries, universities, research hospitals, advertising agencies, and corporate headquarters. New York's bankers and stockbrokers made Manhattan an island of prosperity in the 1980s. Pittsburgh, with major universities and corporate headquarters, made the transition to the information economy even while its steel industry failed. A good benchmark of a brain-powered economy is whether more than a quarter of the adults (people aged 25 or over) have finished college. The District of Columbia, with its high-priced lawyers and lobbyists, ranked first in 2007, with 48 percent. Next was Massachusetts (38 percent), followed closely by Maryland, Colorado, Connecticut, and New Jersey.

The rise of the service economy had political consequences. Rapid expansion of jobs in state and local government triggered popular revolts against state taxes that started in 1978 with passage of California's Proposition 13, which limited property taxes, and continued into the 1990s. Another growth industry was health care. Spending on medical and health services amounted to 15 percent of the gross domestic product in 2000, up from 5 percent in 1960. The need to share this huge expense fairly was the motivation for Medicare and Medicaid in the 1960s and the search for a national health insurance program in the 1990s and beyond.

## The High-Tech Sector

The epitome of the "sunrise" economy was electronics, which grew hand-in-glove with the defense budget. The first computers in the 1940s were derived in part from wartime code-breaking efforts. In the 1950s, IBM got half its revenues from air defense computers and guidance systems for B-52 bombers. "It was the Cold War that helped IBM make itself the king of the computer business," commented the company's president, Thomas J. Watson. Employment in computer manufacturing rose in the mid-1960s with the expansion of mainframe computing. Large machines from IBM, Honeywell, NCR, and other established corporations required substantial support facilities and staff and were used largely by universities, government agencies, and corporations. In the 1970s, new companies began to build smaller, specialized machines for such purposes as word processing. One cluster of firms sprang up outside Boston around Route 128, benefiting from proximity to MIT and other Boston-area universities. California's **Silicon Valley**, north of San Jose, took off with corporate spinoffs and civilian applications of military technologies and benefited from proximity to Stanford University.

**Silicon Valley** The region of California between San Jose and San Francisco that holds the nation's greatest concentration of electronics firms.

Extraordinary improvements in computing capacity drove the electronics boom. At the start of the microcomputer era, Intel cofounder Gordon Moore predicted that the number of transistors on a microchip would double every eighteen months, with consequent increases in performance and drops in price. "Moore's Law" worked, at least through the opening of the new century, as producers moved from chips with 5,000 transistors to ones with 50 million. The practical result was a vast increase in the capacities and portability of computers.

Personal computers and consumer electronics became part of everyday life in the 1990s. Automakers built computers into their cars to diagnose engine problems; high-end models added global positioning systems for drivers too hurried to unfold a map. New buildings came with "smart" climate-control systems. In 2005, 80 percent of adults reported that they had Internet access at home or work, up from around 14 percent in 1996. Although it had taken radio thirty-eight years and television thirteen years before 50 million Americans tuned in, the Internet reached the same level of use in four years. The most networked state was Alaska, where computers helped to make up for vast distances and isolating winters.

## An Instant Society

The spread of consumer electronics helped to create an "instant society." Americans in the 1990s learned to communicate by e-mail and to look up information on the **World Wide Web**. The United States was increasingly a society that depended on instant information and expected instant results.

**World Wide Web** A part of the Internet designed to allow easier navigation of the network through the use of graphical user interfaces and hypertext links between different addresses.

31.1

31.2

31.3

31.4

31.5

31.6

The Internet grew out of concerns about defense and national security. Its prototype was ARPAnet (for Advanced Research Projects Agency of the Defense Department), intended to be a communication system that could survive nuclear attack. As the Internet evolved into a system that connected universities and national weapons laboratories, the Pentagon gave up control in 1984 (when there were only 1,000 Internet-connected devices rather than the billion of 2008). Through the 1980s, it was used mainly by scientists and academics to share data and communicate by e-mail. The World Wide Web, created in 1991, expanded the Internet's uses by allowing organizations and companies to create websites that placed political and commercial information only a few clicks away from wired consumers.

Instant satisfaction was one of the principles behind the boom of dotcom businesses in 1998, 1999, and 2000. Many were services that repackaged information for quick access. Others were essentially online versions of mail-order catalogs, but capable of listing hundreds of thousands of items. Still others were instant-delivery services designed to save consumers a trip to the video store or minimart. Although many of the dotcom companies crashed in 2001, they can be viewed as extensions of ongoing trends in retailing and services. For one example, automatic teller machines had been a convenience when introduced in the early 1980s, but were a necessity twenty years later, when Americans expected to be able to pull cash from their bank accounts 168 hours a week rather than find a bank open perhaps 30 hours a week.

Mobile phones were part of the same instant society. They exploited under-utilized radio bands and communication satellites to allow wireless conversations among cells—geographic areas linked by special microwave broadcasting towers. Technological changes again drove demand. The chunky car phone built into a vehicle gave way to sleek handheld devices the size of *Star Trek* communicators and then to smart phones. Wireless phone companies originally sold their phones as emergency backups and business necessities, just as wired telephones had been sold in the first years of the twentieth century. The 5 million American cell phone subscribers of 1990 had exploded to 332 million in 2011—more phone subscriptions than people of all ages.

## In the World Market

Instant access to business and financial information accelerated the globalizing of the American economy (see Figure 31.1). Expanding foreign commerce had become a deliberate goal of national policy with the General Agreement on Tariffs and Trade (GATT) in 1947. GATT regularized international commerce after World War II and helped to secure one of the goals of World War II by ensuring that world markets remained open to American industry. The Trade Expansion Act in 1962 authorized President Kennedy to make reciprocal trade agreements to cut tariffs by up to 50 percent so as to keep American companies competitive in the new European Common Market.

With the help of national policy and booming economies overseas, the value of U.S. imports and exports more than doubled, from 7 percent of the gross domestic product in 1965 to 16 percent in 1990—the largest percentage since World War I. Americans in the 1970s began to worry about a "colonial" status, in which the United States exported food, lumber, and minerals and imported automobiles and television sets. By the 1980s, foreign economic competitiveness and trade deficits, especially with Japan, became issues of national concern that continued into the new century, when China and India were emerging as the newest competitors.

The effects of international competition were more complex than "Japan-bashers" acknowledged. Mass-production industries, such as textiles and aluminum, suffered from cheaper and sometimes higher-quality imports, but many specialized industries and services, such as Houston's oil equipment and exploration firms, thrived. Globalization also created new regional winners and losers. In 1982, the United States began to do more business with Pacific nations than with Europe.

31.1

31.2

31.3

31.4

31.5

31.6

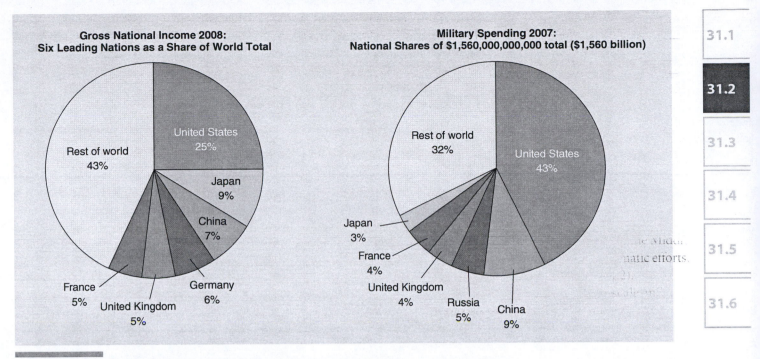

**FIGURE 31.1 THE UNITED STATES IN THE GLOBAL ECONOMY** The United States remained the single largest national economy in the early twenty-first century despite rapid economic growth in Asia.

SOURCES: World Bank, *World Development Report 2009;* Center for Arms Control and Non-Proliferation (www.armscontrolcenter.org)

**The Politics of Trade.** More recent steps to expand the global reach of the U.S. economy were the **North American Free Trade Agreement (NAFTA)** in 1993 and a new worldwide GATT approved in 1994. Negotiated by Republican George H. W. Bush and pushed through Congress in 1993 by Democratic Bill Clinton, NAFTA combined 25 million Canadians, 90 million Mexicans, and 250 million U.S. consumers in a single "common market" similar to that of western Europe. This enlarged free-trade zone was intended to open new markets and position the United States to compete more effectively against the European Community and Japan. The agreement may have been a holdover from the Bush years, but it matched Clinton's ideas about reforming the American economy.

NAFTA was a hard pill for many Democrats, and it revived the old debate between free traders and protectionists. Support was strongest from businesses and industries that sought foreign customers, including agriculture and electronics. Opponents included organized labor, communities already hit by industrial shutdowns, and environmentalists worried about lax controls on industrial pollution in Mexico. In contrast to the nineteenth-century arguments for protecting infant industries, new industries now looked to foreign markets, whereas uncompetitive, older firms hoped for protected domestic markets. The readjustments from NAFTA have produced obvious pain in the form of closed factories or farms made unprofitable by cheaper imports, while its gains have been less visible—a new job here, larger sales there.

The **World Trade Organization (WTO)**, which replaced GATT in 1996, became the unexpected target of a global protest movement. Seattle officials, committed to promoting Seattle as a world-class city, lobbied hard to get the 1999 WTO meeting. With finance and foreign affairs ministers and heads of government expected to attend, it would give Seattle world attention. Instead, it gave the city a headache. Fifty thousand protesters converged on the meeting, held from November 30 to December 4, 1999.

Protesters were convinced that the WTO is a tool of transnational corporations that flout local labor and environmental protections in the name of "free trade" that benefits only the wealthy nations and their businesses. WTO defenders pointed to the long-term effects of open trade in raising net production in the world economy and thereby making more wealth available for developing nations. Opponents asserted, in turn, that such wealth never reaches the workers and farmers in those nations.

**North American Free Trade Agreement (NAFTA)** Agreement reached in 1993 by Canada, Mexico, and the United States to substantially reduce barriers to trade.

**World Trade Organization (WTO)** International organization that sets standards and practices for global trade, and the focus of international protests over world economic policy in the late 1990s.

31.1

31.2

31.3

31.4

31.5

31.6

American opponents demanded that U.S. firms, such as sportswear companies, that make their products overseas make sure that their overseas workers have decent living conditions and wages.

# Broadening Democracy

**31.3** What gains did women and minorities make in national politics in the 1990s?

Closely related to the changes in the American economy were the changing composition of the American people and the continued emergence of new participants in U.S. government. Bill Clinton's first cabinet, in which three women and four minority men balanced seven white men, recognized the makeup of the American population and marked the maturing of minorities and women as distinct political constituencies. The first cabinet appointed by George W. Bush in 2001 included four minority men and four women, one of whom was Asian American. In both administrations, the new prominence of women and minorities in the national government followed years of growing success in cities and states.

## Americans in 2000

The federal census for the year 2000 found 281.4 million Americans in the fifty states, District of Columbia, and Puerto Rico (and probably 2–3 million more residents were not counted). The increase from 1990 was 13.2 percent, or 32.7 million. It was the largest ten-year population increase in U.S. history, evidence of the nation's prosperity and its attractiveness for immigrants. More than 12 percent of Americans had been born in other countries, the highest share since 1920 (see Table 31.2). One-third of all Americans lived in four states: California, Texas, New York, and Florida. These were the key prizes in presidential elections. Their regulations and consumer preferences conditioned national markets for products ranging from automobiles to textbooks.

The West grew the fastest. The super-boom states were Nevada (66 percent growth), Arizona (40 percent), Colorado (31 percent), Utah (30 percent), and Idaho (29 percent). Fast growth implies young populations, and the states with the lowest average ages were all western: Utah, Alaska, Idaho, and Texas. The Southwest and South also had the fastest-growing metropolitan areas. Las Vegas topped them all with an increase of 83 percent. Among large metro areas with more than 500,000 people in 2000, all twenty of the fastest-growing were in the West and Southeast.

In contrast, parts of the American midlands grew slowly. Rural counties continued to empty out in Appalachia and across the Great Plains as fewer and fewer Americans were needed for mining and farming or for the small towns associated with those industries.

Another important trend was increasing ethnic and racial diversity. Hispanics were the fastest-growing group in the U.S. population. Although immigrants concentrated in the coastal and border states, Hispanics and Asian Americans were also spreading into interior states. Asians and Hispanics who had been in the United States for some time showed substantial economic success. Non-Hispanic whites are now a minority in California at 47 percent, in the District of Columbia, in Hawaii, and in New Mexico.

The changing ethnicity of the American people promises to be increasingly apparent in coming decades. Immigrants tend to be young adults who are likely to form families, and birthrates have been high among Hispanics and Asian Americans. The result is a sort of multiethnic baby boom. In 1972, at the peak of the post–World War II baby boom, 80 percent of elementary and high school students were non-Hispanic whites. By 1999, the figure was 63 percent and falling. Over the coming decades, the effects of ethnic change will be apparent not only in schools but also in the workplace, popular culture, and politics.

## TABLE 31.2  IMMIGRANTS 1991–2007, BY CONTINENT AND BY TWENTY MOST IMPORTANT COUNTRIES OF ORIGIN

| (persons obtaining permanent legal resident status) | |
| --- | --- |
| Total | 16,281,000 |
| **North America** | 6,410,000 |
| Mexico | 3,450,000 |
| Dominican Republic | 535,000 |
| El Salvador | 412,000 |
| Cuba | 375,000 |
| Haiti | 323,000 |
| Jamaica | 294,000 |
| Canada | 261,000 |
| Guatemala | 225,000 |
| **Asia** | 5,363,000 |
| Philippines | 920,000 |
| China | 872,000 |
| India | 856,000 |
| Vietnam | 636,000 |
| Korea | 318,000 |
| Pakistan | 222,000 |
| **Europe** | 2,352,000 |
| Poland | 261,000 |
| Ukraine | 260,000 |
| Russia | 241,000 |
| United Kingdom | 246,000 |
| **South America** | 1,157,000 |
| Colombia | 302,000 |
| Peru | 204,000 |
| **Africa** | 909,000 |
| **Oceania** | 90,000 |

SOURCE: *Statistical Abstract of the United States.*

31.1
31.2
31.3
31.4
31.5
31.6

# Women from the Grass Roots to Congress

The increasing prominence of women and family issues in national politics was a steady, quiet revolution that bore fruit in the 1990s, when the number of women in Congress more than doubled. In 1981, President Reagan appointed Arizona judge Sandra Day O'Connor to be the first woman on the U.S. Supreme Court. In 1984, Walter Mondale chose New York Congresswoman Geraldine Ferraro as his vice presidential candidate. In 1993, Clinton appointed the second woman to the Supreme Court, U.S. Appeals Court judge Ruth Bader Ginsburg. Clinton appointee Janet Reno was the first woman to serve as attorney general, and Madeleine K. Albright the first to serve as secretary of state. George W. Bush continued to break new ground by naming Condoleezza Rice as his national security advisor in 2001 and as secretary of state in 2005.

Political gains for women at the national level reflected their growing importance in grassroots politics. The spreading suburbs of postwar America were "frontiers" that required concerted action to solve immediate needs like adequate schools and decent parks. Because pursuit of such community services was often viewed as "woman's work" (in contrast to the "man's work" of economic development), postwar metropolitan areas offered numerous opportunities for women to engage in volunteer civic work, learn political skills, and run for local office. Moreover, new cities and suburbs had fewer established political institutions, such as political machines and strong

31.1

31.2

31.3

31.4

31.5

31.6

As leadership opportunities for African Americans have increased in recent decades, they have gained positions of influence in a growing range of activities. In the field of foreign policy, for example, President George W. Bush chose Colin Powell as secretary of state and Condoleezza Rice as national security advisor. Here Powell (right) and Rice (second from right) participate in a White House meeting between Bush and British Prime Minister Tony Blair.

parties; their politics were open to energetic women. Most women in contemporary politics have been more liberal than men—a difference that political scientists attribute to women's interest in the practical problems of schools, neighborhoods, and two-earner families. But women's grassroots mobilization, especially through evangelical churches, has also strengthened groups committed to conservative social values.

Regional differences have affected women's political gains. The West has long been the part of the country most open to women in state and local government and in business. Westerners have been more willing than voters in the East or South to choose women as mayors of major cities and as members of state legislatures. Many of the skills learned from politics were also useful as women played a growing role in professional and managerial occupations.

In 1991, the nomination of Judge Clarence Thomas, an African American, to the U.S. Supreme Court ensured that everyone knew that the terms of U.S. politics were changing. Because of his conservative positions on social and civil rights issues, Thomas was a controversial nominee. Controversy deepened when law professor Anita Hill accused Thomas of harassing her sexually while she served on his staff at the Equal Employment Opportunity Commission. The accusations led to riveting hearings before a U.S. Senate committee. Critics tried to discredit Hill with vicious attacks on her character, and the committee failed to call witnesses who could have supported her claims. The public was left with Hill's plausible but unproved allegations and Thomas's equally vigorous but unproved denials. The Senate confirmed Thomas to the Supreme Court. Partisans on each side continued to believe the version that best suited their preconceptions and agendas.

Whatever the merits of her charges, Hill's badgering by skeptical senators angered millions of women. In the shadow of the hearings, women made impressive gains in the 1992 election, which pushed women's share of seats in the fifty state legislatures above 20 percent. The number of women in the U.S. Senate jumped from two to seven (and grew further to twelve Democrats and five Republicans in 2011). The number of women serving as federal judges grew from 48 in 1981 to more than 200—roughly a quarter of the total.

Women have influenced national politics as voters as well as candidates and cabinet members. Since the 1980s, voting patterns have shown a gender gap. Women in the 1990s identified with the Democratic Party and voted for its candidates at a higher rate than men. The reasons include concerns about the effect of government spending cuts and interest in measures to support families rather than in conservative rhetoric. This gender gap has helped keep Democrats competitive and dampened the nation's conservative swing on social issues.

## Minorities at the Ballot Box

The changing makeup of the American populace also helped black and Latino candidates for public office to increased success. After the racial violence of the 1960s, many African Americans turned to local politics to gain control of their own communities. The first black mayor of a major twentieth-century city was Carl Stokes in Cleveland in 1967. The 1973 election brought victories for Tom Bradley in Los Angeles, Maynard Jackson in Atlanta, and Coleman Young in Detroit. By 1983, three of the nation's four largest cities had black mayors. In 1989, Virginia made Douglas Wilder the first African American governor in any state since Reconstruction.

The election of a minority mayor was sometimes more important for its symbolism than for the transfer of real power. Efforts to restructure the basis of city council elections, however, struck directly at the balance of power. Most mid-sized cities stopped electing city councils by wards or districts during the first half of the twentieth century. Voting at large shifted power away from geographically concentrated ethnic groups. It favored business interests that claimed to speak for the city as a whole but could assign most of the costs of economic growth to older and poorer neighborhoods.

In the 1970s, minority leaders and community activists realized that a return to district voting could convert neighborhood segregation from a liability to a political resource. As amended in 1975, the federal Voting Rights Act allowed minorities to use the federal courts to challenge at-large voting systems that diluted the impact of their votes. Blacks and Mexican Americans used the act to reestablish city council districts in the late 1970s and early 1980s in city after city across the South and Southwest.

The political rebalancing meant that local leaders faced strong pressures to ensure equitable distribution of the benefits and burdens of growth. Newly empowered minorities began to press for a fair share of an expanding economic pie. In San Antonio and Denver, for example, young Hispanic politicians brought new ideas into city government in the 1980s. Henry Cisneros of San Antonio defeated a representative of the downtown establishment in 1981, and in Denver, Federico Peña ousted a sixteen-year incumbent with the help of an army of volunteers. Both men ran on platforms of planned growth and later served in Clinton's cabinet. Progressive African American mayors in other cities included Andrew Young in Atlanta in the 1980s and Dennis Archer in Detroit in the 1990s, leaders who won on positive platforms of growth and equity and who mended fences with business leaders.

At the national level, minorities gradually increased their representation in Congress. Ben Nighthorse Campbell of Colorado, a Cheyenne, brought a Native American voice to the U.S. Senate in 1992. The number of African Americans in the House of Representatives topped forty after 1992, with the help of districts drawn to concentrate black voters. Even after a series of Supreme Court cases invalidated districts drawn with race as the "predominant factor," however, African Americans held most of their gains, while the number of Latino members of Congress rose rapidly to thirty-one by 2011 (see Table 31.3).

31.1

31.2

31.3

31.4

31.5

31.6

31.1

31.2

31.3

31.4

31.5

31.6

📖 **Read the Document**  Nancy Pelosi, Inaugural Address (2007)

TABLE 31.3  **MINORITIES AND WOMEN IN CONGRESS, 1941–2012**  The number of women and minorities in Congress began to grow substantially in the 1980s, as the result of changing attitudes, the Voting Rights Act of 1965, decades of grassroots activism, and the nation's changing demographics.

| | Women | African Americans | Latinos | Asian and Pacific Americans | American Indians |
|---|---|---|---|---|---|
| 1941–1942 | 10 | 1 | 2 | | |
| 1951–1952 | 11 | 2 | 2 | | |
| 1961–1962 | 20 | 4 | 4 | 3 | 1 |
| 1971–1972 | 15 | 14 | 7 | 4 | |
| 1981–1982 | 23 | 19 | 8 | 8 | |
| 1991–1992 | 33 | 27 | 14 | 7 | 1 |
| 2001–2002 | 75 | 39 | 19 | 9 | 1 |
| 2011–2012 | 94 | 44 | 31 | 10 | 1 |

SOURCE: Congressional Research Service reports. Exact numbers may have varied within each Congress because of resignations, deaths, and/or special elections.

## Rights and Opportunities

In struggling for political influence, recent immigrants have added new panethnic identities to their national identities. Hispanic activists revived the term "Chicano" to bridge the gap between recent Mexican immigrants and Latinos whose families had settled in the Southwest before the American conquest in 1848. Great gaps of experience and culture separated Chinese, Koreans, Filipinos, and Vietnamese, but they gained political recognition and influence if they dealt with other Americans as "Asians." Native Americans have similarly downplayed tribal differences in efforts to secure better opportunities for Indians as a group.

The increasing presence of Latinos and African Americans in public life highlighted a set of troublesome questions about the proper balance between equal rights and equal opportunities. Was government justified in seeking to equalize outcomes as well as starting points? More broadly, was the United States to be a unitary society in which everyone assimilated to a single culture and adhered to a single set of formal and informal rules, or might it be a plural society in which different groups accepted different goals and behaviors? The debates at the end of the twentieth century replayed many of the questions that European immigration raised at the century's beginning.

**Illegal Immigration and Bilingual Education.**  One issue is the economic impact of illegal immigration. Advocates of tight borders assert that illegal immigrants take jobs away from legal residents and eat up public assistance. Many studies, however, find that illegal immigrants fill jobs that nobody else wants. Over the long run, high employment levels among immigrants mean that their tax contributions through sales taxes and Social Security taxes and payroll deductions more than pay for their use of welfare, food stamps, and unemployment benefits, which illegal immigrants are often afraid to claim for fear of calling attention to themselves. Nevertheless, high immigration can strain local government budgets even if it benefits the nation as a whole. Partly for this reason, 60 percent of California voters approved **Proposition 187** in 1994, cutting off access to state-funded public education and health care for illegal immigrants.

The issue of illegal immigration simmered in the 1990s, but exploded in the new century. As the total of undocumented immigrants reached 11 to 12 million by best estimates, many Americans became increasingly concerned about a porous southern border. Unlike early eras of concern about immigration that had usually coincided with economic downturns, the new immigration worries came in an era of economic prosperity. In 2007, the president and leaders in both political parties were blindsided when

**Proposition 187** California legislation adopted by popular vote in California in 1994 that cuts off state-funded health and education benefits to undocumented or illegal immigrants.

31.1

31.2

31.3

31.4

31.5

31.6

In November 2002, Linda Sanchez (left) and Loretta Sanchez celebrate Linda's election to Congress from Los Angeles County. Loretta had won a congressional seat from Orange County in 1996, and Linda's victory made them the first sisters to serve simultaneously in the House of Representatives.

a carefully constructed compromise over immigration policy failed because of public outcry over provisions that many voters interpreted as amnesty for rule-breaking.

**Affirmative Action.**   An equally divisive issue was a set of policies that originated in the 1960s as **affirmative action**, a phrase that first appeared in executive orders issued by presidents Kennedy and Johnson. The initial goal was to require businesses that received federal contracts to "take affirmative action to ensure that applicants are employed, and that employees are treated during employment without regard for their race, creed, color, or national origin." By the 1970s, many states and cities had adopted similar policies for hiring their own employees and choosing contractors and extended affirmative action to women as well as minorities. Colleges and universities used affirmative-action policies in recruiting faculty and admitting students.

As these efforts spread, the initial goal of nondiscrimination evolved into expectations and requirements for active ("affirmative") efforts to achieve greater diversity among employees, students, or contractors. Government agencies began to set aside a small percentage of contracts for woman-owned or minority-owned firms. Cities actively worked to hire more minority police officers and firefighters. Colleges made special efforts to attract minority students. The landmark court case about affirmative action was *University of California v. Bakke* (1978). Alan Bakke was an unsuccessful applicant to the medical school at the University of California at Davis. He argued that the university had improperly set aside 16 of 100 places in its entering class for minority students, thereby engaging in reverse discrimination against white applicants. In a narrow decision, the U.S. Supreme Court ordered Bakke admitted because the only basis for his rejection had been race. At the same time, the Court stated that race or ethnicity

**affirmative action**  A set of policies to open opportunities in business and education for members of minority groups and women by allowing race and sex to be factors included in decisions to hire, award contracts, or admit students to higher education programs.

***University of California v. Bakke***  United States Supreme Court case in 1978 that allowed race to be used as one of several factors in college and university admission decisions but made rigid quotas unacceptable.

937

31.1

31.2

31.3

31.4

31.5

31.6

could legally be one of several factors considered in college and university admissions, as long as a specific number of places were not reserved for minorities.

In 1996, California voters took grassroots action, approving a ballot measure to eliminate state-sponsored affirmative action. One effect was to prohibit state-funded colleges and universities from using race or ethnicity as a factor in deciding which applicants to admit. In the same year, the Supreme Court let stand a lower-court ruling in *Hopwood v. Texas*, which had forbidden the University of Texas to consider race in admission decisions. The number of black freshmen in the University of Texas dropped by half in 1997 and the number of blacks and Hispanics among first-year law students by two-thirds.

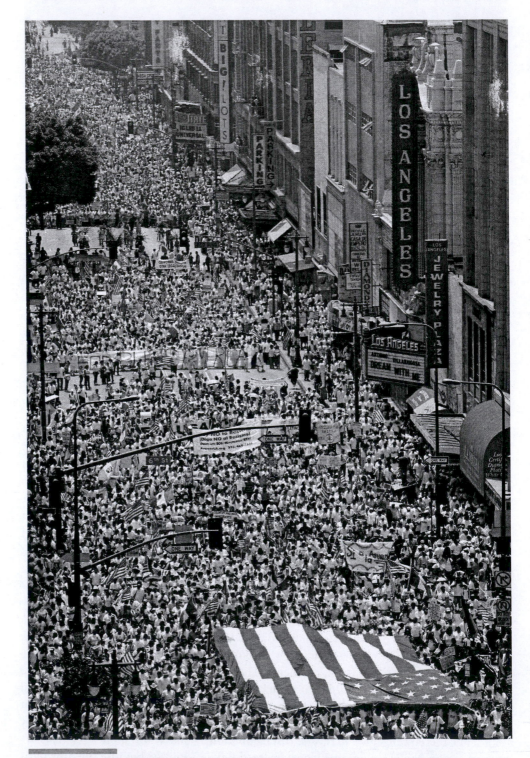

On May 1, 2006, at least 400,000 people turned out for an immigrants' rights march in Los Angeles. Equal numbers marched in Chicago and smaller crowds in many other cities.

In 2003, the Supreme Court affirmed the basic principle of affirmative action in two cases involving admission to the University of Michigan. Aided by supporting statements filed by major corporations and by members of the U.S. military, the Court found that promoting ethnic and racial diversity among students constitutes a compelling state interest, and it approved narrowly tailored affirmative-action programs that weigh race and ethnicity along with other admissions criteria on an individual basis. But four years later, a different majority on the Court rejected public school plans in Lexington, Kentucky, and Seattle that took race into account in deciding how to match students and schools, leaving the larger issue for further court cases.

# Edging into a New Century

31.1

31.2

31.3

31.4

31.5

31.6

**31.4** What were the key goals of George W. Bush's presidency?

On the evening of November 7, 2000, CBS-TV made the kind of mistake that journalists dread. Relying on questions put to a sample of voters after they cast their ballots in the presidential contest between Albert Gore, Jr., and George W. Bush, the CBS newsroom first projected that Gore would win Florida and likely the election, and then reversed itself and called the election for Bush, only to find that it would be days or even weeks before the votes in several pivotal states, including Florida, could be certified.

The miscue was reminiscent of the premature *Chicago Tribune* headline in November 1948 that proclaimed "Dewey Beats Truman" when the actual results were the reverse. The inability to predict the outcome in 2000 was an indication of the degree to which Americans were split down the middle in their political preferences and their visions for the future. The United States entered the twenty-first century both divided and uneasily balanced, with extremes of opinion revolving around a center of basic goals and values.

## The 2000 Election

On November 8, 2000, the day after their national election, Americans woke up to the news that neither Republican George W. Bush nor Democrat Albert Gore, Jr., had a majority of votes in the electoral college. Although Gore held a lead in the popular vote (about 340,000 votes out of more than 100 million cast), both candidates needed a majority in Florida to win its electoral votes and the White House. After protracted protests about voting irregularities and malfunctioning voting equipment, politically divided Floridians engaged in an on-again off-again recount in key counties. The U.S. Supreme Court finally preempted the state process and ordered a halt to recounting on December 12 by the politically charged margin of 5 to 4. The result was to make Bush the winner in Florida by a few hundred votes and the winner nationwide by 271 electoral votes to 267.

The heart of the controversy involved how to read Florida's punch-card ballots. Americans learned a new word, *chad,* for the little paper ovals that get punched out. How should election officials count dangling chads that were partially detached? What should they do with ballots where the chad was dimpled but not punched through? Until the Supreme Court put an end to the discussion, teams of officials struggled through recounts. Both parties put their own spin on the process. Republicans framed the issue as "following the rules," while Democrats framed it as "making every vote count." It is difficult to know who "really" won Florida. There is good evidence that African American voters, who strongly favored Gore, were turned away in disproportionate numbers because of technical challenges to their registration. In one county, a ballot with a particularly poor design probably caused several thousand mistaken votes

31.1
31.2
31.3
31.4
31.5
31.6

# ✳ Explore the 2000 Election on MyHistoryLab

## WHY DID DISAGREEMENT SURROUND THE 2000 PRESIDENTIAL ELECTION?

In 2000, the United States saw one of its closest presidential elections. The margin of victory between Republican George W. Bush and Democrat Al Gore was razor thin. In Florida especially, the popular vote was extremely close, and whichever candidate won the state would also win its electoral college votes and the national election itself. Numerous recounts were held in Florida and controversy ensued over what constituted a valid vote. The decision on who would be president

Republican presidential candidate George W. Bush campaigns at this Oxnard, California train station in 2000. Although ultimately the electoral college victor over Democrat Al Gore, Bush did not win the popular vote.

centered on questions such as whether so-called "hanging chads"—incompletely punched-through holes on punch-card ballots—should be legal votes. The results ended up before the Supreme Court, which decided in favor of Bush who officially won Florida and the election with a majority of electoral college votes while his opponent Gore had more popular votes.

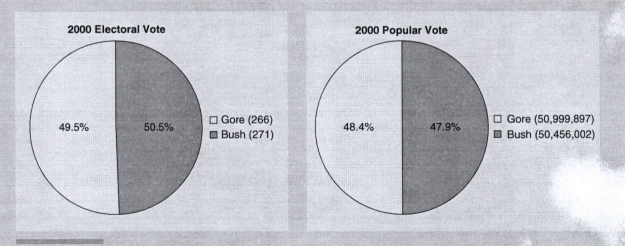

**2000 Electoral Vote**

49.5% / 50.5%
☐ Gore (266)
■ Bush (271)

**2000 Popular Vote**

48.4% / 47.9%
☐ Gore (50,999,897)
■ Bush (50,456,002)

2000 Presidential Election Results Summary
SOURCE: "2000 Presidential Electoral and Popular Vote," *FEC.gov*, http://www.fec.gov/pubrec/fe2000/elecpop.htm.

**KEY QUESTIONS** Use **MyHistoryLab** *Explorer* to **answer** these **questions:**

**Analysis ▶▶▶** *What voting patterns influenced the 2000 election?*
Map the trends that still largely shape voting today.

**Response ▶▶▶** *How did the election controversies in 2000 in Florida play out?*
Consider various socioeconomic factors and their correlations in the recounts.

**Comparison ▶▶▶** *In what ways do various socioeconomic patterns correspond to American voting behavior?*
Chart such relationships to see their influence on elections.

31.1

31.2

31.3

**31.4**

31.5

31.6

for a minor candidate rather than Gore. But recounts by teams of newspaper reporters came to different conclusions about who might have won, depending on what criteria were used to accept or reject disputed punch-card ballots. In the aftermath, each side could claim to have won, but the Supreme Court ruling and Bush's inauguration made the point irrelevant.

Both Bush, governor of Texas and son of President George H. W. Bush (1989–1993), and Gore, vice president for the previous eight years, targeted their campaigns at middle Americans. Each offered to cut taxes, downsize the federal government, and protect Social Security, differing in the details rather than the broad goals. In trying to claim the political middle, they reflected the successful political message of the Clinton administration.

## Reaganomics Revisited

Despite the message of stability, the Bush administration took the Republican return to executive power as an opportunity to tilt domestic policy abruptly to the right. Following the example of Ronald Reagan, Bush made massive tax cuts the centerpiece of his first months in office. By starting with proposals for ten-year cuts so large that two generations of federal programs were threatened, Bush and congressional Republicans forced the Democrats to "compromise" on reductions far higher than the economy could probably support, creating a political crisis at the end of 2012. The resulting cuts to income taxes and estate taxes were projected to total $1,350 billion over the decade, with one-third of the benefits going to families earning more than $200,000. The federal budget quickly plunged into the red, undoing the careful political balancing and fiscal discipline of the Clinton administration with soaring Bush deficits.

The Bush team also moved quickly to deregulate the economy. It opened many of the environmental and business regulations of the last two decades to reconsideration—from arsenic standards in drinking water to the pollution controls required of electric utilities. In many cases, the administration proposed to rely on the market through voluntary compliance and incentives to replace regulations. Vice President Dick Cheney developed a new production-oriented energy policy in consultation with energy companies but not with environmental or consumer groups. The collapse of the energy-trading company Enron in a hailstorm of criticism over deceptive accounting and shady market manipulations, creating an energy crisis in California in early 2000, slowed the push to deregulate. In turn, Enron proved to be the first of many companies that had to restate earnings in 2002, depressing the stock market and raising questions about the ethics of big business and business accounting practices. Stock market declines and the evaporation of retirement savings for many workers raised doubts about the solidity of the 1990s boom and helped to hold down economic growth for a third year (see Table 31.4).

Education policy, a centerpiece of Bush's image as an innovator from his service as governor of Texas, was another legislative front. Tough battles with Congress resulted in compromise legislation, reminiscent of the 1990s, that included national testing

**TABLE 31.4 ECONOMIC INEQUALITY: 2010**

|  | Percent below Poverty Line | Median Household Income |
|---|---|---|
| White, non-Hispanic | 9.9 | $54,620 |
| African American | 27.4 | $32,068 |
| Asian | 12.1 | $64,308 |
| Hispanic origin | 26.6 | $37,759 |
| Native-born | 14.4 | $50,288 |
| Foreign-born | 19.9 | $43,750 |

SOURCE: U.S. Bureau of the Census, Current Population Reports, *Income, Poverty, and Health Insurance Coverage in the United States, 2010.*

31.1

31.2

31.3

31.4

31.5

31.6

standards, as Bush wanted, balanced by more federal funding. More important for both education and religion was the narrow decision by the Supreme Court in *Zelman v. Simmons-Harris* (2002) to uphold the use of taxpayer-funded assistance, or vouchers, to help students attend religious schools. By declaring that both religious and secular institutions can compete for government money as long as it is channeled through individuals who made "true private choices" about how to spend it, the Court continued a two-decade trend to narrow the constitutional prohibition on the "establishment of religion."

## Downsized Diplomacy

Strong conservatives had long criticized subordinating U.S. authority and freedom of action to international agreements. The new Bush administration heeded this criticism and brought a revolutionary approach to foreign affairs. The administration repeatedly adopted unilateral or bilateral policies in preference to the complexities of negotiations with an entire range of nations.

In his first eighteen months, Bush opted out of a series of treaties and negotiations on global issues, sometimes despite years of careful bargaining. In each case, he pointed to specific flaws or problems, but the goal was to reduce restrictions on U.S. business and its military. The administration undercut efforts to implement the Convention on Biological Warfare because of possible adverse effects on drug companies. It refused to sign on to efforts to reduce the international trade in armaments, declined to acknowledge a new International Criminal Court designed to try war criminals, and ignored an international compact on the rights of women in deference to cultural conservatives. Most prominently, it refused to accept the Kyoto Protocol agreement, aimed at combating the threat of massive environmental change through global warming resulting from the carbon dioxide released by fossil fuels, dismissing a growing scientific consensus on the problem.

In the field of arms control, Bush entered office with the intention of ending the 1972 treaty that had limited the deployment of antimissile defenses by the United States and Russia in order to stabilize the arms race. The treaty had been a cornerstone of national security policy. Despite the objection of Russia, Bush formally withdrew from the treaty in December 2001. In its place, he revived Ronald Reagan's idea of a Strategic Defense Initiative with proposals for new but unproven technologies to protect the United States against nuclear attacks by "rogue states." This argument was supported in 2002 by North Korea's revelation that it was pursuing a nuclear weapons program, even though it had agreed not to do so in 1994. Bush also decided not to implement the Strategic Arms Reduction Treaty (START II) which had been one of the major accomplishments of his father's term as president. In its place, he worked directly to improve relations with Russia and negotiated a bilateral agreement to reduce substantially the number of nuclear warheads that Russia and the United States actively deploy (while pressing for the development of new tactical nuclear weapons). A new U.S. policy that explicitly claimed the right to act militarily to preempt potential threats confirmed the go-it-alone approach.

# Paradoxes of Power

**31.5**  How did the terrorist attacks of September 11, 2001, change foreign policy for the following decade?

The United States in the twenty-first century faced the paradox of power: The enormous economic, military, and technological capacity that allowed it to impose its will on other nations did not extend to an ability to prevent anti-American actions by deeply enraged individuals.

In the 1990s, the U.S. economy had surged while Japan stagnated, Europe marked time, and Russia verged on economic collapse. The U.S. economy in the early twenty-first century was twice the size of Japan's; California alone had economic capacity equal to France or Britain. America's lead was nurtured by research and development spending equal to that of the next six countries combined. The U.S. military budget exceeded the total military spending of the next dozen nations. The United States had the world's only global navy and a huge edge in military technology.

But the United States remained vulnerable. Huge trade deficits, massive oil imports, and a falling dollar in the early years of the new century underlined its economic vulnerability. Overseas, terrorist attacks in the 1990s, which had shown that the nation was at risk, were premonitions of disaster to come. Islamic radicals killed nineteen American soldiers at military housing in Saudi Arabia in 1996 and seventeen sailors on the destroyer *Cole* while in port in the Arab nation of Yemen in 2000. Bombs at the U.S. embassies in Kenya and Tanzania in 1998 killed more than 200 people. These bombings followed the detonation of explosives in the basement garage of the World Trade Center in New York in February 1993, killing six people. New acts of terror remained a constant threat—realized in an appalling manner on September 11, 2001.

## September 11, 2001

On September 11, 2001, terrorists hijacked four commercial jetliners. They crashed one plane into the Pentagon and one into each of the twin towers of the World Trade Center, 110-story buildings that housed 50,000 workers at the peak of the workday. Tens of millions of Americans were jolted out of morning routines by riveting television coverage of the burning towers and watched in horror as first one tower and then the other disintegrated into itself. September 11 was an occasion for terror and courage. Passengers on the fourth plane fought the hijackers and made sure that it crashed in the Pennsylvania mountains rather than hit a fourth target. Altogether, 479 police officers, firefighters, and other emergency workers died in the collapse of the towers. Thousands of volunteers rushed to assist rescue efforts or contribute to relief efforts. The total confirmed death toll was 2,752 in New York, 184 at the Pentagon, and 40 in Pennsylvania.

The hijackers were part of the al-Qaeda network of terrorists coordinated by Osama bin Laden. A Saudi Arabian businessman who had turned against the United States because of its military presence in the Middle East and its support for Israel, bin Laden was probably the brains behind the attacks on the U.S. military and on diplomats overseas and the earlier blast at the World Trade Center. Operating from exile in Afghanistan, he now masterminded the new and spectacular assault.

The events of September 11 were an enormous shock to the American people, but worries about escalating terrorism were not new. Security specialists such as Defense Secretary William Cohen had been sounding the alarm through the 1990s. The U.S. Commission on National Security/21st Century, appointed by President Clinton, had included detailed warnings in its February 2001 report, although the new administration had ignored its recommendations to reorganize federal homeland security. The problem, however, had been to connect broad concerns to specific threats. It is always enormously difficult to separate and correlate key points in the vast flood of information that flows through law-enforcement and intelligence agencies, separating "signals" from "noise." It is much easier to read the warnings after an event has occurred than to pick out the essential data before the unexpected happens—something as true about the attack on Pearl Harbor, for example, as about the attack of 9-11.

## Security and Conflict

On September 12, President George W. Bush called the Pentagon and World Trade Center attacks "acts of war." Three days later, Congress gave the president sweeping powers "to use all necessary and appropriate force against those nations, organizations, or persons he determines planned, authorized, committed, or aided the terrorist attacks that occurred on September 11, 2001." Only one member voted against the resolution—the same level of agreement that the nation showed after December 7, 1941.

The government response in the United States was a hodgepodge of security measures and arrests. Federal agents detained more than 1,000 terrorist suspects, mostly men

31.1

31.2

31.3

31.4

31.5

31.6

31.1

31.2

31.3

31.4

31.5

31.6

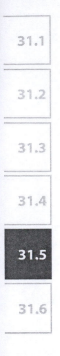

((•  📖 Read the Document   Osama bin Laden, World Islamic Front Statement (1998)

Flames shoot from the South Tower of the World Trade Center in New York as it is struck by hijacked United Airlines flight 15 on the morning of September 11, 2001. Smoke pours from the North Tower, which had been hit sixteen minutes earlier by another hijacked aircraft.

**PATRIOT Act** Federal legislation adopted in 2001, in response to the terrorist attacks of September 11, intended to facilitate antiterror actions by federal law enforcement and intelligence agencies.

from the Middle East, releasing some but holding hundreds without charges, evidence, or legal counsel. President Bush also declared that "enemy combatants" could be tried by special military tribunals, although domestic and international protest caused the administration to agree to more legal safeguards than originally planned. Congress passed the **PATRIOT Act** (Providing Appropriate Tools Required to Intercept and Obstruct Terrorists) in late October, which gave federal authorities substantial new capacity to conduct criminal investigations, in most provisions for the next three to five years. These included the power to request "roving" wiretaps of individuals rather than single telephones, obtain nationwide search warrants, tap information in computerized records, and detain foreigners without filing charges for up to a week. These measures raised a number of concerns about the protection of civil liberties, as noted by the several dozen members of Congress who voted against the act. The law was renewed in 2006 with a few added provisions to protect basic constitutional and political rights.

In November 2002, Congress approved a massive reorganization of the federal government to improve security at home. The new **Department of Homeland Security** includes immigration, customs, border patrol, the Coast Guard, Secret Service, Federal Emergency Management Agency, and Transportation Security Administration. It is the second-largest federal agency, after the Defense Department. In 2004, Congress adopted a package of reforms to improve intelligence gathering and analysis, creating the position of director of national intelligence to oversee the CIA and report directly to the president.

In contrast to the suppression of dissent during World War I or the internment of Japanese Americans during World War II, Americans in 2001 and 2002 were careful on the home front. The leaders and supporters of the War on Terror reacted to dissenting voices, particularly those from a pacifist tradition, with caustic remarks rather than repression. Violations of civil liberties have affected individuals rather than entire groups. President Bush made an important gesture soon after September 11 by appearing at a mosque and arguing against blanket condemnation of Muslims. Ethnic profiling has resulted in heightened suspicion and surveillance of Muslims, selective enforcement of immigration laws on visitors from twenty Muslim nations, and detention of several hundred U.S. residents of Middle Eastern origin, rather than incarceration of entire ethnic groups.

In the months after 9-11, the military response overseas focused on Afghanistan, where the ruling **Taliban** regime was harboring bin Laden. Afghanistan had been wracked by civil war since the invasion by the Soviet Union in 1979. The Taliban, who came to power after the Soviet withdrawal and civil war, were politically and socially repressive rulers with few international friends. United States bombing attacks on Taliban forces began in early October 2001, and internal opposition groups in Afghanistan threw the Taliban out of power by December. Bin Laden, however, escaped with the aid of mountainous terrain and the confusion of war. The United States and NATO allies were left with an uncertain commitment to rebuild a stable Afghanistan, which remained an active war zone where resurgent Taliban activity in 2007 and 2008 threatened previous gains. On May 2, 2011, on the orders of President Barack Obama, U.S. forces would bring some closure to the past decade when they conducted a raid that found and killed Osama bin Laden inside a private residence in Abbottabad, Pakistan.

## Iraq and Conflicts in the Middle East

Even while the United States was intervening in Afghanistan, the administration was extending its attention to other nations that supported or condoned anti-American terrorists or had the potential to produce chemical, biological, or nuclear **weapons of mass destruction**. George Bush named North Korea, Iran, and Iraq as an "axis of evil" for these reasons, and then focused on Iraq. After the Gulf War, Iraq had grudgingly accepted a United Nations (UN) requirement that it eliminate such weapons, but gradually made UN inspections impossible. This resistance caused Bush to make the overthrow of Iraq's ruthless dictator, Saddam Hussein, the center of foreign policy. In effect, he declared one small, possibly dangerous nation to be the greatest menace the United States faced.

In addition to the direct fallout from the Persian Gulf War, the background to the deep-seated tensions in the Middle East included U.S. support of Israel amidst the deterioration of relations between Israel and the Arab Palestinians in territories occupied by Israel since 1967. The United States has consistently backed Israel since the 1960s. The cornerstones of U.S. policy have been the full endorsement of Israel's right to exist with secure borders and agreement on the right of Palestinians to a national state—in effect, a policy of coexistence. The United States helped to broker an Israeli-Egyptian peace agreement in 1977 and agreements pointing toward an independent Palestinian state in the 1990s. But hard-line Israeli governments have taken advantage of U.S. support from the 1980s in Lebanon (see Chapter 30) to the present.

In 2001–2002, the United States watched from the sidelines as agreements for transition to a Palestinian state fell apart. Palestinian extremists and suicide bombers and an Israeli government that favored military responses locked each other into a downward spiral that approached civil war. As a result, many Arabs identified the United States

31.1

31.2

31.3

31.4

31.5

31.6

**Department of Homeland Security** Federal superagency created in 2002 with responsibility for border control and transportation security.

**Taliban** Muslim fundamentalist political organization that has contested for control of Afghanistan in opposition to the United States.

**weapons of mass destruction** Weapons such as nuclear bombs and biological agents capable of inflicting massive casualties on civilian populations.

31.1

31.2

31.3

31.4

31.5

31.6

as an enemy of Arab nations and peoples. Israel's decision in 2005 to withdraw from the Gaza Strip and transfer authority there to the Palestinian government was a step toward resolution that unfortunately led to radical takeover there in 2007–2008. The deep and long unsolvable Israeli-Palestinian conflict helps to explain anti-American terrorism among Arabs, and sometimes other Muslims.

In the spring and summer of 2002, the administration escalated threats of unilateral intervention to change the Iraqi regime and began preparations for a second war in the Persian Gulf region. On October 10, Congress authorized preemptive military action against Iraq. However, international pressure from unenthusiastic allies and from other Arab nations persuaded Bush to put diplomacy ahead of war and devote two months to making his case at the United Nations. On November 8, the UN Security Council unanimously adopted a compromise resolution that gave Iraq three and a half months to allow full and open inspections before military action might be considered. In the following months, UN inspectors searched Iraqi military sites while the United States built up forces in the Middle East in preparation for war. On March 17, 2003, Bush suspended further diplomatic efforts, and on March 19, a full-scale U.S.-British invasion of Iraq began (see Map 31.2).

The war to overthrow Saddam Hussein was a success as a large-scale military operation. Heavy bombing disrupted the communications and command systems for Iraq's armed forces, while the technological superiority of the U.S. armed forces overwhelmed them. United States troops took control of Baghdad without the door-to-door

**MAP 31.2 U.S. MILITARY INVOLVEMENT IN WESTERN ASIA** Beginning in 2001, the United States engaged in major and continuous military operations in western Asia. Operation Enduring Freedom in late 2001 deposed the Taliban regime in Afghanistan and installed a democratic government in Kabul and vicinity, although the mountainous southeastern border of Afghanistan remained insecure. The United States, Britain, and other coalition allies invaded Iraq in March 2003 and defeated the regular Iraqi military in less than a month. However, guerrilla insurgency and terrorism continued to challenge the U.S. presence.

31.1

31.2

31.3

31.4

31.5

**31.6**

fighting that many had feared. On May 1, 2003, President Bush declared "mission accomplished"—that U.S. and British forces now controlled Iraq and major combat operations in Iraq were over.

Peace proved far more difficult than war. Reconstruction of damaged bridges, roads, water systems, and electrical systems took far longer than expected, and many basic services were still fragile or nonexistent four years after the U.S. invasion. Meanwhile, American troops and relief workers were the continuing targets of car bombs, booby-trapped highways, mortar attacks, and similar guerrilla resistance.

By 2007, a consensus had emerged among both critics of the war and realistic supporters that the United States had overthrown Saddam without any clear plan for next steps. Because of decisions by Secretary of Defense Donald Rumsfeld, the occupation force was inadequate in size from the start. United States officials dismantled the Iraqi army and police, putting 650,000 unemployed but armed men onto the streets. The decision to shut down state industries and purge members of Saddam's political party from low-level government jobs like schoolteachers created massive unemployment. The result was the decimation of Iraq's middle class, a collapse of living standards, and the creation of roughly 2 million refugees who fled Iraq's new chaos for neighboring nations. However, a "surge" of additional U.S. forces in 2007 did help to stabilize Iraq, paving the way for gradual transfer of authority to the reconstructed Iraqi government over the next years.

President Obama was finally able to end U.S. combat operations in Iraq in 2011. Nine years of war and occupation cost 4,488 American lives and more than $750 billion directly, with large delayed costs such as care for veterans yet to be counted. It left Iraq a tenuous but independent democracy struggling to reconcile competing ethnic and religious groups. By comparison, the U.S. war effort in Iraq was substantially smaller than that in Vietnam, with roughly 1 million members of the armed forces doing tours of duty in Iraq compared with 2.7 million in Vietnam.

The aftermath of the war also created political problems for George Bush. A systematic search found no active production facilities or stockpiles for chemical, nuclear, or biological weapons of mass destruction. In October 2004, the final report of the U.S. bomb hunters concluded that Saddam had disbanded his chemical and nuclear weapons efforts after 1991, refuting one of the basic justifications for the war. The continuing necessity to mobilize National Guard and reserve units met heavy criticism. The need to keep an occupying army in Iraq stretched the military close to the breaking point at the same time that the United States remained embroiled in Afghanistan well into the second decade of the century.

# Turmoil At Home

**31.6** How did the government and the American people respond to the repeated domestic crises and economic challenges of the twenty-first century?

Wars past and present were the pivotal issue in the 2004 election. George W. Bush argued for staying the course with the same administration. Democratic candidate John Kerry had a liberal voting record as a Massachusetts senator and decorations for meritorious service in Vietnam, but central to the Republican campaign were attacks on the veracity of his war record. A wild card was the issue of same-sex marriage. Courts in Massachusetts and politicians in Oregon and San Francisco decided that legal marriage could not be denied to same-sex couples. Their actions mobilized religious and cultural conservatives and led to successful ballot measures banning same-sex marriage in eleven states.

Bush won a solid although not overwhelming victory that helped Republicans extend their lead in Congress. Commentators liked to talk about a nation divided on issues of morality between Democratic "blue states" and Republican "red states" (colors drawn from television maps of election results). In fact, many states remained closely divided and only three shifted from one party to the other (New Hampshire to Kerry, and Iowa and New Mexico to Bush). Pundits also claimed that Bush used the issue of

31.1

31.2

31.3

31.4

31.5

**31.6**

"moral values," including opposition to same-sex marriage, to mobilize voters, but he did not do any better among regular churchgoers in 2004 than in 2000.

## Hurricane and Financial Storm

As the nation worried about the open-ended commitment in Iraq, it received a devastating reminder of vulnerability when Hurricane Katrina devastated the Gulf Coast at the end of August 2005. The storm first seemed to spare New Orleans, much of which lies below sea level, but its backlash breached levees that protected the city. Much of the city and its surroundings flooded. Tens of thousands of residents who had not evacuated found themselves trapped in homes or huddled in overcrowded shelters. The slowness and inadequacy of the emergency response raised serious doubts about the effectiveness of the Department of Homeland Security and its Federal Emergency Management Agency and revealed the deep fault lines that still separated the poor from the larger society—exacerbated in New Orleans by the fact that most of the poor residents were African American.

In the immediate aftermath of the storm, the number of residents within the city limits fell by more than 50 percent. Residents in the flooded neighborhoods listened to experts suggest permanent downsizing while they wondered about rebuilding their lives. During the next several years, the city did make a partial recovery. The tourist business came back strong and many residents returned, but seven years later substantial areas were still not rebuilt and the population was still well under its starting point in 2005.

Then came the crash of 2008: A financial meltdown up-ended the political jockeying within a closely divided Congress with a series of stunning financial blows. The national economy began to weaken in 2007 because of pressure on housing prices. Especially in the Southwest and Southeast, housing values had inflated beyond the actual level of demand as buyers counted on the ability to resell at a high price. So-called subprime mortgage lending added to the bubble as lenders abandoned conservative practices to make incautious loans to buyers without adequate incomes and resources. Bundling these loans together and reselling them as "black box" investments added further instability. Through 2007 and into 2008, mortgage defaults increased and housing prices plummeted, knocking out one of the main props of extraordinarily high stock market indexes.

By mid-2008, declining real estate values and rising unemployment threatened the banking system, because many banks held now worthless mortgages as part of their required assets. Big investment banks and insurance companies tottered or failed, and stock market indices dropped by close to 50 percent from their highs (including a plunge of 22 percent during the second week of October), wiping out individual nest eggs and retirement accounts. Only a huge influx of government cash and guarantees saved banking from the effects of "toxic" assets, largely through the **Troubled Asset Relief Program (TARP)** that Congress approved in October 2008. TARP authorized up to $700 billion for government purchase or guarantee of illiquid and difficult-to-value mortgages and other bank assets. The federal government also used TARP funds to buy preferred stock in major banks as an additional way to shore them up. Despite being deeply unpopular with the public, who saw it as rewarding bad behavior, this quick action saved the national—and probably international—financial system from a catastrophic meltdown. Only $410 billion of the $700 billon was actually used, and the federal government has recovered nearly all of its investment.

Another vital but unpopular intervention was direct government involvement in the troubled automobile industry. Chrysler, always the smallest of the three Detroit automakers, had been acquired by the German auto giant Daimler from 1998 to 2007. In June 2009, after large infusions of federal aid failed to stem its cash flow problems, the company reorganized with the Italian automaker Fiat as 20 percent owner, the United States and Canadian governments as 10 percent owners, and the rest owned by the United Auto Workers health care trust. General Motors (GM) also went through bankruptcy in July 2009, despite massive infusions of cash from both the Bush and Obama administrations. The company shed its overseas brands (Saab, Opel) and

**Troubled Asset Relief Program (TARP)** Federal program in 2008 to purchase or guarantee shaky bank assets to protect the economy from widespread bank failures.

several domestic makes (Pontiac, Saturn, Hummer). Chevrolet, Buick, Cadillac, and GMC were sold to a new General Motors Company in which the U.S. government took a majority share and the Canadian government, UAW, and bondholders the rest. With this help, GM returned to profitability with positive spillover effects for the entire economy by 2011. Chrysler paid back most of its loans, and the government stood to recoup more than three-fourths of its investment.

## The Obama Phenomenon

With the economy shedding jobs and two wars still unresolved, 2008 was not a promising year for either recent college graduates looking for work or Republicans running for office. In this context that favored Democrats, Americans in 2008 faced a presidential election campaign with two improbable candidates. The Republicans nominated John McCain, an Arizona senator who had been a prisoner of war during the Vietnam War and who cultivated a reputation as a maverick. Nevertheless, he outlasted more mainstream candidates to win his party's nomination. Democrats had a hard-fought contest between Hillary Rodham Clinton, who hoped to be the first woman nominated for president by a major party, and Barack Obama, an Illinois senator who became the first African American nominee. Although Obama won the nomination with surprising ease, Democrats would have made history with either candidate.

Democrats capitalized on Republican problems with the more effective campaign. McCain divided his potential supporters by choosing Alaska governor Sarah Palin as his vice presidential running mate. A conservative suburban politician, Palin's short political resume and home state gave her populist appeal but left her unprepared for the national spotlight. Obama meanwhile generated enthusiasm among younger, often first-time voters as well as middle-class independents. The result was a solid victory in which Democrats added swing states like Virginia, North Carolina, Iowa, and Colorado to their northern and West Coast strongholds (see Table 31.5 and Map 31.3).

The United States passed a tremendously important step in its national maturity by electing an African American as president, but the enthusiasm of Obama's inauguration was not enough to overcome the realities of political deadlock. Obama secured a substantial economic stimulus package to fight the deep recession, his administration began to reinvigorate protections for workers and the environment, and he tapped Sonya Sotomayor to be the first Latina on the Supreme Court. He showed his pragmatic approach by carefully assessing the situation in Afghanistan and authorizing a cautious expansion of the U.S. commitment there. Reform measures that extended health insurance to tens of

**TABLE 31.5** CORE SUPPORT FOR REPUBLICANS AND DEMOCRATS IN 2008 AND 2012

|  | Republicans | Democrats |
|---|---|---|
| Age | 60 and older | 18–29 years old |
| Religion | White Protestants | Jews |
|  | Evangelicals |  |
|  | Regular churchgoers |  |
| Education |  | Less than high school |
|  |  | Postgraduate education |
| Family Income |  | Under $50,000 |
| Sex |  | Women |
| Race and Ethnicity | Whites | African Americans |
|  |  | Latinos |
|  |  | Asian Americans |
| Geography | South Central states | Pacific Coast |
|  | Appalachian states | Northeast |
|  |  | Great Lakes states |
| Size of Community | Rural areas and small towns | Large cities |

31.1

31.2

31.3

31.4

31.5

31.6

31.1

31.2

31.3

31.4

31.5

31.6

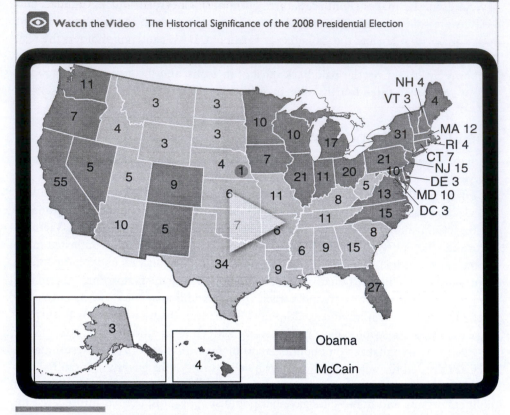

Watch the Video   The Historical Significance of the 2008 Presidential Election

**MAP 31.3  THE ELECTION OF 2008**  In 2008, Barrack Obama won the presidency by holding the reliably Democratic Northeast and Pacific Coast and winning swing states in the Rocky Mountains (Colorado, New Mexico), the Midwest (Ohio, Indiana, Iowa), and the Southeast (Virginia, North Carolina, Florida).

millions of Americans nearly stalled on three-way disagreement among Republicans, conservative Democrats, and liberal Democrats. With great perseverance, Obama in March 2010 was able to sign landmark legislation that promised to have the long-run effect of reducing economic inequality as well as improving access to medical care. However, deep opposition to the legislation's "individual mandate," a requirement that everyone obtain health insurance, made it a continuing political issue. In June 2012, the Supreme Court upheld the mandate, ending the lawsuits but not the controversy.

The economy also remained troubled. In his first months in office, Obama persuaded Congress to adopt a set of spending measures to increase demand and get the economy moving. This stimulus package prevented a plunge into a deep depression and prevented disastrous job losses, but it was not large enough to trigger much new employment. The banking system stabilized in 2009 and the stock market regained about half of its losses (it would make close to a full recovery by 2012). However, the succession of financial crises and the virtual shutdown of private construction left the United States mired in what people began to call the Great Recession. Small businesses found it hard to secure credit, and unemployment peaked above 10 percent in October 2009 before a slow economic recovery began in 2010 and 2011.

## Partisan Politics

Barrack Obama, although moderate in his approach to public issues, inspired intense hostility from a fragment of the American people. Conservatives claimed, with no substantiation, that he was following a blueprint to convert the United States to socialism. Significant numbers of Americans continued to believe that he was a Muslim, despite his past membership in Christian churches and his family's regular attendance at Christian services. Others remained convinced that he was not a natural-born citizen of the United States, and thus not qualified for the presidency, although the evidence was overwhelming that he was born on August 4, 1961, in the state of Hawaii.

The Obama family brought youthful energy to the White House reminiscent of the Kennedy family in the 1960s and Theodore Roosevelt's family in the first years of the twentieth century.

31.1

31.2

31.3

31.4

31.5

31.6

Even leaders in the Republican Party were sometimes unwilling to directly refute these inaccurate beliefs, presumably for the political advantage of mobilizing extremely conservative voters.

More directly impacting national politics was a paralyzing debate over the federal budget that effectively deadlocked Congress for much of 2010, 2011, and 2012. In particular, the mid-term elections in 2010 swept several dozen deeply conservative Republicans into Congress and gave them an effective veto over national policy. Often associated with the "Tea Party" movement, these newcomers to politics focused on the single issue of reducing the admittedly large and growing federal budget deficit. Their preferred solution was to slash federal spending while holding or reducing tax rates. Democrats countered by defending federal programs and pointing to the increasing inequality of wealth in the United States. Their solution to the deficit included limited program cuts along with new taxes on the wealthy—ideas that were unacceptable to many Republicans.

## Election 2012

The remarkable 2012 presidential election pitted two candidates from groups that had historically been marginalized in American society—Mormon Mitt Romney for the Republicans and African American Barack Obama for the Democrats. The significance of this new inclusiveness, however, was obscured by a bitter campaign that highlighted the differences that had divided the nation in the previous four years, especially over health care and the economy.

The result was a surprisingly comfortable reelection victory for Obama, whose margin in the popular vote was 3.2 million (nearly 51 percent of all votes to 48 percent for Romney), making him one of only three Democratic presidents to take a majority of

31.1
31.2
31.3
31.4
31.5
31.6

## From Then to Now
# America's Mission to the World

O n April 2, 1917, President Woodrow Wilson addressed Congress and asked for a declaration of war against Germany. Germany's decision to engage in unrestricted submarine warfare had made that nation the enemy of international law and morality.

Wilson argued the need for the United States to protect its citizens, but he also proclaimed a crusade to make "the world safe for democracy." Wilson's idealism echoed repeatedly through the twentieth century—in Franklin Roosevelt's proclamation of the Four Freedoms, in John Kennedy's claim that Americans would "bear any burden" in the defense of liberty, in Jimmy Carter's emphasis on advancing human rights in other nations.

But the clearest echo came in January 2005, in the second inaugural address of George W. Bush. Like Wilson, Bush proclaimed that the United States has a mission and destiny

In April 1917, two months after Germany initiated unrestricted submarine warfare, president Woodrow Wilson asked Congress to formalize a state of war and also promised "a firm hand of stern repression" against any disloyalty at home—a prelude to substantial curtailment of free speech in the United States for the duration of the war.

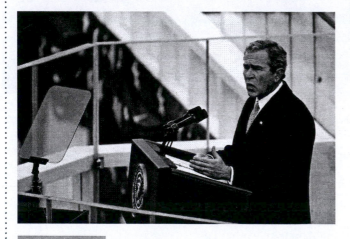

United States president George W. Bush delivers his inauguration speech in January 2005.

to actively and tirelessly extend democracy throughout the world. "It is the policy of the United States to seek and support the growth of democratic movements and institutions in every nation and culture, with the ultimate goal of ending tyranny in our world. America's influence is considerable and we will use it confidently."

**Question for Discussion**

- In what circumstances might a sense of mission enhance the effectiveness of U.S. foreign policy? When might it create problems?

the popular vote in successive elections. Those votes translated into 332 electoral votes for Obama and 206 for Romney. Congress remained divided, with Democrats a majority in the Senate and Republicans retaining their edge in the House of Representatives. Continued political conflict and deadlock over key economic issues seemed a likely prospect.

Analysis of the election showed Obama gaining votes among the nation's growing Latino and Asian American populations and holding his advantage among women and younger votes, although by smaller margins than in 2008. Much of the campaigning, from candidate appearances to television advertising and grassroots organizing, focused on fewer than ten "battleground states" or "toss-up states" such as Ohio, Virginia, Colorado, and Florida. Obama's ability to carry all but one of these states, even if only by narrow margins, returned him to the White House.

# Conclusion

If a dominant theme ran through the changes and challenges of the 1990s and the new century, it was interconnection. The Internet and cell phones brought instant communication. Corporate mismanagement affected far more people than before because of pensions and savings invested in the stock market. Whether by television or Twitter, information—and sometimes real news—traveled faster than ever before.

Despite what some might have wished, Americans also found themselves deeply connected with the rest of the world (see Figure 31.1). The nation undertook military commitments first in Europe and then in Asia and North Africa. International connection also had economic and environmental implications. Americans enjoyed the benefits of open trade and cheap imports, but hovering in the background were global environmental concerns such as global warming caused or accelerated by massive use of fossil fuels. Climate change is a truly international problem that cannot be solved within national boundaries or politics. The same will be true of the necessity to adjust to a world in which petroleum will become increasingly scarce.

Americans have seldom made their personal journeys in isolation. We have depended on our communities, and we see the consequences when the failure of community support throws us on our own, as happened to some in New Orleans in 2005. We welcome refugees from tyranny and journey across oceans to help others. In the coming decades, our community will increasingly span the entire globe as we face the challenges of economic, environmental, and political change. We—the authors of this book—look forward to learning and writing about these new journeys in the years to come.

**For Suggested Readings go to MyHistoryLab.**

31.1

31.2

31.3

31.4

31.5

31.6

# Chapter Review

## Politics of the Center

**31.1** How did Bill Clinton try to capture the political center? p. 919

President Clinton successfully pursued neoliberal policies that emphasized economic growth. However, his personal indiscretions led to deeply partisan politics and an impeachment trial in the later years of the 1990s.

## A New Economy?

**31.2** What role did new information technologies play in the economic boom of the 1990s? p. 927

Growing international trade and the explosive growth of computer technology and instant communications fueled a decade of prosperity that brought employment gains, reduced the federal budget deficit, and reestablished the United States as dominant in the world economy.

## Broadening Democracy

**31.3** What gains did women and minorities make in national politics in the 1990s? p. 932

Women, African Americans, and Latinos all gained significantly in their political roles and influence. However, those very gains helped to deepen divisions over immigration policy, affirmative action, and other policies that were directly connected to the nation's racial differences.

## Edging into a New Century

**31.4** What were the key goals of George W. Bush's presidency? p. 939

The initial goals of the Bush administration were conservative in two ways, intending to limit the role of the federal government in domestic affairs and to reduce the involvement of the United States in multilateral foreign policy involving international cooperation.

## Paradoxes of Power

**31.5** How did the terrorist attacks of September 11, 2001, change foreign policy for the following decade? p. 942

The United States responded to terrorist attacks on the World Trade Center and Pentagon by engaging in a permanent "war on terror." The attacks also paved the way for the nation to wage protracted wars in Afghanistan and Iraq.

## Turmoil at Home

**31.6** How did the government and the American people respond to the repeated domestic crises and economic challenges of the twenty-first century? p. 947

American public life showed contradictory tendencies. A deep partisan division limited the ability of either Republicans or Democrats to achieve their agendas, even while the election and reelection of Barrack Obama reflected the possibility of fundamental political realignment.

# Timeline

**1992**
Politics of the Center—Bill Clinton elected president
`1992`

`1993`
**1993**
New Economy—Congress approves the North American Free Trade Agreement (NAFTA)

**1999**
Politics of the Center—Senate acquits Clinton of impeachment charges
`1999`

`2000`
**2000**
Edging into a New Century—George W. Bush defeats Al Gore in nation's closest presidential election

**2001**
Edging into a New Century—Congress passes massive ten-year tax reduction
`2001`
**Paradoxes of Power**—Terrorists crash airliners into World Trade Center and Pentagon

`2003`
**2003**
Paradoxes of Power—U.S. and British troops invade Iraq and topple government of Saddam Hussein

**2005**
Turmoil at Home—Hurricane Katrina devastates New Orleans
`2005`

`2008`
**2008**
Turmoil at Home—Financial collapse ushers in the Great Recession; Barack Obama elected president

**2010**
Turmoil at Home—Congress expands health insurance coverage
`2010`

# The Declaration of Independence

When in the course of human events it becomes necessary for one people to dissolve the political bands which have connected them with another and to assume, among the powers of the earth, the separate and equal station to which the laws of nature and of nature's God entitle them, a decent respect to the opinions of mankind requires that they should declare the causes which impel them to the separation.

We hold these truths to be self-evident, that all men are created equal; that they are endowed by their Creator with certain unalienable rights; that among these are life, liberty, and the pursuit of happiness. That, to secure these rights, governments are instituted among men, deriving their just powers from the consent of the governed; that, whenever any form of government becomes destructive of these ends, it is the right of the people to alter or to abolish it, and to institute a new government, laying its foundation on such principles, and organizing its powers in such form, as to them shall seem most likely to effect their safety and happiness. Prudence, indeed, will dictate that governments long established should not be changed for light and transient causes; and, accordingly, all experience hath shown that mankind are more disposed to suffer, while evils are sufferable, than to right themselves by abolishing the forms to which they are accustomed. But when a long train of abuses and usurpations, pursuing invariably the same object, evinces a design to reduce them under absolute despotism, it is their right, it is their duty, to throw off such government and to provide new guards for their future security. Such has been the patient sufferance of these colonies, and such is now the necessity which constrains them to alter their former systems of government. The history of the present King of Great Britain is a history of repeated injuries and usurpations, all having, in direct object, the establishment of an absolute tyranny over these States. To prove this, let facts be submitted to a candid world:

He has refused his assent to laws the most wholesome and necessary for the public good.

He has forbidden his governors to pass laws of immediate and pressing importance, unless suspended in their operation till his assent should be obtained; and, when so suspended, he has utterly neglected to attend to them.

He has refused to pass other laws for the accommodation of large districts of people, unless those people would relinquish the right of representation in the legislature, a right inestimable to them and formidable to tyrants only.

He has called together legislative bodies at places unusual, uncomfortable, and distant from the depository of their public records, for the sole purpose of fatiguing them into compliance with his measures.

He has dissolved representative houses, repeatedly for opposing, with manly firmness, his invasions on the rights of the people.

He has refused, for a long time after such dissolutions, to cause others to be elected; whereby the legislative powers, incapable of annihilation, have returned to the people at large for their exercise; the state remaining, in the meantime, exposed to all the danger of invasion from without and convulsions within.

He has endeavored to prevent the population of these States; for that purpose, obstructing the laws for naturalization of foreigners, refusing to pass others to encourage their migration hither, and raising the conditions of new appropriations of lands.

He has obstructed the administration of justice by refusing his assent to laws for establishing judiciary powers.

He has made judges dependent on his will alone for the tenure of their offices and the amount and payment of their salaries.

He has erected a multitude of new offices and sent hither swarms of officers to harass our people and eat out their substance.

He has kept among us, in time of peace, standing armies, without the consent of our legislatures.

He has affected to render the military independent of, and superior to, the civil power.

He has combined with others to subject us to a jurisdiction foreign to our Constitution and unacknowledged by our laws, giving his assent to their acts of pretended legislation—

For quartering large bodies of armed troops among us;

For protecting them by mock trial, from punishment for any murders which they should commit on the inhabitants of these States;

For cutting off our trade with all parts of the world;

For imposing taxes on us without our consent;

For depriving us, in many cases, of the benefit of trial by jury;

For transporting us beyond seas to be tried for pretended offences;

For abolishing the free system of English laws in a neighboring province, establishing therein an arbitrary government, and enlarging its boundaries, so as to render it at once an example and fit instrument for introducing the same absolute rule into these colonies;

For taking away our charters, abolishing our most valuable laws, and altering, fundamentally, the powers of our governments.

For suspending our own legislatures and declaring themselves invested with power to legislate for us in all cases whatsoever.

He has abdicated government here by declaring us out of his protection and waging war against us.

He has plundered our seas, ravaged our coasts, burnt our towns, and destroyed the lives of our people.

He is, at this time, transporting large armies of foreign mercenaries to complete the works of death, desolation, and tyranny already begun with circumstances of cruelty and perfidy scarcely paralleled in the most barbarous ages, and totally unworthy the head of a civilized nation.

He has constrained our fellow citizens, taken captive on the high seas, to bear arms against their country, to become the executioners of their friends and brethren, or to fall themselves by their hands.

From *The American Journey*, Seventh Edition. Goldfield, Abbott, Anderson, Argersinger, Argersinger and Barney Copyright © 2014 by Pearson Education, Inc. All rights reserved.

He has excited domestic insurrections amongst us and has endeavored to bring on the inhabitants of our frontiers, the merciless Indian savages, whose known rule of warfare is an undistinguished destruction of all ages, sexes, and conditions.

In every stage of these oppressions, we have petitioned for redress in the most humble terms; our repeated petitions have been answered only by repeated injury. A prince whose character is thus marked by every act which may define a tyrant is unfit to be the ruler of a free people.

Nor have we been wanting in attention to our British brethren. We have warned them, from time to time, of attempts made by their legislature to extend an unwarrantable jurisdiction over us. We have reminded them of the circumstances of our emigration and settlement here. We have appealed to their native justice and magnanimity, and we have conjured them, by the ties of our common kindred, to disavow these usurpations, which would inevitably interrupt our connections and correspondence. They, too, have been deaf to the voice of justice and consanguinity. We must, therefore, acquiesce in the necessity which denounces our separation, and hold them, as we hold the rest of mankind, enemies in war, in peace, friends.

We, therefore, the representatives of the United States of America, in general Congress assembled, appealing to the Supreme Judge of the world for the rectitude of our intentions, do, in the name and by the authority of the good people of these colonies, solemnly publish and declare, that these united colonies are, and of right ought to be, free and independent states: that they are absolved from all allegiance to the British Crown, and that all political connection between them and the state of Great Britain is, and ought to be, totally dissolved; and that, as free and independent states, they have full power to levy war, conclude peace, contract alliances, establish commerce, and to do all other acts and things which independent states may of right do. And, for the support of this declaration, with a firm reliance on the protection of Divine Providence, we mutually pledge to each other our lives, our fortunes, and our sacred honor.

# The Articles of Confederation and Perpetual Union*

Between the states of New Hampshire, Massachusetts-bay Rhode Island and Providence Plantations, Connecticut, New York, New Jersey, Pennsylvania, Delaware, Maryland, Virginia, North Carolina, South Carolina, and Georgia.

## Article 1

The Stile of this Confederacy shall be "The United States of America."

## Article 2

Each state retains its sovereignty, freedom, and independence, and every power, jurisdiction, and right, which is not by this Confederation expressly delegated to the United States, in Congress assembled.

## Article 3

The said States hereby severally enter into a firm league of friendship with each other, for their common defense, the security of their liberties, and their mutual and general welfare, binding themselves to assist each other, against all force offered to, or attacks made upon them, or any of them, on account of religion, sovereignty, trade, or any other pretense whatever.

## Article 4

The better to secure and perpetuate mutual friendship and intercourse among the people of the different States in this Union, the free inhabitants of each of these States, paupers, vagabonds, and fugitives from justice excepted, shall be entitled to all privileges and immunities of free citizens in the several States; and the people of each State shall have free ingress and regress to and from any other State, and shall enjoy therein all the privileges of trade and commerce, subject to the same duties, impositions, and restrictions as the inhabitants thereof respectively, provided that such restrictions shall not extend so far as to prevent the removal of property imported into any State, to any other State of which the owner is an inhabitant; provided also that no imposition, duties or restriction shall be laid by any State, on the property of the United States, or either of them.

If any person guilty of, or charged with, treason, felony, or other high misdemeanor in any State, shall flee from justice, and be found in any of the United States, he shall, upon demand of the Governor or executive power of the State from which he fled, be delivered up and removed to the State having jurisdiction of his offense.

Full faith and credit shall be given in each of these States to the records, acts, and judicial proceedings of the courts and magistrates of every other State.

## Article 5

For the most convenient management of the general interests of the United States, delegates shall be annually appointed in such manner as the legislatures of each State shall direct, to meet in Congress on the first Monday in November, in every year, with a power reserved to each State to recall its delegates, or any of them, at any time within the year, and to send others in their stead for the remainder of the year.

No State shall be represented in Congress by less than two, nor by more than seven members; and no person shall be capable of being a delegate for more than three years in any term of six years; nor shall any person, being a delegate, be capable of holding any office under the United States, for which he, or another for his benefit, receives any salary, fees or emolument of any kind.

Each State shall maintain its own delegates in a meeting of the States, and while they act as members of the committee of the States.

In determining questions in the United States in Congress assembled, each State shall have one vote.

Freedom of speech and debate in Congress shall not be impeached or questioned in any court or place out of Congress, and the members of Congress shall be protected in their persons from arrests or imprisonments, during the time of their going to and from, and attendence on Congress, except for treason, felony, or breach of the peace.

## Article 6

No State, without the consent of the United States in Congress assembled, shall send any embassy to, or receive any embassy from, or enter into any conference, agreement, alliance or treaty

*Agreed to in Congress November 15, 1777; ratified March 1781.

with any King, Prince or State; nor shall any person holding any office of profit or trust under the United States, or any of them, accept any present, emolument, office or title of any kind whatever from any King, Prince or foreign State; nor shall the United States in Congress assembled, or any of them, grant any title of nobility.

No two or more States shall enter into any treaty, confederation or alliance whatever between them, without the consent of the United States in Congress assembled, specifying accurately the purposes for which the same is to be entered into, and how long it shall continue.

No State shall lay any imposts or duties, which may interfere with any stipulations in treaties, entered into by the United States in Congress assembled, with any King, Prince or State, in pursuance of any treaties already proposed by Congress, to the courts of France and Spain.

No vessel of war shall be kept up in time of peace by any State, except such number only, as shall be deemed necessary by the United States in Congress assembled, for the defense of such State, or its trade; nor shall any body of forces be kept up by any State in time of peace, except such number only, as in the judgement of the United States in Congress assembled, shall be deemed requisite to garrison the forts necessary for the defense of such State; but every State shall always keep up a well-regulated and disciplined militia, sufficiently armed and accoutered, and shall provide and constantly have ready for use, in public stores, a due number of filed pieces and tents, and a proper quantity of arms, ammunition and camp equipage.

No State shall engage in any war without the consent of the United States in Congress assembled, unless such State be actually invaded by enemies, or shall have received certain advice of a resolution being formed by some nation of Indians to invade such State, and the danger is so imminent as not to admit of a delay, till the United States in Congress assembled can be consulted; nor shall any State grant commissions to any ships or vessels of war, nor letters of marque or reprisal, except it be after a declaration of war by the United States in Congress assembled, and then only against the Kingdom or State and the subjects thereof, against which war has been so declared, and under such regulations as shall be established by the United States in Congress assembled, unless such State be infested by pirates, in which case vessels of war may be fitted out for that occasion, and kept so long as the danger shall continue, or until the United States in Congress assembled shall determine otherwise.

## Article 7

When land forces are raised by any State for the common defense, all officers of or under the rank of colonel, shall be appointed by the legislature of each State respectively, by whom such forces shall be raised, or in such manner as such State shall direct, and all vacancies shall be filled up by the State which first made the appointment.

## Article 8

All charges of war, and all other expenses that shall be incurred for the common defense or general welfare, and allowed by the United States in Congress assembled, shall be defrayed out of a common treasury, which shall be supplied by the several States in proportion to the value of all land within each State, granted to or surveyed for any person, as such land and the buildings and improvements thereon shall be estimated according to such mode as the United States in Congress assembled, shall from time to time direct and appoint.

The taxes for paying that proportion shall be laid and levied by the authority and direction of the legislatures of the several States within the time agreed upon by the United States in Congress assembled.

## Article 9

The United States in Congress assembled, shall have the sole and exclusive right and power of determining on peace and war, except in the cases mentioned in the sixth article; of sending and receiving ambassadors; entering into treaties and alliances, provided that no treaty of commerce shall be made whereby the legislative power of the respective States shall be restrained from imposing such imposts and duties on foreigners, as their own people are subjected to, or from prohibiting the exportation or importation of any species of goods or commodities whatsoever; of establishing rules for deciding in all cases, what captures on land or water shall be legal, and in what manner prizes taken by land or naval forces in the service of the United States shall be divided or appropriated; of granting letters of marque and reprisal in times of peace; appointing courts for the trial of piracies and felonies committed on the high seas and establishing courts for receiving and determining finally appeals in all cases of captures, provided that no member of Congress shall be appointed a judge of any of the said courts.

The United States in Congress assembled shall also be the last resort on appeal in all disputes and differences now subsisting or that hereafter may arise between two or more States concerning boundary, jurisdiction or any other causes whatever; which authority shall always be exercised in the manner following. Whenever the legislative or executive authority or lawful agent of any State in controversy with another shall present a petition to Congress stating the matter in question and praying for a hearing, notice thereof shall be given by order of Congress to the legislative or executive authority of the other State in controversy, and a day assigned for the appearance of the parties by their lawful agents, who shall then be directed to appoint by joint consent, commissioners or judges to constitute a court for hearing and determining the matter in question: but if they cannot agree, Congress shall name three persons out of each of the United States, and from the list of such persons each party shall alternately strike out one, the petitioners beginning, until the number shall be reduced to thirteen; and from that number not less than seven, nor more than nine names as Congress shall direct, shall in the presence of Congress be drawn out by lot, and the persons whose names shall be so drawn or any five of them, shall be commissioners or judges, to hear and finally determine the controversy, so always as a major part of the judges who shall hear the cause shall agree in the determination: and if either party shall neglect to attend at the day appointed, without showing reasons, which Congress shall judge sufficient, or being present shall refuse to strike, the Congress shall proceed to nominate three persons out of each State, and the secretary of Congress shall strike in behalf of such party absent or refusing; and the judgement and sentence of the court to be appointed, in the manner before prescribed, shall be final and conclusive; and if any of the parties shall refuse to submit to the authority of such court, or to appear or defend their claim or cause, the court shall nevertheless proceed to pronounce sentence, or judgement, which shall in like manner be final and decisive, the judgement or sentence and other proceedings being in either case transmitted to Congress, and lodged among the acts of Congress for the security of the parties concerned: provided that every commissioner, before he sits in judgement, shall take an oath to be administered by one of the judges of the supreme or superior court of the State, where the cause shall be tried, "well and truly to hear and determine the matter in question, according to the best of his judgement, without favor, affection or hope of reward:" provided also, that no State shall be deprived of territory for the benefit of the United States.

All controversies concerning the private right of soil claimed under different grants of two or more States, whose jurisdictions as they may respect such lands, and the States which passed such grants are adjusted, the said grants or either of them being at the same time claimed to have originated antecedent to such settlement of jurisdiction, shall on the petition of either party to the Congress of the United States, be finally determined as near as may be in the same manner as is before prescribed for deciding disputes respecting territorial jurisdiction between different States.

The United States in Congress assembled shall also have the sole and exclusive right and power of regulating the alloy and value of coin struck by their own authority, or by that of the respective States; fixing the standards of weights and measures throughout the United States; regulating the trade and managing all affairs with the Indians not members of any of the States; provided that the legislative right of any State within its own limits be not infringed or violated; establishing or regulating post offices from one State to another, throughout all the United States, and exacting such postage on the papers passing through the same as may be requisite to defray the expenses of the said office; appointing all officers of the land forces in the service of the United States, excepting regimental officers; appointing all the officers of the naval forces, and commissioning all officers whatever in the service of the United States; making rules for the government and regulation of the said land and naval forces, and directing their operations.

The United States in Congress assembled shall have authority to appoint a committee, to sit in the recess of Congress, to be denominated "A Committee of the States," and to consist of one delegate from each State; and to appoint such other committees and civil officers as may be necessary for managing the general affairs of the United States under their direction; to appoint one of their members to preside, provided that no person be allowed to serve in the office of president more than one year in any term of three years; to ascertain the necessary sums of money to be raised for the service of the United States, and to appropriate and apply the same for defraying the public expenses; to borrow money, or emit bills on the credit of the United States, transmitting every half year to the respective States an account of the sums of money so borrowed or emitted; to build and equip a navy; to agree upon the number of land forces, and to make requisitions from each State for its quota, in proportion to the number of white inhabitants in such State; which requisition shall be binding, and thereupon the legislature of each State shall appoint the regimental officers, raise the men and cloath, arm and equip them in a soldierlike manner, at the expense of the United States; and the officers and men so cloathed, armed and equipped shall march to the place appointed, and within the time agreed on by the United States in Congress assembled; but if the United States in Congress assembled shall, on consideration of circumstances judge proper that any State should not raise men, or should raise a smaller number of men than the quota thereof, such extra number shall be raised, officered, cloathed, armed and equipped in the same manner as the quota of each State, unless the legislature of such State shall judge that such extra number cannot be safely spared out in the same, in which case they shall raise, officer, cloath, arm and equip as many of such extra number as they judge can be safely spared. And the officers and men so cloathed, armed, and equipped, shall march to the place appointed, and within the time agreed on by the United States in Congress assembled.

The United States in Congress assembled shall never engage in a war, nor grant letters of marque or reprisal in time of peace, nor enter into any treaties or alliances, nor coin money, nor regulate the value thereof, nor ascertain the sums and expenses necessary for the defense and welfare of the United States, or any of them, nor emit bills, nor borrow money on the credit of the United States, nor appropriate money, nor agree upon the number of vessels of war, to be built or purchased, or the number of land or sea forces to be raised, nor appoint a commander in chief of the army or navy, unless nine States assent to the same: nor shall a question on any other point, except for adjourning from day to day be determined, unless by the votes of the majority of the United States in Congress assembled.

The Congress of the United States shall have power to adjourn to any time within the year, and to any place within the United States, so that no period of adjournment be for a longer duration than the space of six months, and shall publish the journal of their proceedings monthly, except such parts thereof relating to treaties, alliances or military operations, as in their judgement require secrecy; and the yeas and nays of the delegates of each State on any question shall be entered on the journal, when it is desired by any delegates of a State, or any of them, at his or their request shall be furnished with a transcript of the said journal, except such parts as are above excepted, to lay before the legislatures of the several States.

## Article 10

The Committee of the States, or any nine of them, shall be authorized to execute, in the recess of Congress, such of the powers of Congress as the United States in Congress assembled, by the consent of the nine States, shall from time to time think expedient to vest them with; provided that no power be delegated to the said Committee, for the exercise of which, by the Articles of Confederation, the voice of nine States in the Congress of the United States assembled is requisite.

## Article 11

Canada acceding to this confederation, and adjoining in the measures of the United States, shall be admitted into and entitled to all the advantages of this Union; but no other colony shall be admitted into the same, unless such admission be agreed to by nine States.

## Article 12

All bills of credit emitted, monies borrowed, and debts contracted by, or under the authority of Congress, before the assembling of the United States, in pursuance of the present confederation, shall be deemed and considered as a charge against the United States, for payment and satisfaction whereof the said United States, and the public faith are hereby solemnly pledged.

## Article 13

Every State shall abide by the determination of the United States in Congress assembled, on all questions which by this confederation are submitted to them. And the Articles of this Confederation shall be inviolably observed by every State, and the Union shall be perpetual; nor shall any alteration at any time hereafter be made in any of them; unless such alteration be agreed to in a Congress of the United States, and be afterwards confirmed by the legislatures of every State.

These articles shall be proposed to the legislatures of all the United States, to be considered, and if approved of by them, they are advised to authorize their delegates to ratify the same in the Congress of the United States; which being done, the same shall become conclusive.

# The Constitution of the United States of America

We the people of the United States, in order to form a more perfect union, establish justice, insure domestic tranquillity, provide for the common defense, promote the general welfare, and secure the blessings of liberty to ourselves and our posterity, do ordain and establish this Constitution for the United States of America.

## Article I

### Section 1

All legislative powers herein granted shall be vested in a Congress of the United States, which shall consist of a Senate and House of Representatives.

### Section 2

1  The House of Representatives shall be composed of members chosen every second year by the people of the several States, and the electors in each State shall have the qualifications requisite for electors of the most numerous branch of the State legislature.

2  No person shall be a representative who shall not have attained to the age of twenty-five years, and been seven years a citizen of the United States, and who shall not, when elected, be an inhabitant of that State in which he shall be chosen.

3  Representatives and direct taxes[1] shall be apportioned among the several States which may be included within this Union, according to their respective numbers, which shall be determined by adding to the whole number of free persons, including those bound to service for a term of years, and excluding Indians not taxed, three fifths of all other persons.[2] The actual enumeration shall be made within three years after the first meeting of the Congress of the United States, and within every subsequent term of ten years, in such manner as they shall by law direct. The number of representatives shall not exceed one for every thirty thousand, but each State shall have at least one representative; and until such enumeration shall be made, the State of New Hampshire shall be entitled to choose three, Massachusetts eight, Rhode Island and Providence Plantations one, Connecticut five, New York six, New Jersey four, Pennsylvania eight, Delaware one, Maryland six, Virginia ten, North Carolina five, South Carolina five, and Georgia three.

4  When vacancies happen in the representation from any State, the executive authority thereof shall issue writs of election to fill such vacancies.

5  The House of Representatives shall choose their speaker and other officers; and shall have the sole power of impeachment.

### Section 3

1  The Senate of the United States shall be composed of two senators from each State, chosen by the legislature thereof,[3] for six years; and each senator shall have one vote.

2  Immediately after they shall be assembled in consequence of the first election, they shall be divided as equally as may be into three classes. The seats of the senators of the first class shall be vacated at the expiration of the second year, of the second class at the expiration of the fourth year, and of the third class at the expiration of the sixth year, so that one third may be chosen every second year; and if vacancies happen by resignation, or otherwise, during the recess of the legislature of any State, the executive thereof may make temporary appointments until the next meeting of the legislature, which shall then fill such vacancies.[4]

3  No person shall be a senator who shall not have attained to the age of thirty years, and been nine years a citizen of the United States, and who shall not, when elected, be an inhabitant of that State for which he shall be chosen.

4  The Vice President of the United States shall be President of the Senate, but shall have no vote, unless they be equally divided.

5  The Senate shall choose their other officers, and also a president pro tempore, in the absence of the Vice President, or when he shall exercise the office of the President of the United States.

6  The Senate shall have the sole power to try all impeachments. When sitting for that purpose, they shall be on oath or affirmation. When the President of the United States is tried, the chief justice shall preside: and no person shall be convicted without the concurrence of two thirds of the members present.

7  Judgment in cases of impeachment shall not extend further than to removal from office, and disqualification to hold and enjoy any office of honor, trust or profit under the United States: but the party convicted shall nevertheless be liable and subject to indictment, trial, judgment and punishment, according to law.

### Section 4

1  The times, places, and manner of holding elections for senators and representatives, shall be prescribed in each State by the legislature thereof; but the Congress may at any time by law make or alter such regulations, except as to the places of choosing senators.

2  The Congress shall assemble at least once in every year, and such meeting shall be on the first Monday in December, unless they shall by law appoint a different day.

### Section 5

1  Each House shall be the judge of the elections, returns and qualifications of its own members, and a majority of each shall constitute a quorum to do business; but a smaller number may adjourn from day to day, and may be authorized to compel the attendance of absent members, in such manner, and under such penalties as each House may provide.

---

[1]See the Sixteenth Amendment.
[2]See the Fourteenth Amendment.

[3]See the Seventeenth Amendment.
[4]See the Seventeenth Amendment.

2  Each House may determine the rules of its proceedings, punish its members for disorderly behavior, and, with the concurrence of two thirds, expel a member.

3  Each House shall keep a journal of its proceedings, and from time to time publish the same, excepting such parts as may in their judgment require secrecy; and the yeas and nays of the members of either House on any question shall, at the desire of one fifth of those present, be entered on the journal.

4  Neither House, during the session of Congress, shall, without the consent of the other, adjourn for more than three days, nor to any other place than that in which the two Houses shall be sitting.

## Section 6

1  The senators and representatives shall receive a compensation for their services, to be ascertained by law, and paid out of the Treasury of the United States. They shall in all cases, except treason, felony, and breach of the peace, be privileged from arrest during their attendance at the session of their respective Houses, and in going to and returning from the same; and for any speech or debate in either House, they shall not be questioned in any other place.

2  No senator or representative shall, during the time for which he was elected, be appointed to any civil office under the authority of the United States, which shall have been created, or the emoluments whereof shall have been increased, during such time; and no person holding any office under the United States shall be a member of either House during his continuance in office.

## Section 7

1  All bills for raising revenue shall originate in the House of Representatives; but the Senate may propose or concur with amendments as on other bills.

2  Every bill which shall have passed the House of Representatives and the Senate, shall, before it become a law, be presented to the President of the United States; If he approves he shall sign it, but if not he shall return it, with his objections, to that House in which it shall have originated, who shall enter the objections at large on their journal, and proceed to reconsider it. If after such reconsideration two thirds of that House shall agree to pass the bill, it shall be sent, together with the objections, to the other House, by which it shall likewise be reconsidered, and if approved by two thirds of that House, it shall become a law. But in all such cases the votes of both Houses shall be determined by yeas and nays, and the names of the persons voting for and against the bill shall be entered on the journal of each House respectively. If any bill shall not be returned by the President within ten days (Sundays excepted) after it shall have been presented to him, the same shall be a law, in like manner as if he had signed it, unless the Congress by their adjournment prevent its return, in which case it shall not be a law.

3  Every order, resolution, or vote to which the concurrence of the Senate and the House of Representatives may be necessary (except on a question of adjournment) shall be presented to the President of the United States; and before the same shall take effect, shall be approved by him, or being disapproved by him, shall be repassed by two thirds of the Senate and House of Representatives, according to the rules and limitations prescribed in the case of a bill.

## Section 8

1  The Congress shall have the power.

1  To lay and collect taxes, duties, imposts, and excises, to pay the debts and provide for the common defense and general welfare of the United States; but all duties, imposts, and excises shall be uniform throughout the United States.

2  To borrow money on the credit of the United States;

3  To regulate commerce with foreign nations, and among the several States, and with the Indian tribes;

4  To establish a uniform rule of naturalization, and uniform laws on the subject of bankruptcies throughout the United States;

5  To coin money, regulate the value thereof, and of foreign coin, and fix the standard of weights and measures;

6  To provide for the punishment of counterfeiting the securities and current coin of the United States;

7  To establish post offices and post roads;

8  To promote the progress of science and useful arts, by securing for limited times to authors and inventors the exclusive right to their respective writings and discoveries;

9  To constitute tribunals inferior to the Supreme Court;

10  To define and punish piracies and felonies committed on the high seas, and offenses against the law of nations;

11  To declare war, grant letters of marque and reprisal, and make rules concerning captures on land and water;

12  To raise and support armies, but no appropriation of money to that use shall be for a longer term than two years;

13  To provide and maintain a navy;

14  To make rules for the government and regulation of the land and naval forces;

15  To provide for calling forth the militia to execute the laws of the Union, suppress insurrections and repel invasions;

16  To provide for organizing, arming, and disciplining the militia, and for governing such part of them as may be employed in the service of the United States, reserving to the States respectively, the appointment of the officers, and the authority of training the militia according to the discipline prescribed by Congress;

17  To exercise exclusive legislation in all cases whatsoever, over such district (not exceeding ten miles square) as may, by cession of particular States, and the acceptance of Congress, become the seat of the government of the United States, and to exercise like authority over all places purchased by the consent of the legislature of the State in which the same shall be, for the erection of forts, magazines, arsenals, dockyards, and other needful buildings; and

18  To make all laws which shall be necessary and proper for carrying into execution the foregoing powers, and all other powers vested by this Constitution in the government of the United States, or any department or officer thereof.

## Section 9

1  The migration or importation of such persons as any of the States now existing shall think proper to admit, shall not be prohibited by the Congress prior to the year one thousand eight hundred and eight, but a tax or duty may be imposed on such importation, not exceeding ten dollars for each person.

2  The privilege of the writ of habeas corpus shall not be suspended, unless when in cases of rebellion or invasion the public safety may require it.

3   No bill of attainder or ex post facto law shall be passed.

4   No capitation, or other direct, tax shall be laid, unless in proportion to the census or enumeration herein-before directed to be taken.[5]

5   No tax or duty shall be laid on articles exported from any State.

6   No preference shall be given by any regulation of commerce or revenue to the ports of one State over those of another: nor shall vessels bound to, or from, one State be obliged to enter, clear, or pay duties in another.

7   No money shall be drawn from the treasury, but in consequence of appropriations made by law; and a regular statement and account of the receipts and expenditures of all public money shall be published from time to time.

8   No title of nobility shall be granted by the United States: and no person holding any office of profit or trust under them, shall, without the consent of the Congress, accept of any present, emolument, office, or title, of any kind whatever, from any king, prince, or foreign State.

## Section 10

1   No State shall enter into any treaty, alliance, or confederation; grant letters of marque and reprisal; coin money; emit bills of credit; make any thing but gold and silver coin a tender in payment of debts; pass any bill of attainder, ex post facto law, or law impairing the obligation of contracts, or grant, any title of nobility.

2   No State shall, without the consent of the Congress, lay any imposts or duties on imports or exports, except what may be absolutely necessary for executing its inspection laws: and the net produce of all duties and imposts laid by any State on imports or exports, shall be for the use of the treasury of the United States; and all such laws shall be subject to the revision and control of the Congress.

3   No State shall, without the consent of the Congress, lay any duty of tonnage, keep troops, or ships of war in time of peace, enter into any agreement or compact with another State, or with a foreign power, or engage in war, unless actually invaded, or in such imminent danger as will not admit of delay.

# Article II
## Section 1

1   The executive power shall be vested in a President of the United States of America. He shall hold his office during the term of four years, and, together with the Vice President, chosen for the same term, be elected, as follows:

2   Each State shall appoint, in such manner as the legislature thereof may direct, a number of electors, equal to the whole number of senators and representatives to which the State may be entitled in the Congress: but no senator or representative, or person holding any office of trust or profit under the United States, shall be appointed an elector.

The electors shall meet in their respective States, and vote by ballot for two persons, of whom one at least shall not be an inhabitant of the same State with themselves. And they shall make a list of all the persons voted for, and of the number of votes for each; which list they shall sign and certify, and transmit sealed to the seat of the government of the United States, directed to the president of the Senate. The president of the Senate shall, in the presence of the Senate and House of Representatives, open all the certificates, and the votes shall then be counted. The person having the greatest number of votes shall be the President, if such number be a majority of the whole number of electors appointed; and if there be more than one who have such majority, and have an equal number of votes, then the House of Representatives shall immediately choose by ballot one of them for President; and if no person have a majority, then from the five highest on the list the said House shall in like manner choose the President. But in choosing the President, the votes shall be taken by States, the representation from each State having one vote; a quorum for this purpose shall consist of a member or members from two thirds of the States, and a majority of all the States shall be necessary to a choice. In every case after the choice of the President, the person having the greatest number of votes of the electors shall be the Vice President. But if there should remain two or more who have equal votes, the Senate shall choose from them by ballot the Vice President.[6]

3   The Congress may determine the time of choosing the electors, and the day on which they shall give their votes; which day shall be the same throughout the United States.

4   No person except a natural born citizen, or a citizen of the United States, at the time of the adoption of this Constitution, shall be eligible to the office of President; neither shall any person be eligible to the office who shall not have attained to the age of thirty-five years, and been fourteen years a resident within the United States.

5   In case of the removal of the President from office, or of his death, resignation, or inability to discharge the powers and duties of the said office, the same shall devolve on the Vice President, and the congress may by law provide for the case of removal, death, resignation or inability, both of the President and Vice President, declaring what officer shall then act as President, and such officer shall act accordingly until the disability be removed, or a President shall be elected.

6   The President shall, at stated times, receive for his services a compensation which shall neither be increased nor diminished during the period for which he shall have been elected, and he shall not receive within that period any other emolument from the United States, or any of them.

7   Before he enter on the execution of his office, he shall take the following oath or affirmation:—"I do solemnly swear (or affirm) that I will faithfully execute the office of President of the United States, and will to the best of my ability, preserve, protect and defend the Constitution of the United States."

## Section 2

1   The President shall be commander in chief of the army and navy of the United States, and of the militia of the several States, when called into the actual service of the United States; he may require the opinion in writing, of the principal officer in each of the executive departments, upon any subject relating to the duties of their respective offices, and he shall have power to grant reprieves and pardons for offenses against the United States, except in cases of impeachment.

---

[5]See the Sixteenth Amendment.

[6]Superseded by the Twelfth Amendment.

2 He shall have power, by and with the advice and consent of the Senate, to make treaties, provided two thirds of the senators present concur; and he shall nominate, and by and with the advice and consent of the Senate, shall appoint ambassadors, other public ministers and consuls, judges of the Supreme Court, and all other officers of the United States, whose appointments are not herein otherwise provided for, and which shall be established by law; but the Congress may by law vest the appointment of such inferior officers, as they think proper, in the President alone, in the courts of laws, or in the heads of departments.

3 The President shall have power to fill up all vacancies that may happen during the recess of the Senate, by granting commissions which shall expire at the end of their next session.

## Section 3

He shall from time to time give to the Congress information of the state of the Union, and recommend to their consideration such measures as he shall judge necessary and expedient; he may, on extraordinary occasions, convene both Houses, or either of them, and in case of disagreement between them with respect to the time of adjournment, he may adjourn them to such time as he shall think proper; he shall receive ambassadors and other public ministers; he shall take care that the laws be faithfully executed, and shall commission all the officers of the United States.

## Section 4

The President, Vice President, and all civil officers of the United States, shall be removed from office on impeachment for, and conviction of, treason, bribery, or other high crimes and misdemeanors.

# Article III

## Section 1

The judicial power of the United States shall be vested in one Supreme Court, and in such inferior courts as the Congress may from time to time ordain and establish. The judges, both of the Supreme and inferior courts, shall hold their offices during good behavior, and shall, at stated times, receive for their services, a compensation, which shall not be diminished during their continuance in office.

## Section 2

1 The judicial power shall extend to all cases, in law and equity, arising under this Constitution, the laws of the United States, and treaties made, or which shall be made, under their authority;—to all cases of admiralty and maritime jurisdiction;—to controversies to which the United States shall be a party;[7]—to controversies between two or more States;—between a State and citizens of another State;—between citizens of different States;—between citizens of the same State claiming lands under grants of different States, and between a State, or the citizens thereof, and foreign States, citizens or subjects.

2 In all cases affecting ambassadors, other public ministers and consuls, and those in which a State shall be party, the Supreme Court shall have original jurisdiction. In all the other cases before mentioned, the Supreme Court shall have appellate jurisdiction, both as to law and fact, with such exceptions, and under such regulations as the Congress shall make.

3 The trial of all crimes, except in cases of impeachment, shall be by jury; and such trial shall be held in the State where the said crimes shall have been committed; but when not committed within any State, the trial shall be such place or places as the congress may by law have directed.

## Section 3

1 Treason against the United States shall consist only in levying war against them, or in adhering to their enemies, giving them aid and comfort. No person shall be convicted of treason unless on the testimony of two witnesses to the same overt act, or on confession in open court.

2 The Congress shall have power to declare the punishment of treason, but no attainder of treason shall work corruption of blood, or forfeiture except during the life of the person attained.

# Article IV

## Section 1

Full faith and credit shall be given in each State to the public acts, records, and judicial proceedings of every other State. And the Congress may by general laws prescribe the manner in which such acts, records and proceedings shall be proved, and the effect thereof.

## Section 2

1 The citizens of each State shall be entitled to all privileges and immunities of citizens in the several States.[8]

2 A person charged in any State with treason, felony, or other crime, who shall flee from justice, and be found in another State, shall on demand of the executive authority of the State from which he fled, be delivered up to be removed to the State having jurisdiction of the crime.

3 No person held to service or labor in one State under the laws thereof, escaping into another, shall, in consequence of any law or regulation therein, be discharged from such service or labor, but shall be delivered up on claim of the party to whom such service or labor may be due.[9]

## Section 3

1 New States may be admitted by the Congress into this Union; but no new State shall be formed or erected within the jurisdiction of any other State, nor any State be formed by the junction of two or more States, or parts of States, without the consent of the legislatures of the States concerned as well as of the Congress.

2 The Congress shall have power to dispose of and make all needful rules and regulations respecting the territory or other property belonging to the United States; and nothing in this Constitution shall be so construed as to prejudice any claims of the United States, or of any particular State.

[7]See the Eleventh Amendment.

[8]See the Fourteenth Amendment, Sec. 1.
[9]See the Thirteenth Amendment.

## Section 4

The United States shall guarantee to every State in this Union a republican form of government, and shall protect each of them against invasion; and on application of the legislature, or of the executive (when the legislature cannot be convened) against domestic violence.

## Article V

The Congress, whenever two thirds of both Houses shall deem it necessary, shall propose amendments to this Constitution, or, on the application of the legislatures of two thirds of the several States, shall call a convention for proposing amendments, which in either case shall be valid to all intents and purposes, as part of this Constitution, when ratified by the legislatures of three fourths of the several States, or by conventions in three fourths thereof, as the one or the other mode of ratification may be proposed by the Congress; Provided that no amendment which may be made prior to the year one thousand eight hundred and eight shall in any manner affect the first and fourth clauses in the ninth section of the first article; and that no State, without its consent, shall be deprived of its equal suffrage in the Senate.

## Article VI

1  All debts contracted and engagements entered into, before the adoption of this Constitution, shall be as valid against the United States under this Constitution, as under the Confederation.[10]

2  This Constitution, and the laws of the United States which shall be made in pursuance thereof; and all treaties made, or which shall be made, under the authority of the United States, shall be the supreme law of the land; and the judges in every State shall be bound thereby, any thing in the Constitution or laws of any State to the contrary notwithstanding.

3  The senators and representatives before mentioned, and the members of the several State legislatures, and all executive and judicial officers, both of the United States and of the several States, shall be bound by oath or affirmation to support this Constitution; but no religious test shall ever be required as a qualification to any office or public trust under the United States.

## Article VII

The ratification of the conventions of nine States shall be sufficient for the establishment of this Constitution between the States so ratifying the same.

Done in Convention by the unanimous consent of the States present the seventeenth day of September in the year of our Lord one thousand seven hundred and eighty-seven, and of the independence of the United States of America the twelfth. In witness whereof we have hereunto subscribed our names.

[Signatories' names omitted]

*Articles in addition to, and amendment of, the Constitution of the United States of America, proposed by Congress, and ratified by the legislatures of the several States, pursuant to the fifth article of the original Constitution.*

## Amendment I

[First ten amendments ratified December 15, 1791]

Congress shall make no law respecting an establishment of religion, or prohibiting the free exercise thereof; or abridging the freedom of speech, or of the press; or the right of the people peaceably to assemble, and to petition the government for a redress of grievances.

## Amendment II

A well regulated militia, being necessary to the security of a free State, the right of the people to keep and bear arms, shall not be infringed.

## Amendment III

No soldier shall, in time of peace be quartered in any house, without the consent of the owner, nor in time of war, but in a manner to be prescribed by law.

## Amendment IV

The right of the people to be secure in their persons, houses, papers, and effects, against unreasonable searches and seizures, shall not be violated, and no warrants shall issue, but upon probable cause, supported by oath or affirmation, and particularly describing the place to be searched, and the persons or things to be seized.

## Amendment V

No person shall be held to answer for a capital or otherwise infamous crime, unless on a presentment or indictment of a grand jury, except in cases arising in the land or naval forces, or in the militia, when in actual service in time of war or public danger; nor shall any person be subject for the same offense to be twice put in jeopardy of life or limb; nor shall be compelled in any criminal case to be a witness against himself, nor be deprived of life, liberty, or property, without due process of law; nor shall private property be taken for public use, without just compensation.

## Amendment VI

In all criminal prosecutions, the accused shall enjoy the right to a speedy and public trial, by an impartial jury of the State and district wherein the crime shall have been committed, which district shall have been previously ascertained by law, and to be informed of the nature and cause of the accusation; to be confronted with the witnesses against him; to have compulsory process for obtaining witnesses in his favor, and to have the assistance of counsel for his defense.

## Amendment VII

In suits at common law, where the value in controversy shall exceed twenty dollars, the right of trial by jury shall be preserved, and no fact tried by a jury shall be otherwise reexamined in any court of the United States, than according to the rules of the common law.

## Amendment VIII

Excessive bail shall not be required, nor excessive fines imposed, nor cruel and unusual punishments inflicted.

## Amendment IX

The enumeration in the Constitution of certain rights shall not be construed to deny or disparage others retained by the people.

---

[10]See the Fourteenth Amendment, Sec. 4.

## Amendment X

The powers not delegated to the United States by the Constitution, nor prohibited by it to the States, are reserved to the States respectively, or to the people.

## Amendment XI [January 8, 1798]

The judicial power of the United States shall not be construed to extend to any suit in law or equity, commended or prosecuted against one of the United States by citizens of another State, or by citizens or subjects of any foreign State.

## Amendment XII [September 25, 1804]

The electors shall meet in their respective States, and vote by ballot for President and Vice President, one of whom, at least, shall not be an inhabitant of the same State with themselves; they shall name in their ballots the person voted for as President, and in distinct ballots, the person voted for as Vice President, and they shall make distinct lists of all persons voted for as President and of all persons voted for as Vice President, and of the number of votes for each, which lists they shall sign and certify, and transmit sealed to the seat of the government of the United States, directed to the President of the Senate;—The President of the Senate shall, in the presence of the Senate and House of Representatives, open all the certificates and the votes shall then be counted;—The person having the greatest number of votes for President, shall be the President, if such number be a majority of the whole number of electors appointed; and if no person have such majority, then from the persons having the highest numbers not exceeding three on the list of those voted for as President, the House of Representatives shall choose immediately, by ballot, the President. But in choosing the President, the votes shall be taken by States, the representation from each State having one vote; a quorum for this purpose shall consist of a member or members from two thirds of the States, and a majority of all the States shall be necessary to a choice. And if the House of Representatives shall not choose a President whenever the right of choice shall devolve upon them, before the fourth day of March next following, then the Vice President shall act as President, as in the case of the death or other constitutional disability of the President. The person having the greatest number of votes as Vice President shall be the Vice President, if such number be a majority of the whole number of electors appointed, and if no person have a majority, then from the two highest numbers on the list, the Senate shall choose the Vice President; a quorum for the purpose shall consist of two thirds of the whole number of Senators, and a majority of the whole number shall be necessary to a choice. But no person constitutionally ineligible to the office of President shall be eligible to that of Vice President of the United States.

## Amendment XIII [December 18, 1865]

### Section 1

Neither slavery nor involuntary servitude, except as a punishment for crime whereof the party shall have been duly convicted, shall exist within the United States, or any place subject to their jurisdiction.

### Section 2

Congress shall have power to enforce this article by appropriate legislation.

## Amendment XIV [July 28, 1868]

### Section 1

All persons born or naturalized in the United States, and subject to the jurisdiction thereof, are citizens of the United States and of the State wherein they reside. No State shall make or enforce any law which shall abridge the privileges or immunities of citizens of the United States; nor shall any State deprive any person of life, liberty, or property, without due process of law; nor deny to any person within its jurisdiction the equal protection of the laws.

### Section 2

Representatives shall be apportioned among the several States according to their respective numbers, counting the whole number of persons in each State, excluding Indians not taxed. But when the right to vote at any election for the choice of electors for President and Vice President of the United States, representatives in Congress, the executive and judicial officers of a State, or the members of the legislature thereof, is denied to any of the male inhabitants of such State, being twenty-one years of age, and citizens of the United States, or in any way abridged, except for participating in rebellion, or other crime, the basis of representation there shall be reduced in the proportion which the number of such male citizens shall bear to the whole number of male citizens twenty-one years of age in such State.

### Section 3

No person shall be a senator or representative in Congress, or elector of President and Vice President, or hold any office, civil or military, under the United States, or under any State, who having previously taken an oath, as a member of Congress, or as an officer of the United States, or as a member of any State legislature, or as an executive or judicial officer of any State, to support the Constitution of the United States, shall have engaged in insurrection or rebellion against the same, or given aid or comfort to the enemies thereof. But Congress may by a vote of two thirds of each House, remove such disability.

### Section 4

The validity of the public debt of the United States, authorized by law, including debts incurred for payment of pensions and bounties for services in suppressing insurrection or rebellion; shall not be questioned. But neither the United States nor any State shall assume or pay any debt or obligation incurred in aid of insurrection or rebellion against the United States, or any claim for the loss or emancipation of any slave; but all such debts, obligations, and claims shall be held illegal and void.

### Section 5

The Congress shall have the power to enforce, by appropriate legislation, the provisions of this article.

## Amendment XV [March 30, 1870]

### Section 1

The right of citizens of the United States to vote shall not be denied or abridged by the United States or by any State on account of race, color, or previous condition of servitude.

## Section 2

The Congress shall have power to enforce this article by appropriate legislation.

## Amendment XVI [February 25, 1913]

The Congress shall have power to lay and collect taxes on incomes, from whatever source derived, without apportionment among the several States, and without regard to any census or enumeration.

## Amendment XVII [May 31, 1913]

The Senate of the United States shall be composed of two senators from each State, elected by the people thereof, for six years; and each senator shall have one vote. The electors in each State shall have the qualifications requisite for electors of the most numerous branch of the State legislature.

When vacancies happen in the representation of any State in the Senate, the executive authority of such State shall issue writs of election to fill such vacancies: Provided, That the legislature of any State may empower the executive thereof to make temporary appointments until the people fill the vacancies by election as the legislature may direct.

This amendment shall not be so construed as to affect the election or term of any senator chosen before it becomes valid as part of the Constitution.

## Amendment XVIII[11] [January 29, 1919]

After one year from the ratification of this article, the manufacture, sale, or transportation of intoxicating liquors within, the importation thereof into, or the exportation thereof from the United States and all territory subject to the jurisdiction thereof for beverage purposes is thereby prohibited.

The Congress and the several States shall have concurrent power to enforce this article by appropriate legislation.

This article shall be inoperative unless it shall have been ratified as an amendment to the Constitution by the legislatures of the several States, as provided in the constitution, within seven years from the date of the submission hereof to the States by Congress.

## Amendment XIX [August 26, 1920]

The right of citizens of the United States to vote shall not be denied or abridged by the United States or by any State on account of sex.

Congress shall have the power to enforce this article by appropriate legislation.

## Amendment XX [January 23, 1933]

### Section 1

The terms of the President and Vice President shall end at noon on the 20th day of January and the terms of Senators and Representatives at noon on the 3rd day of January, of the years in which such terms would have ended if this article had not been ratified; and the terms of their successors shall then begin.

### Section 2

The Congress shall assemble at least once in every year, and such meeting shall begin at noon on the 3rd day of January, unless they shall by law appoint a different day.

[11]Repealed by the Twenty-first Amendment.

### Section 3

If, at the time fixed for the beginning of the term of President, the President-elect shall have died, the Vice President-elect shall become President. If a President shall not have been chosen before the time fixed for the beginning of his term, or if the President-elect shall have failed to qualify, then the Vice President-elect shall act as President until a President shall have qualified; and the Congress may by law provide for the case wherein neither a President-elect nor a Vice President-elect shall have qualified, declaring who shall then act as President, or the manner in which one who is to act shall be selected, and such person shall act accordingly until a President or Vice President shall have qualified.

### Section 4

The Congress may by law provide for the case of the death of any of the persons from whom, the House of Representatives may choose a President whenever the right of choice shall have devolved upon them, and for the case of the death of any of the persons from whom the Senate may choose a Vice President whenever the right of choice shall have devolved upon them.

### Section 5

Sections 1 and 2 shall take effect on the 15th day of October following the ratification of this article.

### Section 6

This article shall be inoperative unless it shall have been ratified as an amendment to the Constitution by the legislatures of three-fourths of the several States within seven years from the date of its submission.

## Amendment XXI [December 5, 1933]

### Section 1

The Eighteenth Article of amendment to the Constitution of the United States is hereby repealed.

### Section 2

The transportation or importation into any State, Territory, or possession of the United States for delivery or use therein of intoxicating liquors in violation of the laws thereof, is hereby prohibited.

### Section 3

This article shall be inoperative unless it shall have been ratified as an amendment to the Constitution by conventions in the several States, as provided in the Constitution, within seven years from the date of the submission thereof to the States by the Congress.

## Amendment XXII [March 1, 1951]

No person shall be elected to the office of the President more than twice, and no person who has held the office of President, or acted as President, for more than two years of a term to which some other person was elected President shall be elected to the office of the President more than once.

But this article shall not apply to any person holding the office of President when this article was proposed by the Congress, and shall not prevent any person who may be holding the office of President, or acting as President, during the term within which this article becomes operative from holding the office of President or acting as President during the remainder of such term.

This article shall be inoperative unless it shall have been ratified as an amendment to the Constitution by the legislatures of three-fourths of the several States within seven years from the date of its submission to the States by the Congress.

## Amendment XXIII [March 29, 1961]

### Section 1

The District constituting the seat of Government of the United States shall appoint in such manner as the Congress may direct.

A number of electors of President and Vice President equal to the whole number of Senators and Representatives in Congress to which the District would be entitled if it were a State, but in no event more than the least populous State; they shall be in addition to those appointed by the States, but they shall be considered, for the purposes of the election of President and Vice President, to be electors appointed by a State; and they shall meet in the District and perform such duties as provided by the twelfth article of amendment.

### Section 2

The Congress shall have power to enforce this article by appropriate legislation.

## Amendment XXIV [January 23, 1964]

### Section 1

The right of citizens of the United States to vote in any primary or other election for President or Vice President, for electors for President or Vice President, or for Senator or Representative in Congress, shall not be denied or abridged by the United States or any State by reason of failure to pay any poll tax or other tax.

### Section 2

The Congress shall have power to enforce this article by appropriate legislation.

## Amendment XXV [February 10, 1967]

### Section 1

In case of the removal of the President from office or of his death or resignation, the Vice President shall become President.

### Section 2

Whenever there is a vacancy in the office of the Vice President, the President shall nominate a Vice President who shall take office upon confirmation by a majority of both Houses of Congress.

### Section 3

Whenever the President transmits to the President pro tempore of the Senate and the Speaker of the House of Representatives his written declaration that he is unable to discharge the powers and duties of his office, and until he transmits to them a written declaration to the contrary, such powers and duties shall be discharged by the Vice President as Acting President.

### Section 4

Whenever the Vice President and a majority of either the principal officers of the executive departments or of such other body as Congress may by law provide, transmit to the President pro tempore of the Senate and the Speaker of the House of Representatives their written declaration that the President is unable to discharge the powers and duties of his office, the Vice President shall immediately assume the powers and duties of the office as Acting President.

Thereafter, when the President transmits to the President pro tempore of the Senate and the Speaker of the House of Representatives his written declaration that no inability exists, he shall resume the powers and duties of his office unless the Vice President and a majority of either the principal officers of the executive departments or of such other body as Congress may by law provide, transmit within four days to the President pro tempore of the Senate and the Speaker of the House of Representatives their written declaration that the President is unable to discharge the powers and duties of his office. Thereupon Congress shall decide the issue, assembling within forty-eight hours for that purpose if not in session. If the Congress, within twenty-one days after receipt of the latter written declaration, or, if Congress is not in session, within twenty-one days after Congress is required to assemble, determines by two-thirds vote of both Houses that the President is unable to discharge the powers and duties of his office, the Vice President shall continue to discharge the same as Acting President; otherwise, the President shall resume the powers and duties of his office.

## Amendment XXVI [June 30, 1971]

### Section 1

The right of citizens of the United States who are eighteen years of age or older to vote shall not be denied or abridged by the United States or by any State on account of age.

### Section 2

The Congress shall have power to enforce this article by appropriate legislation.

## Amendment XXVII[12] [May 7, 1992]

No law, varying the compensation for services of the Senators and Representatives, shall take effect until an election of Representatives shall have intervened.

---

[12]James Madison proposed this amendment in 1789 together with the ten amendments that were adopted as the Bill of Rights, but it failed to win ratification at the time. Congress, however, had set no deadline for its ratification, and over the years—particularly in the 1980s and 1990s—many states voted to add it to the Constitution. With the ratification of Michigan in 1992 it passed the threshold of three-fourths of the states required for adoption, but because the process took more than 200 years, its validity remains in doubt.

# PRESIDENTIAL ELECTIONS

| Year | Number of States | Candidates | Party | Popular Vote* | Electoral Vote† | Percentage of Popular Vote |
|------|------|------------|-------|------------|------------|------------|
| 1789 | 11 | GEORGE WASHINGTON | No party designations | | 69 | |
| | | John Adams | | | 34 | |
| | | Other Candidates | | | 35 | |
| 1792 | 15 | GEORGE WASHINGTON | No party designations | | 132 | |
| | | John Adams | | | 77 | |
| | | George Clinton | | | 50 | |
| | | Other Candidates | | | 5 | |
| 1796 | 16 | JOHN ADAMS | Federalist | | 71 | |
| | | Thomas Jefferson | Democratic-Republican | | 68 | |
| | | Thomas Pinckney | Federalist | | 59 | |
| | | Aaron Burr | Democratic-Republican | | 30 | |
| | | Other Candidates | | | 48 | |
| 1800 | 16 | THOMAS JEFFERSON | Democratic-Republican | | 73 | |
| | | Aaron Burr | Democratic-Republican | | 73 | |
| | | John Adams | Federalist | | 65 | |
| | | Charles C. Pinckney | Federalist | | 64 | |
| | | John Jay | Federalist | | 1 | |
| 1804 | 17 | THOMAS JEFFERSON | Democratic-Republican | | 162 | |
| | | Charles C. Pinckney | Federalist | | 14 | |
| 1808 | 17 | JAMES MADISON | Democratic-Republican | | 122 | |
| | | Charles C. Pinckney | Federalist | | 47 | |
| | | George Clinton | Democratic-Republican | | 6 | |
| 1812 | 18 | JAMES MADISON | Democratic-Republican | | 128 | |
| | | DeWitt Clinton | Federalist | | 89 | |
| 1816 | 19 | JAMES MONROE | Democratic-Republican | | 183 | |
| | | Rufus King | Federalist | | 34 | |
| 1820 | 24 | JAMES MONROE | Democratic-Republican | | 231 | |
| | | John Quincy Adams | Independent-Republican | | 1 | |
| 1824 | 24 | JOHN QUINCY ADAMS | Democratic-Republican | 108,740 | 84 | 30.5 |
| | | Andrew Jackson | Democratic-Republican | 153,544 | 99 | 43.1 |
| | | William H. Crawford | Democratic-Republican | 46,618 | 41 | 13.1 |
| | | Henry Clay | Democratic-Republican | 47,136 | 37 | 13.2 |
| 1828 | 24 | ANDREW JACKSON | Democrat | 647,286 | 178 | 56.0 |
| | | John Quincy Adams | National Republican | 508,064 | 83 | 44.0 |
| 1832 | 24 | ANDREW JACKSON | Democrat | 687,502 | 219 | 55.0 |
| | | Henry Clay | National Republican | 530,189 | 49 | 42.4 |
| | | William Wirt | Anti-Masonic | 33,108 | 7 | 2.6 |
| | | John Floyd | | | 11 | |
| 1836 | 26 | MARTIN VAN BUREN | Democrat | 765,483 | 170 | 50.9 |
| | | William H. Harrison | Whig | | 73 | |
| | | Hugh L. White | Whig | | 26 | |
| | | Daniel Webster | Whig | 739,795 | 14 | 49.1 |
| | | W. P. Mangum | Whig | | 11 | |
| 1840 | 26 | WILLIAM H. HARRISON | Whig | 1,274,624 | 234 | 53.1 |
| | | Martin Van Buren | Democrat | 1,127,781 | 60 | 46.9 |
| 1844 | 26 | JAMES K. POLK | Democrat | 1,338,464 | 170 | 49.6 |
| | | Henry Clay | Whig | 1,300,097 | 105 | 48.1 |
| | | James G. Birney | Liberty | 62,300 | | 2.3 |

*Percentage of popular vote given for any election year may not total 100 percent because candidates receiving less than 1 percent of the popular vote have been omitted.

†Prior to the passage of the Twelfth Amendment in 1904, the electoral college voted for two presidential candidates; the runner-up became Vice-President. Data from Historical Statistics of the United States, Colonial Times to 1957 (1961), pp. 682–683, and The World Almanac.

| Year | Number of States | Candidates | Party | Popular Vote* | Electoral Vote† | Percentage of Popular Vote |
|------|------|------------|-------|------------|--------------|------------|
| 1848 | 30 | ZACHARY TAYLOR | Whig | 1,360,967 | 163 | 47.4 |
|  |  | Lewis Cass | Democrat | 1,222,342 | 127 | 42.5 |
|  |  | Martin Van Buren | Free Soil | 291,263 |  | 10.1 |
| 1852 | 31 | FRANKLIN PIERCE | Democrat | 1,601,117 | 254 | 50.9 |
|  |  | Winfield Scott | Whig | 1,385,453 | 42 | 44.1 |
|  |  | John P. Hale | Free Soil | 155,825 |  | 5.0 |
| 1856 | 31 | JAMES BUCHANAN | Democrat | 1,832,955 | 174 | 45.3 |
|  |  | John C. Frémont | Republican | 1,339,932 | 114 | 33.1 |
|  |  | Millard Fillmore | American ("Know Nothing") | 871,731 | 8 | 21.6 |
| 1860 | 33 | ABRAHAM LINCOLN | Republican | 1,865,593 | 180 | 39.8 |
|  |  | Stephen A. Douglas | Democrat | 1,382,713 | 12 | 29.5 |
|  |  | John C. Breckinridge | Democrat | 848,356 | 72 | 18.1 |
|  |  | John Bell | Constitutional Union | 592,906 | 39 | 12.6 |
| 1864 | 36 | ABRAHAM LINCOLN | Republican | 2,206,938 | 212 | 55.0 |
|  |  | George B. McClellan | Democrat | 1,803,787 | 21 | 45.0 |
| 1868 | 37 | ULYSSES S. GRANT | Republican | 3,013,421 | 214 | 52.7 |
|  |  | Horatio Seymour | Democrat | 2,706,829 | 80 | 47.3 |
| 1872 | 37 | ULYSSES S. GRANT | Republican | 3,596,745 | 286 | 55.6 |
|  |  | Horace Greeley | Democrat | 2,843,446 | * | 43.9 |
| 1876 | 38 | RUTHERFORD B. HAYES | Republican | 4,036,572 | 185 | 48.0 |
|  |  | Samuel J. Tilden | Democrat | 4,284,020 | 184 | 51.0 |
| 1880 | 38 | JAMES A. GARFIELD | Republican | 4,453,295 | 214 | 48.5 |
|  |  | Winfield S. Hancock | Democrat | 4,414,082 | 155 | 48.1 |
|  |  | James B. Weaver | Greenback-Labor | 308,578 |  | 3.4 |
| 1884 | 38 | GROVER CLEVELAND | Democrat | 4,879,507 | 219 | 48.5 |
|  |  | James G. Blaine | Republican | 4,850,293 | 182 | 48.2 |
|  |  | Benjamin F. Butler | Greenback-Labor | 175,370 |  | 1.8 |
|  |  | John P. St. John | Prohibition | 150,369 |  | 1.5 |
| 1888 | 38 | BENJAMIN HARRISON | Republican | 5,447,129 | 233 | 47.9 |
|  |  | Grover Cleveland | Democrat | 5,537,857 | 168 | 48.6 |
|  |  | Clinton B. Fisk | Prohibition | 249,506 |  | 2.2 |
|  |  | Anson J. Streeter | Union Labor | 146,935 |  | 1.3 |
| 1892 | 44 | GROVER CLEVELAND | Democrat | 5,555,426 | 277 | 46.1 |
|  |  | Benjamin Harrison | Republican | 5,182,690 | 145 | 43.0 |
|  |  | James B. Weaver | People's | 1,029,846 | 22 | 8.5 |
|  |  | John Bidwell | Prohibition | 264,133 |  | 2.2 |
| 1896 | 45 | WILLIAM MCKINLEY | Republican | 7,102,246 | 271 | 51.1 |
|  |  | William J. Bryan | Democrat | 6,492,559 | 176 | 47.7 |
| 1900 | 45 | WILLIAM McKINLEY | Republican | 7,218,491 | 292 | 51.7 |
|  |  | William J. Bryan | Democrat; Populist | 6,356,734 | 155 | 45.5 |
|  |  | John C. Woolley | Prohibition | 208,914 |  | 1.5 |
| 1904 | 45 | THEODORE ROOSEVELT | Republican | 7,628,461 | 336 | 57.4 |
|  |  | Alton B. Parker | Democrat | 5,084,223 | 140 | 37.6 |
|  |  | Eugene V. Debs | Socialist | 402,283 |  | 3.0 |
|  |  | Silas C. Swallow | Prohibition | 258,536 |  | 1.9 |
| 1908 | 46 | WILLIAM H. TAFT | Republican | 7,675,320 | 321 | 51.6 |
|  |  | William J. Bryan | Democrat | 6,412,294 | 162 | 43.1 |
|  |  | Eugene V. Debs | Socialist | 420,793 |  | 2.8 |
|  |  | Eugene W. Chafin | Prohibition | 253,840 |  | 1.7 |

*Because of the death of Greeley, Democratic electors scattered their votes.

# PRESIDENTIAL ELECTIONS (CONTINUED)

| Year | Number of States | Candidates | Party | Popular Vote* | Electoral Vote† | Percentage of Popular Vote |
|------|------|------------|-------|-------------|---------------|-----------|
| 1912 | 48 | WOODROW WILSON | Democrat | 6,296,547 | 435 | 41.9 |
|      |    | Theodore Roosevelt | Progressive | 4,118,571 | 88 | 27.4 |
|      |    | William H. Taft | Republican | 3,486,720 | 8 | 23.2 |
|      |    | Eugene V. Debs | Socialist | 900,672 | | 6.0 |
|      |    | Eugene W. Chafin | Prohibition | 206,275 | | 1.4 |
| 1916 | 48 | WOODROW WILSON | Democrat | 9,127,695 | 277 | 49.4 |
|      |    | Charles E. Hughes | Republican | 8,533,507 | 254 | 46.2 |
|      |    | A. L. Benson | Socialist | 585,113 | | 3.2 |
|      |    | J. Frank Hanly | Prohibition | 220,506 | | 1.2 |
| 1920 | 48 | WARREN G. HARDING | Republican | 16,143,407 | 404 | 60.4 |
|      |    | James M. Cox | Democrat | 9,130,328 | 127 | 34.2 |
|      |    | Eugene V. Debs | Socialist | 919,799 | | 3.4 |
|      |    | P. P. Christensen | Farmer-Labor | 265,411 | | 1.0 |
| 1924 | 48 | CALVIN COOLIDGE | Republican | 15,718,211 | 382 | 54.0 |
|      |    | John W. Davis | Democrat | 8,385,283 | 136 | 28.8 |
|      |    | Robert M. La Follette | Progressive | 4,831,289 | 13 | 16.6 |
| 1928 | 48 | HERBERT C. HOOVER | Republican | 21,391,993 | 444 | 58.2 |
|      |    | Alfred E. Smith | Democrat | 15,016,169 | 87 | 40.9 |
| 1932 | 48 | FRANKLIN D. ROOSEVELT | Democrat | 22,809,638 | 472 | 57.4 |
|      |    | Herbert C. Hoover | Republican | 15,758,901 | 59 | 39.7 |
|      |    | Norman Thomas | Socialist | 881,951 | | 2.2 |
| 1936 | 48 | FRANKLIN D. ROOSEVELT | Democrat | 27,752,869 | 523 | 60.8 |
|      |    | Alfred M. Landon | Republican | 16,674,665 | 8 | 36.5 |
|      |    | William Lemke | Union | 882,479 | | 1.9 |
| 1940 | 48 | FRANKLIN D. ROOSEVELT | Democrat | 27,307,819 | 449 | 54.8 |
|      |    | Wendell L. Willkie | Republican | 22,321,018 | 82 | 44.8 |
| 1944 | 48 | FRANKLIN D. ROOSEVELT | Democrat | 25,606,585 | 432 | 53.5 |
|      |    | Thomas E. Dewey | Republican | 22,014,745 | 99 | 46.0 |
| 1948 | 48 | HARRY S. TRUMAN | Democrat | 24,105,812 | 303 | 49.5 |
|      |    | Thomas E. Dewey | Republican | 21,970,065 | 189 | 45.1 |
|      |    | J. Strom Thurmond | States' Rights | 1,169,063 | 39 | 2.4 |
|      |    | Henry A. Wallace | Progressive | 1,157,172 | | 2.4 |
| 1952 | 48 | DWIGHT D. EISENHOWER | Republican | 33,936,234 | 442 | 55.1 |
|      |    | Adlai E. Stevenson | Democrat | 27,314,992 | 89 | 44.4 |
| 1956 | 48 | DWIGHT D. EISENHOWER | Republican | 35,590,472 | 457* | 57.6 |
|      |    | Adlai E. Stevenson | Democrat | 26,022,752 | 73 | 42.1 |
| 1960 | 50 | JOHN F. KENNEDY | Democrat | 34,227,096 | 303† | 49.9 |
|      |    | Richard M. Nixon | Republican | 34,108,546 | 219 | 49.6 |
| 1964 | 50 | LYNDON B. JOHNSON | Democrat | 42,676,220 | 486 | 61.3 |
|      |    | Barry M. Goldwater | Republican | 26,860,314 | 52 | 38.5 |
| 1968 | 50 | RICHARD M. NIXON | Republican | 31,785,480 | 301 | 43.4 |
|      |    | Hubert H. Humphrey | Democrat | 31,275,165 | 191 | 42.7 |
|      |    | George C. Wallace | American Independent | 9,906,473 | 46 | 13.5 |
| 1972 | 50 | RICHARD M. NIXON‡ | Republican | 47,165,234 | 520** | 60.6 |
|      |    | George S. McGovern | Democrat | 29,168,110 | 17 | 37.5 |

*Walter B. Jones received 1 electoral vote.

†Harry F. Byrd received 15 electoral votes.

‡Resigned August 9, 1974: Vice President Gerald R. Ford became President.

**John Hospers received 1 electoral vote.

# PRESIDENTIAL ELECTIONS

| Year | Number of States | Candidates | Party | Popular Vote* | Electoral Vote† | Percentage of Popular Vote |
|------|------------------|------------|-------|---------------|-----------------|----------------------------|
| 1976 | 50 | JIMMY CARTER | Democrat | 40,828,929 | 297*** | 50.1 |
|      |    | Gerald R. Ford | Republican | 39,148,940 | 240 | 47.9 |
|      |    | Eugene McCarthy | Independent | 739,256 | | |
| 1980 | 50 | RONALD REAGAN | Republican | 43,201,220 | 489 | 50.9 |
|      |    | Jimmy Carter | Democrat | 34,913,332 | 49 | 41.2 |
|      |    | John B. Anderson | Independent | 5,581,379 | | |
| 1984 | 50 | RONALD REAGAN | Republican | 53,428,357 | 525 | 59.0 |
|      |    | Walter F. Mondale | Democrat | 36,930,923 | 13 | 41.0 |
| 1988 | 50 | GEORGE H. W. BUSH | Republican | 48,901,046 | 426**** | 53.4 |
|      |    | Michael Dukakis | Democrat | 41,809,030 | 111 | 45.6 |
| 1992 | 50 | BILL CLINTON | Democrat | 43,728,275 | 370 | 43.2 |
|      |    | George Bush | Republican | 38,167,416 | 168 | 37.7 |
|      |    | H. Ross Perot | United We Stand, America | 19,237,247 | | 19.0 |
| 1996 | 50 | BILL CLINTON | Democrat | 45,590,703 | 379 | 49.0 |
|      |    | Robert Dole | Republican | 37,816,307 | 159 | 41.0 |
|      |    | H. Ross Perot | Reform | 7,866,284 | | 8.0 |
| 2000 | 50 | GEORGE W. BUSH | Republican | 50,459,624 | 271 | 47.9 |
|      |    | Albert Gore, Jr. | Democrat | 51,003,328 | 266 | 49.4 |
|      |    | Ralph Nader | Green | 2,882,985 | | 2.7 |
| 2004 | 50 | GEORGE W. BUSH | Republican | 62,040,610 | 286***** | 50.7 |
|      |    | John F. Kerry | Democrat | 59,028,444 | 251 | 48.3 |
| 2008 | 50 | BARACK H. OBAMA | Democrat | 69,456,897 | 365 | 52.9 |
|      |    | John McCain | Republican | 59,934,814 | 173 | 45.7 |
| 2012 | 50 | BARACK H. OBAMA | Democrat | 65,446,032 | 332 | 51.0 |
|      |    | Mitt Romney | Republican | 60,589,084 | 206 | 47.1 |

***Ronald Reagan received 1 electoral vote.
****Lloyd Bentsen received 1 electoral vote.
*****John Edwards received 1 electoral vote.

# Glossary

**acquired immunodeficiency syndrome (AIDS)** A complex of deadly pathologies resulting from infection with the human immunodeficiency virus (HIV).

**affirmative action** A set of policies to open opportunities in business and education for members of minority groups and women by allowing race and sex to be factors included in decisions to hire, award contracts, or admit students to higher education programs.

**Alliance for Progress** Program of economic aid to Latin America during the Kennedy administration.

**Allies** In World War I, Britain, France, Russia, and other belligerent nations fighting against the Central Powers but not including the United States, which insisted upon being merely an associated nation. In World War II, the Allies fighting the Axis Powers included the United States as well as the Soviet Union, Great Britain, France, China, and other nations.

**American Federation of Labor (AFL)** Union formed in 1886 that organized skilled workers along craft lines and emphasized a few workplace issues rather than a broad social program.

**American Indian Movement (AIM)** Group of Native American political activists who used confrontations with the federal government to publicize their case for Indian rights.

**Americans with Disabilities Act** Legislation in 1992 that banned discrimination against physically handicapped persons in employment, transportation, and public accommodations.

**Atlanta Compromise** Booker T. Washington's policy accepting segregation and disfranchisement for African Americans in exchange for white assistance in education and job training.

**Atlantic Charter** Statement of common principles and war aims developed by President Franklin Roosevelt and British Prime Minister Winston Churchill at a meeting in August 1941.

**Australian ballot** Secret voting and the use of official ballots rather than party tickets.

**Axis Powers** The opponents of the United States and its allies in World War II. The Rome-Berlin Axis was formed between Germany and Italy in 1936 and included Japan after 1940.

**Baker v. Carr** U.S. Supreme Court decision in 1962 that allowed federal courts to review the appointment of state legislative districts and established the principle that such districts should have roughly equal populations ("one person, one vote").

**Battle of the Atlantic** The long struggle between German submarines and the British and U.S. navies in the North Atlantic from 1940 to 1943.

**Battle of the Little Bighorn** Battle in which Colonel George A. Custer and the Seventh Cavalry were defeated by the Sioux and Cheyenne under Sitting Bull and Crazy Horse in Montana in 1876.

**Bay of Pigs** Site in Cuba of an unsuccessful landing by 1,400 anti-Castro Cuban refugees in April 1961.

**Berlin blockade** A 300-day Soviet blockade of land access to U.S., British, and French occupation zones in Berlin, 1948–1949.

**Berlin Wall** Wall erected by East Germany in 1961 that isolated West Berlin from the surrounding areas in Communist-controlled East Berlin and East Germany.

**black codes** Laws passed by states and municipalities denying many rights of citizenship to free blacks before the Civil War. Also, during the Reconstruction era, laws passed by newly elected southern state legislatures to control black labor, mobility, and employment.

**Black Panthers** Political and social movement among black Americans, founded in Oakland, California, in 1966 and emphasizing black economic and political power.

**Black Power** Philosophy emerging after 1965 that real economic and political gains for African Americans could come only through self-help, self-determination, and organizing for direct political influence.

***blitzkrieg*** German war tactic in World War II ("lightning war") involving the concentration of air and armored firepower to punch and exploit holes in opposing defensive lines.

**Bolshevik** Member of the Communist movement in Russia that established the Soviet government after the 1917 Russian Revolution.

**Bonus Army** A group of unemployed veterans who demonstrated in Washington for the payment of service bonuses, only to be dispersed violently by the U.S. Army in 1932.

***Brown v. Board of Education of Topeka*** Supreme Court decision in 1954 that declared that "separate but equal" schools for children of different races violated the Constitution.

**Bureau of Reclamation** Federal agency established in 1902 providing public funds for irrigation projects in arid regions.

**Camp David Agreement** Agreement to reduce points of conflict between Israel and Egypt, hammered out in 1977 with the help of U.S. President Jimmy Carter.

**carpetbaggers** Pejorative term to describe northern transplants to the South, many of whom were Union soldiers who stayed in the South after the war.

**Central Intelligence Agency (CIA)** Agency that coordinates the gathering and evaluation of military and economic information on other nations, established in 1947.

**Central Powers** Germany and its World War I allies in Austria, Turkey, and Bulgaria.

**chain migration** Process common to many immigrant groups whereby one family member brings over other family members, who in turn bring other relatives and friends and occasionally entire villages.

**Chisholm Trail** The route followed by Texas cattle raisers driving their herds north to markets at Kansas railheads.

**Civil Rights Act of 1964** Federal legislation that outlawed discrimination in public accommodations and employment on the basis of race, skin color, sex, religion, or national origin.

**Cold War** The political and economic confrontation between the Soviet Union and the United States that dominated world affairs from 1946 to 1989.

**collective bargaining** Representatives of a union negotiating with management on behalf of all members.

**Colored Farmers' Alliance** An organization of southern black farmers formed in Texas in 1886 in response to the Southern Farmers' Alliance, which did not accept black people as members.

**Committee on Public Information (CPI)** Government agency during World War I that sought to shape public opinion in support of the war effort through newspapers, pamphlets, speeches, films, and other media.

**Compromise of 1877** The congressional settling of the 1876 election that installed Republican Rutherford B. Hayes in the White House and gave Democrats control of all state governments in the South.

**Congressional Reconstruction** Name given to the period 1867–1870 when the Republican-dominated Congress controlled Reconstruction era policy.

It is sometimes known as Radical Reconstruction, after the radical faction in the Republican Party.

**Congress of Industrial Organizations (CIO)** An alliance of industrial unions that spurred the 1930s organizational drive among the mass-production industries.

**Congress of Racial Equality (CORE)** Civil rights group formed in 1942 and committed to nonviolent civil disobedience.

**conservation** The efficient management and use of natural resources, such as forests, grasslands, and rivers, as opposed to preservation or uncontrolled exploitation.

**containment** The policy of resisting further expansion of the Soviet bloc through diplomacy and, if necessary, military action, developed in 1947–1948.

**Contract with America** Platform proposing a sweeping reduction in the role and activities of the federal government on which many Republican candidates ran for Congress in 1994.

**Council of Economic Advisers** Board of three professional economists established in 1946 to advise the president on economic policy.

**counterculture** Various alternatives to mainstream values and behaviors that became popular in the 1960s, including experimentation with psychedelic drugs, communal living, a return to the land, Asian religions, and experimental art.

**Coxey's Army** A protest march of unemployed workers, led by Populist businessman Jacob Coxey, demanding inflation and a public-works program during the depression of the 1890s.

**Dawes Act** An 1887 law terminating tribal ownership of land and allotting some parcels of land to individual Indians with the remainder opened for white settlement.

**D-Day** June 6, 1944, the day of the first paratroop drops and amphibious landings on the coast of Normandy, France, in the first stage of Operation OVERLORD during World War II.

**Declaration of London** Statement drafted by an international conference in 1909 to clarify international law and specify the rights of neutral nations.

**deindustrialization** The process of economic change involving the disappearance of outmoded industries and the transfer of factories to new low-wage locations, with devastating effects in the Northeast and Midwest, especially in the 1970s and 1980s.

**Department of Homeland Security** Federal superagency created in 2002 with responsibility for border control and transportation security.

**deregulation** Reduction or removal of government regulations and encouragement of direct competition in many important industries and economic sectors.

*détente* (French for "easing of tension") Used to describe the new U.S. relations with China and the Soviet Union in 1972.

**disfranchisement** The use of legal means to bar individuals or groups from voting.

**Dixiecrats** Southern Democrats who broke from the party in 1948 over the issue of civil rights and ran a presidential ticket as the States' Rights Democrats.

**dollar diplomacy** The U.S. policy of using private investment in other nations to promote American diplomatic goals and business interests.

**Eastern Front** The area of military operations in World War II located east of Germany in eastern Europe and the Soviet Union.

**Economic Recovery and Tax Act of 1981 (ERTA)** A major revision of the federal income tax system.

**Eighteenth Amendment** Constitutional revision, adopted in 1919, that prohibited the production and sale of alcohol in the United States.

**Environmental Protection Agency (EPA)** Federal agency created in 1970 to oversee environmental monitoring and cleanup programs.

**Espionage Act** Law whose vague prohibition against obstructing the nation's war effort was used to crush dissent and criticism during World War I.

**Fair Employment Practices Committee (FEPC)** Federal agency established in 1941 to curb racial discrimination in war production jobs and government employment.

**Farmers' Alliance** A broad mass movement in the rural South and West during the late nineteenth century, encompassing several organizations and demanding economic and political reforms; helped create the Populist Party.

**fascist government** Subscribing to a philosophy of governmental dictatorship that merges the interests of the state, armed forces, and big business; associated with the dictatorship of Italian leader Benito Mussolini between 1922 and 1943 and also often applied to Nazi Germany.

**Federal Deposit Insurance Corporation (FDIC)** Government agency that guarantees bank deposits, thereby protecting both depositors and banks.

**Federal Highway Act of 1956** Measure that provided federal funding to build a nationwide system of interstate and defense highways.

**Federal Reserve Act** The 1913 law that revised banking and currency by extending limited government regulation through the creation of the Federal Reserve System.

**Federal Trade Commission (FTC)** Government agency established in 1914 to provide regulatory oversight of business activity.

**Field Order No. 15** Order by General William T. Sherman in January 1865 to set aside abandoned land along the southern Atlantic coast for 40-acre grants to freedmen; rescinded by President Andrew Johnson later that year.

**Fifteenth Amendment** Passed by Congress in 1869, guaranteed the right of American men to vote, regardless of race.

**fireside chats** Speeches broadcast nationally over the radio in which President Franklin Roosevelt explained complex issues and programs in plain language, as though his listeners were gathered around the fireside with him.

**Fourteenth Amendment** Constitutional amendment passed by Congress in April 1866 incorporating some of the features of the Civil Rights Act of 1866. It prohibited states from violating the civil rights of their citizens and offered states the choice of allowing black people to vote or losing representation in Congress.

**Freedmen's Bureau** Agency established by Congress in March 1865 to provide social, educational, and economic services, advice, and protection to former slaves and destitute whites; lasted seven years.

**Freedom Summer** Voter-registration effort in rural Mississippi organized by black and white civil rights workers in 1964.

**free silver** Philosophy that the government should expand the money supply by purchasing and coining all the silver offered to it.

**Free Speech Movement (FSM)** Student movement at the University of California, Berkeley, formed in 1964 to protest limitations on political activities on campus.

**fundamentalists** Religious conservatives who believe in the literal accuracy and divine inspiration of the Bible.

**Gentlemen's Agreement** A diplomatic agreement in 1907 between Japan and the United States curtailing but not abolishing Japanese immigration.

**GI Bill of Rights** Legislation in June 1944 that eased the return of veterans into American society by providing educational and employment benefits.

**Gilded Age** Term applied to late-nineteenth-century America that refers to the shallow display and worship of wealth characteristic of that period.

*glasnost* Russian for "openness," applied to Mikhail Gorbachev's encouragement of new ideas and easing of political repression in the Soviet Union.

**Gospel of Wealth** Thesis that hard work and perseverance lead to wealth, implying that poverty is a character flaw.

**grandfather clauses** Rule that required potential voters to demonstrate that their grandfathers had been eligible to vote; used in some southern states after 1890 to limit the black electorate.

**Granger laws** State laws enacted in the Midwest in the 1870s that regulated rates charged by railroads, grain elevator operators, and other middlemen.

**Great Depression** The nation's worst economic crisis, extending throughout the 1930s, producing unprecedented bank failures, unemployment, and industrial and agricultural collapse and prompting an expanded role for the federal government.

**Greater East Asia Co-Prosperity Sphere** Japanese goal of an East Asian economy controlled by Japan and serving the needs of Japanese industry.

**Great Migration** The mass movement of African Americans from the rural South to the urban North, spurred especially by new job opportunities during World War I and the 1920s.

**Great Society** Theme of Lyndon Johnson's administration, focusing on poverty, education, and civil rights.

**Great Uprising**   Unsuccessful railroad strike of 1877 to protest wage cuts and the use of federal troops against strikers; the first nationwide work stoppage in American history.

**Greenback Party**   A third party of the 1870s and 1880s that garnered temporary support by advocating currency inflation to expand the economy and assist debtors.

**Gulf of Tonkin Resolution**   Request to Congress from President Lyndon Johnson in response to North Vietnamese torpedo boat attacks in which he sought authorization for "all necessary measures" to protect American forces and stop further aggression.

**Harlem Renaissance**   A new African American cultural awareness that flourished in literature, art, and music in the 1920s.

**Helsinki Accords**   Agreement in 1975 among NATO and Warsaw Pact members that recognized European national boundaries as set after World War II and included guarantees of human rights.

**Holocaust**   The systematic murder of millions of European Jews and others deemed undesirable by Nazi Germany.

**Homestead Act**   Law passed by Congress in 1862 providing 160 acres of land free to anyone who would live on the plot and farm it for five years.

**Hooverville**   Shantytown, sarcastically named after President Hoover, in which unemployed and homeless people lived in makeshift shacks, tents, and boxes. Hoovervilles cropped up in many cities in 1930 and 1931.

**Horatio Alger stories**   A series of best-selling tales about young rags-to-riches heroes first published in 1867 stressing the importance of neat clothes, cleanliness, thrift, and hard work. The books also highlighted the importance of chance in getting ahead and the responsibility of those better off to serve as positive role models.

**horizontal integration**   The merger of competitors in the same industry.

**House Un-American Activities Committee**   Congressional committee (1938–1975) that investigated suspected Nazi and Communist sympathizers.

**Hull House**   Chicago settlement house that became part of a broader neighborhood revitalization project led by Jane Addams.

**Immigration and Nationality Act of 1965**   Federal legislation that replaced the national quota system for immigration with overall limits of 170,000 immigrants per year from the Eastern Hemisphere and 120,000 per year from the Western Hemisphere.

**imperialism**   The policy and practice of exploiting nations and peoples for the benefit of an imperial power either directly through military occupation and colonial rule or indirectly through economic domination of resources and markets.

**initiative**   Procedure by which citizens can introduce a subject for legislation, usually through a petition signed by a specific number of voters.

**Intermediate-Range Nuclear Forces (INF) Treaty**   Disarmament agreement between the United States and the Soviet Union under which an entire class of missiles would be removed and destroyed and on-site inspections would be permitted for verification.

**International Monetary Fund (IMF)**   International organization established in 1945 to assist nations in maintaining stable currencies.

**Internet**   The system of interconnected computers and servers that allows the exchange of e-mail, posting of websites, and other means of instant communication.

**Interstate Commerce Act**   The 1887 law that expanded federal power over business by prohibiting pooling and discriminatory rates by railroads and establishing the first federal regulatory agency, the Interstate Commerce Commission.

**Interstate Commerce Commission (ICC)**   The first federal regulatory agency, established in 1887 to oversee railroad practices.

**Irreconcilables**   Group of U.S. senators opposed to ratification of the Treaty of Versailles after World War I.

**island hopping**   In the Pacific Theater during World War II, the strategy in which U.S. forces seized selected Japanese-held islands while bypassing and isolating other islands held by Japan.

**Jazz Age**   The 1920s, so called for the popular music of the day as a symbol of the many changes taking place in the mass culture.

**Jim Crow laws**   Segregation laws that became widespread in the South during the 1890s.

**Kellogg-Briand Pact**   A 1928 international treaty that denounced aggression and war but lacked provisions for enforcement.

**Knights of Labor**   Labor union founded in 1869 that included skilled and unskilled workers irrespective of race or gender.

**Korean War**   War between North Korea and South Korea (1950–1953) in which the People's Republic of China fought on the side of North Korea and the United States and other nations fought on the side of South Korea under the auspices of the United Nations.

**Ku Klux Klan**   Perhaps the most prominent of the vigilante groups that terrorized black people in the South during Reconstruction Era, founded by Confederate veterans in 1866.

**laissez-faire**   The doctrine that government should not intervene in the economy, especially through regulation.

**League of Nations**   International organization created by the Versailles Treaty after World War I to ensure world stability.

**League of Women Voters**   League formed in 1920 advocating for women's rights, among them the right for women to serve on juries and equal-pay laws.

**Lend-Lease Act**   Program begun in 1941 through which the United States transferred military equipment to Britain and other World War II allies.

**Levittown**   Any of three large suburban housing developments built in New York, Pennsylvania, and New Jersey in the late 1940s and 1950s.

**Liberty Bonds**   Interest-bearing certificates sold by the U.S. government to finance the American World War I effort.

**Limited Test Ban Treaty**   Treaty, signed by the United States, Britain, and the Soviet Union, outlawing nuclear testing in the atmosphere, in outer space, and under water.

**Lost Cause**   The phrase many white southerners applied to their Civil War defeat. They viewed the war as a noble cause and their defeat as only a temporary setback in the South's ultimate vindication.

**lynchings**   Executions, usually by a mob, without trial.

**Mahanism**   The ideas advanced by Alfred Thayer Mahan, stressing U.S. naval, economic, and territorial expansion.

**Manhattan Project**   The effort, using the code name Manhattan Engineer District, to develop an atomic bomb under the management of the U.S. Army Corps of Engineers during World War II.

**Marshall Plan**   The European Recovery Program (1948–51), which provided U.S. economic assistance to European nations; named for Secretary of State George Marshall.

**massive retaliation**   Popular name for the military doctrine adopted in the 1950s, whereby the United States promised to respond to any attack on itself or its allies with massive force, including nuclear weapons.

**McCarthyism**   Anti-communist attitudes and actions associated with Senator Joe McCarthy in the early 1950s, including smear tactics and innuendo.

**Medicaid**   Supplementary medical insurance for the poor, financed through the federal government; program created in 1965.

**Medicare**   Basic medical insurance for the elderly, financed through the federal government; program created in 1965.

**Model Cities Program**   Effort to target federal funds to upgrade public services and economic opportunity in specifically defined urban neighborhoods between 1966 and 1974.

**muckraking**   Journalism exposing economic, social, and political evils, so named by Theodore Roosevelt for its "raking the muck" of American society.

**Mugwumps**   Elitist and conservative reformers who favored sound money and limited government and opposed tariffs and the spoils system.

**multinational corporations**   Firms with direct investments, branches, factories, and offices in a number of countries.

**National Aeronautics and Space Administration (NASA)**   Federal agency created in 1958 to manage American space flights and exploration.

**National American Woman Suffrage Association**   The organization, formed in 1890, that coordinated the ultimately successful campaign to achieve women's right to vote.

**National Association for the Advancement of Colored People (NAACP)**   Interracial organization cofounded by W. E. B. Du Bois in 1910 dedicated to restoring African American political and social rights.

**National Origins Act of 1924** Law sharply restricting immigration on the basis of immigrants' national origins and discriminating against southern and eastern Europeans and Asians.

**National Security Council (NSC)** The formal policymaking body for national defense and foreign relations, created in 1947 and consisting of the president, the secretary of defense, the secretary of state, and others appointed by the president.

**National Security Council Paper 68 (NSC-68)** Policy statement that committed the United States to a military approach to the Cold War.

**Nation of Islam** Religious movement among black Americans that emphasizes self-sufficiency, self-help, and separation from white society.

**nativism** Favoring the interests and culture of native-born inhabitants over those of immigrants.

**neoconservatives** A group of intellectuals who revived and updated conservative political ideas in the 1980s.

**neoliberal** Advocate or participant in the effort to reshape the Democratic Party for the 1990s around a policy emphasizing economic growth and competitiveness in the world economy.

**New Deal** The economic and political policies of the Roosevelt administration in the 1930s.

**New Federalism** President Richard Nixon's policy to shift responsibilities of government programs from the federal level to the states.

**New Freedom** Woodrow Wilson's 1912 program for limited government intervention in the economy to restore competition by curtailing the restrictive influences of trusts and protective tariffs, thereby providing opportunities for individual achievement.

**New Frontier** John F. Kennedy's domestic and foreign policy initiatives, designed to reinvigorate a sense of national purpose and energy.

**New Nationalism** Theodore Roosevelt's 1912 program calling for a strong national government to foster, regulate, and protect business, industry, workers, and consumers.

**Niagara Movement** African American group organized in 1905 to promote racial integration, civil and political rights, and equal access to economic opportunity.

**Nineteenth Amendment** Constitutional revision that in 1920 established women citizens' right to vote.

**Nisei** United States citizens born of immigrant Japanese parents.

**Nixon Doctrine** President Nixon's new American policy (1969) toward Asia in which the United States would honor treaty commitments but would gradually disengage and expect Asian nations to handle military defense on their own.

**North American Free Trade Agreement (NAFTA)** Agreement reached in 1993 by Canada, Mexico, and the United States to substantially reduce barriers to trade.

**North Atlantic Treaty Organization (NATO)** Military alliance of the United States, Canada, and European nations created in 1949 to protect Europe against possible Soviet aggression.

**Office of Economic Opportunity (OEO)** Federal agency that coordinated many programs of the War on Poverty between 1964 and 1975.

**Omaha Platform** The 1892 platform of the Populist Party repudiating laissez-faire and demanding economic and political reforms to aid distressed farmers and workers.

**Open Door** American policy of seeking equal trade and investment opportunities in foreign nations or regions.

**open shop** Factory or business employing workers whether or not they are union members; in practice, such a business usually refuses to hire union members and follows antiunion policies.

**Operation Desert Storm** Code name for the successful offensive against Iraq by the United States and its allies in the Persian Gulf War (1991).

**Operation OVERLORD** United States and British invasion of France in June 1944 during World War II.

**Organization of Petroleum Exporting Countries (OPEC)** Cartel of oil-producing nations in Asia, Africa, and Latin America that gained substantial power over the world economy in the mid- to late 1970s by controlling the production and price of oil.

**PATRIOT Act** Federal legislation adopted in 2001, in response to the terrorist attacks of September 11, intended to facilitate antiterror actions by federal law enforcement and intelligence agencies.

**Pendleton Civil Service Act** An 1883 law that reformed the spoils system by prohibiting government workers from making political contributions and creating the Civil Service Commission to oversee their appointment on the basis of merit rather than politics.

**Pentagon Papers** Classified Defense Department documents on the history of the U.S. involvement in Vietnam, prepared in 1968 and leaked to the press in 1971.

**perestroika** Russian for "restructuring," applied to Mikhail Gorbachev's efforts to make the Soviet economic and political systems more modern, flexible, and innovative.

**Persian Gulf War** War (1991) between Iraq and a U.S.-led coalition that followed Iraq's invasion of Kuwait and resulted in the expulsion of Iraqi forces from that country.

**Platt Amendment** A stipulation the United States had inserted into the Cuban constitution in 1901 restricting Cuban autonomy and authorizing U.S. intervention and naval bases.

**Plessy v. Ferguson** Supreme Court decision holding that Louisiana's railroad segregation law did not violate the Constitution as long as the railroads or the state provided equal accommodations.

**pogroms** Government-directed attacks against Jewish citizens, property, and villages in tsarist Russia beginning in the 1880s; a primary reason for Russian Jewish migration to the United States.

**poll taxes** Taxes imposed on voters as a requirement for voting.

**Populist Party** A major third party of the 1890s, also known as the People's Party. Formed on the basis of the Farmers' Alliance and other reform organizations, it mounted electoral challenges against the Democrats in the South and the Republicans in the West.

**Populist Party** A major third party of the 1890s, formed on the basis of the Southern Farmers' Alliance and other organizations, mounting electoral challenges against Democrats in the South and the Republicans in the West.

**Potsdam Declaration** Statement issued by the United States during a meeting of U.S. president Harry Truman, British prime minister Winston Churchill, and Soviet premier Joseph Stalin held at Potsdam, near Berlin, in July 1945 to plan the defeat of Japan and the future of Eastern Europe and Germany. In it, the United States declared its intention to democratize the Japanese political system and reintroduce Japan into the international community and gave Japan an opening for surrender.

**preparedness** Military buildup in preparation for possible U.S. participation in World War I.

**preservation** Protecting forests, land, and other features of the natural environment from development or destruction, often for aesthetic appreciation.

**Progressive Era** An era in the United States (roughly between 1900 and 1917) in which important movements challenged traditional relationships and attitudes.

**prohibition** A ban on the production, transportation, and sale of liquor, achieved temporarily through state laws and the Eighteenth Amendment.

**Prohibition Party** A venerable third party still in existence that has persistently campaigned for the abolition of alcohol but has also introduced many important reform ideas into American politics.

**Proposition 187** California legislation adopted by popular vote in California in 1994 that cuts off state-funded health and education benefits to undocumented or illegal immigrants.

**Reagan Doctrine** The policy assumption that Soviet-influenced governments in Asia, Africa, and Latin America needed to be eliminated if the United States was to win the Cold War.

**recall** The process of removing an official from office by popular vote, usually after using petitions to call for such a vote.

**Redeemers** Southern Democrats who wrested control of governments in the former Confederacy from Republicans, often through electoral fraud and violence, beginning in 1870.

**redlining** Restricting mortgage credit and insurance for properties in neighborhoods defined as being high risk.

**Red Scare** Post–World War I anti-Bolshevik hysteria in the United States directed against labor activists, radical dissenters, and some ethnic groups.

**referendum** Submission of a law, proposed or already in effect, to a direct popular vote for approval or rejection.

**Reservationists** Group of U.S. senators opposing approval of the Treaty of Versailles, without significant amendments.

**Roe v. Wade** U.S. Supreme Court decision in 1973 that disallowed state laws prohibiting abortion during the first three months (trimester) of pregnancy and established guidelines for abortion in the second and third trimesters.

**Roosevelt Corollary** President Theodore Roosevelt's policy asserting U.S. authority to intervene in the affairs of Latin American nations; an expansion of the Monroe Doctrine.

**Sagebrush Rebellion** Political movement in the western states in the early 1980s that called for easing of regulations on the economic issue of federal lands and the transfer of some or all of those lands to state ownership.

**Sand Creek Massacre** The near annihilation in 1864 of Black Kettle's Cheyenne band by Colorado troops under Colonel John Chivington's orders to "kill and scalp all, big and little."

**scalawags** Southern whites, mainly small landowning farmers and well-off merchants and planters, who supported the southern Republican Party during Reconstruction for diverse reasons; a disparaging term.

**search and destroy** U.S. military tactic in South Vietnam, using small detachments to locate enemy units and then massive air, artillery, and ground forces to destroy them.

**Securities and Exchange Commission (SEC)** Federal agency with authority to regulate trading practices in stocks and bonds.

**Sedition Act of 1918** Broad law restricting criticism of America's involvement in World War I or the American government, flag, military, taxes, or officials.

**segregation** A system of racial control that separated the races, initially by custom but increasingly by law, during and after Reconstruction.

**Selective Service Act of 1917** The law establishing the military draft for World War I.

**Selective Service System** Federal agency that coordinated military conscription before and during the Vietnam War.

**self-determination** The right of a people or a nation to decide its own political allegiance or form of government without external influence.

**settlement houses** A multipurpose structure in a poor neighborhood that offered social welfare, educational, and homemaking services to the poor or immigrants, usually under private auspices and directed by middle-class women.

**Seventeenth Amendment** Constitutional change in 1913 that established the direct popular election of U.S. senators.

**sharecropping** Labor system that evolved during and after Reconstruction whereby landowners furnished laborers with a house, farm animals, and tools and advanced credit in exchange for a share of the laborers' crop.

**Sheppard-Towner Maternity and Infancy Act** The first federal social-welfare law, passed in 1921, providing federal funds for infant and maternity care.

**Sherman Antitrust Act** The first federal antitrust measure, passed in 1890; sought to promote economic competition by prohibiting business combinations in restraint of trade or commerce.

**Silicon Valley** The region of California between San Jose and San Francisco that holds the nation's greatest concentration of electronics firms.

**Sixteenth Amendment** Constitutional revision in 1913 that authorized a federal income tax.

**Slaughterhouse cases** Group of cases resulting in one sweeping decision by the U.S. Supreme Court in 1873 that contradicted the intent of the Fourteenth Amendment by decreeing that most citizenship rights remained under state, not federal, control.

**Social Darwinism** The application of Charles Darwin's theory of biological evolution to society, holding that the fittest and wealthiest survive, the weak and the poor perish, and government action is unable to alter this "natural" process.

**Social Gospel movement** Movement created by reform-minded Protestant ministers seeking to introduce religious ethics into industrial relations and appealing to churches to meet their social responsibilities.

**Solid South** The one-party (Democratic) political system that dominated the South from the 1890s to the 1950s.

**sound money** Misleading slogan that referred to a conservative policy of restricting the money supply and adhering to the gold standard.

**Southeast Asia Treaty Organization (SEATO)** Mutual defense alliance signed in 1954 by the United States, Britain, France, Thailand, Pakistan, the Philippines, Australia, and New Zealand.

**Southern Christian Leadership Conference (SCLC)** Black civil rights organization founded in 1957 by Martin Luther King Jr. and other clergy.

**Southern Farmers' Alliance** The largest of several organizations that formed in the post-Reconstruction South to advance the interests of beleaguered small farmers.

**Southern Homestead Act** Largely unsuccessful law passed in 1866 that gave black people preferential access to public lands in five southern states.

**Southern Manifesto** A document signed by 101 members of Congress from southern states in 1956 that argued that the Supreme Court's decision in *Brown v. Board of Education of Topeka* itself contradicted the Constitution.

**spheres of influence** Regions dominated and controlled by an outside power.

**Stonewall Rebellion** On June 27, 1969, patrons fought back when police raided the gay Stonewall Inn in New York; the name refers to that event and to the increase in militancy by gay Americans that it symbolizes.

**Strategic Arms Limitation Treaty (SALT)** Treaty signed in 1972 by the United States and the Soviet Union to slow the nuclear arms race.

**Strategic Defense Initiative (SDI)** President Reagan's program, announced in 1983, to defend the United States against nuclear missile attack with untested weapons systems and sophisticated technologies.

**Student Nonviolent Coordinating Committee (SNCC)** Black civil rights organization founded in 1960 and drawing heavily on younger activists and college students.

**Students for a Democratic Society (SDS)** The leading student organization of the New Left of the early and mid-1960s.

**subtreasury plan** A program promoted by the Southern Farmers' Alliance in response to low cotton prices and tight credit. Farmers would store their crop in a warehouse until prices rose, in the meantime borrowing up to 80 percent of the value of the stored crops from the government at a low interest rate.

**Sunbelt** The states of the American South and Southwest.

**Sussex Pledge** Germany's pledge during World War I not to sink merchant ships without warning, on the condition that Britain also observe recognized rules of international laws.

**Swann v. Charlotte-Mecklenburg Board of Education** U.S. Supreme Court decision in 1971 that upheld cross-city busing to achieve the racial integration of public schools.

**sweatshops** Small, poorly ventilated shops or apartments crammed with workers, often family members, who pieced together garments.

**Taft-Hartley Act** Federal legislation of 1947 that substantially limited the tools available to labor unions in labor-management disputes.

**Taliban** Muslim fundamentalist political organization that has contested for control of Afghanistan in opposition to the United States.

**Teller Amendment** A congressional resolution adopted in 1898 renouncing any American intention to annex Cuba.

**Temporary Assistance for Needy Families (TANF)** Federal program tying benefits to work requirements and time limits; created in 1996 to replace earlier welfare programs to aid families and children.

**tenements** Four- to six-story residential dwellings, once common in New York, built on tiny lots without regard to providing ventilation or light.

**Tennessee Valley Authority (TVA)** Federal regional planning agency established to promote conservation, produce electric power, and encourage economic development in seven southern states.

**Tenure of Office Act** Passed by the Republican-controlled Congress in 1867 to limit presidential interference with its policies, the act prohibited the president from removing certain officeholders without the Senate's consent. President Andrew Johnson, angered at what he believed to be an unconstitutional attack on presidential authority, deliberately violated the act by firing Secretary of War Edwin M. Stanton. The House responded by approving articles of impeachment against a president for the first time in American history.

**Treaty of Fort Laramie** The treaty acknowledging U.S. defeat in the Great Sioux War in 1868 and supposedly guaranteeing the Sioux perpetual land and hunting rights in South Dakota, Wyoming, and Montana.

**Treaty of Versailles** The treaty ending World War I and creating the League of Nations.

**Troubled Asset Relief Program (TARP)** Federal program in 2008 to purchase or guarantee shaky bank assets to protect the economy from widespread bank failures.

**Truman Doctrine** President Harry Truman's statement in 1947 that the United States should assist other nations that were facing external pressure or internal revolution; an important step in the escalation of the Cold War.

**trusts** A combination of corporations cooperating in order to reduce competition and control prices.

**Underwood-Simmons Tariff Act** The 1913 reform law that lowered tariff rates and levied the first regular federal income tax.

**Union League** A Republican Party organization in northern cities that became an important organizing device among freedmen in southern cities after 1865.

***United States v. Cruikshank*** Supreme Court ruling of 1876 that overturned the convictions of some of those responsible for the Colfax Massacre, ruling that the Enforcement Act applied only to violations of black rights by states, not individuals.

***University of California v. Bakke*** United States Supreme Court case in 1978 that allowed race to be used as one of several factors in college and university admission decisions but made rigid quotas unacceptable.

**vertical integration** The consolidation of numerous production functions, from the extraction of the raw materials to the distribution and marketing of the finished products, under the direction of one firm.

**Viet Cong** Communist rebels in South Vietnam who fought the pro-American government established in South Vietnam in 1954.

**Volstead Act** The 1920 law defining the liquor forbidden under the Eighteenth Amendment and giving enforcement responsibilities to the Prohibition Bureau of the Department of the Treasury.

**Voting Rights Act** Legislation in 1965 that overturned a variety of practices by which states systematically denied voter registration to minorities.

**War Industries Board (WIB)** The federal agency that reorganized industry for maximum efficiency and productivity during World War I.

**War on Poverty** Set of programs introduced by Lyndon Johnson between 1963 and 1966 designed to break the cycle of poverty by providing funds for job training, community development, nutrition, and supplementary education.

**Warsaw Pact** Military alliance of the Soviet Union and Communist nations of Eastern Europe from 1955 to 1989.

**Watergate** A complex scandal involving attempts to cover up illegal actions taken by administration officials and leading to the resignation of President Richard Nixon in 1974.

**weapons of mass destruction** Weapons such as nuclear bombs and biological agents capable of inflicting massive casualties on civilian populations.

**welfare capitalism** A paternalistic system of labor relations emphasizing management responsibility for employee well-being.

**Whitewater** A failed Arkansas land development for which Bill and Hillary Clinton were accused of fraud but not indicted because of lack of evidence.

**Wobblies** Popular name for the members of the Industrial Workers of the World (IWW).

**Women's Christian Temperance Union (WCTU)** Women's organization whose members visited schools to educate children about the evils of alcohol, addressed prisoners, and blanketed men's meetings with literature.

**World Bank** Officially the International Bank for Reconstruction and Development, an international organization established in 1845 that assists governments around the world in economic development efforts.

**World Trade Organization (WTO)** International organization that sets standards and practices for global trade, and the focus of international protests over world economic policy in the late 1990s.

**World Wide Web** A part of the Internet designed to allow easier navigation of the network through the use of graphical user interfaces and hypertext links between different addresses.

**Wounded Knee Massacre** The U.S. Army's brutal winter massacre in 1890 of at least 200 Sioux men, women, and children as part of the government's assault on the tribe's Ghost Dance religion.

**Yalta Conference** Meeting of U.S. president Franklin Roosevelt, British prime minister Winston Churchill, and Soviet premier Joseph Stalin held in February 1945 to plan the final stages of World War II and postwar arrangements.

**yellow-dog contracts** Employment agreements binding workers not to join a union.

**yellow press** A deliberately sensational journalism of scandal and exposure designed to attract an urban mass audience and increase advertising revenues.

# Credits

**CHAPTER 16** Stephens, H. L. (Henry Louis), 1824-1882/Library of Congress Prints and Photographs Division; 450: Library of Congress Prints and Photographs Division [LC-DIG-cwpbh-00952]; 455: North Wind Picture Archives; 458: The Granger Collection, NYC; 462: The Granger Collection, NYC; 464: Library of Congress; 466T: Office of Congressman Hakeem Jeffries; 466B: Schomburg Center, NYPL/Art Resource, NY; 469: The Granger Collection, NYC; 471: Library of Congress; 472: Library of Congress Prints and Photographs Division [LC-DIG-pga-01366]

**CHAPTER 17** Library of Congress; 482: Library of Congress Prints and Photographs Division [LC-DIG-fsa-8a26761]; 485: Library of Congress; 496: Library of Congress Prints & Photographs Division [LC-USZC4-4647]; 497: Everett Collection Inc./Alamy; 501: Advertising Archive/Everett Collection; 504: The Granger Collection, NYC; 506L: Greg Campbell/AP Images; 506R: Library of Congress

**CHAPTER 18** Library of Congress Prints and Photographs Division; 510: North Wind Picture Archives/Alamy; 513: The Museum of the City of New York/Art Resource, NY; 519R: The Museum of the City of New York/Art Resource, NY; 519L: Museum of the City of New York/Byron Collection/Archive Photos/Getty Images; 524: Nebraska State Historical Society; 525: Library of Congress Prints and Photographs Division [LC-USZ62-107167]; 526: Library of Congress Prints and Photographs Division [LC-USZC4-1584]; 529: The New York Public Library/Art Resource, NY; 534: Bettmann/Corbis; 536: Library of Congress Prints and Photographs Division [LC-USZ62-107838 ]; 538T: AP Images; 538B: nik wheeler/Alamy

**CHAPTER 19** akg-images/Newscom; 542: National Archives and Records Administration; 547: George Bull Child, Hide Painting, 1930s Denver Art Museum Collection: The L. D. and Ruth Bax Collection, 1985.106 Photograph (c)Denver Art Museum; 549: Western History Collections, University of Oklahoma Libraries; 551: Western History Collections, University of Oklahoma Libraries; 554: Library of Congress Prints and Photographs Division; 557: Library of Congress Prints and Photographs Division; 558: Archive Images/Alamy; 561: Courtesy Palace of the Governors Photo Archive (NMHM/DCA), Negative No: 22468.; 562: Nebraska State Historical Society; 564L: Bettmann/Corbis; 564R: Library of Congress Prints and Photographs Division[LC-DIG-ppmsc-02511]

**CHAPTER 20** Picture History/Newscom; 568: Library of Congress Prints and Photographs Division, [LC-DIG-cwpbh-04797]; 574: The Granger Collection, NYC; 578: Stock Montage, Inc. Historical Pictures Collection; 580 (verse): *Atlanta Journal Constitution*; 582L: Keppler, Joseph Ferdinand/Library of Congress Prints and Photographs Division [LC-USZC4-2835]; 582R: George Frey/Corbis; 585: Everett Collection Inc/Alamy; 587: Library of Congress Prints and Photographs Division [LC-DIG-ppmsca-25438]; 588: The Granger Collection, NYC; 592: Everett Collection Inc/Alamy; 593: Everett Collection Inc/Alamy

**CHAPTER 21** The Denver Public Library; 598: National Archives and Records Administration; 601: Library of Congress Prints and Photographs Division [LC-USZ62-23743]; 608: Library of Congress; 613: INDIANA HISTORICAL SOCIETY, M0513.; 614: Library of Congress

Prints and Photographs Division [LC-USZ62-132968]; 616: Library of Congress Prints and Photographs Division [LC-USZ62-30776]; 621L: Jewel Samad/AFP/Getty Images; 621R: Bettmann/Corbis; 622: Paris Pierce/Alamy; 626: Library of Congress Prints and Photographs Division [LC-USZ62-20570]

**CHAPTER 22** Library of Congress Prints and Photographs Division [LC-U5Z62-55429]; 630: Library of Congress Prints and Photographs Division [LC-USZ62-104479]; 633: Library of Congress Prints and Photographs Division [LC-DIG-ppmsca-02904]; 637: Bettmann/Cprbis; 641: Library of Congress Prints and Photographs Division; 642: Library of Congress Prints and Photographs Division [LC-USZC4-5392]; 643: Ivy Close Images/Alamy; 649: Hamilton, Grant E/Library of Congress Prints and Photographs Division [LC-DIG-ppmsca-25887]; 651: The Granger Collection, NYC; 652L: John Moore/AP Images; 652R: Library of Congress Prints and Photographs Division [LC-USZ62-75561]

**CHAPTER 23** Swim Ink 2, LLC/Fine Art/Corbis; 658: National Archives and Records Administration; 663: Library of Congress Prints and Photographs Division; 667: Everett Collection/Newscom; 668: National Archives and Records Administration; 669: Library of Congress Prints and Photographs Division [LC-USZC4-2950]; 674L: U.S. Department of Defense; 674R: U.S. Department of Defense; 675: American Stock/Archive Photos/Getty Images; 677: National Archives and Records Administration; 678: Library of Congress Prints and Photographs Division [LC-USZ62-115013]; 682: The Granger Collection, NYC

**CHAPTER 24** Swim Ink 2, LLC/Fine Art/Corbis; 686: Bettmann/Corbis; 690: Rykoff Collection/Corbis; 696: Library of Congress Prints and Photographs Division; 697: Los Angeles Public Library; 698: Karen Kent/Corbis Super RF/Alamy; 704: The Denver Public Library; 706: AP Images; 709L: Stephen Boitano/Reuters/Corbis; 709R: David McNew/Getty Images News/Getty Images

**CHAPTER 25** AP Images; 714: Library of Congress Prints and Photographs Division; 719: Library of Congerss Prints and Photographs Division; 720: Picture History/Newscom; 721: Lee, Russell, 1903-1986/Library of Congress Prints and Photographs Division; 721 (quote): Anna Arnold Hedgeman, *The Trumpet Sounds: A Memoir of Negro Leadership*, published by Holt, Rinehart and Winston, 1964. Copyrighted by Anna Arnold Hedgeman; 723: Culver Pictures, Inc/Superstock; 724: National Archives and Records Administration; 726 (quote): Address at Oglethorpe University in Atlanta, GA, May 22, 1932; Papers of Franklin D. Roosevelt; Franklin D. Roosevelt Library, Hyde Park, NY; 728: Picture History/Newscom; 730: Library of Congress Prints and Photographs Division [LC-USF34- 016269-C]; 731 (quote): State of the Union Address Speech to the 74th Congress, 1st Session, January 4, 1935; Papers of Franklin D. Roosevelt; Franklin D. Roosevelt Library, Hyde Park, NY; 733T: Woman getting a tattoo, c.1934 (b/w photo), Rhoads, Harry Mellon (1880/81-1975)/Denver Public Library, Western History Collection/The Bridgeman Art Library; 733B: Mark Wilson/Getty Images News/Getty Images; 734: Hulton Archive/Getty Images; 738: Library of Congress Prints and Photographs Division [LC-USW3- 014843-C]; 743: Popperfoto/Getty Images; 743 (caption): The Goebbels Diaries, 1942-1943, translated by Louis L. Lochner, Doubleday, 1948

# Index

efforts to reduce rate of, 843
urban, 518–520
Poverty, increase in, 893
Powderly, Terence V., 521
*The Power Elite* (Mills), 821
Powers, Francis Gary, 826
Prayer, 915
Preparedness, for war, 662–663
*The Presbyterian Banner,* 641
Presbyterian Church of the United States, 839, 912
Preservation, of natural resources, 619, 621
Presidency, office of, 618
in the late nineteenth century, 575
Presidential Commission on the Status of Women (1961), 857
President's Organizat ion for Unemployment Relief, 722
Presley, Elvis, 818, 819
Pressure groups, 573
Prisons, 924–926
Progressive Era, 597–628
the environmental movement, 621
major laws and constitutional amendments of, 606
overview of, 599
Progressive Party, 623, 624, 693–694
Progressivism
in the 1920s, 692–694
belief in efficiency by leaders, 603
government and, 617–618
influences on European, 604
in New Zealand, 604
origins of, 600
prohibition and, 611
prostitution and, 611
rise of labor unions under, 603
socialism and, 604–605
social justice and, 606–613
women and, 603–604
Prohibition, 611, 667–668, 705
Prohibition Party, 573
*The Promised Land* (Antin), 510
Promontory Summit, Utah, 541, 543
Propaganda, 670, 765–766
Proposition 187 (California 1994), 936
Prosperity, 688, 813–821, 905–906, 928
Prostitution, 550, 555, 611
Protectionists, 931
Protestantism, 912
Protests
at 1968 Democratic Convention, 866
antiwar, 853
international, 866
in Seattle, Washington, 931
social, during the Great Depression, 722
Students for a Democratic Society (SDS) and, 855
Provident Hospital, 530
Public education, 717
Public policy
women's rights and, 910–911
Public-safety committees, during World War I, 671
Public Works Administration (PWA), 727
Pueblos, 544
Puerto Rico, 640
U.S. rule in, 646, 648
Pulitzer, Joseph, 534
Pullman, George, 522

Pullman strike (1894), 522, 590
Punk music, 891
Punk rock, 891
Pure Food and Drug Act (1906), 606, 621

# Q

Quotas, immigration, 907

# R

Race
voting rights and, 466
Race relations, 494–495, 791
Racism, 528–530
education of Native Americans and, 609
in the Filipino-American War, 644
in the Great Depression, 720–721
immigration and, 609
imperialism and, 632
prohibition and, 611
scientific, 500
violence and, 469–470
Radar, development of, 761
Radicalism, 703
Radical Republicans, 463
Radio industry, 689, 700
*Ragged Dick* (Alger), 520
Railroad Administration, 665
Railroads, 691
growth of corporate-owned, 514
in the New South, 486–487
promotion of frontier settlement by, 560
regulation and, 580–581
segregation by law on, 498
and timber, 553
transcontinental, 543, 558
Ranching, open-range, 555–556
Randolph, A. Philip, 767
Range-cattle industry, 555–557
Rap, 891
Rape, 857
Rap music, 891
Rationing
gasoline, 872
during World War II, 760
Rauschenbusch, Walter, 602
Ray, James Earl, 865
Rayner, John B., 586
Reagan, Ronald, 621, 806
background of, 884, 885
Cold War and, 896–898
election of 1976 and, 874
election of 1980 and, 884, 885
foreign policy and, 897–898
as host of *General Electric Theater,* 813
Iran-Contra Affair and, 899
neoconservatism and, 886
personal appeal of, 885
as president, 884–885
Soviet Union and, 896, 897
Strategic Defense Initiative (SDI) and, 897
Reagan Democrats, 866, 922
Reagan Doctrine, 897
Reaganomics, 887–888, 941–942
*Rebel Without a Cause* (film), 818
Recall, 617
Recession, economic, of 1937, 741
Reconstruction, 449–479
abandonment of, 473–478
African-Americans and, 453–458
Andrew Johnson and, 460–463

Congress in conflict with president over, 460–463
Congressional, 463–465
constitutional amendments and federal legislation of, 475
effects of, in the South, 451–453
federal, 459–468
radical, 463
the South and, 477–478
southern republican government during, 465, 467–468
views on, 459, 465
Reconstruction Finance Corporation (RFC), 723
*Redbook,* 821
Red Cloud, 548
Redeemers, 473, 477
Redlining, neighborhoods, 786
Red Power, 861–862
Red Scare (1919–1920), 681–683
Red Scare (1947–1957), 804–809
Red Spring, 865
Referendums, 617
Reform movements
in the 1920s, 694
civil service, 577–579
grassroots, 855
moral, 610–612
Native Americans and, 548
in New Zealand, 604
origins of progressive, 600–605
political and governmental, 573, 585–586, 613–618
in rural areas, 610
social, 602, 606–613
socialism and, 604–605
urban, 606–607
Regulation
early arguments for, 603
environmental, 887–888
and the federal government, 582
of railroads, 580–581
Republican Party and curtailment of, 693, 941
Theodore Roosevelt and corporate, 620–622
Relief programs, during the Great Depression, 722–723, 732–734, 736
Religion, 705
in the 1950s, 819–820
in the 1980s, 911–912
African-Americans and faith, 457–458
social reform movements based on, 602
subjugation of Native American, 543
Religious beliefs, 839, 921
civil rights and, 839
Religious groups, 491, 913
Religious persecution, 522
Reno, Janet, 933
Republican Party
ascendancy of, in the 1920s, 692–693
constituencies in southern, 464, 465
Contract with America and, 923
election of 1896 and, 592–593
election of 1916 and, 663
election of 1920 and, 683
election of 1928 and, 710–711
election of 1948 and, 813
election of 1964 and, 842–843
election of 1992 and, 922

election of 1996 and, 924
election of 2000 and, 939, 941
election of 2008 and, 949–950
election of 2012 and, 951–952
free labor system and, 456
Liberal, 470–471
McKinley, William and, 591, 592
reconstruction and, 459–463, 467–468
Red Scare (1947–1957) and, 804–805, 809
self-identifying characteristics of, 572–573
strength and appeal of, 572
Sunbelt and, 905
under Taft, 622–623
tariff debates and, 579–580
Republic Steel Company, 736
Reservationists, 679
Reservations, for Native Americans, 548–549, 559, 620, 861–862
Resettlement Administration, 731
Revenue Act (1935), 731
Revenue sharing, 869
Revivalism
in the 1950s, 819
Rhee, Syngman, 801, 803
Rice, 502
Rice, Condoleezza, 933
Rice, Thomas, 495
Riis, Jacob, 518, 519, 609
Riots
Chicago, Illinois, 859, 866
international, 866
in Los Angeles, California, 859, 895–896
urban, 858–859
Riverside, Illinois, 537
Road construction, 699, 717, 727, 733
*The Robe* (film), 819
Roberts, Oral, 913
Robertson, Pat, 909–910, 913
Robinson, Jackie, 787, 838
Rockefeller, John D., 486, 515
*Roe v. Wade* (1973), 910
Rome-Berlin Axis, 751
*Romer v. Evans* (1996), 915
Rommel, Erwin, 757
Romney, Mitt, 951–952
Roosevelt, Eleanor, 715, 724, 734, 735, 737
Roosevelt, Franklin D., 840
Atlantic Charter and, 754
Black Cabinet of, 737
declaration of war against Japan, 755
economic collapse and, 715
economic recession of 1937 and, 741
election of 1932 and, 723–725
election of 1936 and, 734–735
election of 1940 and, 753
Fair Employment Practices Committee and, 767
Lend-Lease Act (1941) and, 754
order for internment of Japanese Americans, 768
preparedness for war and, 744
radio address excerpt, 1934, 713, 715
Supreme Court and, 741
World War II and, 752–753, 755, 772
Yalta Conference and, 777

Strategic Arms Limitation Treaty (SALTI, 1972), 869, 901
Strategic Arms Reduction Treaty (START I, 1991), 901
Strategic Arms Reduction Treaty (START II, 1993), 901
Strategic Defense Initiative (SDI), 897
Strategic Offensive Reductions, 901
Strikes
  in the cattle industry, 557
  coal industry, 784
  garment industry, 603
  labor, 520–522
  New Deal, 729
  post-World War I, 680–681
  United Mine Workers (1902), 618–619
Stuart's Stranglers, 556
Student Nonviolent Coordinating Committee (SNCC), 837
Students for a Democratic Society (SDS), 855, 865
Subtreasury plan, of Macune, 491
Subtreasury system, 584, 588
Suburbanization, 815
  interstate highways and, 815
  post-World War II, 783
Suburbs, 532–533, 699
  federal revenue sharing in, 869
  growth of, in 1970s, 862–863
Suez Canal, 755, 757, 826
Sunbelt, 905–909
Sunday, Billy, 605, 703
Superfund program, 871
Supreme Court (U.S.)
  affirmative action and, 937–938
  all-white primary elections and, 832
  apportionment of legislative seats and, 863
  as champions of business interests, 590, 693
  civil rights and, 915
  discrimination in housing and, 786
  education vouchers and, 942
  election of 2000 and, 939, 941
  equal protection and, 813
  evangelical Christians and, 820
  Franklin D. Roosevelt and, 741
  internment and, 769
  interstate commerce and, 580
  labor and, 520, 605, 607
  reproductive rights and, 910
  right to privacy and, 910
  school busing and, 863
  school prayer and, 820
  segregation and, 813
  voting rights and, 466, 478
Sussex Pledge, 662
Swann v. Charlotte-Mecklenburg Board of Education (1971), 863
Sweatshops, 517
Swift, Gustavus, 515

## T

Tabloids, 534
Taft, Robert, 793
Taft, William Howard, 622, 645, 651, 693
Taft-Hartley Act of 1947, 784, 791
Taliban, 945
Tariffs, 579–580, 584, 623, 624, 625

Taverns, 537
Tax cuts, 941
Taxes
  George H. W. Bush and, 896
  income, 623, 624
  need to raise state, during Reconstruction, 467–468
  poll, 499
  property, 717
  in urban environments, 858
Taylor, Frederick W., 603, 688
Teaching profession, women in, 518
Tea Party movement, 951
Technology. see also Science and technology
  agriculture on the plains and, 563
  in an instant society, 929–930
  impact of, on mining, 551–552
Teenagers, in 1950s, 817–818
  music and, 818
Telephones, 930, 944
Televangelists, 913
Television, 891
Teller Amendment, 639, 648
Temperance movement, 575
Temperance reform, 493
Temporary Assistance to Needy Families (TANF), 924
The Ten Commandments (film), 819
Tenements, 518–519, 606–607
Tennessee Valley Authority (TVA), 739, 740
Ten Percent Plan, 459
Tenure of Office Act (1867), 463
Termination policy, 814
Terrell, Mary Church, 505
Terrorism, 899, 924
Terrorist attacks, September 11, 2001, 943
Tet Offensive, 863–864
Texas, 555
Texas Oil Company (Texaco), 515
Textile industry, 485–486, 487, 692
The Grapes of Wrath (Steinbeck), 731
The Great Gatsby (Fitzgerald), 702
Third World, 824
Thirteenth amendment, 475
38th parallel, 801, 803
Thomas, Clarence, 934
Thompson, Cyrus, 491
Thomson, Elihu, 514
369th Infantry Regiment (U. S.), 672, 677
Three Mile Island, 876
Thurmond, Strom, 791
Tijerina, Reies López, 860
Tilden, Samuel J., 475, 476
Tillamooks, 544
Tillman, Benjamin R., 477
Tilyou, George C., 537
Timber, 553
Time, 819
Title IX, 910
Tobacco industry, 484–486, 488, 499
Townsend, Francis, 729
Townsend Plan, 729
Trade
  before the Great Depression, 717
  protection and expansion of foreign, 634
  spheres of influence and, 645
Trade Expansion Act (1962), 930
Treaties, 544–546. see also under individual title keywords
Triangle Shirt Company, 601

Tripartite Pact, 751
Troubled Asset Relief Program (TARP), 948
Truman, Harry S., 824
  character of, 791
  election of 1944 and, 770
  election of 1948 and, 790
  Fair Deal policies of, 792–793
  foreign policy and, 795
  Korean War and, 803, 804
  loyalty program and, 805
  nuclear weapons and, 799
  Potsdam Declaration and, 777
  reasons for dropping atomic bomb, 778
Truman Doctrine, 795
Trump, Donald, 891
Trusts, 515
Tugwell, Rexford, 731
Turner, Henry McNeal, 502
Tuskegee Institute, 505
Twain, Mark, 511
Tweed, William M., 470
Typewriters, 518

## U

U-2 spy plane, 826
Underwood-Simmons Tariff Act (1913), 606, 624
Unemployment
  in the 1920s, 691
  1925–1945, 718
  in the 1990s, 928
  aid for victims of, 722
  before the Great Depression, 716–717
  during Great Depression, 719
Unequal opportunity, 857
The Unheavenly City (Banfield), 886
Union Leagues, 467
Union Pacific Railroad, 541, 542
United Auto Workers (UAW), 735, 789, 805
United Church of Christ, 912
United Daughters of the Confederacy (UDC), 493
United Farm Workers (UFW), 849, 860
United Fruit Company, 825
United Methodist Church, 912
United Mine Workers, 681
United Nations (UN), 777, 794, 803, 945, 946
United States Housing Authority, 742
The United States Investor, 641
United States v. Cruikshank (1876), 466, 478
United States v. E. C. Knight Company (1895), 590
Universal Negro Improvement Association (UNIA), 696
University of California v. Bakke (1978), 937
Urbanization, 531–532, 695
  environmental conservation and, 537
  in the New South, 484–485, 488–489
Urban League, 814
Urban renewal, 814–815
U.S. Army's winter attack (1870), 547
U.S. Commission on National Security, 943

## V

Values, 548
Vanzetti, Bartolomeo, 703
Vardaman, James, 612
Veiller, Lawrence, 607
Venezuela, 637
Versailles, Treaty of (1919), 676, 679, 749
Vertical integration, 514, 515
Veterans Administration (VA), 786, 815
Vicksburg, Mississippi, 474
Viet Cong, 829, 842, 849–850, 863, 866, 868
Vietnamization, 867–868
Vietnam Moratorium, 866
Vietnam War, 821, 842
  1969–1975, 866–868
  bombing in, 850
  cease-fire, 868
  justifications for, 864
  protests against, 852–853
  search and destroy strategy in, 850
  Tet Offensive in, 863–864
Villa, Francisco "Pancho," 653
Violence
  against African-Americans, 468–470, 473–474, 495–496
  after death of Martin Luther King Jr., 865
  between blacks and whites, 768
  in the cattle industry, 556
  in cow towns, 555
  fear of, in the 1990s, 924
  against Hispanics in the Southwest, 561–562
  Ku Klux Klan and, 704
  against Mexican Americans, 768
  mining and, 550, 552
  against Native Americans, 546
  in range-cattle industry, 556
  riots and, 858–859
  against unionization, 736
VISTA (Volunteers in Service to America), 841
Vital center, strategy of, 790, 886
A Voice from the South (Cooper), 483, 504
Volkswagen, 789
Volstead Act (1920), 705
Voluntarism, failure of, 722–723
Volunteer military, 763
Voter turnout, 570
Voting, by district, 935
Voting rights, 464
  African-Americans and, 466, 499
  grandfather clauses for, 499
  women, 613–614, 624
  women and, 493, 574, 674, 694
Voting Rights Act (1965), 466, 842
Voting Rights Act (1975), 935

## W

Wabash, St. Louis, and Pacific Railway Company (1886) v. Illinois, 580
Waco raid, 924
Wade-Davis Bill, 459
Wages
  in the 1920s, 691
  during Great Depression, 718
  in manufacturing jobs, 516
  in the New South, 487
  office work and, 893

# U.S. Map

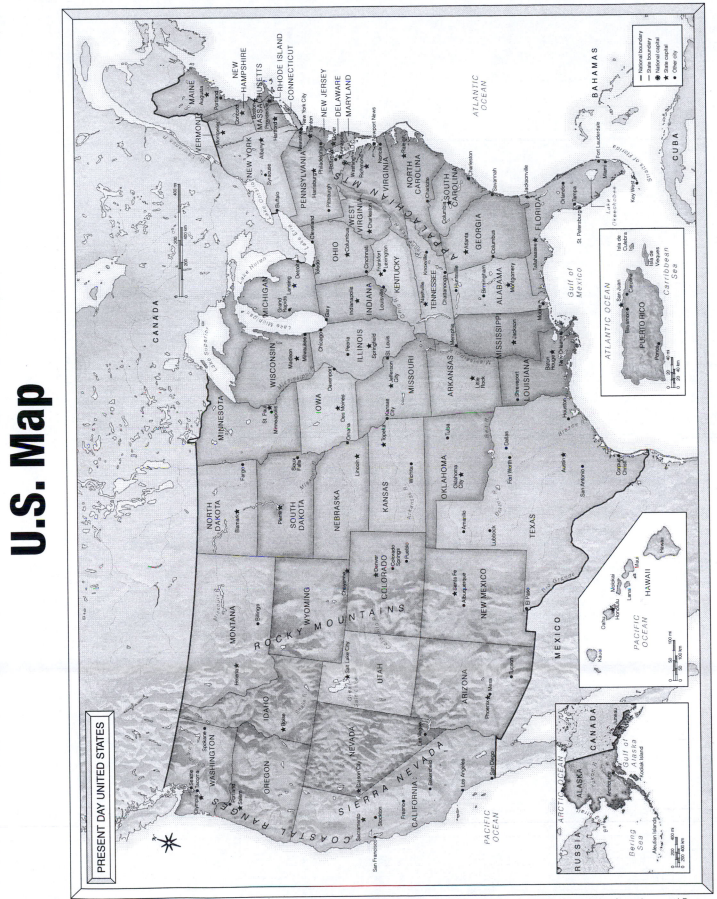

PRESENT DAY UNITED STATES

From The American Journey, Seventh Edition. Goldfield, Abbott, Anderson, Argersinger, Argersinger and Barney.

# World Map

PRESENT DAY WORLD

From The American Journey, Seventh Edition. Goldfield, Abbott, Anderson, Argersinger, Argersinger and Barney.